Commercial Law

This innovative textbook examines commercial law and the social and political context in which it develops. Topical examples, such as funding for terrorism, demonstrate this fast-moving field's relevance to today's concerns. This wide-ranging subject is set within a clear structure, with part and chapter introductions setting out the student's course of study. Recommendations for further reading at the end of every chapter point the reader to important sources for advanced study, and revision questions encourage understanding. The extensive coverage and detailed commentary has been extensively market tested to ensure that the contents are aligned with the needs of university courses in commercial law.

Nicholas Ryder is an associate professor in law at the University of the West of England, Bristol. He is currently Director of the Commercial Law Research Unit and co-convener for the Banking and Finance Stream for the Society of Legal Scholars.

Margaret Griffiths is Professor Emeritus at the University of Glamorgan. She is a specialist in consumer law, having taught and researched the area for over thirty years.

Lachmi Singh is a senior lecturer in law at the University of the West of England Bristol, where she specialises in contract law, international trade and carriage of goods by sea.

The authors discuss why Commercial Law: Principles and Policy is required reading at www.cambridge.org/commerciallaw

Follow the authors on Twitter at @DrNicRyder; @LachmiSingh; @ProfMGriffiths

Commercial Law

Principles and Policy

NICHOLAS RYDER
MARGARET GRIFFITHS
LACHMI SINGH

CAMBRIDGE
UNIVERSITY PRESS

CAMBRIDGE UNIVERSITY PRESS
Cambridge, New York, Melbourne, Madrid, Cape Town,
Singapore, São Paulo, Delhi, Mexico City

Cambridge University Press
The Edinburgh Building, Cambridge CB2 8RU, UK

Published in the United States of America by Cambridge University Press, New York

www.cambridge.org
Information on this title: www.cambridge.org/9780521760645

First published 2012

Printed in the United Kingdom at the University Press, Cambridge

A catalogue record for this publication is available from the British Library

Library of Congress Cataloguing in Publication data
Ryder, Nicholas.
  Commercial law: principles and policy / Nicholas Ryder, Margaret Griffiths, Lachmi Singh.
    p.   cm.
  Includes bibliographical references and index.
  ISBN 978-0-521-76064-5 (hardback) – ISBN 978-0-521-75802-4 (pbk.)
  1. Commercial law – England.   I. Griffiths, Margaret.   II. Singh, Lachmi.   III. Title.
  KD1629.R93   2012
  346.4207–dc23   2012007319

ISBN 978-0-521-76064-5 Hardback
ISBN 978-0-521-75802-4 Paperback

Contents

Preface

The principal objective of this book is to provide a detailed analytical overview of the vast array of areas of commercial law and the policies that lie behind these areas of law. The book is divided into seven parts and has been written with the relevant policies in mind. Part 1 of the book deals with one of the most traditional aspects of commercial law, the law of agency. This part is divided into three chapters and provides a detailed review of the scope of an agent's authority, the obligations owed by a principal to an agent and the Commercial Agency Regulations 1993. The second part of the book deals with another central tenant of the commercial law syllabus, the sale of goods. This is divided into five parts and considers such topics as the historical development and policy underlying the sale of goods, before addressing the integral areas of the implied conditions in the sale of goods, and the passage of title to goods combined with delivery and payment. The last two chapters address the provisions of the supply of goods and services and finally the rise of e-commerce. The third part of the book deals with international trade and sales law. In particular, it concentrates on standard trade terms, the Vienna Convention on the International Sale of Goods, payment in international sales and carriage of goods by sea. Part four looks at tortious liability for defective products, dealing initially with the law of negligence and the rise of product liability and thereafter looking in detail at the provisions of the Consumer Protection Act 1987. The next part of the book consists of three chapters looking at the issue of unfair commercial practices, which has seen a major reform of the previous piecemeal approach towards criminal liability for goods and services. The first chapter looks at the policy underlying the reforms and the role of the European Union in this area. The second chapter considers in detail the provisions of the Consumer Protection from Unfair Trading Regulations 2008, which have adopted a more holistic approach to the entire issue of the liability of traders for goods and services. The final chapter addresses the Business Protection from Misleading Marketing Regulations 2008 and the controls they exercise over misleading and comparative advertising.

As set out above, this book deals with the traditional areas of commercial law, including the law of agency and the sale of goods. However, as there is an artificial divide between consumer law and commercial law, this book also considers other areas that could be viewed as on the periphery of the modern day interpretation of commercial law, namely banking and finance law in Part 6 and consumer credit law in Part 7.

Uniquely, the book provides an interesting overview of the recent policy initiatives introduced by successive British governments that have and will continue to have a fundamental influence on the evolution of commercial law. For example, the British economy has faced almost unprecedented levels of uncertainty since the start of the 'credit crunch' in 2007. The subsequent global banking crisis has necessitated a radical rethink from the government as to its consumer credit and banking strategies. In essence, this resulted in the introduction of, at times, radical legislation aimed at not only protecting consumers and businesses, but also encouraging the growth of the economy. The new consumer protection methods, such as the Consumer Credit Directive, the Consumer Protection from Unfair Trading Regulations 2008, the reforms in sale of goods due to the introduction of the Consumer Rights Directive and the Financial Services Bill (2011), will all have a monumental impact on commercial businesses into the future.

Dr Nicholas Ryder
Professor Margaret Griffiths
Lachmi Singh
August 2011

Abbreviations

AML	anti-money laundering
APR	annual percentage rate
BBA	British Bankers Association
BCCI	Bank of Credit Commerce International
BIS	Bank of International Settlements
BPMM	Business Protection from Misleading Marketing Regulations 2008
CIF	cost, insurance, freight
CISG	UN Convention on Contracts for the International Sale of Goods
CMI	Comité Maritime International
CPMA	Consumer Protection and Markets Authority
CPUT	Consumer Protection from Unfair Trading Regulations 2008
CTF	counter-terrorist financing
DBERR	Department for Business, Enterprise and Regulatory Reform
DBIS	Department for Business, Innovation and Skills
DTI	Department of Trade and Industry
DWP	Department of Work and Pensions
EBA	European Banking Authority
ECHR	European Convention on Human Rights
ECJ	European Court of Justice
EEA	European Economic Area
EMP	Energy Markets Participants
ERL	expected readiness to load
EU	European Union
FAS	free alongside ship
FATF	Financial Action Task Force
FOB	free on board
FOS	Financial Ombudsman Service
FPC	Financial Policy Committee
FSA	Financial Services Authority
FSC	Financial Stability Committee
FSCS	Financial Services Compensation Scheme
FSF	Financial Stability Forum

FSMA	Financial Services and Markets Act 2000
GDP	gross domestic product
IBRD	International Bank for Reconstruction and Development
ICC	International Chamber of Commerce
ICSID	International Centre for the Settlement of Investment Disputes
IDA	International Development Association
IFC	International Finance Corporation
IMF	International Monetary Fund
IOSC	International Organisation of Securities Commission
MIB	Marketing of Investments Board
MIGA	Multilateral Investment Guarantee Agency
MLRO	Money Laundering Reporting Officer
MPC	Monetary Policy Committee
NACAB	National Association of Citizens Advice Bureau
NCA	National Crime Agency
OFT	Office of Fair Trading
PRA	Prudential Regulation Authority
PSC	point of single contact
RPB	recognised professional body
SEU	Social Exclusion Unit
SFO	Serious Fraud Office
SIB	Securities and Investments Board
SRO	self-regulating organisation
UCP	Uniform Customs and Practice of Documentary Credits
UCTA	Unfair Contract Terms Act 1977
UN	United Nations
UNCITRAL	UN Commission on International Trade Law
UNCTAD	UN Conference on Trade and Development
UNIDROIT	International Institute for the Unification of Private Law
URC	Uniform Rules for Collections

Table of Statutory Provisions

Statutory Instruments

European Legislation

International Legislation

Statutory Instruments

Table of Cases

Part 1
Agency

Introduction

The first part of this book considers one of most important and traditional aspects of any commercial law undergraduate course, the law of agency. Chapter 1 begins by attempting to define the law of agency by providing several examples from commercial law scholars. Indeed, Part 1 as a whole illustrates the difficulty experienced by the courts in England and Wales in defining the term 'agency'. The next part of Chapter 1 deals with the nature and characteristics of agency, followed by a brief outline of the different types of agents that exist in the United Kingdom. Chapter 2 provides a detailed commentary on the different types of authority that relate to an agency agreement, including actual authority. Chapter 3 seeks to provide an overview of the legal obligations that an agent owes to his principal. These include, for example, the duty to carry out contractual obligations; to obey the principal's instructions; that the agent must not exceed his authority; the performance of contractual duties; that the agent must exercise due care and skill; the duty not to make a secret profit; not to allow any conflict of interest; and the fiduciary duties not to take a bribe or make a secret profit and to account. The chapter also outlines the rights of an agent, beginning with a discussion of the implications of a disclosed agency, a situation where the third party knows of the existence of the principal, and then dealing with an undisclosed agency, a situation where the agent acts for a principal who is not disclosed to the third party.

Part 1 Chapter 1

Agency: An Introduction

Contents

1 Introduction

Part 1 considers one of most important and traditional aspects of any commercial law undergraduate course, the law of agency. Chapter 1 begins by attempting to define the law of agency by providing several examples from commercial law scholars, illustrating the difficulty experienced by the courts in England and Wales in defining the term 'agency'. The next part of the chapter deals with the nature and characteristics of agency, followed by a brief outline of the different types of agents that exist in the United Kingdom.

2 What is agency?

It is virtually impossible to provide a clear all-embracing definition of agency.[1] Rather unsurprisingly this has resulted in many commentators arguing that the courts have given it an extremely broad and flexible interpretation.[2] The breadth of the interpretation of the term 'agency' is illustrated by the following quotation from an article by Gorton:

> In law the concept of 'agency' may have different meanings. Whereas in common law 'agency' is a wide concept covering the law related to 'authority' and 'power to

---

[1] R. Munday, *Agency: Law and Principles* (Oxford University Press, Oxford, 2010) 1.
[2] R. Bradgate, *Commercial Law* (Oxford University Press, Oxford, 2005) 126.

bind', the agent in, e.g. Scandinavian law is a particular kind of intermediary. In English law the concept of 'agent' may appear in different contexts: 'commercial agent', 'general agent', 'del credere agent', agent of necessity'.[3]

Professor Bradgate defined an agent as 'a person recognised by law as having power to affect legal rights, liabilities and relationships of another person ("the principal")'.[4] Similarly, Bowstead, in perhaps the most definitive guide on the law of agency, defined the term as 'the relationship which exists between two persons, one of whom expressly *consents* that the other should impliedly act on his behalf' (emphasis added).[5] It is important to note here the importance of the term 'consent', as the law of agency is based on this very important concept. The importance of consent in the legal relationships created by the law of agency was highlighted by Brown, who took the view that 'the common law's philosophy is that agency is a *consensual* relationship, with all authority emanating, in some form, from the principal' (emphasis added).[6] Several commentators have argued that the concept of 'consent' is the central tenant of the law of agency.[7] Its influence will be outlined throughout the first part of this book. A similar and very useful definition of agency was offered by Billins, who described it as 'the relationship by which a principal entrusts a transaction or aspect of his business to another (without there being a relationship of employer and employee) in which the most important elements of the relationship are the representation by the agent of the principal's interest and the scope of the agent's authority'.[8]

One of the most utilised definitions of agency is provided by the American Law Institute's Restatement of the Law: Agency, which defines agency as 'the fiduciary relationship that arises when one person (a principal) manifests assent to another person (an agent) that the agent shall act on the principal's behalf and subject to the principal's control, and the agent manifests assent or otherwise consents so to act'.[9] Halsbury's Laws of England defines an agent as 'an agent primarily means a person employed for the purpose of placing the principal in contractual or other relations with a third party'.[10] Dobson and Stokes defined agency as 'a relationship between one person, the principal, and another, the agent, under which the agent will fulfil the intentions of the principal and act on his behalf, generally through the creation, modification or termination of contracts with a third party'.[11]

---

[3] L. Gorton, 'Ships management agreements' (1991) *Journal of Business Law* (Nov.) 562 at 563–4.
[4] Bradgate, above n. 2, at 126.
[5] *Bowstead on Agency* (15th edn, Sweet and Maxwell, London, 1985) 1.
[6] I. Brown 'The agent's apparent authority: paradigm or paradox?' (1995) *Journal of Business Law* (Jul.) 360 at 360–1.
[7] B. Markesinis and R. Munday *An Outline of the Law of Agency* (Butterworths, London, 1992) 4.
[8] R. Billins, *Agency Law* (Sweet and Maxwell, London, 1993).
[9] As cited in Munday, above n. 1, at 1.
[10] As cited in Gorton, above n. 3, at 562.
[11] P. Dobson and R. Stokes, *Commercial Law* (Sweet and Maxwell, London, 2008) 425.

These academic definitions of agency refer to a number of important points, in particular the existence of a legal agreement that consists of three parties: an agent, a principal and a third party. Furthermore, the definitions often refer to a contractual agreement (often described as an agency agreement) and the scope of an agent's authority. The difficulty of defining the term 'agent' has also been recognised by the judiciary. For example, Lord Herschell took the view in *Kennedy* v. *De Trafford*:

> No word is more commonly and constantly abused than the word 'agent'. A person may be spoken of as an 'agent', and no doubt in the popular sense of the word may properly be said to be an 'agent', although when it is attempted to suggest that he is an 'agent' under such circumstances as create the legal obligations attaching to agency that use of the word is only misleading.[12]

Further evidence of the problems associated with defining the term 'agency' is provided by the following quote from Sir John Donaldson in *Potter* v. *Customs and Excise Commissioners*:

> The use of the word 'agent' in any mercantile transaction is, of itself, wholly uninformative of the legal relationship between the parties, and the use of the words 'independent agent' takes the matter no further. Either is consistent with a self-employed person acting either as a true agent who puts his principal into a contractual relationship with a third party or with such a person acting as principal.[13]

In the case of *Garnac Grain Co. Inc.* v. *H. M. F. Faure and Fairclough Ltd*,[14] Lord Pearson stated that 'the relationship of principal and agent ... can only be established by the consent of the principal and agent'. However, Lord Peterson stated they the agent and principal could be deemed to have consented 'if they have agreed to what in law amounts to such a relationship, even if they do not recognise it themselves ... but the consent must have been given by each of them, either expressly or by implication from their words and conduct'.[15] In *Boardman* v. *Phipps*, the House of Lords stated that an agency agreement existed despite no consent by the principal.[16] *Chitty on Contracts* states 'at common law the word "agency" can be said to represent a body of general rules under which one person, the agent, has the power to change the legal relations of another, the principal'.[17] Therefore, an agency agreement includes three parties: first, the 'principal' who empowers the agent to act on his behalf and follow a particular set of instructions; secondly, the 'agent' who, whilst representing the principal, confers with a third party to agree a contract between the principal and third

[12] [1897] AC 180, 188 as cited in Munday, above n. 1, at 1. For a brief discussion of this case see P. Omar, 'A delicate balance of interests: the power of sale and the duty to maximise asset values' (2005) *Conveyancer and Property Lawyer* (Sep./Oct.) 380.
[13] [1985] STC 45, 51, as cited in Munday, above n. 1, at 2.
[14] [1968] AC 1130n.   [15] [1968] AC 1130.   [16] [1967] 2 AC 46.
[17] *Chitty on Contracts* (29th edn, Sweet and Maxwell, London, 2004) vol. I, General Principles.

party; thirdly, the 'third party', who enters into an agreement with the principal based on representations and negotiations with the principal's agent. Agency comprises three legal relationships: first, there is the internal relationship between the agent and the principal; secondly, there is the external relationship between the agent and the third party; finally, there is the potential relationship between the principal and the third party.[18] Therefore, agency is the process by which a contractual agreement is arranged between a principal and a third party, based on the actions and representations of the agent. Agents play a very important role in the commercial world,[19] and their role is to 'negotiate and conclude contracts on behalf of someone else: the principal.'[20]

Q1 *What is agency?*

3 Nature and characteristics of agency

An agency can be created by a wide range of legal mechanisms. For example, *Chitty on Contracts* notes that the association between a principal and agent can be established by an express or implied agreement; by ratification of the agent's actions by the principal; by law; and by the case of agency of necessity. The text adds that 'the principal may be bound under the doctrines of apparent authority or in some cases under the general doctrine of estoppel.'[21]

Agency can, for example, be created by express formation, which involves a contractual agreement or agency agreement between agent and principal. Munday noted that 'the agreement between a principal and his agent may either be express or implied. The great majority of agency agreements will in fact be contractual.'[22] Nonetheless, the court in *Yasuda Fire & Marine Insurance Co. of Europe Ltd* v. *Orion Marine Insurance Underwriting Agency Ltd* determined that:

> Although in modern commercial transactions agencies are almost invariably founded upon a contract between principal and agent, there is no necessity for such a contract to exist. It is sufficient if there is consent by the principal to the exercise by the agent of authority and consent by the agent to his exercising such authority on behalf of the principal.[23]

---

[18] Dobson and Stokes, above n. 11, at 425.
[19] Bradgate, above n. 2, at 126.   [20] *Ibid.*
[21] *Chitty on Contracts,* above n. 17, Creation of Agency, 31–020.
[22] As cited in Munday, above n. 1, at 35.
[23] *Yasuda Fire & Marine Insurance Co. of Europe Ltd* v. *Orion Marine Insurance Underwriting Agency Ltd* [1995] QB 174. For a more detailed discussion of this case see E. Fennell, 'Yasuda Fire & Marine Insurance Co. of Europe Ltd v Orion Marine Insurance Underwriting Agency Ltd and another: case comment' (1995) 3(4) *Journal of Financial Regulation and Compliance* 391 and S. Honeyball and D. Pearce, 'Contract, employment and the contract of employment' (2006) 35(1) *Industrial Law Journal* 30. In this case the court relied on the statement of Lord Pearson in *Garnac Grain Co. Inc.* v. *H.M.F. Faure & Fairclough Ltd* [1968] AC 1130, 1137.

If a contract or agency agreement exists between the agent and principal, the agent will be granted what is referred to as actual authority. This term will be discussed in greater detail below. An agency can also be created by an agreement which could be classified as an implied agreement. Furthermore, it can also be established by estoppel. Such instances traditionally relate to instances where a principal implies that another person is acting as their agent, which person will then be deemed to be acting with apparent authority.

In order for an agency to be created by estoppel a number of circumstances must exist. These include that there must be a representation that the authority as agent exists. The representation must be of fact and not law, made by the principal to a third party, and must be to the effect that the agent is permitted to operate as an agent. The third party must have authentic knowledge of the representation and depend on the representation from the agent and therefore agree to enter into a contract with the agent.

Ratification is another mechanism by which an agency can be created. Here, the agency is created even if the early actions of the agent were not authorised by the principal and in such instance the principal could acquire rights and be subjected to liabilities by retrospectively endorsing the agency. In order for the unsanctioned actions of the agent to be ratified, several requirements must be met. These include the existence of an agreement between the agent and principal; the principal must have the competence to act and have been in existence at the time of the contract; the principal must ratify the actions within a reasonable time and the ratification must be undeniable.

An agency can also be created under certain statutory provisions including the Consumer Credit Act 1974, Bills of Exchange Act 1882,[24] Limitation Act 1980,[25] Trustee Delegation Act 1999 and Trustee Act 2000.[26]

Perhaps the most important and controversial part of the law of agency is the notion or concept of 'authority'. This refers to 'the scope of the agent's ability to affect the legal position'.[27] Generally, there are three different types of authority. First, express actual authority, which has been defined as established by the principal on the agent. This type of authority is often supported by a further type of actual authority, which is referred to as 'implied actual authority'.[28] The second type of authority is usual authority, which has been defined as meaning 'an agent will be deemed to have the authority that an agent in his position would normally have'.[29] Finally, apparent authority has been defined as where 'an agent who acts outside his actual authority will still be able to bind his principal where the principal has made a representation to the third party that the agent is acting within his authority'.[30] Each of the different types of authority will be discussed in more detail below.

---

[24] Bills of Exchange Act 1882, ss.22–26.
[25] Limitation Act 1980, s.24.
[26] Trustee Act 2000, ss.11–23.
[27] Dobson and Stokes, above n. 11, at 426.
[28] *Ibid.*   [29] *Ibid.*   [30] *Ibid.*

Q2 Who are the main parties involved in an agency agreement?

4 The different types of agency

Professor Bradgate, in his seminal book *Commercial Law*, stated that there are a wide range of agents who are not specifically referred to as agents by name or title. For example, he refers to company directors, partners, employees, professionals and finance companies. However, he goes on to note that via judicial precedent and commercial practice, a number of specific types of agents have been created.

(a) General and special agents

A general agent, as the title suggests, is appointed by the principal and is given a very broad remit to perform a 'general' set of duties. Conversely, a special agent is often appointed by the principal to perform a very special or specific task. However, Bradgate noted that this distinction is no more than a merely historical difference and the appointment of a special agent is not commercially attractive.[31]

(b) Mercantile agent

A mercantile agent is often associated with the industrialisation that occurred during the Industrial Revolution in the eighteenth and nineteenth centuries in the United Kingdom. This resulted in a significant proportion of the country's trade being processed through agents, who were also called factors, on behalf of their principals. Merrett stated that 'from the eighteenth century onwards, it had become common for merchants wishing to sell goods to entrust them to agents. An agent who was entrusted with possession of goods was often referred to as a factor'.[32] In many circumstances, the factor was regarded as a 'professional agent who traded in goods'.[33] The position and role of a factor is succinctly commented on in *Chitty on Contracts*:

> The distinction between these was important in nineteenth-century commerce and is still important for the understanding of old cases. A factor was an agent entrusted with the possession and control of goods to be sold by him for his principal. In this respect he differed from a broker, the latter not having generally such possession or control, but being a mere negotiator empowered to effect contracts of sale or purchase for others. A factor was therefore entitled to contract in his own name and to receive payment, and his lien over the goods gave him a special contractual right, which should probably now be explained as based on

---

[31] Bradgate, above n. 2, at 413.
[32] L. Merrett, 'The importance of delivery and possession in the passing of title' (2008) 67(2) *Cambridge Law Journal* 376 at 379.
[33] Bradgate, above n. 2, at 413.

a collateral contract, entitling him to sue in priority to his principal. He might also sell goods which he had bought; and the third party would not always know whether he was doing this, or selling for his principal. These propositions were not normally true of brokers, who negotiated and often concluded contracts in respect of goods which they did not hold at all, and might be assumed to be dealing for others. The term 'factor' is however not used in this sense in England nowadays, and the term 'broker' has subsequently been applied to a much wider range of occupations, starting with stockbrokers but extending much further.[34]

Factors were also referred to as 'commission agents or commission merchants, although these expressions were frequently used in practice for purchasing agents'.[35] Prior to the introduction of the Factors Act 1889, the courts offered some guidance on the definition of a factor. For example, in the case of *Stevens* v. *Biller*, Cotton LJ defined a factor as 'an agent, but an agent of a particular kind. He is an agent entrusted with the possession of goods for the purpose of sale. That is the true definition of a factor.'[36] As a result of the introduction of a number of Factors Acts which 'were partly a confirmation and partly an alteration of the law',[37] the first of which was introduced in 1823, a mercantile agent can be defined as follows:

> Where a mercantile agent is, with the consent of the owner, in possession of goods or of the documents of title to goods, any sale, pledge, or other disposition of the goods, made by him when acting in the ordinary course of business of a mercantile agent, shall, subject to the provisions of this Act, be as valid as if he were expressly authorised by the owner of the goods to make the same; provided that the person taking under the disposition acts in good faith, and has not at the time of the disposition notice that the person making the disposition has not authority to make the same.[38]

Bradgate took the view that mercantile agents are agents 'whose business is to dispose of goods on behalf of principals and who are given possession of the goods for that purpose'.[39] The Factors Act 1889 gave mercantile agents an extensive array of powers to pass title to goods that belong to the principal which are in the agent's possession.[40] Munday took the view that the Act 'confers a wide authority upon certain classes of agent to transfer good title in their principal's goods to third parties, even though they have no express authority'.[41]

(c) Broker

A broker has been referred to as an important historical type of agent, and the term is rarely used in modern commercial practices. Nonetheless, a broker has

---

[34] *Chitty on Contracts*, above n. 17, Factors and Brokers, 31–009.
[35] D. Ward and J. Jones, 'Agents as permanent establishments under the OECD Model Tax Convention' (1993) 5 *British Tax Review* 341 at 362.
[36] (1883) 25 Ch. D 31, 37.   [37] Merrett, above n. 32, at 378.
[38] Factors Act 1889, s.2(1).   [39] Bradgate, above n. 2, at 312.
[40] As cited in Munday, above n. 1, at 5.
[41] Markesinis and Munday, above n. 7, at 21.

been defined as an agent who 'negotiates contracts for the sale and purchase of goods and other property but does not have possession of the goods'.[42]

(d) *Del credere* agent

This type of agent is normally involved with credit insurance and in some cases is an agent who 'guarantees the price of goods purchased by a third party'.[43] Bradgate stated that this type of agent 'negotiates contracts for a principal and guarantees to the principal that the third party will pay any sums due under that contract; this may be important where the third party is not known to the principal. The del credere agent charges the principal an extra commission for providing the guarantee.'[44] This type of agency traditionally occurs when an agent has consented to a 'specially agreed commission to undertake to act as surety in respect of due performance of contracts he has entered into on behalf of his principal. *Chitty on Contracts* provides an excellent summary of the role and function of a *del credere* agent:

> An agent for the sale of goods sometimes acts under a *del credere* commission; that is, for a special commission, he becomes responsible to his principal for the solvency of the buyer; or, in other words, he guarantees to his principal, in cases of sale, the payment of the price of the goods sold, when ascertained and due. His liability is, however, limited to ascertained sums which become due as debts: the principal may not litigate with a *del credere* agent disputes arising out of contracts made by the agent. Nor does an agent as such become responsible to the third party for due performance by his principal. A *del credere* agency may be implied, or inferred from a course of conduct, and does not need to be evidenced in writing because, being merely incidental to another transaction, it is not a promise to answer for the debt, default or miscarriage of another within s.4 of the Statute of Frauds, i.e. not a guarantee. In modern commerce, such agency could involve enormous liabilities, and it has largely been superseded by credit guarantees, confirmations and the like.[45]

(e) Auctioneer

A very common type of agent is an auctioneer who is to a 'limited degree an agent of the buyer, he may well have a contractual relationship with him'.[46]

---

[42] Bradgate, above n. 2, at 132.
[43] *Mercantile International Group plc* v. *Chuan Soon Huat Industrial Group plc* [2002] 1 All ER (Comm) 788, as cited in Munday, above n. 1, at 5. For a brief discussion of this case see F. Randolph, 'Recent cases involving the Commercial Agents Regulations' (2001) 12(4) *International Company and Commercial Law Review* 127 at 129.
[44] Bradgate, above n. 2 at 132. For an illustration of the approach adopted by the courts to this type of agent see *Dowling and H.G. Hamilton Pty Ltd and Kelly* v. *Rae* (1927) 39 C.L.R. 363, as cited in A. Phipps, 'Resurrecting the doctrine of common law forbearance' (2007) 123 *Law Quarterly Review* (Apr.) 286 at 294.
[45] *Chitty on Contracts*, above n. 17, Del Credere Agents, 31–010.
[46] F. Meisel, 'Auctioneers and buyers: a special relationship?' (2005) 21(4) *Professional Negligence* 250.

An auctioneer has been described as an agent to sell at an open sale, who has, however, no authority to provide a warranty unless the auctioneer has been expressly permitted to do so.

(f) Confirming house

A confirming house is an agent traditionally employed during international contracts, usually to act on behalf of international clients who are keen to import certain goods.[47] A confirming house acts for a principal by purchasing goods and introducing them into the UK market and then reselling them to its clients.

(g) Estate agent

An estate agent is employed by the seller of a property to find a buyer for the property.[48] This is a very limited type of agency and the estate agent's authority is limited to merely providing a description of the property and its value to potential purchasers of the property. The duties owed by an estate agent were illustrated in the Privy Council decision in *Kelly* v. *Cooper*.[49] The Estate Agents Act 1979, section 1(1) provides a very useful interpretation and definition of an estate agent:

> things done by any person in the course of a business (including a business in which he is employed) pursuant to instructions received from another person (in this section referred to as 'the client') who wishes to dispose of or acquire an interest in land:
>
> (a) for the purpose of, or with a view to, effecting the introduction to the client of a third person who wishes to acquire or, as the case may be, dispose of such an interest; and
> (b) after such an introduction has been effected in the course of that business, for the purpose of securing the disposal or, as the case may be, the acquisition of that interest.[50]

(h) Gratuitous agent

A gratuitous agent can best be described as a non-contractual agent. These types of agencies are in the minority when compared to written agency. In

---

[47] For an illustration of the use of a confirming house in an agency agreement see E. Ellinger, 'The drawer's right of subrogation revisited' (1996) *Journal of Business Law* (Sep.) 399.
[48] For an interesting discussion of the law relating to estate agents see P. Morris, 'The ombudsman for corporate estate agents' (1994) 13 *Civil Justice Quarterly* (Oct.) 337.
[49] [1992] 3 WLR 936. For a more detailed discussion see I. Brown, 'Divided loyalties in the law of agency' (1993) 109 *Law Quarterly Review* (Apr.) 206.
[50] Estate Agents Act 1979, s.1(1).

Yasuda Fire & Marine Insurance Co. of Europe Ltd v. *Orion Marine Insurance Underwriting Agency Ltd,* Colman J outlined the importance of non-contractual agreements:

> Although in modern commercial transactions agencies are almost invariably founded upon a contract between principal and agent, there is no necessity for such a contract to exist. It is sufficient if there is consent by the principal to the exercise by the agent of authority and consent by the agent to his exercising such authority on behalf of the principal.[51]

(i) Commercial agent

A commercial agent was created by the provisions of the Commercial Agents (Council Directive) Regulations 1993.[52] This Statutory Instrument was based on the Commercial Agents Directive introduced by the European Union in 1986.[53] Gardiner noted that the purpose of the Directive was to:

> Harmonise the laws of the Member States so as to address the problem of differences in national laws concerning the conclusion and operation of commercial agency contracts. According to the preamble, such differences are detrimental to the protection available to commercial agents and to the security of commercial transactions, and substantially inhibit the conclusion and operation of commercial representation contracts where principal and agents are established in different Member States. The Directive set out to provide for minimum rules to establish a common level of protection to commercial agents.[54]

The Commercial Agents Directive defines a commercial agent as 'a self-employed intermediary who has continuing authority to negotiate the sale or purchase of goods on behalf of another person, hereinafter called the "principal", or to negotiate and conclude such transactions on behalf of and in the name of that principal'.[55] A commercial agent is defined in the 1993 Regulations as 'a self-employed intermediary who has continuing authority to negotiate the sale or purchase of goods on behalf of another person (the "principal"), or to negotiate and conclude the sale or purchase of goods on behalf of and in the name of that principal'.[56]

Q3 How many different types of agents can you think of? What is the role of each agent?

---

[51] [1995] QB 174, as cited in Munday, above n. 1, at 35.
[52] SI 1993/3053.
[53] Council Directive 86/653/EC of 18 December 1986 on the co-ordination of the laws of Member States relating to self-employed commercial agents, [1986] OJ L382/17.
[54] C. Gardiner, 'The EC (Commercial Agents) Directive: twenty years after its introduction, divergent approaches still emerge from Irish and UK courts' (2007) *Journal of Business Law* (June) 412.
[55] Article 1(2).
[56] Commercial Agents (Council Directive) Regulations 1993, SI 1993/3053, reg. 2(1).

Q4 What is the definition of a commercial agent?

5 Conclusion

This chapter has provided a very brief overview of the essential requirements for the existence of an agency agreement between three parties, the agent, the principal and the third party. It has also discussed the different and common features and the interpretation of several key phrases that will provide a useful reference for the remaining chapters in Part 1.

6 Recommended reading

Bradgate, R. *Commercial Law* (3rd edn, Oxford University Press, Oxford, 2000)

Brown, I. 'The agent's apparent authority: paradigm or paradox?' (1995) *Journal of Business Law* 360.

Dobson, P. and Stokes, R. *Commercial Law* (7th edn, Sweet and Maxwell, London, 2008) 425

Markesinis, B. and Munday, R. *An Outline of the Law of Agency* (Butterworths, London, 1992) 4

Munday, R. *Agency: Law and Principles* (Oxford University Press, Oxford, 2010)

Part 1 Chapter 2

The Authority of an Agent

Contents

1 Introduction

The purpose of Part 1 Chapter 2 is to provide a detailed commentary on the different types of authority that relate to an agency agreement, including actual authority.

2 The authority of an agent

Chapter 1 highlighted the problems associated with defining the terms 'agent' and 'agency'. Somewhat unsurprisingly, the same problem arises with respect to the different categories of authority. Bradgate pointed out that 'one of the great difficulties of the law of agency is that terminology is not used consistently'.[1] For the purposes of this chapter, we will look at actual authority (both express and implied), apparent authority and usual authority.

(a) Actual authority

The actual authority of an agency is granted by an agreement with the principal, which could be classified either as 'implied' or 'express' authority. This was a point famously referred to by Lord Denning MR in *Hely-Hutchinson* v. *Brayhead Ltd*:

---

[1] R. Bradgate, *Commercial Law* (Oxford University Press, Oxford, 2005) 140.

actual authority may be express or implied. It is express when it is given by words, such as when a board of directors pass a resolution which authorises two of their number to sign cheques. It is implied when it is inferred from the conduct of the parties and the circumstances of the case, such as when the board of directors appoint one of their number to be managing director. They thereby impliedly authorise him to do all such things as fall within the usual scope of his office.[2]

Several commentators have offered very similar definitions of actual authority. For example, Munday stated that 'actual authority refers to authority the agent possesses either because the principal has expressly conferred that authority upon him (express actual authority) or because the law regards the authority as having been conferred upon the agent by necessary implication (implied actual authority)'.[3] Writing in 1992, Markesinis and Munday took the view that 'actual authority is the authority the agent actually has pursuant to the consensual agreement which has been reached between himself and his principal. It is, in other words, real authority.'[4] More recently, Dobson and Stokes described this as follows:

> certainly the most straightforward situation is that where the agency relationship is created by express agreement. In such a case, the agreement will, to some extent at least, dictate the scope of the agent's authority. This is called 'actual authority': the agent can properly do anything detailed within the agreement.[5]

Actual authority may be 'express' or 'implied', and has also been referred to as 'usual' and even 'customary' authority.[6] Indeed, Stone went so far as to argue that there were six different phrases that could be used:

> an agent's ability to bind his principal exceeds his actual authority, *viz.* 'implied authority', 'usual authority', 'customary authority', 'ostensible authority', 'apparent authority', and 'agency by estoppel'. Very roughly, the first three are used to describe the situation where the agent's authority arises from the nature of the job or position which he holds. The last three apply where the principal has made some representation of the agent's authority, which he is then not allowed to retract.[7]

The English and Welsh courts have on several occasions attempted to define actual authority. One of the most famous attempts was made by Diplock LJ in *Freeman & Lockyer (a firm)* v. *Buckhurst Park Properties (Mangal) Ltd*:

> An 'actual' authority is a legal relationship between principal and agent created by a consensual agreement to which they alone are parties. Its scope is to be

---

[2] [1968] 1 QB 549, 583.

[3] R. Munday, *Agency: Law and Principles* (Oxford University Press, Oxford, 2010) 41.

[4] B. Markesinis and R. Munday, *An Outline of the Law of Agency* (Butterworths, London, 1992) 21.

[5] P. Dobson and R. Stokes, *Commercial Law* (7th edn, Sweet and Maxwell, London, 2008) 429.

[6] See Bradgate, above n. 1, at 140.

[7] R. Stone, 'Usual and ostensible authority: one concept or two?' (1993) *Journal of Business Law* (Jul.) 325.

ascertained by applying ordinary principles of construction of contracts, including any proper implications from the express words used, the usages of the trade,
or the course of business between the parties. To this agreement the contractor
is a stranger; he may be totally ignorant of the existence of any authority on the
part of the agent. Nevertheless, if the agent does enter into a contract pursuant to
the 'actual' authority, it does create contractual rights and liabilities between the
principal and the contractor. It may be that this rule relating to 'undisclosed principals', which is peculiar to English law, can be rationalized as avoiding circuity of
action, for the principal could in equity compel the agent to lend his name in an
action to enforce the contract against the contractor, and would at common law
be liable to indemnify the agent in respect of the performance of the obligations
assumed by the agent under the contract.[8]

However, it is important to note that the degree of authority granted to the
agency is heavily dependent on the terms of the agreement.[9]

(b) Implied actual authority

Implied authority can be created by implication, and it will be governed by the
general law of contract.[10] For example, in the famous case of *Hely-Hutchinson* v.
Brayhead Ltd, a company's directors permitted its chairman to act as if he was
its managing director. Here, the Court of Appeal determined that the chairman
had implied actual authority to act in the capacity of the company's managing
director.[11] In *Garnac Grain Co. Inc.* v. *H. M. F. Faure and Fairclough Ltd*, Lord
Pearson stated that:

> The relationship of principal and agent can only be established by the consent
> of the principal and the agent. They will be held to have consented if they have
> agreed to what amounts in law to such a relationship, even if they do not recog-
> nise it themselves and even if they have professed to disclaim it.[12]

Furthermore, actual authority could be implied by the conduct of the parties, the conditions of the case, trade or custom.[13] However, it has been argued
that the relationship between the agent and principal does not have to be contractual.[14] Indeed, Bradgate noted that 'as a general rule no formalities are
required for the appointment of an agent … [therefore] the agreement …
may be express or implied, and if express, may be made orally, in writing, or
by deed'.[15] Nonetheless, if the agency accord is governed by the Commercial
Agents (Council Directive) Regulations 1993,[16] the principal and agent are permitted to request a written statement outlining the rights and obligations of the

---

[8] [1964] 2 QB 480, 502.
[9] Dobson and Stokes, above n. 5, at 430.   [10] *Ibid.*
[11] [1967] 3 All ER 98.   [12] [1967] 2 All ER 353, 358, HL.
[13] Munday, above n. 3, at 1.   [14] See Bradgate, above n. 1, at 141.
[15] *Ibid.*   [16] SI 1993/3053.

signatories,[17] the remuneration[18] and the conclusion and termination of the contract.[19] Sasse and Whittaker stated that:

> the Commercial Agents (Council Directive) Regulations 1993 came into force on 1 January 1994 and implement European Council Directive 86/653 of 18 December 1986 designed to harmonise the laws of the Member States relating to commercial agents. The Regulations have retrospective effect and will mean that agents appointed under new or existing contracts will automatically have much better legal protection.[20]

They added:

> Before the Regulations came into force it had long been a tradition of UK law that, although certain terms were implied into agency arrangements by common law, agents and principals were to a large extent free to agree whatever terms they wished. The effect of the Regulations will be to impose a statutory framework on many types of commercial agency agreements where an agent performs duties on behalf of his principal anywhere in the United Kingdom, a point clarified in the final text. Many of the Regulations are mandatory and, as a result, even if the agreement is silent on a particular point or if the parties wish to agree terms to the contrary, the provisions of the Regulations will still apply and may override the wishes of the parties.[21]

Importantly, the 1993 Regulations require the principal and agent to undertake certain obligations. For example, a principal is required to act in good faith and provide agents with all of the relevant paperwork. Furthermore, the principal is required to notify the agent of any acceptance or rejection of any order agreed by the agent.[22] Amongst the most controversial aspects of the 1993 Regulations were its provisions that related to the compensation or indemnity of agents.[23] Connal stated that:

> article 17 provides for a potential payment to an agent on his … agency coming to an end. The agent is either to be 'indemnified', a concept said to be derived from provisions in German law, or 'compensated for damage', a provision said to be derived from provisions of French law. The Directive allowed Member States the freedom to adopt either approach. In implementing the Directive the UK determined that the choice of option would in turn be left to parties to a contract. In the absence of specific contractual provision – which might of course arise if parties did not turn their attention to this particular matter or indeed did not know

---

[17] *Ibid.* reg. 3–5.   [18] *Ibid.* regs. 13–20.   [19] *Ibid.* regs. 21–23.

[20] S. Sasse and J. Whittaker, 'An assessment of the impact of the UK Commercial Agents (Council Directive) Regulations 1993' (1994) 5(3) *International Company and Commercial Law Review* 100.

[21] *Ibid.*   [22] Sasse and Whittaker, above n. 20.

[23] SI 1993/3053, reg. 17. For a detailed illustration of these measures see *Accentuate Ltd* v. *Asigra Inc.* [2010] 2 All ER (Comm) 738 as cited in H. Dundas, 'Case comment: EU law versus New York Convention – who wins? Accentuate Ltd v Asigra Inc' (2010) 76(1) *Arbitration* 159.

that their contract was a regulated commercial agency – the default position was to be compensation.[24]

(c) Express actual authority

Express actual authority is traditionally granted by the principal to the agent via an agency agreement. Bradgate noted that as there are no formal requirements for the appointment of an agent, the agreement could be express, implied, in writing, made orally or by deed.[25] In the case of *Heard* v. *Pilley,* the court determined that a contract entered into for the purchase of land by the agent could be enforced even though the agent was not appointed in writing.[26] In cases where the agent is appointed by deed, the customary strict rules for the execution of deeds apply.[27]

Q1 What is actual authority?

(d) Apparent or ostensible authority

Apparent authority is also referred to as ostensible authority, and it 'arises where a third party is induced to enter into a transaction with a principal by a party who appears to have authority to act but who in fact lacks such authority'.[28] Apparent authority is the authority granted to an agent via estoppel. Bradgate stated that 'a principal is bound by the authorised acts of his agents because he has consented to them and to be bound. A person may also be bound by acts done by another on his behalf without his consent, or even in breach of an express prohibition, if his words or actions give the impression that he has authorised them.'[29] Apparent authority was famously defined by Doplock LJ in *Freeman & Lockyer (a firm)* v. *Buckhurst Park Properties (Mangal) Ltd* as follows:

> An 'apparent' or 'ostensible' authority, on the other hand, is a legal relationship between the principal and the contractor created by a representation, made by the principal to the contractor, intended to be and in fact acted upon by the contractor, that the agent has authority to enter on behalf of the principal into a contract of a kind within the scope of the 'apparent' authority, so as to render the principal liable to perform any obligations imposed upon him by such contract. To the relationship so created the agent is a stranger. He need not be (although he generally is) aware of the existence of the representation but he must not purport to make the agreement as principal himself. The representation, when acted upon

---

[24] R. Connal, 'Compensation under the Commercial Agents (Council Directive) Regulations 1993' (2007) 28 *Scots Law Times* 211.

[25] See Bradgate, above n. 1, at 141.

[26] (1868–69) LR 4 Ch. App. 548. The decision in *Heard* v. *Pilley* was subsequently applied in *McLaughlin* v. *Duffill* [2008] EWCA Civ 1627; [2010] Ch. 1.

[27] Markesinis and Munday, above n. 4.

[28] Munday, above n. 3, at 59.   [29] See Bradgate, above n. 1, at 144.

by the contractor by entering into a contract with the agent, operates as an estoppel, preventing the principal from asserting that he is not bound by the contract. It is irrelevant whether the agent had actual authority to enter into the contract.[30]

In *ING Re (UK) Ltd* v. *R & V Versicherung AG*, Toulson J took the view that:

> The doctrine of apparent or ostensible authority is based on estoppel by representation. Where a principal (P) represents or causes it to be represented to a third party (T) that an agent (A) has authority to act on P's behalf, and T deals with A as P's agent on the faith of that representation, P is bound by A's acts to the same extent as if A had the authority which he was represented as having.[31]

Ostensible authority refers to the authority of an agent that he 'seems' to have. Byles J in *Totterdell* v. *Fareham Blue Brick and Tile Co. Ltd* stated that:

> a principal is bound, not only by such acts of the agent as are within the scope of the agent's actual authority, but by such acts as are within the larger margin of an apparent or ostensible authority derived from the representations, acts, or default of the principal.[32]

Similarly, Lord Keith of Kinkel in *Armagas Ltd* v. *Mundogas SA* stated:

> ostensible authority comes about where the principal, by words or conduct, has represented that the agent has the requisite actual authority, and the party dealing with the agent had entered into a contract with him in reliance on that representation.[33]

Dobson and Stokes noted that 'the first situation where an agency relationship can be formed despite there being no express agreement to that effect is that where estoppel is established'.[34] In essence, this means that where the principal directs the third party to believe that the other person is acting as his agent 'the courts can find that there is an agent-principal-third party agreement accordingly'.[35] Reynolds took the view that:

> The agent may also bind his principal under the doctrine of apparent authority. This doctrine, which may depend on estoppel but is probably better based on the same reasoning as that which holds contracting parties to the objective appearances of intention which they create, is said to depend on a manifestation (or 'holding out') by the principal to the third party that the agent has authority. The third party is normally entitled to assume that the agent had the authority

---

[30] [1964] 2 QB 480, 502. For a critical review of this case and the issue of apparent authority see I. Brown, 'The significance of general and special authority in the development of the agent's external authority in English law' (2004) *Journal of Business Law* (Jul.) 391.

[31] [2006] 2 All ER (Comm) 870 at para. 99. This case dealt with the question of whether or not a reinsurer was bound by a quota share treaty that had not been approved by the reinsurer and had been entered into by an agent with no actual or ostensible authority. For a brief discussion of this case see A. Street, 'Ostensible authority and ratification' (2006) 119 *Insurance and Reinsurance Law Briefing* (Sept.) 1.

[32] (1865–66) LR 1 CP 674, 677–8.   [33] [1986] AC 717.

[34] Dobson and Stokes, above n. 5, at 432.   [35] *Ibid.*

which would normally be implied under the circumstances, in accordance with the principles of implied authority summarised in the previous paragraph, unless he knows or is to be taken as knowing (another controversial point in the doctrine) that the authority has in fact been withheld.[36]

In *Rama Corp.* v. *Proved Tin and General Investment Ltd*, the court decided that a person who entered into a contract with a company, who had no knowledge of the company's articles of association, could not rely on them as bestowing ostensible or apparent authority on the agent of the company.[37] Here, Slade J said that ostensible authority was a kind of estoppel, and that, therefore, what was needed was '(i) a representation, (ii) a reliance on the representation, and (iii) an alteration of your position resulting from such reliance'.[38] Diplock LJ in *Freeman & Lockyer (a firm)* v. *Buckhurst Park Properties (Mangal) Ltd* stated that:

> An 'apparent' or 'ostensible' authority, on the other hand, is a legal relationship between the principal and the contractor created by a representation, made by the principal to the contractor, intended to be and in fact acted upon by the contractor, that the agent has authority to enter on behalf of the principal into a contract of a kind within the scope of the 'apparent' authority, so as to render the principal liable to perform any obligations imposed upon him by such contract.[39]

This definition has attracted some criticism from several commentators. For example, Brown took the view that 'it is arguable that this archetype of apparent authority is both inadequate and inapt when applied to the complexities of organisational behaviour in the late twentieth century where agents act on behalf of transnational, impersonal corporations'.[40]

Q2 What is apparent authority?

(e) Usual authority

Usual authority can be classified as either actual authority or apparent authority. Dobson and Stokes took the view that 'usual authority is primarily a sub-division of actual, implied authority and thus emanates from, and enlarges the scope of, the actual authority which exists in its own right as an independent category of authority'.[41] However, 'difficulty is caused by a small group of cases dating mainly from the nineteenth century, which do not fit easily into the framework of actual and apparent authority'.[42] The leading case is *Watteau* v. *Fenwick*.[43] This has been described by many commentators

---

[36] F. Reynolds, 'Case comment: apparent authority' (1994) *Journal of Business Law* (Mar.) 144.
[37] [1952] 2 QB 147. See C. Noonan and S. Watson, 'Examining company directors through the lens of de facto directorship' (2008) 7 *Journal of Business Law* 587 at 619–20.
[38] [1952] 2 QB 147.   [39] [1964] 2 QB 480, 502.
[40] Brown, above n. 30, at 362.   [41] Dobson and Stokes, above n. 5, at 432.
[42] See Bradgate, above n. 1, at 151.   [43] [1893] 1 QB 146.

as 'problematic',[44] and in *Rhodian River Shipping Co. SA and Rhodian Sailor Shipping Co. SA* v. *Halla Maritime Corp.*,[45] Bingham J expressed his dissatisfaction with the decision in *Watteau* and took the view that 'I would myself be extremely wary of applying this doctrine, if it exists'.[46] In *Watteau*, the defendants, who were a firm of brewers, appointed a manager of a public house and a licence was taken out in the manager's name. The manager and the defendants reached an agreement that the manager was not permitted to purchase specific items for the purpose of the business, which were to be supplied by the defendants. In breach of this agreement, the manager purchased articles from the plaintiff, in this instance cigars, to utilise in the business. On discovering that the manager was not the owner of the premises, the plaintiff sued the defendants for the value of the goods. The court held that the plaintiff was successful and that the defendants were responsible for the actions of the manager as agent which were within the authority usually conferred upon an agent of this particular character. Wills J stated:

> the principal is liable for all the acts of the agent which are within the authority usually confided to an agent of that character, notwithstanding limitations, as between the principal and the agent, put upon that authority. It is said that it is only so where there has been a holding out of authority – which cannot be said of a case where the person supplying the goods knew nothing of the existence of a principal. But I do not think so. Otherwise, in every case of undisclosed principal, or at least in every case where the fact of there being a principal was undisclosed, the secret limitation of authority would prevail and defeat the action of the person dealing with the agent and then discovering that he was an agent and had a principal.[47]

Stone noted that:

> He [Wills J] thought that this could not be the case, because it was clearly established in partnership law that no limitation of authority as between dormant and active partner will protect the dormant partner as to things within the ordinary authority of a partner. Since the law of partnership is on this issue simply a branch of the general law of agency, the same approach should apply in situations other than partnership.[48]

It has been argued that Wills J was swayed by the fact that the principal in *Watteau* was undisclosed and that if the principal was disclosed 'the principal would have been liable on contracts made by his agent'.[49]

3 Agency by ratification

In most circumstances, an agent's level of authority will be granted by the principal before the agent acts. When this position is reversed, the agent's

---

[44] See Stone, above n. 7, at 327.   [45] [1984] 1 Lloyd's Rep. 373.

[46] [1984] 1 Lloyd's Rep. 373, 379.

[47] *Watteau* v. *Fenwick* [1893] 1 QB 146, 249–349.

[48] See Stone, above n. 7, at 328.   [49] Dobson and Stokes, above n. 5, at 436.

authority is ratified. Ratification was defined by Tindal CJ in *Wilson* v. *Tumman* as follows:

> That an act done, for another, by a person, not assuming to act for himself, but for such other person, though without any precedent authority whatever, becomes the act of the principal, if subsequently ratified by him, is the known and well established rule of law. In that case the principal is bound by the act, whether it be for his detriment or his advantage, and whether it be founded on a tort or a contract, to the same extent as by, and with all the consequences which follow from, the same act done by his previous authority.[50]

Munday took the view that:

> the doctrine of ratification is concerned with acts performed without authority by an agent in the name of a principal. If someone acts without the authority of a principal, either (i) because he exceeds the bounds of his actual authority, his apparent authority or any authority conferred by operation of law or (ii) because he was never employed as the principal's agent in the first place, the would-be principal may nevertheless be entitled to ratify a transaction effected in his name by the agent.[51]

In *Keighly, Maxsted & Co.* v. *Durant*, Lord Macnaghten stated:

> And so by a wholesome and convenient fiction, a person ratifying the act of another, who, without authority, has made a contract openly and avowedly on his behalf, is deemed to be, though in fact he was not, a party to the contract.[52]

According to Dobson and Stokes, the 'courts have imposed fairly restrictive requirements which must all be satisfied in order for ratification to be effective'.[53] The courts have imposed four particular requirements.[54]

For the first requirement to be met, it is essential that at the time the agent undertook or performed the unofficial business deal he professed to have acted on behalf of the principal who then ratifies the unofficial transaction. Bradgate stated that the 'principal can only ratify acts which were done in his name … an undisclosed principal can enforce a contract made with his authority, but an undisclosed principal can never ratify a contract'.[55] In *Keighley Maxsted & Co.* v. *Durant*,[56] Mr Roberts was authorised by the appellants to purchase wheat on a joint account for the appellants and himself at a particular price. Roberts entered into the contract using his own name, but intended it to be in respect of the joint account as agreed with the appellants, however the third party was not made aware of this. Subsequently, the appellants agreed with Roberts to accept the wheat on the joint account but failed to take delivery of the wheat. The third party resold the wheat at a loss and sued the appellants for the loss suffered. The House of Lords determined that the appellants were unable to

---

[50] (1843) 6 Manning and Granger 236, 242.
[51] Munday, above n. 3, at 105.   [52] [1901] AC 240, 247.
[53] Dobson and Stokes, above n. 5, at 432.   [54] *Ibid.* 438.
[55] See Bradgate, above n. 1, at 155.   [56] [1901] AC 240.

ratify the contract because the agent Roberts had not acknowledged that he was acting on the appellants' behalf when the contract was made. This can be viewed as a very restrictive decision, and Brown argued that it was 'peremptory and short-sighted'.[57] A change in approach was signalled by the decision in *Spiro* v. *Lintern*.[58] In this case, a husband was leaving his wife and wanted to sell his house. He asked his wife to make the necessary arrangements for an estate agent to locate a buyer for the property – however, it is important to note that the husband did not provide the wife with the authority to sell the property. The wife made arrangements with an estate agent to find a buyer for the property (the plaintiff), who entered into a written agreement with the wife to buy the property. The husband at no point stated that the wife had acted without his authority or that he was unwilling for the sale to progress, and the plaintiff was allowed to employ an architect and a gardener to undertake work on the house. The husband also informed the plaintiff's solicitor that he would not engage in any transactions with the house without informing the plaintiff. The husband granted his wife power of attorney to complete the sale of the property and signed a transfer of the property to the plaintiff before he left the country. The signed transfer of the property was never handed over to the plaintiff, and the wife subsequently sold the property to third party. The Court of Appeal found that the plaintiff had acted under a mistaken belief that the wife was under a duty to sell the house to him. Accordingly, the husband was under a duty to disclose to the plaintiff that the wife had acted without his authority and that 'his failure to do so amounted to a representation by conduct that she had his authority'. It was therefore held that the plaintiff had acted on the husband's representation and had suffered damage, and the husband was estopped from claiming that the contract had been entered into without his authority.[59]

The decision in *Keighley Maxsted & Co.* v. *Durant* has also been distinguished where an agent wrongly stated that he was acting on behalf of a principal. In such circumstances, the principal is permitted to ratify the contract entered into on their behalf by the agent.[60]

To satisfy the second requirement, the principal must be in existence at the time of the agent's action. This applies to agents who are acting on behalf of a company. Busch and Macgregor took the view that:

> A contract that purports to be made by or on behalf of a company at a time when the company has not been formed has effect, subject to any agreement to the

---

[57] Brown, above n. 30, at 394.   [58] [1973] 1 WLR 1002.

[59] Buckley LJ applied the principle of estoppel in this case and famously stated: 'If A sees B acting in the mistaken belief that A is under some binding obligation to him and in a manner consistent only with such an obligation, which would be to B's disadvantage if A were thereafter to deny the obligation, A is under a duty to B to disclose the non-existence of the supposed obligation' ([1973] 1 WLR 1002, 1011).

[60] See, e.g., *In re Tiedermann and Ledermann* v. *Freres* [1899] 2 QB 66.

contrary, as one made with the person purporting to act for the company or as agent for it, and he is personally liable on the contract accordingly.[61]

Legislation provides that if an agent for a company enters into a contract prior to its incorporation, the company is not permitted to ratify the agreement. Specifically, Companies Act 2006, section 51(1) stipulates:

> A contract that purports to be made by or on behalf of a company at a time when the company has not been formed has effect, subject to any agreement to the contrary, as one made with the person purporting to act for the company or as agent for it, and he is personally liable on the contract accordingly.[62]

Mayson, French and Ryan noted that this section applies even where a company was never registered, to a contract that was made by or on behalf of a company that was registered outside the United Kingdom, and even where the company was never incorporated.[63] The court was asked to consider the consequences of this section in *Phonogram Ltd* v. *Lane*.[64] This case related to a series of discussions for the financing of a new music group. During the negotiations, the plaintiffs considered creating and registering a company that would manage the new pop group and enter into contracts on their behalf. An agreement was signed by the defendant 'for and on behalf of' the proposed company and an early payment was made by the plaintiffs. The payment was refundable if the recording contract was entered into within one month. The proposed company was never formed and no recording contract was ever entered into. At first instance, the plaintiffs claimed the return of the sum advanced and the court decided that the defendant was personally liable. This decision was confirmed by the Court of Appeal because the contract was made by a company that had not been formed.[65] This case can be contrasted with the situation where an agent represents a company which has been bought 'off the shelf'. In such a situation, the company already exists and the actions of its agent can be ratified provided the agent clearly states he was acting on behalf of the company.[66]

To satisfy the third requirement, it is essential that the principal was competent to perform the contract at the time the agent supposedly acted on their behalf. One of the best examples of the operation of this rule is *Boston Deep Sea Fishing & Ice Co. Ltd* v. *Farnham (Inspector of Taxes)*.[67] In this case the

---

[61] D. Busch and L. Macgregor, 'Apparent authority in Scots law: some international perspectives' (2007) 11(3) *Edinburgh Law Review* 349 at 354.

[62] Companies Act 2006, s.51(1). This provision was based on the earlier provisions contained in Companies Act 1985, s.36C and Companies Act 1989, s.130(4).

[63] D. French, S. Mayson and C. Ryan, *Mayson, French and Ryan on Company Law* (Oxford University Press, Oxford, 2010) 626.

[64] [1982] QB 938.

[65] For a more detailed discussion of this case see J. Savirimuthu, 'Pre-incorporation contracts and the problem of corporate fundamentalism: are promoters proverbially profuse?' (2003) 24(7) *Company Lawyer* 196.

[66] N. Bourne, *Bourne on Company Law* (Routledge Cavendish, Abingdon, 2011) 46.

[67] [1957] 3 All ER 204.

appellants, who owned 49 per cent of the shares in a French company, were a company of trawler owners who had taken control of a trawler that was owned by the French company. The appellants had no authority from the French company for their actions but were granted permission by the Minister of War Transport and the Fisheries Section of the French Naval Forces to send the trawler to sea. The appellants were never appointed manager of the trawler but kept records of the ship's income and expenses. After the end of the Second World War, the trawler returned to France and the French company approved the appellants' actions. The court held that, at the time when the appellants acted as an agent of the French company, the French company was an alien enemy at common law, and therefore its attempted ratification was invalid.

The final requirement is that it must be possible to establish the identity of the principal at the time when the act was done. This point was explained in *Watson* v. *Swann*, where Willes J stated:

> To entitle a person to sue upon a contract, it must clearly be shown that he himself made it, or that it was made on his behalf by an agent authorised to act for him at the time, or whose act has been subsequently ratified and adopted by him. The law obviously requires that the person for whom the agent professes to act must be a person capable of being ascertained at the time. It is not necessary that he should be named; but there must be such a description of him as shall amount to a reasonable designation of the person intended to be bound by the contract.[68]

Therefore, it is essential that the specific principal who the agent represents must be ascertainable at the time of the agent's actions.[69]

Q3 What is the difference between actual and apparent authority?

4 Agency of necessity

Agency of necessity often arises when a person acts in an emergency, for example to protect the property interests of another person. This will result in the agent being authorised, even though there is no actual authority. In *China-Pacific SA* v. *Food Corporation of India (the Winson)*,[70] Lord Diplock discussed two different aspects of the law of agency of necessity: first, 'where an agent enters into a contract with a third party on behalf of the principal, consequently binding the principal contractually to the third party'; and secondly, 'where a person acts for another and subsequently seeks reimbursement or an indemnity from him'.[71] Whereas under an agency of necessity, privity of contract arises between the principal and third party, even where a person acts to

---

[68] (1862) 11 Common Bench Reports (New Series) 756; 142 ER 993.
[69] See Bradgate, above n. 1, at 155.
[70] [1982] AC 939.
[71] Dobson and Stokes, above n. 5, at 436–7.

preserve the property of a complete stranger, that person is unable to claim for reimbursement.[72]

Munday noted that 'there exist a number of situations in which the law will impose the incidents of agency where one party has acted on behalf of another in the course of an emergency. This occurs when one party (the agent) is confronted with an emergency that poses such an imminent threat to the property or other interests of another person (the principal) that there is insufficient time for the former to seek the latter's authority or instructions before acting.'[73] In the case of *Springer* v. *Great Western Railway Company*, the court determined that agency of necessity will only arise in extreme circumstances.[74] The court held that there must be 'an actual and definite commercial necessity' for the agent's action.[75] Bradgate noted that four requirements must be satisfied for the agency of necessity to arise. First, there must be an emergency. Secondly, as a result of the emergency it must be impossible to obtain instructions from the principal. Thirdly, the agent must have acted bona fide in the interests of the principal. Finally, the agent must have acted reasonably.[76] Dobson and Stokes took the view that 'in certain, strictly controlled, circumstances the law will impose an agency relationship or where such a relationship already exists, extend an agent's authority to act by virtue of an emergency.'[77]

5 Conclusion

This chapter has outlined the different types of authority that are available to an agent and has commented on how each affects the relationship between the agent, principal and third party. The next chapter will outline the obligations owed by an agent to a principal and by the principal to the agent.

6 Recommended reading

Bradgate, R. *Commercial Law* (Oxford University Press, Oxford, 2005)
Brown, I. 'The agent's apparent authority: paradigm or paradox?' (1995) *Journal of Business Law* (Jul.) 360
   'The significance of general and special authority in the development of the agent's external authority in English law' (2004) *Journal of Business Law* (Jul.) 391
Busch, D. and Macgregor, L. 'Apparent authority in Scots law: some international perspectives' (2007) 11(3) *Edinburgh Law Review* 349
Dobson, P. and Stokes, R. *Commercial Law* (7th edn, Sweet and Maxwell, London, 2008)
French, D., Mayson, S. and Ryan, C. *Mayson, French and Ryan on Company Law* (Oxford University Press, Oxford, 2010)
Markesinis, B. and Munday, R. *An Outline of the Law of Agency* (Butterworths, London, 1992)

---

[72] See Bradgate, above n. 1, at 155.
[73] Munday, above n. 3, at 91.   [74] [1921] 1 KB 257.
[75] See Bradgate, above n. 1, at 153.   [76] *Ibid.*
[77] Dobson and Stokes, above n. 5, at 436–7.

Munday, R. *Agency: Law and Principles* (Oxford University Press, Oxford, 2010)

Noonan, C. and Watson, S. 'Examining company directors through the lens of de facto directorship' (2008) 7 *Journal of Business Law* 587 at 619–20

Reynolds, F. 'Case comment: apparent authority' (1994) *Journal of Business Law* (Mar.) 144

Stone, R. 'Usual and ostensible authority: one concept or two?' (1993) *Journal of Business Law* (Jul.) 325

Street, A. 'Ostensible authority and ratification' (2006) 119 *Insurance and Reinsurance Law Briefing* (Sept.) 1

Part 1 Chapter 3

Relations between a Principal and Agent

Contents

1 Introduction

The purpose of this chapter is to provide an overview of the legal obligations that an agent owes to his principal. These include, for example, the duty to carry out contractual obligations; the duty to obey the principal's instructions; that the agent must not exceed his authority; the performance of contractual duties; that the agent must exercise due care and skill; the duty not to allow any conflict of interest; the fiduciary duties, not to take a bribe or make a secret profit; and the duty to account. The chapter then outlines the rights of an agent, before moving on to discuss the implications of a disclosed agency, a situation where the third party knows of the existence of the principal, and of an undisclosed agency, a situation where the agent acts for a principal who is not disclosed to the third party. Finally, the chapter deals with termination of the agency.

2 Duties of an agent

An agent acting for a principal is subject to a wide range of legal obligations, which are imposed either expressly within an agency agreement or impliedly. The duties owed by an agent to his principal have been classified into two very wide categories, those that arise from the contract between the two parties, and those that arise in equity, which has a strong influence over the duties of agents.[1] The duties imposed on an agent were succinctly summarised in *Armstrong* v. *Jackson* by McCardie J, who stated:

> The position of principal and agent gives rise to particular and onerous duties on the part of the agent, and the high standard of conduct required from him springs from the fiduciary relationship between his employer and himself. His position is confidential. It readily lends itself to abuse. A strict and salutary rule is required to meet the special situation. The rules of English law as they now exist spring from the strictness originally required by Courts of Equity in cases where the fiduciary relationship exists.[2]

(a) To obey the principal's instructions

One of the most obvious duties of an agent relates to his obligation to perform the instructions or directions provided by the principal. The operation of this duty was illustrated in *Turpin* v. *Bilton*,[3] a case that concerned a claim made against an insurance broker who breached his principal's instructions to arrange for the insurance of the plaintiffs' ship, which subsequently became lost at sea. The court held that the agent was liable for not following the principal's instructions.[4] An agent is not required to follow the instructions of his principal if they would be void under the common law or under primary legislation.[5] Watts noted that:

> An agent who has been authorised to act illegally, but has not yet acted, plainly has no rights against the principal to so act. Any contract conferring such a mandate would itself be unenforceable for illegality. Not only would the principal have its normal power to withdraw its mandate, but there could be no liability on an unenforceable agreement. Equally, a principal could not *oblige* an agent to act illegally. Where terms as to illegal conduct can be severed from a contract of agency, the respective positions of the principal and agent will be governed by the remainder of the contract.[6]

There have been two significant recent cases on the effect of illegality of an agent's conduct, *Stone & Rolls Ltd* v. *Moore Stephens (a firm)*[7] and *Safeway Stores Ltd* v. *Twigger*.[8] In the first case, Mr. Stojevic, the beneficial owner and sole directing mind of Stone and Rolls Ltd ('Rolls'), had used Rolls as a vehicle for defrauding banks, and the principal victim of the frauds ('the claimant')

---

[1] R. Munday, *Agency: Law and Principles* (Oxford University Press, Oxford, 2010) 149.

[2] [1917] 2 KB 822, 826.   [3] (1843) 5 Man. & G 455.

[4] Also see *Dufresne* v. *Hutchinson* (1810) 3 Taunt. 117 and *Williams* v. *Evans* (1866) LR 1 QB 352, as cited in Munday, above, n. 1, at 151.

[5] See, e.g., *Cohen* v. *Kittell* (1889) 22 QBD 680 and *Cheshire & Co.* v. *Vaughan Bros & Co.* [1920] 3 KB 240.

[6] P. Watts, 'Illegality and agency law: authorising illegal action' (2011) 3 *Journal of Business Law* 213, 216.

[7] [2009] UKHL 39; [2009] 1 AC 1391.

[8] [2010] EWCA Civ 1472.

had successfully sued Rolls for deceit. The claimant had been awarded substantial damages, but neither Rolls nor Stojevic could satisfy the judgment
and Rolls had gone into liquidation. Its liquidators brought an action in negligence against Moore Stephens, a firm of accountants, contending that they had
been negligent whilst undertaking a series of audits between 1996 and 1998 in
not detecting fraudulent transactions carried out by Stojevic, and seeking to
recover losses suffered by Rolls caused by the fact that, but for Moore Stephens'
negligence, the frauds would have been discovered earlier. Rolls' liquidators
based their case on the claim that Rolls' liability for Stojevic's frauds was vicarious liability only. However, the House of Lords struck out the liquidators'
claim on the grounds that Rolls was primarily rather than vicariously liable for
the frauds, as it was common ground that Stojevic was the directing mind of
the corporation and his fraudulent conduct was to be treated as the conduct of
Rolls.

A similar claim was made in the second case. In *Safeway Stores Ltd* v. *Twigger*,
the Office of Fair Trading (OFT) had imposed financial penalties on Safeway in
respect of alleged anti-competitive actions under the Competition Act 1998.[9]
Safeway brought a claim to recover the amount of the penalties from its directors and employees who were involved in the anti-competitive behaviour,
arguing that the directors and employees were in breach of their contracts of
employment and/or breach of their fiduciary duties owed to Safeway. The Court
of Appeal dismissed the action on the grounds that Safeway's liability was not
vicarious, as the undertaking was personally liable to pay the penalties and the
1998 Act did not impose liability of any kind on the directors or employees for
which Safeway could be vicariously liable.

Bradgate notes that it is important to draw a distinction between contractual
and gratuitous agency.[10] Where there is of a contractual agreement between the
agent and principal, the agent is obligated to execute the obligations under the
agreement. Failure to do so will result in breach of contract and the agent could
be personally liable for the resulting damages or loss suffered by the principal.
Conversely, if the agency is of a non-contractual nature, the agent will not be
under a duty to do anything. Nonetheless, it is possible for the agent to be held
liable under the law of tort.[11]

(b) To exercise due care and skill

An agent is required to exercise due care and skill. This rule was illustrated
in *Solomon* v. *Barker*, where brokers were held liable for failing to obtain the
best price for the principal.[12] The common law rules have been supported by

---

[9] The OFT alleged that Safeway was in breach of Competition Act 1998, s.2(1).
[10] R. Bradgate, *Commercial Law* (Oxford University Press, Oxford, 2005) 189.
[11] For a more detailed discussion of this case see S. Whittaker, 'The application of the "broad
principle of *Hedley Byrne*" as between parties to a contract' (1997) 17(1) *Legal Studies* 169.
[12] (1862) 2 F & F 726.

primary legislation, including, for example, the Sales of Goods and Services
Act 1982.

(c) To perform contractual obligations

Where there is an explicit contract between a principal and an agent, the
duties and responsibilities of both parties are regulated by this agreement. In
this situation, the obligations imposed on the agent are very strict; there is little scope for the obligations to be varied and if the instructions from the principal are not carried out by the agent, he will be liable for damages. However,
if the instructions provided by the principal to the agent are in vague terms,
the agent may not be held liable if 'he acts on a reasonable interpretation of
them'.[13] Nonetheless, if the instructions are unclear, the agent is required to
ask the principal to elucidate the instructions.[14] Bradgate took the view that
'an agent acting under a contract is contractually obliged to perform his
duties undertaken under that contract and is liable for breach of contract if
he fails to perform'.[15] The impact of this rule was illustrated in *Turpin* v. *Bilton*,
where an action was brought against an insurance broker for not insuring
the plaintiff's ship. It was alleged that the broker failed to insure the ship as
requested by the principal, which was subsequently lost at sea.[16] The court
held that the broker was financially accountable for the monetary value of the
ship. Another case that illustrates this point is *Bertrom, Armstrong & Co.* v.
Godfray.[17] In this case an agent was instructed by the principal to sell shares
'when the funds should be at 85 per cent, or above that price'. Sir John Leach,
MR stated that:

> When an agent acts under a general authority he is bound to act for his principal
> as he would act for himself; when he acts under a particular authority, and for a
> special purpose, he has no discretion. If he thinks fit to accept such a commis-
> sion, he must perform that commission according to his duty.[18]

An agent is generally not allowed to delegate his obligations, unless the
principal has agreed for this act of delegation to occur. This is commonly
referred to as *delegatus non potest delegare;* according to Mortimer 'even
where a person in a fiduciary position is authorised to delegate, he cannot
authorise sub-delegation unless his power of delegation specifically allows
for that'.[19] It is important to note, however, that this maxim is only a '*prima*

---

[13] See *Ireland* v. *Livingstone* (1872) LR 5 HL 395.
[14] *European Asian Bank AG* v. *Punjab & Sind Bank (No. 2)* [1983] 2 All ER 508.
[15] Bradgate, above n. 11.   [16] (1843) 5 Man. & G 455.
[17] (1830) i Knapp 381.   [18] (1830) i Knapp 383.
[19] A. Mortimer, 'Trustees and investment management: Part 2' (1994) 3 *Private Client Business* 160,
      164. Also see Alan W. Eccles 'Legislative comment: investing in the future' (2006) 5 *Scots Law
      Times* 23, 25–6.

facie rule which can be overridden if the enabling legislation so permits'.[20] Furthermore, the agent is permitted to delegate the execution of his duties provided he has the consent of the principal. This issue arose in the decision of Court of Appeal in *De Bussche* v. *Alt*.[21] In this case, the agent was employed to sell a ship in the Far East, delegated this role to a sub-agent, who purchased the ship for herself and then sold it for a large profit. The court decided that there was privity of contract between the principal and sub-agent, who was therefore under a contractual obligation to remit her financial gain to the principal.[22] Thesiger LJ took the view that the maxim *delegatus non potest delegare* has a twofold application. First, an agent is prevented 'from establishing the relationship of principal and agent between his own principal and a third person' and secondly, 'an agent cannot, without authority from his principal, devolve upon another obligations to the principal which he has himself undertaken to personally fulfil'.[23] There are, however, a number of exceptions to this rule, including 'exigencies of business'.[24] Thesiger LJ went on to state:

> [Such an exception] may and should be implied where, from the conduct of the parties to the original contract of agency, the usage of trade, or the nature of the particular business which is the subject of the agency, it may reasonably be presumed that the parties to the contract of agency originally intended that such authority should exist, or where, in the course of the employment, unforeseen emergencies arise which impose upon the agent the necessity of employing a substitute.[25]

(d) Not to allow any conflict of interest

An agent is under a strict obligation not to allow his interests to conflict with those of his principal. This is a fiduciary duty owed to the principal. This point has been emphasised by the courts on numerous occasions. For example, in *Aberdeen Railway Co.* v. *Blaikie Bros*, Lord Cranworth stated:

> It is a rule of universal application that no one, having [fiduciary] duties to discharge, shall be allowed to enter into engagements in which he has, or can have, a personal interest conflicting, or which possibly may conflict, with the interest of those who he is bound to protect.[26]

---

[20] *Allingham* v. *Minister of Agriculture* [1948] 1 All ER 780, DC.
[21] (1878) 8 Ch. D 286.
[22] A. Tettenborn, 'Principals, sub-agents and accountability' (1999) 115 *Law Quarterly Review* (Oct.) 655, 657. Also see G. McCormack, 'Conflicts of interest and the investment management function' (1999) 20(1) *Company Lawyer* 2, 5.
[23] (1878) 8 Ch. D 286, 310.
[24] P. Dobson, and R. Stokes, *Commercial Law* (7th edn, Sweet and Maxwell, London, 2008), 455.
[25] (1878) 8 Ch. D 286, 310–11.
[26] (1854) 1 Macq. 461, 471, HL, cited in Bradgate, above n. 11.

Dowrick noted that the judges:

> did not pretend to be giving effect to what they might presume to have been the common intention of the parties in the particular case, nor did they seek for the elements of a valid contract between the parties before enforcing these rules. On the contrary, the judges imposed these duties and disabilities on agents generally … only if it happens in a particular case of agency that the parties expressly or tacitly agree on these very duties, and there exists a contract between them, do these incidents acquire the character of contractual terms.[27]

The operation of this rule was illustrated in *McPherson* v. *Watt*.[28] In this case, Watt, who was an advocate, was instructed to sell a property by his principal. He did not disclose to his principal that he had in fact arranged for his brother to purchase the house for himself. Unsurprisingly, the principal refused to complete the contract.

The purpose of the rule is also to promote a better level of conduct between the agent and principal, a point emphasised in *Rhodes* v. *Macalister:* 'the more that principle is enforced the better for the honesty of commercial transactions … it cannot be repeated too often to commercial men – that in matters of agency they must act with strict honesty'.[29] In *Rhodes*, the agent acted on the instructions of his principal to find someone who would be willing to sell mineral rights to the principal and informed the principal that suitable properties could be found for between £8,000 and £10,000. The agency agreement specified that provided the agent was able to find a seller willing to sell for less than £19,000, he was entitled to keep the difference. The agent located a seller of suitable properties for £6,625 and claimed the difference. However, the agent had negotiated with the seller for an additional commission based on the sale. Banks LJ took the view as follows:

> [w]hat was [the agent's] position and what was his duty[?] Of course, as long as he was acting for the vendors of these properties only he was perfectly entitled to suggest to them that they should fix a price which would include a commission to himself, and he would be perfectly justified in receiving that commission or putting forward the price to an intending purchaser as the only price which he could persuade the vendors to give, so long as that was his real opinion. But the moment he accepted the position of agent for the intending purchasers his entire position in law changed. He could no longer consistently with his duty, unless he disclosed the facts, act as agent for the vendors to procure purchasers with the result of some commission or payment to himself. He could not retain that position consistently with his duty to the purchasers of obtaining these properties at as low a price as he possibly could … the moment he accepted the position of agent to procure these properties as cheap as possible for the intending purchasers his interest and duty conflicted, and he could no longer act honestly towards the intending purchasers without disclosing to them that in that figure

27 F. Dowrick, 'The relationship of principal and agent' (1954) 17(1) *Modern Law Review* 24, 31.
28 (1877) 3 App. Cas. 254.   29 (1923) 29 Com. Cas. 19, 28.

of £8,000 to £10,000 which he had mentioned as the probable price of these properties he had included a figure which he intended should cover a commission to himself.[30]

The facts in *Rhodes* were similar to those in *Andrews* v. *Ramsay*,[31] where the agent had been instructed by his principal to sell his home for £2,500. The agent located a buyer, who was prepared to pay £2,100 for the principal's property, and paid £100 deposit to the agent. The agent gave the seller half of the deposit and kept the other half for himself; and in addition, the agent had received an undisclosed commission of £20 from the purchaser. The seller brought an action against the agent for return of the commission the seller had paid to the agent. The court stated that a principal:

> is entitled to have an honest agent, and it is only the honest agent who is entitled to any commission. In my opinion, if an agent directly or indirectly colludes with the other side, and so acts in opposition to the interest of his principal, he is not entitled to any commission. That is, I think, supported both by authority and on principle; but if, as is suggested, there is no authority directly bearing on the question, I think that the sooner such an authority is made the better.[32]

One of the most complicated areas of the duty to avoid a conflict of interest is where the agent represents two principals.[33] In *Kelly* v. *Cooper*,[34] the plaintiff instructed a firm of estate agents to sell his property (named 'Caliban') and agreed to pay them a commission. The owner of a neighbouring property (named 'Vertigo') then also instructed the estate agents to sell his property.[35] The estate agents exhibited both properties to a potential purchaser, who made an offer which was accepted to buy 'Vertigo'. The prospective purchaser subsequently made an offer which was accepted on the plaintiff's house, 'Caliban'. The agents decided not to inform the plaintiff of their agreement to sell the neighbouring house, and the plaintiff accepted the offer for his property. As a result both properties were sold, however the plaintiff commenced legal proceedings against the estate agents asserting they had had a conflict of interest. The agents counterclaimed for the payment of their commission, as they argued they had successfully completed their contractual agreement with the plaintiff principal to sell his property. At first instance, the court ruled in favour of the plaintiff and granted an award of damages and further ruled that the estate agents were not entitled to their commission. This decision was overturned on appeal, and the plaintiff appealed to the Privy Council, who upheld the decision of the appellate court and rejected the appeal. In particular, the Privy Council determined that:

> the fact of [the purchaser's] attempted simultaneous purchase of both houses was a material fact which could have affected the sale price but … [the purchaser's] proposed purchase of 'Vertigo' was confidential information acquired in the

---

[30] *Ibid.* 23.   [31] [1903] 2 KB 635.   [32] *Ibid.* 642.
[33] Bradgate, above n. 11, 198.   [34] [1993] AC 205.
[35] F. Reynolds, 'Fiduciary duties of estate agents' (1994) *Journal of Business Law* (March) 147, 148.

course of the separate agency to sell that house and, consequently, the facts could not be disclosed to the plaintiff for then the defendants would be in breach of duty to … the owner of 'Vertigo'.[36]

Nolan took the view that:

The logic of the judgment is that the contract between broker and client is the foundation of their relationship. It is, practically speaking, inconceivable that the contract should oblige the broker to disclose to that client information imparted to the broker in confidence by another client. The fiduciary relationship between client and broker must 'accommodate itself' to the terms of the contract between them, so that the fiduciary duties to which the broker becomes subject never include a duty to make disclosure of information to a client, where such disclosure would involve breach of a duty of confidentiality owed to another client.[37]

Therefore, the estate agents could not be prevented from acting for other principals.[38]

(e) Not to make a secret profit

It is a very strict rule of agency that an agent or trustee must not make a secret profit. This was illustrated in *Boardman* v. *Phipps*.[39] In this case, a will trust had a very large holding of 8,000 shares in a private company. The trustees of the trust were the elderly widow, the testator's daughter and an accountant; Boardman was their solicitor. The trustees were unhappy with the company's accounts and Boardman and one of the testator's sons were appointed proxies under proxy forms signed by the daughter and the accountant and attended the company's annual general meeting. Shortly afterwards, Boardman and the son decided to purchase 22,000 £1 shares in the company. This would have enabled them to control the company and make a repayment of capital to the shareholders. The accountant agreed with this decision and the daughter was informed of it, but not the elderly widow. During the discussions to buy the shares, Boardman and the son made use of the information they had received at the company's annual general meeting, and were further able to gain a comprehensive awareness of the financial assets of the company in their role representing the trustees. After the negotiations, Boardman and the son agreed to purchase 14,567 shares and the transaction proved to be very profitable. Boardman then wrote to the beneficiaries of the trust, including the daughter and another son of the testator who had hitherto known nothing of the negotiations (the plaintiff), outlining the negotiations and asking them whether they had any objection to his personal interest in the purchase. The plaintiff brought an action claiming an account of

---

[36] I. Brown, 'Divided loyalties in the law of agency' (1993) 109 *Law Quarterly Review* (April) 206, 207.

[37] R. Nolan, 'Conflicts of duty: helping hands from the Privy Council?' (1994) 15(2) *Company Lawyer* 58, 59.

[38] For a more detailed commentary on the decision by the Privy Council, see Brown, above n. 36.

[39] [1967] 2 AC 46.

the profits made by Boardman and the son personally from the dealings in the shares. At first instance, Wilberforce J held that Boardman and the son were liable to account for the profit attributable to the plaintiff's share in the trust fund, minus expenses. On appeal, the House of Lords dismissed the appeal on the ground that the appellants had placed themselves in position of a fiduciary character and that had enabled them to obtain the prospect of making a profit. The appellants had acted openly, but in a way that was very advantageous to them. In relation to the issue of the making of a secret profit, the court determined that where an agent makes such a profit, he is in breach of the duty of good faith that is owed to the principal, and the profit is therefore recoverable by the principal.

An agent may also be deemed to make a secret profit even if he has no confidential information about the principal's property. In *Hippisley* v. *Knee Bros*,[40] the plaintiff employed the defendants as auctioneers to sell goods at auction. The terms of the agreement were that the defendants were to be paid a lump sum, or commission, as well as expenses. In due course, the defendants began to sell the plaintiff's goods and reclaimed the full amount of their expenses, even though the defendants had been in receipt of several discounts in respect of the expenses without the plaintiff's knowledge. The court held that the defendants were in breach of their duty to the principal and could not be allowed to keep the discounts.

However, it is important to note that the agent will not be in breach of his duty if all of the relevant information is disclosed to the principal and the principal consents to the agent keeping the profit.

***Q1 What is the significance of the decision in* Broadman *v.* Phipps?**

(f) To act as a fiduciary

In addition to the duties that are contained in the agency agreement, the agent is also treated as a fiduciary.[41] This means that the agent will owe the principal 'strict duties in equity'.[42] The fiduciary duty was outlined by the court in *Bristol & West Building Society* v. *Mathew*:

> the distinguishing obligation of a fiduciary is the obligation of loyalty. The principal is entitled to the single-minded loyalty of the fiduciary. This core liability has several facets. A fiduciary must act in good faith: he must not make a profit out of his trust; he must not place himself in a position where his duty and his interest may conflict; he may not act for his own benefit or for the benefit of a third person without the informed consent of his principal. This is not intended to be an exhaustive list ... they are the defining characteristics of the fiduciary.[43]

---

[40] [1905] 1 KB 1.   [41] Munday, above n. 1, at 157.
[42] *Ibid.*   [43] [1998] Ch. 1, 18.

It is important to note that the fiduciary duties owed by an agent to his principal do not arise from the agency agreement, but are based on trust. For an agent to be in breach of a fiduciary duty, there is no need for the agent's behaviour to be dishonest, but his behaviour must be deliberately intentional and involve an element of falseness. An agent is under a duty not to place himself in a situation where his interests conflict with those of the principal. This rule has been confirmed by the judiciary on numerous occasions and has been described as one of an agent's most important obligations.[44] For example, Lord Cairns LC stated emphatically in *Parker* v. *McKenna*:

> Now, the rule of this Court, as I understand it, as to agents, is not a technical or arbitrary rule. It is a rule founded upon the highest and truest principles of morality. No man can in this Court, acting as an agent, be allowed to put himself into a position in which his interest and his duty will be in conflict.[45]

Lord Cranworth LC adopted a similar robust approach toward this duty in *Aberdeen Railway Co.* v. *Blaikie Bros,* quoted above.[46]

(g) Not to take a bribe

Agents are also under a duty not to accept bribes or a secret commission.[47] If an agent does accept a bribe or secret commission, he will be in breach of a fiduciary duty and must account for it to the principal.[48] In *Wilson* v. *Hurstanger Ltd*, the court considered if a secret commission amounted to a breach of duty by the agent.[49] In this case, the defendants (the principals) borrowed £8,000 to pay off the debt on their mortgage, the agent broker's fee of £1,000 and to use the remainder for their own personal use. The lender agreed to pay the broker an arrangement fee and a commission of £240. The defendants defaulted on their mortgage payments and in the following court proceedings the defendants counterclaimed that the loan agreement was void or voidable because of the payment of a commission. In relation to the issue of a secret profit, the court held that the payment was not a secret commission.

A bribe has been defined as a 'secret profit',[50] or a 'commission or other inducement which is given by a third party to an agent ... which is secret from the principal'.[51] Slade J stated that the definition of a bribe in a civil law context

---

[44] B. Markesinis and R. Munday, *An Outline of the Law of Agency* (Butterworths, London, 1992) 109.

[45] (1874) LR 10 Ch. App. 96, 118. See M. Conaglen, 'Public-private intersection: comparing fiduciary conflict doctrine and bias' (2008) *Public Law* (Spring) 58, 62.

[46] {1854} Macq. 461, 471. Other cases that have adopted a similar stance include *Bentley* v. *Craven* (1853) 18 Beav. 75, 76 and *Oliver* v. *Court* (1820) 8 Price 127.

[47] A bribe was famously defined in *Industries and General Mortgage Co. Ltd* v. *Lewis* [1949] 2 All ER 573, 575.

[48] Munday, above n. 1 at 68.

[49] [2007] EWCA Civ 299; [2007] 1 WLR 2351, CA (Civ Div).

[50] Bradgate, above n. 11, at 202.

[51] *Anangel Atlas Compania Naviera SA* v. *Ishikawajima-Harima Heavy Industries Ltd* [1990] 1 Lloyd's Rep. 167, 171.

has three important aspects: first, 'that the person making the payment makes it to the agent of the other person with whom he is dealing'; secondly, 'that he makes it to that person knowing that that person is acting as the agent of the other person with whom he is dealing'; thirdly, 'that he fails to disclose to the other person with whom he is dealing that he has made that payment to the person whom he knows to be the other person's agent'.[52]

Lord Romer in *Hovenden and Sons* v. *Millhoff* stated that:

> If a gift be made to a confidential agent with the view of inducing the agent to act in favour of the donor in relation to transactions between the donor and the agent's principal and that gift is secret as between the donor and the agent – that is to say, without the knowledge and consent of the principal – then the gift is a bribe in the view of the law.[53]

The courts have also determined that it is irrelevant whether the bribe influenced the activities or decisions of the agent.[54] In *Rhodes* v. *Macalister*, Bankes LJ took the view that:

> There seems to be an idea prevalent that a person who is acting as agent or servant of another is committing no wrong to his employer in taking a commission or bribe from the other side, provided that in his opinion his employer or principal does not have to pay more than if the bribe were not given. There cannot be a greater misconception of what the law is, or what the duty of a servant or agent towards his master or principal in reference to such matters is, and I do not think the rule can too often be repeated or its application more frequently insisted upon.[55]

This was illustrated in *Boston Deep Sea Fishing and Ice Co* v. *Ansell*.[56] In this case, Ansell was employed as Boston Deep Sea Fishing's managing director over a five year period. He was also secretly a director of a boat-building company and placed several orders with the boat-building company in exchange for bonuses and a financial commission for an additional contract he made with that company. Boston Deep Sea Fishing brought an action against Ansell for an account of the secret commission and bonuses received by him and the court held that acceptance of the bonuses and commission was grounds for dismissal and that Ansell must account to the company for the money received.[57]

In *Lister* v. *Stubbs*, the plaintiffs, who were a manufacturing company, employed the defendant to purchase certain types of material the plaintiffs used for their business. Under a 'corrupt bargain', the defendant took large sums by way of commission from one of the firms from which he purchased

---

[52] *Industries and General Mortgage Corp.* v. *Lewis* [1949] 2 All ER 573, 575.
[53] (1900) 83 LT 41, 43.
[54] See, e.g., *Hovenden and Sons* v. *Millhoff* (1900) 83 LT 41 and *Anangel Atlas Compania Naviera*, above n. 51.
[55] (1923) 29 Com. Cas. 19, 20.
[56] (1888) 39 Ch. D 339.
[57] This decision was later approved in *Sinclair* v. *Neighbour* [1967] 2 QB 279.

materials, a percentage of which he reinvested. Subsequently, the plaintiffs commenced an action against the defendant to recover the moneys paid to him and sought an injunction to prevent the defendant from dealing with the investments. The court held that the relationship between the defendant and the plaintiffs was one of debtor and creditor, and not that of a trustee and beneficiary, and therefore the plaintiffs' claim was unsuccessful.[58] Devonshire took the view that this decision 'cast a long and enduring shadow on legal thinking, inhibiting the dispensation of relief in situations where property could, and probably would, be spirited away from the grasp of a meritorious claimant'.[59] The decision in Lister has also been described as 'unhelpful and shaky'.[60]

The position in *Lister* v. *Stubbs* was reassessed in *Attorney General for Hong Kong* v. *Reid* by the Privy Council,[61] which 'refused to follow the *Lister* principle'.[62] Here, the respondent, whilst employed as a Crown Servant in Hong Kong, accepted bribes which enabled him to purchase two properties in New Zealand, which were conveyed to him via his wife and solicitor. The respondent was convicted and sentenced to eight years' imprisonment and ordered to pay the Crown the value of the assets, approximately US$12.4 million. At first instance, the High Court of New Zealand held that the Attorney General of Hong Kong had no equitable interest in the property. This decision was upheld by the New Zealand Court of Appeal and subsequently reversed by the Privy Council. The court stated that a gift received by a person who is in a fiduciary position as an inducement for breach of his duty constituted a bribe. The fiduciary accordingly became a debtor for the amount of the bribe to the person to whom the duty was owed, in this case the Crown, for whom he also held the property on constructive trust.[63]

If an agent accepts a bribe or secret commission, there are several legal courses of action available to the principal. In particular, the principal could bring an action to hold the agent liable in the tort of deceit and make a claim for the amount of the bribe.[64] In *Mahesan*, the Privy Council held that under the common law, the principal was allowed to recover from the bribed agent either the total amount of the bribe, or compensation for the loss actually suffered.[65] The courts have also determined that an agent who accepts a bribe is not permitted either to receive or to claim the commission he would have received if the terms of the agency agreement had been satisfied.[66] Furthermore, an agent

---

[58] (1890) LR 45 Ch. D 1, CA.

[59] P. Devonshire, 'Pre-emptive orders against evasive dealings: an assessment of recent trends' (2004) *Journal of Business Law* (May) 355, 359.

[60] H. Johnson, 'Dealing with bribes' (1994) 12(9) *International Banking and Financial Law* 94, 95.

[61] [1994] 1 AC 324.

[62] D. Cowan, 'Lister & Co. v. Stubbs: who profits?' (1996) *Journal of Business Law* (January) 22, 23.

[63] For a more detailed discussion of this case see G. McCormack, 'The remedial constructive trust and commercial transactions' (1996) 17(1) *Company Lawyer* 3.

[64] See the decision of the Privy Council in *Mahesan S/O Thambiah* v. *Malaysia Government Officers' Co-operative Housing Society Ltd* [1979] AC 374.

[65] *Ibid.* 382A–D, 383F–H, 384D–E.   [66] *Andrews* v. *Ramsay* [1903] 2 KB 635.

may be subject to criminal proceedings for payment of a bribe under the Public Bodies Corrupt Practices Act 1889, the Prevention of Corruption Act 1906, or the Prevention of Corruption Act 1916. Under Public Bodies Corrupt Practices Act 1889, section 1(1):

> Every person who shall by himself or by or in conjunction with any other person, corruptly solicit or receive, or agree to receive, for himself, or for any other person, any gift, loan, fee, reward, or advantage whatever as an inducement to, or reward for, or otherwise on account of any member, officer, or servant of a public body as in this Act defined, doing or forbearing to do anything in respect of any matter or transaction whatsoever, actual or proposed, in which the said public body is concerned, shall be guilty of a [criminal offence].[67]

Under Prevention of Corruption Act 1906, section 1:

> If any agent corruptly accepts or obtains, or agrees to accept or attempts to obtain, from any person, for himself or for any other person, any gift or consideration as an inducement or reward for doing or forbearing to do, or for having after the passing of this Act done or forborne to do, any act in relation to his principal's affairs or business, or for showing or forbearing to show favour or disfavour to any person in relation to his principal's affairs or business; or
>
>   If any person corruptly gives or agrees to give or offers any gift or consideration to any agent as an inducement or reward for doing or forbearing to do, or for having after the passing of this Act done or forborne to do, any act in relation to his principal's affairs or business, or for showing or forbearing to show favour or disfavour to any person in relation to his principal's affairs or business; or
>
>   If any person knowingly gives to any agent, or if any agent knowingly uses with intent to deceive his principal, any receipt, account, or other document in respect of which the principal is interested, and which contains any statement which is false or erroneous or defective in any material particular, and which to his knowledge is intended to mislead the principal
>
>   he shall be guilty of a [criminal offence].[68]

It was generally accepted by a majority of commentators that these laws were ineffective and were inconsistent with the Organisation of Economic Co-operation and Development's Bribery Convention 1998.[69] These deficiencies resulted in the publication by the Law Commission of a consultation paper in 2007,[70] which resulted in the introduction of the Bribery Act 2010. The Act was designed to be 'the toughest anti-corruption legislation in the world'.[71] The Bribery Act 2010 criminalises bribery under three categories: general bribery

---

[67] Public Bodies Corrupt Practices Act 1889, s.1(1).
[68] Prevention of Corruption Act 1906, s.1.
[69] See, e.g., T. Pope and T. Webb, 'The Bribery Act 2010 (Legislative Comment)' (2010) 25(10) *Journal of International Banking Law and Regulation* 480.
[70] Law Commission, *Reforming Bribery*, Consultation Paper No. 18532 (London, 2007).
[71] B. Breslin, D. Ezickson and J. Kocoras, 'The Bribery Act 2010: raising the bar above the US Foreign Corrupt Practices Act (2010) 31(11) *Company Lawyer* 362.

offences; bribery of foreign public officials; and the failure of commercial organisations to prevent bribery.[72] In particular, section 1 of the 2010 Act provides that a person is guilty of bribery if he 'offers, promises or gives a financial or other advantage to another person, and that person intends the advantage (i) to induce a person to perform improperly a relevant function or activity, or (ii) to reward a person for the improper performance of such a function or activity';[73] or if he 'offers, promises or gives a financial or other advantage to another person, and the person knows or believes that the acceptance of the advantage would itself constitute the improper performance of a relevant function or activity'.[74]

Furthermore, an agent is under a duty not to exploit or take advantage of his position for a personal gain. One of the leading and seminal cases here is *Keech v. Sandford*,[75] which involved the lease of Rumford Market, which was developed by a trustee for the advantage of a minor. Just before the lease was due to terminate the trustee requested the renewal of the lease on behalf of the trust estate. The landlord declined as he was dissatisfied with the guarantee for the rent, which resulted in the trustee personally renewing the lease. Later, the minor sought an assignment of the lease and a percentage of the profits. King LC stated that:

> I must consider this as a trust for the infant; for I very well see, if a trustee, on the refusal to renew, might have a lease to himself, few trust-estates would be renewed to *cestui que* use; though I do not say there is a fraud in this case, yet he should rather have let it run out, than to have had the lease to himself. This may seem hard, that the trustee is the only person of all mankind who might not have the lease: but it is very proper that rule should be strictly pursued, and not in the least relaxed; for it is very obvious what would be the consequence of letting trustees have the lease, on refusal to renew to *cestui que* use.[76]

Therefore, the underlying principle of this case is 'one of public policy. It reflects a desire to dissuade parties from unscrupulously using their fiduciary position to their own personal advantage.'[77]

(h) To account

An agent is under a duty to account to the principal for the property of the principal in his possession, or if he receives goods or money from or on behalf of

---

[72] D. Aaronberg and N. Higgins, 'The Bribery Act 2010: all bark and no bite…?' (2010) 5 *Archbold Review* 6.

[73] Bribery Act 2010, s.1(2).

[74] *Ibid.*, s.1(3). For an excellent commentary on the offences created by the Act see S. Gentle, 'Legislative comment: the Bribery Act 2010, Part 2: the corporate offence' (2011) 2 *Criminal Law Review* 101.

[75] (1726) Sel. Cas. Ch. 61.   [76] *Ibid.* 62.

[77] Markesinis and Munday, above n. 44, at 117. For an excellent discussion of this case see A. Hicks, 'The remedial principle of *Keech* v. *Sandford* reconsidered' (2010) 69(2) *Cambridge Law Journal* 287 and R. Lee, 'Rethinking the content of the fiduciary obligation' (2009) 3 *Conveyancer and Property Lawyer* 236.

his principal.[78] This duty has been described as a personal duty.[79] It has been argued by some commentators that the duty to account arises due to the agent's fiduciary position.[80] However, case law suggests that this is not always the position.[81] In terms of this duty, an agent who accepts money or goods for his principal must keep them isolated from the agent's own property. In *Foley* v. *Hill*, Lord Cottenham LC stated:

> So it is with regard to an agent dealing with any property; he obtains no interest himself in the subject-matter beyond his remuneration; he is dealing throughout for another, and though he is not a trustee according to the strict technical meaning of the word, he is *quasi* a trustee for that particular transaction for which he is engaged; and therefore in these cases the Courts of Equity have assumed jurisdiction.[82]

It is possible for the agency agreement to contain clauses as to how the money will be held.

This duty also requires an agent to keep and deliver a full set of accounts to the principal. In *Yasuda Fire and Marine Insurance Company of Europe Ltd* v. *Orion Marine Insurance Underwriting Agency Ltd,* Colman J said:

> That obligation to provide an accurate account in the fullest sense arises by reason of the fact that the agent has been entrusted with the authority to bind the principal to transactions with third parties and the principal is entitled to know what his personal contractual rights and duties are in relation to those third parties as well as what he is entitled to receive by way of payment from the agent. He is entitled to be provided with those records because they have been created for preserving information as to the very transactions which the agent was authorised by him to enter into. Being the participant in the transactions, the principal is entitled to the records of them.[83]

In this case, the defendant had acted as an underwriting agent for the principal under several agreements. The court held that because the defendant had acted as an agent, he was under a duty to provide financial records to the principal and that, therefore, the principal was entitled to inspect the records of the underwriting agent following the termination of the agency agreement.[84] This approach can be traced back to the decision in *Turner* v. *Burkinshaw,* where Lord Chelmsford took the view that 'it is the first duty of an agent … to be constantly ready with his accounts … this must mean that the agent must be ready to render his accounts when they are demanded'.[85]

---

[78] Markesinis and Munday, above n. 44, at 103.
[79] Bradgate, above n. 11, at 126.   [80] Munday, above n. 1, at 181.
[81] See, e.g., *Coulthard* v. *Disco Mix Club Ltd* [2000] 1 WLR 707.
[82] (1848) 2 HL Cas. 28, 35–6.   [83] [1995] 3 All ER 211, 219.
[84] For a more detailed discussion of this case see E. Fennell, 'Yasuda Fire & Marine Insurance Co. of Europe Ltd v. Orion Marine Insurance Underwriting Agency Ltd and another' (1995) 3(4) *Journal of Financial Regulation and Compliance* 391. Also see S. Honeyball and D. Pearce, 'Contract, employment and the contract of employment' (2006) 35(1) *Industrial Law Journal* 30.
[85] (1867) LR 2 Ch. App. 488.

Q2 What are the obligations and duties of an agent?

3 Rights of an agent

As previously stated, the agent relationship is often regarded as a fiduciary one. This simply means that the agent owes a number of duties to both the principal and any third party, which can be contrasted with the rights the agent has against the principal. Essentially, under the common law an agent has three rights:

(1) the right to remuneration;
(2) the right to indemnity; and
(3) the right to lien.

(a) Commission and remuneration

One of the most obvious obligations owed by a principal to his agent relates to payment, which if agreed as part of a contract between the parties, the principal is bound to pay. However, where there is no express agreement between the principal and agent, there is an implied agreement that the principal will pay reasonable compensation. The issue of reasonable compensation was discussed by the House of Lords in *Way* v. *Latilla*.[86] In this case, the plaintiff had been asked by the defendant to acquire gold mining concessions in Africa that were worth approximately £1 million. The plaintiff argued that his services were provided as part of an agency agreement with the defendant, which entitled him to a percentage of the concessions. At first instance, the court determined that a contract existed between the plaintiff and defendant and awarded the plaintiff £30,000.[87] However, the House of Lords overturned the decision because in its opinion the agreement had not been completed and the plaintiff was awarded a quantum meruit of £5,000 for the work he had performed for the defendant. The court thus determined that an agent is entitled to a reasonable payment on a restitutionary basis.[88] Williams and Levine took the view that this case:

> demonstrate[s] that restitution in *quantum meruit* can be claimed on the basis that there had been full performance of the work, the benefit of that work had been accepted by the other party and it would be unjust in the circumstances to allow the other party to retain the benefit of that work without paying compensation.[89]

---

[86] [1937] 3 All ER 759, HL.
[87] A. Lodder, '*Benedetti* v. *Sawiris*: unjust enrichment and the assessment of quantum meruit awards' (2010) 126 *Law Quarterly Review* (Jan.) 42, 45.
[88] See A. Burrows, 'Free acceptance and the law of restitution' (1988) 104 *Law Quarterly Review* (Oct.) 576, 595.
[89] J. Williams and M. Levine, 'Restitutionary quantum meruit: the crossroads' 8(3) *Construction Law Journal* 244, 246.

An agent may be entitled to payment from the principal if a particular event occurs. In such a case, the agent must have been the 'effective cause of the event he was employed to bring about'.[90]

In *Rhodes* v. *Forwood*, the important question was whether or not a principal was able to preclude an agent receiving payment. The agent and principal had agreed 'in consideration of the services and payments to be mutually rendered', that for a period of seven years, or as long as the agent decided to carry on his business, he should act exclusively as the principal's agent. The principal sold his business and the agent attempted to claim damages because the principal had decided to close down his business before the seven years had expired. However, the court dismissed the agent's claim.[91]

Luxor (Eastbourne) Ltd v. *Cooper* is a significant case in this area of law.[92] The agent sued the principals for a commission, which the principals had agreed to pay him for successfully introducing a buyer for a property owned by the principals. The agent asserted that he had met his contractual obligations and produced a buyer who was willing to purchase the property, even though the sale did not take place. The agent claimed to be entitled, not to the agreed commission in the absence of a sale, but to damages of the same amount he would have earned if the principals had not broken an implied term of the contract entitling the agent to payment in these circumstances. The House of Lords held that there was no implied term in the contract and the agent was unable to claim the payment. However, this decision can be contrasted with that in *Alpha Trading Ltd* v. *Dunnshaw-Patten Ltd*.[93]

(b) Indemnity

Importantly, the agent has a right of indemnity, which arises if he incurs any financial liabilities whilst executing instructions from the principal. Munday noted that an agent is entitled to be reimbursed any expenses he has incurred whilst acting in the course of an agency and for any losses and liabilities.[94] If the agent and principal have agreed a contract, the indemnity is either an implied or express term of the contract. Where there is no contract between the principal and agent, the agent will receive a restitutionary indemnity.[95]

(c) Lien

In some circumstances, an agent will acquire a lien over property that belongs to the principal which is in the possession of the agent. Munday noted that 'to facilitate recovery by the agent of sums owed to him by the principal, the law

---

[90] Bradgate, above n. 11, at 183. See, e.g., *Coles* v. *Enoch* [1939] 3 All ER 327, CA.
[91] (1875–76) LR 1 App. Cas. 256.
[92] [1941] AC 108.   [93] [1981] QB 290.
[94] Munday, above n. 1, at 206.   [95] Bradgate, above n. 11, at 183.

grants the agent a possessory lien on the goods and chattels of his principal in respect of all claims arising out of his employment'.[96] A lien can be defined as a right to keep hold of or to hold on to property until a debt is paid off and a 'right to retain possession of the goods of another as security for a debt, or other obligation'.[97] A good example of this can be found in *West of England Bank* v. *Batchelor*.[98] Millet LJ in *Re Cosslett (Contractors) Ltd,* stated that 'in the case of a lien the creditor retains possession of goods previously delivered to him for some other purpose'.[99] Stephens stated that:

> Lien is a complex type of security right. It can be viewed from the perspective of contract law, as it arises typically in the context of reciprocal obligations. Equally, it can be seen as part of property law because it is a right relating to a thing which is effective in insolvency. As with many other areas of private law, there is a relatively large nineteenth-century case law, but little in modern times.[100]

There are two different types of lien: general and particular. A general lien has been defined as 'a lien over property which can be retained until payment of the whole of the indebtedness of the owner to the person in possession on any account whatsoever'. However, such liens can rarely be established.[101] It 'also confers on the agent a right to retain the principal's goods until the general balance of account between the principal and agent is settled'.[102] The courts have adopted a very sceptical view toward the use of general liens, as illustrated by Lord Campbell LC in *Bock* v. *Gorrissen*:

> The law of England does not favour general liens, and I apprehend that a general lien can only be claimed as arising from dealings in a particular trade or line of business, such as wharfingers, factors and bankers, in which the custom of a general lien has been judicially proved and acknowledged, or upon express evidence being given that, according to the established custom in some other trade or line of business, a general lien is claimed and allowed.[103]

The other type of lien is a particular lien, which is 'a lien over property which can be retained only until payment of a particular debt due in respect of it is paid'.[104] A particular lien 'means that the agent's right to retain possession of his principal's goods can only be exercised in order to assist in recovery of monies owed to him in respect of those particular goods'.[105] However, it has been argued that there are five different types of particular lien, including statutory, common, maritime, equitable and contractual.[106] It is important to

---

[96] Munday, above n. 1, at 212.
[97] G. McBain, 'Repealing the Bill of Sale Act' (2011) 5 *Journal of Business Law* 475, 487.
[98] Munday, above n. 1, 213.   [99] [1998] Ch. 495, 508.
[100] S. Steven, 'Property issues in lien' (2010) 14(3) *Edinburgh Law Review* 455.
[101] S. Frieze, 'Accountant's lien' (1990) 3(6) *Insolvency International* 45.
[102] Markesinis and Munday, above n. 44, at 105.
[103] (1860) 2 De Gex, Fisher & Jones 434, as cited in Munday, above n. 1, at 213.
[104] Frieze, above n. 101.   [105] *Ibid.*, at 145.
[106] G. McBain, 'Repealing the Bill of Sale Act' (2011) 5 *Journal of Business Law* 475, 487.

note that once an agent has acquired a lien, he is not entitled to sell or dispose of the goods. The agent is merely allowed to retain the goods or property in his possession.

In order for an agent to acquire a lien, a number of requirements have to be met. First, the agent must be in possession of the principal's goods. This is illustrated in *Bryans* v. *Nix*,[107] in which a carrier was employed by the principal to transport a cargo of oats to his agent in Dublin. The principal gave the carrier a series of documents in which it was stated that the carrier was to keep the goods for the agent. The court decided that, in this instance, the agent was in possession of the goods in transit, and had a lien over them. In particular, the court declared 'it is an inference of law and not a presumption of fact that the contract for the safe carriage is between the carrier and the consignee and the latter has the legal right of action even if the consignor pays the freight'.[108]

Another requirement that has to be met is that the agent must have acquired the possession of the goods by lawful means. The court in *Taylor* v. *Robinson* was faced with this particular question.[109] The case related to an agent who had been instructed by his principal to buy a large number of staves, which were to be stored on the seller's property. The principal had agreed with the seller to pay rent whilst his goods were stored on the seller's premises. Unbeknown to the principal, the seller instructed the agent to remove the goods from his premises, which the agent did without the principal's authority. The court held, unlike the decision in *Bryans* v. *Nix* above, that the principal had retained possession of the goods because the agent had exceeded his authority by removing the goods from the seller's property. Burrough J stated that 'it is uncumnent on factors who claim a lien, to prove their possession of the property on which the lien is claimed. Possession is a matter of fact'.[110] Therefore, if the agent gains possession of the principal's goods via an unlawful act, this will prevent him from acquiring any lien rights.

The next requirement is that the agent must have acquired the property whilst acting in his capacity as an agent. For example, in *Muir* v. *Fleming*,[111] the court held that if the principal merely leaves the goods with the agent for safe-keeping, the agent is deemed not to have gained possession of them. For the agent to acquire a lien over the principal's property or goods, the claim or action must relate to the agency agreement which resulted in the agent acquiring the goods. This rule was illustrated in *Dixon* v. *Stansfield*, where an agent who normally only sold goods for the principal under the agency agreement acted as an insurance broker on one occasion and obtained insurance of a ship's cargo. The

---

[107] (1839) 4 M & W 775.
[108] As cited in C. Cashmore, 'Case comment: theft by subcontractors, interpretation of exclusion clauses, parties to a contract of carriage (land)' (1989) *Journal of Business Law* (Jan.) 78, 80.
[109] (1818) 9 Taunt. 648.   [110] Munday, above n. 1, at 216.
[111] (1822) Dowl. & Ry. N.P. 29; 171 ER 906.

court held that, in this instance, the agent had not gained a lien over the insurance policy.[112]

There is one further requirement which needs to be satisfied if the agent is to obtain a lien over the principal's property: the agency agreement must not exclude this right either expressly or impliedly. In *Re Bowes*, a client deposited a life insurance policy with his banker with an express stipulation that he was not to be levied with an overdraft that exceeded £4,000.[113] The court held that the communication between the client and the banker prevented the latter from acquiring a lien.

The agent will lose any lien he possesses over the principal's goods or property when the principal pays any outstanding monies owed to the agent. Markesinis and Munday noted that there are two other situations in which an agent may lose his lien: first, the agent may elect to waive his rights;[114] secondly, the agent will lose the right if he chooses to part with the property.[115]

Q3 What are the rights of an agent?

4 Commercial agents and principals

As outlined above, the Commercial Agents (Council Directive) Regulations 1993, SI 1993/3053, impose compulsory obligations on a commercial agent. The Regulations define a commercial agent as 'a self-employed intermediary who has continuing authority to negotiate the sale or purchase of goods on behalf of another person (the "principal"), or to negotiate and conclude the sale or purchase of goods on behalf of and in the name of that principal'.[116] The Regulations specify that a commercial agent does not include '(i) a person who, in his capacity as an officer of a company or association, is empowered to enter into commitments binding on that company or association; (ii) a partner who is lawfully authorised to enter into commitments binding on his partners; (iii) a person who acts as an insolvency practitioner'.[117] Under the 1993 Regulations, a principal owes the commercial agent the following duties, which must be exercised dutifully and in good faith:

> a principal must (a) provide his commercial agent with the necessary documentation relating to the goods concerned; (b) obtain for his commercial agent the information necessary for the performance of the agency contract, and in particular notify his commercial agent within a reasonable period once he anticipates that the volume of commercial transactions will be significantly lower than

---

[112] The principle was also followed in *Houghton* v. *Matthews* (1803) 3 B. & P 485, as cited in Markesinis and Munday, above n. 44, at 147.

[113] *Re Bowes, Earl of Strathmore* v. *Vane* (1886) 33 Ch. D 586.

[114] See, e.g., *Weeks* v. *Goode* (1859) 6 CBNS 367 and *Forth* v. *Simpson* (1849) 13 QB 680.

[115] Markesinis and Munday, above n. 44, at 149.

[116] SI 1993/3053, reg. 2(1).

[117] An insolvency practitioner is defined in Insolvency Act 1986, s.388.

that which the commercial agent could normally have expected … A principal shall, in addition, inform his commercial agent within a reasonable period of his acceptance or refusal of, and of any non-execution by him of, a commercial transaction which the commercial agent has procured for him.[118]

The 1993 Regulations also impose a series of obligations on the commercial agent, who is required to:

look after the interests of his principal and act dutifully and in good faith … in particular, a commercial agent must (a) make proper efforts to negotiate and, where appropriate, conclude the transactions he is instructed to take care of; (b) communicate to his principal all the necessary information available to him; (c) comply with reasonable instructions given by his principal.[119]

It is important to note that neither the principal nor the commercial agent is entitled to derogate from the respective duties they owe to each other.[120] Furthermore, the principal and commercial agent are entitled to 'receive from the other, on request, a signed written document setting out the terms of the agency contract including any terms subsequently agreed'.[121]

The 1993 Regulations also specify minimum periods of notice for the termination of the agency agreement by either party. Under regulation 15, 'where an agency contract is concluded for an indefinite period either party may terminate it by notice'. The period of notice required is:

(a) one month for the first year of the contract; (b) two months for the second year commenced; (c) three months for the third year commenced and for the subsequent years; and the parties may not agree on any shorter periods of notice.

Under the Regulations, where there is no agreement between the parties regarding the payment of the commercial agent, the agent will be permitted such payment as is normally provided for such agents, and where no such practice exists, the commercial agent is entitled to a reasonable level of compensation.

The 1993 Regulation provide for a commercial agent to be indemnified or compensated as a result of termination of the agency agreement.[122] In particular, the Regulations state that a commercial agent is entitled to indemnity if and to the extent that:

(a) he has brought the principal new customers or has significantly increased the volume of business with existing customers and the principal continues to derive substantial benefits from the business with such customers; and (b) the payment of this indemnity is equitable having regard to all the circumstances and, in particular, the commission lost by the commercial agent on the business transacted with such customers.[123]

---

[118] SI 1993/3053, reg. 4.   [119] *Ibid.* reg. 3.
[120] *Ibid.* reg. 5.   [121] *Ibid.* reg. 13.
[122] *Ibid.* reg. 17.   [123] *Ibid.* reg. 17.

If the commercial agent is granted indemnity, he is still entitled to seek damages from the principal.[124] The commercial agent is permitted to seek compensation for damage suffered as a result of the termination of the agreement and relations with the principal. In particular, the 1993 Regulations provide that:

> such damage shall be deemed to occur particularly when the termination takes place in either or both of the following circumstances, namely circumstances which (a) deprive the commercial agent of the commission which proper performance of the agency contract would have procured for him whilst providing his principal with substantial benefits linked to the activities of the commercial agent; or (b) have not enabled the commercial agent to amortise the costs and expenses that he had incurred in the performance of the agency contract on the advice of his principal.[125]

However, compensation will not be payable to the commercial agent where:

> (a) the principal has terminated the agency contract because of default attributable to the commercial agent which would justify immediate termination of the agency contract; or (b) the commercial agent has himself terminated the agency contract, unless such termination is justified (i) by circumstances attributable to the principal, or (ii) on grounds of the age, infirmity or illness of the commercial agent in consequence of which he cannot reasonably be required to continue his activities; or (c) the commercial agent, with the agreement of his principal, assigns his rights and duties under the agency contract to another person.[126]

Q4 What are the obligations and duties of a commercial agent?

5 Disclosed agency

A disclosed agency can take different forms.[127] The principal may be classified as a 'disclosed principal', which means that the third party is aware of the identity of the principal; or, the principal may be referred to as an 'unnamed principal', meaning that the third party may be aware of the principal's existence but be uninformed of the principal's precise identity. A disclosed principal could also be one who has ratified the unofficial act of his agent.[128]

The general rule is that where an agent enters into a contract and discloses the existence of an agency, this could result in the principal being sued on the contract he has authorised.[129] A similar position arises where the agent exceeds his actual authority, but nonetheless has apparent authority, and the principal ratifies the agreement.[130] Cheng-Han stated:

> In cases of disclosed agency, where the agent has acted within the scope of his authority, it is clear that the acts in question are to be treated in certain respects

---

[124] *Ibid.* reg. 17(5).   [125] *Ibid.* reg. 17(7).   [126] *Ibid.* reg. 18.
[127] Munday, above n. 1, at 226.   [128] *Ibid.*
[129] Bradgate, above n. 11, at 161.   [130] *Ibid.*

as if they were acts of the principal. Accordingly, where the agent has entered into a contract with a third party within the scope of his authority, the contract is treated as that of the principal.[131]

In determining the obligations and liability of the disclosed principal, it is very important to consider the ambit of the agent's authority.[132] For example, in *Camillo Tank Steamship Co. Ltd* v. *Alexandria Engineering Works*, the House of Lords construed the term 'approve' to mean that the agent's authority included his ability to agree to the debt on behalf of his principal,[133] therefore holding that the 'principal could not evade liability to the third party'.[134] Conversely, if the agent operates outside the extent of his authority and the principal has not ratified his actions, the principal will be prevented from commencing legal proceedings or being subject to them.[135]

If it is possible to prove that the third party did have notice of the agent's lack of authority, the principal will not be bound by the actions of his agent. For example, in *Jordan* v. *Norton,* a father wanted to purchase a horse on behalf of his son, and wrote to the seller stating that the horse must come with a warranty that it was 'sound, and quiet in harness'. The son took delivery of the horse, but there was no assurance from the seller that the horse was 'sound, and quiet in the harness'. The court determined that the father was allowed to disclaim the agreement because the son had been ordered to take delivery of the horse only if it was accompanied by a warranty. Markesinis and Munday took the view that as the 'owner failed to give the warranty, but delivered the mare to the son … the father was not bound by the son's acts'.[136]

The discussion above has set out the general rules of a disclosed agent. However, there are a number of exceptions to these rules, some of which will be briefly discussed below.

(a) Foreign principals

There was at one time a general rule that if an agent entered into a contract for a foreign principal, the agent and not the principal would obtain rights and liabilities.[137] However, this position was emphatically overruled by the Court of Appeal in *Teheran-Europe Co. Ltd* v. *S. T. Belton (Tractors) Ltd,*[138] which has been followed in *Novasen SA* v. *Alimenta SA.*[139]

---

[131] T. Cheng-Han, 'Undisclosed principals and contract' (2004) 120 *Law Quarterly Review* (Jul.) 480, 488.

[132] Munday, above n. 1, at 226.   [133] (1921) 9 Ll. L Rep. 307.

[134] Munday, above n. 1, at 226.

[135] See, e.g., the decision in *Comerford* v. *Britannic Assurance Co. Ltd* (1908) 24 TLR 593.

[136] Markesinis and Munday, above n. 44, at 157.

[137] See *Elbinger AG fur Fabrication von Eisenbahn Material* v. *Claye* (1873) LR 8 QB 313.

[138] [1968] 2 QB 545.

[139] [2011] EWHC 49 (Comm); [2011] 1 Lloyd's Rep. 390.

(b) Agent a party to the contract

If an agent enters into a contract which provides that he is a party to the contract, the agent will be jointly legally responsible. Conversely, where there is no such express declaration, the agent's liability depends on the interpretation and construction of the contract.[140]

(c) Deeds

If a contract is entered into under seal, there are a number of special rules. If a principal is not named as party to such a contract or it is not executed in his name, the principal may not sue or be sued for breach of contract.[141] However, if the agent executes the deed, he is liable under it and is also able to enforce it to the exclusion of the principal. An exception to this rule relates to the execution of deeds via a power of attorney.[142]

(d) Bills of exchange

If an agent signs a bill of exchange, he may become liable under it, as the Bills of Exchange Act 1882 provides that the person who signs the bill becomes personally liable. Section 23 of the Act provides that:

> no person is liable as drawer, indorser, or acceptor of a bill who has not signed it as such: provided that (1) where a person signs a bill in a trade or assumed name, he is liable thereon as if he had signed it in his own name; (2) the signature of the name of a firm is equivalent to the signature by the person so signing of the names of all persons liable as partners in that firm.

However, the signatory will not be liable if he is acting in a representative capacity:

> Where a person signs a bill as drawer, indorser, or acceptor, and adds words to his signature, indicating that he signs for or on behalf of a principal, or in a representative character, he is not personally liable thereon; but the mere addition to his signature of words describing him as an agent, or as filling a representative character, does not exempt him from personal liability.[143]

(e) Custom

It is possible for an agent to acquire liability on a contract if there is a trade custom to that effect.

---

[140] Bradgate, above n. 11, at 163.
[141] See, e.g., *Re International Contract Co.*; *Pickering's Claim* (1870–71) LR 6 Ch. App. 525. For an illustration of this rule in operation see *Shack* v. *Anthony* (1813) 1 M & S 573 and *Harmer* v. *Armstrong* [1934] Ch. 65.
[142] See, e.g., Power of Attorney Act 1971, s.7.
[143] Bills of Exchange Act 1882, s.26(1).

(f) Agent the real principal

It is possible for an agent to enter into a contract for his own benefit. The agent can then enforce the contract and will be liable for any breaches of the contract.

(g) Collateral contracts

In a limited number of circumstances, it is possible for an agent to enter into a collateral contract with a third party who is already subject to the contract with the agent's principal. In such a situation, the agent could incur liability and/or instigate legal proceedings. Rights and liabilities under a collateral contract are of course separate from the rights and obligations of the principal.[144]

Q5 What is a disclosed agency?

6 Undisclosed agency

An undisclosed agency arises where the agent, for one of a number of reasons, does not make the third party aware that he is working for a principal. This might arise, for example, where the principal deliberately intends to remain unknown, or where in the course of a dealing, no one divulges the existence of the principal to the third party.[145] It is important to note that the third party is under no legal obligation to ask whether the other party to a contract is acting as an agent; however, case law requires actual notice that the agent is representing a principal for the undisclosed principal doctrine not to be applied.[146] Cheng-Han stated that 'in the case of undisclosed agency, the acts of the undisclosed principal's agent should *prima facie* be those of the principal in as much as the agent acts within the scope of the agent's actual authority'.[147] He added that 'in undisclosed agency, as the agent has been authorised by the principal to enter into the contract with the third party, the contract should be the principal's since the agent has only acted within the scope of the mandate given to him'.[148] The doctrine of undisclosed agency has been described as 'anomalous',[149] and was famously outlined by Lord Lindley in *Keighly, Maxsted & Co.* v. *Durant*:

> The explanation of the doctrine that an undisclosed principal can sue and be sued on a contract made in the name of another person with his authority is, that the contract is in truth, although not in form, that of the undisclosed principal himself. Both the principal and the authority exist when the contract is made; and the person who makes it for him is only the instrument by which the principal acts. In allowing him to sue and be sued upon it, effect is given, so far as he is

---

[144] Bradgate, above n. 11, at 163.   [145] Munday, above n. 1, at 239.
[146] See, e.g., *Oystertec* v. *Barker* [2003] RPC 29, para. 5, as cited in Munday, above n. 1, at 239.
[147] Cheng-Han, above n. 131, at 488.   [148] *Ibid.*
[149] See, e.g., *Welsh Development Agency* v. *Export Finance Corp.* [1992] BCLC 148, 173, 182, CA.

concerned, to what is true in fact, although that truth may not have been known to the other contracting party.[150]

He added:

as a contract is constituted by the concurrence of two or more persons and by their agreement to the same terms, there is an anomaly in holding one person bound to another of whom he knows nothing and with whom he did not, in fact, intend to contract. But middlemen, through whom contracts are made, are common and useful in business transactions, and in the great mass of contracts it is a matter of indifference to either party whether there is an undisclosed principal or not. If he exists it is, to say the least, extremely convenient that he should be able to sue and be sued as a principal, and he is only allowed to do so upon terms which exclude injustice.[151]

Further helpful guidance on undisclosed agency was provided by the Privy Council in *Siu Yin Kwan* v. *Eastern Insurance Co. Ltd*, in which Lord Lloyd of Berwick stated:

For present purposes the law can be summarised shortly. (1) An undisclosed principal may sue and be sued on a contract made by an agent on his behalf, acting within the scope of his actual authority. (2) In entering into the contract, the agent must intend to act on the principal's behalf. (3) The agent of an undisclosed principal may also sue and be sued on the contract. (4) Any defence which the third party may have against the agent is available against his principal. (5) The terms of the contract may, expressly or by implication, exclude the principal's right to sue, and his liability to be sued. The contract itself, or the circumstances surrounding the contract, may show that the agent is the true and only principal.[152]

An undisclosed principal is normally allowed to commence and be the subject of legal proceedings in respect of the actions of his agent. The most often quoted authority for this is the famous statement of Diplock LJ in *Tererhan-Europe Co. Ltd* v. *ST Belton (Tractors) Ltd*:

Where an agent has such actual authority and enters into a contract with another party intending to do so on behalf of his principal, it matters not whether he discloses to the other party the identity of his principal, or even that he is contracting on behalf of a principal at all, if the other party is willing or leads the agent to believe that he is willing to treat as a party to the contract anyone on whose behalf the agent may have been authorised to contract. In the case of an ordinary commercial contract such willingness of the other party may be assumed by the

---

[150] [1901] AC 240, 261.
[151] *Ibid.* 262. For a critical review of the decision of the House of Lords, see I. Brown, 'The significance of general and special authority in the development of the agent's external authority in English law' (2004) *Journal of Business Law* (July) 391.
[152] [1994] 2 AC 199, 207. For a more detailed discussion of this case, see A. Tettenborn, 'Insurers and undisclosed agency: rough justice and commercial expediency' (1994) 53(2) *Cambridge Law Journal* 223.

agent unless either the other party manifests his unwillingness or there are other circumstances which should lead the agent to realise that the other party was not so willing.[153]

Q6 What is an undisclosed agency?

7 Termination of agency

Under common law, an agency may be terminated by mutual consent, by the operation of law and by the unilateral act of the principal or agent.[154] It is important that the revocation is communicated to the other party, as set out by Lord Wilberforce in *Heatons Transport (St Helens) Ltd* v. *Transport and General Workers' Union*:

> To be effective in law a withdrawal or curtailment of an existing actual authority of an agent must be communicated by the principal to the agent in terms which the agent would reasonably understand as forbidding him to do that which he had previously been authorised to do on the principal's behalf.[155]

If there is an agency agreement or contract between the agent and principal, the relationship can be discharged by agreement. Furthermore, if the agent is appointed to perform a specific task or appointed for a certain period of time, the agency will be terminated once the task has been performed or the period of time has expired. One problematic issue as regards the termination of an agency agreement is where both parties seek to terminate the contract unilaterally. If an agency agreement contains provision for termination by notice, the agent and principal will be required to provide the requisite period of notice. However, if the agency agreement contains no specific notice period, the courts will imply a term permitting termination on reasonable notice. In *Martin Baker Aircraft Co. Ltd* v. *Canadian Flight Equipment Ltd*, the plaintiffs entered into an agreement under which the defendants were permitted to 'manufacture, sell and exploit' all of the plaintiffs' goods on the American Continent. The plaintiffs wanted to terminate the agreement but the defendants argued that the agreement was only terminable by mutual consent. The court held that 'the agreement was not one which the parties could have intended to be permanent, and, accordingly, there being nothing in the contract inconsistent with that view, the agreement was, on its true construction, determinable unilaterally on reasonable notice'.[156] The decision in *Martin* was followed by the court in *Stenborough Corp.* v. *Cooke Sons & Co.*[157] In this case, an agreement was entered into by the local authority and the defendant to regulate the release of the defendant's trade effluents into the public sewerage system that belonged to the local authority. The agreement

---

[153] [1968] 2 QB 545, 555.   [154] Bradgate, above n. 11, at 206.
[155] [1973] AC 15, 100, per Lord Wilberforce.
[156] [1955] 2 QB 556.   [157] [1968] Ch. 139.

included a termination period of three months. A new agreement was entered into by the same parties in 1951 that replaced and changed the original agreement, and made no reference to express provision for the determination of the agreement. In 1966, the local authority gave the defendant 12 months' notice of termination which was contested by the defendant. As the contract in question was for an indefinite duration and did not contain any express provision for its termination, the court determined that the agreement could be terminated by reasonable notice.

Consent is of central importance in the law of agency, and one party to an agency agreement cannot terminate it without the consent of the other party. This point was emphasised by Viscount Simon LC in *Heyman* v. *Darwins Ltd*: 'repudiation by one party standing alone does not terminate the contract. It takes two to end it, by repudiation, on the one side, and acceptance of the repudiation, on the other.'[158] It is important to note that if an agency is terminated, this does not necessarily bring to an end the operation of all the terms of the agreement. It was held at first instance in *Yasuda Fire & Marine Insurance Co. of Europe Ltd* v. *Orion Marine Insurance Underwriting Agency Ltd,* that 'certain clauses remain alive and kicking despite the termination of a contract for repudiatory breach'.[159]

An agency agreement can be terminated by the operation of law. Bradgate noted that this can occur through various trigger events.[160] An agency contract will be terminated by frustration if the performance of the agency becomes either illegal or impossible.[161] An agency agreement will also be terminated by the death of either the agent or the principal. In *Campanari* v. *Woodburn*, the court considered the impact of the death of the principal on the agency agreement.[162] In this case, prior to the agent fulfilling his obligations under the agency agreement, the principal died. The unscrupulous agent, although aware of the death of his principal, went on to fulfil his obligations and attempted to claim his commission. The court permitted the agent to recover some compensation on a quantum meruit basis for the services rendered. However, the court concluded that the agent was not permitted to claim the commission under the agency agreement, which had terminated on the death of the principal.

An agency relationship will also be terminated by operation of law if one of the parties is declared insane or becomes bankrupt. In *Drew* v. *Nunn*, a husband, who was represented by his wife, became insane but later recovered his sanity. During his period of insanity, his wife purchased goods from the third party, who had no knowledge of the husband's mental condition. After the husband made a full recovery, he refused to pay the third party for the goods

---

[158] [1942] AC 356, 361.   [159] [1995] QB 174.
[160] Bradgate, above n. 11, at 209.
[161] See, e.g., *Marshall* v. *Granville* [1917] 2 KB 87.
[162] (1854) 15 CB 400.

purchased by his wife. The court decided that the husband was liable for the price of the goods. Brett LJ took the view that:

> The principal is bound, although he retracts the agent's authority, if he has not given notice and the latter wrongfully enters into a contract upon his behalf. The defendant became insane and was unable to withdraw the authority which he had conferred upon his wife: he may be an innocent sufferer by her conduct, but the plaintiff, who dealt with her bonâ fide, is also innocent, and where one of two persons both innocent must suffer by the wrongful act of a third person, that person making the representation which, as between the two, was the original cause of the mischief, must be the sufferer and must bear the loss. Here it does not lie in the defendant's mouth to say that the plaintiff shall be the sufferer.[163]

In *Yonge* v. *Toynbee*, the Court of Appeal was faced with a set of circumstances where a firm of solicitors had been instructed by a client to represent him in proceedings brought against him. However, prior to the instigation of the legal proceedings, the client was certified as being of unsound mind. The solicitors, in ignorance of the state of mind of their client, delivered a defence against the cause of action. Subsequently, the plaintiff in the action made an application that the proceedings should be struck out and the defendant should be compelled to pay the plaintiff's costs because the defendant's solicitors had acted devoid of any authority. The court held that, as the defendant's solicitors had continued to act for their client, they had 'impliedly warranted that they had authority to act' and accordingly were personally liable.[164] It has been argued that the decision in this case is extremely unfair to agents and, as a result, the Power of Attorney Act 1971 now provides an element of protection.[165] Section 5 of the Act relates to protection of the donee and third persons where a power of attorney is revoked. Section 5(1) provides:

> A donee of a power of attorney who acts in pursuance of the power at a time when it has been revoked shall not, by reason of the revocation, incur any liability (either to the donor or to any other person) if at that time he did not know that the power had been revoked.

Under section 5(2):

> Where a power of attorney has been revoked and a person, without knowledge of the revocation, deals with the donee of the power, the transaction between them shall, in favour of that person, be as valid as if the power had then been in existence.

In *Collen* v. *Wright*, the defendant professing to act as an agent for a third party, made an agreement with the plaintiff for the lease of a property that was owned by the third party. However, the defendant had no authority to lease the

---

[163] (1879) 4 QBD 661, 667–8.   [164] [1910] 1 KB 215.
[165] See, e.g., A. Martin, 'Powers of attorney: peace of mind or out of control?' (2008) 1 *Conveyancer and Property Lawyer* 11.

property and the plaintiff successfully sued the agent for the cost of his unsuccessful action against the third party. Of particular relevance here is the following passage in which Wiles J stated:

> The fact that the professed agent honestly thinks that he has authority affects the moral character of his act; but his moral innocence, so far as the person whom he has induced to contract is concerned, in no way aids such person or alleviates the inconvenience and damage which he sustains. The obligation arising in such a case is well expressed by saying that a person, professing to contract as agent for another, impliedly, if not expressly, undertakes to or promises the person who enters into such contract, upon the faith of the professed agent being duly authorized, that the authority which he professes to have does in point of fact exist.[166]

Evans noted that:

> The principal reason justifying the doctrine appears to be that the agent is better placed to know about his authority than the third party. That reason has considerable weight. A solicitor will know whether his correspondence with the client gives him express authority to commence or defend litigation, whereas the third party will not. Such cases are likely to be very rare. In the slightly less unusual case of a client lacking capacity, the solicitor will have contact with the client and be able to form a view from their discussions of the case as to whether there should be any concerns as to his capacity. If the solicitor does have concerns, he should be able to insist on a medical examination. The third party has none of these advantages.[167]

As outlined above, the Commercial Agents (Council Directive) Regulations 1993 include a minimum period of notice which must be given to terminate the agency agreement.[168] The Regulations also provide that 'if the parties agree on notice periods longer than the prescribed minima, the notice period to be observed by the principal must not be shorter than that to be observed by the commercial agent'.[169] These measures have been described as 'significant and novel'.[170] It is important to note that if a commercial agent's agreement is terminated he is entitled to compensation; this has been described as 'one of the most important protective features of the Directive ... [giving] commercial agents, on termination of the agency relationship, the right to claim a lump sum payment'.[171] The rights contained in regulation 17 of the 1993 Regulations have

---

[166] *Collen* v. *Wright* [1910] 1 KB 215.

[167] H. Evans, 'Warranty of authority in litigation' (2010) 26(2) *Professional Negligence* 96.

[168] SI 1993/3053, reg. 15.

[169] P. Ellington and B. Carr, 'Legislative comment: the UK Commercial Agents Regulations 1993 (Council Directive 86/653/EC)' (1995) 1 *International Business Law Journal* 51, 58.

[170] C. Bankes, 'Termination of agreements with commercial agents: the effect of the Commercial Agents Directive in the United Kingdom' (1994) 5(7) *International Company and Commercial Law Review* 247.

[171] S. Saintier, 'Final guidelines on compensation of commercial agents' (2008) 124 *Law Quarterly Review* (Jan.) 31. For an illustration of this regulation in practice see *Claramoda Ltd* v. *Zoomphase Ltd (t/a Jenny Packham)* [2009] EWHC 2857 (Comm).

been tested on several occasions. In *Moore* v. *Piretta PTA Ltd*,[172] a commercial agent contracted with a principal under several agency contracts that began in 1988. When the last contract, entered into in 1994, was terminated by the principal, the agent claimed an indemnity under the terms of regulation 17(3), which allowed a commercial agent to be granted an indemnity if 'and to the extent that (a) he has brought the principal new customers or has significantly increased the volume of business with existing customers from whom the principal continues to derive substantial benefits …; and (b) the payment of this indemnity is equitable having regard to all the circumstances and, in particular, the commission lost by the commercial agent on the business transacted with such customers'. The court held, in favour of the agent, that for the purposes of regulation 17, an 'agency contract' meant 'the agency' and, accordingly, the indemnity was to cover the entire period of the agency.[173]

Q7 On what grounds may an agency agreement be terminated?

8 Recommended reading

Bradgate, R. *Commercial Law* (Oxford University Press, Oxford, 2005)

Brown, I. 'Divided loyalties in the law of agency' (1993) 109 *Law Quarterly Review*, (April) 206

Cowan, D. 'Lister & Co. v. Stubbs: who profits?' (1996) *Journal of Business Law* (Jan.) 22, 23

Dobson, P. and Stokes, R. *Commercial Law* (Sweet and Maxwell, London, 2008)

Dowrick, F. 'The relationship of principal and agent' (1954) 17(1) *Modern Law Review* 24, 31

Munday, R. *Agency: Law and Principles* (Oxford University Press, Oxford, 2010)

Nolan, R. 'Conflicts of duty: helping hands from the Privy Council?' (1994) 15(2) *Company Lawyer*, 58, 59

Tettenborn, A. 'Principals, sub-agents and accountability' (1999) 115 *Law Quarterly Review* (Oct.) 655, 657

Watts, P. 'Illegality and agency law: authorising illegal action' (2011) 3 *Journal of Business Law* 213, 216

---

[172] [1999] 1 All ER 174.

[173] For a brief comment on this case see C. Gardiner, 'The EC (Commercial Agents) Directive: twenty years after its introduction, divergent approaches still emerge from Irish and UK courts' (2007) *Journal of Business Law* (June) 412.

Part 2
Sale of Goods and Services

Introduction

Part 2 analyses the law relating to the sale and supply of goods and services, often considered to be at the heart of commercial law, many other strands of which depend upon the provision of goods and services and, hence, upon the existence of a relevant contract. In addition to these two specific types of contract, other contracts, such as hire contracts, involving the supply of goods are heavily dependent upon sale of goods legislation, often having some similar, if not identical provisions, particularly in relation to implied conditions regarding description and quality. These ancillary contracts will be referred to as appropriate in this part of the text.

Part 2 is divided into five chapters. The first deals with the policy issues underlying the development of sale of goods legislation and thus considers both its origins and the way that it has developed in the last century. It analyses the equality of bargaining power between the seller and the buyer and how the rise of consumerism in the last fifty years has affected the development of the law in this area. It also considers the impact of the European Union in the field of sale of goods both as regards remedies and the measures to regulate Internet trading. Finally, it looks at the distinction between contracts for the sale of goods and other contracts involving the transfer of the property or possession of goods.

Chapter 2 concentrates on the implied conditions relating to the right to sell, sale by description, satisfactory quality and fitness for purpose, and sales by sample. It analyses the various aspects of each of the implied conditions before moving on to consider limitations and exclusions of liability, the concept and impact of acceptance on the rights of the buyer and the available remedies.

Chapter 3 moves on to consider the passage of property and risk under Sale of Goods Act 1979, sections 16–20, an issue of increasing importance in these recessionary times when the ownership of property and the risk attached to it may be crucial in determining rights and liabilities if a business goes into liquidation. Following on from this is a section explaining the rule of *nemo dat* and the valid exceptions to it under which an innocent purchaser acting in good faith will acquire good title to the goods even against the true owner.

The chapter continues by looking at the related topic of delivery and payment, which, in the absence of a dispute, is usually of more concern to both parties to the contract. The buyer is primarily interested in receiving the goods while the seller is primarily concerned with receiving the payment. The chapter concludes by reviewing the remedies available to seller and buyer if delivery and payment do not take place properly.

The supply of services is the focus of the fourth chapter, which looks, initially, at the Provision of Services Regulations 2009[1] and the requirements contained in it as regards what information must be supplied to the recipient of services and the provision of dispute resolution and complaints systems. Thereafter, the chapter considers the Supply of Goods and Services Act 1982 and the implied conditions therein relating to goods supplied under a contract for services, together with the implied terms regarding the duty of care and skill and the time of performance imposed on the supplier and the responsibility on the customer to pay reasonable consideration for the services. The chapter concludes by looking at the role of codes of practice for services.

The final chapter in this Part addresses the impact of Internet trading and other forms of distance trading. It looks specifically at the provisions of the Electronic Commerce (EC Directive) Regulations 2002[2] and the controls they exert over trading on the Web. Thereafter, it analyses the provisions of the Consumer Protection (Distance Selling) Regulations 2000[3] as they apply to differing forms of distance selling.

---

[1] SI 2009/2999.   [2] SI 2002/2013.   [3] SI 2000/2334.

Part 2 Chapter 1

Sale of Goods Policy

Contents

1 Introduction

This chapter looks at the law relating to the sale of goods, a central plank of commercial law. It is of crucial importance to both business purchasers and consumer buyers and provides the framework through which millions of goods are bought and sold.

Section 2 of this chapter outlines the role and breadth of sale of goods legislation. Section 3 details the development of sale of goods legislation from the passage of the Sale of Goods Act 1893 to the present day.

Section 4 discusses the equality of bargaining power between seller and buyer and the mechanisms that the law uses to attempt to maintain an appropriate balance. These include the Unfair Contract Terms Act 1977, the Unfair Terms in Consumer Contracts Regulations 1999 and the Sale of Goods Act 1979, section 15A.

Section 5 looks at the impact of the European Union on the recent development of sale of goods legislation. Section 6 analyses what constitutes a contract for the sale of goods. Section 7 considers contracts for non-monetary consideration, including the status of part-exchange contracts, and section 8 discusses other contracts for the transfer of property or possession that are not classed as contracts for the sale of goods. These include contracts of hire, hire-purchase contracts, leaseback, contracts for the provision of goods and services and the supply of computer programs.

2 Background

The sale and supply of goods and services lies at the very heart of commercial law. The buying and selling, or related supply and acquisition, of goods and services is the fundamental transaction at the centre of commerce both between traders and between traders and consumers. Other aspects of commercial law, such as the insurance of and the financing of goods or services, are dependent upon the main supply contract and would not exist without it. Equally, agency contracts are often created for the express purpose of bringing about the main contract of sale or supply.

Of immediate note is the breadth of transactions that the law governing the sale and supply of goods seeks to control. It is applicable to multimillion-pound international contracts between traders that lie at the centre of international commerce[1] yet is equally applicable to a contract by which a consumer buys a packet of sweets in a local shop. This diversity necessarily presents a challenge to both the law and legislators to ensure that the law remains relevant to the market and encompasses changes to that market, such as the phenomenal growth in distance selling during the last twenty years brought about by the development of the Internet and the ease with which purchasers, both commercial and consumer, can now transact across borders for a wide variety of goods and services. This has necessarily brought about a pan-European review of aspects of the law governing the sale of goods and the ways in which those contracts can be enforced.

Q1 Consider the developments in the market for the supply of goods in the last thirty years and analyse the impact of those changes.

3 Development of the sale of goods

The Sale of Goods Act 1979 (as amended), which came into force in January 1980, provides the current framework for contracts for the sale of goods, the statutory genesis of which lies in the Sale of Goods Act 1893, which itself codified the pre-existing common law as well as seeking to assimilate Scottish law on the subject. Sir Mackenzie Chalmers, who drafted the 1893 Act, stated that, acting on Lord Herschell's advice, the Bill 'endeavoured to reproduce as exactly as possible the existing law, leaving any amendments that might seem desirable

---

[1] This would naturally depend on whether the contracting parties had chosen to have their contract governed by the laws of England.

to be introduced in Committee on the authority of the legislature'.[2] The status of pre-1893 case law would be that those 'decisions which formed the basis of the various sections and which were intended to be reproduced in the Act'.[3] would remain relevant where the law was unchanged.

In the period between 1893 and 1979, the 1893 Act was both statutorily amended and the subject of a plethora of case law. Statutory amendments included the passage of the Law Reform (Enforcement of Contracts) Act 1954, section 2 of which abolished the need for sale of goods contracts with a value of £10 or more to be evidenced by 'a note or memorandum in writing' as previously required by section 4(1) of the 1893 Act. This rendered contractual arrangements less formal, a move now encapsulated in secton 4(1) of the 1979 Act, which provides that contracts of sale can be made in writing (with or without seal), by word of mouth, by a combination of the two, or may be implied from the conduct of the parties. A further significant reform came with the passage of the Supply of Goods (Implied Terms) Act 1973 which changed sale of goods legislation by altering the validity and applicability of clauses seeking to exclude the liability of a seller under sections 12–15 of the Sale of Goods Act 1893. The 1973 Act inserted a new section 55 into the 1893 Act forbidding any exclusion of liability under section 12 and rendering void any clause that purported to exclude liability under the implied conditions of sections 13–15 of the 1893 Act 'in the case of a consumer sale'.[4] Exclusion clauses in other contracts would be unenforceable to the extent that it would not be fair or reasonable to allow reliance on them. This amendment threw into sharp relief the potential for differing regimes for consumer buyers and non-consumer buyers, the development of which has continued since[5] and has given rise to debate as to whether we have now reached the point where two distinct, yet overlapping, regimes of commercial law and consumer law exist.[6]

The 1979 Act is but the latest stage of the development of this area of law and has itself been subject to amendment in 1994, 1995 and 2002. After consideration of the topic by the Law Commission,[7] the Sale and Supply of Goods Act 1994 replaced the familiar implied condition of 'merchantable quality' with the more modern and relevant term 'satisfactory quality'; while the Sale of Goods (Amendment) Act 1994 abolished the historical market overt rule from the

---

[2] To be found in the 'Introduction' to the 1st edn of *Chalmers Sale of Goods* (1894) and reproduced in subsequent editions, see M. Mark, *Chalmers Sale of Goods* (18th edn, Butterworths, London, 1981).

[3] *Ibid.*

[4] This amendment was itself amended so that the current s.55(1) permits exclusion clauses but only to the extent allowed under the Unfair Contract Terms Act 1977.

[5] For example, the Unfair Contract Terms Act 1977, the Unfair Terms in Consumer Contract Regulations 1999 (SI 1999/2083) and the Sale and Supply of Goods to Consumers Regulations 2002 (SI 2002/3045), all of which will be discussed later.

[6] For an interesting discussion of this relationship see R. Bradgate, *Commercial Law* (3rd edn, Butterworths, London, 2000)

[7] Law Commission, *Sale and Supply of Goods* (Report No. 160, 1987).

nemo dat exceptions.[8] The following year, the Sale of Goods (Amendment) Act 1995 addressed the issue of the passage of title in an undivided bulk of unascertained goods by allowing prepaying purchasers to acquire an undivided interest in those goods.[9]

While the Sale of Goods Act 1979 provides the framework for contracts of sale, some of its provisions can be amended by the express agreement of the contracting parties.[10] Chalmers made clear that the Act does not prevent contracting parties agreeing their own contractual terms, thus making whatever bargain they feel is appropriate to their needs. The object of the Act is to 'lay down clear rules for the case where the parties have either formed no intention, or failed to express it'.[11] Thus, while being prescriptive in some areas of the contract, it allows for flexibility in others.

At root, a contract for the sale of goods is simply a specialised form of contract, with certain of the common law rules relating to such contracts being brought together in a statute. It follows that, as the provisions of the statute are not all encompassing, other sources of law may be called upon to fill in the gaps. Indeed, section 62(2) of the 1979 Act itself makes clear that other sources of law are both pertinent and expressly applicable.

> The rules of the common law, including the law merchant, except in so far as they are inconsistent with the provisions of this Act, and in particular the rules relating to the law of principal and agent and the effect of fraud, misrepresentation, duress or coercion, mistake or other invalidating cause, apply to contracts for the sale of goods.

This section underpins the fact that the Act is a flexible framework as opposed to a rigid set of rules and can be inclusive in approach. The express inclusion of mercantile law facilitates the incorporation of the trade usages and practices into the law governing the sale of goods, reflecting the origins of the Act which was introduced during the reign of Queen Victoria to help facilitate trade. The usage of the term 'merchantable quality' in section 14, when codifying the implied condition relating to the quality of goods, spoke to the fact that the Act originally governed relations between merchants, the term 'consumer' still being several decades away from common usage and from the overt recognition that the Act would also be a cornerstone of consumer protection. It is noteworthy that there was no attempt to define 'merchantable quality' statutorily until 1979 when the notion of consumerism was developing steadily.

---

[8] Sale of Goods (Amendment) Act 1994, s.1.

[9] Sale of Goods (Amendment) Act 1995, s.1(3).

[10] Some provisions of the Sale of Goods Act 1979 can be varied by agreement between the seller and the buyer, e.g., s.20 on the passage of risk, s.28 governing the concurrent nature of the terms on delivery and payment, s.31 on instalment deliveries and s.36 stipulating that the buyer is not normally bound to return rejected goods. For a fuller discussion of these provisions see Part 2 Chapter 3.

[11] See the 'Introduction' to the 1st edn of *Chalmers Sale of Goods* (1894) reproduced in subsequent editions, see Mark, above n. 2.

Sale of goods legislation must reflect both changes in the market and the manner of contracting if it is to remain facilitative rather than obstructive. Arguably, the most significant alteration to the market in the last twenty years has been the development of the Internet, which revolutionised contracts of sale by permitting sellers and buyers to contract both nationally and internationally at the click of a button. This has necessarily brought about a new emphasis on the regulation of distance contracts where the contracting parties will never meet and raises issues such as protection of the parties and the choice of applicable law.[12]

It is against this background of shifting markets, EU developments, different legislative approaches and the rise of consumerism that sale of goods legislation has developed over the last hundred years. Naturally, it will continue to develop as appropriate both to address new situations and to remain relevant to the myriad contracts, both national and international, business-to-business, business-to-consumer and consumer-to-consumer that rely upon its provisions for the successful pursuit and management of contracts of sale.

Q2 Consider how the development of the law governing the sale of goods has reflected the rise of consumerism.

4 Equality of bargaining power: non-consumers and consumers

Many factors influence the market within which the Sale of Goods Act 1979 is used and, naturally, have an impact on the way that both it and its predecessors have developed over the years. Thus, for example, English contract law is based on the notion of equality of bargaining power such that the seller and buyer are presumed to have an equal influence over the content of any contract to which they are a party. While this might have been the case in pre-industrial Britain when contracts were largely made between people in the immediate locality, it is naive in the extreme to imagine that this is true in the modern trading world. Nowadays, contracts may take place between businesses of significantly different sizes, such as a multinational company selling goods to a small retail outlet or, equally, in the consumer market, by a major chain store providing goods to the man on the street. In both of these examples, the seller is in a position largely to be able to dictate the terms of the contract with the buyer having very little power or influence.

While in both of the previous examples, the stronger party is the seller, this is not necessarily the case and circumstances can arise, particularly in business-to-business contracts, where the buyer is in the more dominant position. Thus, for example, large producers such as car manufacturers regularly buy component parts from small component manufacturers who are not in a position to have any real influence over the content of the relevant contract of sale. Equally,

---

[12] Distance contracts, including e-contracts, are discussed in detail in Part 2 Chapter 5.

major high street retailers such as supermarkets source their supplies from a large number of small producers who cannot influence the terms of the supply contract. Such small producers may be driven to sell their produce at a low price with a very small profit margin because of their inherent weakness when agreeing the terms of the contract. Indeed, in the not uncommon situation where a small producer is selling all of his produce to one major retail company, he has no control at all over the terms of the contract of sale as, without an alternative buyer, he has no choice but to accept the terms upon which the retail company chooses to buy from him.

This potential inequality of bargaining power between the parties has been partially, though not necessarily successfully, addressed through three different legislative routes, namely the use of the Unfair Contract Terms Act (UCTA) 1977, the passage of the Unfair Terms in Consumer Contracts Regulations 1999[13] and the provision of different remedies for consumer and non-consumer buyers under the Sale of Goods Act 1979. All of these mechanisms impact upon the bargaining power and rights of the respective parties. However, they also reflect the rise of consumerism in the last fifty years as they provide a higher level of protection for consumer buyers as opposed to non-consumer buyers, the assumption being that consumers are more vulnerable and thus in need of greater statutory protection.

(a) Unfair Contract Terms Act 1977

Section 3 of the UCTA 1977 introduced controls over standard form contracts. These contracts, though eminently sensible from a business perspective as they negate the need to continually negotiate terms in each individual contract, present the person imposing the terms with a potential opportunity to impose unfair terms on the other, usually weaker, party. This is a particular problem when the purchaser is a consumer who will not be contracting on their own standard terms and will be powerless to affect those imposed upon him by the business seller. A business-to-business sale raises a different issue as, when each usually contracts on their own standard terms, there may be a disagreement as to whose standard terms govern the contract. This has given rise to the so-called 'battle of the forms'[14] when both seller and buyer seek to use their respective standard form contracts, and it will ultimately be up to the court to decide whose terms will prevail. In practice, it will depend on the facts of the particular case[15] and, if there is no clear evidence as to which terms are paramount, those implied by the Sale of Goods Act 1979 will take effect.[16]

---

[13] SI 1999/2083.
[14] *Butler Machine Tool Co. v. Ex-Cell-O Corp.* [1979] 1 All ER 965.
[15] *Rimeco Riggelsen & Metal Co. v. Queenborough Rolling Mill Co.* [1995] CL 110.
[16] *GHSP Inc. v. AB Electronic Ltd* [2010] EWHC 1828 (Comm).

However, section 3(2)(a) of the UCTA 1977 provides that, when contracting on standard terms, the person whose terms they are cannot use them to exclude or limit his contractual liability for breach unless the exclusion or limitation satisfies the requirement of reasonableness.[17] Further, section 3(2)(b) provides that that person cannot use the contract terms to allow him either to render contractual performance that differs substantially from that which was reasonably expected of him or, alternatively, to render no performance at all, unless in either instance the contract term would satisfy the test of reasonableness. These provisions clearly help the weaker contractual party by restricting the opportunity for the stronger party to abuse that position.

While section 3 applies to all standard term contracts, the cross-over between contracts for the sale of goods, other related contracts for the acquisition of goods and the control of unfair contract terms is explicit in sections 6 and 7 of the UCTA 1977. It is in these sections that we also see the second legislative technique used to protect an overtly weaker contractual party, namely a consumer.

Section 6 of the UCTA 1977 lays out controls over any attempt to exclude or restrict liability for a breach of the implied conditions contained in sections 12–15 of the Sale of Goods Act 1979.[18] Section 6(1)(a) of the UCTA 1977 prohibits absolutely any term that seeks to exclude or restrict the liability of the seller for a breach of section 12 of the Sale of Goods Act 1979, namely the implied condition that the seller will have the right to sell the goods at the time that the property is due to pass. Section 6(1)(b) makes similar provision in respect of any term that seeks to exclude liability for a breach of section 8 of the Supply of Goods (Implied Terms) Act 1973 in respect of hire-purchase contracts.[19] This control exists irrespective of whether the buyer is a business or a consumer.

The divergence between business buyers and consumer buyers becomes apparent when looking at sections 6(2)and (3) of the UCTA 1977, which deal with attempts to exclude or restrict liability for breaches of sections 13–15 of the Sale of Goods Act 1979 or sections 9–11 of the Supply of Goods (Implied Terms) Act 1973. Where the buyer deals as a consumer,[20] a contract term

---

[17] The 'reasonableness' test applicable here is set out in the UCTA 1977, s.11(1), which states that the relevant term must 'have been a fair and reasonable one to be included having regard to the circumstances which were, or ought reasonably to have been, known to or in the contemplation of the parties when the contract was made'.

[18] The implied conditions in Sale of Goods Act 1979, ss.12–15 cover the right to sell, sale by description, satisfactory quality, fitness for purpose and sale by sample. These implied conditions are considered in detail in Part 2 Chapter 2.

[19] The property in the goods in a hire-purchase contract does not pass until the hirer exercises the option to purchase at the end of the agreement either when the agreement has run its full term or at such earlier time as the hirer pays off the total amount owing and brings the agreement to an early end. The title will not pass if the hirer terminates the agreement before the final payment is due or goes into breach.

[20] A person is 'dealing as a consumer' for these purposes when he does not make the contract in the course of a business nor holds himself out as doing so, the other party does make the contract

cannot be used to exclude or restrict liability for a breach of those provisions, while it can be if the buyer is not dealing as a consumer on condition that the term satisfies the test of reasonableness.

Section 7 of the UCTA 1977 puts in place similar provisions regarding any attempt to exclude or restrict liability for a breach where the possession or ownership of goods passes under a contract other than those governed by contracts of sale or hire-purchase. This would include, for example, contracts of barter and contracts of hire. Again, there is a distinction drawn between consumer buyers and non-consumer buyers.

(b) Unfair Terms in Consumer Contracts Regulations 1999

The Unfair Terms in Consumer Contracts Regulations 1999[21] reflect the assumption that consumers will be the weaker of the two contracting parties and thus are in need of a greater level of protection as regards the potential inequality of bargaining power. Regulation 5(1) provides that a contract term that has not been negotiated individually between the seller and buyer shall be regarded as unfair if it causes a significant imbalance between the rights of the contracting parties to the detriment of the consumer. For this purpose, a term will be regarded as not having been negotiated individually when it has been drafted in advance and the consumer has not had the opportunity to influence the terms of the contract.[22] Indeed, even if an individual term has been negotiated individually, the 1999 Regulations will still apply to the rest of the contract if all the evidence suggests that it is a preformulated standard contract.[23]

Regulation 6 provides that, when assessing whether a term is unfair, regard must be had to the nature of the goods or services for which the contract was concluded, the circumstances surrounding the conclusion of the contract and all of the other terms of the contract or of any other contract upon which it is dependent. Further, Schedule 2 to the 1999 Regulations provides an indicative and non-exhaustive list of seventeen different contract terms which are automatically assumed to be unfair.

If a term is found to be unfair, it is not binding on the consumer[24] but the rest of the contract subsists and will be binding on the consumer if it is capable of continuing without the unfair term.[25] Further, any qualifying body within the meaning of the 1999 Regulations can apply for an injunction against any person who appears to be using or recommending the use of an unfair term for general use in consumer contracts.

---

in the course of a business and the goods are of a type ordinarily supplied for private use or consumption: see UCTA 1977, s.12(1). The buyer will not be classed as a consumer for these purposes if he is an individual buying second-hand goods at a public auction which individuals can attend in person: see UCTA 1977, s.12(2).

[21] SI 1999/2083. The Regulations were passed to give effect to the Unfair Terms in Consumer Contracts Directive 93/13/EC.

[22] SI 1999/2083, reg. 5(2).   [23] *Ibid.* reg. 5(3).

[24] *Ibid.* reg. 8(1).   [25] *Ibid.*, reg. 8(2).

These 1999 Regulations will be affected by the Consumer Rights Directive,[26] which broadly reflects the provisions of the previous Directive and thereby of the current Regulations. A proposal has been made to introduce a black list and a grey list of unfair contract terms, those terms which will always be considered unfair or that will be presumed to be unfair unless the trader can prove that the individual term is fair in accordance with the general principles laid out in the Directive.

(c) Sale of Goods Act 1979 section 15A

The provision of different rules for consumer buyers and non-consumer buyers reflecting their essential differences are also to be found in the Sale of Goods Act 1979 itself. Thus, for example, section 15A restricts the remedies available to a non-consumer buyer for a breach of sections 12–15 of the 1979 Act while preserving the right of the consumer buyer to reject the goods following a breach. A person not dealing as a consumer cannot exercise a right to reject the goods if the breach is so slight that it would be unreasonable for him to reject them[27] unless there is a contrary provision, either express or implied, in the contract.[28] The breach will be treated as a breach of warranty instead of being viewed as a breach of condition. As such, the remedy will be a claim for damages as opposed to a right to reject the goods and claim a full refund of the contractual price. A further example exists in section 20(4) of the 1979 Act. Generally, in the absence of an agreement to the contrary, the risk in goods passes with the property irrespective of whether delivery has taken place. However, section 20(4) provides that where the buyer is a consumer, the goods remain at the risk of the seller until they are delivered to the buyer.[29]

Q3 Consider how legislation has been used to differentiate between business purchasers and consumer buyers. Is this legislative distinction valid?

5 Impact of the European Union

While the dichotomy between consumer buyers and non-consumer buyers has increasingly been a feature in the application of rights under the Sale of Goods Act 1979, the other major change in the market of recent times has been the growth in distance sales via the Internet. Of significance here is both the

---

[26] In 2008, the European Commission proposed a Consumer Rights Directive 2008/0196 (COD). In June 2011, the EU Parliament adopted the Directive, with the publication of the new Directive scheduled for 2011 and the transposition of the new rules into national laws to be completed by the end of 2013.

[27] Sale of Goods Act 1979, s.15A(1)(b).

[28] *Ibid.* s.15A(2).

[29] For a full discussion of the passage of property, risk and delivery, see Part 2 Chapter 3.

potential for the cross-border sales and supply of goods and services and also the issues that necessarily result in respect of identifying and enforcing the rights of the buyer in that enlarged market. This brings the regulation of e-commerce to the fore and the enforceability of the rights of the buyer when the seller is in breach of his obligations. The European Union has introduced controls over the workings of e-commerce in the EU with the passage of Directive 2000/31/EC on Electronic Commerce.[30] The provisions of that Directive largely relate to the information that a buyer must receive about the seller with whom he is going to do business, which, of course, allows the buyer the opportunity to contact the seller and ultimately sue him if the latter should be in breach of the contract. The requirements include a provision that the seller must provide the buyer with the terms and conditions upon which he is prepared to do business and that they must be available in a durable form which the buyer can access and retain. Of course, this does not permit the buyer to affect the terms and conditions other than to decide that he will or will not purchase and, if the seller has a monopoly on the market, that choice is effectively non-existent if the buyer needs the goods or services being offered. Assuming that the buyer does purchase and that a breach occurs, the enforcement of his rights raises issues regarding which laws will apply and through which courts the buyer may seek a remedy.

The enforcement of legal rights, even if seller and buyer are in the same jurisdiction, can be problematic. We have already referred to situations in which the seller and buyer may be of significantly different size such that the seller can effectively force his terms and conditions on the buyer. This imbalance continues in respect of enforcement as the small business or consumer may feel unable to take on a big corporate seller in court for fear of losing the case and becoming liable for the costs of the seller. The difference between the buyer knowing his rights under the Sale of Goods Act and being able to enforce them may, in practice, be significant.

Mention has already been made of the role of the European Union in controlling the market for the sale and supply of goods and services on the Internet. However, its role in respect of contracts of sale has gone wider than that and will continue to play a part in the future. Traditionally, amendments to sale of goods legislation have been made by Parliament as a result of ongoing debate and Law Commission reports.[31] However, the most recent amendment to the Sale of Goods Act 1979 affecting consumer contracts resulted from the passage of Directive 1999/44/EC on certain aspects of the sale of consumer goods and associated guarantees.[32] This Directive introduced a new regime of remedies for situations when the goods supplied under the contract are not in conformity with

---

[30] This Directive was given effect in the United Kingdom by the Electronic Commerce (EC Directive) Regulations 2002 (SI 2002/2013). These Regulations are discussed in detail in Part 2 Chapter 5.

[31] For example, the change from merchantable quality to satisfactory quality and the other provisions of Law Commission, *Sale and Supply of Goods* (Report No. 160, 1987).

[32] This Directive was given effect in the United Kingdom by the Sale and Supply of Goods to Consumers Regulations 2002 (SI 2002/3045).

the contract in that, for example, they do not comply with the contract description or are not fit for their purpose. These new remedies are to be found in sections 48A-48F of the Sale of Goods Act 1979 but exist alongside the previously existing remedy of rescission for a contractual breach of that nature. That fact, in itself, reveals one of the difficulties associated with minimum harmonisation Directives in that the Directive expressly permitted Member States to retain or adopt more stringent provisions than those demanded by the Directive.[33] While this has worked to the benefit of UK consumers, where alternative more stringent remedies were already available, allowing differing provisions across the European Union militates against the development of cross-border trade. It is significant that the proposed Consumer Rights Directive,[34] if passed, will impose maximum harmonisation in the areas it addresses with the specific purpose of promoting cross-border trade involving consumers. It is hoped that this will encourage greater use of the Internet for cross-border contracts.

In addition to its intended impact on unfair contract terms in consumer contracts as previously mentioned, the Directive revisits, among other things, the quality and fitness for purpose of goods and the passage of title. As it is applicable only to business-to-consumer contracts, its adoption may further widen the gap between the rights of business purchasers and those of consumer buyers. This could result in two parallel systems unless the United Kingdom adopts the new provisions relating to quality and fitness for all contracts for the sale of goods. A significant aspect of these provisions will be the available remedies as discussed below.

Q4 Consider the impact of the European Union in the continuing development of the law governing the sale of goods.

6 Contract of sale

At the heart of the law of sale of goods is, of course, the requirement that there is a contract of sale, as defined, from which the rights and responsibilities of both the seller and buyer will emanate.

A contract of sale is defined in section 2(1) of the Sale of Goods Act 1979 as being:

> a contract by which the seller transfers or agrees to transfer the property in the goods to the buyer for a money consideration, called the price.

This basic definition makes clear the essential elements of a sale of goods contract, namely, that it is a consensual agreement between two parties, the seller and the buyer, that it must involve the transfer of the property in the goods and not merely their possession and that the consideration must be

---

[33] Directive 1999/44/EC on certain aspects of the sale of consumer goods and associated guarantees, Art. 8.2.
[34] COM(2008)614 final.

money. The section goes on to stipulate that there can be sales between one part owner and another,[35] that a sale may be absolute or conditional,[36] and that where the transfer of the property is to take place at some future time or when some precondition to the sale has been satisfied, the contract will be termed an agreement to sell.[37]

This definition distinguishes contracts for the sale of goods from other similar contracts under which purchasers may acquire goods such as contracts of bailment, contracts of barter and contracts for works and materials. While the distinctions remain important, if only to ensure that any legal action is taken under the correct statutory provision dependent upon the nature of the contract, in practice the statutes are very similar in many respects and the case law under one statute can be called upon in a dispute arising under a different statute. An obvious example of these parallel provisions would be the implied conditions relating to title, description, quality and sale by sample contained in sections 12–15 of the Sale of Goods Act 1979 and which also appear, sometimes verbatim, in the corresponding provisions of other statutes,[38] although it should be remembered that the Acts may develop at differing rates and there may be a time lag between an amendment to the Sale of Goods Act and similar amendments to other statutes.

Nonetheless, it remains important to recognise the differences between the varying types of contract under which a purchaser may acquire ownership, or at least possession, of goods. These alternative contracts fall into two main groups: those where the consideration is something other than money, and those where the buyer may only be acquiring possession of the goods with, in some instances, an option to acquire the property in the goods at a later stage or where the transfer of the property occurs as an integral part of a different category of contract. A further, more modern issue, arises in respect of contracts for computer software.

7 Contracts for non-monetary consideration

Section 2(1) of the Sale of Goods Act 1979 requires that the goods are transferred for 'a money consideration, called the price'. Money in this context would include cash and cheques but would not include credit or some other form of consideration. Two alternative forms of contract can easily be identified as belonging here, contracts of barter or exchange and contracts of gift.

Contracts of barter or exchange include contracts where no money changes hands at all but is less certain where a combination of goods and money are used as consideration for the contract. Whether the parties have attributed a

---

[35] Sale of Goods Act 1979, s.2(2).
[36] *Ibid.* s.2(3).   [37] *Ibid.* s.2(5).
[38] For example, Part I of the Supply of Goods and Services Act 1982 dealing with contracts for the transfer of goods and contracts of hire, and the Supply of Goods (Implied Terms) Act 1973, which deals with the implied conditions in contracts of hire-purchase.

monetary value to the goods to be used as payment may be a factor in deciding whether the resultant contract is one of sale or one of barter but is not conclusive on the point, and whether any given contract is properly classed as a contract of sale may depend ultimately on the intention of the parties rather than on what percentage of the purchase price is to be paid in money as opposed to goods. In *Aldridge* v. *Johnson*,[39] the parties exchanged 32 bullocks valued at £192 for 100 quarters of barley valued at £215, the balance of £23 being paid in cash, it being held that the parties intended the arrangement to be for reciprocal sales of the goods, effectively two contracts of sale with the proceeds being offset against each other. In the most common modern example of part-exchange, namely, the part-exchange of motor vehicles whereby the purchaser of a new car will use his old car and cash to constitute the consideration for the new car, the courts have assumed that it is a contract of sale if that appears to be the intention of the parties. However, it was held by the Irish Supreme Court in *Flynn* v. *Mackin*[40] that where no monetary value had been attached to either the new vehicle or the one to be provided in part-exchange, it was a contract of barter rather than sale.[41]

The provision of a 'free gift' raises a different issue as regards consideration. If there is truly no consideration provided for the gift, then clearly there cannot be a contract of sale or, indeed, any other contract. However, the situation is different where the provision of the gift is dependent upon the purchaser entering a contract for the purchase of something else, as is often the case in marketing campaigns. The precise nature of the contract under which the 'free gift' is provided was considered by the House of Lords in the much quoted decision in *Esso Petroleum Ltd* v. *Commissioners of Customs and Excise*.[42] The case related to the provision by garages of a free commemorative coin bearing the likeness of an England World Cup football player with every four gallons of petrol purchased. Lord Simon was of the opinion that this constituted a collateral contract in which the consideration for the free coin was the purchase of the petrol, a view shared by Lord Wilberforce. However, this view was not shared by all of the Law Lords.

Q5 Analyse the various ways in which non-monetary consideration can be provided.

8 Contracts for the transfer of property or possession

The transfer of the possession of goods, as opposed to the property in them, may occur both in situations where there is no intention that the property will ever pass, e.g., hire contracts, and also where there is no intention to pass

[39] (1857) 7 E & B 885, Court of Queen's Bench.
[40] [1974] 1 IR 101.   [41] This decision has been criticised.
[42] [1976] 1 All ER 117.

property immediately but where there is the potential for it to pass at some point in the future but with no certainty that it ever will, e.g., hire-purchase contracts. These contracts, while similar in appearance to contracts of sale and may indeed attract similar rights and responsibilities, are not classed as contracts for the sale of goods and are governed by other statutes.

(a) Contracts of hire

In the former situation, a contract of bailment will exist under which the bailor will allow the bailee to take possession of the goods with no intention that the latter will ever acquire title to the goods. This cannot be a sale of goods because of the fundamental requirement that a sale of goods contract requires the seller to transfer the property in the goods. In many respects, however, the bailee in such a contract will obtain rights very similar to those bestowed upon a buyer under the Sale of Goods Act 1979, i.e., compliance with description, satisfactory quality,[43] etc., although, naturally the bailor does not warrant that he has the right to sell the goods at the time that the contract takes effect, merely that he has the right to transfer possession of them.[44]

(b) Hire-purchase contracts

Hire-purchase contracts, in which the likelihood is that the property in the goods will ultimately pass to the buyer but where there is no certainty that that will be the case, are not contracts for the sale of goods.[45] Rather, they are contracts of hire followed by an option to purchase at the end of the hire period. While the majority of hirers exercise that option and ultimately purchase the goods, the hirer is under no obligation to purchase the goods. If the hirer so chooses he could exercise the contractual and statutory[46] right to terminate the contract before its conclusion and return the goods to the hire-purchase company. This lack of certainty of sale is fatal to any suggestion that a contract of sale has taken place. By contrast, however, where the contract intends that the property in the goods will pass at the start of the contract but with payment deferred to regular instalments, it will not be a contract of hire-purchase but a credit sale.

(c) Leaseback

'Leaseback' involves a further situation in which the ownership of the goods and possession of them are in separate hands. Typically, the owner of goods

---

[43] The implied conditions in hire contracts appear in the Supply of Goods and Services Act 1982, ss.7–10.

[44] *Ibid.* s.7.   [45] Per Lord Herschell in *Helby* v. *Matthews* [1895] AC 471.

[46] Consumer Credit Act 1974, s.99.

sells them to a finance company and then leases them back from the company in exchange for a regular monetary payment, with the provision that the finance company can seize the goods back should the lessee fail to pay. The issue that the courts face in this scenario, which they need to address on every occasion that a case comes before them, is whether this is a legitimate arrangement in which the sale and lease documents truly represent the intention of the parties and should be enforced as such, or whether it is really merely a device for lending money to the owner of the goods, using those goods as security for the loan. If the latter is the case, then the arrangement would fall under the Bills of Sale Acts and would need to be registered if it is to be enforceable. The court must decide whether the documents reflect the true intention of the parties and should be enforced as such or whether they are a sham which should be put to one side.[47] It is, of course, extremely difficult to determine whether the documents are a sham and thus courts tend to interpret and enforce the documents at face value. However, this allows the unusual situation to arise whereby the 'seller' of the goods can hold the finance company liable for the quality of goods that he sold them as, technically, they are leasing the goods to him and will be liable under the Supply of Goods and Services Act 1982[48] for their quality.[49]

(d) Contracts for the provision of goods and services

Goods may, of course, be acquired as an integral part of a different category of contract with the property in the goods being transferred thereby. An obvious example is contracts for the provision of services, sometimes referred to as contracts for works and materials, in which the contractual performance necessitates the provision of some goods. Thus, an artist commissioned to paint a portrait will ultimately produce the picture and transfer it to the client[50] but the essence of the contract is 'an undertaking by the artist to exercise such skill as he was possessed of in order to produce for reward a thing which would ultimately have to be accepted by the client'.[51] Similarly, when a builder employed a sub-contractor to construct the roof on a building, including the purchase of the requisite roof tiles, it was held that the contract was one for services despite the purchase of the materials.[52] However, it would be wrong to suggest that the line between contracts for the sale of goods and contracts for the provision of services is an easy one to draw, despite the *dicta* in *Robinson* v. *Graves*[53] that the

---

[47] See *Kingsley* v. *Sterling Industrial Securites Ltd* [1967] 2 QB 747; *Snook* v. *London and West Riding Investments Ltd* [1967] 2 QB 786.

[48] Supply of Goods and Services Act 1982, s.9.

[49] For a thorough analysis of the leaseback arrangement and its relationship to sale of goods, see P.S. Atiyah, J.N. Adams and H. MacQueen, *The Sale of Goods* (11th edn, Pearson Education Ltd, Harlow, 2005).

[50] *Robinson* v. *Graves* [1935] 1 KB 579.

[51] *Ibid.* 584 per Greer LJ.

[52] *Young and Martens* v. *McManus Childs* [1969] 1 AC 454.

[53] *Robinson* v. *Graves* [1935] 1 KB 579, 588 per Greer LJ.

determining factor is the 'substance' of the contract. Arguably, the distinction is less significant than it was since the abolition of the requirement that contracts of sale valued at £10 or over must be in writing,[54] a requirement not needed in contracts for services. Also, the passage of the Supply of Goods and Services Act 1982, which implied conditions regarding quality similar to sections 12–15 of the Sale of Goods Act 1979 into contracts for the transfer of goods has lessened the significance of the distinction. Nonetheless, it may still be important in respect of terms as to the quality of the service element of the contract. If a contract is held to be a contract for services, there will be a statutory implied term that the supplier will carry out the service with reasonable care.[55] By contrast, if the contract is deemed to be one of sale, the remedy for any deficiency in the service element will be determined under the law of negligence. In practice, though, this may make little difference as both tests will turn on the exercise of reasonable care and skill.

(e) Supply of computer programs

While much of the law surrounding what constitutes a contract of sale has long since been established, the issue has re-emerged as a result of developments in modern technology, leaving the courts to consider whether the sale of a computer program is indeed a sale of goods. This position is far from resolved. It may depend on whether the computer program is supplied in a tangible form such as a diskette or CD-ROM or supplied in a purely intangible form such as a download from a website. Sir Iain Glidewell in the leading case of *St Albans City and District Council* v. *International Computers Ltd*[56] assumed that if the program is supplied on a diskette, it will constitute a sale of goods with the consequence that if the program is faulty, an action will lie under section 14 of the Sale of Goods Act 1979 for a breach of the conditions of satisfactory quality and fitness for purpose. In coming to this conclusion, he drew a comparison with a car maintenance manual, arguing that if such a manual contained incorrect instructions, it would be unsatisfactory and not fit for its purpose. By contrast, if the software is supplied as a download from the Internet, it cannot be a contract of sale as there are no tangible goods. Yet, in both instances the buyer is primarily concerned with acquiring the computer program, the manner of its transition being of secondary importance. In that context, the distinction is pedantic and arguably of limited effect as, in practice, the common law would be likely to imply terms of fitness for purpose similar to those in section 14 of the 1979 Act into contracts for computer downloads.[57]

---

[54] Law Reform (Enforcement of Contracts) Act 1954, s.2.
[55] Supply of Goods and Services Act 1982, s.13.
[56] [1996] 4 All ER 481.
[57] See *Watford Electronics Ltd* v. *Sanderson* [2001] 1 All ER (Comm) 696.

An alternative analysis was expounded by Lord Penrose in the Scottish decision of *Beta Computers (Europe) Ltd* v. *Adobe Systems Ltd*,[58] in which he drew attention to the intellectual property aspect of the transaction and the fact that, irrespective of the way that the software is acquired, the user will require a licence from the owner of the intellectual property rights.

Q6 Analyse the various categories of contract under which a purchaser or hirer can acquire the property in or possession of goods while not being subject to the Sale of Goods Act 1979.

9 Recommended reading

Atiyah, P.S., Adams, J.N. and MacQueen, H. *The Sale of Goods* (11th edn, Pearson Education Ltd, Harlow, 2005)

The Sale of Goods (12th edn, Pearson Education Ltd, Harlow, 2010)

Bradgate, R. *Commercial Law* (3rd edn, Oxford University Press, Oxford, 2000)

Bridge, M. *The Sale of Goods* (Oxford University Press, Oxford, 1997)

Dobson, P. and Stokes, R. *Commercial Law* (7th edn, Sweet & Maxwell, London, 2008)

European Commission Proposal for a Directive of the European Parliament and the Council on consumer rights, COM(2008)614 final (Brussels, 2008)

Howell, G. and Weatherill, S. *Consumer Protection Law* (2nd edn, Ashgate Publishing Ltd, Aldershot, 2005)

Macleod, J. *Consumer Sales Law* (2nd edn, Routledge-Cavendish, Abingdon, 2007)

Mark, M. *Chalmers Sale of Goods* (18th edn, Butterworths, London, 1981)

Sealy, L.S. and Hooley, R. *Commercial Law : Text, Cases and Materials* (4th edn, Oxford University Press, Oxford, 2009)

Singleton, S. 'Draft Consumer Rights Directive and Unfair Terms' (2008/2009) *Consumer Law Today* (Dec.) 8

The background to sale of goods and the policy underlying it is addressed in most standard works on the topic, such as Atiyah's *The Sale of Goods*. Reading the relevant sections in a selection of the books referred to above will give the reader a good understanding of the topic. Having been relatively static for a considerable period, sale of goods law is now progressing due to the influence of the European Union, the current area of activity being the Consumer Rights Directive. Readers would benefit from reading the Commission's proposal.

---

[58] 1996 SLT 604.

Part 2 Chapter 2

The Implied Conditions in Sale of Goods Contracts

Contents

1 Introduction

This chapter looks in detail at the implied conditions in the law governing the sale of goods which are of equal importance whether the purchaser is a business or a consumer. As such, they are an extremely important aspect of both commercial contracts and consumer contracts, although there are differences between the two, the significance of which will become apparent from the discussion below.

Section 2 looks at the background to sections 12–15 of the Sale of Goods Act 1979 and considers some of the differences in the impact of the provisions dependent upon the nature of both seller and buyer.

Section 3 analyses the implied condition as to the right to sell contained in section 12 of the 1979 Act and considers the section 12(1) implied condition and the section 12(2) implied warranties.

Section 4 deals with the implied condition that requires that goods that are sold by description must comply with that contractual description, and considers the ambit of the condition; what constitutes a 'sale by description'; compliance with description and the relationship between section 13 and section 14.

Section 5 analyses the most well-known of the implied conditions, namely, that goods supplied under a sale of goods contract must be of a satisfactory quality. The section breaks down the analysis of this topic as follows: sale in the course of a business; merchantable quality; the introduction of 'satisfactory quality'; the statutory exceptions to the requirement for satisfactory quality; the goods included in the requirement for satisfactory quality; the meaning of satisfactory quality; and the section 14(2B) criteria.

Section 6 addresses the implied condition in section 14(3) that goods supplied must be fit for their intended purpose. This subsection, which to some extent overlaps with the section 14(2) requirement regarding satisfactory quality, addresses the particular purpose or purposes for which the buyer purchased the goods and the role of his reliance on the skill and judgement of the seller.

Section 7 considers the section 15 requirement that goods that are sold by reference to a sample must comply with that sample.

Section 8 looks at the extent to which it is possible to exclude or limit the liability of a seller for a breach of any of the implied conditions. It draws particular attention to the extent to which the nature of the buyer, i.e., business or consumer, affects the ability of the seller to exclude or limit his liability. Section 9 considers the concept of acceptance and its impact on the remedies available to the buyer, and section 10 analyses the remedies available to both business buyers and consumer buyers for a breach of any of the implied conditions.

2 Background

The implied conditions,[1] originally introduced by the Sale of Goods Act 1893 but now to be found in sections 12–15 of the Sale of Goods Act 1979, are at the heart of the statutory controls over the right to sell, sale by description, satisfactory quality and fitness for purpose of goods and compliance with sample in contracts of sale.[2] As these sections are implied into all contracts of sale, it follows that they apply irrespective of the monetary value of the goods in question or their nature and character. Thus, it applies equally to a business-to-business contract worth millions of pounds and a contract by which a consumer buys a box of matches from a small corner shop. In both instances, the seller must have the right to sell the goods and they must be in conformity with the contract.

---

[1] The provisions in Sale of Goods Act 1979, ss.12–15 refer to implied terms. However, while this terminology is appropriate in Scotland, ss.13–15 make clear that in England and Wales the implied terms contained in those sections are conditions, see s.13(1A), s.14(6) and s.15(3). Further, s.12(5A) stipulates that the implied term regarding the right to sell contained in s.12(1)is a condition in England and Wales, while the other implied terms in s.12 are implied warranties.

[2] See the Supply of Goods (Implied Terms) Act 1973 for the equivalent provisions in respect of contracts of hire-purchase and the Sale and Supply of Goods Act 1982, Part I for the equivalent provisions for contracts for the transfer of goods other than by sale and for contracts of hire.

While the conditions are implied, at least in part, into all contracts of sale, the application of each individual condition will depend to some extent upon the nature of the seller and the nature of the buyer. Thus, for example, while the implied conditions in sections 12, 13 and 15 apply to all contracts irrespective of the status of the seller, the implied conditions in section 14 relating to satisfactory quality and fitness for purpose apply only when the sale is 'in the course of a business'. Thus, in due course, the meaning and context of the phrase 'in the course of a business' must be examined so as to accurately understand the ambit of that section and the protection it offers to purchasers. Equally, it is important to differentiate between consumer buyers and non-consumer buyers as, while the former have the right to reject the goods and repudiate the contract in the event of any breach of an implied condition, the latter cannot reject the goods if the breach is so slight as to render rejection unreasonable.[3] In that instance, the breach of condition will be treated as a breach of warranty, which would attract a remedy of damages rather than rejection.[4]

The existence of the implied conditions does not prevent the seller and buyer including other conditions or warranties governing quality, etc., into any given contract of sale but, clearly, such additional contractual terms cannot conflict with the statutory implied conditions, which, by their very nature, will take precedence. Hence, while it is impossible to introduce express terms that undermine the implied conditions, it is possible for the contracting parties to include express terms which provide for a higher level of protection than that encompassed in statute.

Q1 Consider how the status of the buyer and seller can affect the application of the implied conditions.

3 Sale of Goods Act 1979, section 12: the right to sell

(a) Section 12(1) implied conditions

Section 12 of the Sale of Goods Act 1979, which is implied into all contracts of sale irrespective of whether the seller is in business or is a private seller; is arguably the most fundamental of the implied conditions, for without the right to sell the goods, the remaining conditions relating to description, quality and compliance with sample cease to be relevant. The right to sell the goods is the starting point. Further, section 12 is the only one of the implied conditions that cannot be the subject of a contract term excluding or restricting liability for breach irrespective of whether the purchaser is a business or a consumer.[5] The rights of the purchaser under section 12 are inalienable. By contrast, the rights of the purchaser under sections 13–15 cannot be excluded or restricted against a person dealing as a consumer[6] but can be excluded or restricted against a

---

[3] Sale of Goods Act 1979, s.15A.   [4] *Ibid.*
[5] Unfair Contract Terms Act 1977, s.6(1).   [6] *Ibid.* s.6(2).

non-consumer buyer to the extent that the contract term satisfies the test of reasonableness.[7]

Section 12(1) covers the well-worn ground of the implied condition[8] that the seller will have the right to sell the goods at the time when the property is due to pass and, further, that where the contract is an agreement to sell, the seller will have the right to sell at the time that the property is due to pass under the agreement. The issues that necessarily arise out of this are what constitutes the right to sell and what remedies are available for a breach of this condition.

The right to sell does not carry with it any implication that the seller is necessarily the owner of the goods. If he is, then it follows that he has the right to sell the goods even though they may be the subject of a registered charge and to the rights of the beneficiary of that charge. It is important, however, to distinguish between the right to sell and the power to sell,[9] which are not the same thing. The seller may have the power to sell the goods because he owns them but not have the right to sell them because to do so would infringe the legal rights of some other person. Arguably, section 12(1) should state that the condition is that the seller has the legal right to sell the goods or the right to sell the goods legally, whichever best encapsulates the position. A commonly quoted case is that of *Niblett* v. *Confectioners' Materials Co.*[10] in which the intended sale of goods by the defendant would have infringed the plaintiff's copyright. The defendants, an American company, had contracted to sell 3,000 tins of Nissly brand condensed milk, which were seized by the customs authorities on their arrival in the United Kingdom as being an infringement of the copyright of the Nestlé company. The Court of Appeal held that the defendants were liable for a breach of section 12(1) as they did not have the legal right to sell the goods in the United Kingdom. There is a clear distinction here between the power to sell the goods, which the defendant clearly possessed being the owners of the goods, and the right to sell them legally, which they could not do in the United Kingdom.

The divergence between the power to sell and the right to sell may be equally apparent in situations where a seller has the power to sell the goods because he has possession of them and innocently believes that he has the ownership of them and hence has the right to sell or otherwise dispose of them as he chooses. Two cases in which this was the case and to which we will return when looking at remedies are *Rowland* v. *Divall*[11] and *Butterworth* v. *Kingsway Motors*.[12] In the former case, the goods had been stolen, while in the latter, the hirer of the goods under a hire-purchase agreement had innocently sold them to a third party with a series of sales then occurring before they ultimately reached the

[7] *Ibid.* s.6(3).

[8] Section 12(1) of the 1979 Act refers to an implied term but s.12(5A) stipulates that it is an implied condition in England and Wales.

[9] Note the discussion of the difference in P.S. Atiyah, J.N. Adams and H. MacQueen, *The Sale of Goods* (11th edn, Pearson Education Ltd, Harlow, 2005).

[10] [1921] 3 KB 387.   [11] [1923] 2 KB 500.   [12] [1954] 1 WLR 1286.

plaintiff. In both cases the defendant seller had the power to sell the goods but not the right, with both plaintiff buyers being able to recover their money.

A similar situation arises under the *nemo dat* exceptions[13] in which the seller of the goods again has the power to sell the goods but not the right. The major distinction, however, between the *nemo dat* exceptions and decisions such as *Rowland* v. *Divall* and *Butterworth* v. *Kingsway Motors* is that in *nemo dat* situations the innocent buyer who buys in good faith will acquire good title to the goods even against the true owner. As such, the *nemo dat* buyer will not have suffered any loss and, while there may have been a breach of section 12(1) by the seller, the buyer will not need a remedy. However, the true owner of the goods may seek to sue the seller for conversion of the goods.[14]

The remedy for a breach of section 12(1) comprises a full refund of the purchase price paid by the buyer, as evidenced in both the *Rowland* and *Butterworth* cases. This is based on the premise that, as the seller did not at any stage have the right to sell the goods, there had hence been a total failure of consideration entitling the buyer to a full refund of the contractual price. What this does not allow for is any benefit that the buyer may have enjoyed during his possession of the goods, and the possibility therefore exists for the buyer effectively to gain a windfall, a situation rarely recognised or tolerated in English law, which traditionally focuses on compensation rather than permitting unjust enrichment. This anomaly was most evident in the *Butterworth* decision. The facts were that the hirer under a hire-purchase agreement wrongly sold the goods, a car, to a second person who sold it to a third person who sold it to the defendants, Kingsway Motors, who in turn sold it to the plaintiff, Butterworth. The car was, of course, owned by the hire-purchase company, as the original hirer only had the possession and not the property of the goods under the terms of the hire-purchase agreement.[15] While wrongly selling the car, the original hirer did continue to make the payments under the agreement, a fact that was to be crucial in the decision. The plaintiff had had use of the car for some eleven and a half months when a letter from the hire-purchase company put him on notice that the defendants had not had the right to sell it to him at the time that they had purported to do so. The plaintiff quickly rescinded the contract and claimed a full refund of the purchase price. One week later, the original hirer completed payments to the hire-purchase company and acquired the title to the car, which fed down the line to the defendants and, but for the speed with which the plaintiff had rescinded the contract, would have fed to the plaintiff. Had this happened, the plaintiff could still have claimed for a breach of section 12(1) in that the title to the goods was delivered late but he would only have received nominal damages as opposed to

---

[13] See Part 2 Chapter 3.

[14] For a discussion of the *nemo dat* rule and the exceptions thereto see Part 2 Chapter 3.

[15] The hirer under a hire-purchase agreement does not acquire title to the goods until he exercises the option to purchase at the end of the hire period. Until that point, the goods belong to the hire-purchase company.

the full refund which he actually received. As he had originally paid £1,275 for the car, while it was only worth £800 when he rejected it, the plaintiff effectively avoided a loss of £475 and had the free use of a car for nearly a year. It is hardly surprising that the court questioned the merits of his case.

A more extreme anomaly as regards remedies is demonstrated by Professor Atiyah's famous example of the crate of whisky.[16] In that example, the seller buys a crate of whisky from a thief and sells it to an innocent buyer who consumes it. On discovering the theft, the buyer might seek to recover the purchase price from the seller for a breach of section 12(1) but, unlike in the *Rowland* case, the buyer cannot return the goods as they no longer exist. But, as Professor Atiyah argued, it is not unreasonable for the buyer to seek compensation for the breach as, in the future, he might be held liable in conversion to the true owner. However, if the true owner cannot be identified or for some other reason does not sue the buyer, the latter will have both the money and the goods. Equally, the seller might lose out if the true owner decided to sue him in conversion, in which case the seller might have to compensate both the buyer and the owner.

Given the potential for the enrichment of a buyer, it would be reasonable to consider how the remedy for a breach of section 12(1) could be amended to take account of any use of the goods by the buyer prior to him rescinding the contract. The Law Commission had considered the matter on a previous occasion,[17] but in their most recent report on the point in 1987[18] decided against any amendment, arguing that, although it is anomalous that a buyer should have the use of goods for a prolonged period without payment, it is no solution to make the buyer pay the seller for the use of property belonging to somebody else. They felt that the introduction of complex provisions governing payment by the buyer in this situation would not benefit either the buyer or the seller.[19]

(b) Section 12(2) implied warranties

Section 12(2) of the 1979 Act adds further warranties regarding the right of the buyer to expect that the goods sold by the seller are free, and will remain free, from any charge or encumbrance not known to the buyer at the time of the contract, and further, that the buyer will enjoy quiet possession of the goods except for any disturbance by a person entitled to a charge or encumbrance already disclosed to the buyer. At first sight, these warranties appear to add little to the remedies already available for a breach of section 12(1) and yet there are situations where this alternative or additional remedy may be relevant. Section 12(2)(a) seems particularly limited in effect as it only impacts in respect of charges or encumbrances that existed at the time that the contract was made,

[16] See Atiyah, Adams, and MacQueen, above n.9.
[17] Law Commission Working Paper No. 65 (1979).
[18] Law Commission *Sale and Supply of Goods* (Report No. 160, 1987) paras. 6.1–6.5.
[19] *Ibid.* para. 6.5.

with limitation periods running from that time. In practice, any encumbrance in favour of a third party will not be binding on the buyer unless the third party was in possession of the goods at the time of sale, in which case the buyer would almost certainly be aware of the interest of the third party, which would then constitute a disclosed encumbrance.

Section 12(2)(b) provides greater opportunity for use. It contains a continuing warranty that the buyer will enjoy quiet possession, with a limitation period running from the date of any interference with that right. It is possible for the seller to be in breach, as in the much quoted decision of *Rubicon Computer Systems Ltd* v. *United Paints Ltd.*[20] The facts were that the seller supplied a computer system to the defendants. During a dispute about payment, the seller, who still had access to the system, installed a time lock, which it subsequently triggered, denying the defendants access to their system. It was held that the seller had breached the section 12(2)(b) warranty of quiet possession.

This leaves the issue of to what extent the seller can be held liable for the interference by a third party with the quiet possession of the buyer. Reason demands that the seller should not be held liable if a third party unlawfully disrupts the quiet possession of the buyer, even though that may give rise to strange situations. Hence, it can be argued that in a *nemo dat* situation, the seller, who would be liable under section 12(1) for not having the right to sell, should not be held liable under section 12(2)(b) if the original owner of the goods seeks to interfere with the rights of the innocent buyer who, having acted in good faith, has acquired valid title to the goods. If liability does not arise for unlawful interference, what of lawful disturbance? It seems that the seller may be liable here as long as the right that the third party is seeking to enforce existed at the time the contract was made. If the right has arisen subsequently, the seller will not be responsible, as held in *The Barenbels*,[21] where the rights of the third party arose from a court case heard after the relevant contract of sale had been concluded.

A harder decision to reconcile with the requirement that the rights of the third party existed at the time of the sale, and one that has been criticised, is that of *Microbeads AG* v. *Vinehurst Roadmarkings Ltd.*[22] Microbeads, a Swiss company, sold a machine for painting white lines on roads to Vinehurst Roadmarkings Ltd. Unknown to both parties, a third party had applied for a patent which covered this machine. When the patent was subsequently granted, it was back-dated by statute and hence held applicable at the time of the sale. Consequently, Microbeads were liable for a breach of section 12(2)(b) because the right of the buyer to the continuing quiet enjoyment of his goods had been breached by the subsequent grant of the patent. However, they were not liable for a breach of section 12(1).

Thus far, it has been assumed that the seller is selling the full title to the goods. However, this is not necessarily the case. Thus, for example, it is not

---

[20] (2000) 2 CLY 899, CA.   [21] [1985] 1 Lloyd's Rep. 528.   [22] [1975] 1 All ER 529.

unusual to sell or buy a share in a racehorse. If the owner of one share wants to sell that share, he cannot be subject to an implied condition that he has the right to sell the whole of the goods. His title is limited to a share in them. Equally, the seller may be selling the title owned by a third party rather than, or in addition to, any title that he possesses himself. Section 12(3) addresses the situation where the contract provides, or it can be inferred from the circumstances, that the seller should only transfer such title as he or a third party possesses. In such a situation, section 12(4) implies a warranty that all charges and encumbrances known to the seller and not known to the buyer have been disclosed to the buyer before the contract is made. Further, section 12(5) creates an implied warranty that the quiet possession of the buyer will not be disturbed by the seller, the relevant third party or anyone claiming under them otherwise than under a disclosed encumbrance.

Q2 Analyse the remit of section 12 and consider whether, in the event of a breach, it is appropriate for the buyer to be able to recover the full contract price of the goods despite the fact that he may have had the use of the goods for some considerable time after purchasing them and before rejecting them.

4 Sale of Goods Act 1979, section 13: compliance with description

(a) Ambit of the condition

The implied condition of compliance with description, found in section 13 of the 1979 Act, applies in all contracts for the sale of goods irrespective of whether the seller is a business or a private seller. Thus, liability will arise in a commercial contract if the goods subject to the contract have been misdescribed but, equally, will arise in a private sale when an individual sells an item through the classified advertisements of the local newspaper. However, the available remedy for breach will vary depending whether the buyer is a consumer or a non-consumer for, as mentioned previously, while the consumer buyer will have a right to reject the goods for a breach of section 13, the non-consumer buyer will be restricted to a claim for damages if the breach is so slight as to render rejection unreasonable.[23]

Section 13(1) stipulates that when goods are sold by description, there is an implied condition[24] that the goods supplied must comply with that description. This raises various issues, in particular, what constitutes a 'sale by description' for the purposes of the Act, the relationship between section 13 and the common law regarding misrepresentation and how to identify which descriptive words will attract liability.

---

[23] Sale of Goods Act 1979, s.15A.
[24] *Ibid.* s.13(1) describes it as an implied term, but it is rendered an implied condition in England and Wales by virtue of s.13(1A). In Scotland, the word 'term' prevails.

(b) What constitutes a 'sale by description'

It has long been accepted that a sale by description will necessarily occur where the buyer has not seen the goods but is relying on a description of them.[25] Thus, it follows that a purchase of 'future goods'[26] or unascertained goods[27] must necessarily involve a sale by description, a fact becoming more significant with the rise of sales on the Internet.[28] Unascertained goods includes goods sold via catalogues, the Internet, advertisements on the television or simply ordered from a seller without the actual item being identified at the time of sale. The sale of 'future goods' encompasses situations in which the item is to be made, to the order of the individual buyer, after the contract has been concluded. This would include personal items such as bespoke tailoring or commercial items such as specially constituted animal feed or purpose-built machinery.

Less clear originally, was the situation if the buyer had, prior to purchase, seen or even examined the actual goods that were to change hands under the contract. Such a sale is a sale of specific goods[29] rather than future or unascertained ones and the issue arose as to whether it could it still be a sale by description if a description had been applied at the time of sale. This situation was clarified in Lord Wright's judgment in *Grant* v. *Australian Knitting Mills*,[30] which confirmed that there is a sale by description:

> even though the buyer is buying something displayed before him on the counter: a thing is sold by description, though it is specific, so long as it is sold not merely as the specific thing but as a thing corresponding to a description.[31]

On that basis, the Court of Appeal held that the plaintiff was entitled to succeed in *Beale* v. *Taylor*[32] even though he had seen and examined the car in question, because a description had also been applied to it in an advertisement. The car had been described as a '1961 Herald' when, unknown to both buyer and seller, the car was a 'cut and shut' in which two halves of two different vehicles had been welded together with only the back half of the vehicle dating from 1961, the front half being from an earlier model.[33] This wider approach has been reinforced by the current section 13(3), which makes clear that:

---

[25] *Varley* v. *Whipp* [1900] 1 QB 513.
[26] Defined in Sale of Goods Act 1979, s.61 as being 'goods to be manufactured or acquired by the seller after the making of the contract of sale'.
[27] Goods are 'unascertained' if the actual goods that will pass from seller to buyer under the terms of the contract cannot be identified at the time that the contract is made. When the goods are ultimately identified they are reclassified as 'ascertained goods'.
[28] For a discussion of Internet sales and what information must be provided to the buyer see Part 2 Chapter 5.
[29] Defined in Sale of Goods Act 1979, s.61 as being 'goods identified and agreed upon at the time a contract of sale is made'.
[30] [1936] AC 85.   [31] *Ibid.* 100.   [32] [1967] 1 WLR 1193.
[33] The court's approach in this case may have been affected by the fact that, as the sale was a private sale, there was no opportunity for the buyer to bring a case under Sale of Goods Act 1979, s.14 (merchantable quality), which might have been a more appropriate action.

A sale of goods is not prevented from being a sale by description by reason only that, the goods being exposed for sale or hire, are selected by the buyer.

While the buyer may not have seen the actual item that he will acquire under the contract, he may have seen and examined a sample of the product. Section 13(2) makes clear that this does not affect the requirement that the goods actually provided under the contract must comply with any description applied to them irrespective of whether they correspond with the sample that the buyer has seen. It provides that:

> If the sale is by sample as well as by description it is not sufficient that the bulk of the goods correspond with the sample if the goods do not also correspond with the description.[34]

It seems, therefore, that virtually all contracts for the sale of goods can fall within section 13(1) as long as a relevant description has been applied and the sale is not one in which the buyer has stipulated that this item and only this item will suffice, irrespective of any description applied to it. A further gloss has been put on this, however, by the judgment of Nourse LJ in the decision of *Harlingdon & Leinster Enterprises Ltd* v. *Christopher Hull Fine Art Ltd*,[35] in which he opined that:

> there cannot be a contract for the sale of goods by description where it is not within the reasonable contemplation of the parties that the buyer is relying on the description.[36]

Thus, in the absence of reliance, a description might be included as part of the pre-contractual negotiations but not be classed as a sale by description for the purposes of section 13 as long as the parties did not intend the description to become a term of the contract. The *Harlingdon* case involved the sale of oil paintings attributed to the German expressionist artist, Gabriele Münter, and described as such in a catalogue. The defendant seller was not an expert in German expressionist painting, a fact he made clear to the plaintiff buyer, who was an expert. The Court of Appeal found for the defendant on the basis that there was no common intention that the description be relied upon and, indeed, the declaration by the seller of his lack of expertise confirmed that view.[37] The description was not intended by the parties to become part of the contract and, as such, was not actionable.

It is important to understand the relationship between section 13, express terms of the contract and contractual misrepresentation. Section 13, being statutory in origin, will, of course, take precedence over any contract term or

---

[34] *Idid.* s.15, which deals with sales by sample, is considered in detail below.

[35] [1991] 1 QB 564.   [36] *Ibid.* 574.

[37] Contrast the decision of *Ojjeh* v. *Waller; Ojjeh* v. *Galerie Moderne* (unreported, 1998) concerning the sale of some Lalique glass in which the seller was the expert and it was intended that the description would be relied upon. The seller was held liable under s.13.

misrepresentation which may conflict with it. That said, the express terms of a contract may include a descriptive term, which, if sufficiently significant to be classed as a condition, has the potential to give rise to a situation whereby the implied condition under section 13 involves compliance with an express condition of the contract. Equally however, express contractual terms that are descriptive in nature but are not classed as 'descriptions' for the purposes of section 13 may still give rise to liability as a contractual warranty or innominate term giving the buyer a right to a remedy, dependent upon the severity and impact of the breach.[38] Naturally, this liability would be in addition to any liability that might arise under section 13 in respect of other descriptions within the contract. Further, it is important to note that section 13 does not affect the common law concept[39] of misrepresentation. An inaccurate description used in pre-contractual negotiations and which does not subsequently become a contractual term can still attract liability as a misrepresentation, with the relevant remedy being dependent on whether it was innocent, negligent or fraudulent.

Fundamental to this discussion of what constitutes a 'sale by description' is an analysis of the criteria by which a contractual description will be judged to determine whether it falls within the ambit of section 13. A useful *dicta* in this regard is that of Lord Diplock in *Ashington Piggeries* v. *Christopher Hill Ltd*,[40] which focused on the issue of identification:

> The 'description' … is, in my view, confined to those words in the contract which were intended by the parties to identify the kind of goods which were to be supplied … the test is whether the buyer could fairly and reasonably refuse to accept the physical goods proffered to him on the ground that their failure to correspond with what was said about them makes them goods of a different kind from those he had agreed to buy. The key to s.13 is identification.[41]

The term 'identification' can support two interpretations, the wider one encompassing, for example, words that allow the location of the specific item to be identified, and a narrower approach which is limited to words that identify a specific factor or characteristic of the goods, such as size, composition or age. The latter approach is to be preferred, as demonstrated in the House of Lords' decision in *Reardon Smith Lines* v. *Hansen Tangen*,[42] in which it was held that descriptive words identifying the shipyard in which a ship was to be built did not fall within section 13 as they were of no real concern to the contracting parties, who were more concerned with the specific attributes of the vessel. This case also reinforces the distinction between contractual descriptions giving rise to section 13 liability and contractual descriptions that give rise to remedies as a breach of warranty or innominate term.

Q3 Analyse the meaning and ambit of the phrase 'sale by description'.

---

[38] *Cehave NV* v. *Bremer Handelgeselschaft (The Hansa Nord)* [1976] QB 44.
[39] *Taylor* v. *Combined Buyers Ltd* [1924] NZLR 627.
[40] [1972] AC 441.   [41] *Ibid.* 503.   [42] [1976] 1 WLR 989.

(c) Compliance with description

Compliance with section 13 requires complete compliance with the contract description. Thus, in *Arcos Ltd* v. *Ronaasen & Son*,[43] the seller was held liable for the sale of wooden staves to be used for making barrels. The contract stipulated that the staves were to be half an inch thick but the majority of them exceeded that size, although they were still found to be merchantable under the contract description. Lord Atkin, in the House of Lords, upholding the right of the buyer to reject the goods under section 13, said:

> If the written contract specifies conditions of weight, measurement and the like, these conditions must be complied with. A ton does not mean about a ton, or a yard about a yard. Still less when you descend to minute measurements does ½ inch mean about ½ inch. If the seller wants a margin he must and in my experience does stipulate for it.[44]

This is not, of course, to undermine the *de minimus* rule. The requirement for exact compliance may, of itself, lead to unsatisfactory decisions such as occurred in *Re Moore & Co. Ltd* v. *Landauer & Co. Ltd*,[45] a case now criticised as being excessively technical,[46] in which the buyer was allowed to reject 3,000 cans of fruit on the basis that they were packed in cartons of 24 tins each instead of the 30 tins stipulated in the contract, despite the volume of the goods and their value being unchanged.

A breach of section 13, being a breach of condition, allows the buyer to reject the goods and recover the full contract price, although this remedy has been limited by the impact of section 15A, which restricts the remedy available to a non-consumer buyer to damages where the breach is so slight as to render rejection unreasonable. Equally, while section 6 of the Unfair Contract Terms Act 1977 prevents the exclusion or limitation of section 13 liability to a buyer dealing as a consumer,[47] such exclusion or limitation is permissible against a non-consumer buyer to the extent that it is reasonable.[48]

(d) Relationship between sections 13 and 14

In practice, liability under sections 13 and 14 of the 1979 Act may arise out of the same set of circumstances and thus it would be relatively easy to assume that the two are closely and inextricably linked. However, while the link may exist in situations where the description applied relates directly to the quality or fitness for purpose of the goods, it would be wrong to assume that they do not exist independently of each other. The example usually quoted of a direct link between the two is the New Zealand case of *Cotter* v. *Luckie*,[49] which

---

[43] [1933] AC 470.   [44] *Ibid.* 479.   [45] [1921] 2 KB 519.
[46] See Lord Wilberforce in *Reardon Smith Lines*, above n. 42.
[47] Unfair Contract Terms Act 1977, s.6(2).
[48] *Ibid.* s.6(3).   [49] [1918] NZLR 811.

related to the sale of a bull described as being a 'pure bred polled Angus bull'. Both seller and buyer knew that the animal was being bought for breeding purposes to produce stock of the same quality. In the event, the bull was unable to breed. The court held it was a sale by description in which the description related to the quality of the animal and its fitness for purpose as a breeding bull, for otherwise the description was meaningless. Hence, it is clearly possible to include a description in the contract which relates directly to the quality and fitness for purpose of the goods such that a breach of the provision could give rise both to an action under section 13 for sale by description and under section 14 for breach of satisfactory quality or fitness for purpose or both, dependent on the facts. However, it is worth noting that the court will not infer statements about quality into contractual descriptions. Thus, in the decision of *Ashington Piggeries Ltd* v. *Christopher Hill Ltd*,[50] animal feed for mink was sold as being 'herring meal'. In the event, it was contaminated with a toxin that was fatal to mink but the House of Lords held that it was still properly described as being 'herring meal' as the statement made no inference as to the quality or nature of the goods.

However, each of the sections is capable of existing independently and liability can arise under the one without the other. Thus, an item can match its description perfectly and yet not be of a satisfactory quality, as happened in the *Ashington* case; and, equally, an item may be perfectly satisfactory and fit for its purpose and yet not be as described. Thus, for example, a car sold as an '1800cc' vehicle will be perfectly satisfactory and fit for the purpose of being used as car despite the fact that the engine capacity might be different. Equally, an item might be of appropriate quality and function perfectly well despite being manufactured by a different manufacturer from the one quoted in any description. In either of these situations, the buyer will have a valid claim for a breach of either section 13 or section 14, as appropriate, without a claim arising in respect of the other.

Two other situations can arise in which the buyer might want to take an action under section 13 for a breach of description where, on the facts, a claim under section 14 might seem more appropriate. The first is when the seller is a private seller and is not selling 'in the course of a business'. As mentioned previously, section 14 only applies when the seller is selling in the course of a business and, as such, a claim about the goods not being of a satisfactory quality or fit for their intended purpose cannot be taken against a private seller and the buyer must resort to other possibilities, such as section 13. This is most graphically demonstrated in the case of *Beale* v. *Taylor*, referred to previously, concerning the sale of the 'cut and shut' car described as being a '1961 Herald', when only one half of the car dated from that year. A claim regarding the quality and fitness for purpose of the vehicle would have made more sense but, as the car was bought in a private sale, that option was not open to the buyer. It is entirely

[50] [1972] AC 441.

possible that, if both halves of the car had dated from 1961, the buyer would not have had any remedy at all.

The second situation in which a buyer might opt for a section 13 claim in preference to one under section 14 would be if the contract contains a valid exclusion clause in respect of liability under section 14 but does not include one in respect of liability under section 13. Naturally, this situation can only arise where the buyer is a non-consumer purchaser, as Unfair Contract Terms Act 1977, section 6(2) prohibits any exclusion of such liability against a consumer. By contrast, exclusion and limitation clauses are permitted against a non-consumer purchaser as long as they satisfy the test of reasonableness.[51]

Q4 Analyse the relationship between sections 13 and 14.

5 Sale of Goods Act 1979, section 14(2): satisfactory quality

Section 14(2) of the 1979 Act details the provisions as to satisfactory quality, both for generic sales of goods and for sales by sample, this latter aspect having been inserted in 1994[52] having previously been contained in section 15. The twin concepts of satisfactory quality and fitness for purpose are inextricably linked if only because of the fact that section 14(2B) identifies fitness for all the purposes for which goods of the kind in question are commonly supplied as one of the factors to be considered when assessing the satisfactory quality of the goods. However, while section 14(2) deals with the fitness of goods for common purposes, section 14(3) deals with the particular purposes for which goods might be required and is dealt with later in this chapter

(a) Sale in the course of a business

The implied conditions in section 14(2) only apply when the goods are sold in the course of a business, unlike the other implied conditions in sections 12, 13 and 15, which apply in all contracts of sale. This business requirement, introduced in 1973,[53] limits the applicability of the section to business dealings and excludes private sales from liability. The interpretation of the section 14 business requirement is considerably wider, however, than the corresponding criminal law approach evident in the now defunct section 1 of the Trade Descriptions Act 1968, which required that the supply in question formed an integral part of the business of the supplier.[54] This had the potential to restrict the applicability of the section when dealing with the first sale by a business,

---

[51] Unfair Contract Terms Act 1977, s.6(3).
[52] Sale and Supply of Goods Act 1994, s.1.
[53] Supply of Goods (Implied Terms) Act 1973, s.3.
[54] *Havering London Borough Council* v. *Stevenson* [1970] 3 All ER 609; *Davies* v. *Sumner* [1984] 3 All ER 831.

where it was not possible to tell whether such a sale was truly integral to the future business of the firm. Equally, occasional sales by businesses such as, for example, selling old unwanted plant, machinery or office furniture fell outside the ambit of the section as not being integral to the business so much as ancillary to it.

It was this latter situation that gave rise to a new approach to the sale of goods, as opposed to criminal law, in the Court of Appeal decision in *Stevenson* v. *Rogers*,[55] which confirms that all sales by businesses constitute 'sales in the course of a business' irrespective of whether it is the first such sale and whether the seller is a regular seller of goods of that type. It had previously been thought that a regularity of sale was required[56] but the Court of Appeal in *Stevenson* has put the matter beyond doubt. The facts were that the claimant, Stevenson, had bought a sea-going fishing trawler from the defendant seller, who was a fisherman. The seller had owned the vessel for three years prior to the sale and had previously sold one other vessel. The vessel was unsatisfactory but, in order to enforce his claim, the buyer needed to prove that the sale had taken place in the course of a business. The judge at first instance held that the sale was not in the course of a business, but this was overruled by the Court of Appeal. Adopting a purposive approach to the interpretation of the section, the Court of Appeal decided that the purpose of the section is to differentiate between sales by businesses and purely private sales. As such, the court decided that any sale by a business is a sale in the course of a business. Further, a seller selling via an agent will be deemed to be selling in the course of a business unless either the buyer knew that this was not the case or reasonable steps had been taken to bring it to his attention.[57]

This leaves the issue of the hobbyist, as in *Blakemore* v. *Bellamy*,[58] in which a postman refurbished cars and then sold them. This raises the vexed issue of at what point an enthusiastic hobbyist indulging his hobby crosses an imaginary line and becomes a business, such that any sale of the items he produces will attract liability under section 14 of the 1979 Act. There is no easy answer to this and every case will turn on its facts.

Finally, section 61 of the 1979 Act defines a business as including 'a profession and the activities of any government department (including a Northern Ireland Department) and any local or public authority'. This reinforces the decision in *Roberts* v. *Leonard*,[59] which held that veterinary surgeons were in the course of a trade or business for the purposes of the now defunct section 1 of the Trade Descriptions Act 1968.

Q5 *Analyse the importance and ambit of the phrase 'in the course of a business' in section 14.*

[55] [1999] 1 All ER 613.
[56] See *R & B Customs Brokers Co. Ltd* v. *United Dominions Trust Ltd* [1988] 1 All ER 847.
[57] Sale of Goods Act 1979, s.14(5).
[58] [1982] RTR 303.   [59] *The Times,* 10 May 1995.

(b) Merchantable quality

The legal need for quality in goods is traceable back into common law with the oft quoted *dicta* of Lord Ellenborough in *Gardiner* v. *Gray*,[60] that a buyer does not buy goods simply 'to lay them on a dunghill'. Adopted into statute law in 1893 as the requirement that the goods be of 'merchantable quality' the condition meant little more than that the goods were commercially saleable. Throughout the next eighty years until the introduction of a statutory definition of the term in 1973,[61] there was no standard interpretation of the phrase 'merchantable quality', although two different approaches developed: the 'acceptability' approach as illustrated in *Grant* v. *Australian Knitting Mills*[62] and the 'usability' approach evidenced in *Kendall* v. *Lillico*.[63] The former depended on whether the buyer:

> fully acquainted with the facts, and therefore knowing what hidden defects exist and not being limited to their apparent condition would buy them without abatement of price obtainable for such goods if in a reasonable sound order and condition and without special terms.[64]

This approach considered quality from the perspective of the reasonable buyer while, by contrast, the usability approach adopted in *Kendall* considered it from the perspective of the use of the goods, such that the House of Lords held that the animal feed in question was merchantable as it was suitable for feeding to cattle even though it was toxic when the plaintiff fed it to his pheasants. Further, the usability approach only required that the goods were merchantable for one of their common purposes,[65] as opposed to the current statutory requirement that the goods are fit for all the purposes for which goods of the kind in question are commonly supplied.[66] It is hardly surprising that neither Parliament nor case law produced an all-encompassing definition of merchantable quality given the breadth of the transactions to which it applied, covering not merely commercial sales but also, until 1979, private sales, and being equally applicable to the purchase of factory machinery, vehicles of all shapes and sizes, household furniture and a box of matches. Indeed, Rougier J opined that any definition, however exhaustive or positive, was likely to be 'put to mockery by some new undreamt of set of circumstances'.[67]

In 1973, however, the first attempt at a statutory definition appeared in section 14(6) of the 1979 Act, showing a clear bias towards the usability approach and stipulating that goods were of a merchantable quality if:

---

[60] (1815) 4 Camp. 144.

[61] Sale of Goods Act 1979, s.14(6), as inserted by Supply of Goods (Implied Terms) Act 1973, s.3.

[62] [1936] AC 85.   [63] [1969] 2 AC 31.

[64] Per Dixon J in *Australian Knitting Mills* v. *Grant* (1933) 50 CLR 387, 418 as quoted in *Kendall* v. *Lillico* [1969] 2 AC 31, 51.

[65] See *Aswan Engineering Establishment Co.* v. *Ludpine Ltd* [1987] 1 All ER 135.

[66] Sale of Goods Act 1979, s.14(2B)(a).

[67] *Bernstein* v. *Pamson Motors (Golders Green) Ltd* [1987] 2 All ER 220, 222.

they are as fit for the purpose or purposes for which goods of that kind are commonly bought as it is reasonable to expect having regard to any description applied to them, the price (if relevant) and all the other relevant circumstances.

Applying this approach, the court in *Aswan Engineering* v. *Ludpine*[68] held that plastic pails ordered for export and used to carry a liquid waterproofing compound were merchantable despite their collapse in the Kuwaiti heat. However, other cases such as *Rogers* v. *Parish (Scarborough) Ltd*,[69] while stating that the statutory definition could be applied without reference to pre-definition case law, nonetheless considered non-usability factors such as appearance and finish in deciding merchantable quality.

(c) Introduction of 'satisfactory quality'

The statutory definition changed, both in emphasis and detail, with the introduction of the current section 14(2) in 1994.[70] While introducing implied conditions about quality and fitness, section 14(1) makes clear that no other implied conditions as to quality or fitness exist other than those in sections 14 and 15 or in any other enactment. Hence, there is no resort to any common law implied conditions and *caveat emptor* will apply to situations not covered by sections 14 and 15. This does not, of course, restrict the right of Parliament to include implied conditions in other legislation, as any attempt to do so would be contrary to parliamentary sovereignty.

The basic requirement is that goods sold in the course of a business must be of a satisfactory quality,[71] being goods which a reasonable person would regard as satisfactory, taking account of any description of the goods, the price (if relevant) and all the other relevant circumstances. The change of the requirement from merchantable quality to satisfactory quality followed on from the deliberations of the Law Commission[72] who recommended a move that would be 'sufficiently flexible to be able to apply to all the many types of sale which can take place'.[73] They advocated a move to a generic term such as 'acceptable' combined with a non-exhaustive list of criteria to be used in assessing the acceptability of the item.[74] In the event, Parliament preferred the term 'satisfactory quality', which is an objective term to be assessed by a reasonable man but has raised comment as to whether, in common parlance, the term 'satisfactory' actually denotes a relatively low standard.[75] On the other hand, concern has been expressed that buyers might accept goods without them really being satisfactory. For example, if buyers were to consistently accept goods with minor

---

[68] [1987] 1 All ER 135.   [69] [1987] QB 933.

[70] Inserted by the Sale and Supply of Goods Act 1994, s.1.

[71] Sale of Goods Act 1979, s.14(2)

[72] Law Commission *Sale and Supply of Goods* (Report No. 160, 1987).

[73] *Ibid*. para. 3.11.   [74] *Ibid*. para. 8.1.(3).

[75] See Atiyah, Adams and MacQueen, above n. 9, at 166, where the authors argue that the term satisfactory 'tends to be associated with mediocrity'.

defects, it could raise a presumption that defective goods are 'acceptable' even if not satisfactory. If this is true, then the requirement for satisfactory quality might actually be more demanding than one for acceptable quality. On balance, satisfactory is the better term.

The basic requirement that the goods be of satisfactory quality is now to be found in section 14(2), with a broad definition contained in section 14(2A) and the non-exhaustive list of factors to be found in section 14(2B). The relevant parts of section 14 read thus:

> (2) Where the seller sells in the course of a business, there is an implied term that the goods supplied under the contract are of a satisfactory quality.
>
> (2A) For the purposes of this Act, goods are of a satisfactory quality if they meet the standard that a reasonable person would regard as satisfactory, taking account of any description of the goods, the price (if relevant) and all the other circumstances.
>
> (2B) For the purposes of this Act, the quality of goods includes their state and condition and the following (among others) are in appropriate cases aspects of the quality of goods:–
>
> (a) fitness for all the purposes for which goods of the kind in question are commonly supplied;
> (b) appearance and finish;
> (c) freedom from minor defects;
> (d) safety; and
> (e) durability.

Q6 Consider the benefits of changing the required quality standard from the trader-orientated 'merchantable quality' to the more generic term 'satisfactory quality'.

(d) Statutory exceptions to requirement of satisfactory quality

While the requirement of satisfactory quality lies at the heart of the implied conditions, section 14(2C) details three situations when the implied condition does not apply, namely:

(a) if the matter has been specifically drawn to the buyer's attention before the contract has been made;
(b) where the buyer has examined the goods, there is no liability for any matter which that examination ought to have revealed; and
(c) in the case of a sale by sample, any matter which would have been apparent on a reasonable examination of the goods.

The first stipulation provides that there is no liability where the defect has been drawn to the attention of the buyer before the contract is made.[76] This is

---

[76] Sale of Goods Act 1979, s.14(2C)(a). See *R & B Customs Brokers* v. *United Dominions Trust* [1988] 1 All ER 847, in which the buyer took possession of a car prior to the contract being

not unreasonable as it would be inequitable to allow a buyer to purchase goods knowing of a defect and then allow him to reject the goods and repudiate the contract for the same defect, although, naturally, knowledge of one defect would not prevent a buyer from rejecting goods if another defect rendering the goods unsatisfactory were to come to light.

The potential for examination of the goods also plays a part in determining whether the implied condition applies, although the test varies depending on whether it involves a sale by sample. Where the contract is one of sale by sample, there is no liability for any defect that would have been apparent on a reasonable examination of the goods[77] and thus the implied condition only relates to inherent defects. This is an objective standard for examination and applies irrespective of whether an examination has actually occurred.

By contrast, in contracts of sale other than sales by sample, the test is subjective, with liability only being excluded where the buyer has examined the goods and, further, only in respect of defects which that particular examination ought to have revealed.[78] Liability remains for latent defects that would not have been apparent on examination.[79] Thus, the extent of the liability of the seller will depend on the quality of the examination, if any, undertaken by the buyer. A cursory examination will result only in an exclusion of liability for defects which that cursory examination would reveal. There is an argument for saying that a buyer should not examine goods at all in order to protect himself from the loss of remedy for any defect which an examination might have revealed, although it is possible that a court might view such wilful ignorance of defects as 'a relevant circumstance' under section 14(2A).[80] Indeed, in *Bramhill* v. *Edwards*,[81] the Court of Appeal allowed the seller to benefit from the protection offered by section 14(2C)(b) when the plaintiff sought to reject a second-hand motor-home which, at an external width of 102 inches, contravened the appropriate UK regulations and thus was not legal for use on UK roads, where the maximum legal width was 100 inches. The buyer had not measured the external size of the vehicle but the decision is nonetheless justifiable as the buyer had measured the internal measurements of the vehicle at 100 inches and so must have known that the external measurements were greater.

Q7 Do the statutory exceptions under section 14(2C) provide for a sensible approach to liability?

---

concluded and was aware of a defect which the seller undertook to repair but did not complete satisfactorily. The Court of Appeal allowed the buyer to reject the goods.

[77] Sale of Goods Act 1979, s.14(2C)(c).

[78] *Ibid.* s.14(2C)(b).

[79] See *Wren* v. *Holt* [1903] 1 KB 610 (arsenic in beer) and *Godley* v. *Perry* [1960] 1 WLR 9 (a defect in a child's plastic catapult).

[80] See J.K. Macleod, *Consumer Sales Law* (2nd edn, Abingdon, Routledge-Cavendish, 2007) ch. 14 n.238.

[81] [2004] 2 Lloyd's Rep. 653, CA.

(e) Goods included in requirement of satisfactory quality

The implied condition[82] under section 14(2) provides that the requirement that goods be of a satisfactory quality applies to 'the goods supplied under the contract'. This does not simply mean the actual goods that were the subject of the contract but includes any containers or the like that are supplied with those goods, irrespective of whether the container is being purchased and will become the property of the buyer or whether it remains the property of the seller and must be returned in due course. Thus, in *Geddling* v. *Marsh*,[83] the defendant manufacturer was liable for the damages caused when a bottle of mineral water burst and injured the plaintiff's hand. The defendant was held liable even though it was a refundable bottle and remained his property throughout. On the same basis, if a glass jar was faulty and pieces of glass found their way into the product, or if a bottle containing carbonated drink were to explode and, in either instance, the buyer was to be injured, he would have a valid claim under section 14(2). Naturally, if the injured person was not the buyer and thus lacked privity of contract, he would have to make a claim under product liability or negligence, as appropriate.[84]

In the same vein, liability will also cover any extraneous matter supplied under the contract. Thus, in *Wilson* v. *Rickett Cockerell Ltd*,[85] the defendant coal merchant supplied the plaintiff with some Coalite, which exploded due to the presence of a detonator in it. The Coalite was merchantable by itself, as was the detonator. However, when combined they became unmerchantable (now unsatisfactory) and the defendant was liable for the resultant damage.

Finally, any item supplied as a free gift with the goods must also be of a satisfactory quality as it has been supplied under the contract.

(f) Meaning of satisfactory quality

Section 14(2) of the 1979 Act makes clear that the goods must reach the standard that a reasonable person would regard as satisfactory, taking account of any description of the goods, the price (if relevant) and all other relevant circumstances. The 'reasonable person' test is, of course, an objective test, which considers what the normal reasonable buyer, as opposed to the subjective actual buyer, would think of the goods supplied under the contract and whether he would consider them to be of a satisfactory quality.

Satisfactory quality and fitness must be assessed by reference to the contract description, an approach echoed in the Sale and Supply of Goods to Consumers Regulations 2002,[86] which, in giving effect to Directive

---

[82] Sales of Goods Act 1979, s.14(2) refers to an implied term but, by virtue of s.14(6), it is an implied condition in England, Wales and Northern Ireland.
[83] [1920] 1 KB 668.
[84] For a discussion of negligence and product liability see Part 4 Chapter 1.
[85] [1954] 1 QB 598.   [86] SI 2002/3045.

1999/44/EC,[87] requires that the goods supplied conform to the contract. This approach is reasonable and allows all goods to be measured against a general standard for the product in question while allowing for the particularities of the item to be assessed. Thus, both ballet shoes and mountain boots would satisfy the description 'footwear' but the ballet shoes, if described as such, will not be deemed unsatisfactory because they cannot withstand the rigours of being used for mountain climbing.

Price may be relevant in determining quality but the mere fact that goods are cheap does not allow them to be unsatisfactory, as held in *Godley* v. *Perry*,[88] in which a cheap plastic catapult was found to be unmerchantable. The plaintiff child, who was injured when the item broke, recovered thousands of pounds in damages for being blinded in one eye. The catapult had cost sixpence in pre-decimal currency (equivalent to two and a half pence in decimal currency). The price paid for an item may raise expectations as to a level of quality and is relevant in deciding value for money. Hence, the price may be indicative of what the buyer has a right to expect from the goods he has purchased, as held in *Rogers* v. *Parish*.[89] However, *caveat emptor* rules as the 1979 Act does not require any particular quality but simply provides for a lower threshold of quality below which goods are not allowed to fall. As Salmond LJ stated in *Taylor* v. *Combined Buyers Ltd* :[90]

> The term 'merchantable' does not mean good, or fair, or average quality. Goods may be inferior or even bad quality but yet fulfil the legal requirement of merchantable quality. For goods may be in the market in any grade, good, bad, or indifferent, and yet all equally merchantable.

While this *dicta* expressly discusses merchantable quality, there is no reason to assume that the underlying philosophy is not equally applicable to the modern notion of satisfactory quality.

'All the other relevant circumstances' provides a catch-all for the courts and now statutorily includes public statements made about the specific characteristics of the goods by the seller, producer or his representative.[91] However, no liability will arise under this latter provision if the seller can show that he was not and could not reasonably have been aware of the statement at the time the contract was made, or that the statement had been withdrawn or corrected in public before the contract was made or that the decision by the buyer to buy could not have been influenced by the statement.[92] 'Relevant circumstances' would also include factors such as whether the goods were second-hand[93] and

---

[87] Directive 1999/44/EC on certain aspects of the sale of consumer goods and consumer guarantees.
[88] [1960] 1 WLR 9.   [89] [1987] QB 933.   [90] [1924] NZLR 627.
[91] Sale of Goods Act 1979, s.14(2D) bringing into effect Art. 2(2)(d) of Directive 1999/44/EC.
[92] Sale of Goods Act 1979, s.14(2E).
[93] *Bartlett* v. *Sydney Marcus Ltd* [1965] 1 WLR 1013; *Crowther* v. *Shannon Motor Co.* [1975] 1 All ER 139.

whether the buyer had complied with instructions for use and safety warnings when using the product.

(g) Section 14(2B) criteria

Section 14(2B) of the 1979 Act provides, for the first time, a non-exhaustive list of five factors which the courts may use in deciding quality issues. They are to facilitate proper evaluation of the requirement for satisfactory quality in a factual situation and, as such, are not absolute requirements in themselves. It is important to note that the courts are not obliged to consider all of the factors every time, only those that are relevant to the case at hand. Equally, as the list is non-exhaustive, the court can consider any other factors that it deems relevant in the circumstances.

These factors have been reproduced in the equivalent legislation covering hire-purchase goods[94] but not in the corresponding 1982 Act dealing with goods transferred other than by sale or hire-purchase and goods subject to contracts of hire.[95] In practice, of course, any case law decided in relation to contracts of sale or hire-purchase will be transferable to contracts for the transfer of goods and contracts of hire and thus the new factors will become applicable by that means.

(i) Fitness for all common purposes

The first factor is fitness for purpose, which serves to reinforce its significance in assessing quality but, unlike the approach adopted previously,[96] the goods must now be fit for all the purposes for which goods of the kind in question are commonly supplied and not merely one of them. It may well be that if *Aswan Engineering* were to be decided now, it would be decided the other way, with the pails being held to be unsatisfactory, as would be the animal feed in *Kendall* v. *Lillico* if feeding it to poultry was a common intended purpose.

Where there is only one purpose, it seems self-evident that the goods must be suitable for that purpose. Thus, a hot water bottle must be fit for the purpose of being filled with hot water and used to warm a bed, a car must be fit to be driven legally on the highway, and food must be fit to be eaten. The approach of the Court of Appeal, when looking at a single use item in *Bramhill* v. *Edwards*, proved interesting. As mentioned previously, the case involved the sale of a motor-home which had an external width of 102 inches, 2 inches more than the legal limit allowed on the roads in the United Kingdom. The evidence was that, in practice, the enforcement authorities ignored the slight excess in width and did not prosecute the users of such vehicles and, equally, insurance companies were prepared to ignore the size issue and insure them. The claimant argued

---

[94] Supply of Goods (Implied Terms) Act 1973, s.10.
[95] Supply of Goods and Services Act 1982, ss.4 and 9.
[96] *Kendall* v. *Lillico* [1969] 2 AC 31, 51.

that the motor-home was unsatisfactory but a unanimous Court of Appeal held that the goods were satisfactory. As discussed by Professor Macleod,[97] this raises the concern that the court has extended the use of the *de minimus* rule from matters of fact to breaches of the law and effectively condoned a proven breach.

The key factor that differentiates the requirement for satisfactory quality under section 14(2) from the fitness for purpose condition in section 14(3) is that section 14(2) relates only to 'common' purposes while section 14(3) deals with the particular purposes intended by the buyer and made known to the seller, either expressly or impliedly. It follows that an item might be satisfactory for its common or normal purpose but not be fit for any particular purpose under section 14(3), a distinction apparent in *Jewson Ltd* v. *Boyham*,[98] in which the defendant had installed boilers in flats belonging to the plaintiff and which the plaintiff wished to resell following their redevelopment. The boilers were installed but proved inefficient as regards energy-rating, which the plaintiff felt would make the flats harder to sell. The Court of Appeal held that the boilers were of satisfactory quality as they satisfied the common purpose as heaters and, further, that in the absence of any information being given to the defendant about the particular purpose for which the plaintiff was buying the boilers, there was no liability under section 14(3) either.

(ii) Appearance and finish

Appearance and finish are now formally recognised as an aspect of quality[99] as advocated by the Law Commission and were recognised judicially in *Rogers* v. *Parish (Scarborough) Ltd,*[100] in which the court held that the appearance of the vehicle and the pride that the buyer might have in its appearance was a factor to be considered. Mustill LJ in the Court of Appeal stated that the purpose for which a car is purchased:

> would include in respect of any passenger vehicle not merely the buyer's purpose of driving the car from one place to another but of doing so with the appropriate degree of comfort, ease of reliability and, one may add, of pride in the vehicle's outward and interior appearance.

The new provision also reinforces the decision of *Jackson* v. *Rotax Motor & Cycle Co.,*[101] in which it was held that scratches and dents on motor horns rendered them unmerchantable when they could not be resold.

However, given that satisfactory quality must be judged by reference to the contract description and the objective assessment of the reasonable man, appearance and finish may vary in different situations. Thus, for example, a scratch on a new car may be unacceptable while a scratch on the back of a wardrobe may not truly affect whether it is satisfactory in the eyes of a reasonable person. Equally,

---

[97] Macleod, above n. 80, ch. 14.   [98] [2003] EWCA 1030.
[99] Sale of Goods Act 1979, s.14(2B)(b).
[100] [1987] 2 All ER 232.   [101] [1910] 2 KB 937.

there will be a difference between new and second-hand goods, as the reasonable buyer has a right to expect new goods to look new, while accepting that the appearance of second-hand goods will reflect the level of wear and tear that they have suffered since being produced and prior to the current purchase. There is also an argument for saying that natural products may vary in appearance in a way that manufactured goods would not. Thus, for example, an apple might not be of an even colour all over or might have a mark on the skin or be slightly misshapen, but a toy manufactured on a production line should match its design perfectly as regards dimensions, constituent material, colour, etc.

(iii) Minor defects

Under the previous law relating to the implied condition of merchantable quality, minor defects could give rise to a right to reject the goods as, of course, any breach of condition carried with it a right to reject the goods. The issue of whether the goods could be repaired easily did not affect this basic premise. Thus, in *Rogers* v. *Parish (Scarborough) Ltd* (above), the buyer was allowed to reject the car some six months after purchase because of a series of repairable minor faults. The court took the same approach in both *Shine* v. *General Guarantee Corp.*,[102] and in *Bernstein* v. *Pamson Motors (Golders Green) Ltd*.[103] The latter case involved the sale of a new Nissan Laurel car in which the engine seized after being used for 140 miles when a lump of sealant caused a block in the oil supply system. Despite the fact that the fault could have been repaired easily, the court held that the car was unmerchantable and that the buyer had a right to reject the car. In the event, however, the buyer had lost the right to reject the goods as the court held that he had accepted them.

The Law Commission recommended the inclusion of minor defects in the statutory definition of satisfactory quality. That said, the existence of a minor defect will not necessarily render goods unsatisfactory. As Howells and Weatherill suggest, a faulty cigarette lighter in a new car would be unlikely to render the car unsatisfactory.[104] Of course, even though the buyer may not be able to reject goods because of a minor defect, a remedy of repair or replacement under section 48B of the 1979 Act might still be available to a consumer buyer if the court interpreted the failure as meaning that the goods were not in conformity with the contract. Further, a commercial buyer will not be able to reject the goods if the breach is so slight as to make rejection unreasonable under section 15A of the 1979 Act.

(iv) Safety

It is a reasonable assumption that goods that are unsafe will not be of a satisfactory quality. This may result from some obvious or inherent defect that poses

---

[102] [1988] 1 All ER 232.   [103] [1987] 2 All ER 220.
[104] G. Howells and S. Weatherill, *Consumer Protection Law* (2nd edn, Ashgate Publishing Ltd, Aldershot, 2005) 178.

a risk of injury to users of the product. Equally, goods may be unsafe because of a lack of appropriate instructions for use. Of course, any claim under section 14(2) based upon the safety of the item must be brought by the buyer as the only person with contractual privity. If someone other than the buyer has been injured by the unsafe and unsatisfactory goods, their claim must be made through product liability or negligence, as relevant.

In addition, unsafe goods may, of course, breach criminal law controls. It is an offence contrary to the General Product Safety Regulations 2005 (SI 2005/1803) for a producer to place a product on the market unless the product is a safe product, or to offer or agree to place a product on the market or expose or possess a product for placement on the market unless it is a safe product.[105] Further, distributors of the product, which would include retailers, can be held criminally liable for a similar range of offences.[106] While it is possible for civil compensation to result from the breach of a criminal offence, the position of the buyer vis-à-vis the unsatisfactory nature of unsafe goods has been strengthened considerably by the inclusion of safety as a factor to be considered under section 14(2B).

(v) Durability

It seems reasonable to expect goods to last for a reasonable period, as discussed by Lord Diplock in *Lambert* v. *Lewis*,[107] where he suggested that goods should remain fit for their purpose 'for a reasonable time after delivery'. What that reasonable period is will, naturally, depend to some extent on the product concerned. A car should last longer than a perishable foodstuff. Equally, whether the product is new or second-hand will play a part, as will the price paid, with the corresponding expectation of value for money as regards the quality and the anticipated life of the product. The presumption in section 48A(3) of the 1979 Act that goods that prove defective within the first six months following delivery are assumed not to have complied with the contract at the time that it was made may also aid the consumer buyer questioning durability, but again issues such as the nature of the product will be relevant.

Q8 Consider how the introduction of the five factors in section 14(2B) will help the court in assessing whether goods supplied under a contract satisfy the requirement of 'satisfactory quality'.

6 Sale of Goods Act 1979, section 14(3): fitness for purpose

The fitness of goods for their common purpose has already been considered as part of satisfactory quality but there remains the issue of liability for the 'particular purposes' to which goods may be put. Liability will arise under section 14(3)

---

[105] General Product Safety Regulations 2005 (SI 2005/1803), reg. 5.
[106] *Ibid.* reg. 9.   [107] [1981] 1 All ER 1185.

of the 1979 Act for any particular purpose for which the goods are being bought, irrespective of whether it is a common purpose, as long as the buyer has made that purpose known to the seller either expressly or impliedly. If goods have only one common purpose, then that will be deemed to be a particular purpose for the purposes of section 14(3), as evidenced in *Priest* v. *Last*[108] concerning a hot water bottle and *Grant* v. *Australian Knitting Mills*[109] regarding underwear. Where goods are multipurpose, the seller must be able to demonstrate that the goods are fit for one of those purposes[110] but would not be liable under section 14(3) if they were not fit for one of those various purposes, unless the buyer had made clear that that particular purpose was the one for which the goods were being acquired.

Particular purpose is wide enough to take into account particular special needs or idiosyncrasies that might affect the buyer, hence the decision in *Griffiths* v. *Peter Conway*,[111] where the seller was held not liable for the buyer suffering dermatitis after wearing a Harris Tweed coat when it was shown that the buyer had unusually sensitive skin and that a normal user would not have suffered any ill-effect from wearing the coat. Had the buyer informed the seller of her particular needs, the result might have been different. In this example, of course, the buyer knew her particular needs while the seller did not, but would it be reasonable to hold the seller liable where neither buyer nor seller knew of the pertinent facts? The House of Lords in *Slater* v. *Finning Ltd*[112] was firmly of the view that no liability would follow in that situation. The defendant, a marine engineer, installed a new camshaft in a fishing boat belonging to the plaintiff. The camshaft failed due to an abnormality in the engine of the boat about which neither party knew. The House of Lords held that it would be unreasonable to hold the seller liable in those circumstances.

Assuming that a particular purpose has been identified to the seller, two further issues arise: the need for reliance to be shown and that the goods supplied were not reasonably fit for that purpose. The current version of the Sale of Goods Act 1979 places the burden on the seller to demonstrate either that there was no reliance or that such reliance was unreasonable, a reversal of the burden of proof from the 1893 Act in which the responsibility lay on the buyer to demonstrate that reliance had taken place.[113] A general assumption of reliance may arise from the fact that a buyer has chosen to purchase the goods from the seller in question, the argument being that the buyer is relying on the seller to have selected his stock carefully.[114]

However, what if the buyer knew that the seller only sold goods of one brand or, alternatively, that while the seller might sell goods produced by various manufacturers, the buyer specified goods by brand name for his purchase?

---

[108] [1903] 2 KB 148.   [109] [1936] AC 85.
[110] *Ashington Piggeries* v. *Christopher Hill* [1972] AC 441.
[111] [1939] 1 All ER 685, CA.   [112] [1996] 3 All ER 398.
[113] Sale of Goods Act 1893, s.14(1).
[114] *Grant* v. *Australian Knitting Mills*, above n. 109.

There is a strong argument here for saying that there has not been any reliance upon the seller but rather a reliance upon the reputation and publicity of the manufacturer. Thus, in *Wren* v. *Holt*,[115] the court failed to find reliance when the buyer purchased beer from a tied house. Of course, the reversal of the burden of proof might now mean that reliance would be assumed on the basis of *Grant* v. *Australian Knitting Mills* (above), with the burden falling on the seller to demonstrate a lack of reliance. Further, it is clear, following the decision in *Cammell Laird & Co. Ltd* v. *Manganese Bronze & Brass Co. Ltd*,[116] that reliance might be partial in that none exists in respect of any specifications for the product laid down by the buyer, but that reliance will be presumed in respect of other aspects of the goods unless the seller demonstrated that even partial reliance did not occur or would have been unreasonable. In that case, the seller was to provide two propellers for two ships. The buyer laid down certain specifications regarding the design but other factors, including the thickness of the blades, were not covered by the specifications. In the event, the propellers were not fit for the purpose because they were not thick enough. The House of Lords held that the seller was liable for any factors not governed by the specifications as, in respect of those, the buyer was relying on the seller's skill and judgement.

As for the suitability of the goods themselves, section 14(3) requires that they are reasonably fit for the intended purpose. This does not provide an absolute guarantee of suitability and factors similar to those considered when assessing satisfactory quality come into play. Hence, things such as age, price and durability must be considered when evaluating fitness for purpose as one cannot reasonably expect second-hand goods to perform as well as new ones and cheaper goods may not last as long as more expensive ones. That said, there is authority that the seller will be held liable in respect of latent defects that render the goods not fit for the purpose even though it may be that the seller could not have discovered the defect even with the exercise of care and skill. Thus, in *Frost* v. *Aylesbury Dairy Co. Ltd*,[117] the seller of milk infected with typhoid was held liable despite the defect being unknowable, a strict approach supported in *Kendall* v. *Lillico*.[118] This approach is to be expected given that the section imposes strict liability and not liability based on care and skill. A different approach to the unknowable defect occurs in tort where, under product liability, the producer of defective products will escape liability using the state of the art defence if the defect was unknowable given the state of scientific and technical knowledge available at the relevant time.[119]

Q9 Analyse the relationship between section 14(2) and (3) as regards liability for the fitness for purpose of goods supplied under a contract. Further, consider the role of reliance in liability under section 14(3).

---

[115] [1903] 1 KB 610.   [116] [1934] AC 402.
[117] [1905] 1 KB 608.   [118] [1969] 2 AC 31.
[119] Consumer Protection Act 1987, s.4.

7 Sale of Goods Act 1979, section 15: sale by sample

The last of the implied conditions relates to a sale by sample, which is defined in section 15(1) as occurring where the contract provides either expressly or impliedly that it is a contract for sale by sample. The mere fact that a sample is provided for the buyer to see will not necessarily mean that the contract is one by sample. In the much quoted *dicta* of Lord Macnaughten in *Drummond* v. *Van Ingen*:[120]

> The office of a sample is to present to the eye the real meaning and intention of the parties with regard to the subject matter of the contract which, owing to the imperfections of language, it may be difficult or impossible to express in words. The sample speaks for itself.[121]

It has been suggested that sales by sample only occur in the business context but Professor Macleod argues[122] that consumers often buy after inspecting a demonstration model and will expect the specific item that they finally receive under the contract to comply with the demonstration model. This approach is more in line with section 11 of the Supply of Goods (Implied Terms) Act 1973 and sections 5 and 10 of the Supply of Goods and Services Act 1982, which refer to relevant contracts being 'by reference to a standard', arguably a less demanding provision than that of section 15.

Provisions about sales by sample are scattered throughout the 1979 Act. The primary section 15(2) provides for two conditions, the previous requirement of section 15(2)(b) having been moved to become section 14(2C)(c) in 1994. What remains are the requirements that the bulk of the goods will comply with the sample[123] and that the goods will be free from any defect which would render them unsatisfactory which would not be apparent upon a reasonable examination of the goods.[124] The requirement for the bulk compliance with the sample does not, of itself, make any statement as to the quality of the goods and it may be that the bulk, and indeed the sample, have an inherent defect that would not have been apparent on examination of the sample without breaching this requirement. As explained previously, by virtue of section 14(2C) there is no liability for defects that would have been apparent on a reasonable examination irrespective of whether one actually takes place. Section 35(2)(b) of the 1979 Act further protects the buyer by providing that, in a contract for sale by sample, the buyer will not be deemed to have accepted the goods until he has had a reasonable opportunity to examine the goods to establish that the bulk complies with the sample.[125] Section 15(2)(c) merely affirms the protection regarding latent defects.

---

[120] (1887) 12 App. Cas. 284.   [121] *Ibid.* 297.
[122] Macleod, above n. 80.   [123] Sale of Goods Act 1979, s.15(2)(a).
[124] *Ibid.* s.15(2)(c).
[125] Until 1994, the right to a reasonable opportunity to compare the bulk with the sample was to be found in Sale of Goods Act 1979, s.15(2)(b).

Sample and description may co-exist. Indeed, one might reasonably construe a sample as a visual description. Section 13(2) makes clear that when goods have been sold both by description and by sample, it is not sufficient merely that the bulk of the goods comply with the sample, they must also correspond with the description.

Q10 Consider the role of sales by sample in modern sale of goods law.

8 Exclusion and limitation of liability

Remedies is an area in which the dichotomy between the position of the commercial buyer and that of the consumer buyer is very apparent, as the protection now available to the latter is significantly more extensive and flexible than that available to the former. However, before examining the availability of remedies, one must, of course, consider whether any liability has been limited or excluded and whether acceptance or affirmation has occurred which would impact on whether the buyer may seek any remedy. This accentuates further the distinction between the consumer buyer and the non-consumer buyer.

Limitation and exclusion is governed by the Unfair Contract Terms Act (UCTA) 1977 and also, for consumers, by the Unfair Terms in Consumer Contract Regulations 1999 (SI 1999/2083). It is the former, however, that is significant in relation to any attempt by the seller to exclude or reduce his liability for breaches of sections 12–15 of the Sale of Goods Act 1979. As is well established, liability for breaches of section 12 cannot be excluded[126] against any buyer, with equal protection being granted in respect of the similar provision in hire-purchase[127] and in other contracts for the transfer of goods.[128] This prohibition applies to all such contracts irrespective of the nature of the buyer, whether business or consumer, and is eminently defensible given the fact that a breach of the 'right to sell' involves a total lack of consideration, allowing the buyer to terminate the contract and seek a full refund of the contract price.[129] By contrast, the ability of the seller to exclude or restrict his liability for breaches of sections 13–15 and the corresponding provisions in other statutes will depend on the nature of the buyer. As against someone dealing as a consumer within the meaning of the UCTA 1977,[130] exclusion or restriction of liability is not permitted by reference to any contract term. Any such term would be void. Against

---

[126] Unfair Contract Terms Act 1977, s.6(1)(a).

[127] *Ibid.* s.6(1)(b).

[128] *Ibid.* s.7(3A) which prohibits the exclusion of liability for breaches under Supply of Goods and Services Act 1982, s.2.

[129] See the discussion on the Sale of Goods Act 1979, s.12 (right to sell) above; also *Rowland* v. *Divall* [1923] 2 KB 500 and *Butterworth* v. *Kingsway Motors* [1954] 1 WLR 1286.

[130] See Unfair Contract Terms Act 1977, s.12 for the criteria to establish whether the buyer is 'dealing as a consumer'.

a non-consumer buyer, however, liability under sections 13–15 and the other corresponding provisions may be excluded or restricted by reference to a contract term but only to the extent that the term satisfies the test of reasonableness laid down in section 11 of the UCTA 1977.[131]

Q11 Consider whether the distinction between business buyers and consumer buyers as regards limitations and exclusions is an appropriate one.

9 Acceptance

Acceptance of the goods or affirmation of the contract[132] are fatal to the remedy of rejection although the buyer may still be able to claim damages for a breach of warranty under section 11 of the 1979 Act. Section 35 of the 1979 Act outlines three main situations in which acceptance will be deemed to have occurred, the first being where the buyer intimates to the seller that he has accepted them, and the second being when the goods have been delivered to the buyer and he does any act with them that is inconsistent with the continued ownership of the seller. Amendments to section 35 have strengthened both of these options from the perspective of the buyer, as the current version of the 1979 Act places limitations on them. Thus, in line with section 34, which takes priority over section 35,[133] the new section 35(2) recognises the right of the buyer to have a reasonable opportunity to examine the goods to ascertain whether they are in conformity with the contract and, in a contract of sale by sample, the opportunity to compare the bulk with the sample.[134] Assuming that the buyer has not examined them previously, only when this opportunity for examination under section 35(2) has occurred will acceptance take place. Thus, the common situation of a buyer being expected to sign a delivery note confirming acceptance of the goods prior to him having an opportunity to examine them will be of no effect. This right to an examination cannot be excluded where the buyer deals as a consumer[135] and is yet another example of the growing divide between the protection offered to consumer buyers and that made available to non-consumer buyers.

The current version of the 1979 Act has also clarified concerns about what behaviour constitutes an act by the buyer that would be inconsistent with the

---

[131] See *ibid.* s.6(3) as regards liability for contracts of sale and hire-purchase contracts and *ibid.* s.7(3) for other contracts under which possession or title to goods passes.

[132] The provisions regarding acceptance to be found in Sale of Goods Act 1979, ss.35 and 35A only apply to contracts for the sale of goods and do not extend to other contracts under which a buyer may acquire goods. Affirmation, having its basis in common law, applies to all contracts for the sale or other transfer of goods.

[133] For a discussion of the relationship between Sale of Goods Act 1979, ss.34 and 35 see Atiyah, Adams and MacQueen, above n. 9, ch. 27.

[134] This approach is in line with the recommendations of the Law Commission who felt that acceptance should not take place prior to the opportunity to examine the goods.

[135] Sale of Goods Act 1979, s.35(3).

continued ownership of the seller. Again, the relationship between sections 34 and 35 caused difficulties in the past, particularly in relation to sub-sales where the buyer might be buying for resale to a sub-buyer without examining the goods himself. If a sub-sale is deemed to be an act inconsistent with the continued ownership of the seller, the situation could arise where a buyer who arranged for the seller to deliver direct to the sub-buyer might be deemed to have accepted them without the opportunity to examine them. Equally, the onward sale of sealed goods raised a similar problem. Clearly, this was an unsatisfactory situation, particularly given the assumed superiority of section 34. The 1994 amendments to the 1979 Act resolved the issue by inserting a new section 35(6)(b) that expressly provides that a sub-sale or other disposition of the goods to another person does not constitute acceptance.

An act inconsistent with the continued ownership of the seller would include situations whereby the buyer has destroyed the character of the item by, for example, reconstituting it as an integral part of another product from which it cannot be recovered. Equally, it can be argued that if a product has been used extensively and so cannot be returned in the same condition in which it was provided, that could constitute acceptance.[136]

Section 35(6) also clarifies another long-standing issue, namely, whether allowing a seller the opportunity to repair faulty goods is tantamount to acceptance, by stipulating that where the buyer asks for, or agrees to, their repair under an arrangement with the seller, this will not be deemed to be acceptance. This may be of greater significance to the whole concept of acceptance given that section 48 has introduced new remedies available to consumer buyers which include a right to ask for a repair when goods are not in conformity with the contract, which is defined as being where there is a breach of sections 13–15 of the 1979 Act.

Acceptance is also deemed to occur when the buyer has retained the goods for a reasonable period without intimating to the seller that he is rejecting them.[137] The reasonable period must include allowing the buyer a reasonable opportunity to examine the goods to ensure conformity with the contract and confirm that a bulk complies with a sample, once again reinforcing the importance of that requirement.[138] The Law Commission rejected any suggestion that there should be a long-term right to reject goods or even a long-term right to reject for latent defects.[139] Amongst other things, they argued that such a right would raise issues about what consideration the buyer should provide for the use and enjoyment he had had from the goods prior to rejection. They felt that no meaningful formula for assessing this could be devised which did not depend 'upon criteria so uncertain as almost to invite dispute'.[140] Equally, they

---

[136] Atiyah, Adams and MacQueen, above n. 9, ch. 27.
[137] Sale of Goods Act 1979, s.35(4).   [138] *Ibid.* s.35(5).
[139] Law Commission *Sale and Supply of Goods* (Report No. 160, 1987).
[140] *Ibid.*

rejected any notion of different fixed periods for the rejection of different classes of goods.[141] Consequently, they recommended the continued use of the 'reasonable time' approach, which, while lacking certainty, facilitates the breadth of situations to which it must be applied. Of course, what constitutes a 'reasonable time' is ultimately a matter of fact for the court to decide but some guidance can be gleaned from case law.

A key issue as regards rejection is whether the goods are being purchased for resale, a situation typically occurring in business sales, or whether they are being sold for use, which will include some business sales and virtually all consumer sales. Two leading cases, *Truk (UK) Ltd* v. *Tokmakidis GmbH*[142] and *J & H Ritchie Ltd* v. *Lloyd Ltd*[143] are instructive here. In the former case, the buyer purchased some lifting equipment for fitting to a vehicle which the buyer intended to resell. A potential sub-buyer noticed that the gear was defective and the buyer immediately notified the seller of the suspected defect. Three months later, when an investigation confirmed the fault, the buyer sought to reject the goods. The court held that the rejection was valid, opining that, when goods are intended for resale, a 'reasonable time' would include the time taken to sell the goods together with an appropriate period for the sub-buyer to examine and try them out. The dealings between buyer and seller need to be considered, including any agreement to allow for a repair so as to permit the seller the opportunity to provide goods that conform to the contract. Further, where payment is to be delayed beyond the date for delivery, it could be argued that the reasonable period should last at least until payment is due.

The House of Lords in *J & H Ritchie Ltd* v. *Lloyd Ltd* considered the impact upon acceptance of permitting repairs to faulty goods, holding that when the buyer has agreed to allow the seller the opportunity to inspect and repair the goods, there is an implied term that the seller will inform the buyer both about the defect and the remedial action taken to repair it so as to allow the buyer the opportunity to make an informed decision as to whether to accept the repaired goods. The refusal of the seller to provide the buyer with such information was a breach entitling the buyer to repudiate the agreement and claim a refund of the purchase price.

Both of these cases related to business contracts. For several years, the leading case in consumer sales was that of *Bernstein* v. *Pamson Motors (Golders Green) Ltd*,[144] which took quite a restrictive approach to acceptance, holding that acceptance had occurred after only three weeks. However, the 1994 amendments to the 1979 Act have invalidated the *Bernstein* decision, which no longer represents the law, a view confirmed by the Court of Appeal in *Clegg* v. *Olle Anderson*.[145] The major issue is that consumer goods are invariably bought for use and it is more difficult to establish what constitutes a reasonable period

---

[141] *Ibid.*   [142] [2000] 1 Lloyd's Rep. 543.
[143] [2007] 1 WLR 670.   [144] [1987] 2 All ER 220.
[145] [2003] EWCA Civ 320.

when the goods are in daily use, particularly if the seller refuses to accept a rejection by the buyer and the latter is forced to continue using them while the dispute is ongoing. Arguably, there will come a point when that continued use may be classed as acceptance and possibly as an act that is inconsistent with the continued ownership of the seller. That said, the court was prepared to allow rejection after the lapse of six months in *Rogers* v. *Parish*[146] and of two months in *Porter* v. *General Guarantee Corp.*,[147] a hire-purchase case decided on common law grounds, there being no statutory equivalent to section 35 of the 1979 Act in hire-purchase legislation.

A significant amendment to the rules on acceptance relates to the insertion in 1994 of section 35A of the 1979 Act dealing with partial acceptance. Until that point, partial acceptance was only permissible in severable contracts, or where the seller had delivered more than the contract amount when the buyer could reject the excess,[148] or where the contract goods had become mixed with goods of a different description.[149] The current section 35A, however, has expanded the opportunity for partial acceptance by extending it to goods in non-severable contracts. Thus, as long as there has been a breach that gives the buyer a right to reject the goods for non-conformity with the contract, he will not lose his right to reject the non-conforming goods just because he has accepted those that are not affected by the breach.[150] Partial acceptance will still be subject to the rule under section 35(7) that prohibits partial acceptance of goods in a 'commercial unit' when the division of the unit would materially impair the value or character of the goods.

Q12 Analyse the methods through which acceptance can occur.

10 Remedies

The classic remedies for a breach of sections 12–15 of the Sale of Goods Act 1979 are the rejection of the goods and repudiation of the contract for a breach of condition, and a claim for damages for a breach of warranty. In respect of the former, it is possible to reject the goods without repudiating the contract if the buyer is prepared to allow the seller a second opportunity to provide goods that comply with the contract. Further, it is possible to repudiate the contract without rejecting the goods if they have not been received.

While these remedies cannot be excluded in consumer contracts, we have already seen that it is possible to exclude or limit liability for breach of sections 13–15[151] and thereby for remedies in non-consumer sales.[152] Remedies

---

[146] [1987] 2 All ER 232.   [147] [1982] RTR 384.

[148] Sale of Goods Act 1979, s.30(2).

[149] *Ibid.* s.30(4) (now repealed).   [150] *Ibid.* s.35A(1).

[151] Liability for a breach of Sale of Goods Act 1979, s.12 cannot be excluded against any buyer, consumer or non-consumer.

[152] Sale of Goods Act 1979, s.15A.

for non-consumer buyers have been restricted further since 1994 and the insertion of section 15A of the 1979 Act, which provides that where the buyer is a non-consumer and the breach of sections 13, 14 or 15 is so slight that it would be unreasonable for the buyer to reject the goods, then the breach will be treated as a breach of warranty instead which will sound in damages only. The parties may contract either expressly or impliedly to overrule this section and, when it is relied upon, the onus is on the seller to demonstrate that the breach is so slight as to render rejection unreasonable.

The distinction between non-consumer buyers and consumer buyers is even more apparent, however, when considering the new remedies introduced by the Sale and Supply of Goods to Consumers Regulations 2002,[153] which took effect from 31 March 2003.[154] The remedies are to be found in section 48A–48F of the 1979 Act and comprise rights of repair, replacement of the goods, reduction of the purchase price and rescission of the contract. The remedies are available where the buyer is dealing as a consumer and the goods do not conform to the contract of sale at the time of delivery. An interesting development is that there is a presumption under section 48A(3) that if the goods do not conform to the contract at any time within six months of delivery to the buyer, they are assumed not to have complied at the time of delivery. This reverses the burden of proof and requires the seller to demonstrate the non-conformity by showing either that the goods did conform at the time of delivery or that six months is incompatible with the nature of the goods or the nature of the non-conformity. Thus, for example, perishable goods with a short life-span would be excluded from this six-month presumption.

These remedies are in addition to those already in existence as, while the United Kingdom was obliged to introduce these remedies to give effect to the Directive on the sale of consumer goods and associated guarantees,[155] the Directive expressly permitted Member States to adopt or maintain more stringent provisions to ensure a higher level of consumer protection.[156] Thus, while a consumer buyer may choose to use one of the additional remedies to request a repair, replacement, etc., the buyer still has the right to reject the goods under the existing regime if there has been an actionable breach of condition. It is clear from the wording of the section that the buyer has the choice of remedy, with section 48B(1) dealing with repair and replacement, and section 48C(1) dealing with reduction of purchase price or rescission, both stating 'the buyer may require the seller…'. This choice of remedy is important to prevent overbearing sellers from forcing weak buyers into accepting a lesser remedy against their wishes when they might really prefer to enforce their traditional right of rejection. The balance is restored by the provision that the buyer cannot force

---

[153] SI 2002/3045.
[154] The Regulations also provide for new controls over consumer guarantees, see SI 2002/3045, reg. 15.
[155] Sale of Goods and Associated Guarantees Directive 99/44/EC.
[156] *Ibid.* Art. 8.

the seller to repair or replace the goods if that is impossible, or disproportionate to the other of those remedies, or disproportionate to a reduction in the
price or a rescission of the contract. A remedy is deemed to be disproportionate if it imposes unreasonable costs on the seller given the value of the goods
had they conformed, the significance of the lack of conformity and whether the
other remedy could be effected without significant inconvenience to the buyer.
Of note is the fact that if the buyer opts for rescission of the contract, he will
not necessarily receive the full value of the goods at the time of delivery, as section 48C(3) provides that reimbursement to the buyer may be reduced to take
account of the use that he has had since the time of delivery. In that situation,
the buyer would be better advised, if possible, to reject the goods and repudiate
the contract under the traditional remedies so that he can recover the full value
of the goods at the time of delivery.

The protected position of the consumer buyer might have changed significantly under proposals for new provisions in the Consumer Rights Directive.[157]
However, in the event, the Consumer Rights Directive as enacted did not make
any changes.

*Q13 Compare and contrast the remedies available to consumer buyers and
non-consumer buyers.*

11 Recommended reading

Atiyah P.S., Adams J. and MacQueen A. *The Sale of Goods* (11th edn, Pearson Education
    Ltd, Harlow, 2005)
Atiyah, P.S., Adams, J.N. and MacQueen, H. *The Sale of Goods* (12th edn, Pearson
    Education Ltd, Harlow, 2010)
Bradgate R. *Commercial Law* (3rd edn, Butterworths, London, 2000)
Bradgate, R. and Twigg-Flesner, C. *Blackstone's Guide to Consumer Sales and Associated
    Guarantees* (Oxford University Press, Oxford, 2003)
Bridge M. *The Sale of Goods* (Oxford University Press, Oxford, 1997)
Department for Business, Enterprise and Regulatory Reform *Consultation on EU
    Proposals for a Consumer Rights Directive* (BERR, London, 2008)
Dobson P. and Stokes R. *Commercial Law* (7th edn, Sweet & Maxwell, London, 2008)
Editorial 'Proving goods are defective: the six month requirement' (2009) 32(2)
    Consumer Law Today 1
  'Satisfactory quality and the right of rejection' (2010) *Consumer Law Today* 1–3 April
European Commission Proposal for a Directive of the European Parliament and the
    Council on consumer rights COM(2008)614 final (Brussels, 2008)
Griffiths M. and Griffiths I. *Law for Purchasing and Supply* (3rd edn, Pearson Education
    Ltd, Harlow, 2002)
Howells, G. and Weatherill, S. *Consumer Protection Law* (2nd edn, Ashgate Publishing
    Ltd, Aldershot, 2005)

---

[157] Proposal for a Directive of the European Parliament and of the Council on consumer rights
    COM(2008)614 final. See now Directive 2011/83/EU on consumer rights.

Law Commission *Sale and Supply of Goods* (Report No. 160 1987)
> *Consumer Remedies for Faulty Goods* Report No. 317, Scottish Law Commission
> Report No. 216 London, 2009)
Law Commission and Scottish Law Commission *Consumer Remedies for Faulty Goods.*
> *A Summary of Responses to Consultation* (London, 2009)
Macleod J. *Consumer Sales Law* (2nd edn, Routledge-Cavendish, Abingdon, 2007)
Mark M. *Chalmers Sale of Goods* (18th edn, Butterworths, London, 1981)
Miller, C.J. and Goldberg, R.S. *Product Liability* (2nd edn, Oxford University Press,
> Oxford, 2004)
Ramsay, I. *Consumer Law and Policy: Text and Materials on Regulating Consumer
> Markets* (2nd edn, Hart Publishing, Oxford, 2007)
Sealy, L.S. and Hooley, R.J.A. *Commercial Law: Text, Cases and Materials* (4th edn,
> Oxford University Press, Oxford, 2009)

The implied conditions are central to sale of goods law. All textbooks that include the sale of goods will include discussion of the implied terms and readers can benefit from reading the relevant parts of standards works such as Atiyah's *The Sale of Goods*, Bradgate's *Commercial Law* and Macleod's *Consumer Sales Law*. This will also allow the reader to gain a broad appreciation of the topic and consider the growing divide between the rights of the consumer buyer and the business buyer. A developing issue relates to available remedies and readers would benefit from reading the Law Commission's consultation on consumer remedies and the editorials from *Consumer Law Today*.

Part 2 Chapter 3

The Passage of Title, Delivery and Payment

Contents

1 Introduction

This chapter considers the issues surrounding the passage of property and risk in goods and the various rules that dictate when the title to the goods moves from the seller to the buyer, a factor that becomes crucial when determining who owns the goods if one of the parties becomes insolvent or the goods are damaged. Allied to this, the chapter also looks at the related topics of the delivery of and payment for goods.

Section 2 provides a background to the topic of the passage of property to goods and the related issue of the passage of risk which dictates who will have to bear the loss if the goods are damaged or destroyed.

Section 3 looks in detail at the rules relating to the passage of property to goods and the statutory rules that exist to determine when the title will pass if the contracting parties have not expressly agreed the matter in the contract. In particular, it looks at Sale of Goods Act 1979, section 17; the section 18 rules; section 19 on reservation of title clauses; and undivided shares in a bulk.

Section 4 considers the passage of risk to the goods and the relationship between the passage of property and the passage of risk.

Section 5 looks at the *nemo dat* exceptions, i.e., those situations in which a seller of goods who has no title to them can nonetheless pass a valid title to those goods to an innocent third party buyer. In particular, it looks at several of the recognised statutory *nemo dat* exceptions, namely, estoppel; mercantile agent; seller in possession; buyer in possession; Hire-Purchase Act 1964, s.27; voidable title; sale under court order; and market overt.

Section 6 looks at the concurrent duties of delivery and payment with the duty being on the seller to deliver the goods and a duty on the buyer to pay the agreed contract price for them. The section looks particularly at three issues relating to delivery and payment, namely, time and place of delivery; delivery of the wrong quantity; and delivery by instalments.

Section 7 considers the remedies that are available to both seller and buyer when delivery and payment has been successfully achieved. Thus, it deals with both monetary remedies and remedies that the seller may have against the goods themselves. The section includes seller's remedies, including real remedies, and personal remedies, and buyer's remedies.

2 Background to the passage of property and risk

In both commercial sales and consumer sales, the transfer of the property to goods is of concern to both seller and buyer, even if only when things go wrong. In a time of recession and economic uncertainty, such as the current recession, when small businesses face difficult times and even high street stores may succumb to financial troubles,[1] the ownership of goods becomes of increasing importance. When a seller goes into liquidation or a buyer becomes bankrupt, the transfer of property will identify who has ownership of the goods, and thus who must bear the loss. This is so irrespective of whether payment has been made, as payment is not linked to transfer of property but rather to delivery. *Prima facie*, the loss will generally fall on the owner. This is due to the rebuttable presumption in section 20 that risk passes with title irrespective of whether delivery has occurred, although this does not necessarily follow, especially in consumer sales where statute provides that the risk remains with the seller until delivery.[2] This provision has been enhanced by the passage of the Consumer Rights Directive,[3] Article 20 of which provides that the risk in the goods will pass to a consumer when he or a third party (other than a carrier and indicated by the consumer) has acquired material possession of the goods.

3 Rules governing the passage of property

The rules governing transfer of property are found in sections 16–19 of the Sale of Goods Act 1979 and depend on whether the goods are specific goods or unascertained, specific goods being defined as those 'identified and agreed on

---

[1] For example, HMV, Focus, etc.
[2] Sale of Goods Act 1979, s.20(4).
[3] Directive 2011/83/EU of the European Parliament and of the Council on consumer rights.

at the time a contract of sale is made'.[4] Hence, where the precise goods cannot be identified at the time of the contract, as in *Kursell* v. *Timber Operators*[5] and *Re Wait*,[6] the goods cannot be classed as specific. As section 61 of the 1979 Act only defines specific goods, it follows that all other goods are necessarily unascertained at the relevant time, becoming 'ascertained' in the course of contractual performance as the identity of the goods to be provided under the contract is finalised. Unascertained goods, when identified, are reclassified as 'ascertained' goods and do not become 'specific' goods within the meaning of the 1979 Act.

(a) Sale of Goods Act 1979, section 17

All transfers of property start with section 17 of the 1979 Act, which stipulates that the passage of property in specific and ascertained goods will pass when the contracting parties intend it to pass, their intention being deduced from the terms of the contract, the conduct of the parties and the circumstances of the case. In short, it is a question of fact. It may be that the parties intend the property to pass straight away, on some specified date, or on the happening of some specific event. This legitimises the use of devices such as reservation of title clauses, as governed by section 19 of the 1979 Act, which are themselves an example of the contracting parties agreeing the time or event at which property is to pass. Section 17 is a prime example of the freedom enjoyed by contracting parties to expressly agree the terms of their contract without undue interference from statute. This reinforces the essential nature of the 1979 Act as being a statutory framework which facilitates and, at times, governs some aspects of contracts of sale, but which is not a straight-jacket controlling every aspect of a contract at the expense of the contractual freedom of the parties. In practice, however, contracts are often silent on the issue of the passage of title to the goods, the seller being more concerned with payment and the buyer with delivery, although stipulating these may be taken as inferring the intention of the parties that property in the goods will pass at the same time.[7]

Given the primacy of section 17, it follows that the remaining provisions governing the passage of property are secondary in nature and fill any vacuum left by the contracting parties not specifically agreeing the time of transfer.[8]

---

[4] Sale of Goods Act 1979, s.61.

[5] [1927] 1 KB 298. The contract involved the sale of timber to be harvested over a period of fifteen years. The timber was to be measured at the time of felling to identify which timber fell within the terms of the contract. Thus, the timber covered by the contract could not be identified at the time that the contract was made, only at various times over the next fifteen years. The timber was not specific goods.

[6] [1927] 1 Ch. 606. This concerned the sale of 500 tonnes of wheat from a bulk cargo of 1,000 tonnes. They were unascertained at the time of the contract but would become ascertained when separated from the remainder.

[7] *Ward* v. *Bignall* [1967] 1 QB 534.

[8] A similar approach is to be found in ss.14–15 of the Supply of Goods and Services Act 1982 dealing with the time of performance in contracts for the provision of services and the consideration due for such contracts. In both sections, the provisions are only applicable where

This is reinforced by the opening words of section 18 of the 1979 Act, which confirm that the rules contained therein apply 'unless a different intention appears', a clear reference to the primacy of any contractual agreement by the parties.

Q1 *Consider the importance of section 17 in reflecting the freedom of contracting parties to agree the terms of any contract that they may conclude.*

(b) Sale of Goods Act 1979, section 18 rules

The section 18 rules divide somewhat naturally into those governing specific goods and those applicable to unascertained goods, specific goods being governed by section 18 rules 1–4 and unascertained goods by section 18 rule 5 with the issue of unidentified shares in a bulk being dealt with separately in section 20A of the 1979 Act. The provisions regarding specific goods are relatively straight-forward with the main issues arising in respect of unascertained goods.

Rules 1, 2 and 3, all of which address the passage of property in specific goods, revolve around the concept of the goods being in a 'deliverable state'. The meaning of this term is defined in section 65(5) of the 1979 Act as being when the goods 'are in such a state that the buyer would under the terms of the contract be bound to take delivery of them'. It follows that if the buyer would not be bound to take delivery, it cannot be said that the goods are in a deliverable state. However, when the goods are available, comply with the terms of the contract and the seller is in a position to pass the property in them to the buyer, such that, under the terms of the contract, the buyer is obliged to take delivery of them, they are in a 'deliverable state' within the meaning of the 1979 Act. Naturally, if something remains to be done to the goods by the seller before delivery and passage of property in them can take place, the goods are not in a 'deliverable state' and the property in them cannot pass until that thing has been done.[9]

(i) Section 18 rule 1

Section 18 rule 1 stipulates that when specific goods under an unconditional contract are in a deliverable state, the property in them will pass at the time that the contract is made, irrespective of whether the time for delivery or payment or both are postponed. This requires an understanding of the term 'unconditional contract' in this context. Theoretically, an unconditional contract could mean one of two things: either that the contract does not contain any conditions, or that it has no preconditions that restrict when it comes into effect. The

---

there is a contractual vacuum because the parties have not expressly agreed the term, it will not be resolved in a manner laid out in the contract and there is no previous course of dealings between the parties.

[9] *Rugg* v. *Minett* (1809) 11 East 210, in which barrels of turpentine were to be topped up by the seller prior to delivery. The goods were destroyed before the task was completed.

first of these options is not sustainable as all contracts will have some terms that are so fundamental as to render them contractual conditions. Indeed, all contracts for the sale of goods will necessarily contain conditions, even if only the implied conditions under sections 12–15 of the 1979 Act. Therefore, an 'unconditional contract' must mean a contract the performance of which is not limited by some precondition, such as the need for the seller to acquire the goods from a third party, before contractual performance can begin. It follows that this would include agreements to sell as defined in section 2(5) of the 1979 Act. Equally, a term specifying that the property in the goods will not pass until payment has been made would be a conditional contract, and hence not subject to section 18 rule 1. In practice, such a contract would be subject to section 19, which governs reservation of title clauses.

It should be noted that if the contract is unconditional and the goods are in a deliverable state, the property in them will pass under rule 1 irrespective of whether the time of delivery or payment, or both, is postponed.[10] Thus, property in the goods can pass to a buyer while the goods are still in the possession of the seller awaiting collection or delivery. Equally, property will pass despite the fact that payment is to be delayed by, for example, the sending of an account for settlement, such as routinely occurs in business-to-business contracts where the goods are provided on normal trade terms such as 'payment within 30 days'.

(ii) Section 18 rule 2

Section 18 rule 2 provides that when the seller needs to do something to put the goods into a deliverable state, the property in them will not pass to the buyer until that thing has been done and the buyer has been notified that it has been done. *Underwood* v. *Burgh Castle Brick & Cement Syndicate*[11] provides a good example of this concept in practice. The sellers contracted to sell a 30-ton condensing machine which, at the time of sale, was bolted to the floor. The contract involved the delivery of the machine, 'f.o.r.' (free on rail), which required the seller to arrange for its removal from its present position and for its safe loading onto a train. The Court of Appeal held that property in the goods could not pass under rule 1 as the goods were not in a deliverable state, as they needed both to be unbolted and removed from their present location and, further, to be delivered and loaded onto the train. Consequently, the passage of property would be governed by rule 2 instead.

Rule 2 requires not only that the goods be put into a deliverable state, but also that the buyer has notice that it has been done. Only then can the property in the goods pass. This raises the question whether the notice required is actual or constructive, to which there is no clear answer. The section does not explicitly require the seller to inform the buyer, merely requiring that the buyer has

---

[10] Article 18(1) of the Consumer Rights Directive, above n. 3, will require delivery in consumer contracts to take place within thirty days of the contract.

[11] [1922] 1 KB 343.

had notice. This suggests that the buyer could have been informed by someone other than the seller.

Q2 Consider the relationship and essential differences between section 18 rules 1 and 2.

(iii) Section 18 rule 3

Section 18 rule 3 is likewise concerned with the actions of the seller, providing that where there is the sale of specific goods in a deliverable state but the seller is bound to weigh, measure, test or do some other thing for the purpose of ascertaining the price, then the property cannot pass until that thing has been done and the buyer has notice of it. Rule 3 is little used, being very precise in its wording. If anyone other than the seller is required to do the weighing, etc.,[12] rule 3 will not apply, with property passing under rule 1 or rule 2 as appropriate.

(iv) Section 18 rule 4

Section 18 rule 4 does not expressly refer to specific goods in the way that rules 1–3 do but is concerned with the passage of property where the goods are provided to the buyer on a sale or return basis. This arguably stretches the use of the term 'buyer' as, clearly, if the person receives the goods on a sale or return basis but does not buy them, he can hardly be termed the 'buyer'.[13] Further, it could be argued that sale or return is not a contract of sale at all but is really an 'agreement to sell' subject to a condition that the 'buyer' decides to buy.[14] However, the rule is more concerned with how the property in the goods might pass rather than with semantics. Property can pass either positively through the buyer accepting the goods or doing an act consistent with adopting them, or negatively by allowing the expiration of the specified return period or, alternatively, a reasonable period without rejecting the goods. Actions that would be deemed to adopt the transactions would include selling them or otherwise using or parting with them in a way that would preclude giving them back to the seller. Thus, giving them away as a gift would suggest adoption, as would destroying the character of the goods by using them as a component in a new product. By contrast, the situation is less clear where the buyer provides them to a sub-buyer also on a sale or return basis. It may well depend on whether the prescribed periods in each contract are such that the buyer could reclaim the goods from the sub-buyer in sufficient time to return them to the seller within the relevant period.[15] The ability to hand them back at the end of the return

---

[12] See *Nanka-Bruce* v. *Commonwealth Trust Ltd* [1926] AC 77, in which the buyer's sub-buyer was to weigh the goods. The Privy Council held that s.18 r.3 did not apply.

[13] As a result of this, it is questionable whether a person in possession of goods under a sale or return contract could pass good title to an innocent third party under Sale of Goods Act 1979, s.25, as he is not truly a person who has 'bought or agreed to buy the goods'.

[14] See P.S. Atiyah, J.N. Adams and H. MacQueen, *The Sale of Goods* (11th edn, Pearson Education Ltd, Harlow, 2005) ch. 19, 329.

[15] See P. Dobson and R. Stokes, *Commercial Law* (7th edn, Sweet & Maxwell, London, 2008).

period is crucial. A provision that the property is not to pass until the goods have been paid for, as in *Weiner* v. *Gill*,[16] would, of course, constitute 'a different intention' on behalf of the parties, lifting the transaction out of section 18 and potentially placing it under the remit of section 19 on reservation of title.

Q3 Analyse the various ways in which property may pass under section 18 rule 4.

(v) Section 18 rule 5: unascertained goods

The passage of property to unascertained goods raises particular issues. As a general rule, property cannot pass until the goods have been ascertained[17] although there is a statutory exception in respect of undivided shares in goods forming part of a bulk[18] introduced by section 3 of the Sale of Goods (Amendment) Act 1995. As with the transfer of specific goods, the intention of the contracting parties is paramount, that being deduced from the contractual terms, the conduct of the parties and other circumstances. In the absence of any express intention, section 18 rule 5 dictates the passage of property and thereby the allocation of risk.

Rule 5 provides both for the situation of unascertained goods in a deliverable state and, since 1995, for unascertained goods forming part of a bulk. The latter provision is a significant addition, providing help to international trade where goods may be transported for a period of weeks in a ship's hold with sellers and buyers wanting to deal with the goods while they are in transit. The net effect is that rule 5 effectively deals with two different yet related situations.

Rule 5(1) provides that when unascertained goods are in a deliverable state and are unconditionally appropriated to the contract, the property in them will pass. This unconditional appropriation may be by the seller with the assent of the buyer or vice versa, with the assent being either express or implied and occurring either before or after appropriation. What matters is that the goods have been irretrievably allocated to the contract with the seller not being able to change his mind and use different goods to fulfil the contract. Thus, the seller putting goods labelled with the name of the buyer to one side and sending a delivery note identifying the particular goods and entitling the buyer to immediate possession would be unconditional appropriation,[19] as would a customer dispensing petrol into his car, the latter being an example of unconditional appropriation of the goods by the buyer with the implied assent of the seller.

Goods may also be unconditionally appropriated by exhaustion when the seller has dispatched goods for more than one buyer by a carrier who is responsible for allocating the goods as each delivery is made. When the last but one

---

[16] [1906] 2 KB 574.   [17] Sale of Goods Act 1979, s.16.   [18] *Ibid.* s.20A.
[19] *Hendy Lennox (Industrial Engines) Ltd* v. *Grahame Puttick Ltd* [1984] 2 All ER 152, but contrast *Carlos Federspiel & Co. SA* v. *Charles Twigg & Co. Ltd* [1957] 1 Lloyd's Rep. 240, in which packing up the goods and putting labels on them was not sufficient to constitute unconditional appropriation as the seller could have substituted other goods if he had so chosen.

delivery is made such that the only goods that remain with the carrier are those intended for the buyer, the goods are unconditionally appropriated at that point.[20] Section18 rule 5(3) reinforces the rule regarding appropriation by exhaustion. It provides that, where there is a contract for the sale of a specified quantity of unascertained goods in a deliverable state forming part of a bulk identified by contract or by subsequent agreement between the parties, then property will pass to the buyer if two conditions are satisfied. These are, first, that the buyer is the only buyer to whom goods are due out of the bulk and, secondly, that the quantity of goods remaining is equal to or less than the quantity of goods due to the buyer. Further, where a single buyer has several contracts for goods to be drawn from an identifiable bulk, the property will pass when the bulk is reduced to, or to less than, the aggregate of goods due to the buyer and he is the only buyer remaining.[21] Note that the goods must not merely be identifiable but must also be in a deliverable state, as per the previous discussion above in respect of other rules.

Given the immense rise in the use of the Internet as a trading forum for both businesses and consumers, it is of considerable importance to analyse the passage of property in this situation. Essentially, when goods are bought on the Internet or by some other form of distance selling, the seller unconditionally appropriates the goods with the implied assent of the buyer when the seller posts them. Alternatively, delivering the goods to a carrier, or other bailee or custodier, to transport to the buyer without the seller reserving a right of disposal will cause unconditional appropriation resulting in the passage of property in the goods,[22] leaving the goods at the risk of the buyer during transit. However, the dichotomy between consumer buyers and non-consumer buyers, apparent in other areas of the sale of goods,[23] raises its head once again. Section 20(4) of the Sale of Goods Act 1979 provides that, in consumer contracts, goods remain at the risk of the seller until delivery to the consumer occurs. This will be reinforced by the Consumer Rights Directive, which seeks to protect consumer buyers by stipulating that the risk in goods will only pass where the consumer or a third party other than the carrier and indicated by the consumer has acquired material possession of the goods.[24] Thus, when goods are purchased via the Internet, property may pass to both non-consumer buyers and consumer buyers when the seller unconditionally appropriates the goods by dispatching them, however, while the risk in them will pass to the non-consumer buyer with title, it will not pass to the consumer buyer until material possession occurs.

Q4 Analyse the scope of the term 'unconditional appropriation' in relation to the passage of property in unascertained goods.

---

[20] *Healy* v. *Howlett & Sons* [1917] 1 KB 337.
[21] Sale of Goods Act 1979, s.18 r.5(4).
[22] *Ibid.* s.18 r.5(2).   [23] For example, remedies under *ibid.* s.15A.
[24] Consumer Rights Directive, above n. 3, Art. 20.

(c) Sale of Goods Act 1979, section 19: reservation of title clauses

Reservation of title clauses involve the contracting parties agreeing the time when the property in the goods is to pass, typically when the buyer pays for the goods and, as such, conforms to the section 17 stipulation that the property will transfer when the parties so intend. Consequently, the section 18 rules will not apply in the presence of a reservation of title clause. Reservation of title clauses blur the divide between specific goods and ascertained goods, applying, as they do, to contracts for both. Thus, section 19(1) governs both specific goods, i.e., goods identified at the time that the contract is made, and ascertained goods, i.e., those goods not identified at the time that the contract is made but which have subsequently been appropriated to the contract. Naturally, a reservation of title clause cannot attach to unascertained goods because of the need to identify the goods that are subject to the clause.

It is possible for the seller to reserve the right of disposal of the goods until certain conditions are satisfied notwithstanding the delivery of the goods to the buyer or a carrier or other bailee or custodian of the goods for transmission to the buyer.[25] Further, when goods are shipped, the seller is presumed to have reserved the right of disposal if the bill of lading renders the goods deliverable to the order of the seller or those of his agent.[26] Equally, where the seller has drawn on the buyer for payment and the seller transmits the bill of lading and the bill of exchange to the buyer, property will not pass if the latter fails to pay and has wrongfully retained the bill of lading.[27]

Reservation of title clauses more usually occur in commercial contracts rather than consumer ones, and it may be that in difficult economic times such as the current recession, their use becomes even more attractive as a way for sellers to protect their position against the inherent risks of a buyer proving insolvent. There are, however, some restrictions on their use in that such clauses are largely restricted to situations in which the buyer is able to return the goods to the seller in their original state, and cannot operate once the goods have lost their identity by being subsumed into another product.[28]

The leading decision on reservation of title clauses is the *Romalpa*[29] case in which the Court of Appeal recognised the ability of a seller to use a reservation clause both to retain the property rights in goods and, where the clause imposes on the buyer a fiduciary relationship with the seller, to have a claim over the proceeds of sale of any goods by the buyer. This is particularly pertinent where both buyer and seller expect that the buyer will resell the goods to a third party. The later decision in *Armour v. Thyssen Edelstahlwerke AG*[30] extended the scope

---

[25] Sale of Goods Act 1979, s.19(1).

[26] *Ibid.* s.19(2).   [27] *Ibid.* s.19(3).

[28] For example, *Borden (UK) Ltd v. Scottish Timber Products* [1981] Ch. 25; *Re Peachdart Ltd* [1984] Ch. 131.

[29] *Aluminium Industrie Vaassen BV v. Romalpa Aluminium Ltd* [1976] 2 All ER 552.

[30] [1991] 2 AC 339.

of reservation clauses by confirming the validity of 'all monies' clauses under which the clause reserves the property in the goods to the seller not merely until monies owing on that particular contract are paid, but until all monies owing by the buyer to the seller under other contracts have been paid. Typically, a reservation of title clause will impose a requirement that the buyer stores the goods separately from those acquired from any other source so that in the event of the liquidation of the buyer, the seller can easily identify his goods and reclaim them.

Such clauses are intended to allow the seller to protect himself from the consequences of any liquidation of the buyer. Were the property in the goods to pass to the buyer, the unpaid seller would merely rank as an unsecured trade creditor and, as such, run the very real risk of receiving nothing at all in the liquidation or, at best, receiving only a proportion of the money that he is owed. Bodies such as banks, who have secured loans against the business assets of the buyer as either fixed or floating charges, would have priority at the expense of the seller.

In some situations, the seller may be required to register their interest as a registerable charge. As mentioned above, the ability of the seller to physically reclaim the goods cannot subsist once the goods have lost their identity by being subsumed within another product. Thus, in *Borden*,[31] the resin supplied by the seller had been irretrievably changed by being mixed with wood chips to make chipboard, while in *Re Peachdart*,[32] the leather had been used to manufacture handbags, the court holding in both instances that the ability of the seller to enforce the clause had ended.

If the seller wants to extend his protection, he may seek to include a clause giving him a right to reclaim manufactured goods produced using his materials, but such a clause would require to be registered if it is to be enforceable.

Q5 Consider the role of retention of title clauses in protecting the position of the seller, particularly in the event of the insolvency of the buyer.

(d) Undivided shares in a bulk

The issue of undivided shares in a bulk raises particular issues of concern in relation to trade generally but especially international trade. Bulk tankers may be carrying a huge volume of one product intended for delivery to a number of identified buyers, potentially from several countries, each of whom has a contract for a given amount of the goods to be drawn from the bulk, with the goods remaining in transit for weeks or even months awaiting delivery. While the goods remain undivided prior to delivery, they are unascertained such that, following traditional contract rules, title in them would not pass until either delivery or exhaustion occurs. However, in 1995, new provisions were introduced

---

[31] [1981] Ch. 25.   [32] [1984] Ch. 131.

that strengthen the position of buyers of undivided shares in an identifiable bulk as regards their ownership rights in the goods during transit.[33] These should facilitate international trade by giving buyers ownership rights which identify goods sufficiently to allow for sub-sales of identifiable goods prior to them being separated from the bulk. However, the application of the provision is closely controlled and does not simply apply to all unascertained goods forming part of a bulk but only those satisfying specified criteria. Thus, it will only apply to sales of a specified quantity of unascertained goods where the goods form part of an identifiable bulk and, further, where the buyer has paid the price for some or all of the relevant goods.[34] Unless the parties agree otherwise, as soon as these conditions have been satisfied, or at such later time as the parties agree, the buyer will acquire property in the undivided share and also be an owner in common in the bulk along with the other buyers.[35] The undivided share that will be protected via this mechanism is that quantity of the goods for which the buyer has paid in relation to the quantity of the goods in the bulk at the time. Where the total of the undivided shares exceeds the bulk, as might occur where part of the bulk has been lost, then the undivided share of the buyers is reduced proportionately so that the total shares equal the bulk available. Further, where the buyer has only paid for part of the goods due to him, that will be treated as payment for a corresponding proportion of the goods and any delivery of goods made to the buyer will relate first to those goods for which he has paid.

The purpose behind this move to allocate some ownership rights is to permit the owners in common to deal with the goods prior to delivery and thereby facilitate trade. This necessitates the co-owners recognising the rights and duties of each other vis-à-vis the goods. Thus, by virtue of section 20A of the Sale of Goods Act 1979, each co-owner is deemed to have consented to the delivery of goods out of the bulk to each of the co-owners as those goods are due to him under the contract – in short, allowing each co-owner to receive delivery of his share.[36] Equally, co-owners are deemed to consent to every other co-owner dealing with or removing, delivering or otherwise disposing of his undivided share of the goods while those goods still form part of the bulk.[37] Under section 20B(1), no cause of action can arise against a co-owner in respect of his legitimate actions when the consent of other co-owners is deemed to have been given under that subsection. Section 20B(3) restricts the impact of section 20A on other legal obligations. Thus, an owner in common has no obligation to compensate any other owner in common for any shortfall in the quantity of goods that the latter receives. Further, sections 20A and 20B will not affect any contractual arrangements between co-owners about any adjustments between

---

[33] Sale of Goods Act 1979, ss.20A and 20B, as inserted by Sale of Goods (Amendment) Act 1995, s.1(3).
[34] Sale of Goods Act 1979, s.20A(1).   [35] *Ibid.* s.20A(2).
[36] *Ibid.* s.20B(1)(a).   [37] *Ibid.* s.20B(1)(b).

themselves and will not affect the rights of any buyer under his contract. Thus, for example, if a buyer has contracted to buy and has paid for 5,000 tons of grain out of an identified bulk sailing on a named ship departing Hamburg on a given day, the seller remains contractually obliged to deliver that quantity, such that if less that 5,000 tons is delivered because, for example, the bulk is insufficient to satisfy all the contracts, the buyer will have a right to contractual damages.

Q6 Analyse how the provisions of sections 20A and 20B of the Sale of Goods Act 1979 have strengthened the position of the buyer of undivided shares in a bulk.

4 Passage of risk

Discussion of contractual remedies necessarily raises the issue of risk, for the party who has the risk in the goods must bear the loss if they are lost or damaged, which may well involve the payment of contractual damages to an injured party. It is important to distinguish here between risk and frustration, for risk involves one party having to bear the loss with the accompanying possibility that they might also have to pay contractual damages to the other party to the contract if they have suffered loss. By contrast, when a contract for the sale of specific goods has been frustrated by the perishing of the goods, without fault of either buyer or seller, before risk passes to the buyer, then the contract is rendered void.[38] As a general rule of thumb, however, risk passes with property, hence knowing when the property will pass is important, particularly in these uncertain financial times. In practice, this comes down to who should insure the goods so as to ensure that if the goods are lost or damaged or one party becomes insolvent, an insurance claim can be made to recover the loss. But, of course, it is not that straight-forward.

Section 20(1) provides that, unless agreed otherwise, the goods remain at the risk of the seller until the property is transferred to the buyer but when the property transfers to the buyer so does the risk, irrespective of whether or not delivery has been made. There are notable exceptions to this, however, as buyers, and in some circumstances sellers, might be forgiven for expecting that risk will attach to physical possession of the goods rather than legal ownership of them. Buyers purchasing specific goods and to whom title will pass by section 18 rule 1, but who have not yet taken delivery of those goods, would not expect that the risk in the goods has passed to them while the goods are still in the hands of the seller. Section 20(1) specifically allows the parties to agree that risk will pass at a time other than the passage of property and gives priority to their wishes. Thus, it is perfectly acceptable for the parties to agree that risk will pass with possession. A prime example would be reservation of title

[38] *Ibid.* s.7.

clauses (discussed above) where the seller retains ownership of the goods pending the payment of the price but the risk in the goods passes to the buyer along with possession of the goods. This idea has been extended to include a situation where the buyer had a right to immediate possession even though actual possession had not passed, and can be illustrated by the difficult and exceptional case of *Sterns Ltd* v. *Vickers Ltd*,[39] in which the risk in a consignment of white spirit was held to have passed to the buyer. He had contracted to buy 120,000 gallons of white spirit out of an undivided bulk of 200,000 gallons. He had been supplied with a delivery note giving him a right to immediate possession but had decided to leave the spirit where it was. It deteriorated before delivery and the Court of Appeal held that the risk had passed to the buyer despite the fact that, as unascertained goods which had not been appropriated, property in the goods had not passed. Under the provisions of section 20A, the buyer in that situation would now be a co-owner if he has paid for the goods, and as an owner with a right to immediate possession, risk would pass to the buyer unless the parties had agreed to the contrary.

Given the norm of property and risk being tied together, it is equally possible for possession to pass to the buyer while risk remains with the seller, as might happen where the goods are being purchased on a sale or return basis. Section 18 rule 4 provides that the property will only pass when the buyer signifies his acceptance to the seller, or does an act adopting the transaction, or the specified return period or a reasonable period has expired, so, unless there is a contrary agreement, the goods are at the risk of the seller despite the obvious fact that possession will have passed to the buyer. It follows that if the goods are lost or damaged during that period, without any fault attributable to the buyer,[40] the seller must bear the loss.

While section 20(1) makes the sweeping generalisation that risk passes with property, the section does go on to provide some exceptions to that tenet. Thus, where delivery of the goods has been delayed through the fault of either buyer or seller, that party must bear the risk as regards any loss that would not have occurred but for that fault.[41] Further, section 20(3) reinforces the point that the section does not affect the normal duties and responsibilities of either seller or buyer when acting as a bailee or custodian of the goods for the other party.

Arguably, the most significant exception to the normal rule that risk passes with property is that contained in section 20(4),[42] which, once again, reinforces the distinction between consumer buyers and non-consumer buyers. It stipulates that subsections (1)–(3) of section 20 do not apply when the buyer deals as a consumer. In that situation, the goods will remain at the risk of the seller

---

[39] [1923] 1 KB 78.
[40] The buyer would, of course, be liable for any damage to the goods caused by his negligence because of his duty as a contractual bailee to take care of the goods while they are in his possession.
[41] Sale of Goods Act 1979, s.20(2); see *Demby Hamilton & Co. Ltd* v. *Barden* [1949] 1 All ER 435.
[42] Inserted by Sale and Supply of Goods to Consumers Regulations 2002 (SI 2002/3045).

until they have been delivered to the buyer. This certainly accords with what the average consumer would expect the position to be. Further, it means actual possession, given that section 32(4) of the 1979 Act, which deals with the delivery of goods to a carrier, makes clear that where the seller is authorised or required to send the goods to a consumer buyer, his delivery of those goods to a carrier does not constitute delivery to the buyer. The position of the consumer will be strengthened further by the passage of the Consumer Rights Directive,[43] which, as mentioned previously, stipulates that the risk of loss or damage to the goods will only pass to the consumer when he or a third party, other than the carrier and indicated by the consumer, acquires material possession of the goods.[44] The Directive is one of full harmonisation and thus will apply to all consumer purchases made within the European Union, a distinct improvement on the previous situation in which the Directives that it replaces were of minimum harmonisation and thus allowed differing standards across the EU. Thus, following the passage of the Directive, a consumer will be able to purchase from anywhere in the EU and know that the same rules about the passage of risk will apply. Hence, whether the consumer buyer purchases goods in a shop with delivery to follow, or over the phone or by Internet from anywhere in the EU, the risk in them will not pass to him despite any passage of title until the buyer or his nominee has physical possession of them. Until the time of delivery, all such goods will remain at the seller's risk and thus it is he who should insure them during this period.

Q7 Analyse the relationship between the passage of property and the passage of risk.

5 The *nemo dat* exceptions

In addition to those situations in which the seller and buyer agree when property is to pass or it has passed under the section 18 rules, there are a number of situations in which property will pass to an innocent buyer acting in good faith, which entitles him to legal ownership of the goods even against the original owner. These are the so-called exceptions to the so-called *nemo dat* principle by which a seller cannot pass better title than he himself possesses, and are largely, though not exclusively, to be found in the Sale of Goods Act 1979 itself. The basic philosophy upholds the sanctity of property and the rights of the original owner by specifying in section 21 that where goods are sold by a person who is not their owner, and who does not sell them with the authority or consent of the owner, then the buyer acquires no better title to them than the seller had. This preserves the basic '*nemo dat quod not habet*' tenet that you cannot give what you do not have and, as such, protects the position of the original owner. Nonetheless, there

---

[43] Consumer Rights Directive, above n. 3.
[44] *Ibid.* Art. 20.

are some statutory exceptions to this principle which allow an innocent third party buying in good faith with no knowledge of the rights of the original owner to acquire good title to the goods even against the original owner.

The basic policy underlying these exceptions seems to be that, when you have two innocent parties with a claim to ownership of particular goods, the innocent buyer should be protected provided certain criteria are satisfied. This is not necessarily as unfair to the original owner as might appear at first sight, especially if he has allowed the situation to arise in which a seller, whether innocently or fraudulently, was able to sell goods belonging to the original owner to an innocent third party. Without this protection, the innocent third party could be liable to the original owner in conversion for wrongly interfering with the right of the owner to deal with his property as he chooses.

Q8 Analyse the basic premise behind the **nemo dat** *exceptions which allow an innocent buyer to defeat the ownership rights of the original owner.*

(a) Estoppel

Many of the *nemo dat* exceptions emanate from normal trading situations of agency, the conduct of the original owner, and the seller or buyer of goods remaining in possession of them after a sale has been concluded. Thus, they might be viewed as mere interpretations of normal trading situations seen from the perspective of the innocent third party buyer acting innocently in good faith. Section 21 itself contains an exception based in agency concepts, stipulating that the basic *nemo dat* tenet can be set aside where the owner of the goods is precluded by his conduct from denying that the seller had his authority to sell the goods; or alternatively, that the conduct of the owner had allowed the third party to think that the seller was himself the owner. Where this has arisen the owner is estopped from denying the right of the seller to sell. This might come about by the owner making a representation, whether by words, conduct or even through negligence, (although, in respect of a negligent misrepresentation, there would be an issue as to whether the owner owes any duty of care to the third party).[45] Thus, to some extent, estoppel overlaps with situations of apparent authority in which the owner may be deemed by his conduct to have clothed the seller with apparent authority, with the original owner becoming an unknowing principal in the sale of his goods. Apparent authority is, of course, binding on the principal in that the contract of sale is enforceable by the innocent third party, with the principal able to sue the 'agent' for recompense. However, for section 21 estoppel to be effective, some definite action or omission by the owner is essential. It is insufficient for the owner merely to have allowed the seller to have possession of the goods. We all allow people to have possession of our goods for repair or simply by lending them without in any

---

[45] See Atiyah, Adams and MacQueen, above n. 14, ch. 21, 380.

way representing that the person in temporary possession would have any right to sell them. The responsibility of the owner stretches as far as not creating a belief in the third party either that the seller owns the goods or, alternatively, that he has a right to sell them. Equally, the owner must correct any misrepresentation about the position of the seller if he is to protect his rights to his own property.

(b) Mercantile agent

Mercantile agency also gives rise to a *nemo dat* exception, but again the original owner must have played a part in facilitating the sale by the mercantile agent. Various criteria must be satisfied if the exception under section 2 of the Factors Act 1889 (which is expressly reserved by Sale of Goods Act 1979, section 21(2)),[46] is to work to the benefit of the innocent third party buyer. The seller must:

  (i)   be an independent mercantile agent with the ability to buy and sell goods in his own right;[47]
 (ii)   be in possession of the goods or document of title, such as a bill of lading, in his capacity as a mercantile agent;[48]
(iii)   be in possession with the consent of the owner;
 (iv)   have been acting in the ordinary course of his business when disposing of the goods.

Further, the buyer must have been acting in good faith without notice of the lack of authority of the agent.

The consent of the owner is crucial and is binding on the owner even if consent was given as a result of a fraud perpetrated by the agent, as long as consent has actually been given. In *Stadium Finance* v. *Robbins*,[49] the agent was asked to obtain offers for a car with the owner retaining the key but accidentally leaving the registration book in the glove compartment. The agent acquired a second key, found the registration book and sold the car. Similarly, in *Pearson* v. *Rose & Young*,[50] the agent obtained the registration document by tricking the owner into leaving it behind with the car. He likewise sold the vehicle. In both instances, the court held that the seller had possession of the goods in his capacity as an agent but in neither case had the consent of the owner been given. In *Stadium Finance*, there was no consent as regards possession of either the car or the document, while in *Pearson*, there was no consent to possession of the registration book. In neither case was the agent able to pass good title to the innocent third party buyer, which may seem unduly harsh on the buyer given

---

[46] Sale of Goods Act 1979, s.21(2).
[47] That is, he must not merely be an employee; he must be capable of buying and selling without disclosing that he is an agent.
[48] He must not have possession in any other capacity, e.g. repairer.
[49] [1962] 2 QB 664.   [50] [1951] 1 KB 275.

that in neither case was there anything that should have put the buyer on notice of the irregularity.

(c) Seller in possession

When possession of the goods and title to them are in different hands, the scope exists for the person in possession, either innocently or fraudulently, to pass possession of the goods to an innocent third party and possibly to pass title to them as well. The two most obvious examples arising out of a contract of sale are the exceptions for the seller in possession of the goods[51] and the buyer in possession of the goods.[52]

   The former involves the seller who, having sold goods to a first buyer, remains in possession of them and then subsequently sells them again to an innocent third party. A situation of deemed agency arises in that the seller will be deemed to be acting with the express authority of the new owner (the first buyer) when selling them to the second buyer. For the exception to be relevant, the property in the goods must have passed to the first buyer and thus, in practice, is most likely to arise with specific goods, although it would be possible for it to apply to ascertained goods which have been unconditionally appropriated before being delivered to the first buyer and are then sold for a second time. Where this occurs, the second buyer acquires title to the goods with the first buyer claiming a full refund of the contract price from the seller. Ultimately, neither buyer loses out financially although the first buyer will not have acquired the goods that they believed they had bought.

(d) Buyer in possession

An allied example exists where a person who has bought or agreed to buy goods takes possession of them with the consent of the seller and then transfers them to an innocent sub-buyer who has no knowledge of any lien or rights of the original seller/owner. Where that is the case, the first 'buyer' will be deemed to be selling as if he were a mercantile agent acting with the consent of the owner, with title passing to the second buyer. The key factor is that the first buyer must satisfy the requirement of being someone who has bought or agreed to buy the goods. It is not sufficient that he has possession of them unless he is contractually committed to buying them. Thus, a person purchasing goods under a conditional sale agreement, whereby possession passes immediately but title will pass at some point in the future pending the payment of sufficient instalments of the price, has not 'bought or agreed to buy,' as it is possible that the relevant payments will not be paid and title will never pass.[53] Equally, the debtor/purchaser under a hire-purchase agreement has not 'bought or agreed

---

[51] Sale of Goods Act 1979, s.24.
[52] *Ibid.* s.25.   [53] *Ibid.* s.25(2).

to buy' the goods as title does not pass until the option to purchase is exercised at the end of the hire period.[54] The debtor has a statutory right to terminate the contract at any time before the final payment is due[55] and hand the goods back to the hire-purchase company, making an appropriate financial settlement.[56] Consequently, an innocent purchaser buying the goods from the debtor/hirer under hire-purchase does not attract the protection of section 25 of the 1979 Act and will not acquire good title to the goods.

The other class of purchasers who have not 'bought or agreed to buy' goods would be those buying on sale or return and who have not informed the seller of their wish to purchase and to whom title has not yet passed under section 18 rule 4. As long as the right remains to return the goods to the original seller, the buyer has not 'bought or agreed to buy' and any sub-buyer buying the goods from him will not gain the protection of section 25 and would be obliged to return the goods to the original owner/seller. Naturally, the sub-buyer would have a right to a refund of the full contract price for a breach of section 12 of the 1979 Act and the total failure of consideration.

(e) Hire-Purchase Act 1964, section 27

There is a valid *nemo dat* exception that works in favour of some innocent purchasers acquiring goods from a hire-purchase debtor but the exception is limited to innocent private purchasers of motor vehicles. Section 27 of the Hire-Purchase Act 1964 stipulates that if an innocent private purchaser of a motor vehicle buys it, not knowing of the existence of the hire-purchase agreement, then the hire-purchase company's title to the goods will be deemed to pass to the hire-purchase debtor immediately before the sale to the innocent private purchaser.[57] Thereafter, title will then pass as normal. Even if the hire-purchase debtor sells directly to a trader, the first private purchaser buying innocently from that trader will acquire the title[58] even though the trader himself would not have been so protected. Once a valid title has passed to the innocent purchaser, it will pass down the line in the usual way to any subsequent purchasers. This protection is particularly valuable to consumers given the high percentage of cars purchased on hire-purchase which are subsequently resold to private individuals through classified advertisements in a newspaper, notices in shops or even sales notices appearing on the vehicles themselves. While traders have the opportunity to check for outstanding hire-purchase though HPI checks[59] and thus are in a position to protect themselves, consumers are more vulnerable.

---

[54] *Helby* v. *Matthews* [1985] AC 471.
[55] Consumer Credit Act 1974, s.99.
[56] *Ibid.* s.100.   [57] Sale of Goods Act 1979, s.27(2).
[58] *Ibid.* s.27(3).
[59] An HPI check is a search of financial information to establish whether a specific vehicle is the subject of a hire-purchase agreement in respect of which there are outstanding payments. This

The application of section 27 was reconsidered in the recent Court of Appeal decision in *Rohit Kulkarni v. Manor Credit (Davenham) Ltd.*[60] The appellant, Kulkarni, contracted to buy a car from a third party, G, knowing that G did not have a car at the time and would need to acquire one to fulfil the contract. G subsequently acquired a car on hire-purchase from the respondent, Manor Credit (Davenham) Ltd, and wrongfully passed the car onto to Kulkarni on the same day. Subsequently, Manor Credit repossessed the car and Kulkarni claimed it, arguing that the title had passed to him as he was a private purchaser protected under the *nemo dat* exception in section 27 of the Hire-Purchase Act 1964. Kulkarni had been given the registration details some three days before delivery to allow him to insure the car but the registration plates were not fixed to the car until the date of delivery. The court confirmed that this meant that the goods were not in a deliverable state under section 18 rule 1 and, hence, the passage of property was not governed by that rule. When Kulkarni took possession of the goods, G was already the hirer under a hire-purchase and Kulkarni was entitled to claim ownership under the *nemo dat* rule in section 27 of the Hire-Purchase Act 1964.

(f) Voidable title

There remains the issue of voidable title. The presumption is that the owner of goods intends to deal with the person in front of them,[61] with any defect in the contract through misrepresentation rendering the title voidable. Consequently, if the owner has parted with possession of the goods to a fraudster who has acquired the goods as the result of a fraud, the fraudster will only acquire a voidable title to the goods. Whether an innocent third party buyer buying the goods from the fraudster will gain title to them will depend on whether the fraudster's voidable title had been validly avoided at the time of the sale to the innocent buyer. The onus is on the owner to act quickly to protect himself by avoiding the sale through informing the fraudster or the police.[62] If the owner has not avoided the sale prior to the goods being sold to an innocent third party buyer, the innocent buyer will acquire title,[63] leaving the owner to try and recover his money from the fraudster. By contrast, if the owner avoids the fraudulent sale before the fraudster sells the goods to the innocent third party buyer, the owner retains title to the goods. The innocent buyer must then return the goods to the owner or face a claim in conversion, and must seek to recover his money from the fraudster. It is only if the identity of the person buying the goods from the owner was crucial to the sale that the contract will be rendered void, with the

---

      would mean that the vehicle is the legal property of the finance company and not of the person in possession of it.

[60]   [2010] EWCA Civ 69.

[61]   *Phillips v. Brooks* [1919] 2 KB 243, *Lewis v. Averay* [1972] 1 QB 198.

[62]   *Car and Universal Finance v. Caldwell* [1965] 1 QB 535.

[63]   Sale of Goods Act 1979, s.23.

owner reclaiming his title to the goods.[64] Once again, an innocent third party who attempts to keep the goods in that situation will be liable in conversion and so must return the goods to the owner and seek compensation from the fraudster.

(g) Sale under court order

Finally, an innocent purchaser may acquire good title to the goods where they have been sold as the result of the High Court ordering their sale or where he has innocently purchased them when, unknown to him, they were subject to a writ of execution.

(h) Market overt

The most colourful of the *nemo dat* exceptions, namely market overt, which protected the innocent buyer purchasing goods from a market overt[65] according to the normal usages of that market and between the hours of sunrise and sunset, has now been abolished. It was repealed in 1995[66] amidst concerns that this exception facilitated the sale of stolen goods causing the innocent owner to lose title to them.

*Q9 Consider whether the **nemo dat** exceptions provide an acceptable balance between the protection of an innocent buyer and the legitimate rights of the true owner.*

6 Delivery and payment

While passage of property governs ownership and risk, two factors which are becoming increasingly important in the prevailing economic climate are delivery and payment, with many sellers and buyers being equally, if not more, concerned by these factors. Buyers want the goods while sellers want the money and, unless something goes wrong, issues of ownership and risk will not really concern them, while delivery and payment will always be important. Unless the parties agree otherwise, delivery and payment are concurrent,[67] such that the seller must be ready and willing to deliver the goods and the buyer must be ready and willing to pay for them in accordance with the contract. Delivery is the 'voluntary transfer of possession from one person to another'[68] and can be by the physical delivery of the goods to the buyer, or by providing him with the

---

[64] *Cundy* v. *Lindsay* (1878) 3 App. Cas. 459.
[65] Retail shops in the City of London plus certain open markets in England. There were no markets overt in Wales or Scotland.
[66] Sale of Goods (Amendment Act) 1994, s.1.
[67] Sale of Goods Act 1979, s.28.   [68] *Ibid.* s.61(1).

means to control the goods. The latter includes, for example, giving the buyer the physical means of control, e.g., the keys for a car, or, alternatively, by giving him the appropriate documents to allow him to control the goods, the most important example of which is undoubtedly bills of lading used in international trade contracts. A further method of delivery occurs when a third party in possession of the goods attorns by acknowledging that the goods are now held to the order of the buyer not the seller.[69] Typically, this third party would be a warehouse or a carrier.

(a) Time and place of delivery

Delivery raises obvious issues as regards the time and place of delivery, delivery of the wrong amount, and in what situations delivery by instalments may be acceptable. Sections 27–33 of the 1979 Act establish the framework within which issues regarding delivery are addressed while preserving the contractual freedom of the parties. Thus, the place of delivery is decided by the parties but with a fallback position that in the absence of agreement whether express or implied, delivery occurs at the seller's place of business or, alternatively, his residence or, in the case of contracts for specific goods known to be at some other place, that place. Given this, delivery charges are acceptable as the seller is providing a service over and above his legal obligation. Further, if the seller agrees to deliver at his risk to a place other than where the goods were at the time of the contract, the buyer remains liable for any deterioration of the goods necessarily due to the transit.[70] Delivery must be made at a reasonable hour and, where the seller has agreed to send them to the buyer, within a reasonable time. In practice, of course, time is likely to be of the essence in a commercial contract with a failure to deliver being an actionable breach of the contract. Likewise, with consumer buyers time will be of the essence if a delivery date is included in the contract but, in the absence of such a term, the Consumer Rights Directive will require delivery to the consumer or a third party of his choosing within a period of thirty days from the conclusion of the contract,[71] with non-compliance entitling the consumer to a full refund if the trader fails to deliver the goods by a second delivery date.[72] Thus, in consumer sales, the status of delivery will be heightened in comparison with the current situation, in which consumers can feel thwarted by an inability to get sellers to deliver goods on time.

The distinction between consumer buyers and non-consumer buyers is again apparent with regard to the use of carriers to transport the goods from seller to buyer. Generally, where the seller is authorised or required to send the goods to the buyer, delivery of the goods to the carrier constitutes delivery to the buyer,[73] but this provision is expressly overruled in consumer contracts where delivery to a carrier

---

[69] *Ibid.* s.29(4).   [70] *Ibid.* s.33.

[71] Consumer Rights Directive, above n. 3, Art. 18(1).

[72] *Ibid.* Art. 18(2).   [73] Sale of Goods Act 1979, s.32(1).

does not constitute delivery to the consumer buyer.[74] Unless otherwise agreed, the seller is obliged to contract with the carrier on behalf of the buyer and is under a duty to make the best contract possible, a failure to do so allowing the buyer to claim damages from the seller if anything happens to the goods.[75] Delivery drivers employed by the seller are not carriers for this purpose. Where carriage is by sea, the goods are likely to be at the risk of the buyer, particularly under an FOB contract,[76] and the buyer must be told of the carriage arrangements to facilitate him insuring the goods during transit,[77] though again the parties are free to agree otherwise.

(b) Delivery of the wrong quantity

Two policies are relevant when considering a delivery of the wrong quantity of goods, namely, the law ignoring trifling breaches and a distinction in remedies available to non-consumer and consumer buyers. The former, evident in common law in *Shipton, Anderson* v. *Weil Bros*,[78] is now encapsulated in section 30(2D) of the 1979 Act, which prevents rejection of the goods unless the shortfall or excess is material. Thus, where the seller has delivered less than the contractual amount, the buyer cannot reject them, and where the seller has delivered too much, the buyer cannot reject all of the goods, unless the shortage or excess is material. In the latter situation, the buyer would still be able to reject the excess while retaining the contractual amount.[79] This position is reinforced, though with a variation for consumer buyers, by section 30(2A), which provides that a non-consumer buyer cannot reject the goods where the shortfall or excess is so slight that it would be unreasonable for him to do so, wording that resonates with the variable remedies in section 15A of the 1979 Act for breach of the statutory implied conditions. The right of the consumer buyer to reject the goods is protected, although this may be largely academic as the average consumer does not typically buy large quantities of loose goods, with the possible exception of DIY enthusiasts ordering sand or gravel by weight or wood or turf by width and length.

(c) Delivery by instalments

Delivery in instalments is relatively rare in consumer contracts. Thus, the rules governing instalment deliveries are primarily of interest in the commercial

[74] *Ibid.* s.32(4).
[75] See *Thomas Young* v. *Hobson* (1949) 65 TLR 365, in which the seller was held liable when the goods were carried at the buyer's risk when the carrier would have carried them at his own risk for the same price.
[76] An FOB (free on board) contract is one under which the buyer arranges for the shipment of the goods and for their insurance cover for the voyage (see Part 3 Chapter 1). The seller's responsibilities for the goods end when they are loaded on board.
[77] Sale of Goods Act 1979, s.32(3).
[78] [1912] 1 KB 574, in which the seller was due to deliver 4,950 tonnes and actually delivered 55lbs excess. It was held that the buyer could not reject the whole consignment.
[79] Sale of Goods Act 1979, s.30(1).

context. There is no obligation on the buyer to accept instalment delivery,[80] although the parties are free to decide otherwise, it then being a matter for the construction of the contract as to whether it is severable or non-severable. If the contract is non-severable, a breach in one instalment does not allow the buyer to repudiate the whole contract unless the problem was with the first instalment. Once the buyer has accepted the first instalment he cannot reject the contract because of a breach in a subsequent instalment. He would need to claim damages instead.[81] However, if the contract is severable, a breach of any instalment may allow the rejection of that instalment without affecting the remainder of the contract,[82] with acceptance of the first instalment not affecting that position. It will depend on how serious the breach is and its impact on the contract as a whole. Ultimately, that is a matter for the court to decide. Equally, the court will decide whether the contract is severable at all with factors such as separate payment for each instalment being persuasive but not conclusive.

Q10 Review the statutory provisions governing the delivery of goods and payment for them.

7 Remedies

In the majority of contracts for the sale of goods, property passes without any difficulty and delivery and payment happen both successfully and on time. Nonetheless, it is in the nature of commerce that there will be some contracts which do not run smoothly and for which the seller or buyer, or both, will seek access to a contractual remedy. It is unsurprising therefore that a breach of the provisions as to delivery and payment give rise to a variety of remedies for both buyer and seller.

(a) Seller's remedies

The remedies available to the seller fall into two categories, real remedies exercisable against the goods and personal remedies involving a monetary claim for the price of the goods and damages.

(i) Real remedies

The real remedies available to the seller involve, in effect, using the goods as a form of security to protect his position. However, the availability of the remedies is restricted to sellers who are classed as an 'unpaid seller' within the meaning of the 1979 Act.[83] Section 38(1) defines an 'unpaid seller' thus:

---

[80] *Ibid.* s.31(1).   [81] *Ibid.* s.11(4).

[82] See *ibid.* s.35A(2) as regards the right of partial rejection in instalment deliveries.

[83] Defined in *ibid.* s.38 as occurring when the whole of the price for the goods has not been paid or tendered or when a bill of exchange or other negotiable instrument has been dishonoured.

An unpaid seller is an unpaid seller within the meaning of this Act:

(a) when the whole of the price has not been paid or tendered;
(b) when a bill of exchange or other negotiable instrument has been received as conditional payment, and the condition on which it was received has not been fulfilled by reason of the dishonour of the instrument or otherwise.

In addition to the seller himself, section 38(2) makes it clear that anyone who is in the position of the seller can bring himself within the definition of 'unpaid seller', most particularly, any agent of the seller to whom a bill of lading has been indorsed or any consignor or agent who has paid, or is responsible for, the price. Thus, an agent who has already paid the price to the seller with the intention of recouping it from the buyer would be classed as an 'unpaid seller' for these purposes.

Section 39 provides the unpaid seller with three rights exercisable against the goods when the property in the goods has already passed,[84] with a further right to withhold delivery of the goods when the property in them has not yet passed.[85] The three remedies exercisable against the goods, even if the property in them has passed, are a lien over them, a right of stoppage in transit when the buyer has become insolvent,[86] and a right of resale within the terms of the 1979 Act. As mentioned previously, where the property has not passed, the seller has a right to withhold delivery of the goods, this right being co-extensive with the other three rights. These remedies all relate to possession of the goods rather than ownership of them and are circumscribed by the statutory controls that govern them.[87]

The seller has a lien over the goods such as to allow him to retain possession of them in three situations, namely:

(a) where the goods have been sold without any stipulation as to credit;
(b) where the goods have been sold on credit but the term of the credit has expired;
(c) where the buyer becomes insolvent.

When any of these situations has occurred, the seller can exercise his lien or a right of retention even if he is in possession as the agent of the buyer.[88] He can retain all or part of the goods unless a previous part delivery of the goods shows an intention on the part of the seller to waive any lien or right of retention.

Naturally, being a right in possession, the lien will terminate automatically if the seller loses possession of the goods. The statute identifies three situations in which the seller will lose his lien or right of retention, namely, if he delivers the goods to a carrier, bailee or custodian of the goods for onward transmission

---

[84] *Ibid.* s.39(1).   [85] *Ibid.* s.39(2).
[86] A remedy that may become increasingly important in the current economic climate.
[87] Unpaid seller's lien (Sale of Goods Act 1979, ss.41–43), stoppage in transit (*ibid.* ss.44–46) and right of resale (*ibid.* ss.47–48).
[88] *Ibid.* s.41(2).

without reserving a right of disposal, or if the buyer or his agent obtain possession of the goods lawfully, or if the seller waives his lien or right of retention.[89] However, the seller does not lose his lien or right of retention purely because he has obtained judgment against the buyer for the money owing.[90] As long as the money is unpaid, the lien or right of retention subsists.

The right of stoppage in transit arises when the buyer has gone into liquidation while the goods are still in transit from the seller to the buyer, i.e., delivery has not been completed. Where this is so, the seller has a right to stop the goods in transit, retaking possession of them and retaining them until the payment or tender of the price.[91] It does not matter whether the property in the goods has passed or not, the seller can still utilise this remedy. However, it has been suggested that the remedy is no longer as useful as when originally developed because of the modern use of payment against documents and payment by banker's commercial credits. These allow the seller to retain control of the goods pending payment and so provide a degree of protection against the buyer's liquidation.[92] Equally, the use of retention of title clauses allows the seller to recover his goods if the buyer has failed to pay for them on condition that the criteria relating to the use of the clause have been satisfied.

Naturally, central to this remedy is an understanding of the duration of the transit and when it comes to an end, as the remedy is only available while the transit subsists and will come to an end automatically when the transit finishes. Essentially, the goods are in transit when they have passed from the possession of the seller into the hands of an independent carrier but have not yet reached the possession of the buyer or his agent.[93] It is important to note that the carrier must be independent and in business on his own account. If the carrier is an employee or agent of the seller, then the seller has not really parted with possession of the goods and can simply recall them if the need arises, exercising his lien over them. The goods are not in transit within the meaning of the 1979 Act and hence the right of stoppage in transit does not arise.

It is relatively easy to establish when the transit has started but more difficult to identify when it ends such as to defeat the use of this remedy. Section 45(2)–(7) of the 1979 Act deal with a variety of situations that may arise and indicate the effect of each on the transit. Thus, section 45(2) makes clear that if the buyer or his agent obtain delivery of the goods before their arrival at their appointed destination, the transit will come to an end. Equally, if after arrival at the appointed destination, the independent carrier retains possession of the goods but acknowledges that he now holds them on behalf of the buyer or his agent, then the transit will come to an end as the seller no longer controls what happens to the goods.[94] However, if the buyer rejects the goods and as a consequence the carrier remains in possession of

---

[89] *Ibid.* s.43(1).   [90] *Ibid.* s.43(2).   [91] *Ibid.* s.44.
[92] See Atiyah, Adams and MacQueen, above n. 14.
[93] Sale of Goods Act 1979, s.45(1).   [94] *Ibid.* s.45(3).

them, the transit will not come to an end even if the seller refuses to receive them back. Delivery has not taken place.[95] As regards carriage by sea on a ship that has been chartered by the buyer, it will be a question of fact whether the master of the ship has taken possession of the goods as an independent carrier or as an agent for the buyer[96] and this will dictate whether delivery has taken place or whether the goods are still in transit while they remain on the ship.

The final two situations involve a wrongful refusal to deliver the goods[97] and partial delivery of them.[98] In respect of the first, note that the refusal to deliver must be wrongful but, if it is, the transit will be deemed to have come to an end. This protects the buyer from the seller exercising a stoppage in transit when the goods should lawfully have been delivered to the buyer and the buyer had a legitimate right to expect delivery to occur. Finally, partial delivery of the goods to the buyer or his agent does not, of itself, prevent the unpaid seller from exercising a right of stoppage in transit against the remainder of the goods. However, the seller will lose the right of stoppage if the circumstances surrounding the partial delivery are such as to show an agreement to give up possession of the whole of the goods.

Having identified the period within which stoppage in transit can take place, the mechanism for exercising the right must be understood. Under section 46 of the 1979 Act, the unpaid seller must either take physical possession of the goods or, alternatively, he can give notice to the carrier, bailee or custodian currently in possession of the goods that he is exercising his right of stoppage in transit. If doing the latter, he can give notice either to the person in actual possession or to his principal. in which case he must allow enough time for the principal to notify the person in actual possession such as to prevent delivery to the buyer. When the person in actual possession has the relevant notice, he must redeliver the goods to the seller, or to his order, with the seller bearing any expenses associated with the redelivery.

The third of the real remedies that the seller can exercise against the goods is the right of resale under section 48, which bestows limited rights upon the seller in this regard. It must be noted that the mere exercise by the seller of his right of lien or stoppage in transit does not cause rescission of the contract of sale. However, where an unpaid seller who has exercised one of those rights resells the goods, the new buyer acquires good title to the goods as against the original purchaser.[99] Particular arrangements are made as regards perishable goods. Under section 48(3), where the seller has given notice to the buyer of his intention to resell the goods and the buyer does not pay or tender payment within

---

[95] *Ibid.* s.45(4).   [96] *Ibid.* s.45(5).
[97] *Ibid.* s.45(6).   [98] *Ibid.* s.45(7).
[99] Note that unlike the *nemo dat* exception under *ibid.* s.24 (seller in possession of the goods) there is no requirement here that the new buyer is acting in good faith and without knowledge of the previous sale.

a reasonable time, the unpaid seller can resell the goods and recover damages from the buyer for any loss resulting from his breach of contract. Finally, section 48(4) stipulates that if the seller has expressly reserved a right of resale upon default by the buyer and duly exercises that right, the original contract is rescinded but the unpaid seller still has the right to sue for contractual damages.

(ii) Personal remedies

In addition to his rights over the goods themselves, the seller can sue to recover either the price or contractual damages for non-acceptance. These remedies are, arguably, less useful than the real remedies already discussed in that those remedies use the goods themselves as a form of security for the debt and can be used when the buyer has gone into liquidation. By contrast, claims for the price or damages for non-acceptance relate to monetary compensation and, consequently, are of no use to the seller if the buyer has gone into liquidation.

The right of the seller to sue for the price is laid out in section 49 and can be used when the property in the goods has passed to the buyer and the latter wrongfully neglects or refuses to pay for them.[100] The key word here is 'wrongfully' for the seller cannot enforce this remedy if the buyer has a legitimate legal reason for refusing payment as, for example, if the goods are faulty and the buyer is seeking to rescind the contract because of the failure of the seller to provide goods that conform with the contract. In that situation, the buyer may be withholding payment legitimately pending the seller providing goods that conform to the contract. Further, as delivery and payment are concurrent duties, it follows that the buyer will not have wrongfully refused to pay for the goods unless the seller is ready and willing to deliver them. However, assuming that the refusal to pay is wrongful, the seller is able to sue. In addition, the seller can also sue for the price irrespective of the lack of passage of title if payment was due on a day certain which has passed.[101] To qualify as a 'day certain', the contract must either specify a precise date or provide a formula that allows the date for payment to be identified. The right to payment in this situation is totally dependent on the date identified by the contract and arises irrespective of delivery. Thus, the fact that delivery has taken place before the 'day certain' does not give the seller the right to claim payment until the 'day certain' arrives.

Allied to the right to sue for payment when property has passed is the right to sue for damages for non-acceptance when the buyer has wrongfully neglected or refused to accept and pay for the goods.[102] Again, the buyer's action must be wrongful for a remedy to follow. Hence, it would not be wrongful to refuse to accept goods that do not comply with the contract. The measure of damages payable to the seller will be the loss directly and naturally resulting from the buyer's breach and, where there is an available market for such goods, it will be the difference between the contract price and the market price at the time when the goods should have been accepted.

---

[100] *ibid.* s.49(1).   [101] *Ibid.* s.49(2).   [102] *Ibid.* s.50(1).

Naturally, as this is a claim for damages, the seller must prove that he has suffered loss and is under a duty to mitigate that loss by seeking to resell the goods. His ability to do this will be effected by supply and demand for the goods at the time of resale. If supply outstrips demand, he may find it impossible to resell the goods and would be quite entitled to claim damages for the profit that he would have made on the contract with the buyer if the latter had not gone into breach. By contrast, if demand exceeds supply, he should have no trouble in reselling the goods, which will be reflected in the amount of damages that he will be likely to recover.

In addition to the right of the seller to sue for the price or claim damages for non-acceptance, he also has an allied claim under section 37 of the 1979 Act. This provides that when the seller is ready and willing to effect delivery of the goods and has requested the buyer to take delivery, then if the buyer does not accept delivery of them within a reasonable time thereafter, the buyer will be liable to the seller for any loss that the seller suffers as a result of the buyer's neglect or refusal to take delivery. The seller can also claim a reasonable charge for the storage and custody of the goods pending delivery. It should be noted that, unlike section 50 of the 1979 Act, this section does not require that the buyer has acted wrongfully in refusing to accept delivery. The right bestowed under section 37 does not impact on the rights of the seller if the buyer's refusal to accept delivery amounts to a repudiation of the contract.

(b) Buyer's remedies

The buyer has three statutory remedies, to be found in sections 51–53 of the 1979 Act, which encompass damages for non-delivery, specific performance and damages for a breach of warranty.[103]

While the seller can sue for non-acceptance, the buyer can sue for non-delivery when the seller has wrongfully neglected or refused to deliver the goods to him.[104] The refusal by the seller to deliver the goods must have been negligent or wrongful. Thus, for example, if the buyer has indicated that he will not pay for the goods, the seller would be entitled to refuse to deliver the goods as the duty to deliver and the duty to pay are concurrent duties.[105] In that situation, the buyer would not be able to bring a claim for non-delivery.

The damages will be 'the estimated loss directly and naturally arising, in the ordinary course of events, from the seller's breach of contract'[106] and includes any special damages that are foreseeable within the rule of *Hadley v. Baxendale*.[107] Naturally, as this is a claim for damages, the buyer is under a duty to mitigate his loss, which is most likely to involve him purchasing replacement goods, if this is possible, as soon as the seller refuses to deliver as

---

[103] Remedies available to the buyer when the goods as delivered are not of a satisfactory quality or fit for their purpose are considered in Part 2 Chapter 2.
[104] Sale of Goods Act 1979, s.51(1).   [105] *Ibid.* s.28.
[106] *Ibid.* at s.51(2).   [107] (1854) 9 Exch. 341.

required under the terms of the contract. Indeed, if the seller commits antici-patory breach by informing the buyer before the due date for delivery that he will not deliver the relevant goods, the buyer can buy alternative goods imme-diately if he so chooses. Section 51(3) stipulates that, if there is an available market for the goods in question, the measure of damages for non-delivery is *prima facie* the difference between the contract price and the market or cur-rent price at the time that the goods should have been delivered. If there was no set date for delivery, then the time of the refusal to deliver is used instead. In practice, this provision allows the buyer to recover any difference in the market value of the goods. Thus, for example, if the contract price was £1,000 and the market price at the time for delivery is £1,200, the buyer is entitled to recover the additional £200. By contrast, if the price of the goods has fallen to £800, the buyer purchases the replacement goods but is permitted to retain the £200 difference in price. As regards claims for special damages within the ambit of *Hadley* v. *Baxendale*, the buyer can recover for losses that were fore-seeable to the seller at the time that the contract was made. The most obvious example would be where the goods have been sold by the buyer to a third party in a sub-contract. If the seller knows that the buyer is committed to using those goods to perform the sub-contract and cannot use replacement goods (because, for example, alternative goods cannot be acquired in time or the goods are unique) then the buyer can recover damages to recompense him for his contractual liability to the sub-buyer for non-performance of the sub-contract.

Damages may not be a sufficient remedy for non-delivery in some situations, most particularly where the contract relates to specific goods that are suffi-ciently unique to mean that replacement goods cannot be obtained easily, or indeed at all. Clearly, money is an inadequate remedy in that situation and the court may resort to the remedy of specific performance, instructing the seller to deliver the goods as per the contract without giving him the option of retaining the goods on payment of damages.[108]

Finally, the buyer may be able to claim damages for any breach of warranty by the seller or any breach of condition that the buyer has elected to treat, or is compelled to treat, as a breach of warranty.[109] Alternatively, he can set up the breach of warranty in diminution of the extinction of the price and the fact that he has done so does not prevent him claiming for the same breach of warranty if he has suffered other damage.[110] As with the other monetary remedies relat-ing to delivery and payment, the measure of damages will be that loss directly and naturally resulting from the breach.[111] In respect of claims for a breach of warranty of quality, the loss is *prima facie* the difference in value between the goods as delivered and the value that they would have had if they had fulfilled the warranty.[112]

---

[108] Sale of Goods Act 1979, s.52(1).   [109] *Ibid.* s.53(1).
[110] *Ibid.* ss.53(2) and (4).   [111] *Ibid.* s.53(2).   [112] *Ibid.* s.53(3).

Q11 Analyse whether the remedies available to the seller and buyer provide appropriate protection for both parties in the event of a breach of contract.

8 Recommended reading

Atiyah, P.S., Adams, J.N. and MacQueen, H. *The Sale of Goods* (11th edn, Pearson Education Ltd, Harlow, 2005)

Bradgate, R. *Commercial Law* (3rd edn, Oxford University Press, Oxford, 2000)

Bridge, M. *The Sale of Goods* (Oxford University Press, Oxford, 1997)

European Commission Proposal for a Directive of the European Parliament and the Council on consumer rights COM(2008)614 final (Brussels, 2008)

Dobson, P. and Stokes, R. *Commercial Law* (7th edn, Sweet & Maxwell, London, 2008)

Griffiths, M. and Griffiths, I. *Law for Purchasing and Supply* (3rd edn, Pearson Education Ltd, Harlow, 2002)

Macleod, J. *Consumer Sales Law* (2nd edn, Routledge-Cavendish, Abingdon, 2007)

Mark, M. *Chalmers Sale of Goods* (18th edn, Butterworths, London, 1981)

Sealy, L.S. and Hooley, R.J.A. *Commercial Law: Text, Cases and Materials* (4th edn, Oxford University Press, Oxford, 2009)

The passage of title, together with delivery and payment, are central to smooth progress of sale of goods contracts. All major textbooks that include sections on the sale of goods will discuss this topic and readers can gain a broader understanding of the issue by reading the relevant section from a selection of the standard texts listed above.

Part 2 Chapter 4

The Supply of Goods and Services

Contents

1 Introduction

This chapter considers the provision of services by traders to both businesses and consumers. It looks at the information that must be provided to potential recipients of services and also the current statutory controls over the quality and fitness for purpose of services provided under a contract.

Section 2 looks at the background to the provision of services and the ambit and limitations to contracts for services.

Section 3 looks in detail at the Provision of Services Regulations 2009 which stipulate what information must be provided to potential recipients of services and the requirement for a suitable complaints system to be established, including authorisation schemes; the provision of information to service recipients; the definition of 'service'; the definition of 'provider' and 'recipient'; Part 2 of the 2009 Regulations; the information that must be provided under regulation 8; information to be provided on request; information regarding dispute resolution; complaints; and enforcement.

Section 4 looks in detail at the provisions of the Supply of Goods and Services Act 1982 incorporating the current implied conditions and terms relating to the provision of contracts for goods and services, including implied conditions under Part I of the 1982 Act; the common law approach; the implied terms regarding care and skill, time for performance and consideration; exclusion of liability; and Codes of Practice.

2 Background

By comparison with contracts for the sale of goods, statutory controls over contracts for the provision of services are a relatively recent phenomenon. The statutory implied terms and conditions date from the Supply of Goods and Services Act 1982, passed some ninety years after those relating to goods entered the statute book. More recently, the Provision of Services Regulations 2009[1] were enacted, giving effect to the EU Services Directive.[2] This requires the providers of services to provide specified information, including contact details, to prospective purchasers prior to the provision of the services. Further, they must provide a suitable complaints system through which purchasers can make legitimate complaints.

Contracts for services include a wide variety of potential services both for business purchasers and consumer purchasers. On the commercial front, this would, for example, include contracts for the provision and maintenance of IT services or the provision of ongoing legal services or commercial insurance. By contrast, for a consumer purchaser, it would include tourist services, hairdressing and estate agents. Naturally, there is potential overlap in the type of services provided to both business purchasers and consumers, e.g, insurance, legal services and transport, with the distinction being not the type of service provided but the scale of it.

One of the essential difficulties in legislating for the provision of services is the wide variety of contracts that might legitimately be termed contracts for the supply of a service. Contracts may be for services in which there are no tangible goods involved, or, alternatively, they can relate to the provision of a service where some goods will change hands as a result of the contract. Thus, the former includes services such as medical services, legal services, financial services and insurance. The latter includes those contracts for works and materials where there is a predominant service element but where the consumer also acquires some goods. This would include, for example, an artist painting a portrait, a double glazing contract and a garage repairing a car. In all of these contracts the consumer acquires goods: the portrait, the central heating system and the car parts used to repair the vehicle. Nonetheless, these contracts are essentially about the provision of the service element of the contract by the supplier. There is no hard and fast rule about when such a contract will be classed as a service contract or merely one for the supply of goods. It depends on the facts of the case and the substance of the contract as to which is the dominant aspect of the agreement.[3]

---

[1] SI 2009/2999.

[2] Directive 2006/123 EEC of the European Parliament and the Council of 12 December 2006 on services in the internal market.

[3] See *Robinson* v. *Graves* [1935] 1 KB 579, CA, in which the painting of a picture was held to be a service and not a sale of goods; *contra Lee* v. *Griffin* (1861) 1 B & S 272, where the supply of false teeth was held to be a sale of goods.

What is beyond dispute is the distinction between a contract for services and a contract of service, primarily contracts of employment. Over the years, this has involved an analysis of the difference between employees and independent contractors and the various legal tests used in employment law to establish that difference. In the classic example, a chauffeur is an employee under a contract of service while a taxi driver would be an independent contractor under a contract for services. In the event of a breach of care and skill, action would be taken against the chauffeur under his contract of employment, while the taxi driver would be sued under a contract for services.

The above example also raises a different principle of liability, namely, that persons providing a service under a contract can also be sued in negligence in respect of the same incident.[4] Thus, for example, if the taxi driver drove negligently causing an accident in which his paying passenger was injured, the passenger could sue both in contract and in negligence, though he could not obtain double compensation. The availability of both causes of action remains important as the limitation periods for the two differ; while the limitation period in a contract claim begins to run from the date of the contract, it only starts to run in tort when the cause of action has accrued.[5] A third party who does not have contractual privity with the service provider but who has been injured by the defective service will need to sue in negligence unless he can bring himself within the provisions of the Contracts (Rights of Third Parties) Act 1999.

Q1 Consider the scope of contracts for the provision of services and analyse which contracts do and do not constitute contracts for the provision of services.

3 Provision of Services Regulations 2009

The EU Services Directive[6] forms part of the EU strategy to promote cross-border trade, the intention of the Directive being to open up the internal market for services. Currently, services account for approximately 70 per cent of EU output and employment, yet they only account for 24 per cent of intra-EU trade and investment.[7] The Directive is intended to address this anomaly and

---

[4] See *Midland Bank Trust Co. Ltd* v. *Hett, Stubbs and Kemp* [1979] Ch. 384, which was expressly approved by the House of Lords in *Henderson* v. *Merrett Syndicates Ltd* [1995] 2 AC 145.

[5] Limitation Act 1980, s.2. Generally, the limitation period is six years from when the cause of action accrued. However, where the claim relates to personal injury suffered by the plaintiff, the time limit is three years from the date that the action accrued or the date of the plaintiff's knowledge of his action, whichever is the later Limitation Act 1980, s.11. This is important in respect of claims such as those in respect of asbestosis or cancers, where the damage caused to the plaintiff may not be obvious for many years after the incident that caused the damage, i.e., after exposure to asbestos or to a carcinogenic substance.

[6] See above n.2.

[7] Department for Business, Innovation and Skills, *Guidance for Business on the Provision of Services Regulations 2009* (October 2009) para. 2.

has also been adopted under the EEA Agreement and thus applies to Iceland, Liechtenstein and Norway in addition to the EU Member States.

The Provision of Services Regulations 2009, SI 2009/2999, which give effect to the Directive, took effect on 28 December 2009. There are two strands within the Regulations that seek to promote and facilitate cross-border trade, the first relating to authorisation schemes and the second to the provision of information about available services to prospective recipients.

(a) Authorisation schemes

Authorisation schemes under Part 3 of the 2009 Regulations deal with the provision by appropriate authorities of any authorisations and licences needed by a service provider to offer their particular services legally in the United Kingdom, whether the service provider is based in the UK or not. Thus, for example, in the provision of food and alcoholic drink, the service provider will need a licence for the sale of alcohol, while those people handling the food will need the appropriate food hygiene qualifications. In practice, there are a plethora of licences and permissions that may be needed depending on the particular service provided.

An authorisation scheme is intended to assist service providers in ensuring that they have the relevant licences, etc., to allow them to get their business up and running legally. There are three conditions attached to the existence of an authorisation scheme:

(a) that the scheme does not discriminate against a provider of a service;
(b) that the need for a scheme is justified by an overriding reason relating to the public interest; and
(c) the objective pursued cannot be attained by a less restrictive measure, in particular because inspection after commencement of the service activity would take place too late to be genuinely effective.[8]

Of course, an authorisation scheme must not be used as a means of discrimination against individual businesses and must not be used in an arbitrary manner. Thus, the criteria used to deal with individual applications must be non-discriminatory, justifiable and proportionate to the public interest objective, clear and unambiguous, objective, made public in advance and be transparent and accessible.[9]

Each country that is a party to the Directive is required to provide a point of single contact (PSC) to enable service providers to apply for and pay for all the relevant authorisations online.[10]

---

[8] SI 2009/2999, reg. 14(2).   [9] *Ibid.* reg. 15.
[10] See DBIS Guidance, above n. 7, Annex C, for a full list of the regulators, local authorities and other bodies who will be competent authorities for the purposes of the 2009 Regulations and, as such, will be available online via the point of single contact.

Q2 Consider the role of authorisation schemes in promoting cross-border trade in the provision of services.

(b) Provision of information to service recipients

For the purposes of prospective recipients of services, the more important strand of the 2009 Regulations is the requirement upon service providers to provide specified information before the contract is entered into and, further, to ensure that a suitable mechanism for dealing with complaints exists. It is hoped that this two-pronged strategy will encourage confidence among prospective purchasers and thereby encourage them to access cross-border services rather than relying wholly upon services available in their own country. In practice, depending on the nature of the service being provided, the manner of its provision and the intended service recipient, it is possible that more than one set of regulations will be relevant to the transaction with an obligation on the service provider to attempt to comply with all of the relevant regulations. Other applicable legislation might include[11] the Companies Act 2006, Consumer Protection (Distance Selling) Regulations 2000,[12] Electronic Commerce (EC Directive) Regulations 2002[13] and the Consumer Protection from Unfair Trading Regulations 2008.[14] Should it prove impossible for a service provider to comply with both the Provision of Services Regulations 2009 and another set of regulations, priority must be given to the other regulations.[15]

(c) Definition of 'service'

In analysing the 2009 Regulations and their impact, it is essential to understand which contracts for services are covered by the Regulations. Not all services fall within their provisions and it is as important to recognise which services are not covered as to identify those that are. The basic definition included in regulation 2(1) is that service means 'any self-employed economic activity normally provided for remuneration'. Thus, it follows that the person providing the service must not be doing so as an employee, So, for example, a chauffeur is employed while a taxi driver would be providing a service. Further, to fall within the ambit of the 2009 Regulations, the service must be performed for remuneration and thus cannot be provided *gratis* with no contractual consideration changing hands. As such, it impacts on businesses providing paid services rather than on individuals providing a service on an unpaid basis. Thus, for example, persons providing unremunerated services for a charity are not covered.[16]

---

11 See DBIS Guidance, above n. 7, para. 116.
12 SI 2000/2334. See also Part 2 Chapter 5.
13 SI 2002/2013. See also Part 2 Chapter 5.
14 SI 2008/1277. See also Part 5 Chapter 2.
15 See DBIS Guidance, above n. 7, para. 120.
16 *Ibid.* para. 11.

The definition of service for the purposes of the 2009 Regulations is narrowed significantly by regulation 2(2), which details all those services to which the Regulations do not apply. The list of excluded services is lengthy and far-ranging, including some financial services; electronic communications services and networks to the extent that they are already subject to other specified EU Directives; some transport services; services of temporary work agencies; some healthcare services; audiovisual services; gambling activities; activities connected with the exercise of official authority; some social services; private security services; and some services provided by notaries and bailiffs.[17]

(d) Definitions of 'provider' and 'recipient'

The 2009 Regulations talk in terms of a service 'provider,' i.e., the supplier of the services, and the service 'recipient,' i.e., the person using the service. Both terms are defined in regulation 4, the interpretation regulation. The service 'provider' is the person who 'provides, or offers to provide, the service'. There is no requirement that the provision is in the course of a business and it is clear that the provider can be a body or an individual,[18] although Parts 3–9 of the 2009 Regulations only apply where that body or individual is established in or is a national of an EEA state.[19] The 2009 Regulations apply to all service providers offering services in the United Kingdom irrespective of whether they are based in the UK or are based in another EEA state. Equally, there is no requirement that the provider has any premises in the UK. However, in respect of Part 2 of the 2009 Regulations (duties of service providers), the Part with which this section is primarily concerned, the Regulations have an even wider impact for they apply to all service providers offering relevant services in the United Kingdom irrespective of where they are based. As such, they apply to providers from around the world to the extent that their services are offered to recipients in the UK, an important protection given the impact of the Internet.[20]

The 'recipient' of a service includes a person, being an individual or a legal person, who 'for professional or non-professional purposes, uses, or wishes to use, the service'. It follows that this includes both businesses and consumers who wish to use the services proffered. However, the recipient must be either an individual who is a national of an EEA state or who otherwise benefits from rights conferred by EU acts, or must be a legal person established in an EEA state.[21] Thus, the service can be either business-to-business or business-to-consumer.

---

[17] For full details of the various exemptions see SI 2009/2999, reg. 2(2)(a)–(k).

[18] See DBIS Guidance, above n. 7, Annex A.

[19] See SI 2009/2999, reg. 5(4).

[20] While Part 2 of the 2009 Regulations applies to providers around the world, enforcement may prove to be very difficult if the provider is based outside the EEA without any base in the United Kingdom and hence, potentially, beyond the jurisdiction of the courts.

[21] See SI 2009/2999, reg. 5(3).

Q3 Analyse how the definitions of 'service', 'provider' and 'recipient' set the parameters for the scope of the Provision of Services Regulations 2009.

(e) Part 2 of the 2009 Regulations

Part 2 of the 2009 Regulations (regulations 7–12) detail the information that must be provided to all recipients of the service, as regards both contact details and other information that must be made available, and also information about dispute resolution and complaints.

Regulation 11 specifies that all of the information provided by a service provider to comply with this Part of the 2009 Regulations must be made available or supplied in a clear and unambiguous manner, which includes the format and style in which it is presented and the clarity of the wording used. Further, it must be provided in good time before the conclusion of the contract. Alternatively, where there is no written contract, the information must be provided before the service is provided. The underlying purpose of these requirements is to allow the recipient to have sufficient time to read and understand the information before committing himself to the service contract. The only exception to this requirement to provide the information before the contract is completed occurs when the service recipient has requested information under regulation 9 after the service has been provided.

Regulation 7 stipulates that the service provider must provide contact details to all users of the service so that they can seek further information about the service or send a complaint about it. The contact details for this purpose must include a postal address, fax number or email address, a telephone number and any official address that the service provider may have. Regulation 7(3) states that an official address is one that the service provider 'is required by law to register, notify or maintain for the purpose of receiving notices or other communications'. The most obvious example of an official address would be the registered office of a limited company.

(f) Information that must be provided under regulation 8

Regulation 8 details the information that must be made available to the recipient of the service, regulation 8(2) providing that it can be made available in a variety of ways. Thus, it can be provided by the supplier on his own initiative, or he can make it accessible to the recipient at the place where the service is to be provided or where the contract for the services is concluded. Alternatively, it can be made accessible to the recipient electronically by means of an address supplied by the service provider, or it can be included in any information document supplied by the service provider to the recipient in which the provider gives a detailed description of the service. Clearly, an inherent risk in relying on electronic delivery alone would be that not all recipients will necessarily have access to electronic facilities and, if the general availability of the service has been advertised in a variety of ways, it would be insufficient to rely only on electronic means to satisfy regulation 8.

The information that the service provider must make available is listed in regulation 8(1). The first few items relate to the name of the business; its legal status and form, i.e., whether it is a limited company, a partnership or a sole trader; the geographic address of the business; and details of how it can be contacted quickly and directly, including, if relevant, an email address or number for text messages. Thereafter, if the business is registered in a trade organisation or public register, details must be provided both of the register and of the identity or registration number of the trader.

The next two items relate to authorisation schemes within the meaning of Part 3 of the 2009 Regulations. Where a service in the United Kingdom is subject to an authorisation scheme, the particulars of the competent authority or the appropriate electronic assistance facility under regulation 38 must be specified. Equally, if the service is in another EEA state and there is an equivalent scheme, the particulars of the relevant authority or point of contact must be provided.

The last two information requirements relating to the set-up of the business are that where the activity concerned is subject to VAT, the service provider must provide his VAT identification number. Also, if the service provider is carrying on a regulated profession, regulation 8(h) requires that he must provide details of any professional body or similar institution with which he is registered, any professional title that he may have and the EEA state in which the title was granted. The example quoted in the official guidance is that an insolvency practitioner practising in the United Kingdom might state 'I am licensed to act as an insolvency practitioner in the UK by the Association of Chartered Certified Accountants'.[22]

The remainder of the information that service providers are required to make available relates more specifically to the individual service, as opposed to the identity, contact details and status of the service provider. Thus, regulation 8(i) requires production of the general terms and conditions, if any, used by the provider, while regulation 8(j) requires details of any contractual term relating to the law applicable to the service contract or competent courts, e.g., that this contract is subject to English law. The next three necessary pieces of information are the existence, if any, of an after-sales guarantee that is not imposed by law; the price of the service where that is predetermined; and the main features of the service if they are not already apparent. Thus, for example, a heating installation company which guarantees to correct any faults that occur within three years of the installation of the heating system would be required to inform the service recipient of that fact. Equally, the provider of a machine allowing customers to

---

[22] See DBIS Guidance, above n. 7, para. 22(h).

print digital photographs from a CD or memory stick must display details of the cost per photo.

Finally, where the provider is required to have any professional liability insurance or guarantee, details of the identity of the insurer or guarantor and the territorial coverage of the insurance or guarantee must be provided.

Q4 Analyse the scope of the information that must be provided to a service recipient under regulation 8.

(g) Information to be provided on request

In addition to the information that must be provided by a service provider under regulation 8, there is other information that he must supply if so requested by a service recipient. Regulation 9 details four categories of further information. The first relates to price, in that if the price of the service was not predetermined such as to bring it within the requirements of regulation 8, then, if requested, the service provider must give the service recipient details of the price of the individual service. If an exact price cannot be given, then the service provider must detail the method for calculating the price so that the recipient can check the price. Alternatively, the service provider can provide a sufficiently detailed estimate of the likely price.

The second additional piece of information relates to regulated professions. Regulation 9(1)(b) requires a service provider who is in a regulated profession to make reference to the professional rules applicable to the service provider in the EEA state in which he is established and how a service recipient can access those rules.

The third requirement relates to any other activities with which the service provider might be involved. It requires him to provide information of any of his other activities that are directly linked to the service in question and the measures that he has taken to avoid any conflict of interest. This information must also be included in any information document in which the provider gives a detailed description of the service.

Finally, if asked, the service provider must provide details of any Codes of Practice to which he is subject and an electronic address from which the service recipient can access the provisions of the Code. The service provider must also specify the language in which the Code is available.

Q5 Consider the scope of the additional information that must be provided to a service recipient on request.

(h) Information regarding dispute resolution

Reference has already been made to the fact that a service provider might be subject to a code of conduct and/or be a member of a professional body or trade association. Where that is so and the relevant code or body provides for redress to a non-judicial dispute resolution procedure in the event of a dispute, certain information requirements come into play under regulation 10. These are that the service provider is required to inform a service recipient of the existence of the dispute resolution procedure and, further, that it must be mentioned in any information document in which the service provider has given a detailed description of the service. With respect to both of these methods of providing information about the dispute resolution system, the service provider must specify how the service recipient can access detailed information about the process.

(i) Complaints

The remaining provisions of this Part of the 2009 Regulations deal with the issue of complaints and their resolution. Complaints are a normal part of business and there can be very few traders who have not had to deal with a complaint at some point. This is as true of service providers as it is of the sellers and suppliers of goods. Regulation 12(1) requires that service providers must respond to complaints from service recipients as quickly as possible and, further, that they must use their best efforts to resolve the complaint in a satisfactory way. There are no specified criteria as to what factors contribute to the complaint being resolved as quickly as possible but obvious ones would include the ease with which the complainant can contact the service provider, the complexity of the complaint, and the ease, or lack thereof, with which evidence as to the complaint can be adduced. This latter factor might include, for example, gaining evidence from a third party or evidence from another EEA state, with the latter also having the potential to raise language issues. In deciding whether a service provider has resolved the complaint as quickly as possible, there can be no hard and fast deadlines. Each case will depend on its facts.

   The requirement to find a satisfactory solution is not always easy, as a solution that is reasonable will not necessarily satisfy the complainant if it is not the result for which he hoped. However, while the 2009 Regulations merely state that the service provider must use his best efforts to find a satisfactory result, the official guidance does reinforce the view that, if a provider has done his best and has found a solution with which the complainant could reasonably be expected to be satisfied, then the provider will have complied with the requirement and no more can be expected from him.[23] The requirement to find a satisfactory resolution does not apply if the complaint is vexatious.[24]

Q6 Analyse the requirements of the 2009 Regulations regarding dispute resolution systems and the requirement for the provision of a complaints system.

---

[23] *Ibid.* para. 32.   [24] SI 2009/2999, reg. 12(2).

(j) Enforcement

Where there has been a breach of the information and complaints requirements of the 2009 Regulations, or where a service provider has breached the prohibition in regulation 30(2) not to discriminate against an individual service recipient on the basis of his place of residence, the injured recipient can enforce the provisions and seek redress. This right of action exists irrespective of whether the service was a business-to-business transaction or a business-to-consumer transaction.

In addition, where the service recipients are consumers, enforcement bodies such as the Office of Fair Trading and Trading Standards Departments can use their enforcement powers under Part 8 of the Enterprise Act 2000. This option is restricted, however, to situations where the breach has affected, or has the potential to affect, the collective interests of consumers. It is not intended for use in an individual complaint unless there is also the potential for it to affect the collective interests of consumers.

Q7 Analyse how the introduction of the Provision of Services Regulations 2009 has improved the position of service recipients.

4 Supply of Goods and Services Act 1982

(a) Introduction

While the Provision of Services Regulations 2009 deal with the provision of information to prospective service recipients, the Supply of Goods and Services Act 1982 deals with the quality and fitness of the service provided. The Act was passed some ninety years after the Sale of Goods Act 1893 and brings together implied conditions about description and quality for contracts other than sale and three implied terms specifically addressing the issue of services.

The 1982 Act's genesis lay in the report by the National Consumer Council entitled *Service Please: Services and the Law, A Consumer View*. The Act came hot on the heels of the report and was perceived as being a temporary measure, since at the same time as passing the statute, the government referred the question of implied terms in services to the Law Commission, who published a report in 1986.[25] In the event, the Law Commission did not recommend any changes on the grounds that its report came too soon after the passage of the 1982 Act and that more time was needed to ascertain whether the Act would achieve its purpose or would require amendment.

(b) Implied conditions under Part I

Prior to the 1982 Act, implied terms for services emanated from the common law and the Act did not seek to alter the law as it stood, but rather to codify

---

[25] Law Commission, *Law of Contract: Implied Terms in Contracts for the Supply of Services* (Report No. 156 1986).

it. Hence, the substance of the law was unchanged and pre-existing case law remains relevant. Part I of the 1982 Act implies conditions about title, description, satisfactory quality, fitness for purpose and sample into contracts that involve the passage of title or possession, as the case may be, in contracts other than sale or hire-purchase.[26] Thus, sections 1–6 deal with contracts for the transfer of goods, such as barter, while sections 6–10 deal with contracts of hire in which the possession of the goods passes but the property in them does not. These provisions closely echo those in sections 12–15 of the Sale of Goods Act 1979 and there is accordingly no need to consider them further here except to note that the list of factors to be found in section 14(2B) of the 1979 Act relating to quality has not been adopted in the 1982 Act. Nonetheless, given the basic similarity of the provisions, it is a reasonable presumption that judicial decisions under sections 12–15 of the Sale of Goods Act 1979 will be equally applicable in decisions under Part I of the 1982 Act. As with the sale of goods, the implied conditions in Part I of the 1982 Act cannot be excluded against a person dealing as a consumer but, with the exception of the condition relating to title, can be excluded against a non-consumer purchaser to the extent that the exclusion is reasonable.[27]

Q8 Compare the implied conditions in Part I of the 1982 Act with those contained in sections 12–15 of the Sale of Goods Act 1979.

(c) Common law approach

The common law approach to liability for services is based in negligence and hence the need to demonstrate a duty of care owed by the supplier of the service to the consumer, a breach of that duty and resultant damage. It is not merely the existence of the duty but also the standard of care to be exercised by the supplier that is pertinent. All service providers must exercise reasonable care and skill irrespective of whether or not they are a professional, or are employed, or volunteer to perform that service.

The standard of care required increases with the professed expertise of the supplier. Thus, a doctor must exercise the medical skills appropriate to a doctor of his standing, a lawyer the legal skills appropriate to his place in the profession, etc., which will far exceed the level of skill to be expected of the 'man on the Clapham omnibus' were he to be faced with the task.[28]

---

[26] The implied conditions regarding description, quality, etc, in hire-purchase contracts are governed by Supply of Goods (Implied Terms) Act 1973, ss.8–11.

[27] Unfair Contract Terms Act 1977, s.7.

[28] See the *dicta* of Lord Denning MR in *Greaves & Co. (Contractors) Ltd* v. *Baynham Meikle and Partners* [1975] 3 All ER 99. However, an error of judgement will not necessarily amount to negligence, as in *Whitehouse* v. *Jordan* [1981] 1 All ER 267, in which a surgeon was held not liable for brain damage caused to a new-born baby by a forceps delivery. Although the decision to deliver the child in that way may have been an error of judgement, the decision was not unreasonable and hence did not constitute negligence.

That said, the requirement that the supplier demonstrates an appropriate level of skill does not equate with a guarantee that he will achieve the desired result. In the much quoted *dicta* of Lord Denning regarding the employment of a professional man:

> The law does not usually imply a warranty that he will achieve the desired result, but only a term that he will use reasonable care and skill. The surgeon does not warrant that he will cure the patient. Nor does the solicitor warrant that he will win the case. But, when a dentist agrees to make a set of false teeth for a patient, there is an implied warranty that they will fit his gums.[29]

This distinction seems rational. It is perfectly reasonable to expect a lawyer or a financial adviser to exercise their professional care and skill when advising their clients, though with no guarantee as to the outcome of the case or the performance of the investment; however, if the consumer has employed a heating contractor to instal central heating or a garage to repair a car, it is reasonable to expect not only that the work will be done professionally but also that the desired result will be achieved in that the central heating works, as does the car. The item produced must be fit for its purpose.

Q9 Review the main requirements of the law of negligence as they apply to services.

(d) Implied terms

In transposing the previous common law into statutory form, the 1982 Act introduced three statutory implied terms, namely, that the supplier will carry out the service with reasonable care and skill; that the service will be carried out within a reasonable time; and that a reasonable charge will be paid for the service. It is important to note that, unlike the statutory provisions relating to goods,[30] these implied terms are not specified as either conditions or warranties. They are statutory innominate terms. As such, the remedy for breach of one of these terms is dependent on the facts of the case and the view of the court as to the severity of the breach. The remedy is dependent on the effect of the breach rather than on its nature. While a breach of condition gives a right of rescission and a breach of warranty only sounds in damages, an innominate term gives the court the flexibility to award whichever remedy is appropriate. This seems eminently sensible in respect of services

---

[29] Per Lord Denning MR in *Greaves & Co. Contractors Ltd* v. *Baynham, Meikle & Partners* [1975] 3 All ER 99, 103, in which the defendant was employed to design a factory, the floor of which would need to be able to support the weight of fork-lift trucks moving barrels of oil. In the event, the floor cracked due to the vibration caused by the trucks when moving around. The defendant was found liable for the damage.

[30] Sale of Goods Act 1979, ss.12–15; Supply of Goods (Implied Terms) Act 1973, ss.7–10; and Supply of Goods and Services Act 1982, Part I.

where the types of service can be so varied and where, unlike strict liability, the culpability of the service provider is a factor in the decision of the court. It would, in practice, have been virtually impossible to introduce strict liability in respect of services.

The implied terms in sections 13–15 of the 1982 Act are not exhaustive as to the duties imposed on the supplier of services. Section 16 expressly provides that nothing in the Act prejudices any other rule of law which may either impose a stricter duty on a supplier[31] or imply other non-inconsistent duties into contracts for services.[32]

(e) Implied term re care and skill

Section 13 of the 1982 Act provides that in a contract for the supply of a service where the supplier is acting in the course of a business, there is an implied term that the supplier will carry out the service with reasonable care and skill. The resonance with the duty of care in negligence is obvious and intentionally so, for, as discussed above, section 13 is essentially a statutory contractual adoption of the law of negligence with all of the relevant case law being equally applicable.[33] However, for section 13 to apply there must have been a contract for the supply of the service so it is of no effect where the service has been provided on a voluntary or non-contractual basis. Further, the contract must have been made in the course of a business. This requirement would be construed in line with the decision in *Stevenson* v. *Rogers,*[34] a sale of goods case, in which it was held that any contract entered into by a business is deemed to be in the course of a business, a much less stringent requirement than the criminal law counterpart, which requires that the action was an integral part of the business.[35] This leaves the court in the same position as under section 14 of the Sale of Goods Act 1979 in having to decide on the facts whether or not a particular contract was entered into as part of a business, and raises the issue of a hobbyist, such as an amateur painter or photographer, and at what point the hobbyist steps over the boundary and becomes a business.

The business requirement means that the injured claimant has to decide which of three claims he should pursue. If he has a contract with a supplier who is in the course of a business, he can sue under section 13 of the 1982 Act, enforce any express provisions of the contract and claim in negligence. If his contract is with a non-business supplier, he cannot sue under the 1982 Act but

---

[31] Supply of Goods and Services Act 1982, s.16(3)(a).

[32] *Ibid.* s.16(3)(b).

[33] For a case decided under the 1982 Act see *Wilson* v. *Best Travel Ltd* [1993] 1 All ER 353, in which a holiday company was held not liable under s.13 when a customer was injured by falling through a glass patio door at a hotel advertised in the defendant's brochure. The defendant had inspected the hotel and confirmed that the glass satisfied the current Greek safety standards.

[34] [1999] 1 All ER 613.

[35] *Havering London Borough Council* v. *Stevenson* [1970] 3 All ER 609; *Davies* v. *Sumner* [1984] 3 All ER 831.

can still enforce the express provisions of the contract and sue in negligence. Finally, if he does not have a contract with the supplier, he will be restricted to a claim in negligence. In practice, claims under the 1982 Act and in negligence are likely to result in the same outcome, though different limitation periods will apply.

Many service contracts actually involve performance by more than one person.[36] Thus building a house will involve brick-layers, plumbers, electricians, etc., while the provision of a package holiday will typically involve the main holiday company, a transport company whether it be an airline for a holiday overseas or a rail or coach company for a holiday in the United Kingdom, and hoteliers. In the first example, it may be that all of the different tradesmen are employed by the main contractor, in which case he will be liable for the quality of the work that they do. However, it is possible that the tradesmen are all self-employed and are sub-contracted by the main building contractor. The issue then arises as to whether the main contractor is liable for their work or whether the injured customer would have to sue the sub-contractors directly if the performance does not reach the correct standard. Equally, in the holiday example, it is probable that the hotelier, and perhaps the transport company, are independent sub-contractors rather than employees of the main holiday company. So, who does the customer sue if the airline or the hotelier does not perform the contract with appropriate care and skill?

The answer is likely to depend on the contractual relationship between the main contractor and the sub-contractor, with the key issue being whether the main contractor is acting as the agent of the sub-contractor. If he is, the normal rules of agency dictate that the role of the agent is to bring about a contract between the principal and the third party. In the example given above of building a house, this would mean that the main contractor is setting up contracts between the various tradesmen and the house purchaser. Equally, in the holiday example, the holiday company as the main contractor would be setting up a contract between the hotelier and the holiday-maker. If that is the case, then agency dictates that, having set up the contracts, the agent drops out of the scene leaving the principal and the third party with a binding contract upon which they can sue and be sued. Thus, if the service was not performed with reasonable care and skill, the customer would have to sue the sub-contractor directly, with the problems that might be involved in so doing, particularly in the holiday scenario where the hotelier might be elsewhere in the European Union[37] or even outside the EU, when the difficulties of enforcing a legal action may be immense and well beyond the ability of the average holiday-maker. It is far more beneficial to the customer and, in practice, more likely that the main contractor is not acting as the agent of the sub-contractor and that he has simply sub-contracted the

---

[36] Not all contracts for services can be sub-contracted. Some contracts necessarily require personal performance by the service provider, e.g., painting a portrait or performing in a concert.

[37] Although the consumer would be able to enforce any legal judgment in that situation.

performance of part of the work for which he has contracted, so that while he has delegated the work, he remains legally responsible for it.

While section 13 lays down the general duty to be imposed on the supplier of services, section 12(2) of the 1982 Act gives the Secretary of State the authority to exclude identified suppliers from the provisions of sections 13–15. There are three relevant Statutory Instruments providing exemptions for advocates, in court or before any tribunal or inquiry and the preliminary work directly affecting the conduct of the hearing;[38] and company directors when acting in that capacity;[39] for building society directors and management committee members of industrial and provident societies;[40] and for arbitrators (including umpires) when acting as such.[41] These exclusions apply in contract only and liability in negligence remains. Of particular note in this regard is the position of barristers and solicitor advocates. Contractual liability has never been an issue with respect to barristers as they do not contract with the person whom they represent in court. The contract is between the client and the solicitor, with the latter then retaining the services of the barrister. There remains the issue of the liability of a barrister in negligence. The traditional view was that no liability was possible as a barrister has 'an overriding duty to the court'[42] and that he must be free to pursue that duty without fear of legal liability. Lord Reid opined that:

> it is in the public interest to retain the existing immunity of barristers from action by clients for professional negligence, at least so far as it relates to their work in conducting litigation.[43]

However, this approach was turned on its head in *Arthur JS Hall & Co.* v. *Simons*,[44] which overruled *Rondel* v. *Worsley*. In the rare situation of the House of Lords overruling one of its previous decisions, their Lordships held that public policy no longer justified the exemption and that we should 'bring to an end an anomalous exception to the basic premise that there should be a remedy for a wrong'.[45] Thus, advocates, including both barristers and solicitor advocates, are now liable in negligence in the same way as other professionals such as doctors.

Service sectors that have caused particular problems may attract additional statutory control, this being expressly permitted under section 16(3) of the 1982 Act. One of the most notable examples is package holidays, which have always prompted a significant number of complaints, perhaps because a holiday is one of the most expensive and eagerly anticipated purchases by the average consumer in any year. Having saved all year for their two weeks in the sun, consumer expectations may be high and thus disappointment is both more

---

[38] Supply of Services (Exclusion of Implied Terms) Order 1982, SI 1982/1771, reg. 2.
[39] *Ibid.*
[40] Supply of Services (Exclusion of Implied Terms) Order 1983, SI 1983/902, reg. 2.
[41] Supply of Services (Exclusion of Implied Terms) Order 1985, SI 1985/1, reg. 2.
[42] Per Lord Reid in *Rondel* v. *Worsley* [1967] 3 All ER 993, 998.
[43] [1967] 3 All ER 993, 1000.   [44] [2000] 3 All ER 673.   [45] *Ibid.* 683 per Lord Steyn.

immediate and more keenly felt should the holiday not provide all it promised. Lord Denning MR in *Jackson* v. *Horizon Holidays Ltd*[46] opined that:

> People look forward to a holiday. They expect the promises to be fulfilled. When it fails they are greatly disappointed and upset. It is difficult to assess in terms of money; but it is the task of the judges to do the best they can.

It is unsurprising, therefore, that, in addition to the 1982 Act, consumers are now protected by the Package Travel, Package Holidays and Package Tours Regulations 1992,[47] although it should be remembered that these Regulations give effect to Council Directive 90/314/EEC and therefore did not originate in the United Kingdom. The regulations provide civil liability for misleading descriptions of holidays,[48] and incorrect price information, and provide for arrangements to be made in the event of the non-provision of a significant proportion of the services[49] and compensation for a failure to provide proper performance of the service.[50] In addition, they also impose criminal liability for a failure to provide the required information about the holiday in a 'legible, comprehensive and accurate manner'.[51]

Q10 Analyse the relationship between the implied term of care and skill under section 13 and the law of negligence.

(f) Implied term re time for performance

The time for performance of a service can be dictated by the terms of the contract, where both parties make time of the essence. If there is an express term as to time, any failure by the service provider to meet that requirement will lay him open to a claim for compensation. In the absence of such a contractual term, section 14 of the 1982 Act steps into the breach. As with section 13, it only applies when the supplier is acting in the course of a business. Further, it only applies when the contract has not stipulated the time for performance or indicated the mechanism by which the time for performance can be calculated, and when there is no previous course of dealings between the parties that could be used to determine the time of performance. Thus, it acts to fill a contractual vacuum. When it does apply, it requires that the service will be carried out within a reasonable time, which will be a question of fact. This term has been adopted from the previous common law rules and requires both that the service will be started within a reasonable time and that it will be completed within a reasonable time. It is not sufficient merely to begin the service within a reasonable time but then be dilatory about completion. The test is objective, with the outcome dependent upon how long a provider of a similar service

---

[46] [1975] 3 All ER 92, CA.   [47] SI 1992/3288.
[48] *Ibid.* reg. 4.   [49] *Ibid.* reg. 14.
[50] *Ibid.* reg. 15.   [51] *Ibid.* reg. 5.

might reasonably expect to take to do the work at hand. The opinion of an independent expert may be needed, particularly if the service is one such as car repairs, which may be beyond the knowledge of the average customer. A leading example of the section in practice was the decision in *Charnock* v. *Liverpool Corporation*,[52] in which the Court of Appeal held a garage liable for taking eight weeks to repair a car when a reasonable period would have been five weeks.

Q11 Consider the factors to be taken into account when deciding whether a service has been provided within a reasonable time.

(g) Implied term re consideration

Unless the services have been provided free of charge, the customer will be expected to pay for them. This is dealt with in section 15, the only one of the three implied terms that does not contain a business requirement. It imposes a duty on all customers under service contracts, irrespective of whether they or the supplier are in business, to pay a reasonable charge for the services provided. As with section 14, this term only applies in a contractual vacuum, i.e., when the contract is silent as to the price, there is no contractually agreed method for calculating it and no previous course of dealings that can be relied upon. What is reasonable is, of course, a question of fact. Given the importance of price in any contract, the parties are unlikely not to have given any thought to it, unless the contract has come about because of an emergency, such as a car breaking down at the side of the road or a water pipe bursting and flooding the premises. Therein lies one of the concerns about price. In an emergency situation, the customer may not have the opportunity to look around to find a reasonable price and may, in all innocence, pay an extortionate price for the services that are provided. However, having paid the bill he will have no redress, for the payment will constitute an agreement that the sum paid is the contract price and, in the absence of duress, the customer has no remedy. The law does not protect customers from bad bargains – *caveat emptor* rules.

The other issue with price is the old chestnut about estimates and quotations. Opinions may vary as to the meaning of the terms. The Vehicle Body Repair Association in their Code of Practice[53] defined an estimate as being the 'anticipated cost for the work being requested' while a quotation is 'an all-inclusive fixed cost for carrying out the work as described and may not be increased'. This accords with the generally held view that an estimate may be adjusted depending upon the work actually done while a quotation is a fixed contractual price. It has been suggested that an unrealistically low estimate might be an unfair commercial practice under the Unfair Commercial

---

[52] [1968] 3 All ER 473. See also *Rickards* v. *Oppenheim* [1950] 1 All ER 420.
[53] Quoted in I. Ramsay, *Consumer Law and Policy: Texts and Materials on Regulating Consumer Markets* (2nd edn, Hart Publishing, Oxford, 2007) 679.

Practices Directive,[54] it having been construed as a misleading action under regulation 5 of the Consumer Protection from Unfair Trading Regulations 2008.[55]

Q12 Consider whether the implied terms of care and skill, time for performance and consideration together provide a suitable level of protection for the users of services.

(h) Exclusion of liability

In the same way that a distinction has been drawn between the strict liability provisions in Part I of the 1982 Act governing the quality of goods and the fault liability in sections 13–15, a similar dichotomy exists in relation to the ability of the supplier to exclude liability. Liability under Part I cannot be excluded against a buyer dealing as a consumer, while it can be excluded against a person not dealing as a consumer to the extent that the exclusion is reasonable.[56] By contrast, liability under sections 13–15 is subject to the main provisions of the Unfair Contract Terms Act 1977, which apply irrespective of the nature of the buyer and instead relate to the type of damage suffered as a result of the breach. This brings exclusion under section 13 in contract in line with exclusion for negligence in tort, which two actions may arise from the same incident and in respect of which two legal claims may be pursued. It is logical that the same approach should be adopted as regards exclusion for both of these potential liabilities. Thus, liability for death and personal injury arising from negligence cannot be excluded by any contract term or notice given to persons generally or to a particular person.[57] It follows that any attempt to use a term in a contract for services will be void to the extent that it seeks to exclude liability for death or personal injury. It would be valid, however, to exclude liability for damage to property to the extent that the exclusion is reasonable within the terms of the Unfair Contract Terms Act 1977.[58] Other exclusions can be agreed between the contracting parties by express agreement or by their course of dealings, or by such usage as binds them both, although such exclusion clauses cannot offend against the 1977 Act.[59] Further, an express term will not negate one of the implied terms in sections 13–15 unless it is inconsistent with it.[60]

Q13 Consider how the provisions of the Unfair Contract Terms Act 1977 impact upon liability for a breach of sections 13–15 of the Supply of Goods and Services Act 1982.

---

[54] *Ibid.* 669.   [55] SI 2008/1277.

[56] Unfair Contract Terms Act 1977, s.7.

[57] *Ibid.* s.2.   [58] *Ibid.* s.11.

[59] *Ibid.* s.16(1). See *Eagle Star Life Assurance Co. Ltd* v. *Griggs, Independent,* 20 October 1997, in which an express provision that the quality of the supply was to be judged by the supplier negated the implied term.

[60] Unfair Contract Terms Act 1977, s.16(2).

(i) Codes of practice

While additional statutory controls to regulate services are an option, alternative non-statutory mechanisms may also prove helpful. The Office of Fair Trading (OFT) considered the introduction of a general duty to trade fairly[61] but nothing ever came of it. Equally, the use of written assurances by traders who engaged in unfair practices proved to be ineffective. Arguably of more interest is that some service industries strive to be self-regulatory through the use of codes of practice, efficient self-regulation often being viewed as preferable to statutory control. One of the most prominent codes of practice is the Association of British Travel Agents (ABTA) Code, which regulates the holiday industry. Codes of practice typically include a requirement that signatories to the code[62] must act in a professional manner and exercise care and skill in their dealings and, additionally, will often provide for a dispute resolution system should the service provider fail to meet the legitimate expected standard. This is intended to provide consumers of services with a second source of protection and guarantee of the quality of services, and with a second avenue for compensation in the event of an unsatisfactory service. Sadly, this has not always proven to be the case. There are inherent weaknesses with codes of practice, of which the most obvious is that such a code only regulates traders who are members of the particular organisation and does not impact on those traders who are not a party to the code. In practice, it may well be the latter who cause problems within any particular industry but who fall outside the voluntary self-regulation promulgated by a code.

Codes of practice have therefore suffered from a poor image, although this hopefully will be improved by the criteria now set out by the OFT for Codes to be included in the Consumer Codes Approval Scheme. The core criteria for approval are stringent and include a commitment to provide customers with adequate information about goods and services; the use of clear and fair contracts; the protection of deposits or prepayments; and low cost, independent dispute resolution if a complaint is not dealt with satisfactorily.[63] In practice, service providers governed by OFT approved codes are likely to be providing a good quality service. While the OFT has invited many sectors to participate in the Consumer Codes Approval Scheme, relatively few codes of practice have met the standards to be OFT approved.[64]

[61] Office of Fair Trading, *A General Duty to Trade Fairly,* Discussion Paper (London, 1986); Office of Fair Trading, *Trading Malpractices: A Report by the Director General of Fair Trading* (London, 1990).

[62] It is an unfair commercial practice for a trader to claim that he is a signatory to a code of conduct when he is not, see SI 2008/1277, Sch.. 1 para. 1.

[63] See 'OFT Approved Codes Explained' at www.oft.gov.uk.

[64] Currently there are ten approved Codes: Bosch Car Service, British Association of Removers Ltd (BAR), British Healthcare Trades Association, Carpet Foundation, Debt Managers Standards Association (DEMSA), Direct Selling Association (DSA), Institute of Profesional Will Writers, Motor Codes Ltd (New Car Code), The Property Ombudsman Ltd (Sales) and Vehicle Builders and Repairers Association Ltd (VBRA), see 'OFT Approved Codes Explained' at www.oft.gov.

Q14 Consider the strengths and weaknesses of codes of practice in promoting good practice among traders and in protecting the users of services.

5 Recommended reading

Bradgate, R. *Commercial Law* (3rd edn, Oxford University Press, Oxford, 2000)

Department for Business, Innovation and Skills *Guidance for Business on the Provision of Services Regulations 2009* (October 2009)

Dobson, P. and Stokes, R. *Commercial Law* (7th edn, Sweet & Maxwell, London, 2008)

Griffiths, M. and Griffiths, I. *Law for Purchasing and Supply* (3rd edn, Pearson Education Ltd, Harlow, 2002)

Law Commission *Law of Contract: Implied Terms in Contracts for the Supply of Services* (Report No. 156, 1986)

Office of Fair Trading *A General Duty to Trade Fairly,* Discussion Paper (London, 1986)
    Trading Malpractices: A Report by the Director General of Fair Trading (London, 1990)

Ramsay, I. *Consumer Law and Policy: Texts and Materials on Regulating Consumer Markets* (2nd edn, Hart Publishing, Oxford, 2007)

The topic of the supply of services divides into two parts. The first relates to the Provision of Services Regulations 2009 and readers would benefit from reading the guidance published by the Department for Business, Innovation and Skills. The second, the Supply of Goods and Services Act 1982, is addressed in Dobson and Stokes, *Commercial Law* and Griffiths and Griffiths, *Law for Purchasing and Supply*. If readers want to learn more about the role of the OFT's Consumer Codes Approval Scheme, this is available on the OFT's website.

uk. In addition, another four Codes have satisfied Stage 1 of the approval process: Motor Sales (Service and Repair), Motor Codes (Vehicle Warranty Products), Renewable Energy Association and Safebuy. The Association of British Travel Agents (ABTA) withdrew from the scheme in 2005 as they were no longer able to satisfy the criteria, see Ramsay, above n. 53, at 472.

Part 2 Chapter 5

E-commerce and Distance Selling

1 Introduction

The sale of goods by some form of distance selling has been in place for many decades, initially through the use of advertisements and catalogues, but more latterly through TV advertising and the Internet. This chapter analyses the current legal controls over distance selling in its various forms.

Section 2 looks at the background to the subject and the rise of Internet selling. Section 3 analyses the requirements of the Electronic Commerce (EC Directive) Regulations 2002 including details of the trader; price; commercial communications; making the contract; placing the order; remedies; and electronic signatures.

Section 4 introduces the Consumer Protection (Distance Selling) Regulations 2000 and considers the provisions relating to information requirements; cancellation rights; and cancellation periods.

2 Background

The major development of the last twenty years in the law relating to the sale and supply of goods and services has been the dramatic move towards the purchase of goods and services via the Internet. Although distance selling occurred before this through the use of catalogues, telephone, etc., it has been the advent of the Internet which has occasioned a major change in the way in which both business buyers and consumers acquire goods and services. Given the prominence of Internet sales now, it seems hard to remember that the World Wide Web was not made public until 1991,[1] with leading online stores not being founded until the mid-1990s.[2] Nowadays, purchasing on the Internet is an integral part of the supply process, whether the purchaser is a business or a consumer. E-commerce has undoubtedly contributed to broadening the purchase options for a buyer, there being no need for seller and purchaser to meet face to face or even be in the same country or continent. Buyers have the ability to access goods and services from all over the world at the touch of a button. Nonetheless, there remains concern that while Internet buying has grown within an individual country, the amount of Internet cross-border trading involving consumers remains low and is an issue that must be addressed in order to promote trade generally.[3]

Despite the advantages brought about by Internet trading, it does pose some problems for traders who, in supplying goods to recipients in a large number of countries, can find themselves required to comply with a significant number of differing local laws relating to goods and services provided in those various countries. Of course, Internet traders are not obliged to do business with everyone who accesses their site and it may be a wise precaution to identify those countries to which their business is limited. Other issues that have arisen include the information that a prospective buyer needs to know to allow them to purchase confidently on the Internet; the role of electronic signatures in verifying the legitimacy of a transaction; and the enforceability process governing the contract should any dispute arise. This includes identifying both the applicable law and which courts have jurisdiction. The location of the information service, which is important in establishing where any legal action between seller and buyer should be commenced, is generally assumed to be the place where the seller pursues his economic activity, i.e., the place where his business is located. The location of the server supporting his e-business is irrelevant for this purpose.

Q1 Consider the impact of Internet trading in the last twenty years and the legislation needed to address this new form of trading.

3 Electronic Commerce (EC Directive) Regulations 2002

The European Union has addressed the regulation of e-commerce by enacting various Directives of which the two most important here are the Directive

---

[1] See. A.R. Lodder and H.W.K. Kaspersen (eds.), *eDirectives: Guide to the European Union Law on E-Commerce* (Kluwer Law International, London, 2002) 1 note 1.

[2] For example, Amazon.com, a leading internet company selling books, DVDs, CDs, etc., started business in 1995: see Lodder and Kaspersen, above n. 1, at 1.

[3] This concern and the wish to promote cross-border trade lies behind the proposed Consumer Rights Directive COM(2008)614 final, which it is hoped will stimulate cross-border trade by ensuring that consumers have the same rights irrespective of where in the EU goods are purchased. This should encourage consumer confidence.

governing electronic signatures[4] and the so-called E-Commerce Directive.[5] In the United Kingdom, the former has been adopted via the Electronic Communications Act 2000 and the Electronic Signatures Regulations 2002[6] while the E-Commerce Directive has been enacted via the Electronic Commerce (EC Directive) Regulations 2002.[7]

The recitals to the E-Commerce Directive postulate that the development of information services plays a vital role in promoting the internal market and 'eliminating the barriers which divide the European peoples'.[8] Consequently, the Directive aims to lay down a clear and general framework for electronic commerce to ensure legal certainty and thereby promote customer confidence. This extends to economic activity which includes the selling of goods and provision of services online and, as such, includes online information, online advertising, online shopping and online contracting.

The 2002 Regulations give effect to the E-Commerce Directive and essentially deal with the information and procedural requirements for contracting online irrespective of whether the buyer is a business or a consumer, although some provisions can be varied by agreement between the service provider and non-consumer buyers.[9] The 2002 Regulations apply to service providers, i.e., those providing 'information society services', which are defined as being:

> any service normally provided for remuneration, at a distance, by means of electronic equipment for the processing (including digital compression) and storage of data, and at the individual request of a recipient of a service.[10]

This would include any request made by a purchaser, whether a business buyer or a consumer, for the supply of goods or services, although doubt has been raised over whether an order from a trader that has been triggered as part of an ongoing relationship with a supplier[11] can truly be classed as an individual request. However, a visit to a website is always an individual request because the prospective purchaser has accessed it either by typing in the web address or by following a link.[12]

---

[4] Directive 1999/93/EC on a Community framework for electronic signatures.

[5] Directive 2000/31/EC on certain legal aspects of information society services, in particular electronic commerce, in the internal market (Electronic Commerce).

[6] SI 2002/318.   [7] SI 2002/2013.

[8] Electronic Commerce Directive, recital 1.

[9] SI 2002/2013, regs. 9 and 11.

[10] *Ibid.* reg. 2, adopting Electronic Commerce Directive, recital 17. See J. Harrington 'Information Society services: what are they and how relevant is the definition?' (2001) *Journal of Business Law* 190.

[11] Suppliers and trade purchasers may utilise EDI (Electronic Data Interchange) and thereby have an ongoing electronic arrangement covering many aspects of their relationship, see M. Chissick, and A. Kelman, *Electronic Commerce Law and Practice* (3rd edn, Sweet & Maxwell, London, 2002) 67. It is questionable whether any request for goods or services processed via EDI can truly be said to be an individual request.

[12] Lodder and Kaspersen, above n. 1, at 72.

(a) Details of the trader

Under regulation 6(1) of the 2002 Regulations,[13] a person providing a service must make specified information available to both the recipient of the service and to any relevant enforcement authority. The information must be in a form and manner which is 'easily, directly and permanently accessible'. Thus, for example, it should be accessible as part of the webpage or by following a link to another page on the site and should be capable of being copied electronically or printed off into a hard copy. The information required by regulation 6(1) essentially requires the service provider to provide a plethora of details about himself that allows the buyer to have confidence about the identity and professional standing of the service provider. Thus, the service provider must provide his name, his geographic address,[14] and his electronic address so as to facilitate a person contacting him rapidly and in a direct and effective manner. In addition to this basic information, certain other professional details are required. Hence, if the service provider is registered in a trade or other publicly available register, details of that register and the registration number of the service provider must be given. Also, details of the supervisory authority of any authorisation scheme must be provided, or the details of any professional body or similar institution with whom the service provider is registered, with his professional title, the Member State where it was granted and a reference to any professional rules applicable to the service provider and how to access them. In addition, where the activity of the provider is subject to VAT, the relevant identification number must be included.

(b) Price

When purchasing goods or services, price is a crucial factor and one on which the decision of whether or not to purchase is often based. It is clearly important that the purchaser knows whether the price quoted includes tax and delivery costs so that the purchaser is not misled and any decision to purchase is made from a position of knowledge. Given that the 2002 Regulations apply to both business and consumer purchasers, the issue of tax is particularly pertinent, as while prices quoted to consumers must be inclusive of tax, it is possible to quote prices exclusive of tax where the trading environment is aimed solely at business buyers. Thus, in trade warehouses it is common for prices to be quoted ex-VAT with the VAT being added on to the bill at the checkout. Regulation 6(2) requires

---

[13] SI 2002/2013, reg. 6(1).

[14] The geographic address is very important, for while the web address of the service provider may allow the country in which he is based to be identified, the geographic address provides a postal address for correspondence with the trader if needed. It also further emphasises the location of the service provider's business and allows the customer to decide whether they are happy to transact with someone in that country given the obvious difficulties of enforcing a contract in another country or continent.

that any statement about prices must be clear and unambiguous and indicate whether they are inclusive of tax and delivery costs.

(c) Commercial communications

Anybody can buy and sell on the Internet and there is a huge volume of sales of goods and services to consumers on sites such as eBay. It is important for purchasers to know whether the person from whom they are buying on the Internet is a trader or a consumer as the legal rights that they have against them will vary depending on that one factor alone. Goods sold in the United Kingdom via the Internet will attract liability under the Sale of Goods Act 1979[15] and thus must be of satisfactory quality and fit for their purpose[16] but only if purchased from someone in the course of a business.[17] Regulation 7 of the 2002 Regulations therefore requires that a service provider must ensure that any commercial communication provided by him is clearly identifiable as such[18] and must identify the person on whose behalf it has been made.[19] Further, any promotional offer, such as a discount, premium or gift, must be identified as such with any conditions attached to qualification for it being clearly and unambiguously presented and easily accessible to the prospective purchaser.[20] Also, any promotional competition or game and the rules governing it must be easy to access and be clear and unambiguous.[21] In addition, regulation 8 requires that the service provider must ensure that any unsolicited commercial communication sent by him by electronic mail is clearly and unambiguously identifiable as being unsolicited as soon as it is received. (In practice, spam filters may achieve this automatically.) An interesting issue is whether an email is unsolicited when a purchaser has previously indicated a general preparedness to receive emails from that service provider or other similar service providers but has not requested the specific email in question. Article 7.2 of the E-Commerce Directive[22] stipulates that Member States which allow unsolicited emails must ensure that service providers consult and respect the opt-out registers on which buyers can register the fact that they do not want to receive any unsolicited emails. However, difficulties obviously arise in respect of service providers who do not have access to such registers and who therefore cannot abide by them. Equally, enforcement authorities cannot enforce the provisions against service providers whose emails originate outside the jurisdiction of the authority.

---

[15] Assuming that the service provider and buyer have chosen to have their contract subject to English law.

[16] Sale of Goods Act 1979, s.14(2) and (3).

[17] *Ibid*. s.14 only applies where the seller is in the course of a business. For a fuller discussion see Part 2 Chapter 2 on the implied conditions in sale of goods.

[18] SI 2002/2013 reg. 7(a).

[19] *Ibid*. reg. 7(b)   [20] *Ibid*. reg. 7(c)   [21] *Ibid*. reg. 7(d)

[22] Electronic Commerce Directive Art. 7(2).

Q2 *Analyse whether the requirements of the Electronic Commerce (EC Directive) Regulations 2002 are adequate to allow a purchaser to identify and contact the person from whom he has bought acquired goods or services and to know whether that person is a trader or a private seller.*

(d) Making the contract

When concluding a contract, it is important for both parties to be fully aware of the point in the negotiations at which the contract comes into existence and to have the opportunity to continue to seek additional information and negotiate terms until that point is reached. Consequently, it is important to recognise what constitutes the contractual offer and acceptance such as to bring about a legally binding contract. English law also deals with the concept of the invitation to treat, and the display on a website of goods and services that the service provider is prepared to supply would constitute an invitation to treat in the same way as goods advertised in a shop window.[23] The placing of the order on a website would constitute the contractual offer and the acceptance of the order by the service provider would be the contractual acceptance that creates the contract. This allows the service provider to accept or reject the offer in line with normal practice as he cannot be forced to enter a contract with a potential customer, it is a matter of free will. In practice, a service provider may choose not to contract with a particular customer if the supplier is no longer in a position to supply the goods because, for example, he underestimated the customer demand for the product concerned and has run out of stock. Equally, given the potential for cross-border contracts as a result of web-based trading, the supplier may choose not to contract with anyone from the country in which the potential customer is domiciled as it may be that his product does not fully comply with the legal requirements of that country.

The 2002 Regulations deal with the statutory requirements in terms of the 'placing of the order' irrespective of whether the placing of the order constitutes the contractual offer.[24] Regulation 9(1) requires that if the contract is to be concluded by electronic means, the service provider must provide certain information prior to the placing of an order unless non-consumer contracting parties have agreed otherwise. This allows the parties in a business-to-business contract to agree other arrangements. The requisite information must be provided in a 'clear, comprehensible and unambiguous manner'. The requirements cover the different technical steps that the customer must follow to conclude the contract; whether the concluded contract will be filed by the service provider and whether it will be accessible; the technical means for identifying and

---

[23] *Fisher* v. *Bell* [1961] 1 QB 394.

[24] SI 2002/2013, reg. 12. However, there are two exceptions to this general rule: reg. 9(1)(c) and reg. 11(1)(b) where the placing of the order will be the contractual offer.

correcting input errors prior to the placing of the order; and the languages offered for concluding the contract. These requirements must be satisfied in addition to any other information requirements that exist in legislation giving effect to Community law.[25] A breach of the regulation 9(1) requirements renders the service provider liable to an action by any recipient of the service for a breach of statutory duty. In practice, websites provide step-by-step guidance as to how to place an order and invariably provide a confirmation of the order with an opportunity for amendment before finally inviting the customer to click the 'order' button.

As for the language in which the contract is to be concluded, it is a reasonable assumption that the contract will be in the language used on the website, with the potential for different languages to be used if the site is available in more than one language. If the contract is to be in a language other than that used for the website, the recipient must be made aware of that fact.[26]

Regulation 9(2) requires that where the service provider is a subscriber to a code of practice, he must provide information on how that code can be accessed electronically. In practice, this can be achieved by web-seals whereby if the recipient of the service clicks on the relevant logo on the service provider's website, he will be transferred automatically to a page containing the details of the relevant code.[27] As under regulation 9(1), non-consumer parties can agree otherwise and choose not to comply with regulation 9(2). This might be appropriate when, for example, both seller and buyer are in the same trade and thus equally familiar with the terms of a code of practice to which both parties may subscribe. To force the service provider to give details of a code of practice with which the recipient is familiar would be otiose.

By contrast with regulation 9(1) and (2), which are subject to some variation, regulation 9(3) applies to all contracts irrespective of the character of the parties and requires that where the service provider provides the recipient of the service with the terms and conditions applicable to the contract, they must be made available in a way that allows the recipient to store and reproduce them, either electronically or by printing them off on hard copy.

Regulation 9(1) and (2) envisage situations in which a large number of potential recipients may access the website and be provided with standard information and terms with no real opportunity to ask individual questions of the service provider. The situation is entirely different where the contractual negotiations are conducted on an individual basis resulting in an opportunity for the recipient to request any additional information that he requires. Given this difference, regulation 9(1) and (2) do not apply where the

---

[25] SI 2002/2013, reg. 10. Thus, e.g., the trader must also comply with the requirements of Directive 97/7/EC on the protection of consumers in respect of distance contracts, which has been given effect in the United Kingdom via the Consumer Protection (Distance Selling) Regulations 2000, SI 2000/2334. Distance selling regulation in the European Union is currently under review and the Directive may be replaced by the proposed Consumer Rights Directive, above n. 3.

[26] See Lodder and Kaspersen, above n. 1, at 84.   [27] *Ibid.*

contract has been concluded exclusively by email or by an equivalent individual communication.[28]

(e) Placing the order

Regulation 11 of the 2002 Regulations deals with the basic requirements to ensure that the recipient of the service has the opportunity to correct any input errors prior to his order being placed and arrangements to ensure that he knows that his order has been received. Regulation 11(1) specifies two requirements, although, as under regulation 9(1) and (2), parties who are not consumers can agree to vary these requirements, and choose to agree arrangements more appropriate to their business needs. The first requirement under regulation 11 is that the service provider must acknowledge receipt of the order to the person placing it without undue delay and by electronic means.[29] Both the order and the acknowledgement of the receipt are deemed to have been received by the person to whom it is addressed when those parties are able to access them. Thus, the supplier of the service is deemed to have received the order when it reaches his system and can be accessed, even though in practice it may be acknowledged automatically and the order is not read by the service provider until some hours or even days later. Websites are accessible 24 hours a day, 365 days of the year, and it follows that customers are able to place orders at any time even when the business is not open in the traditional sense. Nonetheless, the order has been legally placed once the provider can access the order. Equally, the receipt of the order takes place once it is accessible to the person who placed it even though he may not actually access the receipt until later. This process negates any argument as to when or even whether an order was placed, which may be important in respect of any later dispute about the alleged non-delivery of any goods that were the subject of the order. Where the order relates to the provision of an information society service, actual provision of that service by the provider is itself deemed to be acknowledgement of the receipt of the order.[30]

Regulation 11(1)(b) deals with the actual mechanics of placing the order. It requires the service provider to make available to the recipient of the service, i.e., the person placing the order, effective and accessible technical means to allow him to identify and correct any input errors before he places the order. This is crucially important for, as explained previously, the placing of the order is a contractual offer which can be accepted by the service provider and would, at that point, become a legally binding contract such as to require the person placing the order to accept the goods or face a claim for damages for non-acceptance of the goods. The central nature of this requirement is underlined by the fact that, if the service provider fails to make available an opportunity for the person placing the order to identify and amend errors in it prior to sending it, any resulting contract can be rescinded by a person who has entered into that

---

[28] SI 2002/2013, reg. 9(4).   [29] *Ibid.* reg. 11(1)(a).   [30] *Ibid.* reg. 11(2)(b).

contract.[31] It remains open to the court, on an application by the service provider, to render the contract valid and hence enforceable.[32]

(f) Remedies

Remedies are provided for breaches of the various requirements referred to above, as the recipient of the service may make a claim for damages for breach of statutory duty against the service provider in respect of any such breach.[33] This applies to breaches of regulations 6 (general information to be provided), 7 (commercial communications), 8 (unsolicited commercial communications), 9(1) (information to be provided when concluding a contract) and 11(1)(a) (acknowledging receipt of an order). When a breach of regulation 9(3) of the 2002 Regulations has occurred (the requirement that the service provider will provide the recipient with the terms and conditions of the contract in a way that he can store and reproduce), the recipient may seek an order from the court requiring the service provider to comply with the statutory requirement and provide the recipient of the service with the contractual terms and conditions in the appropriate format.[34]

(g) Electronic signatures

The parties to the contract may wish to enhance the security of the contract by using an electronic signature, which authenticates the identity of the person using it. In the United Kingdom, electronic signatures are subject to the provisions of the Electronic Communications Act 2000 and the Electronic Signatures Regulations 2002.[35] The need to provide the three digit security number from the reverse of a credit card when using the card to place an order on the Internet would be deemed to be confirmation that the person placing the order has access to the card. One of the most significant uses of electronic signatures in commercial law is to be found in the Consumer Credit Act 1974 (Electronic Communications) Order 2004,[36] which now facilitates the making of consumer credit agreements by electronic means.

Q3 Do the Electronic Commerce (EC Directive) Regulations 2002 ensure that, when contracting online, both parties have sufficient information to know both whether a contract has been concluded and, if so, upon what terms and conditions?

4 Distance selling

Distance selling, by which the seller or supplier and the buyer transact at a distance, encompasses not merely Internet trading but also includes other

---

[31] *Ibid.* reg. 15.   [32] *Ibid.*
[33] *Ibid.* reg. 13.   [34] *Ibid.* reg. 14.   [35] SI 2002/318.
[36] SI 2004/3236, which was made under the Electronic Communications Act 2000, s.8.

situations such as buying from catalogues or newspapers and contracting by phone. The common factor in these situations is, of course, that the contracting parties never meet. Where the parties are both acting in the course of a business, normal contractual principles such as *caveat emptor* and freedom of contract apply and the parties have the flexibility to decide what information they need about each other and about the subject matter of the contract, including the contractual terms and conditions. If contracting via the Internet, traders will need to comply with the Electronic Commerce (EC Directive) Regulations 2002 as set out above, although, where the purchaser is a non-consumer, the parties can agree to set aside some of the provisions[37] if they so choose. Apart from these controls regarding Internet sales, the parties in a business-to-business contract are free to contract as they see fit.

Consumers present a different case, however, because in the majority of such trading situations there is no equality of bargaining power between the business supplier and the consumer buyer. As a result, consumers are perceived as being vulnerable, this being particularly true when they are contracting at a distance. Consequently, additional protection for the consumer in business-to-consumer distance contracts[38] is provided through the Consumer Protection (Distance Selling) Regulations 2000,[39] which specify information requirements in distance contracts and legislate for cancellation periods. When purchasing goods or services via the Internet, the protection for consumers under these Regulations will be in addition to that provided by the Electronic Commerce (EC Directive) Regulations 2002. The Consumer Protection (Distance Selling) Regulations 2000 apply to all distance contracts other than those which are excepted contracts under regulation 5[40] and those in respect of which the Regulations only apply in part.[41]

---

[37] See SI 2002/2013, regs. 9(1), (2) and 11(1).

[38] The Consumer Protection (Distance Selling) Regulations 2000, SI 2000/2334, do not extend to consumer contracts. Hence, a consumer buying goods from another consumer whether via the Internet or through the small ads in a paper or magazine, would not be protected and the normal principle of *caveat emptor* would apply.

[39] SI 2000/2334. These Regulations give effect to Directive 97/7/EC on the protection of consumers in respect of distance contracts. For a discussion of the background to this Directive, see Lodder and Kaspersen, above n. 1 at 11.

[40] The excepted contracts are those for the sale or other disposition of an interest in land, except for rental agreements; the construction of a building where the contract provides for the sale or other disposition of the land on which the building is constructed, except for rental agreements; contracts relating to financial services; contracts concluded via vending machines or automated commercial premises; contracts concluded with a telecommunications operator through the use of a public pay-phone; and contracts concluded at an auction.

[41] SI 2000/2334, reg. 6 provides that the Regulations only apply in part to timeshare agreements under the Timeshare Act 1992 and contracts for a 'package' holiday under the Package Travel, Package Holidays and Package Tours Regulations 1992, SI 1992/3288.

(a) Information requirements

Regulations 7 and 8 detail the information requirements, the time within which the information must be provided and the format in which some of it must be provided. In a provision not dissimilar to provisions under the Electronic Commerce (EC Directive) Regulations 2002, regulation 7(1) of the Consumer Protection (Distance Selling) Regulations 2000 requires that a supplier must provide the following information to a consumer 'in good time prior to the conclusion of the contract'. The provision of the information at this point ensures that the consumer can make an informed decision about whether to contract with the identified supplier for the particular goods or services.

The first required information is the identity of the supplier and, where payment in advance is required, his geographic address.[42] This requirement to specify the address where prior payment is intended ensures that the buyer can contact the supplier in the event of the goods or services not arriving when they should or not complying in some way with the contract, e.g., not being of satisfactory quality. Arguably, the need to specify the supplier's address is less urgent when the consumer is not due to pay for the goods or services until after he has received them and has had the opportunity to inspect them to ensure compliance with the contract.[43]

The next five information requirements relate to aspects of the goods or services, delivery and cancellation.[44] They require a description of the main characteristics of the goods or services;[45] the price of the goods or services, including all taxes and delivery costs where appropriate;[46] arrangements for payment, delivery or performance; and the existence of a right of cancellation, except for those cases referred to in regulation 13 of the 2000 Regulations.[47] The net effect of these provisions is to ensure that the buyer has a comprehensive understanding of the goods or services that he will be acquiring and the contractual rights and liabilities that accompany the purchase. The underlying importance of this is demonstrated by the requirement in regulation 8 that this information must be provided to the consumer in writing or in some other durable medium that is available and accessible to the consumer, either prior to the conclusion of the contract or thereafter in good time or, in any event, during the performance of any contract for services, or no later than the time of delivery for goods where

---

[42] SI 2000/2334, reg. 7(1)(a)(i).

[43] For a discussion of the buyer's right to a reasonable examination of the goods see Part 2 Chapter 2.

[44] SI 2000/2334, reg. 7(1)(a)(ii)–(vi).

[45] For a non-exhaustive list of the 'main characteristics of the product' under criminal trading law, see the Consumer Protection from Unfair Trading Regulations 2008, (SI 2008/1277) reg. 5(5). See also Part 4 Chapter 2 of this text.

[46] A supplier may make delivery charges for delivering goods to the buyer's home, as the Sale of Goods Act 1979, s.28 provides that, in the absence of any express of implied term in the contract, the normal place of delivery is the seller's place of business or, failing that, his residence. See Part 2 Chapter 3 for a full discussion of the law relating to delivery of goods.

[47] These exceptions will be dealt with below when looking in detail at cancellation rights in distance contracts.

the goods are not for delivery to a third party.[48] However, it should be noted that this requirement does not apply where any contract for services are performed through the use of distance communication[49] and are either only supplied once or are invoiced by the operator through distance communication.[50]

While the information requirements of regulation 7(1)(a)(i)–(vi) of the 2000 Regulations are of primary importance such as to justify them being provided to the consumer in a durable form, regulation 7(1) also specifies three other pieces of information that must be provided prior to the conclusion of the contract but which do not have to be provided in a durable form. These are the cost of using the means of distance communication if it is to be charged at other than the basic rate;[51] the period for which the offer remains valid; and, where appropriate, the minimum duration of the contract where the contract in question provides for the supply of goods and services which are to be provided either permanently or recurrently.[52] Thus, for example, if a consumer contracted over the Internet or by phone for the provision of a new mobile phone service, he would be entitled to be told if the contract of supply for the phone service was subject to a minimum duration, e.g., twelve months.

Ordering goods by distance contract without any direct contact between supplier and buyer may result in the prospective buyer making a contractual offer for goods that the supplier is no longer able to supply because, for example, he has run out of stock. In that situation, the supplier could simply reject the contractual offer but it may be that he would prefer to supply an alternative product that may prove acceptable to the prospective buyer, although the latter would not be obliged to accept the alternative goods as they are not the ones which he offered to buy. If the supplier intends to offer alternative goods or services or ones of equivalent quality and price to those ordered, he must inform the consumer of that fact and make clear that the supplier would bear the cost of returning the substitute goods to the supplier if the consumer chose to reject them.[53]

When providing any of the information required by regulation 7(1), the supplier is under a duty to make clear his commercial purpose[54] which, in the case of a telephone conversation, will be satisfied by the supplier identifying himself and the commercial nature of the call at the outset of the conversation.[55] Whatever the nature of the distance communication used in the making of the contract, the supplier must ensure that all of the information required under regulation 7(1) is provided in a clear and comprehensible manner appropriate to the distance communication being used and with due regard to the principles

---

[48] SI 2000/2334, reg. 8(1).
[49] This would include, e.g., the provision by the supplier of a computer program.
[50] SI 2000/2334, reg. 9(1).
[51] This would include, e.g., the cost of premium phone lines or any additional cost attached to using a mobile phone.
[52] SI 2000/2334, reg. 7(1)(a)(vii)–(ix).   [53] *Ibid.* reg. 7(1)(b) and (c).
[54] *Ibid.* reg. 7(3).   [55] *Ibid.* reg. 7(4).

of good faith[56] in commercial transactions and protection of those unable to give consent for themselves,[57] e.g., minors or vulnerable adults.

In addition to providing the information required by regulation 7(1) in a durable medium, regulation 8(2)(b) of the 2000 Regulations details other information that must be supplied to the consumer either in writing or in another durable medium available and accessible to the consumer. This includes information about the buyer's cancellation rights under regulation 10;[58] the geographical address of the supplier's business;[59] information about any after-sales services and guarantees;[60] and the conditions under which the buyer can exercise any cancellation rights if the contract either exceeds one year in duration or is of an unspecified duration.[61] With respect to cancellation rights under regulation 10 of the 2000 Regulations, the information that must be provided is whether the consumer must return the goods to the supplier when cancelling the order; whether it is the supplier or the consumer who must pay the cost of returning the goods; and, in the case of a contract of services, the effect of the consumer agreeing to allow performance to begin before the expiry of the cancellation period.[62]

Q4 Consider whether the information requirements of the Consumer Protection (Distance Selling) Regulations 2000 are sufficiently comprehensive to allow the consumer to contract with confidence.

(b) Cancellation rights

Regulation 10 of the 2000 Regulations details cancellation rights, with regulations 11 and 12 prescribing the relevant cancellation periods within which those rights may be exercised. Essentially, the consumer can validly cancel the contract by giving a notice in writing or in some other accessible and durable medium, either to the supplier or to any other person that the supplier has indicated is able to receive such notification on his behalf. There is no specific requirement as to the content of the cancellation notice other than that it must make clear the intention of the consumer to cancel. When validly served, the effect of the notice is to render the contract as if it had never existed. Valid service requires that the notification has been left or posted to the supplier at his last known address, or faxed to the supplier's business fax number, or sent to him via electronic mail at his last known email address.[63] It follows that, in an

---

[56] The statutory use of the concept of 'good faith' on the part of the trader when protecting consumers is becoming more common in legislation that gives effect to EU Directives. See the definition of 'professional diligence' in SI 2008/1277, reg. 2, which depends on the 'general principles of good faith in the trader's field of activity'. Those Regulations give effect to Directive 2005/29/EC concerning unfair business-to-consumer commercial practices in the internal market. See also Part 4 Chapter 2 of this text.

[57] SI 2000/2334, reg. 7(2).   [58] *Ibid.* reg. 8(2)(b).

[59] *Ibid.* reg. 8(2)(c).   [60] *Ibid.* reg. 8(2)(d).

[61] *Ibid.* reg. 8(2)(e).   [62] *Ibid.* reg. 8(2)(b).   [63] *Ibid.* reg. 10.

Internet-based contract, valid cancellation could take place by the consumer sending an email to the trader.

However, not all distance contracts include cancellation rights. Regulation 13(1)(b)–(f) of the 2000 Regulations provides some straight-forward exceptions to the provisions of regulation 10. These excepted contracts comprise contracts for the supply of goods and services, the price for which depends on fluctuations in financial markets that cannot be controlled by the supplier; for the supply of goods which have been made to the consumer's specifications or are personalised; for the supply of goods that cannot be returned because they will deteriorate or perish rapidly; for the supply of audio and video recordings and computer software when the consumer has broken the seal on the goods concerned; for the supply of newspapers, periodicals or magazines; and contracts for betting or lottery services. All of these contracts are easily identifiable, dealing as they do with very specific situations and creating reasonable exceptions to the regulation 10 rights.

The remaining exception is under regulation 13(1)(a) and is of more general effect. It relates to contracts for the supply of services, which may be many and varied. The exception deals with the situation where the performance of the contract has begun before the end of the relevant expiry period for notice and, further, where the supplier has supplied the relevant information under regulation 8(2) to the consumer. Given the range of potential service contracts, covering everything from hiring a car to downloading computer programs to having double glazing installed, it is very important for the consumer to be aware that allowing performance to start may affect his cancellation rights. If it does, the consumer will be bound by the contract.

(c) Cancellation periods

The period during which cancellation can occur is dependent upon whether the supplier has provided the information required under regulation 8. In practice, prolonging cancellation periods can be a very effective way of encouraging suppliers to provide the requisite information at the correct time. Cancellation periods for goods and services do vary although there is a commonality of approach in setting them. For both goods and services, the cancellation period starts on the day that the contract is concluded.[64] Thereafter, in respect of contracts for goods, the cancellation period expires seven days after the consumer receives the goods on condition that the supplier has complied with the regulation 8 information requirements.[65] However, if the supplier is late in providing the relevant information, but nonetheless does so within three months of the contract being concluded, the cancellation period expires after seven working days beginning with the day after the one on which the consumer received the information.[66] Finally, if the supplier does not supply the requisite information

---

[64] *Ibid.* regs.11(1) and 12(1), respectively.
[65] *Ibid.* reg. 11(2).   [66] *Ibid.* reg. 11(3).

at all, the cancellation period will expire after three months and seven days beginning with the day after which the consumer received the goods.[67]

The cancellation periods for contracts for services are the same as those for goods, when the regulation 8 information was provided either when the contract was concluded or within a period of three months thereafter or, alternatively, was never provided at all.[68] The difference in respect of contracts for services comes when performance of the contract has started, because, at that point, the consumer will have derived some benefit from the contract, which, unlike goods, cannot be returned following cancellation. Once performance has started, it is impossible for the contracting parties to return to the prior status quo. This necessarily places a duty on the consumer to consider his position carefully before allowing performance of the contract to start. It is, of course, possible for performance to begin before the supplier has provided the relevant regulation 8 information, so the consumer should be wary. Regulation 12(3A) of the 2000 Regulations covers the situation where performance has started with the consent of the consumer within seven working days starting with the day after the one on which the contract was concluded and the supplier has provided the regulation 8 information in good time during performance, though not necessarily before performance started. In that situation, the cancellation period expires after seven working days beginning the day after the consumer receives the information or, alternatively, if the performance finishes before that period has expired, then on the day that the performance is completed.

The right to cancel a contract for goods or services brings with it other rights and obligations. The supplier must reimburse any money that he has received under the contract[69] together with any part-exchange goods,[70] while the consumer is under a duty to take care of any goods that he has received under the contract and return them to the supplier.[71] Further, cancellation of the contract will also bring about the automatic cancellation of any related credit agreement,[72] with regulation 16 of the 2000 Regulations stipulating the method for concluding the financial arrangements.

The Directive underpinning these Regulations[73] has been replaced along with three other Directives with the passage of the Consumer Rights Directive.[74] This Directive will introduce maximum harmonisation provisions for distance contracts[75] and hence it is hoped will promote cross-border trading, particularly via the Internet.

---

[67] *Ibid.* reg. 11(4).   [68] *Ibid.* reg. 12(2), (3) and (4).   [69] *Ibid.* reg. 14
[70] *Ibid.* reg. 18(1). If, however, the supplier cannot return the part-exchange goods because he no longer has them, he must pay the consumer a sum equal to the part-exchange allowance. This would be a typical situation in respect of cars provided in part-exchange, as the supplier is likely to dispose of the part-exchange vehicle through the trade very soon after receiving it.
[71] *Ibid.* reg. 17.   [72] *Ibid.* reg. 15.
[73] Directive 97/7/EC on the protection of consumers in respect of distance contracts.
[74] See above n. 3.
[75] As opposed to the minimum harmonisation provisions that exist currently.

Q5 Review the cancellation provisions of the Consumer Protection (Distance Selling) Regulations 2000 and analyse whether they achieve an appropriate balance between the protection of the consumer and the rights of the trader.

5 Recommended reading

Butler, M. and Darnley, A. 'Consumer acquis: proposed reform of B2C regulation to promote cross-border trading' (2007) *Computer and Telecommunications Law Review* 109

Chissick, M. and Kelman, A. *Electronic Commerce Law and Practice* (3rd edn, Sweet & Maxwell, London, 2002)

Department for Business, Enterprise and Regulatory Reform *Consultation on EU Proposals for a Consumer Rights Directive* (London, 2008)

Dobson, P. and Stokes, R. *Commercial Law* (7th edn, Sweet and Maxwell, London, 2008)

Hall, E. 'Cancellation rights in distance-selling contracts for services: exemptions and consumer protection' (2007) *Journal of Business Law* 683

Harrington, J. 'Information society services: what they are and how relevant is the definition?' (2001) *Journal of Business Law* 190

Lodder, A.R., and Kaspersen, H.W.K. (eds.) *eDirectives: Guide to the European Union Law on E-Commerce* (Kluwer Law International, London, 2002)

Kono, T., Paulus, C.G., and Rajak, H. (eds.) *Selected Legal Issues of E-Commerce* (Kluwer Law International, The Hague, 2002)

Howells, G. and Weatherill, S., *Consumer Protection Law* (2nd edn, Ashgate Publishing Ltd, Aldershot, 2005)

Singleton, S. *eCommerce: A Practical Guide to the Law* (Gower Publishing Ltd, Aldershot, 2003)

'Proposed Consumer Rights Directive' (2008) 31 *Consumer Law Today* 10(8)

'Proposed changes to distance-selling rules' (2009) *Consumer Law Today* (Feb.) 8

'Proposed new EU laws: Consumer Rights Directive' (2008) 16 *IT Law Today*, 10(1)

Warner, J. 'The new E.C. Regulations' (2002) *Company Lawyer* 313

Distance selling divides into two parts, traditional distance selling via magazines, advertising, etc., and the increasing market of selling via the Internet. The book edited by Lodder and Kaspersen and the one by Singleton provide a good discussion of controls over e-commerce.

Part 3
International Trade and Sales

Introduction

Part 3 deals with the issues relating to international trade and sales. Every day, many business people rely on the certainty of the laws and rules relating to international trade to govern their obligations, provide remedies and resolve disputes.

Chapter 1 deals with the relevance of standard trade terms in international contracts. Trade terms such as CIF and FOB will be examined along with the relevance of INCOTERMS. These terms, which have developed through practice and customs have been recognised and given legal effect by the English courts. They have served a useful purpose over the years as they reflect the intent of the parties and help to determine the rights and obligations of the buyer and seller, as well as rules relating to the passing of property and risk.

Chapter 2 examines the role of the UN Convention on Contracts for the International Sale of Goods 1980 (CISG). This Convention has been widely used and recognised by many countries, including important trading nations such as the United States, China and most of the European Union. The CISG has been hailed as a success in that it strives to achieve a balance between the interests of the buyer and seller in sale of goods transactions. This chapter will examine the scope of the Convention, the obligations of the parties as well as the available remedies.

Chapter 3 looks at the various methods of payment available to the parties to finance international trade. As these transactions usually involve large sums of money with parties unknown to each other, located in different countries, rules governing the method of payment and other aspects of these transactions are essential. This chapter looks at the rules surrounding letters of credit as well as other means of payment such as factoring and forfaiting.

Chapter 4 examines the importance of carriage of goods by sea in international trade. We examine various types of contracts of affreightment such as charterparties and bills of lading. Legislative instruments such as the Hague-Visby Rules, which have been incorporated in the United Kingdom through the Carriage of Goods by Sea Act 1971, will be discussed. This chapter also looks at the role of freight in sea carriage and the emergence of electronic bills.

Part 3 Chapter 1

Standard Trade Terms

Contents

1 Introduction

Standard trade terms have long been used by tradesmen to establish the duties of the buyer and seller. This chapter will examine two of the main standard trade terms in use in international trade, mainly CIF (cost, insurance, freight) and FOB (free on board). We will also examine variants of these terms, as well as the relevance of INCOTERMS, a series of commercial terms developed and published by the International Chamber of Commerce (ICC), which are widely used in international commercial transactions. First published in 1936, the latest set of these rules was published in 2010.

2 CIF contracts

As stated above, CIF contracts have long been part of the mainstream of international sales transactions. In *Ross T Smyth & Co. Ltd* v. *TD Bailey, Son & Co. Ltd*[1] Lord Wright summarises the characteristics of a CIF contract as follows:

> the price is to include cost, insurance and freight. It is a type of contract which is more widely and more frequently in use than any other contract used for purposes of seaborne commerce. An enormous number of transactions, in value

---

[1] [1940] 3 All ER 60.

amounting to untold sums, are carried out every year under cif contracts. The essential characteristics of this contract have often been described. The seller has to ship or acquire after that shipment the contract goods, as to which if unascertained he is generally required to give a notice of appropriation. On or after shipment he has to obtain proper bills of lading and proper policies of insurance. He fulfils his contract by transferring the bills of lading and the policies to the buyer. As a general rule he does so only against payment of the price, less the freight, which the buyer has to pay. In the invoice which accompanies the tender of the documents on the 'prompt', that is, the date fixed for payment, the freight is deducted for this reason. In this course of business the general property in the goods remains in the seller until he transfers the bills of lading.[2]

(a) What is a CIF contract?

In a CIF contract the seller will quote the buyer the contractual price; this price will include the cost of the goods, the cost of insuring the goods, as well as the cost of freight for the carriage of the goods. The CIF contract will be most suitable for buyers and sellers who are located in different countries, where the buyer may not have any agents or brokers to act on his behalf. The seller will bear the risk of any fluctuations in the market rate of insurance or transport once he has entered into the contract of sale with the buyer. The buyer will pay the contractual price against tender of the documents. The CIF contract will state the port of destination, for example 'CIF Antwerp', however the seller in a CIF contract is not guaranteeing the physical arrival of the goods to the named port. Rather, the seller's duties are to procure the goods, arrange the contract of affreightment as well as the contract of insurance, and tender these documents to the buyer. Thus, the documents represent the buyer's interests in the goods.

CIF contracts usually involve more than one buyer and seller in a string sale; in many cases the goods are bought and sold while they are afloat. As stated by Scrutton J in *Arnold Karberg & Co. v. Blythe, Green Jourdain & Co.*:[3]

> It is not a contract that goods shall arrive, but a contract to ship goods complying with the contract of sale, to obtain, unless the contract otherwise provides, the ordinary contract of carriage to the place of destination and the ordinary contract of insurance of the goods on that voyage, and to tender these documents against payment of the contract price.[4]

(b) Sale of documents

The CIF contract is often described as a sale of documents rather than a sale of goods. While this may be true to some extent, the obligation to deliver the goods still remains in the contract of sale. As Lord Wright in *Ross T Smyth & Co. Ltd* v. *T D Bailey, Son & Co.*[5] stated:

---

[2] *Ibid.* 68.   [3] [1915] 2 KB 379.
[4] *Ibid.* 388.   [5] [1940] 3 All ER 60, 70.

one peculiarity of the cif contract … is that the sale can be completed after the loss of the goods by the transfer of the shipping documents. That does not mean that a cif contract is a sale of documents, and not of goods. It contemplates the transfer of actual goods in the normal course, but, if the goods are lost, the insurance policy and bill of lading contract – that is, the rights under them – are taken to be, in a business sense, the equivalent of the goods.

Perhaps the most practical approach is to consider the buyer's obligation under a CIF contract as twofold: first, he has an obligation to pay against the tender of documents which conform to the contract, and secondly, he has the obligation to take delivery of the goods if they conform to the contractual description.

(c) Duties of the seller

The duties of the seller under a classic CIF contract were best summarised by Lord Atkinson in *Johnson* v. *Taylor Bros & Co. Ltd*:[6]

> First, to make out an invoice of the goods sold. Second, to ship at the port of shipment goods of the description contained in the contract. Third, to procure a contract of affreightment under which the goods will be delivered at the port contemplated by the contract. Fourth, to arrange for an insurance upon the terms current in the trade which will be available for the benefit of the buyer. Fifthly, with all reasonable despatch to send forward and tender to the buyer these shipping documents, namely, the invoice, bill of lading and policy of assurance, delivery of which to the buyer is symbolical of delivery of the goods purchased, placing the same at the buyer's risk and entitling the seller to payment of the price.[7]

The seller's first obligation in relation to procuring the necessary documents is in relation to the invoice. The invoice should contain information relating to the contractual price of the goods, the insurance premiums paid, as well as the cost of freight credited to the buyer.

The seller is also responsible for procuring the bill of lading as this will allow the goods to be bought and sold during transit.[8] It is essential that goods are shipped in good order and condition so that the master of the ship can issue a clean bill of lading. The buyer, in most cases, will only be willing to pay against a clean bill of lading; a clean bill will also be required by the bank before a letter of credit will be opened.[9] The bill of lading must be issued to cover the whole of the voyage[10] as well as having the correct date of shipment. Failure to do so entitles the buyer to reject such documents as non-conforming. In *James Finlay & Co. Ltd* v. *Kwik Hoo Tong HM*,[11] the CIF contract stated that shipment was to take place in September, and the bill of lading inaccurately stated

---

[6] [1920] AC 144.   [7] *Ibid.* 155–6.

[8] Must be a 'to order' bill to make it negotiable. See Part 3 Chapter 4 for a more in depth discussion.

[9] See Part 3 Chapter 3 for further discussion.

[10] *Hansson* v. *Hamel & Horley Ltd* [1922] 2 AC 36.

[11] [1929] 1 KB 400.

that the shipment did indeed take place in September. However, some time later the bills were rejected by sub-buyers after the inaccuracy was discovered. The buyer was awarded damages for his loss of the right to reject the non-conforming documents. It some cases, the parties may substitute a delivery order for the bill of lading, for example, where the goods are shipped in bulk and need to be apportioned. Such substitution will not result in the contract no longer being on CIF terms. In *Comptoir d'Achat et de Vente du Boerenbond Belge S/A* v. *Luis de Ridder Ltda (The Julia)*[12] it was stated by Lord Porter:

> The strict form of c.i.f. contract may, however, be modified: a provision that a delivery order may be substituted for a bill of lading or a certificate of insurance for a policy would not, I think, make the contract concluded upon something other than cif terms, but in deciding whether it comes within that category or not all the permutations and combinations of provision and circumstance must be taken into consideration.[13]

The seller is also under a duty to procure a contract of insurance for the goods. The insurance should be appropriate cover against the risks for the length of the voyage as well as the type of goods. In most cases the contract of sale will contain clauses as to the nature of the insurance policy, for example, whether the policy should cover all risks as embodied in the Institute Cargo Clauses A. Failure on the part of the seller to obtain a suitable contract of insurance will be a breach of his obligations under the contract and he will be liable for any loss or damage that occurs. Unless the contract states otherwise, it is the policy itself that must be tendered to the buyer and not merely a certificate of insurance.[14]

It is generally accepted in international sales that where export licences are necessary in order to ship the goods, this will be the responsibility of the seller while import licences are the responsibility of the buyer.[15] In the absence of any express contractual stipulations, the seller is only required to take reasonable steps to procure the licence.[16]

The seller may have additional documents to procure under the terms of the contract. For example, it is common for the buyer to ask for a certificate of quality that guarantees the goods are of a specific class or grade. However, the statements given in a certificate of quality are not to be confused with the order in which the goods were shipped. In *Cremer* v. *General Carriers SA (The Dona Mari)*,[17] Kerr J stated:

> Generally speaking, if a contract contains distinct provisions relating respectively to quality and to condition, then the parties will be taken to have intended to draw a distinction between those two characteristics. That is so in the present

---

[12] [1949] AC 293.   [13] *Ibid.* 309.

[14] *Diamond Alkali Export Corp.* v. *Fl Bourgeois* [1921] 3 KB 443.

[15] *Mitchell Cotts and Co. (Middle East Ltd)* v. *Hairco Ltd* [1943] 2 All ER 552.

[16] *Anglo-Russian Merchant Traders Ltd* v. *Batt* [1917] 2 KB 679.

[17] [1974] 1 All ER 1.

case, with the added factor that the provision relating to quality also contains a conclusive evidence provision by stipulating that a certificate as to quality is to be final. It must therefore be construed restrictively so that full effect must be given to the incorporation of [the clause] which provides distinctly and expressly that shipment is to be made in good condition.[18]

In some cases the buyer may demand that the seller procure a certificate of origin; this may be required if there are prohibitions in place in the buyer's country which may prevent import of goods from certain countries.

(d) Tender of documents

The seller is under a duty to tender the documents, namely the invoice, insurance policy and bill of lading, in addition to any other documentation required by the contract as soon as he is able to do so. If there is a time for tender stipulated in the contract the seller must comply with this time limit. Failure to do so gives the buyer the right to reject the late documents. If the seller tenders non-complying documents and there is still time left to run, he may retender the documents before the date of tender has passed.[19] In the absence of any expressed time the seller must take all reasonable steps to tender the documents as soon as possible. In *Sanders* v. *Maclean*,[20] Brett MR stated:

> The stipulations which are inferred in mercantile contracts are always that the party will do what is mercantilely reasonable. What, then, is the contract duty which is to be imposed by implication on the seller of goods at sea with regard to the bill of lading? I quite agree that he has no right to keep the bill of lading in his pocket, and when it is said that he should do what is reasonable it is obvious the reasonable thing is that he should make every reasonable exertion to send forward the bill of lading as soon as possible after he has destined the cargo to the particular vendee or consignee. If that be so, the question of whether he has used such reasonable exertion will depend upon the particular circumstances of each case. If there is a perishable cargo or one upon which heavy charges must surely be incurred, the reasonable thing for him to do is to make even a greater exertion than he would in the case of another cargo. That is one of the circumstances which has to be considered. Another circumstance would be from whence is the shipment? How near is the consignor to the ship so as to enable him to get possession of the bill of lading?[21]

(e) Passing of property

There are two main rules in relation to the passing of property in a CIF contract. If the goods shipped are specific or ascertained goods, section 17(1) of the Sale of Goods Act 1979 provides:

---

[18] *Ibid.* 14.
[19] *Borrowman, Phillips & Co.* v. *Free and Hollis* (1878) 4 QBD 500.
[20] (1883) 11 QBD 327.   [21] *Ibid.* 337.

(1) Where there is a contract for the sale of specific or ascertained goods the property in them is transferred to the buyer at such time as the parties to the contract intend it to be transferred.

In such a case property will therefore pass when the parties intend it to pass, which will be determined from the terms of the contract as well as the surrounding circumstances. However, in most CIF contracts, the type of goods shipped will not be specific goods. Section 18(5) of the 1979 Act provides that in the case of unascertained goods, property will not pass until the goods have been unconditionally appropriated to the contract. Under section 19, the seller may reserve the right of disposal over the goods until certain conditions have been met, which can include payment by the buyer. In *Re Wait*,[22] the seller sold 500 ton of wheat to the buyers, however, before the documents were tendered but after the buyers had paid for the goods, the seller was declared bankrupt. The buyers claimed ownership of the goods but it was held that as their 500 tonnes of wheat was in an unidentified portion of the bulk, no property had passed.

In a CIF contract if the goods have been ascertained[23] there are several different stages at which property in the goods can pass.

First, property may pass on shipment of the goods; however, if the seller retains the bill of lading in his own name, property will not pass. As stated earlier, the seller may choose to reserve the right of disposal until he has secured payment for the goods. Some *dicta* indicate that property may pass on shipment; for example, in *Biddell Bros* v. *E Clemens Horst Co.*,[24] Kennedy LJ stated:

> the property in the goods has passed to the purchaser, either conditionally or unconditionally. It passes conditionally where the bill of lading for the goods, for the purpose of better securing payment of the price, is made out in favour of the vendor or his agent or representative … It passes unconditionally where the bill of lading is made out in favour of the purchaser or his agent or representative, as consignee.[25]

However, it is unlikely that property will pass on shipment in most CIF contracts as the seller would have no security over the goods in the event the buyer fails to make payment.

The second stage at which property could pass is when the documents are tendered to the buyer for payment. This is the most common method in CIF contracts; the documents represent a conditional ownership of the goods by the buyer, but if the goods arrive and are found to be physically non-conforming then the buyer can reject the goods.[26]

However, these situations concern ascertained goods. As stated above, most goods will be shipped in bulk and property will not pass until they are

---

[22] [1927] 1 Ch. 606.   [23] Sale of Goods Act 1979, s.16.
[24] [1911] 1 KB 934.   [25] *Ibid.* 959.
[26] *Kwei Tek Chao* v. *British Traders & Shippers Ltd* [1954] 2 QB 459

unconditionally appropriated to the contract. This approach has led to unfair results, as seen in *Re Wait* (above), and to alleviate this harsh approach the Sale of Goods (Amendment) Act 1995 inserted sections 20A and 20B in the Sales of Goods Act 1979. These provisions allow the buyer to become tenant in common, in proportion to the quantity paid, in an unidentified bulk.

(f) Passing of risk

Section 20 of the Sale of Goods Act 1979 provides that risk will pass when property is transferred to the buyer. However, in a CIF contract risk passes on shipment, whereas property is usually transferred to the buyer at a later stage, i.e., payment against the documents or when goods are ascertained. In *Biddell Bros v. E. Clemens Horst Co.*,[27] Kennedy LJ stated:

> Two further legal results arise out of the shipment. The goods are at the risk of the purchaser, against which he has protected himself by the stipulation in his cif contract that the vendor shall, at his own cost, provide him with a proper policy of marine insurance intended to protect the buyer's interest, and available for his use, if the goods should be lost in transit.

Thus, where the goods are sold while afloat, the risk passes to the buyer retrospectively. If the goods are lost or damaged at the time they are sold this does not prevent the buyer from accepting the documents; he can recover his losses either from the contract of carriage or the policy of insurance. In *Manbre Saccharine Co. Ltd* v. *Corn Products Co. Ltd.*[28] it was stated by McCardie J:

> If the vendor fulfils his contract by shipping the appropriate goods in the appropriate manner under a proper contract of carriage, and if he also obtains the proper documents for tender to the purchaser, I am unable to see how the rights or duties of either party are affected by the loss of ship or goods, or by knowledge of such loss by the vendor, prior to actual tender of the documents. If the ship be lost prior to tender but without the knowledge of the seller it was, I assume, always clear that he could make an effective proffer of the documents to the buyer. In my opinion, it is also clear that he can make an effective tender even though he possess at the time of tender actual knowledge of the loss of the ship or goods. For the purchaser in case of loss will get the documents he bargained for; and if the policy be that required by the contract, and if the loss be covered thereby, he will secure the insurance monies. The contingency of loss is within and not outside the contemplation of the parties to a cif contract.[29]

However, if the cause of loss is not covered by an exception or the policy of insurance the buyer will bear the losses.[30]

---

[27] [1911] 1 KB 934, 937.   [28] [1919] 1 KB 198.
[29] *Ibid.* 203.   [30] *C. Groom Ltd* v. *Barber* [1915] 1 KB 316.

Q1 What are the basic duties of a seller under a CIF contract? Explain in light of the decision in The Julia.

Q2 How are risks allocated under a CIF contract? Does this approach favour one party to the contract?

(g) Seller's remedies

The seller is afforded a number of remedies under the Sale of Goods Act 1979. This applies to both CIF and FOB contracts. Section 49 provides that the seller can bring an action for the price where property has passed to the buyer and the buyer refuses to make payment for the goods.

Section 50 of the 1979 Act provides the seller the right to claim for damages for non-acceptance of the goods:

(1) Where the buyer wrongfully neglects or refuses to accept and pay for the goods, the seller may maintain an action against him for damages for non-acceptance.

(2) The measure of damages is the estimated loss directly and naturally resulting, in the ordinary course of events, from the buyer's breach of contract.

(3) Where there is an available market for the goods in question the measure of damages is *prima facie* to be ascertained by the difference between the contract price and the market or current price at the time or times when the goods ought to have been accepted or (if no time was fixed for acceptance) at the time of the refusal to accept.

The seller may also exercise a lien over the goods under section 41 of the 1979 Act, however the goods must be in his possession to do so. Section 44 gives the seller the right to stop the goods in transit, however he may only do so if the buyer is insolvent and the goods are still in transit.

(h) Duties of the buyer

It is the duty of the buyer under a CIF contract to make payment against the tender of documents. The buyer must pay the price if the documents are conforming to the contract and cannot delay payment until he has examined the goods. If the buyer knows that the goods are not in conformity with the contract, the general rule is that he must nevertheless pay against documents if they are conforming. The buyer must make payment in accordance with the terms of the contract. Failure to do so may give the seller the right to reject performance, for example, the buyer may be under an obligation to open a letter of credit in favour of the seller.[31]

The buyer is also under an obligation to take delivery of the goods. He has the right to inspect the goods on arrival and may reject them if he can prove that

---

[31] See Part 3 Chapter 3 for further discussion.

the goods did not conform when they were shipped by the seller. Alternatively, if the loss or damage was caused after the time of shipment the buyer must look either to the carrier or to his insurance to claim damages.

(i) Buyer's remedies

The buyer's right of rejection under a CIF contract is twofold. First, he may reject the documents if they do not conform to the contract, for example, a wrongly dated bill of lading. However if the documents on their face conform to the contract, he must accept them even if he suspects the goods may be non-conforming. If the goods on arrival are indeed found to be non-conforming the buyer can then reject the goods. However, the right to reject the goods can only apply if the buyer accepts the documents. In *Kwei Tek Chao* v. *British Traders & Shippers Ltd*,[32] Devlin J stated:

> there is a right to reject documents, and a right to reject goods, and the two things are quite distinct. A cif contract puts a number of obligations upon the seller, some of which are in relation to the goods and some of which are in relation to the documents. So far as the goods are concerned, he must put on board at the port of shipment goods in conformity with the contract description, but he must also send forward documents, and those documents must comply with the contract. If he commits a breach the breaches may in one sense overlap, in that they flow from the same act. If there is a late shipment, as there was in this case, the date of the shipment being part of the description of the goods, the seller has not put on board goods which conform to the contract description, and therefore he has broken that obligation. He has also made it impossible to send forward a bill of lading which at once conforms with the contract and states accurately the date of shipment. Thus the same act can cause two breaches of two independent obligations.[33]

Under section 51 of the Sale of Goods Act 1979, the buyer may claim damages in respect of non-delivery by the seller, under both CIF and FOB contracts. Where there is an available market for the goods in question, the measure of damages is *prima facie* to be ascertained by the difference between the contract price and the market or current price of the goods at the time or times when they ought to have been delivered or (if no time was fixed) at the time of the refusal to deliver.[34]

Section 53 of the 1979 Act gives the buyer the right to claim damages in respect of any breaches of warranty by the seller. In the case of breach of warranty of quality, such loss is *prima facie* the difference between the value of the goods at the time of delivery to the buyer and the value they would have had if they had fulfilled the warranty.[35]

---

[32] [1954] 2 QB 459.   [33] *Ibid.* 481.
[34] Sale of Goods Act 1979, s.51(3).   [35] *Ibid.* s.53(3).

**Q3 *The right of rejection under a CIF contract is 'separate and successive'.
Explain in light of the case law.***

(j) CIF and INCOTERMS 2010

INCOTERMS 2010 came into force on 1 January 2011 and contain some modifications on the definition of CIF found in English law.

CIF under INCOTERMS requires that the seller deliver the goods on board the vessel or procures goods which have already been delivered. The risk of loss or damage to the goods passes when the goods are placed on board the vessel. The seller must arrange for and pay the costs and freight necessary to bring the goods to the port of destination. The seller will also arrange for insurance cover against the buyer's risk of loss or damage to the goods during the carriage. The seller is required to obtain insurance only on minimum cover. If the buyer wishes to have greater insurance protection, it will have to be expressly provided for in the contract or the buyer will have to make his own insurance arrangements.

The CIF trade terms should only be used when goods are transported by sea or inland waterway. The terms should not be used where there is any other form of transport involved in the carriage. The documents which the seller and buyer are required to provide may be supplied electronically 'if agreed between the parties or customary'.

3 FOB contracts

FOB trade terms are one of the oldest trade terms used in both domestic as well as international trade, with their origins dating back almost 200 years. Unlike CIF contracts, which are primarily used in sea carriage, FOB is used to cover all types of transport. FOB is commonly used where the buyer requires a certain type of ship and it is convenient to nominate or charter his own ship. FOB is often described as a 'flexible' instrument, however its core principles remain the same; the seller at his expense places the goods on board the vessel for delivery to the buyer, and property and risk will pass at this stage.[36] The price paid to the seller will include all expenses up to the loading of the goods on board the ship nominated by the buyer, while from there on all expenses will be the buyer's responsibility. In *Pyrene Co. Ltd* v. *Scindia Steam Navigation Co. Ltd*,[37] Devlin J attempted to set out the various types of FOB contracts. This is summarised by Donaldson J in *The El Amria and The El Minia*:[38]

> In the first, or classic type, the buyer nominates the ship and the seller puts the goods on board for account of the buyer, procuring a bill of lading. The seller is then a party to the contract of carriage and if he has taken the bill of lading to his

---

[36] Usually described as 'over the ship's rail'.
[37] [1954] 2 QB 402.   [38] [1982] 2 Lloyd's Rep. 28.

order, the only contract of carriage to which the buyer can become a party is that contained in or evidenced by the bill of lading which is endorsed to him by the seller. The second is a variant of the first, in that the seller arranges for the ship to come on the berth, but the legal incidents are the same. The third is where the seller puts the goods on board, takes a mate's receipt and gives this to the buyer or his agent who then takes a bill of lading. In this latter type the buyer is a party to the contract of carriage *ab initio*.[39]

Q4 What are the various types of FOB contracts? Why is a FOB contract described as a 'flexible instrument'?

(a) Duties of the seller

In a classic FOB contract, the seller arranges for the goods to be put on board the vessel and procures a bill of lading. The seller may act as the buyer's agent if he enters into the contract of affreightment. Under a FOB 'with additional services' the seller nominates the vessel and enters into the contract of affreightment as principal; he may also be asked to arrange for insurance. In a 'strict' FOB contract the buyer or his agent nominates the vessel and enters into the contract of carriage with the ship-owner. The seller loads the goods on board and collects mate's receipts from the vessel and gives them to the buyer or his agent, who obtains a bill of lading from the master in exchange for the receipts.[40]

Section 13 of the Sale of Goods Act 1979 places an obligation on the seller that the goods must correspond to their contractual description. This obligation extends to the packaging of the goods.[41] The buyer may reject the goods on arrival if they are found to be non-conforming.

The seller must ship the goods from the port of loading specified in the contract. Failure to ship from the specified port is a breach of condition that entitles the buyer to terminate the contract. In *Peter Turnbull & Co.* v. *Mundas Trading Co.*[42] the contract called for shipment 'FOB Sydney', however the sellers contended that they could not ship from Sydney and sought to substitute Melbourne instead. The buyer refused, and the sellers were held liable for failing to ship from the stipulated port of shipment.

The seller is also under a duty to deliver the goods by putting them on board the ship at his expense, within the stipulated period for shipment. Any failure to do so will amount to a repudiatory breach. The courts tend to treat this obligation as strict.[43]

---

[39] *Ibid.* 32.
[40] *President of India* v. *Metcalfe Shipping Line* [1970] 1 QB 289.
[41] *George Wills & Sons Ltd* v. *Thomas Brown & Sons* (1922) 12 Ll. L Rep. 292.
[42] [1954] 2 Lloyd's Rep. 198.
[43] *All Russian Cooperative Society Ltd* v. *Benjamin Smith* (1923) 14 Ll. L Rep. 351.

Similarly to CIF contracts, it is the seller who procures the necessary export licences.[44] The seller is also under an obligation to give the buyer all the necessary documentation for him to take control of the goods; this is usually satisfied by a mate's receipt that the goods have been put on board the vessel. Under section 28 of the Sale of Goods Act 1979, which provides '[U]nless otherwise agreed, delivery of the goods and payment of the price are concurrent conditions, that is to say, the seller must be ready and willing to give possession of the goods to the buyer in exchange for the price and the buyer must be ready and willing to pay the price in exchange for possession of the goods', the seller would be entitled to demand payment when the documents are given to the buyer.

(b) Duties of the buyer

Under a classic FOB contract it is the buyer's duty to nominate a port of shipment. This can be a specific port or a range of ports, however the buyer must inform the seller of his choice in time for the seller to load the goods. If there is a date stipulated in the contract for making a nomination, failure to do so amounts to a breach of a condition precedent to the seller's duty to load.[45]

The buyer is also under a duty to book shipping space or to charter a vessel for the carriage of the goods. He must do so with sufficient time for the seller to load the goods. Failure to do so may result in the buyer bearing the costs of warehouse charges. However, if the seller delivers the goods too early for loading and they deteriorate the buyer will not be liable.[46]

The buyer is permitted to substitute another vessel if the first nomination is no longer suitable, as long as it still gives the seller enough time to load the goods in accordance with the contract.[47]

Finally the buyer is under a duty to pay for the goods in accordance with the terms of the contract. He must do so at the time and place stipulated, usually when goods are loaded on board, however the seller may retain the bill of lading until payment is made.

Q5 What are the seller's responsibilities under a FOB contract? What are the buyer's corresponding duties?

(c) Passing of property

Property under a FOB contract will most commonly pass when the goods are placed on board the vessel.[48] However, if the seller has reserved the right of disposal under section 19 of the Sale of Goods Act 1979, by retaining the bill of

---

[44] *AV Pound & Co. Ltd* v. *MW Hardy* [1956] AC 588.
[45] *Gill & Duffus* v. *Societe pour l' Exportation* [1985] 1 Lloyd's Rep. 621.
[46] *Cunningham* v. *Munro* (1922) 28 Com. Cas. 42.
[47] *Agricultores Federados Argentinos* v. *Ampro SA* [1965] 2 Lloyd's Rep. 290.
[48] *Carlos Federspiel* v. *Charles Twigg* [1957] 1 Lloyd's Rep. 240.

lading in his own name, then property will pass at a later stage, normally against payment of the goods. Goods, if shipped in bulk, must be ascertained for the purposes of section 16 of the 1979 Act before property will pass.

(d) Passing of risk

In a FOB contract, risk will pass on shipment even if property may not have passed at the same time. In *Stock* v. *Inglis*,[49] a cargo of sugar was shipped 'FOB Hamburg', however the bags were not appropriated to the contract; when the ship and goods were lost it was held that the cargo was at the risk of the buyer even though property had not passed.

Q6 In what circumstances can the FOB buyer substitute a nominated ship?

(e) FOB and INCOTERMS 2010

Under INCOTERMS 2010, FOB is varied from its meaning under English law. Although the seller is not under an obligation to the buyer to make a contract of carriage, INCOTERMS provide that if requested by the buyer or if it is commercial practice and the buyer does not give any contrary instructions, the seller 'may' arrange for carriage of the goods on the usual terms; this will be at the buyer's risk and expense. If the seller declines to perform this duty he must notify the buyer.

There is no obligation for the seller to arrange for insurance of the goods, however he must provide any information that the buyer needs to obtain insurance.

The seller is under a duty to pack the goods; the cost of any pre-shipment inspection required before export can take place will be at the seller's expense. Delivery will consist of placing the goods on board the vessel as opposed to 'over the ship's rail'; risk will pass at this time as well.

4 Ex Works

The trade term 'Ex Works' places the least amount of responsibility on the seller, with the buyer performing most of the duties under the contract. When a contract is made subject to the term 'Ex Works', the place of delivery is usually the seller's place of business. It is the buyer's duty to collect the goods from the seller's premises on the date of delivery. The buyer will bear the cost of transporting the goods to their destination as well as the risk of any loss or damage. The seller is usually not required to load the goods for transport, however parties are free to make any express contractual stipulations to this effect.

---

[49] (1884) 12 QBD 564.

5 FAS contracts

FAS (free alongside ship) is similar to FOB with the exception that the goods are delivered when they are placed alongside the ship. The seller must provide the goods and the documents, in conformity with the contract of sale. The seller must obtain at his own expense any export licences necessary to facilitate shipment. The buyer is under an obligation to name a port of shipment and to nominate a vessel. He must take delivery of the goods and pay the contract price. Once delivery is made alongside the vessel, risk will pass to the buyer.

6 Conclusion

As we can see, standard trade terms fulfil a useful function in international trade. They set out the obligations of the buyer and seller as well as determining when risk and property will pass. Parties to the contract can choose to incorporate INCOTERMS to provide a set definition of their obligations under the contract. Courts will give effect to these trade terms if the parties make an express stipulation to that effect.

7 Recommended reading

Atiyah, P.S., Adams, J. and MacQueen, A. *The Sale of Goods* (11th edn, Pearson Education Ltd, Harlow, 2005)

Bridge, M. *The International Sale of Goods* (Oxford University Press, 2007)

Evans, P. 'FOB and CIF contracts' (1993) *ALJ* 844

Gower, S., 'FOB contracts' (1955) 19 *MLR* 417

Ramberg, J. *Guide to INCOTERMS 1990* (ICC, 1991)

Sassoon, D.M. 'Application of FOB and CIF sales in common law countries' (1981) *ETL* 50

Treitel, G.H. 'Rights of rejection under CIF sales' (1984) *LMCLQ* 565

Part 3 Chapter 2

The Vienna Convention on the International Sale of Goods 1980 (CISG)

Contents

1 Introduction and background

Due to the effects of increased trade amongst states in the late twentieth century, the need for a harmonised instrument of international sales law was expressed. It was envisaged that a harmonising measure would increase international trade, promote fairness and reduce the negotiation cost of transactions.

In 1929, Ernst Rabel working with the International Institute for the Unification of Private Law (UNIDROIT), sought to establish a uniform law governing transactions of sale. This resulted in two Hague Conventions in 1964: the Uniform Law for the International Sale of Goods (ULIS), and the Uniform Law on the Formation of Contracts for the International Sale of Goods (ULF). These Conventions came into force in 1972, but they had limited success as uniform law, because they were generally considered too wide-ranging in scope and thought to favour industrialised nations. They were therefore only ratified by nine countries, predominately European nations.

The failure of these Conventions led to the recognition that more effort was needed to create a uniform sales law that could be applied in all states regardless of their legal, social or economic backgrounds. In 1966, the General Assembly of the United Nations established the United Nations Commission on International Trade Law (UNCITRAL). This working group sought to review ULIS and ULF in order to create a new Convention, and the result of their efforts were completed in 1978. The UN Convention on Contracts for the International Sale of Goods (CISG) was signed in Vienna in 1980, and came into force in 1988 upon gaining the required number of ratifications. As of 1 August 2011, UNCITRAL reports that seventy-seven states have adopted the CISG.[1]

2 Structure and scope

When the Convention is ratified by a Contracting State, this results in the CISG taking precedence over domestic law and choice of law rules with regard to international sale of goods. The CISG has 101 Articles and is divided into four principal parts. Part I deals with the Convention's scope and contains general provisions applicable to the rest of the Convention. Part II is concerned with rules for the formation of contracts of sale, and Part III with the rules governing the seller's and buyer's substantive obligations. Part IV contains the final provisions on adherence to and ratification of the Convention by Contracting States, including the reservations that may be made at one of several stages to the Convention's applicability to a Contracting State.

Under Article 1(1)(a), the Convention applies to contracts of sale of goods between parties whose places of business are in different states. The CISG will also apply when the rules of private international law lead to the application of the law of a Contracting State.[2]

It is important to note that the CISG is a set of rules for business not consumer transactions. In addition to this, certain types of contracts are specifically excluded under the Convention.[3] Questions involving the validity of the contract are also outside the Convention, as is the effect which the contract may have on property in the goods sold,[4] and any liability of the seller for defective goods causing death or personal injury to any person.[5] One of the notable features of the Convention is that it allows contracting parties the ability to derogate from[6] or exclude its provisions altogether.[7]

Q1 Describe the scope and purpose of the CISG. When will it apply?

(a) Trade usages

CISG, Article 9 addresses the relevance of trade usages under the Convention. It provides:

> (1) The parties are bound by any usage to which they have agreed and by any practices which they have established between themselves.

---

[1] See www.uncitral.org/uncitral/en/uncitral_texts/sale_goods/1980CISG_status.html.
[2] CISG, Art. 1(1)(b).
[3] *Ibid.* Art. 2 provides that contracts involving the sale of securities, ships, vessels, hovercraft or aircraft, and electricity are not governed by the Convention.
[4] *Ibid.* Art. 4.   [5] *Ibid.* Art. 5.
[6] Under CISG, Art. 6 derogation under the Convention is permitted, with the one exception of CISG, Art. 12.
[7] *Ibid.*

(2) The parties are considered, unless otherwise agreed, to have impliedly made applicable to their contract or its formation a usage of which the parties knew or ought to have known and which in international trade is widely known to, and regularly observed by, parties to contracts of the type involved in the particular trade concerned.

Usages have long been a part of the *lex mercatoria*, and are commonly made up of uncodified customs and general principles of commercial law. International trade usages gain normative force though their use by parties who believe it falls within their obligations to follow the meaning attached to the usage. Throughout the course of history, usages have played an important role in trade, for example, the 'law merchant' system used customs and practice to protect the expectations of parties. Under the law merchant system, merchants from a particular mercantile community would employ a set of principles and regulations which were customary practice to resolve disputes. However, when this system was superseded by the common law, the role of usages declined and tradesmen sought to use their own dispute mechanisms instead of those used by the courts.

CISG, Article 9(1) refers to those usages which the parties have agreed; this can include actions and types of behaviour and can exist even though they are not widely known in international trade. Therefore, under the provisions of Article 9(1), local, regional and national usages will be applicable in accordance with the party's agreement. However, these patterns of conduct can only be established as 'practices' when they have been carried out over a certain length of time and have resulted in a number of contracts. In a case involving a Swiss seller and an Italian buyer for the sale of white urea, the courts held that the seller's contention that there was an established practice between the parties under which the buyer was bound to pay at the seller's bank was unfounded. In the court's decision it stated that, under Article 9(1), two previous contractual relationships were not sufficient to establish a practice between the parties.[8]

CISG, Article 9(2) concerns usages which the parties have impliedly made applicable to their contract. These usages can be invoked in two different ways. The first is when the parties knew or ought to have known of the usage in question, and the second is when the usage is one which is widely in international trade and is widely known to, and regularly observed by, parties to contracts of the type involved in the particular trade concerned. In *Libyan Arab Foreign Bank* v. *Bankers Trust Co.*[9] the plaintiffs kept a Eurodollar call account in a London branch of the defendant's bank and a demand account in an American branch of the defendant's bank. The US government imposed a freeze order on all Libyan property in the United States. When the plaintiffs called for their money, the defendants tried to argue that it was a usage of the Eurodollar deposit market that transfers from outside the United States in US currency

[8] Civil Court, Basel, 3 December 1997.   [9] [1989] QB 728.

could only be made through a CHIPS or Fedwire system which was located in New York and therefore they could not process the order because of the government ban. However, this argument failed on the grounds that while it may have been regular practice in this market for Eurodollars to be transferred through either of these two systems, this did not amount to a usage as it was not the only option available to the plaintiff.

Therefore, the usage must be one which is regularly observed in the type of trade the parties are involved in; the usage must be regularly observed in the relevant type of contract for that trade, and the usage must be one which is widely known in international trade. It will be for the party who is alleging that the usage exists to prove that it meets the burden of proof set out in Article 9(2). In a case heard by the German Appellate Court, it was decided that the buyer had not proved that an international trade usage existed under which silence in response to a commercial letter of confirmation was sufficient for the contract to be concluded.[10]

Q2 What is the position of the CISG on trade usage? When will a usage be implied?

(b) Interpretation

CISG, Article 7 provides:

> (1) In the interpretation of this Convention, regard is to be had to its international character and to the need to promote uniformity in its application and the observance of good faith in international trade.
> (2) Questions concerning matters governed by this Convention which are not expressly settled in it are to be settled in conformity with the general principles on which it is based or, in the absence of such principles, in conformity with the law applicable by virtue of the rules of private international law.

CISG, Article 7(1) requires regard to be had to:

(a) the Convention's international character;
(b) the need to promote uniformity in its application; and
(c) the observance of good faith in international trade.

The solution to the problem of filling in any gaps which may be evident in the Convention was provided for in Article 7(2), which creates a hierarchical system for judges and arbitrators to adhere to. In order to resolve gaps in matters governed by the Convention but not expressly settled in it, one must first look to its internal principles, and only when this method is exhausted can external principles, such as laws applicable by virtue of private international law, be looked to as a last resort.

---

[10] Appellate Court, Dresden, 9 July 1998.

Given the language in Article 7(1) regarding how interpretation should be carried out, judges should as far as possible abstain from resorting to a domestic definition of a provision or term which could be in conflict with the CISG. Instead, decision-makers should strive to keep in mind the purpose for which the Convention came into existence, thus any deviation from its 'international character' would undermine its legitimacy. One example of a court using domestic concepts to interpret the CISG can be seen in *Beijing Metals* v. *American Business Center*,[11] in which it was stated *obiter* that the parole evidence rule would apply even if that case was governed by the CISG.[12] No further explanation or analysis is given as to why this conclusion was reached by the court even though a contrary decision was reached in an earlier case.[13]

The Convention stresses the need to promote uniformity when interpreting its provisions. The Preamble to the Convention raises the issue of uniformity as one of its aims is stated to be that, 'the adoption of uniform rules which govern contracts for the international sale of goods and take into account the different social, economic and legal systems would contribute to the removal of legal barriers in international trade and promote the development of international trade'.

The treatment of the concept of 'good faith' in the Convention is a reflection of the tension amongst countries of varying social, legal and economic backgrounds. The extent to which commercial law should emulate and uphold standards of morality is a subject of much debate. The reconciling of morality with the law has been approached in opposing ways by civil and common law systems. The common law contingent appears to have 'won' from the fact that in the CISG good faith was not imposed as a legal obligation on contracting parties. Instead, good faith was shifted to the interpretation of the Convention, which requires that the observance of good faith in international trade be taken into account.

Q3 Critically analyse the role of good faith in the CISG. How does this concept lead to uncertainty?

(c) Obligations of the seller

CISG, Article 30 provides:

> The seller must deliver the goods, hand over any documents relating to them and transfer the property in the goods, as required by the contract and this Convention.

---

[11] US Federal Appellate Court (5th Circuit), 15 June 1993.

[12] This case, whilst cited in *MCC-Marble Ceramic Center* v. *Ceramica Nuova D'Agostino*, US Federal Appellate Court (11th Circuit), 29 June 1998, was not followed and instead *Filanto SpA* v. *Chilewich International Corp.* below n. 13 was confirmed as the correct decision with regard to the parole evidence question.

[13] *Filanto SpA* v. *Chilewich International Corp.* US Federal District Court (New York), 14 April 1992.

The seller may also be required to perform additional duties to complete his contractual obligations, for example, the seller's duty to hand over the goods could be qualified by the use of trade terms such as INCOTERMS.[14] The seller is also responsible for handing over documents to the buyer; the Convention is silent as to the nature of these documents, however they can include transport documents, quality certificates as well as insurance policies.

CISG, Article 34 sets out the seller's obligations in relation to the documents:

> If the seller is bound to hand over documents relating to the goods, he must hand them over at the time and place and in the form required by the contract. If the seller has handed over documents before that time, he may, up to that time, cure any lack of conformity in the documents, if the exercise of this right does not cause the buyer unreasonable inconvenience or unreasonable expense. However, the buyer retains any right to claim damages as provided for in this Convention.

While the seller is bound to hand over documents relating to the goods he is not bound to arrange for them to be issued, unless expressly stated in the contract or implied by trade usage. The Convention does not cover matters relating to the property in the goods and such matters are left to be decided by the rules of private international law.

CISG, Article 31 deals with the obligation to deliver:

> If the seller is not bound to deliver the goods at any other particular place, his obligation to deliver consists:
> (a) if the contract of sale involves carriage of the goods – in handing the goods over to the first carrier for transmission to the buyer;
> (b) if, in cases not within the preceding subparagraph, the contract relates to specific goods, or unidentified goods to be drawn from a specific stock or to be manufactured or produced, and at the time of the conclusion of the contract the parties knew that the goods were at, or were to be manufactured or produced at, a particular place – in placing the goods at the buyer's disposal at that place;
> (c) in other cases – in placing the goods at the buyer's disposal at the place where the seller had his place of business at the time of the conclusion of the contract.

CISG, Article 31 addresses three different situations in which different rules apply. If the contract involves carriage of the goods, delivery obligations are fulfilled when the goods are handed over to the first carrier. In a case involving a Swiss buyer and an Italian seller for the supply of art books which were to be sold at an exhibition, in order to have the catalogues available on time, the seller commissioned a forwarding company which guaranteed timely delivery of the goods. Nevertheless, the catalogues arrived too late. The court held that pursuant to CISG, Article 31, the seller was only obliged to arrange for transport, i.e., to hand the goods over to the first carrier to have them transmitted to the buyer. Therefore the seller had duly performed his obligations and was not liable for

---

[14] *Laborall* v. *Matis* Appellate Court, Paris, 4 March 1998.

the carrier's lateness in delivery.[15] If the conditions of Article 31(b) are met, the seller is required to place the goods at the buyer's disposal at the particular place the goods are produced.[16] Where Article 31(c) applies, the seller must put the goods at the buyer's disposal at the place where the seller had his place of business when the contract was concluded.

Q4 What are the seller's obligations with respect to documents?

CISG, Article 35(1) deals with conformity of the goods. It provides that the seller is required to deliver goods that are of the quantity, quality and description prescribed in the contract, and that any breach of these duties represents a breach of contract. Except where the parties have agreed otherwise, goods do not conform to the contract if they are not fit for ordinary use, or for the particular use by the buyer which the seller knew or should have known of; or do not conform to samples; or finally are not properly packaged in a manner usual for such goods.

Q5 Discuss the CISG's requirement as to the conformity of the goods. Does this provide equal protection to the buyer and seller?

(d) Obligations of the buyer

CISG, Article 53 provides:

> The buyer must pay the price for the goods and take delivery of them as required by the contract and this Convention.

The buyer has two main obligations under the Convention, namely, to take delivery of the goods and pay the price for the goods. The latter part of the wording of this provision would indicate that the party's intentions and express stipulations in the contract will prevail over the Convention. This would be consistent with the provisions of CISG, Article 6, which allow for party autonomy and derogation under the Convention. The contract may stipulate other duties which the buyer must perform, which may include such things as supplying the seller with contractual specifications for goods being produced.

Under CISG, Article 60:

> The buyer's obligation to take delivery consists:
> (a) in doing all the acts which could reasonably be expected of him in order to enable the seller to make delivery; and
> (b) in taking over the goods.

---

[15] *Art Books* case, Commercial Court, Zürich, 10 February 1999.
[16] *Electronic Hearing Aid* case, District Court, Aachen, 14 May 1993.

The buyer is expected to co-operate with the seller to ensure delivery of the goods; this could mean, for example, letting the seller enter the buyer's premises to deliver the goods. Article 60(b) provides that the buyer has to take over the goods when they are delivered by the seller. In a case involving a German seller and Italian buyer for the sale of electronic hearing aids, the buyer was liable for damages for breach of contract when he failed to take delivery despite the additional period of time set by the seller for the buyer to take delivery.[17]

The buyer is entitled to reject the goods if the seller makes delivery before the fixed date[18] and if the seller delivers a greater quantity of goods than was stipulated in the contract.[19] The buyer also has the right to reject the goods if the seller commits a fundamental breach of contract.[20]

CISG, Article 38 deals with the buyer's obligation to examine the goods. It provides:

> (1) The buyer must examine the goods, or cause them to be examined, within as short a period as is practicable in the circumstances.
>
> (2) If the contract involves carriage of the goods, examination may be deferred until after the goods have arrived at their destination.
>
> (3) If the goods are redirected in transit or redispatched by the buyer without a reasonable opportunity for examination by him and at the time of the conclusion of the contract the seller knew or ought to have known of the possibility of such redirection or redispatch, examination may be deferred until after the goods have arrived at the new destination.

Article 38 provides that the buyer must make examination of the goods within a short period of time, however if the contract involves carriage of goods then he can wait until the goods are delivered to their final destination. If the goods are found to be defective, CISG, Article 39 requires the buyer to give notice of the defect to the seller. Under the provision of Article 39(1), the buyer loses the right to rely on a lack of conformity if he does not give notice to the seller specifying the nature of the lack of conformity within a reasonable time after he discovered it or ought to have discovered it. The period for examination of the goods under Article 38 and the period for giving notice under Article 39 must be distinguished and kept separate, even when the facts of the case would permit them to be combined into a single period for giving notice.[21] The CISG Advisory Council suggests that the reasonable time for giving notice after the buyer discovered or ought to have discovered the lack of conformity will differ depending on the relevant factors. In some cases, notice should be given within a few days; in other cases, a longer time-frame may be suitable. No fixed period should be regarded as reasonable without taking into consideration the

---

[17] *Ibid.*   [18] CISG, Art. 52(1).

[19] *Ibid.* Art. 52(2).   [20] *Ibid.* Art. 25.

[21] CISG Advisory Council, 'Examination of the Goods and Notice of Non-Conformity Articles 38 and 39 Opinion No. 2', available at www.cisg.law.pace.edu/cisg/CISG-AC-op2.html.

circumstances of the case. These can include the nature of the goods, the nature of the defect, the situation of the parties and relevant trade usages. Article 39(2) specifies that, in any event, the buyer must give the seller notice of the lack of conformity within two years of the date on which the goods were actually handed over to the buyer, unless this time limit is inconsistent with a contractual period of guarantee.

Q6 What are the rules as regards the buyer's obligation to pay the price? Where must the buyer make payment?

(e) Passing of risk

CISG, Article 67 deals with the passing of risk. It provides:

(1) If the contract of sale involves carriage of the goods and the seller is not bound to hand them over at a particular place, the risk passes to the buyer when the goods are handed over to the first carrier for transmission to the buyer in accordance with the contract of sale. If the seller is bound to hand the goods over to a carrier at a particular place, the risk does not pass to the buyer until the goods are handed over to the carrier at that place. The fact that the seller is authorized to retain documents controlling the disposition of the goods does not affect the passage of the risk.

(2) Nevertheless, the risk does not pass to the buyer until the goods are clearly identified to the contract, whether by markings on the goods, by shipping documents, by notice given to the buyer or otherwise.

Under the provisions of Article 67, risk passes either when the goods are handed over to the carrier for delivery to the buyer, or if the contract expressly stipulates, at a particular place. Although this rule is in accordance with most other international rules on the passing of risk, the parties can still override this provision by opting for trade usages under CISG, Article 9. Thus, in a case involving a French seller and a German buyer for the sale of frozen chickens, the court held that although the goods were handed over to the carrier for transmission to the buyer, the use of the term 'free delivery'[22] meant that the seller was bound to deliver the goods at the buyer's place of business and concurrently risk would then pass to the buyer.[23] If the seller retains the documents relating to the goods this does not affect the passing of risk.

Article 67(2) requires that the goods be clearly identified to the contract before risk is passed to the buyer. This requirement can be fulfilled by the description of the goods in the shipping documents. CISG, Article 68 deals with

---

[22] The court noted that the term 'free delivery' had to be interpreted under German law, as the seller had used a clause common in German commerce, drafted in German and with a German buyer. The German doctrine and the jurisprudence show that this clause is generally interpreted as a rule dealing with costs as well as with the passing of risks.

[23] *Frozen Chicken* case, Appellate Court, Karlsruhe, 20 November 1992.

goods that are sold while in transit. In this case risk will pass on conclusion of the sale; alternatively, if circumstances indicate, risk could also pass on delivery to the carrier, however the seller is prevented from doing so if he knew that the goods were lost or damaged at the time of contracting.

(f) Remedies

There are a number of remedies available to the parties in the event a breach occurs.

(i) Avoidance

One of the most important remedies available to the buyer and seller is the remedy of avoidance. CISG, Article 64 deals with the seller's right to avoid the contract. It provides:

(1) The seller may declare the contract avoided:

(a) if the failure by the buyer to perform any of his obligations under the contract or this Convention amounts to a fundamental breach of contract; or

(b) if the buyer does not, within the additional period of time fixed by the seller in accordance with paragraph (1) of article 63, perform his obligation to pay the price or take delivery of the goods, or if he declares that he will not do so within the period so fixed.

(2) However, in cases where the buyer has paid the price, the seller loses the right to declare the contract avoided unless he does so:

(a) in respect of late performance by the buyer, before the seller has become aware that performance has been rendered; or

(b) in respect of any breach other than late performance by the buyer, within a reasonable time:

(i) after the seller knew or ought to have known of the breach; or

(ii) after the expiration of any additional period of time fixed by the seller in accordance with paragraph (1) of Article 63, or after the buyer has declared that he will not perform his obligations within such an additional period.

The buyer's right of avoidance can be found in CISG, Article 49, which provides:

(1) The buyer may declare the contract avoided:

(a) if the failure by the seller to perform any of his obligations under the contract or this Convention amounts to a fundamental breach of contract; or

(b) in case of non-delivery, if the seller does not deliver the goods within the additional period of time fixed by the buyer in accordance with paragraph (1) of article 47 or declares that he will not deliver within the period so fixed.

(2) However, in cases where the seller has delivered the goods, the buyer loses the right to declare the contract avoided unless he does so:

(a) in respect of late delivery, within a reasonable time after he has become aware that delivery has been made;

(b) in respect of any breach other than late delivery, within a reasonable time:

    (i) after he knew or ought to have known of the breach;

    (ii) after the expiration of any additional period of time fixed by the buyer in accordance with paragraph (1) of article 47, or after the seller has declared that he will not perform his obligations within such an additional period; or

    (iii) after the expiration of any additional period of time indicated by the seller in accordance with paragraph (2) of article 48, or after the buyer has declared that he will not accept performance.

The primary mechanism necessary to trigger avoidance in both provisions is the occurrence of a fundamental breach.[24] CISG, Article 25 defines fundamental breach as follows:

> A breach of contract committed by one of the parties is fundamental if it results in such detriment to the other party as substantially to deprive him of what he is entitled to expect under the contract, unless the party in breach did not foresee and a reasonable person of the same kind in the same circumstances would not have foreseen such a result.

In order for a breach to be 'fundamental', the breach must cause a 'detriment' that substantially deprives the non-breaching party of its expectations. The CISG, however, does not define the term 'detriment'. The purpose of including the requirement of detriment is to exclude those breaches where they may have occurred but caused no harm to the buyer. For example, taking the case of an ante-dated bill of lading, although the seller would be committing a fundamental breach of his obligations, if the breach does not cause the buyer any injury, it can be argued that detriment does not occur. The remedy of avoidance is not suited to minor breaches and it is applied as such by the courts. In a case involving an Italian seller and a German buyer for the sale of shoes,[25] the seller demanded partial payment against the quantity of goods that were delivered even though the quantity was less than contractually agreed. The buyer sought to claim damages for non-performance and the right to suspend payment until delivery of the missing quantity was made. The court held in favour of the seller, the reason being that the buyer had no grounds to avoid the contract,[26] and the partial delivery of goods by the seller in this case did not amount to a fundamental breach within the meaning of Article 49(1)(a).

The test of foreseeability as set out in Article 25 is meant to preclude a fundamental breach where the substantial detriment occurs unforeseeably; it is a mechanism which allows the party in breach to evade avoidance of the contract. Since it is improbable that the party in breach will acknowledge that

---

[24] CISG, Arts. 64(1)(a), 49(1)(a).

[25] Appellate Court, Düsseldorf, 24 April 1997.

[26] This is a right essential to a claim of damages.

they foresaw the detriment in question, the 'reasonable person standard' was established. Thus, where substantial detriment is deemed to exist, the party in breach, in order to escape avoidance, has to show that he did not foresee the negative result, nor would a reasonable person have foreseen it. Foreseeability would also need to be determined within the meaning of CISG, Article 74, as this is the provision dealing with damages, providing that:

> damages may not exceed the loss which the party in breach foresaw or ought to have foreseen at the time of the conclusion of the contract, in the light of the facts and matters of which he then knew or ought to have known, as a possible consequence of the breach of contract.

The burden of proving unforeseeability rests with the party in breach.

Q7 Discuss the problems inherent in the concept of fundamental breach.

Q8 Why is it important to determine when the time of foreseeability should apply?

(ii) Additional time

CISG, Article 47 gives the buyer the right to fix an additional time for performance. It states:

> (1) The buyer may fix an additional period of time of reasonable length for performance by the seller of his obligations.
> (2) Unless the buyer has received notice from the seller that he will not perform within the period so fixed, the buyer may not, during that period, resort to any remedy for breach of contract. However, the buyer is not deprived thereby of any right he may have to claim damages for delay in performance.

The seller has a corresponding right under CISG, Article 63.

CISG, Articles 64(1)(b) and 49(1)(b), respectively, allows the parties to fix an 'additional time' for performance. Under the Convention the parties do not have to fix an additional time; however, given the strict criterion of establishing a fundamental breach, it may be in their best interests to do so. It is important to note that whereas under the CISG's predecessor, the ULIS, the buyer could convert any breach of contract, however minor, into a fundamental breach by allowing an additional time for performance, under the CISG, only in cases of non-delivery or non-payment can the time-fixing mechanism be used to make a non-fundamental breach into a fundamental breach. Under the Convention, the additional time must be determined by indicating a given date or a period of time; this helps to bring certainty with regard to the party's interest in performance of the contract, in addition to a possibility of avoiding the contract. Thus, in order to determine an additional period of reasonable length, considerations such as the extent and the cost of the delay have to be taken into account. In one case, the courts decided that an additional period of two weeks was not suitable for a delivery of three printing machines from Germany to Egypt and an additional period of seven weeks would have been more appropriate.[27]

Articles 64(2) and 49(2) deal with the circumstances under which parties may lose the right to avoid the contract. Paragraph (2)(a) of each Article deals with the issue of late payment or late delivery, respectively. A party must declare the contract avoided within a reasonable time after he has discovered that performance has been rendered; the breach must be a fundamental breach of contract, as in the case where time is of the essence, or a delivery after the additional period set by the other party has expired. For any breach other than late delivery, paragraph (2)(b) of each Article stipulates that avoidance must be carried out within a reasonable time.

(iii) Cure

Under the CISG, the seller has the right to cure any defects in his performance. Article 37 states that the seller has the right to cure defects in the quality or quantity of the goods before the date of delivery. It further stipulates that the seller may, up until the end of an agreed period of time for performance:

> deliver any missing part or make up any deficiency in the quantity of the goods delivered, or deliver goods in replacement of any non-conforming goods delivered or remedy any lack of conformity in the goods delivered, provided that the exercise of this right does not cause the buyer unreasonable inconvenience or unreasonable expense.

The Convention offers no guidance on what is meant by the term 'unreasonable'. However, the expenses incurred by the buyer may not play a role in whether the seller should be allowed to cure any defects in performance. If the buyer can reclaim the expenses under the damages provision in the Convention, then arguably a request to cure should not be unreasonable. It should be noted while it is the seller who bears the expense of curing the defect, and it is for him to decide whether it is worth the expense, he cannot insist that the buyer present the sum of money necessary to cure the defect, up front, then proceed to repay that amount in damages.

Another point worth noting is that under CISG, Article 52(1) the buyer is not required to take delivery of the goods prior to the delivery date. The extent to which refusal of early delivery will be limited by the observance of good faith and trade usages remains to be seen as there are no reported cases on this issue.

CISG, Article 48 contains the more controversial provision on curing defects. This Article addresses the seller's right to cure defects in the quality or quantity of the goods after the date of delivery. It provides:

> (1) Subject to Article 49, the seller may, even after the date for delivery, remedy at his own expense any failure to perform his obligations, if he can do so without unreasonable delay and without causing the buyer unreasonable inconvenience

---

[27] Appellate Court, Celle, 24 May 1995.

or uncertainty of reimbursement by the seller of expenses advanced by the buyer. However, the buyer retains any right to claim damages as provided for in this Convention.

(2) If the seller requests the buyer to make known whether he will accept performance and the buyer does not comply with the request within a reasonable time, the seller may perform within the time indicated in his request. The buyer may not, during that period of time, resort to any remedy which is inconsistent with performance by the seller.

(3) A notice by the seller that he will perform within a specified period of time is assumed to include a request, under the preceding paragraph, that the buyer make known his decision.

(4) A request or notice by the seller under paragraph (2) or (3) of this Article is not effective unless received by the buyer.

Article 48 states that it is subject to Article 49, the buyer's right to avoid the contract. However, in many cases the seller's right to cure prevails over the buyer's right to avoid the contract. Thus, if a replacement can be made without undue delay even after the date for performance has passed there cannot be any substantial detriment to the buyer such as is required to produce a fundamental breach. In one decision of a Swiss court it was held that:

> According to this Article [CISG, Article 25], the condition for a fundamental breach of contract is an especially weighty impairment of the buyer's interest in the performance. Yet, besides the objective weight or importance of a defect, it is decisive of the substantiality of a breach of contract, whether the defect can be removed by subsequent repair or substitute delivery. The UN Sales Law proceeds from the fundamental precedence of preservation of the contract, even in case of an objective fundamental defect. When in doubt, the contract is to be maintained even in case of fundamental defects, and an immediate contract avoidance should stay exceptional. Because, as long as and so far as (even) a fundamental defect can still be removed by remedy or replacement, the fulfilment of the contract by the seller is still possible and the buyer's essential interest in the performance is not yet definitively at risk.[28]

When a seller does not deliver the goods in a timely manner or presents non-conforming goods, Article 48 permits the seller to cure the defective performance if it does not result in unreasonable delay, unreasonable inconvenience or unreasonable uncertainty of reimbursement by the seller of expenses advanced by the buyer. Article 48(2) states that if the seller requests the buyer to communicate whether he will agree to a cure and the buyer does not respond within a reasonable time, the seller may carry out performance within the time-line specified in his request. The buyer cannot, during this time, decide to choose another remedy which would affect performance by the seller. There are numerous circumstances which can hinder or delay the buyer's

---

[28] Commercial Court des Kantons, Aargau, 5 November 2002.

ability to respond to a request to cure defects: for example, it may depend on the nature of the goods in question, or the buyer may need to weigh his options to decide whether curing is advantageous to his situation. Therefore, if the buyer is silent on the issue and this period constitutes an unreasonable amount of time, then the seller's right to cure the defect takes precedence and the buyer cannot resort to any other remedies under the Convention. This can be seen in a decision of a German court where the buyer failed to reply to the seller's request to cure – in this case to make an additional delivery; therefore, the seller was entitled to perform the contract and the buyer could not resort to avoidance.[29] Furthermore, it is worth noting that CISG, Article 50 precludes the buyer from declaring a reduction of price if he refuses to have the defect cured by the seller. This was illustrated in one case where the buyer refused to allow the seller to cure the defect in a delivery of blankets, of which five were missing, and the court held that the buyer was not entitled to a reduction in price in accordance with Article 50.[30]

Q9 Discuss how the seller's right to cure defects in performance may create uncertainty in international trade.

(iv) Specific performance

CISG, Article 46 deals with the buyer's right to demand specific performance of the contractual obligations. It provides:

> (1) The buyer may require performance by the seller of his obligations unless the buyer has resorted to a remedy which is inconsistent with this requirement.
> (2) If the goods do not conform with the contract, the buyer may require delivery of substitute goods only if the lack of conformity constitutes a fundamental breach of contract and a request for substitute goods is made either in conjunction with notice given under Article 39 or within a reasonable time thereafter.
> (3) If the goods do not conform with the contract, the buyer may require the seller to remedy the lack of conformity by repair, unless this is unreasonable having regard to all the circumstances. A request for repair must be made either in conjunction with notice given under Article 39 or within a reasonable time thereafter.

The seller's corresponding right can be found in CISG, Article 62, which provides:

> the seller may require the buyer to pay the price, take delivery or perform his other obligations, unless the seller has resorted to a remedy which is inconsistent with this requirement.

---

[29] Lower Court, Nordhorn, 14 June 1994.
[30] Appellate Court, Koblenz, 31 January 1997.

Both Articles provide that the parties cannot resort to a remedy which would be inconsistent with requiring performance; for example, the parties cannot declare avoidance of the contract nor fix an additional time for performance. Furthermore, CISG, Article 28 states that a court is not bound to order specific performance on behalf of a party, if the court would not do so under its domestic law. As specific performance is not a generally accepted remedy in most common law jurisdictions, this could restrict the availability of this remedy.

(v) Price reduction

As mentioned earlier, CISG, Article 50 permits the buyer to request a reduction in price if the goods do not conform to their contractual quantity, quality and description within the meaning of CISG, Article 35. The buyer may reduce the price in proportion to the reduced value of the goods, however he is prevented from doing so if the seller offers to cure the defects. The buyer must have given notice of the non-conformity within the requirements of CISG, Article 39.

Q10 What is the nature and purpose of the remedy of price reduction?

(vi) Damages

CISG, Article 74 deals with a party's right to claim damages. It provides:

> Damages for breach of contract by one party consist of a sum equal to the loss, including loss of profit, suffered by the other party as a consequence of the breach. Such damages may not exceed the loss which the party in breach foresaw or ought to have foreseen at the time of the conclusion of the contract, in the light of the facts and matters of which he then knew or ought to have known, as a possible consequence of the breach of contract.

Under this provision, the party can claim all losses suffered as a result of the breach, including loss of profits. Recoverability is limited by the requirement of foreseeability at the time the contract was concluded. CISG, Article 78 provides that, '[i]f a party fails to pay the price or any other sum that is in arrears, the other party is entitled to interest on it'.

3 UNIDROIT Principles of International Commercial Contracts

The International Institute for the Unification of Private Law (UNIDROIT) is an independent intergovernmental organisation, whose purpose is to study needs and methods for modernising, harmonising and co-ordinating private and in particular commercial law between states and groups of states. The UNIDROIT Principles were drafted and discussed by legal scholars from different nations, whose opinions did not bear the official representation of any one country. This approach precluded the need to adopt diplomatic solutions in the formulation of rules, and the consequent need to obscure important issues with compromise formulae. Thus, the unequal bargaining conditions that may exist in international treaties between parties with different levels of education and technical skills were not present in the drafting of UNIDROIT Principles. The UNIDROIT Principles set out rules for international commercial contracts and will be applicable when parties have agreed that their contract be governed by them. The Principles may also apply when parties have decided their contract should be governed by general principles of law such as the *lex mercatoria*, or alternatively have not chosen a law to govern the contract.

4 Conclusion

The CISG has proved to be one of the most successful international Conventions of its kind. The Convention offers parties a useful compromise in that it may decrease the time and legal costs otherwise involved in research of foreign laws, and it will have a degree of familiarity to both parties, thus putting each on an equal footing with the other with no unfair advantage to either party. Other 'soft law' instruments, such as the UNIDROIT Principles, are often times used as a means of supplementing the provisions of the CISG. It is more advantageous to use the UNIDROIT Principles as a means of 'gap filling' instead of domestic law if the international character, uniformity and good faith of the Convention are to be protected. In using the UNIDROIT Principles, the settlement of the dispute is kept within its international legal habitat, and ensures fairness to the parties as they will both have equal access to its provisions.

5 Recommended reading

Babiak, A. 'Defining fundamental breach under the United Nations Convention on Contracts for the International Sale of Goods' (1992) 6 *Temple Int'l and Comp. LJ* 113

Bailey, J. 'Facing the truth: seeing the Convention on Contracts for the International Sale of Goods as an obstacle to a Uniform Law of International Sales' (1999) 32 *Cornell International Law Journal* 273

Bianca, C.M. and Bonell, M.J. (eds.) *Commentary on the International Sales Law: the 1980 Vienna Sales Convention* (Giuffre, Milan, 1987)

Dimatteo, L. 'The CISG and the presumption of enforceability: unintended contractual liability in international business dealings' (1997) 22 *Yale Journal of International Law* 111

Farnsworth, A. 'The Eason-Weinmann Colloquim on International and Comparative Law: duties of good faith and fair dealing under the UNIDROIT principles, relevant international Conventions, and national laws' (1995) 3 *Tulane Journal of International and Comparative Law* 54

Lee, R. 'The UN Convention on Contracts for the International Sale of Goods: OK for the UK?' (1993) 37 *Journal of Business Law* 131

Murray, J. 'An essay on the formation of contracts and related matters under the United Nations Convention on Contracts for the International Sale of Goods' (1988) 8 *Journal of Law and Commerce* 11

Schlechtriem, P. *Commentary on the UN Convention on the International Sale of Goods (CISG)* (2nd edn, Clarendon Press, Oxford, 1998)

Van Alstine, M. 'Dynamic treaty interpretation' (1998) 146 *University of Pennsylvania Law Review* 687

Part 3 Chapter 3

Payment in International Sales

Contents

1 Introduction and background

The role of payment in international trade is complicated by many factors. International trade, particularly sales of goods transactions, often involve long periods of transit, multiple buyers and sellers who are unfamiliar to each other, different currencies and different laws. For these reasons the method of payment chosen by the parties will be crucial to the contract of sale. As many sellers will require payment to procure the goods from suppliers and arrange for transport of the goods, the buyer's creditworthiness will be necessary to ensure the seller is paid for his goods and services. This chapter will examine some of the most common methods of payment in international transactions, each having inherent risks as well as benefits to the parties. In particular, we will be examining payment by open account, bills of exchange, documentary collections, letters of credit, factoring and forfaiting.

2 Open account

Open account as a means of payment in international trade is usually seen where the buyer and seller have done business in the past and may continue to do so on a frequent basis. This particular method of payment carries with it a very high risk to the exporter as he will usually ship the goods in advance of payment. The buyer will usually pay the seller within thirty days of receiving the goods. Open accounts benefit the importer enormously as he is able to obtain the goods without restricting his cash flow. It is recommended that the exporter only use this method of payment when he is certain of the creditworthiness of the buyer. It does offer some benefit to the exporter as he will be able to increase his ability to stay competitive in the market. The exporter can protect himself from non-payment by the buyer if he takes out export credit insurance.

3 Bills of exchange

In English law, a bill of exchange is defined by the Bills of Exchange Act 1882 as an unconditional order in writing addressed by one person to another, signed by the person giving it, requiring the person to whom it is addressed to pay on demand or at a fixed or determinable future time a certain sum in money to or to the order of a specified person, or to the bearer.[1] The person who draws the bill is referred to as 'the drawer'. He gives the order to pay money to the third party. The party upon whom the bill is drawn is called 'the drawee'. He is the person to whom the bill is addressed and who is ordered to pay the amount stated in the bill. A bill of exchange, sometimes referred to as a draft, is a negotiable instrument whereby it is transferable on delivery to the transferee and the transferee can enforce the bill in his own right. If transferred in good faith for value it will be without defects to the transferee. In *Crouch* v. *Credit Foncier of England*,[2] it is stated in the judgment of Blackburn J:

> It may therefore be laid down as a safe rule that where an instrument is by the custom of trade transferable, like cash, by delivery, and is also capable of being sued upon by the person holding it *pro tempore*, then it is entitled to the name of a negotiable instrument, and the property in it passes to a bona fide transferee for value, though the transfer may not have taken place in market overt.[3]

The bill of exchange offers a benefit to the seller as it is treated as having the same effect as being paid in cash. However, if the buyer chooses to dishonour the bill and not pay upon presentation the seller may be liable for the sums owed to the holder of the bill. In *Jade International Steel Stahl und Eisen GmbH & Co. KG* v. *Robert Nicholas (Steels) Ltd.*[4] the bill of exchange was indorsed by the plaintiff and discounted to their bank in Germany, which then transferred the bill through another bank to the Midland Bank. It was accepted by the defendant buyers, but dishonoured on presentation for payment. It was stated in the judgment of Donaldson J:

> The bill was for payment in the future, and the plaintiffs indorsed the bill to their bankers in order to obtain cash … the only reason why the plaintiffs have the

---

[1] Bills of Exchange Act 1882, s.3(1).   [2] (1873) LR 8 QB 374.
[3] *Ibid.* 381.   [4] [1978] QB 917.

bill in their possession is because of the activities ... of the defendants thereafter in dishonouring the bill. The bankers have taken advantage of their rights of compulsory recovery against the plaintiffs to place the bill in the hands of the plaintiffs and debit the plaintiffs' account. The plaintiffs stand in the shoes of the banks, each of which have the undoubted right not only to judgment but also to immediate payment against the defendants without the possibility of being met by any set off or counterclaim.[5]

The United Nations Convention on International Bills of Exchange and International Promissory Notes was adopted in 1988.[6] The aim of the Convention is to harmonise the approach taken to bills of exchange. Article 1(1) stipulates that the Convention will apply when the heading and text of the bill contain the words 'International bill of exchange (UNCITRAL Convention)'. The Convention is not yet in force as actions taken by ten states are required for it to take effect. Accordingly, most transactions are governed by domestic laws.

Q1 Discuss payment options such as open accounts and bills of exchange. Is there an unfair advantage to one party in these transactions?

4 Documentary collections

A documentary collection is a method of payment where the seller's bank takes collection of the payment on his behalf. The seller's bank will send the documents relating to the goods and instructions for payment to the buyer's bank. The bank will issue a draft upon which the buyer may pay either on sight of the documents or on a future date. The draft will stipulate the documents necessary for transfer of title of the goods. The banks therefore facilitate the exchange process of the payment and title of the goods. Although this process is somewhat similar to a letter of credit, it is much more straight-forward and less expensive. However, there are no verification mechanisms for the documents nor is there any security against non-payment.

The Uniform Rules for Collections (URC) is the internationally recognised codification of rules unifying banking practice regarding collection operations for drafts and for documentary collections. These rules have been developed and revised by the International Chamber of Commerce (ICC). The latest version of the rules was published in 1995.[7]

5 Introduction to letters of credit

Letters of credit are one of the most important mechanisms in international payments. We will examine the different types, functions and rules relating

[5] *Ibid.* 921.
[6] See www.uncitral.org/uncitral/en/uncitral_texts/payments/1988Convention_bills_status.html.
[7] ICC Brochure No. 522 (ICC, 1995).

to letters of credit. Historically, letters of credit or documentary credits have served a useful purpose in international trade and have been referred to as 'the life blood of international commerce'.[8] With a vast amount of trade being conducted by parties in different countries, in many cases where the buyer and seller are unknown to each other, letters of credit allow the parties an essential element of security in the payment of the contractual price. Letters of credit also serve a useful purpose when one party does not possess adequate financial history, assets or credit to support good faith credit terms.

(a) Law governing letters of credit

There are no specific laws governing the letter of credit transaction in international trade. However, the rules developed by the ICC on the Uniform Customs and Practice of Documentary Credits (UCP) have been the closest step towards a unified approach on letters of credits. First issued in 1933 to deal with the problems encountered by conflicting laws in different countries, the UCP rules have met with limited success. Nevertheless, the latest revision of the rules, the UCP 600, which was approved by the ICC Banking Commission and came into effect in 2007, has met with widespread approval by many in the international banking community. The UCP rules are supplemented by the ICC International Standard Banking Practice (ISBP) for the Examination of Documents under Documentary Credits. The ISBP sets out various procedures for document checkers to consult when examining the documents presented under letters of credit; the latest version was published in 2007 to coincide with the UCP 600. The UCP 600, which consists of thirty-nine articles, offers significant improvements over its predecessor, the UCP 500.[9] Whereas the UCP 500 was criticised as being too ambiguous, the new revised rules contain articles that provide interpretation and definitions of the terms used within.[10]

For example, article 2 of the UCP 500 defined the term 'credit' as 'any arrangement however named or described, whereby the bank (the "Issuing Bank") acts at the request and on the instructions of a customer (the "Applicant") or on its own behalf'. The scope of this definition was very broad and covered all documentary promises to pay. In contrast, the UCP 600, article 2, defines 'credit' as 'any arrangement, however named or described, that is irrevocable and thereby constitutes a definite undertaking of the issuing bank to honour a complying presentation'. Thus, the UCP 600 will only apply to irrevocable letters of credit. The UCP 500, in fact, offered only a definition of the meaning of the term 'credit' in its provisions, while the UCP 600 goes further to eliminate any confusion that was caused by its predecessor in providing definitions for terms such as 'honor', 'negotiation' and 'presentation'. Article 3 of the UCP 600 provides an interpretative function in that it lends greater clarity to commonly

[8] Per Kerr LJ in *Hardbottle (RD) (Mercantile) Ltd* v. *National Westminster Bank Ltd* [1978] QB 146, 155.
[9] Came into effect in 1994.   [10] UCP 600, arts. 2 and 3.

used terms which are often misconstrued. For example, it states 'the expression "on or about" or similar will be interpreted as a stipulation that an event is to occur during a period of five calendar days before until five calendar days after the specified date, both start and end dates included'.[11] The UCP 500 had no counterpart in its provisions.

As mentioned above, even though the UCP rules have received widespread recognition for the useful function they serve in international trade, they are by no means considered part of the *lex mercatoria* or a customary trade usage. Parties have to agree to incorporate the rules into their contracts. UCP 600, Article 1 states that the rules will apply 'when the text of the credit expressly indicates that it is subject to these rules'.

In the absence of parties failing to stipulate the UCP rules or any other laws to govern the letter of credit transaction, the English courts will determine the applicable law by referring to the EEC Convention on the Law Applicable to Contractual Obligations 1980 ('Rome Convention'). The Convention was replaced by Regulation 593/2005 ('Rome I'), which applies to contracts concluded after 17 December 2009. Under these provisions, the letter of credit transaction will be governed by the laws of the country to which it is most closely connected, specifically the country in which the party who is to carry out the performance that is essential to the contract is located. However identifying this location in the letter of credit transaction is not entirely straightforward as there are at least four main parties involved in the transaction: the applicant, the beneficiary, the issuing bank and the advising bank, all of whom may be located in different countries. Thus, it would be prudent of the parties to nominate a set of rules in the event that a dispute should arise. It is important to note that the UCP rules do not address every contingency that may arise, so that issues such as fraud or insolvency in the letter of credit will be governed by the common law.

Q2 How has the UCP 600 improved the law on letters of credit in comparison with its predecessor?

(b) Stages of a letter of credit

There are several stages involved in a letter of credit transaction. A typical documentary letter of credit will operate in the following way: once the buyer has concluded the contract of sale with the seller, the parties will agree that payment is to be made by the opening of a letter of credit. In some cases, the seller may request that the buyer open the letter of credit before the goods will be shipped. In *Kronos Worldwide Ltd* v. *Sempra Oil Trading SARL*,[12] the buyer, for the supply of oil, was under an obligation to promptly open an irrevocable letter of credit. The issue that arose was whether the laytime for loading the goods should begin

---

[11] *Ibid.* art. 3.   [12] [2003] 1 Lloyd's Rep. 567.

to run after the opening of the letter of credit. It was stated in the judgment that the opening of the letter of credit could in some circumstances be viewed as a condition precedent to the seller's obligation to load the cargo; however, this would depend on the wording of the contract.[13]

The next step in the process is that the buyer (the 'applicant') will request his bank (the 'issuing bank') to open a letter of credit in favour of the seller (the 'beneficiary'). The buyer will stipulate the documents required; these can include invoices, insurance policies and transport documents. The UCP 600 makes provisions for a wide range of transport documents, such as multimodal transport,[14] bills of lading,[15] non-negotiable sea waybills[16] and charterparty bills of lading.[17]

The issuing bank, in order to fulfil this request, sends the letter of credit details to the seller's bank (the 'advising bank'). The advising bank endorses the letter of credit and sends the beneficiary (seller) the details. The seller examines the details of the letter of credit to make sure that they are correct. If needed, the seller will contact the buyer and ask for the necessary amendments to be made. Once the seller is satisfied with the conditions of the letter of credit, the goods are shipped and the seller presents the documents to the advising bank. The advising bank examines the documents against the details on the letter of credit and, if applicable, the UCP 600 rules or any other governing laws. If the documents are in order, the advising bank will send them to the issuing bank for payment. If the details are not correct, the advising bank informs the seller and waits for the documents to be corrected. The issuing bank examines the documents from the advising bank and, if they are in order, pays the amount as promised. If the details are not correct, the issuing bank contacts the buyer for authorisation to pay or accept the documents. If acceptable, the issuing bank releases the documents to the buyer, and makes payment as agreed. The buyer receives the documents from the issuing bank and collects the goods. The seller receives the payment through the advising bank. The advising bank notifies the seller that payment has been made.

It is perhaps most helpful to view the letter of credit process as three separate obligations. The first obligation is found in the contract for the sale of goods, which sets out the responsibilities of the buyer and seller. The second obligation is between the buyer (applicant) and his chosen bank (issuing bank), whereby the bank agrees to ensure the creditworthiness of the buyer. The final obligation is found in the letter of credit itself, in which the issuing bank promises to pay the seller the contractual sum upon tendering of documents.

(c) Characteristics of letters of credit

There are two main characteristics that define letters of credit: first, the principle of autonomy, and secondly the doctrine of strict compliance.

---

[13] *Ibid.* 568.   [14] UCP 600, art. 19.
[15] *Ibid.* art. 20.   [16] *Ibid.* art. 21.   [17] *Ibid.* art. 22.

(i) Principle of autonomy

One of the doctrines upon which letters of credit are built is the principle of autonomy. This means that the responsibility on the part of the issuing bank to pay the seller under the terms and conditions of the letter of credit is a separate obligation and is entirely severed from the contract of sale between the buyer and seller. Therefore, the issuing bank *must* honour the payment under the letter of credit irrespective of any problems or disputes that arise under the contractual transaction for the sale of goods, the only exception to this rule being where fraud can be proven.[18] This principle is embodied in articles 4 and 5 of the UCP 600, which emphasise that the banks are in no way concerned or bound by the underlying sales contract.[19] An example of this principle can be seen in *Hamzeh Malas & Sons* v. *British Imex Industries Ltd*,[20] where it was stated:

> We have been referred to a number of authorities, and it seems to be plain enough that the opening of a confirmed letter of credit constitutes a bargain between the banker and the vendor of the goods, which imposes upon the banker an absolute obligation to pay, irrespective of any dispute there may be between the parties as to whether the goods are up to contract or not.[21]

It is often the case that buyers will try to halt the payment from the issuing bank once they are aware that the goods do not conform to the contract; this is usually in the form of an injunction. However, the courts are reluctant to grant such injunctions as this would undermine the function of the letter of credit in international trade. In *Discount Records Ltd* v. *Barclays Bank Ltd*,[22] the plaintiffs were purchasers of a consignment of records and cassettes. Although the documents tendered were in conformity with the contract, some of the boxes delivered were empty or only partially filled, while others were filled only with rubbish. The buyers' attempt to restrain the bank from paying the seller by asking for an injunction was refused by the courts. Megarry J stated that:

> I would be slow to interfere with bankers' irrevocable credits, and not least in the sphere of international banking, unless a sufficiently grave cause is shown;

---

[18] David C. Howard, 'The Application of Compulsory Joinder, Intervention, Impleader and Attachment to Letter of Credit Litigation' (1984) 52 *Fordham Law Review* 957.

[19] Article 4: 'Credits v. Contracts: (a) A credit by its nature is a separate transaction from the sale or other contract on which it may be based. Banks are in no way concerned with or bound by such contract, even if any reference whatsoever to it is included in the credit. Consequently, the undertaking of a bank to honour, to negotiate or to fulfil any other obligation under the credit is not subject to claims or defences by the applicant resulting from its relationships with the issuing bank or the beneficiary. A beneficiary can in no case avail itself of the contractual relationships existing between banks or between the applicant and the issuing bank. (b) An issuing bank should discourage any attempt by the applicant to include, as an integral part of the credit, copies of the underlying contract, proforma invoice and the like.' Article 5: 'Documents v. Goods/Services/Performances. Banks deal with documents and not with goods, services or performance to which the documents may relate.'

[20] [1958] 2 QB 127.   [21] *Ibid.* 129.

[22] [1975] 1 Lloyd's Rep. 444.

for interventions by the Court that are too ready or too frequent might gravely impair the reliance which, quite properly, is placed on such credits.[23]

Q3 Explain why the courts are reluctant to interfere with the letter of credit mechanism. Does this leave the innocent party without a remedy?

(ii) Principle of strict compliance

The second principle that the letter of credit system is based on, and arguably the most important, is the principle of strict compliance. The rules governing this principle state that if the seller wishes to be paid under the letter of credit transaction, then documents that comply with the letter of credit must be tendered. Similar to the principle of autonomy as presented above, once documents which on their face conform to the terms and conditions of the letter of credit are tendered then the issuing bank must honour their obligation to pay. This rule is strict in the sense that presentation of documents which almost conform will not be sufficient to justify payment. If the issuing bank chooses to pay under these circumstances, it does so at its own risk and may not be reimbursed by the buyer.

While the rules of strict compliance are not explicitly mentioned in the UCP 600,[24] the principle has for many years been embodied in judicial decisions, both in the English courts and in the United States. This is illustrated, for example, in cases such as *Equitable Trust* v. *Dawson Partners*,[25] where Lord Sumner stated that, 'there is no room for documents which are almost the same or which will do just as well'. This was supported by the decision in *Fidelity National Bank* v. *Dade County*,[26] in which it was held that '[c]ompliance with the terms of a letter of credit is not like pitching horseshoes. No points are awarded for being close.'

The UCP 600 provides in article 14(a) that:

> A nominated bank acting on its nomination, a confirming bank, if any, and the issuing bank must examine a presentation to determine, on the basis of the documents alone, whether or not the documents appear on their face to constitute a complying presentation.

In *Seaconsar Far East* v. *Bank Markazi Jomhouri Islami Iran*,[27] it was held that the bank was correct in rejecting the non-conforming documents even though the discrepancy in question was trivial. The reasoning behind this strict approach is evident, as banks do not have expertise in the goods, rather they are concerned with the aspect of finance.[28] In *J.H. Rayner and Co. Ltd* v. *Hambros Bank Ltd*,[29] the description of the goods in the letter of credit stated

---

[23] *Ibid.* 448.   [24] UCP 600, art. 14(b).
[25] (1927) 27 Ll. L Rep. 49, 52.   [26] 371 So. 2d 545, 546 (1979).
[27] [1993] 1 Lloyd's Rep. 236.   [28] This is supported by UCP 600, art. 5.
[29] [1943] 1 KB 37.

'Coromandel groundnuts', whereas the bill of lading referred to the goods as 'machine-shelled kernels'. Although the two terms have the same meaning in the trade, the bank rejected the documents as being non-conforming. In his judgment Mackinnon LJ stated:

> The words in that bill of lading clearly are not the same as those required by the letter of credit … The bank, if they had accepted that proposition, would have done so at their own risk. I think on pure principle that the bank were entitled to refuse this sight draft on the ground that the documents tendered, the bill of lading in particular, did not comply precisely with the terms of the letter of credit which they have issued.[30]

However, this does not mean the document will be deemed non-conforming if it fails to dot every 'i' or cross every 't' or contains obvious typographical errors. This can be seen in *Hing Yip Fat Co.* v. *Diawa Bank Ltd*,[31] where it was held that the use of the word 'industrial' rather than 'industries' on a letter of credit application was an obvious typographical error. Also, in *New Braunfels National Bank* v. *Odiorne*,[32] it was held that strict compliance can mean something other than absolute or perfect compliance. Therefore, the courts will have to decide whether the typographical error in question has the potential to have severe repercussions for the transaction.

The letter of credit process is very technical and there are many things that can potentially go wrong. Indeed, in commercial reality the letter of credit process can be revised many times before it is deemed to be in conformity with the documents identifying the contractual terms. In a study undertaken in the United Kingdom by the Midland Bank and SITPRO[33] in the mid 1980s, the amount of letter of credit transactions that failed upon first presentation of documents was staggering.[34] Out of 1,143 presentations, 51.4 per cent failed to meet the strict compliance standard, however most were accepted upon retender.[35] Furthermore, 23.7 per cent of those that failed were due to discrepancies in transport documentation. In other studies carried out in countries such as Hong Kong and Australia, the failure rate was as high as 90 per cent in some cases.[36] These numbers have not decreased; in a more recent study undertaken it was found that documents did not conform to the letter of credit 73 per cent of the time.[37] Some experts have asserted that courts should apply a legal test rather than a commercial one when examining non-conforming documents; specifically they should inquire whether there is a substantial, and more to the point a *real* discrepancy.[38] The strictness of this rule has been somewhat

---

[30] *Ibid.* 40.   [31] [1991] 2 HKLR 35.   [32] 780 SW 2d 313 (1989).

[33] The Simplification of International Trade Procedures Board.

[34] Clive M. Schmitthoff 'Discrepancy of documents in letter of credit transactions' in Chia-Jui Cheng (ed.), *Select Essays on International Trade Law* (Kluwer, The Hague, 1988) 431–49.

[35] *Ibid.*   [36] *Ibid.*

[37] Ronald J. Mann, 'The role of letters of credit in payment transactions' (2000) 98 *Michigan Law Review* 2495.

[38] Schmitthoff, above n. 34, at 437.

alleviated by the UCP 600 rules. For example, although article 18(c) states that 'the description of the goods, services or performance in a commercial invoice must correspond with that appearing in the credit', article 14(e) permits that in 'documents other than the commercial invoice, the description of the goods, services or performance, if stated, may be in general terms not conflicting with their description in the credit'. Also, article 30 allows for some tolerance in credit amount, quantity and unit prices. For example, in relation to quantity of the goods, in the absence of the letter of credit stating the quantity by a stipulated number, a tolerance of not more or less than 5 per cent will be permitted.[39]

(d) Fraud exception

As mentioned above, the only exception to the bank's obligation to pay against conforming documents is where fraud is present. However, it is not sufficient that fraud be alleged, rather it must be proven.[40] In *United City Merchants (Investments) Ltd* v. *Royal Bank of Canada*,[41] which concerned a confirmed irrevocable letter of credit, the loading brokers had falsely backdated a bill of lading to reflect an earlier 'shipped on' date. The sellers were unaware of this fraud; however, the bank, on becoming aware of the discrepancy, refused to pay the seller. The court held that if the seller had no knowledge of the fraud he cannot be deprived of payment. Although the aim of public policy is to limit or control instances of fraud, the courts tend to construe the fraud exception narrowly to protect the utility of the letter of credit transaction. The UCP 600 does not expressly deal with the issue of fraud and such matters are left to be determined by the applicable laws of the forum state. However, UCP 600, article 34 states that:

> A bank assumes no liability or responsibility for the form, sufficiency, accuracy, genuineness, falsification or legal effect of any document, or for the general or particular conditions stipulated in a document or superimposed thereon

Thus, the risk of payment for devalued or even worthless documents will remain on the buyer.

Q4 'The UCP 600 fails to provide adequate protection in cases of fraud.' Critically analyse this statement with reference to the case law.

(e) Types of letters of credit

(i) Documentary letters of credit and standby letters of credit

There are two main types of letters of credit, documentary letters of credit and standby letters of credit. Documentary letters of credit are the most common,

---

[39] UCP 600, art. 30(b).
[40] *Discount Records Ltd* v. *Barclays Bank Ltd* [1975] 1 Lloyd's Rep. 444.
[41] [1983] 1 AC 168.

and are used on an individual transaction, order or invoice basis. They generally have specific conditions applied to them, such as being irrevocable by the
buyer and confirmed by the bank. Standby letters of credit are used as a back-up
should the buyer fail to pay the contract price as agreed upon. Thus, a standby
letter of credit allows the buyer to ensure the security of the transaction with
the seller by showing that it can uphold its promise to pay the price. Standby letters of credit are covered by the UCP 600, as well as by the ISP98 International
Standby Practices.

(ii) Revocable letters of credit and irrevocable letters of credit

The UCP 600 defines the term 'credit' as being only that which is irrevocable.[42]
This means that it cannot be altered or withdrawn without the consent of the
parties to the letter of credit transaction. Therefore, once all the terms are complied with the issuing bank gives its assurance to the seller that payment will
be made. Unlike the revised rules, the UCP 500 allowed for credit terms to be
negotiated as revocable, meaning credit could be withdrawn at any time by the
bank without notice to the seller.[43] In *Cape Asbestos Co. Ltd* v. *Lloyds Bank Ltd*,[44]
it was held that in the case of revocable letters of credit, the risk of not being
paid will remain on the seller as the banks have no duty to notify that credit has
been withdrawn.

(iii) Confirmed and unconfirmed letters of credit

A letter of credit may also be confirmed or unconfirmed by the advising bank,
which is usually located in the beneficiary's country. If the letter of credit is
unconfirmed, this means that the advising bank has not given its undertaking
to the seller that it will make payment in the event that the buyer or its bank
should default on payment, rather it has simply verified that the letter of credit
is in conformity with the requirements requested. In contrast, with a confirmed
letter of credit, the advising bank gives an undertaking that if the documents
are conforming then payment will be made. This undertaking will prevail if
the buyer or the issuing bank fails to make payment. This type of credit is commonly used where the buyer is situated in a country that may be politically or
economically unstable, however the cost of opening such a letter of credit will
increase with the risk involved.

(iv) Revolving letters of credit

In cases where the buyer and seller regularly conduct transactions, a revolving
letter of credit may be used. This helps to avoid the time and cost of opening a
new letter of credit for each transaction. A revolving credit operates either on
the basis of 'time' or 'value'. If it is on the basis of time, then once this is used up
it will continue to be renewed until it is revoked. If the credit is made on a value
basis then once the amount has been paid, it will be re-instated.

---

[42] UCP 600, art. 2.   [43] UCP 500, art. 8(a).   [44] (1921) WN 274.

(v) Transferable letters of credit

In a typical letter of credit transaction, the credit will be payable to the seller (the 'beneficiary'). However in some transactions there will be a 'middleman' involved, and the beneficiary may request that credit be made available to this third party. An example of this is where the seller or exporter has purchased the goods from a third-party supplier and will need to use a portion of this credit to repay the supplier.

(vi) Back-to-back letters of credit

An alternative to a transferable letter of credit is a back-to-back letter of credit. In this case, the beneficiary asks that the advising bank issue a second letter of credit to the supplier instead of transferring the original credit. However, most banks refrain from this practice as it involves a higher amount of risk, whereas a transferable letter of credit will not be any higher a risk than was undertaken in the original letter of credit.

(f) Electronic documents

The advancement of technology and modern transport has introduced the need for electronic documents to aid in the efficient running of international transactions. The ICC released the eUCP V1.1 in 2007 to supplement the UCP 600 rules. The eUCP was designed to deal with presentations of electronic documents, either on their own or with corresponding paper documents. An 'electronic record' is defined in article e3(b)(i) as:

(a) data created, generated, sent, communicated, received or stored by electronic means;
(b) that is capable of being authenticated as to the apparent identity of a sender and the apparent source of the data contained in it, and as to whether it has remained complete and unaltered; and
(c) is capable of being examined for compliance with the terms and conditions of the eUCP credit.

This mechanism has been very helpful for business people and banks to provide clarity in a sometimes uncertain 'virtual' marketplace. The eUCP provides helpful guidelines on terms such as 'electronic signature'[45] and determining what is meant by the term 'received'.[46]

6 Factoring

Factoring is one of the oldest methods of financing international trade and offers an alternative option to businesses to finance international transactions.

---

[45] eUCP V1.1, art. e3(b)(ii).   [46] *Ibid.* art. e3(b)(v).

The process of factoring entails the exporting business or creditor assigning the benefit of the sale contract over to a third party. The third party will usually be a financing organisation and is referred to as the 'factor'. The factor will assess the value of the contract and advance a portion of that value to the exporter, who in turn will use the money to pay for goods and services. The importer or debtor will pay the sums owed under the contract of sale to the factor. This method of payment serves a useful purpose in international trade as it liquidates working capital and avoids delays in payments for goods supplied or services rendered. It serves to facilitate purchasing of raw materials, making payments to suppliers, expansion of market shares and maintaining a range of goods.

(a) Types of factoring

There are different types of factoring transactions; for example, factoring can either be disclosed or undisclosed, on a recourse or non-recourse basis. In disclosed factoring, the debtor is informed by the creditor about the existence of the factoring contract. In this case, the debtor transfers the money to the factor's account, in most cases on a non-recourse basis whereby if the debtor fails to present payment the creditor will not be liable to the factor, thus the risk remains with the factor. If, however, the outstanding debt is on a recourse basis the creditor will be liable for such sums. If the factoring agreement is on a non-disclosed basis then the debtor will pay the outstanding sums directly to the creditor. The creditor will hold such sums as trustee for the factor.

(b) Two factor system

In a domestic factoring system there are usually only three parties involved: the creditor, the debtor and the factor. However, due to the increasing complications associated with international transactions, such as different languages, currency and financial laws, there are usually two factors involved, one located in the creditor's country and one in the debtor's country. The export factor will obtain the relevant information about the sales contract from the exporter and contact the import factor to negotiate the terms of the factoring agreement. There are three main agreements in the two factor system: first, between the exporter and the importer; secondly, between the exporter and his factor; and thirdly, between the import and export factor. The import factor will bear the risk of any default in payment; however, the export factor will bear the risk if on a recourse basis.

This system offers several benefits to the parties involved in international trade. First, factor organisations provide a valuable financial and collection service, to enable the parties to liquidate their assets to finance current and future transactions. Secondly, it provides a credit risk element whereby parties may be protected in the event of default of payment by the other party. Thirdly, it provides a consultancy function to assess the financial stability of the parties and to give advice on conducting the transaction.

Q5 Discuss the nature and purpose of factoring as a means of financing international trade. What types of transactions is this method of payment most suited to?

(c) Laws governing factoring

The UNIDROIT Convention on International Factoring was drafted by the International Institute for the Unification of Private Law in May 1988 in Ottawa, Canada. The purpose of the Convention was to harmonise international factoring transactions, reduce uncertainties and to promote international trade. The Convention has been ratified, most noticeably by France, Germany and Italy.[47]

Article 2 states that the Convention will apply when parties have their places of business in different states. Article 3 states that the parties may exclude the application of the Convention. Article 8 sets out the duty of the debtor to pay the factor for the receivables once they have been assigned to him. Article 6 (which was the result of much compromise at the drafting of the Convention) provides that:

> the assignment of a receivable by the supplier to the factor shall be effective notwithstanding any agreement between the supplier and the debtor prohibiting such assignment.[48]

However, Article 6(2) allows states which make a declaration under Article 18[49] to circumvent this provision. This is further qualified by Article 6(3), which stipulates:

> Nothing in paragraph 1 shall affect any obligation of good faith owed by the supplier to the debtor or any liability of the supplier to the debtor in respect of an assignment made in breach of the terms of the contract of sale of goods.

This presents a concern over the certainty of the factoring transaction for the parties involved. The Convention also presents limitations in its scope, as it does not address issues such as insolvency of the parties or conflict of laws.

7 Forfaiting

The term 'forfait' derives from the French 'a forfait' which means to surrender one's rights. Forfaiting is another mechanism used to finance international trade and is most commonly seen in Europe. The forfaitor will purchase the

---

[47] See www.unidroit.org/english/implement/i-88-f.pdf.
[48] UNIDROIT Convention, Art. 6(1).
[49] A Contracting State may at any time make a declaration in accordance with Art. 6(2) that an assignment under Art. 6(1) shall not be effective against the debtor if, at the time of conclusion of the contract of sale of goods, it has its place of business in that state.

receivable from the exporter at a discount. This will be evidenced by a promissory note, a bill of exchange, a deferred payment letter of credit or a letter of guarantee. The transaction will be without recourse to the exporter, which means that the forfaitor will assume the risks inherent in the transaction. Forfaiting differs from factoring in that forfait can be used for the entire contract value and is usually used for longer maturity dates of one to five years.

The process of forfaiting works in the following way. The exporter and importer negotiate the terms of the commercial contract, the exporter sends the details to the forfaitor, and the forfaitor then agrees a discounted rate for the receivable. The exporter and importer enter into the commercial contract. The exporter ships the goods to the importer, and the promissory note or bill of exchange is sent to the forfaitor and endorsed without recourse. Once this is verified payment is made to the exporter. The forfaitor will present the bill or promissory note to the importer on the date of maturity and payment of the debt will be made to the forfaitor.

Forfaiting offers several benefits in that it creates liquidity and reduces risks to the exporter. It also benefits the importer by giving him a longer period to repay the debt at a fixed rate. However, forfaiting is not suitable for transactions involving small sums or short periods of time. It is also unsuitable in countries that are financially weak.

Q6 Identify the main differences between factoring and forfaiting. In what circumstances will the parties choose the latter option?

8 Conclusion

The smooth running of international trade transactions depends on the ability of the parties to make timely payments for goods. We have examined the benefits and drawbacks of various methods of international financing, including factoring and forfaiting. As seen above, letters of credit continue to serve as an important tool in international trade. They can provide efficiency as well as security to buyers and sellers located in different countries. However, the rigorous procedures and strict compliance guidelines often result in the letter of credit being rejected by the banks. The UCP 600 rules have alleviated some of these problems, however it is only applicable through incorporation by the parties. In addition to this, the UCP 600 does not address issues such as insolvency or fraud and the parties can often find themselves at risk in the transaction. Until there is a harmonised international measure to govern letter of credit transactions, parties are advised to exercise care in drafting their contracts.

9 Recommended reading

Arora, A. 'The dilemma of an issuing bank: to accept or reject documents under a letter of credit' (1984) *LMCLQ* 81

Buckley, R.P. 'Potential pitfalls with letters of credit' (1996) 70 *ALJ* 217

Creed, N. 'The governing law of letter of credit transactions' (2001) 16 *JIBL* 41

Dolan, J. 'Strict compliance with letters of credit: striking a fair balance' (1985) *BLJ* 18

Ellinger, E.P. 'The uniform customs and practice for documentary credits (UCP): their development and the current revisions' (2007) *LMCLQ* 152

Enonchong, N. 'The autonomy principle of letters of credit: an illegality exception?' (2006) *LMCLQ* 404

Kozolchyk, B. 'Strict compliance and the reasonable document checker' (1990) 56 *BLR* 48

Ortego, J. and Krinick, E. 'Letters of credit: benefits and drawback of the independence principle' (1998) 115 *BLJ* 487

Salinger, F. 'International factoring and conflicts of law' (2007) 1(1) *LFMR* 7

Ward, G. 'The legal context of forfaiting trade finance' (1991) 12(2) *BLR* 47

Part 3 Chapter 4

Carriage of Goods by Sea

Contents

1 Introduction

The subject of carriage of goods by sea is one of paramount importance to international trade. Despite the existence of other forms of transport such as rail, road and air, sea carriage remains the most practical and often most financially viable option for traders. This is especially true where the buyer and seller are located in different countries. In 2009, world seaborne trade fell overall by 4.5 per cent following the economic collapse of 2008.[1] The total goods loaded in 2009 amounted to 7.8 billion tons; this was down from 8.2 billion tons loaded in 2008.[2] Although these figures may initially seem disappointing and indicate a lack of demand for seaborne transport, this is not the case. In its 2010 trend report, the United Nations Conference on Trade and Development (UNCTAD) stated that the figures for 2009 were not indicative of the overall picture for the future. Rather, statistics showed that developing countries (mainly those in Asia) continued to increase the amount of trade conducted despite the global economic upheavals. Asia holds a 41 per cent share in goods loaded

---

[1] *Maritime Transport Review* (UNCTAD, 2010) 6.   [2] *Ibid.*

worldwide.[3] Also, the ever-growing demand for crude oil resulted in an upsurge in the tanker trade. Dry bulk cargoes, in particular ore used for steel, continued to drive demand in this area as well.

There are many issues to be considered when shipping goods by sea, including the parties involved in the process, the nature of the cargo, the type of vessel to be used, as well as the most suitable type of contract for the voyage.

(a) Cargoes

There are a wide variety of cargoes shipped internationally every day. These include raw materials as well as manufactured cargoes. It is the nature and amount of cargo to be shipped which will decide what type of contract of carriage the parties will choose. If there is a large quantity of bulk cargo the shipper may choose to charter an entire vessel, whereas with smaller cargoes it may be more suitable to use liner trades which run on a fixed schedule. Dry bulk cargoes comprise two distinctions: major dry bulks, which include iron ore, coal, grain, bauxite/alumina and phosphate rock, and the minor bulk trades, which include manufactures, agribulks, metals and minerals. Within the category of dry bulk cargo there is a wide variation in the characteristics of these goods. For example, cargoes such as grain intended to be sold for consumption will require holds which are free of any type of contamination. Other types of cargo, such as coal, may be susceptible to inherent vice[4] and may require storage in holds with cooler temperatures. Some agricultural goods such as potatoes may deteriorate in damp conditions or where the hold is likely to take in water. Goods may also be classed as dangerous and require special handling when loading or unloading.[5]

Cargoes such as liquid bulk cargo, mainly oil, will require special equipment to be transferred onto the tankers for transport. Once these cargoes reach their destination they will be discharged into terminals, and the oil is then pumped through a pipeline to a refinery for processing.

Not all cargoes will be large enough to require use of the entire ship; such cargoes will be shipped separately, using dunnage[6] to store and secure them in the hold. Most modern transport methods however employ the use of containers to transport separate items; this helps to protect the goods, as well as speeding up the process of loading and unloading the goods.

(b) Vessels

For the purposes of transporting goods in international trade there are several different types of vessels; the type and amount of cargo will usually determine

---

[3] *Ibid.* 7.   [4] When goods react naturally to their environment.
[5] See the International Maritime Dangerous Goods Code.
[6] Materials such as wood, burlap or matting used to protect goods.

the kind of vessel employed. One of the most common types are container ships; these ships, which carry most of the world's manufactured goods and products, are usually operated through scheduled liner services. Container ships carry their containers both on and below deck.

Bulk carriers are another type of vessel used in the shipping industry. These vessels transport raw materials such as iron ore and coal. They are usually identifiable by the hatches raised above deck level which cover the cargo holds.

Tankers are used to transport crude oil, chemicals and petroleum products. Tankers are similar in appearance to bulk carriers, however the deck will be covered by oil pipelines and vents.

(c) Parties

There are many parties who play a role in the international transport of goods by sea. Some parties will play a primary role while others are ancillary to the process. Typically, the buyer and seller in the sale contract will play a prominent role in the carriage process. The responsibilities of each party will depend on the applicable law or set of rules to the contract. For example, a seller in a CIF contract[7] will be tasked with arranging for carriage as well as insurance for the goods. As the buyer and seller are located in different countries they may employ agents or brokers to conduct business on their behalf.

Another important party to the carriage transaction is the carrier; the carrier will enter into the contract of carriage with the shipper. The carrier can be someone employed in the liner trade or may be a charterer. On board the vessel there will be members of the crew responsible for undertaking the voyage; the most important member of the crew is the master who issues commands to the other members. He is also given the responsibility of signing bills of lading presented to indicate acceptance of the goods on board the vessel. The consignee will be the person named in the bill of lading to whom the goods should be delivered at the port of discharge. Most modern shipping practices employ the use of stevedores to load and unload the goods; such persons are usually treated as independent contractors and not as servants of the ship-owner.

(d) Contracts

There are two main types of contracts of affreightment: bills of lading and charterparties. For shippers with only a small quantity of cargo, chartering an entire vessel will not be a practical option, instead they will choose to use liner services, which operate between major ports on a fixed schedule or tramp vessels, which sail from port to port in search of cargo.

---

[7] See Part 3 Chapter 1 for further discussion.

The bill of lading serves several different functions: it can act as a receipt for the goods, evidence of the contract of carriage, as well as a negotiable document of title. In the United Kingdom, bills of lading are subject to statutory regimes, namely, the Carriage of Goods by Sea Act (COGSA) 1971, which imposes a limitation of liability under the Hague-Visby Rules on bills of lading issued in the United Kingdom. The Carriage of Goods by Sea Act 1992 allows the lawful holder of the bill of lading and other sea carriage documents to have rights of suit.

The shipper will prefer to charter a vessel when the whole or a large part of the ship is used to carry the goods. There are two types of charterparties: voyage charterparties and time charterparties. The voyage charter is used for a single or series of voyages. The charterer is obligated to provide cargo; he will pay freight and can be bound to pay for any laytime or demurrage depending on how risk is allocated between the ship-owner and the charterer. When the ship is used for a period of time a time charter is used. The ship-owner places the ship for the charterer's use for a specified period of time. The charterer pays a hire cost and is responsible for the operation of the ship, although in most cases the crew will be employed by the ship-owner. The charterer will issue the bills of lading. Charterparties are not subject to any statutory regime, unless they are incorporated into the charterparty, such as, for example, the Hague-Visby Rules.

Q1 What is the main factor in deciding what type of contract to use?

2 Hague and Hague-Visby Rules

There are several legal regimes which can govern carriage of goods by sea. Before the enactment of laws to govern carriage of goods by sea, under the common law carriers were allowed widespread freedom to draft extensive exclusion clauses in their contracts. This practice meant that shippers as well as consignees of the goods had little or no say as to the terms of the contract. In order to rectify the situation, the Hague Rules (officially titled the International Convention for the Unification of Certain Rules of Law relating to Bills of Lading) was initially adopted by the United Kingdom and given effect in the Carriage of Goods by Sea Act 1924.

The Hague-Visby Rules (i.e., the Hague Rules, as amended by a Protocol agreed in Visby) were formally signed in Brussels in February 1968. The Visby amendments were enacted by the United Kingdom in the Carriage of Goods by Sea Act 1971. The Act came into effect on 23 June 1977 once the Protocol was ratified by ten states with sufficient flagged tonnage. Although the Hague Rules, and their successor the Hague-Visby Rules have enjoyed a wide measure of success, it has been argued that a more comprehensive measure was needed to balance the interests of the carrier and consignee of the goods.

(a) Application of rules

The application of the Hague-Visby Rules to the contract of affreightment can either be mandatory[8] or by agreement, in which case parties will include a 'clause paramount' into the contract stipulating that the Rules are to apply. Article III(8)[9] will, however, only take effect where the Rules are applied mandatorily. COGSA 1971, section 1(6) provides that if the Rules are incorporated into a bill of lading it shall have the 'force of law'. This therefore expands the scope of the Rules, making them applicable to those bills which have fallen outside the ambit of the COGSA 1971. However, the position in relation to Article III(8) may remain the same in the case of charterparties which incorporate the Rules.[10]

Article I(b) of the Rules states that they apply to contracts of carriage covered by a bill of lading or any similar document of title, insofar as such document relates to the carriage of goods by sea.[11] The Rules do not apply to waybills or any other non-negotiable documents of title.[12] The Rules also do not apply to bills of lading issued under a charterparty if the bill remains in the hands of the charterer, however the Rules will apply when the bill is indorsed to a third party.[13] The Rules may also apply where it was the parties' intention that the contract of carriage be covered by a bill of lading even if one had not been issued.[14] In *Pyrene* v. *Scindia*, a cargo of fire tenders was awaiting loading on board the vessel when one of the tenders fell as it was being loaded on board the ship and as a result was damaged. The bill of lading made no mention of the damaged tender. When the carrier invoked Article IV(5) to limit his liability, the shipper tried to argue that the Hague Rules should not apply because the damaged tender was not mentioned in the bill of lading. It was held that the Rules did apply. Devlin J stated:

> In my judgment whenever a contract of carriage is concluded, and it is contemplated that a bill of lading will, in due course, be issued in respect of it, that contract is from its creation 'covered' by a bill of lading, and is therefore in its inception a contract of carriage within the meaning of the Rules and to which the Rules apply.[15]

---

[8] COGSA 1971, s.1(2).

[9] Hague-Visby Rules, Art. III(8): 'Any clause, covenant, or agreement in a contract of carriage relieving the carrier or the ship from liability for loss or damage to, or in connection with, goods arising from negligence, fault, or failure in the duties and obligations provided in this article or lessening such liability otherwise than as provided in these Rules, shall be null and void and of no effect. A benefit of insurance in favour of the carrier or similar clause shall be deemed to be a clause relieving the carrier from liability.'

[10] *The Strathnewton* [1983] 1 Lloyd's Rep. 219. See also COGSA 1971, Sch. 1.

[11] This is supported by COGSA 1971, s.1(4).

[12] For the exception of straight bills of lading, *The Rafaela S* [2005] 1 Lloyd's Rep. 347.

[13] Hague-Visby Rules, Art. I(b).

[14] *Pyrene Co. Ltd* v. *Scindia Navigation Co.* [1954] 2 QB 402.

[15] *Ibid.* 419.

Article X of the Hague-Visby Rules provides that they apply to:

every bill of lading relating to the carriage of goods between ports in two different States if:

(a) the bill of lading is issued in a contracting State, or
(b) the carriage is from a port in a contracting State, or
(c) the contract contained in or evidenced by the bill of lading provides that these Rules or legislation of any State giving effect to them are to govern the contract,

whatever may be the nationality of the ship, the carrier, the shipper, the consignee, or any other interested person.

Section 1(3) of the COGSA 1971 extends the Rules to also cover coastal trade within the United Kingdom. The wording of Article X states that the Rules will apply when the carriage of goods takes place between two different states if the bill is issued in a Contracting State, or where the carriage is from a port in a Contracting State, or alternatively where the bill expressly stipulates that the Rules will apply. In relation to Article X(b) there may be some ambiguity as to the automatic application of the Rules. For example, parties may avoid the rules by using a non-negotiable document of title, which would detract from the intention of the drafters that the Rules should not be excluded. The courts in these cases tend to look at whether the parties intended to issue a bill of lading at some stage in the voyage.[16]

Section 1(6)(b) of the COGSA 1971 further extends the Rules to any receipt which is a non-negotiable document marked as such if the contract provides that the Rules are to govern the contract.

(b) Types of cargo

The Hague-Visby Rules under Article I(c) specifically exclude the carriage of live animals and deck cargo.[17] The reason for such exclusions is evident given the risk involved in transporting cargo of this kind. Article IV states that in such cases:

a carrier, master or agent of the carrier and a shipper shall in regard to any particular goods be at liberty to enter into any agreement in any terms as to the responsibility and liability of the carrier for such goods, and as to the rights and immunities of the carrier in respect of such goods, or his obligation as to seaworthiness, so far as this stipulation is not contrary to public policy, or the care or diligence of his servants or agents in regard to the loading, handling, stowage, carriage, custody, care and discharge of the goods carried by sea, provided that in this case no bill of lading has been or shall be issued and that the terms agreed

---

[16] *Mayhew Foods Ltd* v. *Overseas Containers Ltd* [1984] 1 Lloyd's Rep. 317.
[17] That is, 'cargo which by the contract of carriage is stated as being carried on deck and is so carried'.

shall be embodied in a receipt which shall be a non-negotiable document and shall be marked as such.

In relation to the carriage of goods on deck, the Rules provide that the bill of lading must disclose that the goods will be carried on deck and that they are in fact carried on deck. The courts tend to apply the exclusion very narrowly. In *Svenska Traktor AB* v. *Maritime Agencies*,[18] a cargo of tractors had been shipped under a bill of lading which gave the carrier the option to transport the tractors on deck. One of the tractors was subsequently lost when it went overboard and the ship-owner relied on the bill of lading to exclude his liability for loss. The ship-owner's claim failed as the courts held that an option to carry deck cargo does not mean it is in fact being carried on deck.

In *Encyclopaedia Britannica* v. *Hong Kong Producer*,[19] a cargo of encyclopaedias was shipped in containers. The bill of lading permitted the carrier to transport the container on deck, and stated that he would only be prevented from doing so if the shipper objected to this in writing and requested that the goods be carried in the holds. Upon arrival the goods were found to be damaged by sea-water. It was held that the carrier could not rely on the exclusion clause in the bill of lading because the bill had to state whether or not the goods were actually being carried on deck or not.

(c) Period of coverage

Article I(e) defines 'Carriage of goods' as covering the period from the time when the goods are loaded on board to the time they are discharged from the ship. This means that the Rules will apply on a 'tackle to tackle' basis from the start of the loading operation to conclusion of discharge. The parties may choose to extend the operation of the Hague-Visby Rules to other contractual operations by express contractual provision.[20]

Q2 'The period of liability under the Hague-Visby Rules is insufficient to deal with the needs of modern transport.' Discuss with reference to the case law.

(d) Contracting out

Article V allows the carrier to give up any of his rights or immunities or to increase his obligations and responsibilities as long as these are included in

---

[18] [1953] 2 QB 295.   [19] [1969] 2 Lloyd's Rep. 536.

[20] Hague-Visby Rules, Art. VII: 'Nothing herein contained shall prevent a carrier or a shipper from entering into any agreement, stipulation, condition, reservation or exemption as to the responsibility and liability of the carrier or the ship for the loss or damage to, or in connection with, the custody and care and handling of goods prior to the loading on, and subsequent to the discharge from, the ship on which the goods are carried by sea.'

the bill of lading; however, the carrier cannot improve his position under the Hague-Visby Rules as this would contravene Article III(8).

Q3 What types of contracts are covered by the Hague-Visby Rules?

(e) Duties of the carrier

(i) Bills of lading

Article III(3)of the Hague-Visby Rules states:

> After receiving the goods into his charge the carrier or the master or agent of the carrier shall, on demand of the shipper, issue to the shipper a bill of lading showing among other things:
>
> (a) the leading marks necessary for identification of the goods as the same are furnished in writing by the shipper before the loading of such goods starts, provided such marks are stamped or otherwise shown clearly upon the goods if uncovered, or on the cases or coverings in which such goods are contained, in such a manner as should ordinarily remain legible until the end of the voyage;
>
> (b) either the number of packages or pieces, or the quantity, or weight, as the case may be, as furnished in writing by the shipper;
>
> (c) the apparent order and condition of the goods.
>
> Provided that no carrier, master or agent of the carrier shall be bound to state or show in the bill of lading any marks, number, quantity or weight which he has reasonable ground for suspecting not accurately to represent the goods actually received, or which he has had no reasonable means of checking.

Under Article III(3) the shipper can demand that the carrier issue a bill of lading showing leading marks, the quantity of the goods and the apparent order and condition of the goods. In practice the carrier may not always be able to verify the accuracy of the information given by the shipper, as in most cases the cargo will be covered by packaging or packed in containers. However, as the bill of lading is a receipt issued by the carrier, it is the carrier and not the shipper that will be liable to the consignee for any discrepancies in the bill of lading. The bill of lading is treated as conclusive evidence as between the carrier and consignee and as *prima facie* evidence as between the carrier and the shipper.[21] Article III(5) requires the carrier to be indemnified by the shipper against any inaccuracies provided in the bill of lading. The carrier is under no duty to issue a bill containing such information unless he is requested to do so by the shipper, and is not required to do so if he has reasonable grounds to believe the information to be inaccurate. In *Ace Imports Pty Ltd* v. *Companhia de Navegacao Lloyd Brasileiro (The Esmeralda)*,[22] the plaintiffs purchased a consignment of cutlery, which was shipped on board the defendant's vessel in

[21] *Ibid.* Art. III(4).   [22] [1988] 1 Lloyd's Rep. 206.

a container. The bill of lading that was issued for the container stated that 'this bill of lading shall be *prima facie* evidence of the receipt by the carrier … of the total amount of … packages … specified on the face hereof'. Upon arrival at the port of discharge there was a shortfall in the quantity received. The defendants claimed that the goods had been missing prior to shipment. It was held that this was not a clean bill of lading, as the defendants were relying on the information supplied by the plaintiffs about the cargo.

(ii) Seaworthiness

Article III(1) of the Hague-Visby Rules provides:

> The carrier shall be bound before and at the beginning of the voyage to exercise due diligence to:
> (a) make the ship seaworthy;
> (b) properly man, equip and supply the ship;
> (c) make the holds, refrigerating and cool chambers, and all other parts of the ship in which goods are carried, fit and safe for their reception, carriage and preservation.

This rule modifies the common law approach of an absolute duty with regard to seaworthiness. It has been incorporated in COGSA 1971, section 3, which states:

> Absolute warranty of seaworthiness not to be implied in contracts to which the Rules apply. There shall not be implied in any contract for the carriage of goods by sea to which the Rules apply by virtue of this Act any absolute undertaking by the carrier of the goods to provide a seaworthy ship.

Article III(1) sets out three main requirements in its provisions: first, the obligation for the carrier to exercise due diligence to make the ship seaworthy; secondly, to properly man and equip the ship; and finally, to make sure the hold and other parts of the ship for which goods are carried are fit for the purpose. In *Actis Co. Ltd* v. *Sanko Steamship Co. Ltd (The Aquacharm)*,[23] the seaworthiness of a vessel was questioned when her draught proved too much for passage through the Panama Canal. Lord Denning stated:

> I think the word 'seaworthy' in the Hague Rules is used in its ordinary meaning, and not in any extended or unnatural meaning. It means that the vessel – with her master and crew – is herself fit to encounter the perils of the voyage and also that she is fit to carry the cargo safely on that voyage … This vessel was so fit. It may be that she had to be lightened to pass through the Panama Canal, but that did not make her unfit … There is no case in which a ship has been held to be unseaworthy merely because she has to lighten in order to get into port. So also, if she has to lighten in order to get through a canal.[24]

---

[23] [1982] 1 WLR 119.   [24] *Ibid.* 122–3.

Q4 What is the nature of the duty to provide a seaworthy vessel?

(iii) Due diligence

The Hague-Visby Rules state that the carrier is obliged to exercise due diligence before and at the beginning of the voyage to make the ship seaworthy. In *Maxine Footwear Co. Ltd* v. *Canadian Government Merchant Marine Ltd,*[25] a fire broke out just before the ship was to sail for Jamaica. This was as a result of the crew attempting to unthaw a frozen pipe with an acetylene torch. The master was forced to order the scuttling of the ship, which resulted in the loss of the cargo. The ship-owners sought to rely on the fire exception contained in the Rules.[26] Their claim failed as it was held that the ship-owners had breached their obligation as to seaworthiness, as Article III(1) covered the period from the beginning of loading of the goods until the ship had sailed. Under the Hague-Visby Rules, the obligation as to seaworthiness is a personal obligation which renders the carrier liable for anyone whose actions caused the unseaworthiness of the vessel.[27]

(iv) Goods

Article III(2) states:

> Subject to the provisions of Article IV, the carrier shall properly and carefully load, handle, stow, carry, keep, care for, and discharge the goods carried.

In *Albacora* v. *Westcott & Laurence Line Ltd,*[28] a cargo of salted fish deteriorated on the voyage from Glasgow to Genoa, Both the shipper and the carrier knew that the holds of the ship were not refrigerated, however neither was aware that the cargo would not be able to withstand the journey without refrigeration. In this case it was held that the ship-owners were not in breach of their duty under Article III(2), as the carrier had fulfilled his duties to care for the cargo in light of all the knowledge he possessed at the time.

Q5 What is the obligation to care for the cargo under Article III(2)? What is the relevance, if any, of the carrier's knowledge?

(v) Deviation

Article IV(4) provides:

> Any deviation in saving or attempting to save life or property at sea or any reasonable deviation shall not be deemed to be an infringement or breach of these Rules or of the contract of carriage, and the carrier shall not be liable for any loss or damage resulting therefrom.

---

[25] [1959] AC 589, PC.   [26] Hague-Visby Rules, Art. IV(2)(b).

[27] *Riverstone Meat Co. Pty Ltd* v. *Lancashire Shipping Co. Ltd (The Muncaster Castle)* [1961] AC 807.

[28] [1966] 2 Lloyd's Rep. 53, HL.

The Hague-Visby Rules offer a wider range of permissible deviations than the common law, as the deviation can be to save life or property or, alternatively, if the deviation is reasonable the ship-owner will not be liable. The aim of Article IV(4) is to reduce the use of liberty clauses only to those which are deemed reasonable. In *Stag Line Ltd* v. *Foscolo, Mango & Co.*,[29] Lord Atkin addressed the question of whether what would be considered reasonable had to be in the interests of both the ship and the cargo:

> deviation may, and often will, be caused by fortuitous circumstances never contemplated by the original parties to the contract and may be reasonable though it is made solely in the interests of the ship or solely in the interest of the cargo or indeed in the direct interest of neither; as for instance where the presence of a passenger or of a member of the ship or crew was urgently required after the voyage had begun, on a matter of national importance; or where some person on board was a fugitive from justice, and there were urgent reasons for his immediate appearance. The true test seems to be, what departure from the contract voyage might a prudent person controlling the voyage at the time make and maintain, having in mind all the relevant circumstances existing at the time, including the terms of the contract and the interests of all parties concerned, but without obligation to consider the interests of any one as conclusive[30]

Q6 What is the obligation not to deviate from the agreed route?

(f) Immunities of the carrier

Article IV(2) states:

> Neither the carrier nor the ship shall be responsible for loss or damage arising or resulting from:
>
> (a) act, neglect, or default of the master, mariner, pilot, or the servants of the carrier in the navigation or in the management of the ship;
> (b) fire, unless caused by the actual fault or privity of the carrier;
> (c) perils, dangers and accidents of the sea or other navigable waters;
> (d) act of God;
> (e) act of war;
> (f) act of public enemies;
> (g) arrest or restraint of princes, rulers or people, or seizure under legal process;
> (h) quarantine restrictions;
> (i) act or omission of the shipper or owner of the goods, his agent or representative;
> (j) strikes or lockouts or stoppage or restraint of labour from whatever cause, whether partial or general;
> (k) riots and civil commotions;
> (l) saving or attempting to save life or property at sea;

---

[29] [1932] AC 328.   [30] *Ibid.* 343–4.

(m) wastage in bulk of weight or any other loss or damage arising from inherent
     defect, quality or vice of the goods;
(n) insufficiency of packing;
(o) insufficiency or inadequacy of marks;
(p) latent defects not discoverable by due diligence;
(q) any other cause arising without the actual fault or privity of the carrier, or
     without the fault or neglect of the agents or servants of the carrier, but the bur-
     den of proof shall be on the person claiming the benefit of this exception to
     show that neither the actual fault or privity of the carrier nor the fault or neg-
     lect of the agents or servants of the carrier contributed to the loss or damage.

Article IV(2) provides a 'list' of immunities available to the carrier. These
exceptions will protect the carrier from liability in the event of a claim by the
shipper or consignee. Article IV(2)(a), which deals with the navigation and
management of the ship, and Article IV(2)(b), which deals with fire, are the
most contentious as they allow for negligence on the part of the carrier and
servants. Navigation refers to damage sustained to the cargo as a result of the
poor piloting of the vessel. This can cover a number of situations, including
collision as seen in *The Xantho*.[31] As regards the issue of management of the
ship the courts are careful to distinguish between acts which affect the ship and
acts which affect the cargo. In *Gosse Millard* v. *Canadian Government Merchant
Marine*,[32] a cargo of tinplate was damaged when the vessel put in for repairs.
The hatch covers were opened and the tarpaulins which covered the cargo were
removed, which resulted in rain-water damaging the cargo. It was held that the
damage was caused by the failure to replace the tarpaulins, which was related to
the care of the cargo and not the management of the vessel.

Article IV(2)(b), which covers the exception of fire, provides that the carrier
will not be liable if the fire is caused by the negligence of his servants or agents,
but would only be liable if he was personally at fault. However, if as a result of
the fire the ship is made unseaworthy, the ship-owner will have to establish due
diligence to escape liability.[33]

It is also worth noting the 'catch all' exception in Article IV(q), which the
carrier can invoke to cover any situations not covered by the listed exceptions.
However, to avail himself of this exception he will need to prove the event was
not caused by the fault or negligence of himself, his servants or agents.

Q7 Why is Article IV(2)(a) considered controversial?

(g) Shipper's obligations

Article III(5) of the Hague-Visby Rules examines the shipper's duty to provide
accurate information about the goods to the carrier. It states:

---

[31] (1887) 12 App. Cas. 503.   [32] [1927] 2 KB 432.
[33] *Maxine Footwear Co. Ltd* v. *Canadian Government Merchant Marine Ltd* [1959] AC 589, PC.

The shipper shall be deemed to have guaranteed to the carrier the accuracy at the time of shipment of the marks, number, quantity and weight, as furnished by him, and the shipper shall indemnify the carrier against all loss, damages and expenses arising or resulting from inaccuracies in such particulars. The right of the carrier to such indemnity shall in no way limit his responsibility and liability under the contract of carriage to any person other than the shipper.

One of the main functions of the bill of lading is to evidence the goods shipped on board the vessel, thus it is important that the shipper provides information that is correct to the master when the goods are loaded on board. Article III(5) specifically deals with information regarding 'marks, number, quantity and weight' of the goods, but it does not cover any information given as to the condition of the goods. In the event that the shipper supplies inaccurate information, the carrier will be entitled to be indemnified for his losses.

Article IV(3) provides:

The shipper shall not be responsible for loss or damage sustained by the carrier or the ship arising or resulting from any cause without the act, fault or neglect of the shipper, his agents or his servants.

Therefore, the shipper will be protected from liability for any damage caused to the carrier or ship as long as the cause of the damage was not the result of an act or negligence on his part or on the part of his agents or servants.

Article IV(6) examines the shipper's obligation with regard to dangerous goods. It states:

Goods of an inflammable, explosive or dangerous nature to the shipment whereof the carrier, master or agent of the carrier has not consented with knowledge of their nature and character, may at any time before discharge be landed at any place, or destroyed or rendered innocuous by the carrier without compensation and the shipper of such goods shall be liable for all damages and expenses directly or indirectly arising out of or resulting from such shipment. If any such goods shipped with such knowledge and consent shall become a danger to the ship or cargo, they may in like manner be landed at any place, or destroyed or rendered innocuous by the carrier without liability on the part of the carrier except to general average, if any.

This provision is twofold. First, if the carrier is unaware that the shipper has shipped goods that are of an 'inflammable, explosive or dangerous nature' he may dispose of such goods without incurring any liability to the shipper. Furthermore, the shipper will be liable for any damages or expenses as a result of the dangerous shipment. Secondly, if the carrier is aware of the nature of the goods and the goods become dangerous to the vessel or other cargo, the carrier can dispose of the dangerous goods without incurring liability, other than for the losses incurred in general average.

The Hague-Visby Rules do not only apply to goods which are physically dangerous. In *The Giannis NK*,[34] a cargo of groundnut pellets infested with Khapra beetles had to be disposed of when it became a danger to the other cargoes aboard the vessel.[35] In his judgment, Lord Steyn held that cargo that is not physically dangerous *can* fall within the meaning of the Rules:

> it would be wrong to apply the *ejusdem generis* rule to the words 'goods of an inflammable, explosive or dangerous nature'. These are disparate categories of goods. Each word must be given its natural meaning, and 'dangerous' ought not to be restrictively interpreted by reason of the preceding words. Secondly, it would be wrong to detract from the generality and width of the expression 'goods of … [a] dangerous nature' by importing the suggested restriction that the goods must by themselves, or by reason of their inherent properties, pose a danger to the ship or other cargo. For my part I would resist any temptation to substitute for the ordinary and non-technical expression 'goods … of a dangerous nature' any other formulation.[36]

Q8 What are the rights and obligations of the parties under the Hague-Visby Rules?

Q9 What is the shipper's obligation with regard to dangerous goods?

(h) Limitation of liability

Article IV(1) *bis* states:

> The defences and limits of liability provided for in these Rules shall apply in any action against the carrier in respect of loss or damage to goods covered by a contract of carriage whether the action be founded in contract or in tort.

The Hague-Visby Rules provide for a maximum limit on the carrier's liability. This is calculated on the basis of special drawing rights as defined by the International Monetary Fund per package or kilogram of gross weight.

Article IV(5)(a) states:

> Unless the nature and value of such goods have been declared by the shipper before shipment and inserted in the bill of lading, neither the carrier nor the ship shall in any event be or become liable for any loss or damage to or in connection with the goods in an amount exceeding the equivalent of 666.67 units of account per package or unit or units of account per kilo of gross weight of the goods lost or damaged, whichever is the higher.

In the case of goods being shipped in containers, Article IV(5)(c) states:

---

[34] [1998] AC 605.
[35] This case was decided under the Hague Rules, Art. IV(6).
[36] [1998] AC 605, 620.

Where a container, pallet or similar article of transport is used to consolidate goods, the number of packages or units enumerated in the bill of lading as packed in such article of transport shall be deemed the number of packages or units for the purpose of this paragraph as far as these packages or units are concerned. Except as aforesaid such article of transport shall be considered the package or unit.

Thus, if the shipper fails to enumerate the packages within the container, the container will be treated as one package.

The carrier will not be able to invoke the package limitation if the damage incurred was caused by his act or omission done with the intent to cause damage, or where he was reckless and it was foreseeable such damage would occur.[37]

(i) Time bar

Article III(6) provides:

Subject to paragraph 6*bis* the carrier and the ship shall in any event be discharged from all liability whatsoever in respect of the goods, unless suit is brought within one year of their delivery or of the date when they should have been delivered. This period may, however, be extended if the parties so agree after the cause of action has arisen

Article III(6) contains a time bar that a claim must be brought within one year from delivery of the goods. If a party fails to bring a suit within one year from delivery of the goods, the claim will be extinguished. This is subject to a variation under Article III(6) *bis*, which states:

An action for indemnity against a third person may be brought even after the expiration of the year provided for in the preceding paragraph if brought within the time allowed by the law of the Court seized of the case

In the event that the goods are never loaded a claim can still be brought within the one-year time limit, in which case it will be determined on the basis of when the goods should have been delivered. Delivery for the purposes of this provision is when the goods are transferred to the consignee.

(j) Hamburg Rules

From the above it can be said that the Hague-Visby Rules were drafted in an attempt to reconcile and balance the interests of the shipper, carrier and cargo-owner. However, in recent years the modernisation of sea transport has resulted in changes which the Rules are unable to address. For example, the Rules were designed to cover bills of lading, and documents such as sea waybills are left out of the scope of its application. The Rules were also not designed to deal with

---

[37] Hague-Visby Rules, Art. IV(5)(e).

multimodal carriage. The Rules have also been criticised for favouring the carrier, citing the burden of proof and the fact that the carrier can escape liability for negligence under Article IV(2)(a) and (b). The Hamburg Rules was a UNCITRAL sponsored regime containing rules more favourable to cargo owners. These Rules were adopted at a diplomatic conference at Hamburg in 1978; however, they have failed to gain any significant measure of acceptance and were not adopted by the United Kingdom.

The Hamburg Rules are applicable to all types of contracts of carriage of goods by sea except for charterparties. Thus, they cover a wider range of contracts rather than just bills of lading. Article 10 of the Hamburg Rules states that the contractual carrier shall remain responsible for the entire carriage of goods even where the carriage is being performed by another carrier. However, this is qualified by Article 11, which allows the contractual carrier to exclude his liability while the goods are in the care of another carrier. Article 4 extends the period of liability to cover the period during which the carrier is in charge of the goods at the port of loading, during the carriage and at the port of discharge, thus a 'port to port' liability. Article 5 provides that once a claimant can prove the loss or damage took place while the goods were in the charge of the carrier, the carrier will be presumed liable for the loss or damage. The carrier will be relieved of liability if he can prove that he, his servants or agents took all measures that could reasonably be required to avoid the occurrence and its consequences.

Q10 '*The system of presumed fault of the carrier has hindered widespread acceptance of the Hamburg Rules.' Analyse and discuss.*

(k) Rotterdam Rules

In an effort to create a uniform law on carriage of goods by sea, the Comité Maritime International (CMI) in 1999 commenced drafting a new Convention. The CMI completed their draft of the instrument in 2001 and the project was then transferred to the remit of UNCITRAL for further development. In 2008, UNCITRAL concluded work on the draft and the UN Convention on Contracts for the International Carriage of Goods Wholly or Partly by Sea ('Rotterdam Rules') was opened for signing in Rotterdam in September 2009.

Instead of 'carrier' the Rotterdam Rules uses the term 'performing party' to cover a wider range of persons. A contract of carriage is one where the carrier takes the goods from one place to another against payment of freight. The Rules provide for carriage by sea as well as other modes of transportation, such as rail or road, which may result in overlap with the liability provisions of other Conventions. Thus, the period of liability under the Rules will cover 'door to door' carriage.

The Rotterdam Rules will cover all types of transport documents, for example waybills and electronic bills, however they will not apply to charterparties. The

Rules apply if the port of loading or acceptance or place of discharge or delivery is a Contracting State. The Rules will apply to all types of cargo including deck cargo and live animals.

The carrier must exercise due diligence to make the ship seaworthy, however this is a continuous obligation from before, beginning and during the voyage. There is a list of exemptions of liabilities for the carrier but this does not include negligence in navigating the ship or the 'catch all' exemption.

Q11 What is the period of liability under the Rotterdam Rules? What are the problems that arise under this approach?

3 Charterparties

Charterparty contracts of affreightment are most commonly used for large quantities of cargo, which may require the use of the entire vessel. We will examine the two main types of charterparties, the voyage charter and the time charter, and the obligations of the parties in these types of contracts.

(a) Voyage charterparty

As mentioned earlier, the voyage charterparty is not subject to any statutory regimes governing carriage of goods by sea, but parties are free to incorporate such rules as they see fit. Most commonly the voyage charterparty will be regulated by the use of a standard form contract, which is particular to the type of goods being shipped.[38]

There are four main stages of the voyage charterparty:

(1) the preliminary voyage to the specified port of loading;
(2) the loading operation: this stage covers both the loading and the stowage of the goods;
(3) the carrying voyage to the port of discharge;
(4) the discharging operation.

The preliminary voyage and the carrying voyage will be the responsibility of the ship-owner, whereas the loading and discharging operation will be a shared operation between the ship-owner and the charterer. The charterparty may contain specific clauses as to which party shall bear the risk of loss or damage during a particular stage of the voyage. If the charterparty is silent on the issue of risk, in such cases the risk will lie on the party responsible for the stage where the loss or damage occurred. It is usually straight-forward to identify when one stage ends and the other stage begins, the area of most contention tending to centre on when the ship becomes an 'arrived ship' for

---

[38] See, e.g., Gencon 1994.

the purposes of laytime. The following sections will examine each of the four stages in the voyage charter.

(b) Preliminary voyage

(i) Nomination of port of loading

The charterer is under an obligation to nominate a port or berth. This may be fixed, for example, 'Le Havre'; alternatively, the charterer may reserve the right to nominate a port from a range of ports in the same geographic area. Once the nomination is given, the ship-owner is under an obligation to proceed to the specified port. The charterer is under an obligation to make a nomination either within a specified time or a reasonable period of time. Failure to make a nomination within a specified time does not entitle the ship-owner to with-draw the vessel, but if the delay is extensive this may result in frustration of the contract. The ship-owner may also be entitled to damages caused by the delays. In *Zim Israel Navigation Co. Ltd* v. *Tradax Export SA (The Timna)*,[39] it was held that the charterers were in breach of their obligation to give orders for the first discharging port, and as a result they were liable in damages from the time when the orders should have been given to when they were in fact given. Once the charterer has nominated a port or berth he cannot change his nomination.[40]

(ii) Voyage to port of loading

In the absence of an express stipulation in the contract, at common law the ship-owner is under an obligation to proceed to the port of loading with all reasonable dispatch. The charterer may claim damages for any losses incurred as a result of any delays, however he may not terminate the charter unless the delay is so extensive as to amount to frustration of the contract. In *Evera SA Commercial* v. *North Shipping Co. Ltd*,[41] the plaintiffs chartered a vessel from the defendants which was already engaged on another charter. The word-ing of the charterparty stated that the vessel was 'now due to arrive in UK to discharge about August 30, estimating fourteen days to discharge, expected ready to load under this charter-party about September 27, 1953' and 'the said steamship ... shall with all convenient speed sail and proceed to Fort Churchill'. The vessel was delayed and could not arrive in Fort Churchill as it was ice-bound. The plaintiffs cancelled the charter and brought a claim for damages. It was held that the wording of the charterparty imposed an abso-lute obligation on the defendants to ensure that the vessel would arrive on or about the expected date.

---

[39] [1971] 2 Lloyd's Rep. 91.
[40] *Anglo-Danubian Transport Co. Ltd* v. *Ministry of Food* [1949] 2 All ER 1068.
[41] [1956] 2 Lloyd's Rep. 367.

(iii) Expected readiness to load

Most charterparty contracts deal with the problem of fixing a date for the arrival of the vessel by having a date fixed for expected readiness to load (ERL), which is then coupled with a cancellation clause which allows the charterer the right to terminate the charter if the vessel has not arrived by the date specified. This is referred to as a 'lay/can' clause. Failure to arrive by the ERL date does not automatically amount to a breach of condition. However, the ship-owner must have reasonable grounds to believe that the vessel will be ready to load on the date given.[42] When a cancellation clause has been included in the wording of the charterparty, the charterer has the freedom to terminate the contract without liability once the date has passed without the arrival of the vessel.

(iv) The 'near to' cause

The ship-owner may qualify his obligation to deliver the vessel at the port of loading by inserting a 'near to' clause. Thus, in the event of any impediments at the port of loading the ship-owner will still be entitled to the payment of full freight. The ship-owner is expected to wait a reasonable period of time before invoking the 'near to' clause. In any event, the courts tend to construe these clauses quite narrowly. In *Metcalfe* v. *Britannia Ironworks*,[43] a cargo of railway bars was shipped under a charterparty from a port in England to Taganrog, in the Sea of Azof. The charterparty included the wording 'or so near thereto as the ship could safely get'. On the arrival of the ship, on 17 December, at Kertch, which was as near as it could then get to Taganrog, the captain found the sea blocked with ice until the following spring. The captain proceeded to discharge the cargo at Kertch. The bill of lading stated that the cargo was deliverable at Taganrog 'freight and other conditions as per charterparty'. No bill of lading was produced at Kertch, and the captain placed the cargo in charge of the custom-house authorities where it was delivered to the agent of the railway company. The captain claimed to retain the goods until the freight was paid. The ship-owner brought a claim against the charterers for freight. It was held that the ship-owner was not entitled to full freight, as the delivery at Kertch was not a delivery within the wording of the charterparty, and secondly, that the plaintiff was not entitled to freight on a pro rata basis, as no new contract for such freight had been agreed.

The ship-owner may also include other additional clauses in the charterparty to protect him from liability and entitle him to payment of freight in the event he cannot reach the specified port. For example, the use of the words 'always afloat' protects the ship from damage due to grounding and allows him to discharge the goods at the nearest port.

---

[42] *Maredelanto Compania Naviera SA* v. *Bergbau-Handel GmbH (The Mihalis Angelos)* [1971] 1 QB 164.
[43] (1876–77) LR 2 QBD 423.

(c) Loading operation

(i) Division of responsibility

When the ship arrives at the port of loading, the ship-owner and the charterer each have certain responsibilities and obligations to perform. The ship-owner has the task of getting the ship to a position where it is ready to receive and load the goods. The charterer has to provide a cargo, and make sure it is alongside the vessel and ready to load. The charterer has the responsibility to bring the cargo alongside the ship such that it can be loaded on board using the ship's tackle.

(ii) Provision of cargo

The charterer has an absolute obligation to provide cargo for loading on board the vessel. The charterparty will stipulate the quantity and type of goods to be shipped on board the vessel. The charterer will not be able to invoke hardship or any other excuse as a reason for not having a full and complete cargo. The charterer will not be able to invoke any clauses or exceptions to protect him from liability for failure to provide cargo, as these clauses are designed to cover delays in the *actual* loading of the goods and not the procuring of the goods.[44] If there is a range of cargo to choose from the charterer must load a cargo that is within this range; failure to do so may entitle the ship-owner to repudiate the contract. The ship-owner may choose to waive the breach and accept another type of cargo, in which case the charterer will be obligated to pay freight at the current rate for cargo of that kind.[45]

Failure to provide a cargo does not automatically entitle the ship-owner to withdraw the vessel; he must wait for laytime to expire. Even upon the expiration of laytime the ship-owner cannot withdraw the vessel until it is evident that the charterer will not be able to provide a cargo for the voyage, or alternatively the delay is to such an extent as to frustrate the contract.[46]

(iii) The arrived ship

Depending on the wording of the charterparty, a vessel can become an 'arrived' ship either as a berth, dock or port charter. Berth and dock stipulations are fairly straight-forward, as the vessel will be deemed 'arrived' when it reaches the designated location. If the vessel fails to reach the designated berth or dock due to congestion, the ship-owner will bear the risk.[47] Port charters tend to pose more of a problem in deciding when the vessel has arrived for the purposes of laytime to run. In the *E.L. Oldendorff & Co. GmbH* v. *Tradax Export SA (The Johanna Oldendorff)*,[48] the vessel was chartered under a port charter to carry bulk grain

---

[44] *Grant* v. *Coverdale* (1884) 9 App. Cas. 470.
[45] *Steven* v. *Bromley* [1919] 2 KB 722.
[46] *Universal Cargo Carriers* v. *Citati* [1957] 2 Lloyd's Rep. 191.
[47] *Reardon Smith Line Ltd* v. *Ministry of Agriculture* [1963] AC 691.
[48] [1974] AC 479.

from the United States to Liverpool/Birkenhead. As there was no berth free on the vessel's arrival, the port authority ordered the vessel to anchor at Mersey Bar, which was seventeen miles from the dock but still within the administrative limits of the port. The ship-owners tendered the notice of readiness to load, however the charterers argued that laytime could not commence as the ship was not an arrived ship for the purposes of loading. Lord Reid stated:

> On the whole matter I think that it ought to be made clear that the essential factor is that before a ship can be treated as an arrived ship she must be within the port and at the immediate and effective disposition of the charterer and that her geographical position is of secondary importance. But for practical purposes it is so much easier to establish that, if the ship is at a usual waiting place within the port, it can generally be presumed that she is there fully at the charterer's disposal.
>
> I would therefore state what I would hope to be the true legal position in this way. Before a ship can be said to have arrived at a port she must, if she cannot proceed immediately to a berth, have reached a position within the port where she is at the immediate and effective disposition of the charterer. If she is at a place where waiting ships usually lie, she will be in such a position unless in some extraordinary circumstances, proof of which would lie in the charterer.[49]

The test laid out in the *The Johanna Oldendorff* has been much criticised, as it remains uncertain whether it covers the situation where a ship may be directed by the port authorities to wait at an area which is outside the port area. It is argued that the test should be whether the ship-owner has done all he can to bring the ship as close as possible to the congested port to wait for a berth to become free so loading can commence.

Q12 In a voyage charterparty, when is the ship deemed an 'arrived' ship? Why is this important?

(iv) Shifting risk

The ship-owner will try to shift the risk of delays on to the charterer using various mechanisms, one being the WIBON clause, meaning time to count whether in berth or not. Therefore, when the vessel arrives in the port the ship-owner can tender the notice of readiness to load even if there is no berth available. The courts tend to construe the application of these clauses quite narrowly so that they can only apply in situations where the vessel is delayed as a result of no available berths.

(v) Readiness to load

Before the commencement of laytime, the ship must be deemed an 'arrived' ship for the purposes of loading the goods, the master of the ship must have tendered a notice of readiness to load to the charterers, and the vessel must

---

[49] *Ibid.* 535.

be physically ready to load. In some cases the master will tender a notice of readiness to load without the vessel actually becoming an arrived ship. Such notices will be invalid, even if the ship then proceeds to berth for the purposes of loading with the co-operation of the charterer; laytime will not commence and the ship-owners will be unable to claim demurrage in the circumstances.[50] However, in *Flacker Shipping Ltd* v. *Glencore Grain Ltd (The Happy Day)*,[51] the charterers accepted the invalid notice and acted upon it without reservation, and it was held that this could amount to waiver. Potter LJ stated:

> In my view the circumstances of the case and the demands of commercial good sense are such that the court should be reluctant to apply or adopt doubts expressed in obiter dicta … so as to arrive at a result whereby, despite the fact that the vessel has arrived, NOR has been tendered and the unloading operation commenced without any reservation expressed in respect of it, the charterers are free of any constraints upon the time which they take in unloading and, despite delays for which they would otherwise be liable for demurrage, they are in fact entitled to despatch.[52]

(vi) Actual readiness to load

When the notice of readiness to load is tendered, the vessel must in fact actually be ready to load. Once in berth the vessel must have cleared the holds of any previous cargo so that loading can commence and all equipment necessary for loading must be in working order.

(vii) Laytime

One of the most important clauses in a voyage charterparty is the laytime clause. Laytime is the length of time for which the ship will be at the charterer's disposal for the purposes of loading and unloading of the cargo. The amount of laytime allowed will be expressly stipulated in the charterparty. If the charterer exceeds the allocated laytime he will be liable for damages to the ship-owner, either in the form of demurrage or damages for detention. There are competing interests, as the ship-owner will want the vessel loaded as swiftly as possible so that he can remain on schedule, whereas the charterer will negotiate for a greater amount of laytime in case any unforeseen circumstances arise which may result in delays to the loading. Laytime will be paid for by the charterer in the freight that is quoted.

Laytime can be expressed either as a specific number of days or hours (e.g., 'five working days'), or alternatively it can be expressed as a fixed rate of loading (e.g., 200 tons per day). If the charter makes no provision for laytime then it will be what is customary for that particular port. In *Van Liewen* v. *Hollis Bros & Co. Ltd (The Lizzie)*,[53] it was stated by Lord Atkinson:

---

[50] *Transgrain Shipping BV* v. *Global Transporte Oceanico SA (The Mexico 1)* [1990] 1 Lloyd's Rep. 507.
[51] [2002] EWCA Civ 1068.   [52] *Ibid.* 77–85.   [53] [1920] AC 239.

If by the terms of the charterparty the charterers have agreed to discharge the chartered ship within a fixed period of time, that is an absolute and unconditional engagement for the non-performance of which they are answerable, whatever be the nature of the impediments which prevented them from performing it, and thereby causing the ship to be detained in their service beyond the time stipulated. If no time be fixed expressly or impliedly by the charterparty the law implies an agreement by the charterers to discharge the cargo within a reasonable time, having regard to all the circumstances of the case as they actually existed, including the custom or practice of the port, the facilities available thereat, and any impediments arising therefrom which the charterers could not have overcome by reasonable diligence[54]

Laytime is usually expressed using the terms 'days' or 'running days', which means an uninterrupted twenty-four-hour period. Some charterparties may state 'Sundays and holidays excepted' or 'working days' or even 'weather working days'. In *Reardon Smith Line Ltd* v. *Ministry of Agriculture, Fisheries and Food*,[55] Lord Devlin summarised the meaning of some of these terms:

> Day: a continuous period of 24 hours which runs from midnight to midnight.
> Conventional day: a period of 24 hours which starts from the time when a notice of readiness expires or in accordance with its instructions.
> Working day: a period of 24 hours, a day for work as opposed to a day for religious observance or for play or rest.
> Weather working day: a day where cargo could be loaded (or discharged) without interference from the weather.

Today, most charterparties will make provision for laytime to be calculated using a daily rate of loading and unloading, e.g., 100 tons per weather working day. Laydays will then be stipulated by dividing the amount of cargo to be loaded by the daily rate.

(viii) Suspension of laytime

In the absence of any fixed laytime, the charterer will be excused from failing to load if there are circumstances that arise which are beyond his control.[56] If laytime is stipulated in the charterparty then the charterer will bear the risk of any supervening events. In *Budgett* v. *Binnington*,[57] a cargo was shipped under a bill of lading in which the laytime was for a specified number of days; neither the bill of lading nor the charterparty contained any exception for strike action. During the discharge of the goods a strike took place and did not end until after the expiry of the laytime. It was held that, as the laytime was fixed, the consignees were liable to pay demurrage.

Q13 What is meant by laytime? In what circumstances would laytime be suspended?

---

[54] *Ibid.* 251.   [55] [1963] AC 691.
[56] *Hick* v. *Raymond and Reid* [1893] AC 22.
[57] [1891] 1 QB 35.

(ix) Completion of loading

The vessel will be at the charterer's disposal for the agreed period of laytime. The ship-owner cannot force the charterer to hasten the loading process. However, once the loading process is completed the charterer cannot detain the vessel even if there is laytime left to run. In *Owners of The Nolisement* v. *Bunge and Born*,[58] the vessel completed its loading with nineteen laydays left to run. The charterers delayed the departure of the vessel for three days as it took that time to decide on a port of discharge. The court held that the charterer was liable for two days' damages for detention.

(x) Demurrage

If the charterer fails to load the cargo within the agreed laytime, this will amount to a breach of contract. Breach in these circumstances will entitle the ship-owner to claim damages, with demurrage being calculated as an agreed rate per day. The courts tend to apply the maxim 'once on demurrage, always on demurrage', meaning that if the parties intend that demurrage should not be payable in certain circumstances this needs to be expressly stated in the contract. In *Marc Rich & Co. Ltd* v. *Tourloti Compania Naviera SA (The Kalliopi A)*,[59] the vessel was chartered for a voyage from Rotterdam to Bombay. The wording of the charterparty stated that the vessel could give notice of readiness whether in berth or not and that 'the act of God, restraint of Princes and Rulers … and all and every other unavoidable hindrances which may prevent the … discharging … always mutually excepted'. On arrival at Bombay, the master tendered the notice, however, due to congestion there was no free berth available. The shipowner claimed demurrage, but the charterer argued that the clause operated so as to relieve them from having to pay. It was held that while the clause could be read so as to exclude liability for demurrage, where the vessel was already on demurrage, the clause could not cover these circumstances.

A breach of failure to load within the specified laytime does not entitle the ship-owner to rescind the contract but to claim damages only. The charterer, however, may not keep the ship indefinitely on demurrage; when the delay is such as to frustrate the contract, the ship-owner can terminate the contract.[60]

(xi) Damages for detention

If there is no agreed rate of damages stated in the charterparty then the charterer will be liable for damages for detention in the event that laytime is exceeded. Damages will be assessed in relation to actual losses suffered, as well as subject to the limitations of remoteness and mitigation.

---

[58] [1917] 1 KB 160.   [59] [1988] 2 Lloyd's Rep. 101.
[60] *Universal Cargo Carriers* v. *Citati* [1957] 2 QB 401.

(xii) Despatch money

As the ship-owner will want to have the ship at his disposal as early as possible, he may offer an incentive to the charterer if loading is completed in a shorter period than was agreed. The general view is that dispatch monies are calculated at half the rate of demurrage and usually include all time saved at the port.[61]

Q14 What are the consequences where the charterer exceeds the allocated laytime? What if the shipper completes his loading duties with laytime remaining?

(d) Carrying voyage

Once loading is completed, the ship-owner has an obligation at common law to proceed with all reasonable dispatch to the port of discharge. When the ship is deemed an 'arrived' ship at the port of discharge, the carrying voyage comes to an end. The ship-owner is under no duty to tender a notice of readiness to discharge, the consignee has to be ready to unload the goods on arrival.[62]

(e) Discharging operation

The discharge operation will begin once the ship becomes an arrived ship. The procedure for discharge involves a division of responsibility on the part of the ship-owner and consignee. The ship-owner is under an obligation to deliver the cargo to the consignee or lawful holder of the bill of lading. If there is no consignee present to take delivery of the goods, the ship-owner must wait a reasonable time before he can warehouse the goods. The consignee will be liable to the ship-owner for such expenses incurred. If the ship-owner is aware of any other claims against the goods he may be liable for the tort of conversion.

   If the goods become mixed with other goods, making them unidentifiable as belonging to the consignee, the ship-owner may be liable unless the event occurred as a result of an exception; for example, if the goods became mixed during a particularly rough sea voyage this may be covered by the perils of the sea exception. In *Spence v. Union Marine Insurance Co.*,[63] Bovill J stated:

> when goods of different owners become by accident so mixed together as to be undistinguishable, the owners of the goods so mixed become tenants in common of the whole, in the proportions which they have severally contributed to it.[64]

In the event that the mixed goods are not covered by an exception, the consignee is not obliged to accept an apportionment of the goods, rather, the ship-owner will be liable to the consignee.[65]

---

[61] *The Themistocles* (1949) 82 Ll. LR 232.
[62] *Houlder* v. *GSN* (1862) 3 F & F 170.
[63] (1868) LR 3 CP 427.   [64] *Ibid.* 437.
[65] *Sandeman* v. *Tyzack* [1913] AC 680.

4 Time charterparty

The time charterparty contract is designed for the use of a vessel for a period of time. The ship-owner agrees to place the ship at the charterer's disposal for the stipulated time period. The time charterer pays a sum referred to as 'hire' for the use of the vessel and is responsible for the day-to-day commercial operation of the ship, however the crew continues to be employed by the ship-owner. The charterer will enter into contracts with shippers for the carriage of goods and will issue bills of lading for those goods.

(a) Description of the vessel

The vessel's physical and other characteristics must be appropriate for the purpose of the time charter. Once the ship has been named and assigned to the time charter it cannot be replaced with an alternative ship even if the ship possesses the same characteristics as the original.[66] In this instance, the charterer can terminate the contract. The nationality of a ship may determine if the ship can enter a particular port. If the ship-owner changes the nationality of the ship, the charterer may be entitled to terminate the contract if the changes cause serious repercussions to the contract.[67]

Vessels are often 'classed' by different independent organisations, for example Lloyd's Register, which undertakes to classify a ship's seaworthiness. A warranty as to the class of the ship is not a continuing warranty, as the classification society may revoke the class given to the vessel. If the classification is revoked and it is shown that the ship-owner breached the classification clause, he may be liable for the unseaworthiness of the vessel and the charterer may be entitled to terminate the contract.[68]

The vessel's specifications as to speed and fuel intake are the most frequent sources of dispute as these factors can have signifiant financial implications for the charter. English courts tended to treat such warranties as being effective at the time the charter was signed. However, in *Cosmos Bulk Transport Inc.* v. *China National Foreign Trade Transportation Co.*,[69] the courts held that the warranty as to speed should apply to the date the vessel was delivered. The measure of damages awarded in such cases would be the difference between market hire rate for a vessel with the requested specifications and the market hire rate of the one that was in fact delivered.

Q15 What are the main characteristics of a time charter?

(i) Period of hire

The length of the time charter may be stated in the form of days, months or even years. In many cases, the cirumstances of the final voyage of the charter may

---

[66] *Société Navale de L'Ouest* v. *RWJ Sutherland & Co.* (1920) 4 Ll. L Rep. 58.
[67] *M. Isaacs and Sons, Ltd* v. *William Mcallum* [1921] 3 KB 377.
[68] *Routh* v. *Macmillan* (1863) 159 ER 310.   [69] [1978] 1 Lloyd's Rep. 52.

make it difficult to guarantee the vessel will have completed the voyage in the given time. The vessel may return early (known as underlap) or it may exceed its time (known as overlap).

The charter may provide a fixed period for the charter, such as 'one year'. In this case, if the vessel is early or exceeds its time the courts tend to imply a margin of 4–5 per cent. Some charters will include a qualification using wording such as 'more or less' or a minimum/ maximum approach. Such qualifications will be treated as absolute in setting the maximum time allowable to the charterer. Once the period of tolerance is exceeded, the charterer will be in breach of contract. The ship-owner can also decide to make time of the essence by expressly stating a specific date for the return of the vessel.[70] Unlike the voyage charter, if the vessel is returned at an earlier date to the ship-owner the charterer is not entitled to a refund of hire.[71]

If the charterer exceeds the time for redelivery and is within the leeway allowed, he will only be liable to pay for time exceeded at the normal rate of hire. However, if the vessel is not redelivered when the period of tolerance has run out, the charterer will be liable for damages at the current market rate. The courts will sometimes apply the 'legitimate last voyage' test to decide if the charterer is in breach; this requires that when the vessel departed for its last voyage it was reasonable to expect the voyage would be completed within the period of hire with the addition of the leeway.[72]

(b) Hire

The wording of the time charter will make express stipulation as to the amount of hire payable. There will also be clauses as to the time of payment, as well as the currency. Payment is usually made on a monthly basis and will include clauses to protect against currency fluctuations. Payment is normally made in cash; this term embodies a wider meaning and can cover banker's drafts and transfers. The general practice is for payment to be made in advance, however the charterer is allowed until midnight to tender payment.[73] The obligation to make timely payment is a strict one and the charterer will be in breach even if failure to pay is not due to his actions.[74]

(i) Off-hire

Time charters normally provide that hire will cease to be payable on the occurrence of certain events for the time lost to the charterer as a result of the event. The charterer will bear the onus of establishing that 'off hire' should apply in the circumstances. 'Off hire' clauses take the form of either a 'period' clause that

---

[70] *Watson* v. *Merryweather* [1913] 12 Asp. 353.
[71] *Reindeer SS Co.* v. *Forslind* (1908) 13 Com. Cas. 214.
[72] *The Democritos* [1976] 2 Lloyd's Rep. 149.
[73] *The Afovos* [1983] 1 Lloyd's Rep. 335.
[74] *Tankexpress* v. *Compagnie Financière Belge des Petroles* (1948) 82 LI. L Rep. 43.

runs from the start until the end of the event, or alternatively, a 'net loss of time' clause which covers the payment of hire for the time lost during the event.

(ii) Deductions from hire

In some circumstances the charterer is permitted to make deductions from hire. These can include where he has made disbursements on behalf of the ship-owner, monies owed from off hire, failure of the vessel to meet specifications or damage to the cargo. Although the English courts were reluctant to accept this approach,[75] in *The Nanfri*[76] Lord Denning reasoned that, where the ship-owner, in breach, deprives the charterer of use of the vessel, there was no reason why a cross-claim could not be set-off from hire.

Q16 When is hire payable? Can the charterer deduct from hire? If so, in what circumstances?

(c) Right of withdrawal

The ship-owner has a right to withdraw a vessel from service if hire is not paid in full or by the due date stipulated in the contract. At common law, however, time is not of the essence and therefore the ship-owner may only withdraw the vessel if it becomes clear that the charterer will not perform his obligations.[77] Therefore, most time charters will contain an express clause as to time of payment for which a breach would entitle the ship-owner to withdraw the vessel. Notice of withdrawal must be given to the charterers, and once the vessel is withdrawn the charter will be terminated. The ship-owner may choose to waive the breach and accept a late payment, however if this is a continued pattern the ship-owner may lose his right to withdraw altogether.[78]

(d) Employment and agency

In a time charter, the charterer will issue orders to the master of the ship and the master must act in accordance with his directions. The charterer has the right to issue bills of lading in relation to the goods taken on board. The master will sign these bills on the charterer's instructions, however this would leave the ship-owner liable to any holders of the bill of lading. To prevent this, the charterer will agree to indemnify the ship-owner against any claims brought by third parties. However, if the master follows instructions he knows are not within the charterer's authority, then the ship-owner is not entitled to rely on the indemnity.[79]

---

[75] *Seven Seas Transportation* v. *Atlantic Shipping* [1975] 2 Lloyd's Rep. 188.
[76] [1978] 2 Lloyd's Rep. 132.
[77] *Cochin Refineries* v. *Triton Shipping* [1978] AMC 444.
[78] *Tankexpress* v. *Compagnie Financière Belge des Petroles* (1948) 82 Ll L Rep. 43.
[79] *Larrinaga SS Co.* v *R* [1945] AC 246.

(e) Redelivery of the vessel

The charterers are under an obligation to redeliver the ship in good order and condition, with the exception of everyday wear and tear. The charterer will be liable in damages if, as a result of any breach of his obligations under the charter, he redelivers the ship in a worse condition than when delivered. The ship-owner cannot refuse to accept the vessel in its damaged state.[80]

5 Common law obligations of the shipper

(a) Obligation to nominate a safe port

The charterer is under an obligation to nominate a port of loading and discharge. It is essential that the nominated ports are deemed 'safe' ports. The ship-owner has no obligation to proceed to a port known to be unsafe. The safety of the port covers a wide list of events that include ice, wars, sandbanks, high winds, wrecks, amongst many others. The courts will consider a range of factors in determining a port to be unsafe, however the risk must be a factual rather than a subjective one. In *The Saga Cob*,[81] the Court of Appeal rejected the argument that the nominated port was unsafe simply because another ship had been attacked in that port at an earlier date. In the judgment of Parker LJ, the relevance of foreseeability by the charterer was not given much weight, rather it was stated:

> If [the fact that it was foreseeable an attack could occur at the port or on the vessel's approach to it] were enough it would seem to follow that, if there were a seaborne guerilla or terrorist attack in two small boats in the coastal waters of a country in which there had been sporadic guerilla or terrorist activity on land and which had many ports, it would become a normal characteristic of every port in that country that such an attack in the port or whilst proceeding to it or departing from it was sufficiently likely to render the port unsafe. This we cannot accept.[82]

When the charterer gives a warranty as to the safety of the port, the warranty takes immediate effect. It is envisaged that the port should remain safe until the vessel has completed its operations. However, the port, although safe when nominated, could have subsequently become unsafe.

In *Kodros Shipping Corp. of Monrovia* v. *Empresa Cubanade Fletes (The Evia) (No. 2)*,[83] the vessel was time-chartered on the terms that it was to be sent to safe ports. The charterers elected the port of Basrah, which, although safe at the time of nomination, became unsafe when hostilities broke out between Iran and Iraq, and as a result the vessel became trapped. In his judgment, Lord Roskill discussed the charterer's obligation in such circumstances. He stated

---

[80] *Wye Shipping Co.* v *Compagnie Paris-Orleans* [1922] 1 KB 617.
[81] [1992] 2 Lloyd's Rep. 545.
[82] *Ibid.* 551.   [83] [1983] 1 AC 736.

that if, while the vessel was in such a port or place, some unexpected or abnormal event suddenly occurred that made it unsafe, then the charterers' contractual nomination did not extend to making the charterers liable for any resulting loss or damage.

In *The Kanchenjunga*, the vessel was under a voyage charter on terms to load at '1/2 safe ports Arabian Gulf'.[84] The charterers nominated the port of Kharg Island; at the time, this port was known to be unsafe as a result of the Iran–Iraq war. The ship-owners accepted this nomination and proceeded to tender a notice of readiness; however, when hostilities broke out the ship-owners asked the charterer to make an alternative nomination. It was held that as the ship-owner accepted a nomination of a port known to be unsafe, this amounted to a waiver of the right to call for another nomination. In most cases, a breach of the duty to nominate a safe port will amount to a breach of warranty entitling the ship-owner to damages.

Q17 What is meant by 'safe ports'? Will any type of hazard render the port unsafe? At what times must the port be safe?

(b) Dangerous goods

The shipper is under an obligation not to ship dangerous goods. Some goods are classified as being 'dangerous' by statute; for example, section 446 of the Merchant Shipping Act 1894 defined dangerous goods as:

> aquafortis, vitriol, naphtha, benzine, gunpowder, lucifer matches, nitro-glycerine, petroleum, any explosives within the meaning of the Explosives Act 1875, and any other goods which are of a dangerous nature.[85]

The Merchant Shipping (Dangerous Goods and Marine Pollutants) Regulations 1997, SI 1997/2367, regulation 2(1) defines 'dangerous goods' as:

> goods classified in the IMDG Code or in any other IMO publication referred to in these Regulations as dangerous for carriage by sea, and any other substance or article that the shipper has reasonable cause to believe might meet the criteria for such classification;
>
> This expression also includes:
>
> (i) residues in empty receptacles, empty tanks or cargo holds which have been used previously for the carriage of dangerous goods unless such receptacles, empty tanks or cargo holds have been cleaned and dried, purged, gas freed or ventilated as appropriate or, in the case of radioactive materials, have been both cleaned and adequately closed; and
> (ii) goods labelled, marked or declared as dangerous goods.

---

[84] [1990] Lloyd's Rep. 391, HL.
[85] This section was repealed by the Merchant Shipping (Registration) Act 1993.

The expression shall not include goods forming part of the equipment or stores of the ship in which they are carried.

However, it is not always straight-forward to determine what goods will be 'dangerous'. In *The Giannis NK*, a cargo of groundnut pellets was shipped under a bill of lading incorporating the Hague Rules.[86] Unknown to the ship-owner, the groundnuts were infested with Khapra beetles, and when the infestation was discovered the ship was not permitted to discharge the cargo at ports in the Dominican Republic or Puerto Rico. The ship-owners were forced to dispose of the cargo at sea at its original port of loading in Dakar. The House of Lords considered the implied duty under the common law whereby the shipper is to notify the ship-owner of any dangerous cargo, and Lord Lloyd *obiter* supported the view that such a duty should be absolute regardless of the shipper's knowledge.[87]

(c) Obligation to provide cargo

The charterer has an obligation to provide a cargo for loading on board the vessel. In *Grant* v. *Coverdale*,[88] the charterers tried to rely on an exception covering, 'frost or floods', as they were unable to obtain the goods from the wharf due to the canal being blocked by ice. It was held that the exception could only be relied upon in the actual loading of the goods, not in delivering the goods to the loading dock.

If the charterer fails to provide cargo, this will not entitle the ship-owner to withdraw the vessel; he must wait for laytime to expire. Even upon the expiration of laytime, the ship-owner cannot withdraw the vessel until it is evident that the charterer will not provide a cargo or the delay is to such an extent as to frustrate the contract.[89]

Q18 What is meant by 'full and complete cargo'? Can an alternative cargo be provided?

(d) Freight

Freight is the payment to the carrier for transporting the goods from the port of loading to the port of discharge. Freight is the type of payment used in voyage charters, as well as bill of lading contracts of affreightment. In most cases, the quantity of cargo will determine the amount of freight payable. The quantity can be measured by weight, number of packages or by cubic measurement.

If the goods are lost or destroyed for any reason, no freight will be payable to the carrier. The courts construe this rule quite narrowly, thus if the contract is

---

[86] [1998] AC 605.   [87] *Ibid*. 619.   [88] (1884) 9 App. Cas. 470.
[89] *Universal Cargo Carriers* v. *Citati* [1957] 2 Lloyd's Rep. 191.

substantially performed albeit the goods are damaged, freight is still payable.[90] The cargo-owner can then bring a separate claim for damages; the cargo-owner cannot deduct from or set-off freight. The reasoning behind this rule can be seen in *The Brede*, where Lord Denning stated:

> The good conduct of business demands that freight should be paid according to the terms of the contract. Payment should not be held up because the goods are alleged to have been damaged in transit. If that were allowed, it would enable unscrupulous persons to make all sorts of unfounded allegations so as to avoid payment. In any case, even with the most scrupulous, it would lead to undesirable delay.[91]

The carrier will not be allowed to claim freight if he is unable to deliver the goods to the port of destination, even if this is due to circumstances beyond his control.[92]

An exception to the rule that there is no deduction from freight is where the goods are so badly damaged on their arrival that they are held to be unmerchantable; this means that they no longer correspond with their commercial description. In *Asfar* v. *Blundell*,[93] a cargo of dates was badly damaged when the ship collided with another vessel and sank. When the ship was bought to the surface the dates were found to be unmerchantable as they were unfit for human consumption.

(e) Types of freight

(i) Advanced freight
In some liner trades it is common for freight to be payable in advance; this is normally stated to take place 'on signing of bill of lading' or 'on sailing of vessel'. In English law, advance freight is not refundable even if the cargo is lost.[94]

(ii) Lump sum freight
Lump sum freight is commonly used when the quantity of goods may be unknown. It is calculated in reference to the space used on the ship, which may be part of or the whole of the ship, rather than the quantity of goods shipped.[95] In the event that some of the goods are not delivered, lump sum freight will still remain payable.[96]

---

[90] *Dakin* v. *Oxley* (1864) 15 CBNS 646.
[91] [1973] 2 Lloyd's Rep 333, 338.
[92] *Metcalfe* v. *Britannia Ironworks Co.* (1877) 2 QB 423.
[93] (1896) 1 QB 123, CA.
[94] *Allison* v. *Bristol Marine Insurance* (1876) 1 App. Cas. 209, HL.
[95] Lump sum freight is different from the obligation to provide a 'full and complete' cargo under a freight rate calculated per unit.
[96] *Williams & Co.* v. *Canton Insurance Office Ltd* [1901] AC 462.

(iii) Pro rata freight

Pro rata freight will be used where the goods have been carried part of the voyage, but the goods have not been able to reach their destination due to circumstances beyond the ship-owner's control. The cargo-owner must voluntarily agree to accept the goods at some alternative location.[97]

(iv) Dead freight

When the charterer fails to provide a full cargo he is obligated to pay dead freight to the carrier. This is usually calculated as the freight which would be payable minus the charges for loading and unloading. The ship-owner is under an obligation to try and mitigate his losses by finding another cargo to fill the space.[98]

(v) Back freight

Back freight is the sum payable to ship the goods back to the port of origin when the goods are refused on arrival. The reason for this refusal can include the outbreak of war, strikes or the cargo-owner's refusal to take delivery.

Q19 What are the advantages and disadvantages of using advanced freight?

6 Common law obligations of the carrier

(a) Seaworthiness

The carrier is under an obligation at common law to make the ship seaworthy. This obligation is absolute, meaning that the owner of the vessel will be liable regardless of fault. The obligation will be assessed in light of the nature of the voyage as well as the cargo being carried on board the vessel. The state of the vessel is linked to its ability to carry the cargo. In *Tattersall* v. *National Steamship Co.*,[99] a cargo of cattle was shipped from London to New York. When the cattle contracted foot and mouth disease on board the ship, it was found that this was as a result of an earlier voyage where the animals on board had carried the disease. Due to negligence on the part of the defendants, the ship was not cleaned and disinfected properly. It was held that these actions resulted in the ship being unseaworthy.

Unseaworthiness can also be caused by the incompetence of the crew if they are not trained or supervised properly.[100] The carrier is also required to have all necessary documentation in order to render the vessel seaworthy. In *Cheikh Boutros Selim El-Khoury* v. *Ceylon Shipping Lines (The Madeleine)*,[101] documentation to certify the ship had been fumigated was not issued until after

---

[97] *Metcalfe* v. *Britannia Ironworks Co.* (1877) 2 QB 423, 427.
[98] *The Storviken* [1927] 2 KB 99.   [99] (1884) 12 QBD 297.
[100] *Standard Oil* v. *Clan Line Steamers* [1924] AC 100.
[101] [1967] 2 Lloyd's Rep. 224.

the date of delivery of the vessel had passed, which resulted in the vessel being unseaworthy.

The carrier's duty as to seaworthiness will attach at the time of loading until the ship has sailed, it is not a continuous duty. The burden will be on the claimant to prove the carrier breached his duty as to seaworthiness.[102]

If the party alleging unseaworthiness is able to prove causation, the most common remedy available to the parties will be the award of damages. Termination of the contract will not be available unless it amounts to frustration of contract.[103]

(b) Deviation

The carrier is under an obligation at common law not to deviate from the agreed route without lawful justification. This rule is justified on the basis that the cargo-owner will not be protected by his policy of insurance on the goods if the vessel deviates from the agreed route. The insurer will fix a premium based on the facts disclosed by the owner of the policy, therefore some routes will incur a higher risk of loss or damage to the vessel or goods. If the ship-owner breaches his obligation not to deviate he will be unable to rely on the excepted perils. If there is no expressly agreed route, it will be the usual geographic route taken from the port of loading to port of discharge.[104]

At common law it is permissible in some circumstances to deviate from the agreed or usual route. The first of these is where the deviation is for the purpose of saving life; this can include saving property if it is in the course of saving lives.[105]

It may also be necessary to deviate from the agreed or usual route where the purpose is to avoid danger to the vessel or to the cargo.[106] Deviation without lawful justification will entitle the party to terminate the contract.[107]

(c) Reasonable dispatch

The carrier is under a duty to perform his contractual obligations with reasonable dispatch. This means that the vessel will proceed on the voyage, load and discharge at the time agreed or within a reasonable time. A breach of the duty to proceed with reasonable dispatch will be remedied by the award of damages. However, if the delay is for an extended period of time, this could amount to frustration of the contract. In *Freeman* v. *Taylor*,[108] a vessel had been chartered

---

[102] *McFadden* v. *Blue Star Line* [1905] 1 KB 697.
[103] *Hong Kong Fir Shipping* v. *Kawasaki Kisen Kaisha* [1962] 2 QB 26, CA.
[104] *Reardon Smith Line* v. *Black Sea and Baltic General Insurance* [1939] AC 562, HL.
[105] It must be for the primary purpose of saving life. See *Scaramanga* v. *Stamp* (1880) 5 CPD 295, CA.
[106] *Phelps, James & Co.* v. *Hill* [1891] 1 QB 605, CA.
[107] 'Held cover' insurance policies have made this less of an issue.
[108] (1831) 8 Bing. 124.

from Cape Town where, after discharging, it was to proceed to Bombay for loading. After discharging the cargo in Cape Town, the master proceeded to Mauritius before calling at Bombay. As a result the vessel was severely delayed and it was held that this was sufficient to frustrate the contract.

7 Bills of lading

The bill of lading is the most commonly used contract of affreightment. The bill of lading serves several different functions: it can act as a receipt for the goods, as evidence of the contract of carriage, as well being a negotiable document of title. In the United Kingdom, bills of lading are subject to statutory regimes, namely, the Carriage of Goods by Sea Act 1971, which imposes a limitation of liability under the Hague-Visby Rules on bills of lading issued in the United Kingdom. The COGSA 1992 allows the lawful holder of the bill of lading and other sea carriage documents to have rights of suit.

(a) Functions of the bill of lading

(i) Bill of lading as receipt for goods

The bill of lading will serve as a receipt for the quantity, condition and leading marks of goods received. Article III(3) of the Hague-Visby Rules states that the shipper can demand the carrier issue a bill of lading, which contains information as to the quantity, order and condition, and leading marks of the goods. Article III(4) provides that such statements in the bill of lading shall be *prima facie* evidence of receipt by the carrier but conclusive evidence once the bill is transferred to a third party in good faith. At common law, a ship-owner could avoid liability even towards a bona fide transferee of the bill of lading if he could prove that the goods were not in fact shipped. This is seen in *Grant* v. *Norway*,[109] where the master signed a bill of lading that twelve bales of silk had been shipped, when in fact they had not been loaded on board the ship. The holders of the bill of lading had no remedy as the master had no authority to sign for goods which were not loaded. This problem was somewhat resolved by the Hague-Visby Rules, Article III(4). However, as the Rules do not apply to all types of bills, section 4 of the COGSA 1994 was enacted, which covers a wider range of bills.

Statements as to the order and the condition of the goods are *prima facie* evidence in favour of the shipper but conclusive once the bill is in the hands of a bona fide purchaser for value. The master of the ship can either issue a bill of lading as 'clean' if the goods are in good order and condition, or 'claused' if the goods contain defects. In *Compania Naviera Vascongada* v. *Churchill*,[110] a cargo of timber became badly stained with petroleum while awaiting shipment. The

---

[109] (1851) 10 CB 665.   [110] [1906] 1 KB 237.

master issued a clean bill of lading but was estopped from disclaiming the truth when a claim was brought by the third-party bill of lading holders. However, the master will only be held liable for statements which he could verify by reasonable inspection of the goods.[111] If the bill of lading discloses the defect in the goods then the master can issue a 'clean' bill of lading.

In some cases, the shipper may promise the master an indemnity against liability from third parties if the master issues a clean bill even though he knows the statements to be untrue. In *Brown, Jenkinson & Co. Ltd v. Percy Dalton*,[112] the master issued a clean bill of lading against an indemnity for a cargo of orange juice even though it was apparent the barrels were leaking. It was held that as the statements were known to be false, the plaintiffs could not enforce the indemnity and were liable in the tort of deceit.

However, in the absence of fraud an indemnity is permitted under Article III(5) in relation to statements as to quantity or leading marks but not as to the condition of goods.

Q20 Explain the shipper's liability for statements made in the bill of lading. What is the effect of such statements on the consignee?

(ii) Bill of lading as evidence of contract of carriage

In practice, the shipper will have concluded the terms of carriage before the bill of lading is issued. While the bill remains in the hands of the shipper, this is evidence of the contract of carriage. When the bill is transferred to a third party, it will be treated as the contract of carriage, meaning it will contain the relevant terms and conditions. Therefore, any oral agreements between the shipper and carrier will not bind the third party.[113]

(iii) Bill of lading as document of title

To be a document of title a bill of lading must be drafted 'to order' and name a consignee. A bill of lading which is drafted without the words 'to order' is known as a straight bill – these are not documents of title.[114]

The bill of lading represents the goods, and possession of the bill is treated as equivalent to possession of the goods which it covers. The transferee of the bill of lading will not acquire a better title to the goods than was held by the previous owner.

(b) The Carriage of Goods by Sea Act 1992

The COGSA 1992 improved the earlier position under the Bills of Lading Act 1855 under which the contract of carriage was governed by rules of privity.

---

[111] *Silver* v. *Ocean Steamship Co.* [1930] 1 KB 416.
[112] [1957] 2 QB 621.   [113] *Leduc* v. *Ward* (1888) 20 QBD 475.
[114] See *The Rafaela S* [2005] 1 Lloyd's Rep. 347.

Under the COGSA 1992, any lawful holder of a bill of lading, sea waybill or delivery order is vested with the right of suit under the contract of carriage. Section 2(1) states:

(a) the lawful holder of a bill of lading;
(b) the person who (without being an original party to the contract of carriage) is the person to whom delivery of the goods to which a sea waybill relates is to be made by the carrier in accordance with that contract; or
(c) the person to whom delivery of the goods to which a ship's delivery order relates is to be made in accordance with the undertaking contained in the order,

shall (by virtue of becoming the holder of the bill or, as the case may be, the person to whom delivery is to be made) have transferred to and vested in him all rights of suit under the contract of carriage as if he had been a party to that contract.

The lawful holder of the bill of lading is defined in section 5(2) as:

(a) a person with possession of the bill who, by virtue of being the person identi-fied in the bill, is the consignee of the goods to which the bill relates;
(b) a person with possession of the bill as a result of the completion, by delivery of the bill, of any indorsement of the bill or, in the case of a bearer bill, of any other transfer of the bill;
(c) a person with possession of the bill as a result of any transaction by virtue of which he would have become a holder falling within paragraph (a) or (b) above had not the transaction been effected at a time when possession of the bill no longer gave a right (as against the carrier) to possession of the goods to which the bill relates;

and a person shall be regarded for the purposes of this Act as having become the lawful holder of a bill of lading whenever he has become the holder of the bill in good faith.

Once a transfer is made, section 2(5) extinguishes the rights of the previous transferee or any other party. However, the shipper can still retain property in the goods. Section 2(4) allows the party with right of suit to exercise that right on behalf of a party who has suffered loss.

Section 3 states that liability will only attach if the party:

(a) takes or demands delivery from the carrier of any of the goods to which the document relates;
(b) makes a claim under the contract of carriage against the carrier in respect of any of those goods; or
(c) is a person who, at a time before those rights were vested in him, took or demanded delivery from the carrier of any of those goods.

The intermediate holder of the bill will no longer incur liability under the contract of carriage once title to sue has been transferred. However, the shipper may still remain liable to the carrier for outstanding freight.

8 Electronic bills of lading

As modern transport and communication increase in speed and efficiency, the use of electronic bills of lading has increased. Section 1(5) of the COSGA 1992 provides a mechanism for the Secretary of State to extend the application of the Act to electronic bills, but this has not yet been exercised. However, the UNCITRAL Model Law on Electronic Commerce and the Model Law on Electronic Signatures have been helpful to provide guidance to parties using electronic bills. The CMI Rules for Electronic Bills of Lading were adopted by the Comité Maritime International (CMI) in 1990. The Rules need to be incorporated into the contract. If the parties agree that the Rules will apply to the contract, the shipper delivers the goods to the carrier who then transmits a receipt message to the shipper's electronic address. The message will contain information pertaining to the name of the shipper, the description of the goods, the date and place of receipt and a private key. The private key is the mechanism that allows for endorsement, negotiation and registration of the electronic bill. It is also a secure means of electronic transmission. The shipper can access material with the private key and control the goods in transit. Once the shipper transfers the goods to the next holder, a new key is issued to the consignee.

Another mechanism is the BOLERO Rules (Bill of Lading Electronic Registry Organization). BOLERO is a project set up by the European Union to study the viability of electronic bills. This is a closed system only accessible by subscribers, who are subject to the BOLERO Rule Book. The system incorporates the use of notification, confirmation and authentication through digital signature. It is unknown how effective the system has been in international trade.

9 Conclusion

In this chapter, we have seen that the process of carriage of goods by sea in international trade is complex. While legal mechanisms such as the Hague-Visby Rules attempt to achieve a balance between the parties, there are still many gaps present in the law. The competing rights of the parties involved mean that the terms negotiated in the contracts have to be as clear and as specific as possible.

10 Recommended reading

Barclay, C. 'Technical aspects of unseaworthiness' (1975) *LMCLQ* 288
Baughen, S. 'Does deviation still matter' (1991) *LMCLQ* 70
  'Defining the limits of the carrier's responsibilities' (2005) *LMCLQ* 153
Clarke, M. 'Seaworthiness in time charters' (1977) *LMCLQ* 493
Dockray, M. 'Deviation: a doctrine all at sea' (2000) *LMCLQ* 76
Grunfeld, C. 'Affreightment – unseaworthiness – causation' (1949)*MLR* 372

Mills, C. 'The future of deviation' (1983) 4 *LMCLQ* 587

Schofield, J. *Laytime and Demurrage* (4th edn, Lloyd's of London, 2000)

Sheppard, J.C. 'The rule against deduction from freight reconsidered' (2006) *JBL* 1

Solvang, T. 'Laytime, demurrage and multiple charterparties' (2001) *LMCLQ* 285

Todd, P. 'The peculiar position of freight' (1989) 8(4) *Int. Bank. L* 56

   'Start of laytime' (2002) *JBL* 217

Part 4
Tortious Liability for Defective Products

Introduction

Part 4 looks at the tortious liability of traders and the rights of users in respect of product-related injuries. The law of tort is, of course, a far wider topic than liability for faulty products, encompassing negligence, trespass and defamation, amongst other areas. However, the parameters of tort as discussed here are limited to tortious liabilities and actions arising from the production of faulty products.

Part 4 is divided into two chapters, the first looking briefly at the law of negligence before moving on to consider the move towards strict product liability, initially in the United States and, since the 1970s, in Europe. This movement in Europe stemmed from three different sources: the United Kingdom, the Strasbourg Convention and, finally, the EC Directive which overtook both of the other two. The second chapter looks expressly at the regime of strict product liability under Part I of the Consumer Protection Act 1987, which gave effect to the EC Directive in the United Kingdom.

It is important to recognise that negligence and strict liability run in tandem since, although product liability has had a significant impact in this area, the law of negligence remains extremely important for a variety of reasons. The strict liability regime under the Consumer Protection Act 1987 only provides rights to consumers, not businesses. Thus, any damage suffered by a business as a result of using a defective product, such as, for example, damage caused to a factory by a negligently manufactured heater catching fire, must be recovered via negligence. Further, consumer rights under Part I of the Consumer Protection Act 1987 are themselves restricted. Thus, claims for property damage of less than £275, damage to the defective item itself and claims that fall outside the limitation period or the ten-year cut-off period are excluded from the auspices of the 1987 Act. Accordingly, claimants in such cases will need to revert to the law of negligence, or contract, as the case demands.

Finally, while there is a tendency to think of product liability as a consumer law subject, it is important to remember that the legislation impacts on all businesses in the way that they produce their goods and the legal liability to which they are subject. Equally, every claim made by an injured user impacts on a defendant business and may affect the reputation of the business, its financial wellbeing and its ability to acquire insurance at a reasonable premium. As such, negligence and strict liability for product-related incidents cannot, and should not, be ignored as an important aspect of commercial practice.

Part 4 Chapter 1

Negligence and the Rise of Product Liability

Contents

1 Introduction

This chapter looks at the development of tort law and its application to prod-uct-related injuries. Thus, it considers both the tort of negligence and the policy lying behind the development of strict liability.

The chapter is structured as follows. Section 2 considers the background to the development of the law of negligence and strict liability and the relationship between the two legal regimes.

Section 3 considers the development of the law of negligence and introduces the essential elements of the tort, namely, (i) the duty of care as enunciated in *Donoghue* v. *Stevenson*,[1] which laid down that the manufacturer of a product owes a duty of care in respect of that product; (ii) the persons to whom the duty is owed as identified through the 'neighbour principle' as laid down by Lord Atkin in *Donoghue* v. *Stevenson*; (iii) the standard of care owed by the manufacturer; (iv) the impact of any intermediate inspection; (v) the need to establish a breach of the duty of care; and (vi) the impact of contributory negligence on liability.

Section 4 introduces the concept of strict liability and the change in emphasis away from the fault of the manufacturer and towards the defectiveness of the product.

---

[1] [1932] AC 562.

Section 5 deals with the different types of defect, namely, manufacturing defects; design defects; and 'duty to warn' defects.

Section 6 looks at the development of strict liability and the policies that led to this movement in liability for product-related injuries. The section considers liability in the United States under the decision in *Greenman* v. *Yuba Power Products*[2] and the Second and Third Restatements of Torts; the approach in the United Kingdom with the recommendations of the Pearson Commission and the Joint Law Commissions; the recommendations of the Strasbourg Convention; the development, underlying policy and impact of the EC Directive on product liability, including a review of the EC Directive since its passage.

2 Background

Tortious liability for injuries caused by defective products is relatively recent when compared with contractual liability. The contractual requirement of merchantable quality was recognised in the early nineteenth century,[3] while negligence only came to the fore with the decision in *Donoghue* v. *Stevenson*[4] in 1932. The advent of strict liability in the United Kingdom in Part I of the Consumer Protection Act 1987 further developed tortious liability and has resulted in the current two-strand regime, namely, negligence and product liability, both of which are important in providing comprehensive protection for both persons and businesses affected by defective products.

Strict liability has not replaced negligence; rather, the two regimes complement each other. Thus, claims for product-related death and personal injury can be made through both regimes, although, it may be preferable to make a claim under strict liability as it merely requires proof of defectiveness and causation without any requirement to prove fault. However, if the ten-year cut-off period for a strict liability claim has expired, the claimant may still be able to claim in negligence, assuming that the claim complies with the applicable time limits.[5] Further, negligence remains crucial in respect of claims for property damage as the two systems diverge in respect of what liability will arise. While damage to personal property over £275 can be claimed under both systems, tortious claims for damage to all business property and personal property of less than £275 can only be made through negligence. Given the potential range of damage that may be caused by a single incident, it is entirely possible that a claim will include both negligence and strict liability. Further, if the injured party purchased the defective product, a claim may also lie in contract for breach of terms relating to satisfactory

---

[2] 377 P.2d 897 (1963), Supreme Court of California.
[3] *Gardiner* v. *Gray* (1815) 4 Camp. 144.   [4] [1932] AC 562.
[5] See the Limitation Act 1980.

quality and fitness for purpose, which would include a claim for the value of the product itself.[6]

Finally, defective products may give rise to criminal liability for unsafe goods under the General Product Safety Regulations 2005, SI 2005/1803, although such liability lies beyond the remit of this text. However, the link is important since, if the criminal law framework succeeds in preventing unsafe goods from reaching the market, the incidence of product-related injuries and claims should be minimised. Unfortunately, this is not always the case as, on the one hand, unscrupulous traders will always seek to make money irrespective of any danger that the products might pose to product users and, on the other, users may be prepared to use a less safe product because it is cheaper.

Q1 Consider the relationship between negligence, product liability and contract as forms of remedy for product-related injuries.

3 Development of negligence

(a) Duty of care

Many product-related injuries are caused by faults that were introduced into the product while it was still under the control of the manufacturer and it is reasonable to expect that the manufacturer will be liable in tort in respect of injuries caused by such faults. Since the days of *Donoghue* v. *Stevenson*, itself a product liability case, a remedy has lain in tort through an action in negligence. Lord Atkin, in his oft-quoted judgment, defined the parameters of a manufacturer's tortious liability thus:

> a manufacturer of products, which he sells in such a form as to show that he intends them to reach the ultimate consumer in the form in which they left him with no reasonable possibility of intermediate examination, and with the knowledge that the absence of reasonable care in the preparation or putting up of the products will result in an injury to the consumer's life or property, owes a duty to the consumer to take reasonable care.[7]

Of course, the decision in *Donoghue* v. *Stevenson* impacted well beyond product liability cases and underpins the whole of the modern law of negligence, with its requirement for the existence of a duty of care, a breach of that duty and a proven causal link between that breach and the damage which ensued. Only by showing the existence of all three and proof that the damage was within the bounds of foreseeability, will the claimant be able to successfully claim compensation. In the current context, however, it is the impact of *Donoghue* v. *Stevenson* on product-related injuries that is of interest. To recap the facts, the

---

[6] Damages for the defective item itself cannot be claimed in strict liability, see Consumer Protection Act 1987, s.5(2).

[7] [1932] AC 562, 599.

claimant claimed damages for having suffered severe gastro-enteritis after consuming some ginger beer, which had been bought by a friend and was packaged in a sealed dark opaque bottle. The allegation was that, after the claimant had consumed part of the drink, the remainder was poured out and found to contain the decomposed remains of a snail. As the friend had purchased the item, the claimant lacked contractual privity and so could not pursue a claim against the café from which the drink had been purchased. Instead, she chose to pursue a claim against the manufacturer. The Court of Session in Scotland (the events having occurred in Paisley) decided that there was no cause of action. The case was then sent to the House of Lords, which held that the manufacturer of goods does owe a duty of care to the ultimate user of those goods. Ironically, given the pre-eminence of this decision, the existence of the snail itself was never proven – when the case left the House of Lords, it was remitted to the Court of Session to apply the judgment to the facts of the case but the manufacturer died before this could happen and the claim was settled by an out-of-court payment of £100.

While Lord Atkin referred specifically to the manufacturer of a product, there is no doubt that the principle includes wholesalers, distributors, assemblers, retailers, and anyone else handling the product, to the extent that their negligent activities contribute to a fault in the product and a consequent injury. Clearly, there is a duty on everyone in the distributive chain to ensure that the goods are handled correctly and stored properly. Thus, for example, chilled food that is meant to be stored in a chill cabinet but is allowed to remain at room temperature will deteriorate faster and may cause actionable food poisoning even if eaten by the specified 'use by' date. In this situation, it will be the person incorrectly storing the food who will be liable and not the original producer who packed it.

Q2 Consider the scope of the duty of care in product liability both in terms of the people who owe the duty and the breadth of situations in which it will arise.

(b) To whom is the duty of care owed?

Donoghue established that the duty of care is owed to those persons who would be classed as your 'neighbours'. In answer to the question 'Who then, in law, is my neighbour?' Lord Atkin opined that it is:

> persons who are so closely and directly affected by my act that I ought reasonably to have them in contemplation as being so affected when I am directing my mind to the acts or omissions which are called into question.[8]

---

[8] [1932] AC 562, 580.

In the context of a manufacturer of goods, there is no doubt that this necessarily includes the ultimate user of the product and anyone else who is sufficiently near to the product to be affected by the fault. Thus, for example, if an indoor firework has been made negligently and explodes when lit, it may injure not merely the person lighting it but also anyone standing close by. The damage might be physical, such as a burn, or property damage if, for example, a fire ensues. But it may go wider than that. If the tyre on a car has been negligently manufactured and an accident results, potential claimants would include the driver of the car together with any passengers but would also include any pedestrians or occupants of other cars that may become embroiled in the accident, as long as this was foreseeable. In respect of claims for nervous shock, it also includes those who come upon the aftermath of the accident and who have a special relationship with an injured party, e.g., the parent of an injured child.[9]

While the examples quoted above all relate to personal injury of foreseeable victims, the duty of care extends well beyond that. Foreseeable 'neighbours' to whom a duty of care would be owed would include businesses and other organisations which might suffer some property damage as a result of the negligent action of the manufacturer of the product or someone else in the distributive chain.

Q3 Does the neighbour principle adequately identify those who should have a valid tortious claim?

(c) Standard of care

Negligence revolves around the concept of holding liable the person who is to blame for the incident and the consequent damage. As such, it is thought to be a moral approach to liability as it requires the defendant to face the consequences of his blameworthy actions. This thus demands identification of the standard of behaviour to be required of the defendant, for only by establishing the requisite level can a failure to meet it be proven. The standard of care in negligence is the standard of the reasonable man, the so-called 'man on the Clapham omnibus'. However, the standard of care to be expected will rise in relation to the professional skills of the defendant, so that, in the words of McNair J:

> The test is the standard of the ordinary skilled man exercising and professing to have that special skill. A man need not possess the highest expert skill … it is sufficient if he exercises the ordinary skill of a competent man exercising that particular art.[10]

---

[9] *White and others* v. *Chief Constable of South Yorkshire* [1998] 3 WLR 1510.
[10] *Bolam* v. *Friern Hospital Management Committee* [1957] 2 All ER 118, 121. For further discussion of the standard of care in the provision of services see Part 2 Chapter 4.

Translating this into a product-related situation, it follows that manufacturers must exercise the skills appropriate to the manufacture of that product range. This requires them to use relevant knowledge and skills to avoid negligent manufacture and thereby ensure that a product will not cause injury.[11] As will be seen later in the chapter, a similar approach underpins strict liability, with its emphasis on the safety of the product. The standard of care applicable in negligence is decided by reference to what it was reasonable to expect of the manufacturer at the time that he manufactured the item, as it would be totally unreasonable to require him to exercise knowledge and skills not available at the time of manufacture. Negligence must be assessed in context – you cannot 'look at [a] 1947 accident with 1954 spectacles'.[12]

(d) Intermediate inspections

Thus far, we have presumed that the product will be transferred from the manufacturer to the ultimate injured user without any intermediate inspection. Indeed, Lord Atkin delineated the duty of the manufacturer on the basis that he intends the goods 'to reach the ultimate consumer in the form in which they left him with no reasonable possibility of intermediate examination'.[13] Where the product is sealed in a tin, bottle or jar, as occurred in *Donoghue* v. *Stevenson* itself, it is clearly the intention of the manufacturer that the product will reach the ultimate user in the form in which it left him and hence liability will follow. It would, in those circumstances, be unreasonable for the manufacturer to assume that any intermediate examination will occur. Consequently, the manufacturer must ensure that the goods have been produced properly and, further, that they do not contain any extraneous substance that might adulterate them or pose a risk to the ultimate user. Where an intermediate examination does occur, the manufacturer will remain liable in respect of latent inherent defects that the examination would not reveal as long as it was his negligence that introduced the fault. If an item is clearly defective and a retailer, knowing that fact, proceeds to supply it and an ultimate user is subsequently injured, the retailer will also be responsible for his negligence in allowing the supply to take place.[14]

---

[11] Failure to manufacture a safe product might also give rise to criminal liability under the General Product Safety Regulations 2005, SI 2005/1803.

[12] *Roe* v. *Minster of Health* [1954] 2 All ER 131, 137, per Denning LJ. The case concerned the adulteration of an anaesthetic in 1947. Denning LJ was at pains to point out in his judgment that negligence must be considered in the context of the knowledge available at the time of the alleged negligence and cannot be judged against knowledge that became available later, even if the new knowledge would affect the defendant's actions if the same situation were to arise again.

[13] [1932] AC 562, 599.

[14] He would also be criminally liable under the General Product Safety Regulations 2005, reg. 8(1)(a), which makes it an offence to 'expose or possess for supply, or offer or agree to supply, or supply a product to any person which he knows or should have presumed, on the basis of the information in his possession and as a professional, is a dangerous product'. The offence is committed by a 'distributor' who is defined in reg. 2 as being 'a professional in the supply chain whose activity does not affect the safety properties of a product'.

(e) Breach of duty and causation

Having established that the defendant owes a duty of care to the claimant, the latter must show that there has been a breach of that duty and that he has suffered recoverable damage as a consequence. In practice, this will involve the claimant proving that the defendant's actions have fallen below the standard of care to be expected of him and that, as a direct consequence of that failure, the claimant has suffered injury either to his person or his property. It is insufficient merely to establish that the defendant has breached the requisite duty of care. It is crucial that the causal link between that breach and the injury suffered by the claimant is proven.

When assessing whether a breach of care has occurred, the essential question is whether the manufacturer has fallen below the standard of care to be expected of him. This will include not merely considering the physical properties of the item but also any instructions for use and warnings that the manufacturer has chosen to provide to prospective users. He has a right to expect that users of products will exercise appropriate care for their own safety and wellbeing and, hence, there is no need to warn of obvious dangers.[15] However, he is required to take into account vulnerable groups who foreseeably may use his product. The most obvious group is children and thus the standard of care to be expected of a manufacturer would include the provision of warnings stipulating a lower age limit for users of the product where appropriate, e.g., 'not suitable for children under 3 years of age'. Equally, foreseeable use or abuse of a product by children might require the use of extra safety devices such as childproof lids on pharmaceutical containers. Of course, children are not the only potentially vulnerable group and manufacturers may need to make extra or alternative provision for the elderly or the disabled and provide them with appropriate warnings. The provision of warnings to a professional person who is going to use the product in a service offered to the ultimate user will often suffice.[16] Thus, warning a doctor of the side-effects of a prescription-only drug would satisfy the requisite standard of care, the duty then moving to the doctor and pharmacist to pass on appropriate warnings to the patient. By contrast, warnings in respect of over-the-counter drugs must be included with the product either on the outer packaging or on a user leaflet in the box. There is no requirement that full details of a warning about a product be included in both places.[17] In that situation, the manufacturer has a right to assume that the user will read the leaflet and not discard it.

---

[15] *Farr* v. *Butters Brothers & Co.* [1931] 2 KB 606.

[16] *Holmes* v. *Ashford* [1950] 2 All ER 76, in which a hairdresser ignored the warning on a bottle of hair dye to do a patch test prior to use. The customer suffered dermatitis from the use of the product but the court held that the warning given to the hairdresser was sufficient to absolve the manufacturer from liability for negligence. The court held that it would be 'unreasonable and impossible' to expect the manufacturer to give a warning in a form that would definitely come to the attention of every customer.

[17] See *Worsley* v. *Tambrands Ltd* (unreported, 3 December 1999), a product liability case involving the use of tampons. A warning of the risk of toxic shock syndrome when using the product was

Q4 Analyse the standard of care and the need to prove a failure to comply with that standard.

(f) Contributory negligence

In assessing liability for negligence, the contributory negligence, if any, of the injured user will be relevant in determining the outcome of the case. Hence, if the user has used a product knowing that it is defective or he has ignored appropriate warnings or not read the instructions for use provided with the product, he must bear his portion of the liability for his injuries with any compensation being reduced by a percentage that recognises his share of the blame.

4 The move to strict liability

The move to strict liability for product-related injuries has been a steady development over many years, involving amendments to the US Restatements of Torts, a report by the Joint Law Commission,[18] the Pearson Report,[19] the Strasburg Convention and, finally, the passage of an EC Directive,[20] which, in the United Kingdom, has been adopted via the Consumer Protection Act 1987, Part 1.

Before proceeding to discuss the development and the detail of the Directive and the 1987 Act, it is important to recognise what is meant by strict liability. Strict liability must be distinguished from absolute liability. The latter renders the defendant liable irrespective of negligence and without the possibility of any defences. The mere doing of the action is enough to make the defendant legally responsible. By contrast, strict liability provides for *prima facie* liability without proof of fault but does typically allow for some defences upon which the defendant can rely to negate liability. Thus, in respect of strict product liability under the Consumer Protection Act 1987, there are six possible defences under section 4 ranging from compliance with mandatory standards to the development risk defence.[21]

The move away from negligence-based liability to strict product liability necessarily requires a different emphasis when considering whether civil

---

given on the box with fuller details being included on a leaflet contained in the box. The court held that this was sufficient. See also Peter Shears, 'The EU Product Liability Directive: twenty years on' (2007) *Journal of Business Law* 884.

[18] Law Commission and Scottish Law Commission, *Liability for Defective Products,* Law Com. No. 82, Scot Law Com. No. 45 (Cmnd. 6831, 1977).

[19] *Royal Commission on Civil Liability and Compensation for Personal Injury* (Cmnd. 7054, 1978) ('Pearson Report').

[20] Council Directive 85/374/EC on the approximation of the laws, regulations and administrative provisions of the Member States concerning liability for defective products.

[21] A full discussion of the statutory defences follows later in this chapter. Strict liability in criminal law is also indicated by the availability of defences. Thus, for example, defendants charged with offences the Consumer Protection from Unfair Trading Regulations 2008, SI 2008/1277 (dealt with in Part 5) can utilise the due diligence defence assuming that they satisfy its requirements.

liability has arisen. Strict liability has supposed advantages over negligence liability, of which the most obvious is that the claimant no longer needs to establish whose negligence is to blame for the defective product. Rather, the claimant needs to demonstrate that the product was 'defective' within the statutory meaning of that word and that there is a causal link between the defective product and the injury or damage he has suffered. In this respect, it can be argued that strict liability has some of the same weaknesses as negligence in that the claimant still needs to identify a potential and viable defendant[22] and doubts have been raised as to whether strict liability is really a significant improvement in this area. A further advantage claimed for strict liability is an economic one; namely, that it facilitates risk spreading through the use of product liability insurance, the premiums for which can be recouped via an added factor to the costs of production and thereby spread among all of the purchasers of the product via the price. The potential danger attached to the practice of risk spreading through insurance is that insurance premiums may become prohibitively expensive, with some manufacturers being forced to 'go bare' and not have product liability insurance at all. This argument underpinned the so-called insurance crisis in the United States but the Presidential Interactive Task Force[23] found that there was no evidence of any real emergency and thus it seems that this risk had been overstated.

Negligence claims revolve around the alleged negligent behaviour of the defendant while, in product liability, it is the defective nature of the product that is key to the potential liability of the defendant. If liability is truly strict the actions or intentions of the defendant are irrelevant. Naturally, this change of emphasis requires a much closer scrutiny of the types of defect that may arise and what will constitute a defective product.

Q5 Analyse the supposed advantages of strict liability over negligence.

5 Types of defect

Defects can generally be divided into three main categories: manufacturing defects, design defects and 'duty-to-warn' defects.[24] While this is the simplest categorisation of defects, other commentators have developed more sophisticated analyses.

---

[22] This is not necessarily the case in some US jurisdictions where the claimant can sue anyone who manufactured the product, who will then be held liable for a percentage of the claim equivalent to their percentage of the market. See *Sindell* v. *Abbott Laboratories,* 26 Cal. 3d 588 (1980).

[23] Set up by President Ford to consider this issue.

[24] For a very comprehensive analysis of types of defects see C.J. Miller and R.S. Goldberg, *Product Liability* (2nd edn, Oxford University Press, 2004). See also M. Griffiths, 'Defectiveness in EEC product liability' (1987) *Journal of Business Law* 222.

(a) Manufacturing defects

At its most basic, a manufacturing defect is the easiest to spot for it exists when an item 'deviates from the norm' of products being produced according to that design or on that production line. It can be proved statistically that a percentage of products, however minimal, in a production run will contain a manufacturing defect irrespective of the production method used or the efficiency of the quality assurance system employed during the manufacturing process. As the statistical frequency of such rogue products can be calculated accurately, the manufacturer can adopt a suitable quality control system to limit the occurrence of such rogues and recoup both the cost of the system and the cost of any injuries caused by defective products that reach the market via the price of the product.

Manufacturing defects can be evidenced in a variety of ways. The defective product may look different from others in the production run or might not perform in the way intended or have all of the characteristics of a perfect product. Equally, it may be that the product is adulterated by the presence of a foreign object such as a caterpillar in a tin of peas[25] or an explosive detonator in a delivery of Coalite.[26] Finally, a defective container is integral to the definition of a manufacturing defect, as, for instance, when a defective bottle containing carbonated drink explodes.

(b) Design defects

A design defect is much more significant than a manufacturing defect and has potentially far wider-reaching consequences due to the fact that it involves not merely a small, statistically identifiable percentage of the production run but, rather, involves the whole of it. The contention is not that the product deviates from the legitimate specifications used by the manufacturer but rather that those specifications or design are themselves defective and present a hazard. The assessment of defectiveness in a design case is much more difficult as it involves considering viable alternatives, the utility of the product, the costs of changing the design, a risk-utility analysis of whether the benefits of the product outweigh the risk and severity of potential injury,[27] and whether the state of scientific and technical knowledge prevailing at the time of production was such as to allow the producer to realise that the design posed unacceptable risks. This raises the vexed question of the unknowable defect which even the most diligent manufacturer cannot identify. The issues of the state of the art and of the availability of a development risk defence is of particular concern

---

[25] *Smedleys v. Breed* [1974] 2 All ER 21.

[26] *Wilson v. Rickett, Cockerill & Co.* [1954] 1 All ER 168.

[27] Thus, the Pasteur Rabies vaccine is an acceptable product as, although it causes serious side-effects, the alternative would be to allow the patient to die from rabies.

in industries such as pharmaceuticals, which depend heavily on research and development to develop new products and to which there is likely to be a risk attached. A prime example of a development risk was the drug Thalidomide, which, when used by pregnant mothers, caused limb damage to the foetus resulting in a large number of children born with deformed or shortened limbs.[28] In the event, their plight acted as a driving force in the demand for strict product liability,[29] as a claim in negligence, the legal regime prevailing at the time, would have failed.[30] Somewhat naturally, manufacturers, particularly in industries such as pharmaceuticals, feel the need for a development risk defence, both to protect them from liability for injuries caused by unknowable defects and also to encourage the research and development of new products. By contrast, consumer bodies argue that such a defence should not be allowed and that a manufacturer who produces a product should be liable for all injuries caused by using it irrespective of whether the manufacturer could have known of the underlying defect. Their argument is that the injured user deserves compensation either way and that if the manufacturer takes the profits from the product, he should also be prepared to accept liability for any injuries caused by it. Needless to say, there is no easy solution to this difference of opinion. It is no surprise that the debate about whether to allow a development risk defence in the EC Directive continued for some years and was ultimately resolved only by allowing Member States the option to choose whether they wished to adopt the defence into their national legislation.[31]

(c) Duty to warn defects

The third type of defect is the so-called 'duty to warn' defect, which occurs when a producer has failed to provide appropriate instructions for the safe use of the product and appropriate warnings about any known risks that the product may

---

[28] We will return to the issue of development risks when we consider the defences permitted under the EU Product Liability Directive.

[29] When establishing the Royal Commission on Civil Liability and Compensation for Personal Injury, the then Prime Minister, Edward Heath, stated 'The Government has been considering proposals made from time to time in the past, which are now particularly relevant in the light of the Report of the Robens Committee on Health and Safety at Work and in connection with the recent concern over the thalidomide cases, that there should be an inquiry into the basis of civil liability in the United Kingdom for causing death or personal injury.'

[30] The Thalidomide victims in the United Kingdom received an out-of-court settlement of £20 million in respect of their claim.

[31] Only Luxembourg and Finland decided against a development risk defence and thus producers in those countries have liability for all products. In Spain, manufacturers are liable for development risks in food and pharmaceutical products, while in France producers are liable for development risks in products derived from the human body. In Germany, producers are liable for development risks in pharmaceutical products as a consequence of the Thalidomide issue. Germany was the country worst affected by this drug, which was known there as Contergan. See *Report from the Commission on the Application of Directive 85/374 on Liability for Defective Products,* COM(2000)893 final and also G. Howells and S. Weatherill, *Consumer Protection Law* (2nd edn, Ashgate Publishing Ltd, Aldershot, 2005).

pose. As discussed earlier, there is no duty to warn of obvious dangers[32] and the producer has a right to assume that users of a product will exercise appropriate care for their own safety and welfare. However, warnings must cater for foreseeable vulnerable product users such as children or the disabled and, equally, must warn of dangers to identifiable groups of idiosyncratic users, which would include, for example, warning of the presence of nuts in foodstuffs given that it is known that a significant percentage of the population are allergic to nuts. The duty to warn is an ongoing one with producers being expected to warn consumers of new risks as they become known. A failure to do this might also give rise to criminal liability under the General Product Safety Regulations 2005.[33]

The duty to provide a warning raises the issue of what should be included, especially given that it has been suggested that providing too many warnings can be counterproductive in that it may encourage users not to read any warnings at all. That said, there is clearly a duty to warn the user of known risks that are both foreseeable and reasonably common. There is no duty to warn of a risk that is so remote and unlikely as not to pose a real risk to the everyday user.[34] However, in warning of some risks, it is important to warn the user of all relevant risks, as to do otherwise might lull the user into a false sense of security in assuming that the product does not pose any risks other than the ones to which the warning refers.[35] Hence, it could be argued that the net effect of an inadequate warning might be that the risk of injury to the user will increase, as he might exercise less care in respect of those facets of the product that, unbeknown to him, pose additional risks. Thus, in *Vacwell Engineering Co. Ltd* v. *BDH Chemicals Ltd,*[36] the defendant was held responsible for the deaths and injuries caused when a warning that the chemical gave off 'harmful vapours' did nothing to warn users of the risk of a violent explosion if the product came into contact with water.

Q6 Analyse the different types of defect and how each might occur.

6 Developments in strict liability

(a) United States

The break-through decision regarding strict product liability in the United States came in the 1963 case of *Greenman* v. *Yuba Power Products.*[37] The case

---

[32] *Farr* v. *Butters Brothers & Co.* [1931] 2 KB 606.

[33] General Product Safety Regulations 2005, SI 2005/1803, reg. 7(3) and reg. 20(2). Enforcement authorities may also issue a 'requirement to warn notice' under reg. 13 requiring specified persons to give warnings to potential users of the product who have been supplied with it, to publish a warning in such a format as to bring the risk to the attention of such people and to ensure that the product carries a warning of the risk in the form specified in the notice.

[34] This is arguably not true in respect of warnings to doctors about the side-effects of pharmaceuticals. Doctors need to be aware of all the risks, however small, so as to be able to make a professional judgement about prescribing the drug to any given patient.

[35] *Vacwell Engineering Co. Ltd* v. *BDH Chemicals Ltd* [1970] 3 All ER 553.

[36] *Ibid.*   [37] 377 P.2d 897 (1963), Supreme Court of California.

involved injuries suffered by the plaintiff when using a combination power tool that had been manufactured by the defendants and purchased by his wife. A piece of wood had flown up from the tool and injured the plaintiff in the eye. In giving judgment, Justice Traynor, on behalf of a unanimous court, declared that:

> A manufacturer is strictly liable in tort when an article he places on the market knowing that it is to be used without inspection for defects, proves to have a defect which causes injury to a human being.

This development was, perhaps, to be expected, as US courts already recognised the liability of manufacturers for both express and implied warranties in non-contractual situations where there was no privity between the manufacturer and the injured party. The former liability had been recognised in 1932[38] in *Baxter* v. *Ford Motor Co.*,[39] in which the Washington Supreme Court contended that it would be unjust to allow a manufacturer to create a demand for his products through the use of express warranties and then absolve himself from liability to the ultimate user because of a lack of privity. The liability of manufacturers for implied warranties followed in 1960 in the decision in *Henningsen* v. *Bloomfield Motors,*[40] a case involving injury to the wife of the purchaser when a defect in the steering mechanism of her car caused it to veer off the road and hit a wall. Commenting on the absence of a need for privity, the Supreme Court opined that:

> an implied warranty of merchantability … extends to the purchaser of the car, members of his family and to others persons occupying it or using it with his consent … In this way, the burden of losses consequent upon the use of defective articles is borne by those who are in a position to either control the danger or make an equitable distribution of the losses when they do occur.

The move to strict tortious liability was an obvious next step. That said, it must be remembered that the United States is not simply one jurisdiction but fifty State jurisdictions, the law of each of which develops separately. In product liability, the three most active jurisdictions are California, New York and New Jersey, with the majority of ground-breaking developments occurring in one of these three States. It does not necessarily follow that the approach to liability in all fifty jurisdictions has developed in the same way or at the same speed.

Greenman v. *Yuba Power Products* was followed only two years later by the Restatement (Second) of Torts (1965), section 402A of which stated:

> (1) One who sells any product in a defective condition unreasonably dangerous to the user or consumer or to his property is subject to liability for physical harm thereby caused to the ultimate user or consumer, or to his property.

---

[38] The same year as *Donoghue* v. *Stevenson.*
[39] 12 P. 2d 409 (1932), Supreme Court of Washington.
[40] 161 A. 2d 69 (1960), Supreme Court of New Jersey.

This liability would apply irrespective of whether the seller had exercised all possible care in the preparation and sale of the product and irrespective of whether the user or consumer had a contract with the seller. This put beyond doubt that the action would exist in tort and, further, that it would involve strict liability, the exercise of care by the seller being irrelevant. In short, there was no need to prove any negligence by the seller. However, there was a rider to section 402A, in that Comment K to that section dealt specifically with unavoidably unsafe products by stipulating that, provided that such a product had been properly prepared and had appropriate warnings and instructions, it would not be classed as defective or unreasonably unsafe.

Some of the decisions that followed on from the *Greenman* decision pushed the boundaries of liability and gave rise to the so-called product liability 'crisis'. The court in *Cronin* v. *Olsen*[41] suggested that there was no need to prove that the defect was 'unreasonably dangerous' as required by the Restatement, the plaintiff only needing to show that there was a defect in design or manufacture which caused harm in normal use, whether the particular manner of the injury was foreseeable or not. Another Californian decision, *Luque* v. *McLean*,[42] effectively required products to be 'idiot-proof', the court reasoning that 'manufacturers who callously ignore patent dangers in their products' should not be allowed to escape liability while 'those who innocently market products with latent defects' remain responsible. A third Californian decision, *Sindell* v. *Abbott Laboratories*,[43] (case involving the 'DES daughters')[44] refined the policy of 'industry-wide liability' by imposing liability on the industry as a whole as opposed to identifiable defendants. Upon proof of injury, each manufacturer would become liable for a percentage of the damages equivalent to his market share, although with the ability to escape liability by proving his innocence by, for example, proving that he was not producing the item at the relevant time. Such cases fuelled concern about the level of liability for manufacturers in the United States, concern that was heightened by the culture of jury decisions about liability resulting in very high awards of damages, and the use of contingency fee arrangements whereby plaintiffs were not liable for any legal costs because lawyers in successful claims would instead receive a percentage of the damages awarded.

In more recent times, however, there has been a shift in the approach to strict liability in the United States. The Restatement (Third) of Torts, section 2 has

---

[41] 104 Cal. Rptr 433 (1972).   [42] 8 Cal. 3d 136 (1972).

[43] 26 Cal. 3d 588, 163 Cal. Rptr 132 (1980).

[44] DES (Dierhylstilbestrol) was a synthetic oestrogen prescribed between 1947 and 1971 to women with problem pregnancies. It was linked to genital tract irregularities in children of both sexes but, most notably, to clear cell adenocarcenoma of the cervix or vagina in females. It also caused vaginal adenosis in females and testicular abnormalities in males. *Sindell* v. *Abbott Laboratories* was a class action by a group of injured daughters of women who had taken DES during pregnancy.

redefined liability for a defective product, with some significant amendments. A product is now being defined as defective if:

> at the time of sale or distribution, it contains a manufacturing defect, is defective in design, or is defective because of inadequate instructions or warnings.

Further, and more significantly, the new definitions do not include any reference to strict liability but have opted to consider liability for each of the three types of defect separately. Strict liability has been retained for manufacturing defects[45] but negligence has effectively been re-introduced for design defects[46] and duty to warn defects[47] by the requirement that the defects involve a 'foreseeable risk of harm', which goes to the liability of the manufacturer for his actions rather than looking merely at the defective nature of the product.[48]

The relevant parts of section 2 provide that a product:

(a) contains a manufacturing defect when the product departs from its intended design even though all possible care was exercised in the preparation and marketing of the product;

(b) is defective in design when the foreseeable risks of harm posed by the product could have been reduced or avoided by the adoption of a reasonable alternative design by the seller or other distributor, or a predecessor in the commercial chain of distribution, and the omission of the alternative design renders the product not reasonably safe;

(c) is defective because of inadequate instructions or warnings when the foreseeable risks of harm posed by the product could be reduced or avoided by the provision of reasonable instructions or warnings by the seller or other distributor, or a predecessor in the commercial chain of distribution, and the omission of the instructions or warnings renders the product not reasonably safe.

The Restatement, published by the American Law Institute, is advisory as opposed to mandatory and does not have the authority of a court decision. It is, however, intended to reflect current practice in the State courts so it is not unreasonable to assume that it will have some influence in future decisions.

Q7 Consider the approach to strict liability taken in the United States and the apparent change in emphasis in the most recent version of the Restatement of Torts.

(b) United Kingdom

Two separate reports on product liability were published in the United Kingdom within a short period of each other: the joint report by the Law Commission

---

[45] Restatement (Third) of Torts, s.2(a).
[46] *Ibid.* s.2(b).   [47] *Ibid.* s.2(c).
[48] For further discussions see G. Howells and S. Weatherill, *Consumer Protection Law* (2nd edn, Ashgate Publishing Ltd, Aldershot, 2005) and C.J. Miller and R.S. Goldberg, *Product Liability* (2nd edn, Oxford University Press, Oxford, 2004).

and Scottish Law Commission on *Liability for Defective Products*[49] and the *Royal Commission on Civil Liability and Compensation for Personal Injury*[50] ('Pearson Report'). As the title suggests, the former was exclusively concerned with product liability while the latter dealt with a much broader range of issues but included one chapter[51] specifically about liability for defective products. Both reports came to essentially the same conclusions, namely, that the existing legal remedies did not provide the level of protection that injured users of defective products deserved and that the existing regimes of contract and negligence should be supplemented by the introduction of strict liability for product-related injuries. In considering the parameters of such proposed liability, the Reports are markedly similar in their conclusions, which perhaps reflects the commonality of view that was becoming more prevalent both in the United Kingdom and in Europe through the Strasbourg Convention[52] and the (then) draft EC Directive.[53] Both the Joint Law Commission Report and the Pearson Report advocated that strict liability should be placed on the producer of a product if the product was put into circulation in the course of a business; but also that own-branders,[54] distributors and the first importer into a jurisdiction should be subject to strict liability as well. There was also a common approach advocating that the concept of defectiveness should be decided by reference to the level of safety which a person is entitled to expect[55] and that the defence of contributory negligence should be available to the producer of a product.[56] Arguably, the most significant proposal was that both reports argued against the inclusion of a development risk defence, taking the view that producers should be liable for all injuries resulting from their products even in industries that are heavily dependent on research and development, such as the motor car industry and the pharmaceutical industry. Indeed, the Joint Law Commission Report expressly stated that the producers of pharmaceuticals should be subject to strict liability,[57] while the Pearson Report commented that:

> to exclude development risks from a regime of strict liability would be to leave a gap in the compensation cover, through which, for example, the victims of another thalidomide disaster might easily slip.[58]

---

[49] Joint Law Commission Report, above n. 18.

[50] Pearson Report, above n. 19.   [51] *Ibid.* ch. 22.

[52] European Convention on Product Liability in regard to Personal Injury and Death.

[53] Council Directive 85/374/EC on the approximation of the laws, regulations and administrative provisions of the Member States concerning liability for defective products.

[54] 'Own-branders' are companies, often but not exclusively supermarkets, who market products under their own in-house label and may, or may not, include the name of the actual producer on the label as well.

[55] Joint Law Commission Report, above n. 18, para. 125(g); Pearson Report, above n. 19, ch.22, para. 1237.

[56] Joint Law Commission Report, above n. 18, para. 125(n); Pearson Report, above n. 19, ch.22, para. 1257.

[57] Joint Law Commission Report, above n. 18, para. 125(j).

[58] Pearson Report, above n. 19, ch.22, para. 1259.

In the event, both of these reports were overtaken by the major debate going on in the EC about the proposed draft Directive on Product Liability, the first draft of which had been published in 1976 just prior to the publication of these two reports.

(c) Strasbourg Convention

The Strasbourg Convention was developed and published by the member states of the Council of Europe and opened for signature in January 1967. Its declared intent was to achieve a greater degree of unity between the member states and to ensure better protection of the public with regard to compensation for personal injury and death while taking into account the legitimate interests of producers.[59] It advocated strict liability in respect of product-related injuries, with liability being placed on producers, own-branders, importers acting in the course of a business, component manufacturers and other suppliers in the chain of distribution unless they identified the person from whom they had acquired the goods. Significantly, the Convention did not include a development risks defence, a significant difference from the final version of the EC Directive, which allowed Member States to opt at national level as to whether or not to include a development risk defence. In the event, insufficient member states of the Council of Europe ratified the Strasbourg Convention and it too was overtaken by developments in the EC. This is hardly surprising given that many of the member states of the Council of Europe are also Member States of the EU and thus were bound to adopt the EC Directive. The Strasbourg Convention was effectively surplus to requirements.

(d) EC Directive

The first draft of the EC Directive was published in 1976, with a second draft published in 1979. However, the final version of the Directive was not passed until 1985 and was only passed then on the basis that there would be three derogations available for individual Member States to adopt at national level. This effectively undermined the declared intention of the Directive to provide approximation of the laws across the EC to address existing divergences that distorted competition, affected the movement of goods and offered differing degrees of protection to consumers injured by defective products. The three derogations related to liability for primary agricultural products, applicable financial limits and the adoption of a development risk defence. The derogation for the first of these, namely, liability for primary agricultural products, was removed in 1999[60] as a direct response to the 'mad cow disease' (BSE) crisis

---

[59] Strasbourg Convention, above n. 52, Preamble.
[60] See Directive 99/34/EC[1999] OJ L141/20. See also *Report from the Commission on the Application of Directive 85/374 on Liability for Defective Products*, COM(2000)893 final, 6.

with the result that strict liability now applies to unprocessed primary agricultural products across the European Union. The other two derogations remain in force and will be discussed in due course.

Directive 85/374/EC ('Product Liability Directive') is a maximum harmonisation Directive and thus Member States are not permitted either to introduce provisions that fail to comply with the Directive or, alternatively, to introduce provisions that provide a higher level of protection to consumers than is specified under the Directive. A failure to comply with the provisions of the Directive results in legal action being taken against the Member State concerned. Thus, in *EC Commission* v. *United Kingdom*,[61] the government of the United Kingdom was challenged over the wording used in section 4(1)(e) of the Consumer Protection Act 1987, the allegation being that that subsection, which gives effect to Article 7(e) of the Directive regarding the development risk defence, does not accurately reflect the wording of the Directive. Article 7(e) states that the producer will not be liable if he proves:

> that the state of scientific and technical knowledge at the time when he put the product into circulation was not such as to enable the existence of the defect to be discovered.

By contrast, section 4(1)(e) of the Consumer Protection Act 1987 states that it will be a defence for a producer to show:

> that the state of scientific and technical knowledge at the relevant time was not such that a producer of products of the same description as the product in question might be expected to have discovered the defect if it had existed in his products while they were under his control

The European Commission argued that this wording did not correctly transpose the meaning of Article 7(e), which clearly imposes strict liability. The Commission argued that the wording used in the 1987 Act introduces negligence into the defence as it considers the actions of the producer by reference to other producers of similar products. In its judgment, the European Court of Justice (ECJ) confirmed that the most advanced level of science and technology is what must be considered; that the defence does not depend on what the individual producer knew but rather on what he should objectively have known, and that it refers only to the knowledge available at the time that the product was put into circulation. In the event, the ECJ held that the Commission had not proved the case against the United Kingdom and, further, that because of the wording of section 1(1)[62] of the 1987 Act, the UK courts would be bound to interpret the defence in accordance with the Directive.[63]

---

[61] C-300/95 [1997] ECR I-2649.

[62] Consumer Protection Act 1987, s.1(1) reads 'This Part shall have effect for the purpose of making such provision as is necessary in order to comply with the product liability Directive and shall be construed accordingly.'

[63] For an in-depth commentary on the decision, see R. Schulze, H. Schulte-Nölke and J. Jones (eds.), *A Casebook on European Consumer Law* (Hart Publishing, Oxford, 2002). Other cases

While the Product Liability Directive is maximal in nature and Member States cannot introduce conflicting provisions, Article 13 specifically retains the rights that an injured person might have under the rules of contractual and non-contractual liability or a special liability system existing at the moment that the Directive was notified. As such, claims under product liability do not replace existing legal remedies, rather they overlay them and are an add-itional means of claiming compensation when applicable. This means that, in the United Kingdom, the laws of contract and negligence remain. Thus, as dis-cussed earlier, the injured user of the product can also sue in negligence and, if he was also the purchaser of it, he can bring an action in contract under the Sale of Goods Act 1979 claiming that the product was not of a satisfactory quality or fit for its purpose. Accordingly, he would be able to claim for all of the direct consequential loss resulting from the incident, i.e., for death, personal injury and property damage, and also for the value of the defective item itself. This has distinct advantages over a claim in product liability where there are limita-tions on claims for property damage and no claim can be made in respect of the defective item itself.

In addition to the retention of pre-existing national legal regimes, Article 13 of the Directive also expressly retains 'special liability systems'. While not of direct consequence in the United Kingdom, this is nonetheless an important provision for some other EU Member States who already had schemes in place to deal with specific product sectors. Thus, Germany, the country worst hit by the Thalidomide[64] crisis, had passed the Medicines Act 1976 to deal with drug-related injuries, while Spain had passed legislation to deal with the implications of a scandal involving adulterated cooking oil.[65] Both Sweden and Finland also have specials arrangements in place to deal with the victims of drug-related injuries.[66]

Q8 Compare and contrast the approaches taken to strict liability in the United Kingdom, the Strasbourg Convention and the EC Directive.

(e) Review of the EC Directive

Under the terms of the Product Liability Directive, the European Commission is required to present a report to the European Council about the workings of the Directive and, if necessary, submit proposals for changes to it.[67] The first

---

relating to non-compliance with the Directive have been brought against France and Greece, see *EC Commission* v. *France* C-52/00 [2002] ECR I-3827 and *EC Commission* v. *Greece* C-154/00 [2002] ECR I-3879. For additional comment see Howells and Weatherill, above n. 48.

[64] Thalidomide was known as Contergan in Germany.

[65] The Spanish government subsequently repealed this Act when introducing a new law giving effect to the EC Directive.

[66] See M. Brahms, '"No fault" in Finland: paying patients and drug victims' (1988) 138 *NLJ* 678.

[67] Product Liability Directive, Art. 21.

report, published in 1995, acknowledged that the Directive is an important piece of legislation but felt that there was insufficient experience of its working and very limited case law, with the result that the Commission concluded that it was not appropriate to make any suggestions for amendments at that stage.

In 1999, a Green Paper on Liability was published seeking views about how the Directive was working in practice and whether any revisions should be made. Following on from the replies that were received,[68] a Report from the Commission was published in January 2001.[69] The key factors coming out of that Report included that the Directive appeared to function well having created a well-balanced and stable framework,[70] which runs alongside separate national regimes. Suggested reasons for the continued use of pre-existing systems are, first, that such systems often provide for remedies where the Directive has gaps, such as claims for damage to business property and claims under €500 and, secondly, that a larger volume of case law means that national legislation is more settled. Such cases as there are appear to be few in number with the vast majority being settled out of court.[71] If this is so, then arguably the system is working well, with businesses settling genuine claims in which they acknowledge liability and only need to agree the amount of compensation payable. Of course, the opposite may also be true, with injured users accepting whatever offer is made rather than undertake a lengthy case through the courts with no certainty of outcome. It is possible, of course, that the low number of cases also indicates that the deterrent effect of the Directive, combined with potential criminal liability under product safety legislation,[72] encourages producers to be more careful about the products they place on the market and to ensure that they have effective quality control systems in place to prevent unsafe or faulty goods reaching the market.

The 2001 Report considered various issues in detail, balancing the contributions from the various bodies that responded to the issues raised by the Green Paper. These included the vexed questions of the development risk defence, financial limits, limitation periods and a possible extension to the liability of suppliers. In all areas, the Report was hampered by a dearth of hard information about the extent to which the Product Liability Directive was being invoked and the impact of its provisions.

---

[68] Approximately 100 comments were received about the Green Paper from national and European consumer organisations, national industry associations and national and European unions representing different sectors of industry, public administrations of Member States and other European countries and bodies specialising in product liability. See European Commission, *Report from the Commission on the Application of Directive 85/374 on Liability for Defective Products*, COM(2000)893 final, para. 1.3.

[69] *Ibid.*   [70] *Ibid.* para. 2.1.1.

[71] According to German and Dutch insurers, this may be as high as 90 per cent of claims, see European Commission, *Report from the Commission on the Application of Directive 85/374 on Liability for Defective Products*, Com(2000)893 final, para. 2.2.

[72] In the United Kingdom, the General Product Safety Regulations 2005, SI 2005/1803 give effect to Directive 2001/95/EC on general product safety.

In all areas of potential liability under the Directive, there is an inherent tension between the demands of the producer lobby to limit their liability to the lowest level possible and to maintain rigorous financial and temporal limits, and the demand from the consumer lobby who, somewhat naturally, want producer liability to be as extensive as possible and thereby give injured users the strongest rights available. Producer bodies argue that increasing consumer rights militates against innovation and product development, as producers will not want to run the risks inherent in new product design and usage, this being particularly true in high risk innovative industries such as pharmaceuticals. By contrast, consumer bodies argue that producers are in the best position to absorb such risks through the costs of production and business insurance and that, as producers make a profit from the supply of products, it is reasonable to expect them to bear the costs of any injuries caused by them.

Nowhere is this conflict more obvious than in relation to the development risk defence, which was introduced originally for a period of ten years,[73] Producers argue that, in the absence of such a defence, scientific progress could be hindered and the production of new products delayed or even prevented. Further, they argue that product liability insurance would be affected as insurers cannot accurately assess the level of the risk that they would be insuring.

There is very little actual data available from the five Member States[74] in which producers are liable either fully or in part for development risks, with some countries reporting either no cases[75] or very few cases[76] involving development risks. Similarly, there is no hard information about the impact, if any, on insurance cover.[77] Further, it is notable that the specialist compensation funds set up to deal with pharmaceuticals, the product most likely to involve development risks, also report few claims, with the German 'Pharmapool' (probably the best known of such compensation funds) only making one compensation payment[78] and subsequently reducing the premiums payable by the pharmaceutical manufacturers.[79] Similarly, the Danish compensation system only reported two cases in the period 1998–2000.[80]

The conclusion of the 2001 Report was that it seemed to be very difficult for producers to establish the development risk defence in any case brought against them. The defence requires that the very highest level of knowledge be used

---

[73] European Commission, *Report on Directive 85/374*, above n. 68, para. 3.2.2.
[74] Finland, Luxembourg, Spain, France and Germany.
[75] Finland.   [76] Germany.
[77] Spain indicated that the impact on insurance companies was unknown, while France reported that although some insurance companies had experienced difficulty with the concept, there was no data available. See European Commission, *Report on Directive 85/374,* above n. 68, para. 3.2.2.
[78] The payment was for DM55 million to compensate haemophiliacs who contracted HIV as a result of contaminated blood products.
[79] Premiums are paid by all pharmaceutical manufacturers, premiums being calculated as a percentage of turnover based on three criteria.
[80] European Commission, *Report on Directive 85/374,* above n. 68, para. 3.2.2.

to assess whether a producer could have known of the risk that occurred and, in practice, it was difficult for a producer to show that the defect could not be detected given the knowledge available at the time that the product was marketed. No change to the defence is therefore being suggested at present.

Producer liability is also restricted by financial and temporal limits but, again, there is no intention to change these provisions at present. The financial limits are twofold: first, claims for property damage are limited to those where the damage has a value of €500; and secondly, the global financial limit for claims caused by identical products is set at €70 million. In respect of the first limit, consumer bodies argue that it should be removed so as to increase the rights of injured users, but the inherent risk in doing so is that it could give rise to a potentially large increase in the number of claims being made for very small amounts of money, which are proportionately more expensive to pursue through the legal system and which might otherwise be covered by household insurance anyway. To abolish this limit might cause more problems than it solves.

The global financial limit differs in that it is one of the three[81] derogations permitted to Member States under the terms of the Product Liability Directive.[82] As with the derogation for the development risk defence, the Directive required that this provision be reviewed after ten years. The perceived problem with a global financial limit for all injuries caused by identical products is that the funds available may not be sufficient to fully compensate all of the legitimate claims occurring during the ten-year cut-off period. If that is likely to be the case, monies can be allocated in one of two ways: either on a first-come first-served basis, in which case some claimants may be left without any compensation; or, alternatively, all claims must be put in abeyance until the end of the ten-year cut-off period, with the money being distributed at the end on a pro rata basis if the claims exceed the available funding. Under the former option, some claimants will be fully compensated while others may receive nothing, while under the second option, all compensation will be delayed with no guarantee that claimants will be fully compensated at the end. Neither is ideal as, if the purpose of a compensation system is to fully compensate legitimate claims, both options may fail to do so. In practice, only three countries, Germany, Spain and Portugal, adopted this derogation and, while data is not available for Portugal, there are no reported cases in either Germany or Spain where the financial limit was insufficient to meet relevant claims.[83] Consequently, no change is considered necessary.

Article 11 of the Directive establishes a ten-year cut-off period from the time when the producer put the product into circulation, with all claims being

---

[81] Now two, after the removal of the derogation for primary agricultural products following the 'mad cow disease' (BSE) crisis.
[82] Product Liability Directive, Art. 16.1.
[83] European Commission, *Report on Directive 85/374*, above n. 68, para. 3.2.3.

extinguished at that point, unless the injured user has already instituted legal proceedings. As with so many of the provisions of the Directive, this cut-off period has both its supporters and its detractors. The pro cut-off period lobby argues that there is a need for legal certainty so that producers can be assured of an end to their legal liability after a reasonable period and, further, that such certainty enables insurers to assess more accurately their potential liability and thereby to better calculate insurance premiums. Opponents of the cut-off period argue that producers should be liable for the effects of defective products irrespective of when the injury occurs or becomes known. They point in particular to injuries caused by foodstuffs and pharmaceuticals, the impact of which may not be known for twenty or thirty years, long after the expiration of the cut-off period. The case of the 'DES daughters' litigation[84] referred to above is a prime example of such a situation where the damage done to the children of women who had used DES during pregnancy did not become obvious until approximately twenty years later. Had that case occurred under the auspices of the Directive,[85] the claim would have failed because of the time delay. Equally, the effects of using other carcinogenic products, or asbestos, may not come to light until after the ten-year cut-off period, denying compensation under strict liability to injured users and forcing them back onto the law of negligence with the need to prove fault.

In addition to the ten-year cut-off period, claimants must institute proceedings within three years from the date when the claimant became aware, or should reasonably have become aware, of the damage, the defect and the identity of the producer.[86] This is very similar to the normal approach to the requirements for a claim in tort under the Limitation Act 1980.[87] The 2001 Report does not propose amending either the ten-year cut-off period or the three-year limitation period.

The remaining issues addressed by the 2001 Report are the liability of suppliers for product-related injuries and whether amendments should be made to the categories of recoverable property damage. Under the Product Liability Directive, suppliers of products are treated as secondary suppliers who will be held liable in limited circumstances, namely, where the producer cannot be identified and where the supplier has then failed to provide the injured user with details of the identity of the person from whom the supplier obtained the goods.[88] The same provision applies in respect of imported goods if the product does not identify the name of the importer even though it may identify the original producer. It was decided that the term 'reasonable time' does not need further definition, as Member States tend to construe it in roughly similar ways and, consequently, there was no need for any further harmonisation

---

[84] *Sindell v. Abbott Laboratories*, above n. 43.
[85] It was a case before the Supreme Court of California in the United States.
[86] Product Liability Directive, Art. 10.1.
[87] Indeed, the Limitation Act 1980 was amended to give effect to this requirement.
[88] Product Liability Directive, Art. 3.3.

of the concept[89] by introducing a maximum period within which the information must be provided. Consideration was given to whether the liability of suppliers should be extended to include defects for which they are responsible, such as defects caused by improper storage or transport. Such an amendment would bring suppliers' product liability into line with the corresponding criminal liability in product safety where suppliers are liable to the extent that their activities affect the safety of the product. However, doing this would effectively introduce fault liability into the Directive and conflict with its underlying strict liability rationale. Consequently, this approach has been rejected.[90] In practice, such fault-based liability on suppliers already exists under the law of negligence.

As regards types of recoverable damage, the Report recommended that no changes be made to the existing Directive. This has ruled out introducing remedies for non-material damage, damage to the defective item itself and compensation for damages to business property, which, in practice, can be recovered by other means and is likely to be covered by business insurance.[91]

One final policy issue considered by the European Commission was whether liability should be extended from products as they are currently defined in Article 2 of the Directive to include real estate property. This idea was rejected.[92]

While the 2001 Report did not support any amendments to the Directive, it did propose some follow-up measures, including the setting up of an expert group on product liability to gather information on various aspects of the workings of the Directive.[93] It also proposed the launch of a study into whether additional steps can and should be taken to further harmonise product liability law by reviewing the continued existence and impact of other national legislation on claims under the Directive[94] and to assess whether the medium term aim should be to introduce a common and sole EU-wide system of product liability.

Q9 Given that the 2001 Report suggested that the EC Directive is working effectively, consider the advantages and disadvantages of using it throughout the European Union to replace all national legislation dealing with product-related claims.

7 Recommended reading

Brahms, M. 'No fault in Finland: paying patients and drug victims' (1988) 138 *New Law Journal* 678

Clark, A.M. 'The conceptual basis of product liability' (1985) 48 *Modern Law Review* 325

European Commission Report from the Commission on the Application of Directive 85/374 on Liability for Defective Products, *COM*(2000)893 final

---

[89] European Commission, *Report on Directive 85/374*, above n. 68, para. 3.2.7.

[90] *Ibid.*   [91] *Ibid.* para. 3.2.9.

[92] *Ibid.* para. 3.2.8.   [93] *Ibid.* para. 4.1.1.

[94] *Ibid.* para. 4.1.2.

Griffiths, M. 'Defectiveness in EEC product liability' (1987) *Journal of Business Law* 222

Howells, G. and Weatherill, S. *Consumer Protection Law* (2nd edn, Ashgate Publishing Ltd, Aldershot, 2005)

Kirkpatrick, J. 'Product Liability Law: from negligence to strict liability in the US' (2009) 30 *Business Law Review* 48

Law Commission and Scottish Law Commission *Liability for Defective Products* Law Com. No. 82, Scot Law Com. No. 45 (Cmnd. 6831, 1977)

Miller, C.J. and Goldberg, R.S. *Product Liability* (2nd edn, Oxford University Press, Oxford, 2004)

Royal Commission on Civil Liability and Compensation for Personal Injury (Cmnd. 7054, 1978)

Schulze, R., Schulte-Nölke, H. and Jones, J. (eds) *A Casebook on European Consumer Law* (Hart Publishing, Oxford, 2002)

Shears, P. 'The EU Product Liability Directive: twenty years on' (2007) *Journal of Business Law* 884

The law of negligence is discussed at length in any of the standard works on the law of tort. In respect of the development of strict product liability via the EC Directive and its adoption in the Consumer Protection Act 1987, readers are directed to the excellent text *Product Liability* by Miller and Goldberg. In addition, readers may benefit from reading the text by Howells and Weatherill and the articles by Griffiths, Kirkpatrick and Shears. For current thinking in the EU, readers are recommended to read the Commission's Report on the workings of the Directive.

Part 4 Chapter 2

Product Liability under the Consumer Protection Act 1987

Contents

1 Introduction

The Product Liability Directive[1] was given effect in the United Kingdom via Part I of the Consumer Protection Act 1987. In passing the Act, Parliament took the opportunity to legislate for both product liability and product safety, reinforcing the indisputable link between the civil law consequences and criminal law liability for defective products. Criminal product safety controls prohibit producers from placing unsafe goods on the market, while compensation under product liability occurs where defective goods have caused injuries to product users. However, this chapter only deals with civil liability under Part I of the 1987 Act, criminal law controls being beyond the remit of this text.

Section 1(1) of the 1987 Act makes clear that Part I of the Act is to be construed so as to comply with the Product Liability Directive. This approach was confirmed in the decision in *EC Commission* v. *United Kingdom*[2] when it was held that the development risk defence in section 4(1)(e) of the Act must be

---

[1] Council Directive 85/374/EC on the approximation of the laws, regulations and administrative provisions of the Member States concerning liability for defective products.

[2] C-300/95 [1997] ECR I-2649.

construed in line with the Directive even though the wording of the Act differs significantly from that of the Directive.[3]

Section 2 looks at the personnel involved in product liability, beginning with the statutory definition of the term 'producer'. The section continues by analysing the potential liability for product-related injuries of producers, own-branders, importers into the European Union and other people in the distributive chain. Section 3 considers the meaning of the term 'product' in the context of the Consumer Protection Act 1987. Section 4 addresses the central issue of defectiveness by considering (a) the classification of defects into manufacturing defects, design defects and duty to warn defects; it also considers the challenge to this traditional classification by the decision in *A* v. *National Blood Authority*;[4] (b) an analysis of the meaning of 'safety' in section 3 of the Consumer Protection Act 1987 and the criteria used in determining whether a product satisfies the requirement for a product to be safe; (c) the need for a claimant to prove that the product is defective and that there is a causal link between the defective product and the injury.

Section 5 considers the six defences that are available to the defendant in a product liability case under section 4 of the Consumer Protection Act 1987. Particular attention is given to the most controversial of the defences, namely, the development risk defence.

Section 6 confirms that contributory negligence is applicable in product liability cases, and Section 7 analyses the types of recoverable damage in product liability cases, namely, death, personal injury and some types of property damage.

Section 8 considers the time limits applicable in product liability claims. In addition to the three-year limitation period there is also a ten-year cut-off period after which no further claims can be made. It also looks at the global financial limit permitted under the Product Liability Directive.

2 Personnel

(a) Definition of a 'producer'

Two key concepts in the Consumer Protection Act 1987 are 'producer' and 'product', as the one is held liable for injuries caused through a defect in the other. The definition of 'producer' covers three types of persons.[5] The first, and most obvious, is the person who manufactured the product.[6] This also includes the manufacturer of any component part to the extent that his component has proven faulty, resulting in the injury to the user.[7] Given the highly technical nature of many of the products now available in the market, a significant

---

[3] Product Liability Directive, Art.7(e).   [4] [2001] 3 All ER 289.
[5] Consumer Protection Act 1987, s.1(2).   [6] *Ibid.* s.1(2)(a).
[7] However, note the defences available to a component manufacturer under *ibid.* s.4(1)(f).

number of individual manufacturers may be liable, in whole or part, in respect of a single end-product.

The second definition of a producer involves the person responsible for the production of substances that have not been manufactured but have been won or abstracted.[8] This includes, for example, companies abstracting coal, gas, water or other minerals from underground but would be broad enough to include catching fish.

The final definition of a producer covers those who, where the product has not been manufactured, abstracted or won, have carried out an industrial or other process which has created essential characteristics of the product.[9] This last definition requires some analysis as to what constitutes an industrial or other process and when a characteristic of a product is deemed to be essential. An industrial process would include, for example, turning timber into chipboard, but what of freezing food? Is a frozen pea a different product from a freshly picked one such as to make both the picker and the frozen food company liable as manufacturers? Arguably, the answer is 'yes', as although both products are peas, they have different storage abilities and thus, if the one is kept frozen, it will remain edible long after the other has perished, In fact, section 1(2)(c) specifically refers to agricultural produce as a product that may be subjected to an industrial or other process. As Professor Miller points out,[10] the discussion is probably an academic one as the Directive does not go into such detail. Rather, it initially limits the definition to manufacturers, producers of raw materials, component manufacturers and own-branders.[11] However, it goes on to provide that anyone importing a product into the Community in the course of his business will be deemed to be a producer and will be responsible as such. Finally, the Directive provides that, when the producer cannot be identified, each supplier of the product will be treated, *prima facie*, as its producer. By contrast, the Consumer Protection Act 1987's definition of producer is restricted to a person who manufactured a product, won or abstracted it or who carried out an industrial process in relation to it. However, this restricted definition does not prevent liability being placed on own-branders and other suppliers of the product.[12]

There is an obvious attraction in interpreting the meaning of producer widely and placing liability upon other persons in the supply chain who have not truly produced the item at all. If an underlying purpose of the legislation is to place liability upon the people who are best able to handle it, then potential liability should extend to all those involved in the supply of the product as they can spread the risk most effectively through the use of insurance. This would mean that product liability has moved away from the basic societal proposition of only

---

[8] *Ibid.* s.1(2)(b).   [9] *Ibid.* s.1(2)(c).
[10] C.J. Miller and R.S. Goldberg, *Product Liability* (2nd edn Oxford University Press, 2004).
[11] Product Liability Directive, Art. 3.1.
[12] Consumer Protection Act 1987, s.2.

holding liable those people who are responsible for an action and extend it to anyone with an interest in the supply of the product. This argument would be particularly relevant in respect of the liability of producers for design defects were it not for the existence of the development risk defence under section 4(1)(e) of the 1987 Act. Of course, product liability is not the only area in which strict liability is imposed; the Sale of Goods Act 1979 holds the seller of goods strictly liable even though he has done nothing other than purchase the goods from a distributor and sell them on to the buyer.

Q1 Consider whether the broader definition of 'producer' helps to promote the underlying rationale of the Directive.

(b) Potential defendants

The Product Liability Directive requires that in order to promote consumer protection, all producers in the production process should be made liable insofar as their finished product, component part or raw material was defective and further, that liability should be extended to the first importer into the community, own-branders and, when the producer cannot be identified, suppliers.[13] In addition to this, comprehensive consumer protection requires that when several people are liable for the same damage, the consumer should be able to claim full compensation from any of them, i.e., that joint and several liability will apply.[14]

Section 2 of the 1987 Act identifies the potential defendants and complies both with the requirements of the Directive and the philosophy contained therein. Thus, section 2(1) requires that liability will fall on the specified individuals when damage has been caused wholly or partly by a defect in a product. The provision of 'wholly or partly' recognises that the defect may have been a contributory factor in the injury-causing incident without necessarily being the only factor. Thus, for example, it may be that the injured person is partly to blame for the injury, a situation acknowledged by the inclusion of contributory negligence as a factor reducing the liability of the defendant.[15]

The primary defendants are detailed in section 2(2) as being the producer of the product as previously defined, own-branders[16] and the first importer into the European Union.

An own-brander is recognised as being someone who puts his name on the product or uses his trade mark or other distinguishing mark in relation to the

---

[13] Product Liability Directive recital, para. 4.   [14] *Ibid.*
[15] Consumer Protection Act 1987, s.6(4).
[16] *Ibid.* s.1(2). There is no overt requirement that the producer or own-brander be acting in the course of a business and thus, technically, there could be *prima facie* liability against a private person. However, that possibility is negated by the fact that s.4(1)(c)(i) provides a defence to anyone who has only supplied the product other than in the course of a business. Thus, in practice, liability is restricted to producers and own-branders who are in business.

product, thereby holding himself out to be the producer. This would obviously include those businesses, often but not exclusively supermarkets, who supply goods under their own brand name when, in reality, they have been produced on their behalf by somebody else. In practice, these own-brand companies often make a better defendant than the company who actually produced them, either because the real producer is a much smaller enterprise[17] or because the real producer is in another country beyond the jurisdiction of the UK courts.[18] An interesting issue arises with regard to the statements actually made on the product packaging. If the only name that appears on the packaging is that of the own-brander, then holding them liable is a straight-forward matter. However, it may be that the packaging, while emphasising the name of the own-brander for marketing purposes, also indicates the name of the real producer, with a statement to the effect that 'this product was produced for ABC Ltd by XYZ Ltd'. In this case, there is an argument for saying that the own-brander, ABC Ltd, should not be liable as the identity of the true producer has been provided. As yet, there is no firm decision on this point. However, to allow an own-brander to evade liability in this way would seem inequitable, as it would permit him to reap all of the benefits of using his market profile to promote and sell the products while not accepting any liability for them. Equally, it would fly in the face of fixing liability on those who are in the best position to face it, and thus providing injured users with the best chance of seeking compensation for their product-related injuries.[19]

The policy of providing multiple potential defendants for the injured user to sue also explains the inclusion of the first importer into the European Union as a potential defendant in any action. Having a legitimate claim against a non-EU producer based outside the jurisdiction of the courts is of no real benefit to an injured user. However, by rendering the first importer liable, the Directive, and hence the Consumer Protection Act 1987, ensures that there is always a potential defendant based within the jurisdiction of the courts against whom any judgment can be enforced. While there always remains the possibility that all of the potential defendants have ceased trading, it would be an extremely unlucky claimant who faced this reality.

As regards the first importer into the European Union, the provision expressly provides that the importation must have been in order for that person, in the course of any business of his, to supply it to another. This business requirement negates the risk, however remote, of a private tourist being held legally responsible in respect of any defective items that they bring back with them from travels outside the European Union.[20] Thus, there is no liability for

---

[17] Typical in food production and retailing

[18] This is often the case in clothing production and retailing where the clothes are often manufactured in workshops in the Far East.

[19] For further discussion on this point see G. Howells and S. Weatherill, *Consumer Protection Law* (2nd edn, Ashgate Publishing Ltd, Aldershot, 2005).

[20] A defendant who has imported goods into the European Union in his private capacity would be able to show that there is no *prima facie* action against him. Equally, he could use the defence in

presents or for items purchased outside the European Union at the express request of someone known to the tourist. The definition of the first importer requires analysis of the phrase 'in the course of any business of his'. Business requirements appear regularly in trading legislation, both civil[21] and criminal,[22] but the wording can vary, and with it the meaning. The phrase 'in the course of any business of his' was considered by the House of Lords in the decision of *Warwickshire County Council* v. *Johnson*[23] when interpreting and applying section 20 of the Consumer Protection Act 1987.[24] They held that the phrase requires that the person is the owner of the business or has a controlling interest in it.[25] This is a relatively narrow construction of the phrase. However, this construction is in line with the ethos of the Product Liability Directive and the 1987 Act, which seek to place liability on those who can exercise a measure of control over defective products as opposed to those who are simply employed in the industry producing and supplying them.

In addition to the primary defendants under section 2(2), liability is also placed upon suppliers by virtue of section 2(3) when the damage has been caused wholly or partly by a defective product. The term supplier is construed widely and is not limited to someone who supplies the product to the injured user. Instead, the approach is to hold responsible anyone who has been involved at any point in the chain of distribution. Thus, it includes not merely someone who supplied the product to the injured user but also anyone who has supplied a product to another person who has then incorporated it into another product, i.e., component manufacturers and anyone who has supplied the product to another person. This latter provision encompasses all suppliers in the whole of the contractual chain of distribution, including the ultimate sale by the retailer to a consumer who will not necessarily be the injured user. This liability extends the number of possible defendants quite significantly as it has the potential to include several people who have been involved in the supply of the product

---

Consumer Protection Act 1987, s.4(1)(c)(i) that the only supply by him had been otherwise than in the course of a business.

[21] See, e.g., Sale of Goods Act 1979, s.14.

[22] Trade Descriptions Act 1968, ss.1 and 14 (now repealed); Consumer Protection Act 1987, s.20(1) (now repealed). More recently, other regulations have introduced a business requirement by placing liability on a 'trader', defined as being a person who 'is acting for purposes relating to his business'. See Consumer Protection from Unfair Trading Regulations 2008 (SI 2008/1277), reg. 2(1).

[23] [1993] 1 All ER 299.

[24] Consumer Protection Act 1987, s.20(1) provides that a person is guilty of an offence 'if, in the course of any business of his, he gives (by any means whatsoever) to any consumers an indication which is misleading as to the price at which any goods, services, accommodation or facilities are available (whether generally or from particular persons)'. This section was repealed and replaced by the Consumer Protection from Unfair Trading Regulations 2008.

[25] The subsequent decision in *Denard* v. *Burton Retail Ltd, The Times*, 19 November 1997 held that goods had been supplied in the course of Burton's business when they were paid for through a till in a store belonging to Burton even though the goods had been supplied by a concession holder in the store who both owned the goods and fixed the prices for them. That said, some of the goods did carry price labels from Burton.

while not producing it. However, given that suppliers, while still making a profit from the goods, are one step removed from their production, the section includes factors that limit the liability of suppliers to situations where they have failed the injured user in some way. Consequently, liability only arises where the injured user has requested the supplier to identify one or more of the producer, own-brander or first importer of the product[26] and the supplier has failed to do so.[27] However, the injured person must have made the request within a reasonable time after the damage occurred and at a time when it was not reasonably practicable for him to identify all of the section 2(2) defendants.[28] There is no definition of reasonable in either context and presumably it will depend on the facts of the case. Assuming that the request has been made within a reasonable time, the supplier must then comply with the request within a reasonable time by either identifying the producer, own-brander or importer or, alternatively, providing details of the person from whom he acquired the product. Again there is no definition of a reasonable time but the European Commission when considering the term in the Directive saw no need for amendment.[29] It is this failure by the supplier to comply with the request within a reasonable time that triggers his liability to the injured user. Assuming, however, that he complies with a valid request, the supplier will escape liability even if the people that he identifies no longer exist, there being no requirement that the supplier provides the user with a viable defendant who is capable of being sued. The supplier's liability is restricted to identifying the relevant people. Given the prevailing economic climate, this is significant as many businesses, particularly in the manufacturing sector, have gone into liquidation and thus are no longer capable of being sued. The net result is that the potential number of prospective defendants available to an injured user may be less than would otherwise be the case, but this is no reason to extend the liability placed on a supplier.

Section 2(5) provides for joint and several liability such that each person who can be held liable under Part I of the 1987 Act is liable for the whole of the damages payable to the injured user. Clearly, this is advantageous to the injured user as he only needs to identify one potential defendant to sue, leaving it to that defendant to identify other potential defendants and either join them in as co-defendants or seek a contribution from them in a separate action. But the benefit to the injured user is not simply that he only needs to sue one person. It also lies in the fact that he can select which of the potential defendants is in the strongest position to pay him the full amount of his compensation, either through a court action or, preferably, via product liability insurance, which will save the delay and cost of pursuing a court case. Hence, for example, in a situation where a small producer produces goods for a large multinational

---

[26] Consumer Protection Act 1987, s.2(3)(a).
[27] *Ibid.* s.2(3)(c).   [28] *Ibid.* s.2(3)(b).
[29] European Commission, *Report from the Commission on the Application of Directive 85/374 on Liability for Defective Products,* COM(2000)893 final, para. 3.2.7.

own-brander, the injured user will opt, in all probability, to sue the own-brander as being the wealthier defendant who is better placed to pay compensation.

Section 2(6) confirms that identifying potential defendants and placing joint and several liability upon them under section 2 does not prejudice any other liability that might arise from the injury. Thus, for example, if the injured user is also the person who bought the goods from a retailer, his contract action will subsist against the retailer even though the latter will escape liability under product liability if he has identified the person from whom he acquired the relevant goods or the producer, own-brander or first importer into the European Union. Equally, actions in negligence will still exist alongside liability under product liability. Hence, a producer who is negligent in the way he produces goods will be liable in negligence in addition to being strictly liable under the 1987 Act. This may be invaluable if, for example, some of the damage cannot be recovered under product liability. Thus, for example, if the injured user has suffered personal injury and damage to business property, he will be able to claim compensation for the personal injury through strict liability and for the damage to business property through negligence. Naturally, the potential multiplicity of legal causes of action cannot be used to gain double compensation.

Against this background of several alternative defendants, the European Commission concluded in its report that there is no justification for introducing a 'market share liability' concept similar to that used in the United States in situations such as occurred in the 'DES daughters' litigation. Indeed, the Commission acknowledged that the use of this policy is limited.[30]

Q2 Does the inclusion of first importers, own-branders and suppliers as potential defendants in a product liability action provide a balanced approach to the protection of consumers? Is it reasonable to allow suppliers of the product to negate their own liability by identifying their supplier?

3 Meaning of 'product'

The definition of a 'product' is clearly of central importance to liability under the 1987 Act. It is defined in section 1(1) as being 'any goods or electricity and includes a product which is comprised in another product, whether by virtue of being a component part or raw material or otherwise'. A rider to this general statement is included in section 1(3), which provides that a person who supplies a product in which other products are comprised, either as component parts or raw materials, will not be deemed to be a supplier of those component parts or raw materials purely by virtue of his supply of the main product.

This definition differs from that contained originally in the Directive, which defined a product as meaning 'all movables, with the exception of primary agricultural products and game, even though incorporated into another movable

---

[30] *Ibid.* para. 3.2.1.

or into an immovable'. The exception for primary agricultural products was removed from the Directive in 1999 as a direct response to the 'mad cow disease' (BSE) crisis in the farming industry.[31] Therefore, agricultural products are now included in the definition of a product and liability will ensue in respect of damage caused by defective products. In practice, though, it may be very difficult for a claimant to prove the causal link between his injury and the agricultural product concerned. Someone contracting an illness from drinking unpasteurised milk may find it relatively easy to establish the identity of the farmer who supplied that product. However, by contrast, it would be extraordinarily difficult for a claimant who has contracted variant Creutzfeldt-Jakob Disease (vCJD)[32] to prove the link between himself and an individual BSE-infected animal.[33]

The Directive definition also expressly states that 'products' are 'movables', a definition which clearly excludes immovables. Thus, land and buildings are not included, a situation that remains unaltered following the European Commission's Report, which recommended that real property should not be included within the meaning of product.[34] However, it is clear that movables that have been incorporated into an immovable item will be classed as products. Thus, liability would arise in respect of windows, central heating systems and electrical circuits if they were to prove defective and cause an injury. Electricity itself is expressly included as a product.[35]

There is no express statement that either includes or excludes blood and other human products. However, in *A v. National Blood Authority*,[36] a case concerning a claim by 114 people who contracted Hepatitis C as a result of being given infected blood during blood transfusions, it was expressly accepted that blood is a product for the purposes of product liability.[37] It is then a small step to argue that other human organs and tissues must likewise be classed as products for this purpose, with liability ensuing if the 'products' have not been stored or prepared properly for a medical procedure.[38] The French government introduced

---

[31] By Directive 1999/34/EC [1999] OJ L141/20.

[32] vCJD is sometimes referred to as a human form of BSE.

[33] In a statement, the Spongiform Encephalopathy Advisory Committee (SEAC) reported that they 'have considered 10 cases of CJD which have occurred in people aged under 42 which have recently been identified by the CJD Surveillance Unit, Edinburgh. The Committee have concluded that the Unit has identified a previously unrecognised and consistent disease pattern. A review of patients' medical histories, genetic analysis to date and consideration of other possible causes, such as increased ascertainment, have failed to explain these cases adequately. Although there is no direct evidence of a link, on current data and in the absence of any credible alternative the most likely explanation at present is that these cases are linked to exposure to BSE before the introduction of the SBO ban in 1989'.

[34] European Commission, *Report on Directive 85/374*, above n. 29, para. 3.2.8.

[35] Product Liability Directive, Art. 2; Consumer Protection Act 1987, s.1(2).

[36] [2001] 3 All ER 289.

[37] *A v. National Blood Authority* is also a key decision in analysing the meaning and assessment of when a product is defective for the purposes of the 1987 Act.

[38] See *Henning Veedfald v. Århus Amtskommune* C-203/99 [2001] ECR I-3569, as discussed in Howells and Weatherill, above n. 19, ch. 4, note 82.

product liability for products derived from the human body[39] so there is a clear precedent within Europe for this line of thinking. In the United Kingdom, the Pearson Commission recommended regarding 'human blood and organs' as products,[40] an approach that would reflect our modern treatment of blood and body parts as commodities.[41]

As is obvious from the definition in section 1(2), component parts and raw materials are deemed to be products for the purposes of the 1987 Act for which the relevant producers can be held liable if those parts or materials prove to be defective and cause an injury. Naturally, such producers will have recourse to the defences in section 4(1)(f) in certain circumstances,[42] notably if the defect is due to the way that a subsequent producer used the component or where the component complied with a defective design that was supplied to the component producer by the producer of the final product.

Q3 Is the definition of a product sufficiently comprehensive to satisfy the underlying purposes of the 1987 Act?

4 Defectiveness

(a) When are goods 'defective'

Liability arises as a result of goods being 'defective,' so what constitutes defectiveness is crucial to the working and application of the 1987 Act. The topic falls into three parts: the factors that contribute to defectiveness in any given product, the standard that products must satisfy and the perspective to be used when assessing defectiveness.

The basic definition in section 3(1) provides that 'there is a defect in a product for the purposes of this Part if the safety of the product is not such as persons generally are entitled to expect'. Safety of a product for this purpose includes the safety of products comprised in the main product, i.e., component parts and raw materials, and also safety in the context of damage to property, as well as in the context of risks of death or personal injury.[43]

---

[39] France expressly included human blood products and products derived from the human body when adopting the Product Liability Directive. However, as Professor Miller points out, given that the Directive is a maximal Directive and Member States are not able to introduce any new provisions that exceed the protection offered by the Directive, this provision could be struck down as not being a correct interpretation of the Directive unless the European Court of Justice were to rule that such products are included within the meaning of Art. 2 of the Directive. See Miller and Goldberg, above n. 10, para. 9.69.

[40] *Royal Commission on Civil Liability and Compensation for Personal Injury* (Cmnd. 7054, 1978) para. 1276 ('Pearson Report').

[41] See also Howells and Weatherill, above n. 19, para. 4.2.4.3 and Miller and Goldberg, above n.10, para. 9.68.

[42] See the discussion of defences below.

[43] Consumer Protection Act 1987, s.3(1).

The choice of safety as the defining criteria emphasises the link between product liability and product safety. As mentioned previously, Parliament took the opportunity in 1987 to use the same piece of legislation both to adopt the requirements of the Directive and to update product safety controls.[44] Further, there is also a link between defectiveness in product liability and unsatisfactory quality in contract, as safety is a factor in determining satisfactory quality under section 14 of the Sale of Goods Act 1979.[45] However, the overlap only works in one direction. Goods that are defective under section 3 of the Consumer Protection Act 1987 and, as such, are unsafe will also be of unsatisfactory quality. However, it does not necessarily work the other way, as goods may be unsatisfactory in contract because they breach one of the other factors in section 14(2B)[46] while not being unsafe within the meaning of either section 14 of the Sale of Goods Act 1979 or section 3 of the Consumer Protection Act 1987.[47] It follows that when a successful claim is made under product liability, the purchaser of the defective item should not have any trouble in recovering the cost of the goods under the Sale of Goods Act 1979.[48]

Traditionally, defects have been categorised as manufacturing defects, design defects and duty to warn defects.[49] This approach is still adopted in the US Restatement (Third) of Torts in which strict liability is imposed for manufacturing defects, with something more akin to negligence being used for design defects and duty to warn defects.[50]

In the United Kingdom, this traditional approach was challenged in the leading decision of *A* v. *National Blood Authority,*[51] in which Burton J revisited the categorisation of defects. He preferred to consider all products as either standard or non-standard, defining the terms by reference to whether the product performs in the way that the producer intends. He opined that:

> [a] standard product is one which is and performs as the producer intends. A non-standard product is one which is different, obviously because it is deficient or inferior in terms of safety, from the standard product; and where it is the harmful characteristic or characteristics present in the non-standard product, but not in the standard product, which has or have caused the material injury or damage.[52]

---

[44] Consumer Protection Act 1987, Part II replaced the criminal controls over safety previously contained in the Consumer Safety Act 1978. While some of the sections of Part II of the Consumer Protection Act 1987 remain extant, the main provisions covering product safety are now to be found in the General Product Safety Regulations 2005, SI 2005/1803.

[45] Sale of Goods Act 1979, s.14(2B)(d).

[46] Fitness for all the purposes for which goods of the kind in question are commonly supplied, appearance and finish, freedom from minor defects and durability.

[47] See also Miller and Goldberg, above n. 10.

[48] The purchaser will have to make a claim in contract in respect of the defective item itself as it is not recoverable in strict product liability, see Consumer Protection Act 1987, s.5.

[49] See Part 4 Chapter 1 for a full discussion of these categories of defect.

[50] See Part 4 Chapter 1.   [51] [2001] 3 All ER 289.   [52] *Ibid.* para. 36.

Applying this terminology, manufacturing defects would be classed as non-standard products as they would differ from what the producer intended by their failure to comply with the design being used on the production run. In short, rogue products would be classed as non-standard products in this context. Burton J ruled that the primary issue in relation to non-standard products is whether:

> the public at large accepted the non-standard nature of the product, i.e., they accept that a proportion of the products is defective … That, as discussed, is not of course the end of it, because the question is of legitimate expectation, and the Court may conclude that the expectation of the public is too high or too low.[53]

In considering non-standard products, Burton J continued that the avoidability of the harmful characteristic, the impracticality, cost or difficulty of taking precautionary measures and the benefit to society or utility of the product should not be taken into account.[54] In respect of the last of these, however, the benefit to society and utility of the product can be considered when the public, with proper knowledge and full information about it, does and ought to accept the risk.[55] Assessing the defect in a non-standard product should be relatively straight-forward with the opportunity for the injured user to prove the causal link to the damage and thereby claim compensation.

Applying this alternative terminology, a product with a design defect would nonetheless be a standard product as the product would be as the producer intended, even though the design itself was deficient. Indeed, Burton J acknowledged that if a standard product is unsafe, it is likely to be as the result of either an alleged design error or an allegedly flawed system.[56] Assessing defectiveness in standard products is likely to be more problematic, and Burton J opined that the harmful characteristic in the goods must be identified, if necessary with the help of experts. The sole question is the safety of the goods for their foreseeable use, with comparison to other goods on the market being appropriate to identify and compare the relevant features of the products concerned. He included price as a significant factor in legitimate expectation and potentially material when comparing products. However, as with non-standard products, he felt that what the producer could have done differently and whether the producer could or could not have done the same as other producers are not relevant factors in this context.[57] Naturally, the inherent risk of taking into account other similar products on the market and comparing the features of those products which the producer could have included in his product is that it would come very close to re-introducing negligence by the back door, as it renders pertinent the actions of the producer by reference to the actions of others. Strict liability is supposed to depend upon the existence of the defect rather than upon whether the producer has failed in some way in allowing the defect to occur.

---

[53] *Ibid.* para. 68.   [54] *Ibid.*
[55] *Ibid.*   [56] *Ibid.* para. 71.   [57] *Ibid.*

A v. *National Blood Authority* involved an action by 114 people who contracted Hepatitis C from blood transfusions and blood products after 1 March 1988 and for which the defendant blood authority was responsible. The claimants argued that the case related to a manufacturing defect in that the blood was defective as it was infected and thus differed from pure blood. By contrast, the defendants argued that it was a design defect and, further, that throughout the period when the blood was being used for transfusions, the Hepatits C infection was either unidentified or could not be detected by the tests available at the time.[58] The risk of the infection was known to the medical profession at the time but not to the general public. Burton J, having proffered his alternative analysis of the types of defect, ruled that the bags of blood 'were non-standard products and were unsafe by virtue of the harmful characteristics which they had and which standard products did not have'.[59] They were defective because:

> the public at large was entitled to expect that the blood transfused to them would be free from infection. There were no warnings and no material publicity, certainly none officially initiated by or for the benefit of the defendants, and the knowledge of the medical profession, not materially or at all shared with the consumer, is of no relevance. It is not material to consider whether any steps or any further steps could have been taken to avoid or palliate the risk that the blood would be infected.[60]

Given his findings, the court found in favour of the plaintiffs, with the defendant being held liable for the defective blood and for the injuries suffered by the plaintiffs.[61] The court also ruled that the claim by the defendant that the defect attracted a development risk defence failed.[62]

It remains to be seen the extent to which the alternative categorisation of defects propounded by Burton J is followed or whether courts continue to use the traditional approach of defining defects as manufacturing, design or duty to warn.[63]

Q4 Compare the traditional categorisation of defects into manufacturing defects, design defects and duty to warn defects with the approach suggested by Burton J in **A v. National Blood Authority.**

(b) Concept of safety

Section 3(1) of the 1987 Act stipulates that there is a defect in a product for the purposes of this Part of the Act when 'the safety of the product is not such as persons generally are entitled to expect'.

---

[58] This raises issues about the development risk defence to which we will return below.
[59] [2001] 3 All ER 289, para. 79.
[60] *Ibid.* para. 80.   [61] *Ibid.* para. 82.
[62] *Ibid.* We will return to the development risk defence below.
[63] For an excellent discussion of the many facets of the decision in *A* v. *National Blood Authority,* see Miller and Goldberg, above n. 10, paras. 10.83–10.100.

This definition clearly indicates the adoption of an objective consumer expectation test as the basis underpinning liability. It therefore demands an analysis of who constitutes 'persons generally'[64] for this purpose and how their legitimate expectations are to be assessed. In practice, the court acts as arbiter in analysing the expectations of the public as 'an informed representative of the public at large'[65] and hence decides what persons generally have a right to expect. However, it is possible that the standard adopted by the court does not accord with what either the public generally or an individual subjective consumer might actually have thought or expected. Burton J considered this aspect in *A v. National Blood Authority*,[66] stating that:

> The Court decides what the public is entitled to expect ... Such objectively assessed legitimate expectation may accord with actual expectation; but it may be *more* than the public actually expects, thus imposing a higher standard of safety, or it may be *less* than the public actually expects. Alternatively, the public may have no *actual* expectation, e.g. in relation to a new product[67]

The standard of safety is what the public is legitimately entitled to expect. This does not require absolute safety any more than product liability imposes absolute liability as opposed to strict liability for the injuries caused. The level of safety provided by the product will be assessed by reference to all the relevant criteria[68] to see whether it satisfies the legitimate expectations of the public, but no more. In *A v. National Blood Authority* itself, Burton J held that the infected blood was defective as the public had a right to expect that the blood was safe and not infected with Hepatitis C. This was so because there was a known risk that blood used for transfusions might be infected even though there was no test to establish whether any individual bag of blood was so contaminated. It was relevant that the risk was not known to the public generally, although it was recognised within the medical profession, but the knowledge of the 'learned intermediary' was not sufficient to avoid liability to the ultimate recipients of the blood.

Q5 Is a consumer expectation test an appropriate test to use when assessing product safety?

While section 3(2) of the 1987 Act raises the issue of the time of production when assessing defectiveness so as to put the incident into context, time plays no part in the expectation of persons generally that the product be safe. Thus, the court in *Abouzaid* v. *Mothercare (UK) Ltd*[69] held that defectiveness

---

[64] It is noteworthy that s.3 refers only to the level of safety expected by persons generally and does not expressly refer to particular categories of users, such as children or the elderly, who may legitimately expect higher levels of safety. Contrast the requirements for a safe product under the General Product Safety Regulations 2005, reg. 2, where categories of consumers at risk are dealt with explicitly.

[65] *A v. National Blood Authority* [2001] 3 All ER 289, para. 31(vii).

[66] *Ibid.*   [67] *Ibid.* para. 31(vii).

[68] Consumer Protection Act 1987, s.3(2).   [69] [2000] All ER (D) 2436.

in a product is to be judged by the expectations of the public rather than by the passage of time. The plaintiff, aged twelve, was helping to fix a 'Cosytoes' fleece-lined sleeping bag to a pushchair used for his younger brother. The Cosytoes was manufactured by the defendant and was affixed using two elasticated straps, which went around the back of the pushchair and fastened with a buckle. While attaching the Cosytoes, one of the straps sprang from the plaintiff's grasp and the buckle on the end of the strap hit him in the left eye, resulting in permanent sight damage. The defendant tried to claim a development risk defence, which the court rejected, deciding that the lack of any previous similar accidents was not sufficient to satisfy the defence.[70] The judge, finding for the plaintiff, opined that the inherent risk in the product arose from the propensity of elastic to spring back. If that propensity constituted a defect in 1999, when the product was considered by a safety expert prior to the court hearing, it was equally a defect in 1990 when the accident occurred. The Court of Appeal upheld this decision and rejected an appeal by the defendant.

In assessing defectiveness in any individual item, section 3(2) of the 1987 Act provides that all the circumstances must be taken into account and proceeds to provide a non-exhaustive list of three specific factors that are relevant. In this respect, it echoes the thrust of the corresponding provision of the Product Liability Directive,[71] although the 1987 Act goes into greater detail, outlining the three criteria thus:

(a) the manner in which, and purposes for which, the product has been marketed, its get-up, the use of any mark in relation to the product and any instructions for, or warnings with respect to, doing or refraining from doing, anything with or in relation to the product;

(b) what might reasonably be expected to be done with or in relation to the product; and

(c) the time when the product was supplied by its producer to another.

The first criterion deals with the presentation of the product and the purpose for which it has been put into the market. It expressly refers to instructions and warnings, reflective of the fact that this criterion deals primarily with duty to warn defects. The get-up or presentation of the product is most unlikely to impact upon either a manufacturing defect or a design defect but may be the major factor in a duty to warn defect. Section 3(2)(a) encompasses a few related issues, the first of which is the manner in which, and purposes for which, the product has been marketed. This allows the court to consider issues such as whether the product is aimed at any particular section of the community such as children or the infirm, and whether any advertising accompanying the product is geared specifically to appeal to that group. This would also be relevant in later consideration of whether instructions and warnings were appropriate

---

[70] The development risk defence under s.4(1)(e) will be discussed in greater detail below.

[71] Product Liability Directive, Art. 6.

to foreseeable product users. The marketing of the product might also indicate whether the product is aimed only at experienced users of such products or the public in general, which would again impact on the instructions and warnings provided with the product.

The purpose for which the product has been marketed delineates the intended use of the product but this will not necessarily negate the liability of the producer if an injury is caused when the product is used for a non-intended purpose, but one that would constitute a reasonably foreseeable misuse. However, much might depend on the warnings provided and the previous known history of the product. As Professor Miller points out,[72] Thalidomide, which has a notorious reputation given its impact on the foetus if used during pregnancy, would not be classed as defective if marketed as, and used solely as, a treatment for leprosy, for which it has proved very effective. This would, of course, depend on it not being prescribed for use by pregnant women. In fact, Thalidomide has received approval by the Food and Drug Administration (FDA) for use in the United States in the treatment of leprosy, all the more remarkable given that the FDA refused to license it originally and thereby avoided the tragic injuries to unborn foetuses that were suffered by children in countries where the drug was used during pregnancy.[73]

The get-up of the product and the use of any mark in relation to it may also contribute to the perception of how safe the product is likely to be. The use of marks would include things such as the BSI Kitemark, which provides a clear statement of compliance of the relevant aspect of the product with safety requirements. However, the inclusion of a mark should not be interpreted as meaning that the product is safe in every regard. Any safety standard must be applied and interpreted in the light of what it seeks to control. Thus, for example, compliance with a BSI Standard that governs the flammability of a product does not address the strength of the item or the constituent substances from which it is made. Further, compliance with a voluntary standard does not necessarily mean that the product is safe, as a standard may not reflect the highest level of safety possible at the time of the incident as opposed to the level acceptable at the time when the standard was published. It follows that a product that complies with a voluntary standard could still be defective for the purposes of the 1987 Act and compliance with that standard would not be a defence. It may, demonstrate the intention of the producer to supply a quality product, but will not protect him from the consequences of supplying a defective item to an injured user.

A similar issue to the voluntary use of a quality mark such as the Kitemark is the compliance of the product with a mandatory standard. Again, the standard will not necessarily reflect the highest level of safety achievable at the time,

---

[72] Miller and Goldberg, above n. 10, para. 10.55.

[73] The FDA official who refused to license Thalidomide originally was subsequently awarded a Congressional medal.

rather it is likely to reflect the lowest common denominator standard that the legislative parties were able to agree upon, a problem that increases the larger the number of legislative partners involved.[74] Compliance with such a standard does not necessarily mean that the product is safe and hence it remains possible for a product that complies with the standard to still be defective for the purposes of section 3. Of course, if the defectiveness is directly caused by compliance with the requisite mandatory standard, the defendant will have access to the defence under section 4(1)(a) of the 1987 Act, which states that it is a defence to show that 'the defect is attributable to compliance with any requirement imposed by or under any enactment or with any Community obligation'.[75]

The latter part of section 3(2)(a) refers to 'any instructions for, or warnings with respect to, doing or refraining from doing, anything with or in relation to the product'. Instructions and warnings complement each other, with instructions providing the positive statements as to how to use the product safely while warnings advise against actions that would adversely affect the safe use of the product. Both instructions and warnings need to be clear and comprehensive and located in a suitable place to ensure that they will come to the attention of the user. For his part, the producer can reasonably expect that the user of the product will both read the instructions and warnings and comply with them. The decision in *Worsley v. Tambrands Ltd*[76] related to the position of the requisite warnings. The claimant suffered toxic shock syndrome from using tampons manufactured by the defendant. She argued that the product was defective because there was no warning about the risk on the outside of the box, although there was a warning on a leaflet inside the box. The court rejected her claim, holding that there was no failure to warn and that the product was not defective.

If warnings are to be effective, they must draw the attention of the user to all of the relevant risks. *Vacwell Engineering Co. Ltd v. BDH Chemicals Ltd*[77] is good authority for the fact that liability will arise in respect of any injury caused by a risk not included in a warning and hence not drawn to the attention of the user. Indeed, a failure to warn of all relevant risks may lull the user into a false sense of security and thereby place him at greater risk than would otherwise be the case.

If the instructions for use and/or the warnings are not sufficient, the product may be deemed to be defective within section 3 and give rise to liability, although it is still open to the defendant to show that the claimant was

---

[74] The derogations in the Product Liability Directive themselves evidence the difficulties faced when a large number of parties are involved in the debate about any legislative provision. The net result will be a lower common standard or even an agreement to disagree as occurred with the derogations.

[75] Defences will be discussed fully. Conformity with UK standards is also relevant to criminal law where compliance with UK rules is evidence that a product is safe as regards aspects of the product governed by those rules. See General Product Safety Regulations 2005, reg. 6.

[76] [2000] PIQR 95.   [77] [1970] 3 All ER 553.

contributorily negligent in using the product in the way that they did and that any damages awarded in respect of the injury should be reduced accordingly.

A related issue is that of any obvious dangers posed by a product, the most common examples being knives, guns, open access to moving parts in machinery, etc. A producer has a right to expect that a product user will exercise care for his own safety and take account of obvious dangers.[78] Nonetheless, it may be that a producer will still choose to protect himself by including warnings about such dangers and there remains the possibility that an injured user may be held contributorily negligent for his injuries.[79]

Q6 Consider whether section 3(2)(a) adequately covers the presentation of the product and any instructions for use.

Section 3(2)(b) of the 1987 Act refers to 'what might reasonably be expected to be done with or in relation to the product'. Arguably, this introduces a degree of negligence into the definition for it requires the producer to consider the ways in which the product may be used and warn accordingly of any risks that such usage might pose. Foreseeability is a concept central to negligence and yet this section necessitates using this to assess liability for both the intended uses and any foreseeable misuse of the product. Having identified the purposes for which the product will be used, the producer must ensure that appropriate instructions and warnings are provided or run the risk of the product being considered defective under section 3(2)(a).

Section 3(2)(c) raises the issue of the time of production, requiring that 'the time when the product was supplied by its producer to another' is taken into account. This effectively requires the court to turn the clock back to the time of production of the individual product and assess the state of the art at that time. This is no easy task for it is potentially very difficult to establish exactly what was known at any point in the production and development of a product, particularly as the court may be looking back over a period of up to ten years given that the cut-off period for liability occurs ten years after the offending product last left the control of the producer, own-brander or importer.[80] This may be complicated further by the fact that the relevant state of the art may have moved on during the period in which products of the type in question were being produced. This would be true of any popular product which is produced over an extended period. The net result is that the court needs to be satisfied as to the development of the state of the art at a given date in the production process for products of that type. The maintenance of production or import

---

[78] A case in point was *B* v. *McDonald's Restaurants Ltd* [2000] EWHC (QB) 490, in which the defendant was not liable for scalding injuries caused to the claimant when drinking a hot drink supplied by the defendant. The expectation of persons generally is that hot drinks will be hot and appropriate care should be taken.

[79] There is also the possibility that *volenti non fit injuria* will apply.

[80] Limitation Act 1980, s.11A.

records identifying batch numbers, and perhaps even the individual product, is crucially important to this process as it allows all parties to identify the relevant date both for the purpose of establishing the state of the art, but also for establishing whether the claim made by the claimant is valid or statute-barred.

Specifying that the relevant time for section 3(2)(c) is the time that the product is supplied by the producer further requires him to be aware of any change in the state of the art during any storage period. If the producer produces an item but does not supply it for another two years, the state of the art that is applicable will be that existing at the time of supply and not the time of production. A product that was in compliance with the state of the art at the date of production may not be so at the time of supply and thereby will fall foul of section 3(2)(c). This problem can be particularly acute during periods of economic slowdown, particularly if they occur unexpectedly, when purchasing may slow down or stop faster that the corresponding production with the result that a higher number of goods than usual enter storage.

The safety of the product will not be assessed by considering whether a later product is safer that the product in question. This makes sense since otherwise producers would not engage in any product development for fear that producing a newer, safer product would leave them open to claims that the previous version of the product was unsafe. Each defective product must be assessed on its own merits by reference to the state of the art prevailing at the relevant time. Hence, in *Roe* v. *Minster of Health*,[81] a case involving the storage of drugs, the court opined that 'we must not look at the 1947 accident with 1954 spectacles', a clear reference to the need to consider things in temporal context.

Q7 Does the application of section 3(2)(c) successfully place the assessment of any individual defect into its temporal context?

(c) Proof of defect

It is for the plaintiff to demonstrate that the defect exists. While the basis of product liability has altered from negligence to strict liability, the burden of proof remains the same.[82] However, the approach of the courts to this burden has caused comment in two of the leading decisions, *Foster* v. *Biosil*[83] and *Richardson* v. *LRC Products Ltd.*[84] In *Foster* v. *Biosil*, the court[85] held that the claimant not only had to prove that the product was defective but must also

---

[81] [1954] 2 All ER 131. The plaintiff suffered injury through the use of drugs that had become adulterated during storage. The evidence showed that the potential for the type of adulteration that occurred had not been recognised at the time.

[82] While the Consumer Protection Act 1987 does not expressly address the burden of proof, the Product Liability Directive provides in Art. 4 that 'The injured person shall be required to prove the damage, the defect and the causal relationship between defect and damage.' This approach accords with the normal burden of proof in English tort law.

[83] (2001) 59 BMLR 178.   [84] [2000] Lloyd's Rep. Med 280.

[85] The case was heard before a Recorder, Cherie Booth QC.

identify the cause of the defect. This approach is more akin to negligence than strict liability as, theoretically, the latter only requires proof of the defect and not how the product came to be defective. In practice, the cause of the defect speaks to the actions of the producer, own-brander or importer, which are not relevant in a strict liability action but would be pertinent if the claim was based in negligence. The whole rationale of strict liability is to absolve the claimant from needing to address the actions of the defendant at all and concentrate instead on proving the defective condition of the goods.

Foster v. *Biosil* related to a claim arising out of the use of two silicone breast implants consequent upon the claimant undergoing a bilateral mastectomy operation. Both implants had to be surgically removed and the claimant alleged that both breast implants had been defective within the meaning of the 1987 Act and sued for damages accordingly. She alleged that the left implant had ruptured prematurely and that the right implant had leaked silicone. It was accepted that the surgeon responsible for inserting the implants had not been negligent and that the matter revolved wholly around the alleged defectiveness of the implants. The claimant argued that she simply had to prove that the product had failed in a way that was unsafe but the court held that she had to prove not merely that the product was defective but also the cause of the defect, in this case a manufacturing fault, a burden that she had not satisfied. The right implant was intact at the time that it was removed and although the left implant had ruptured there was no evidence as to why this had occurred. Indeed, the evidence was that ruptures of this type are rare and that no other implants from this batch had ruptured. The court held that the claimant had failed to establish that the rupture had occurred because of a defect within the meaning of section 3 of the 1987 Act.

Richardson v. *LRC Products Ltd* related to a claim arising from an unwanted pregnancy resulting from the failure of a condom. The teat end of the condom had become detached and was not found. Evidence showed that the condom had suffered ozone damage and the defendant company acknowledged that it would be liable if this defect had been present at the time that the condom had left its control and had been the cause of the failure of the condom during use. However, the court held that the more likely explanation was that the ozone damage had occurred during storage of the condom while awaiting the court hearing, and that the fracturing of the teat from the main body of the condom had not been caused by the ozone damage. Further, the evidence was that condoms can fail in use and that the manufacturer had not suggested that his product was 100 per cent reliable. The product was not defective within the meaning of section 3 and complied with the level of safety expected by persons generally.

The net result of these cases is to reinforce the point that the claimant must prove defectiveness within the meaning of section 3 and the mere fact that a product has failed will not necessarily mean that the product is defective such as to give rise to a cause of action.

Q8 Analyse the approach of the courts to proving defectiveness within section 3.

(d) Need for causation

While strict liability has altered both the basis of liability and the range of potential defendants, it has not affected the requirement that the claimant proves the causal link between the defective product and the damage caused. Indeed, the Product Liability Directive expressly states that the injured person is 'required to prove the damage, the defect and the causal relationship between defect and damage'.[86] Producers can still rely on the defence that, while the claimant used their product, it was not their product that caused the damage and that some other factor is responsible for the injuries sustained by the claimant. There is no reversal of proof and thus the burden lies on the claimant to prove the causal link rather than on the defendant to disprove it. Causation may be very difficult to prove, particularly in cases involving pharmaceuticals and medical products, leading to suggestions that such injuries should be dealt with via a no-fault compensation scheme, such as that in New Zealand, or through an industry-based scheme like the German Pharmapool. Given that most, if not all, pharmaceuticals have side-effects and are designed to impact physiologically upon the user, it is very difficult to establish causation in any individual case. Each person has a different metabolism, which, combined with differences of ill-health, age, sex, weight, etc., can lead to differing reactions to the same product. The net result is that causation may be difficult to prove unless there is a proven link between the pharmaceutical in question and the type of injury suffered by the claimant, as occurred in the Thalidomide situation.

It must also be acknowledged that the fact that the claimant can prove a causal link does not automatically mean that the product is defective. It may be that the claimant is an idiosyncratic user whose reaction to the product is abnormal. Thus, for example, nuts are not rendered defective because a person who is allergic to nuts becomes ill after eating them. In respect of pharmaceuticals, a risk-benefit analysis comes into play and the incidence of a relatively minor side-effect would not make a product defective if the benefit it bestows is to save the life of the user. Causation was specifically addressed in *X* v. *Schering*,[87] a case in which the user suffered a thrombosis allegedly caused by the use of a third generation contraceptive pill. The plaintiff, the lead claimant in a group action, had used the contraceptive Femodene, a third generation COC, which was manufactured by the defendant. The plaintiff had suffered a deep vein thrombosis while others in the group litigation had suffered various cardiovascular disorders, which, in some instances, had proved fatal. The claimant alleged that the third generation COCs carried more than twice the risk of the second generation equivalent, a fact she needed to prove to establish causation. In giving judgment for the defendant, Mackay J held

[86] Product Liability Directive, Art. 4.   [87] (2003) 70 BMLR 88.

that the plaintiff had failed to demonstrate this increased risk and that the evidence of expert witnesses and epidemiological studies confirmed that the probability was that there was no increased relative risk in using this third generation pill.

Q9 Consider the relationship between proof of defectiveness and the need to prove causation.

5 Defences

The Consumer Protections Act 1987 has introduced strict product liability and not absolute liability. The former allows for appropriate defences to be made available to the defendant while absolute liability would not allow any such concession. The use of strict liability in consumer law is common to both civil law and criminal law, where the imposition of strict liability offences is mitigated by the use of statutory defences, the most significant of which is the due diligence defence. This allows the defendant to avoid criminal liability by proving that he took all reasonable precautions and used all due diligence to avoid the commission of the offence.[88]

The six statutory defences to a product liability claim are to be found in section 4 of the 1987 Act. Five of them are relatively straight-forward, while the sixth, the development risk defence, is considerably more complex and will be discussed in greater detail below.

(a) Compliance with a mandatory standard

The first defence is one that is most unlikely to occur in practice. Section 4(1)(a) provides that it is a defence to show that the defect is attributable to compliance with any requirement imposed by or under any enactment or Community obligation. Thus, if the injury-causing defect is directly attributable to compliance with a mandatory standard, the defendant will not be held liable. However, this is quite a narrow defence, as the defendant must demonstrate that the defect is a direct and unavoidable consequence of his compliance with the legal enactment. If it is possible for him to comply with the enactment without the defect occurring by, for example, changing his production process, the defence will not apply. The whole tenor of the defence is that the defendant was forced to market a defective product. Naturally, this is most unlikely to happen as the whole raison d'être of safety regulations is to promote and ensure the production of safe products, so the likelihood of a safety regulation actually causing a

---

[88] The relevant offences are contrary to General Product Safety Regulations 2005, reg. 20. For current purposes, the most pertinent example of the due diligence defence is to be found in *ibid.* reg. 29, which provides a defence for persons charged with offences under those Regulations relating to the supply of unsafe goods.

defect is remote, to say the least. The producer remains liable for any defect in any aspect of the product that is not covered by the regulatory requirements. It must also be noted that the defence only covers compliance with mandatory standards and thus a defect occasioned by compliance with a voluntary standard, such as a BSI Kitemark, will not be covered.

(b) Product not supplied by the defendant

The second defence is that the defendant did not supply the product to another person. This encompasses two situations. The first is where the producer, having produced the product, decides not to market it. This might be because the item contains a manufacturing defect and has failed the quality control process or, alternatively, it could be that the product has been in storage and would now be deemed to be defective because of safety developments that have occurred during the storage period. In either instance, the product would be classed as defective if the producer was to put it into circulation and, hence, he would be liable for any injuries suffered by a user of that product. Having made his decision not to put the product into circulation, the responsibility is on the producer to ensure that the product is destroyed and cannot find its way to the market. Nonetheless, there are two ways in which it might still reach the market, one of which will render the producer liable. Assuming that he is an employer and not a sole trader working alone, the producer will be liable for the actions of his employees during the course of their employment. It follows that if an employee allows a product to be put into circulation, even contrary to the instructions of the producer, the latter will be responsible as supply will have occurred, even if accidentally or unintentionally. In the event of an unintended supply such as this, the producer should arrange for a product recall as soon as possible, thereby limiting the possibility of a user being injured and hence limiting his exposure to damages in respect of such an injury.[89] The other way in which defective goods might reach the market despite quality controls by the producer and his decision not to market them, would be if they were stolen from his factory prior to their destruction. In practice, this is probably the less likely of the two possibilities but theoretically could happen. In this situation, the producer would not be responsible as clearly he had no control over the circulation of the product.

The second, and arguably more common, situation in which the defendant could validly claim this defence will be if he did not produce the goods at all. There is a ready market for cheap counterfeit goods, from which no producer is

---

[89] If a producer knows that he has put unsafe goods into the market, he is obliged to inform the relevant enforcement authority in writing of that fact and the action that he has taken to prevent risk to the consumer and, if relevant, the identity of each Member State in which, to the best of his knowledge, the product has been supplied or marketed: see General Product Safety Regulations 2005, reg. 9(1). A failure to comply with this requirement is an offence under *ibid.* reg. 20(2). If the producer fails to arrange for a product recall, the enforcement authority can order him to do so under *ibid.* reg. 15.

exempt. Any high street name or, more particularly, designer label is liable to be copied by a counterfeiter who will then supply the product through markets at a knock-down price.[90] Anyone can wear a fake Rolex watch or carry a fake Gucci handbag if they so choose.[91] If a counterfeit product is defective and causes an injury to the user, the genuine producer will not be liable and will be able to raise a defence under section 4(1)(b). Theoretically, the producer would have a claim in passing off against anyone producing counterfeit goods that confuse a purchaser as to their true origin but, in practice, such a claim would generally be pointless, both in terms of the ability to pursue the counterfeiter successfully and since purchasers buying cheap counterfeit goods often do so knowingly and have not been misled.

(c) Supply otherwise than in the course of a business

The third defence is designed to protect private sellers. It requires both that the only supply by the defendant was 'otherwise than in the course of a business'[92] of that person and, further, either that section 2(2) does not apply to him or only applies to him in respect of things done without a view to a profit. This means that any voluntary non-profit-making organisation can claim the protection of this defence. This allows bodies such as the Women's Institute or the Scout movement to be able to produce and sell items for the purpose of fund-raising to support their organisations without falling foul of the requirements of the 1987 Act. The position of charities is arguably more precarious, as their raison d'être is to make money, although, as it is ploughed back into the cause for which they are raising the funds, it can be argued that they are not truly acting 'in the course of a business' as they are not sharing profits among share-holders or other owners of the organisation.[93] The phrase 'in the course of a business of that person's' implies a degree of ownership and control over the enterprise in question.[94] Consequently, employees can also claim the protection

[90] The person producing the counterfeit goods could be held liable for a criminal offence under the Trade Marks Act 1994. It might also be an unfair commercial practice under the Consumer Protection from Unfair Trading Regulations, SI 2008/1277, reg. 5(3)(a), breach of which is an offence under *ibid.* reg. 9. See Part 5 for a full discussion of unfair commercial practices.

[91] If a consumer is found in possession of counterfeit goods, enforcement staff in France and Italy can seize the counterfeit goods, with the consumer then being liable to pay a fine double the value of the real item. Thus, if a consumer is found to be carrying a counterfeit handbag, which is a copy of a handbag that retails at €1,000, the consumer is liable to a fine of €2,000 in addition to having the fake bag seized. *BBC News*, 22 August 2009.

[92] A business is defined for this purpose as including 'a trade or profession and the activities of a professional or trade association or of a local authority or other public authority': Consumer Protection Act 1987, s.45(1).

[93] Professor Miller comments that organisations such as universities, schools, nursing homes and hospices may be able to satisfy the requirement that any application of s.2(2) of the 1987 Act to them is otherwise than with a view to a profit. This would allow them to claim the protection of the defence in s.4(1)(c). See Miller Goldberg, above n. 10, para. 13.12.

[94] This phrase would be similar in effect to the phrase 'in the course of a business of his' used elsewhere in consumer protection legislation and would be construed accordingly.

of this defence as the business within which they work would not be classed as theirs for this purpose, and thus any supply by them would not have been made 'in the course of a business of that person's'. As regards the owner of the business, the issue will be whether the supply in question was within the course of that business, as to which the decision in *Stevenson* v. *Rogers*[95] is pertinent, the thrust of that decision being that any activity undertaken by the business will be deemed to be in the course of that business even if it is the first such transaction. The borderline between businesses and hobbies is also relevant, as hobbyists benefit from the protection of the defence while businesses do not. There is no hard and fast rule about when a hobby becomes a business, as is evidenced by the difficulties faced by the courts in deciding criminal liability under the (now, largely defunct) Trade Descriptions Act 1968.[96] The balance is always a delicate one to draw, in which facts will alter cases. Some useful examples on the point were provided by the Joint Law Commission Report when distinguishing between a man who sells apples to his neighbour as opposed to a small-scale market gardener or, equally, a woman who makes home-made jam for the church as opposed to someone providing home-made teas for tourists during the summer.[97] A hobbyist will not have acted in the course of a business of his and, although he might technically be a producer within the meaning of section 2(2), he will attract the protection of the defence as his activities were undertaken otherwise than with a view to a profit.

(d) Defect not present at the relevant time

The fourth defence, contained in section 4(1)(d), is triggered when the defendant can demonstrate that the defect did not exist in the product at the relevant time. The relevant time for this purpose means the time at which the producer, own-brander or first importer supplied the product to another person.[98] In respect of claims against any section 2(2) defendants, this is the logical point to choose as it would be totally unreasonable, not to say inequitable, to attempt to hold them liable for a defect that arose after the product left their control. It might be, for example, that the defect has been introduced into the product through inadequate storage by someone further down the chain of distribution. However, the same time-frame is used when the defendant is not the producer, own-brander or first importer but some other person, such as a distributor or retailer who falls within section 2(3). This means that those persons cannot be

---

[95] [1999] QB 1028.

[96] See, e.g., *Blakemore* v. *Bellamy* [1982] RTR 303. The remaining major offences under s.1 and s.14 of the Trade Descriptions Act 1968 were repealed and replaced by the Consumer Protection from Unfair Trading Regulations 2008, SI 2008/1277.

[97] Law Commission and Scottish Law Commission, *Liability for Defective Products,* Law Com. No. 82, Scot Law Com. No. 45 (Cmnd. 6831, 1977) para. 43, as referred to in Miller and Goldberg, above n. 10, para. 13.12.

[98] Consumer Protection Act 1987, s.4(2).

held strictly liable for any injuries caused by a defect in the product that arose after it left the producer, own-brander or first importer and, as such, cannot be held strictly liable in respect of injuries caused by a defect for which they are themselves responsible, an interesting lacuna in the protection provided by the statute. In this scenario, the injured user is left without any claim in strict liability and will be forced to pursue any claim that he may have against the retailer, distributor, etc. in the tort of negligence, with all the difficulties that involves and which strict liability under the 1987 Act was intended to circumvent.

Q10 Analyse whether the first four statutory defences provide an appropriate level of protection for innocent defendants who are being sued for alleged breaches of product liability requirements.

(e) Development risk defence

Without doubt, the most significant and contentious defence in the 1987 Act[99] is the development risk defence contained in section 4(1)(e), which provides:

> that the state of scientific and technical knowledge at the relevant time was not such that a producer of products of the same description as the product in question might be expected to have discovered the defect if it had existed in his products while they were under his control.

As previously discussed,[100] the UK government was taken to the European Court of Justice over the wording of this defence as it differs to a significant extent from the wording in the corresponding provision of the Product Liability Directive,[101] Article 7(e) of which reads:

> that the state of scientific and technical knowledge at the time when he put the product into circulation was not such as to enable the existence of the defect to be discovered.

The distinction is clear, the UK version of the defence referring to the knowledge 'of producers of products of the same description' in a way that the Directive does not. The suggestion was that this limits the potential liability of the producer by allowing him to use the knowledge of similar producers as his touchstone rather than the knowledge available within the wider community. Nonetheless, the ECJ decided in *EC Commission* v. *United Kingdom*[102] that

---

[99] Equally, it is the most contentious defence in the Product Liability Directive and was ultimately included in the Directive to satisfy the demands of some of the Member States, including the United Kingdom, and thereby allow the Directive to be passed. The development risk defence was one of the three derogations originally contained in the Directive allowing Member States to choose whether to allow a development risk defence within their own jurisdictions. The United Kingdom chose to include it. For a fuller discussion of this aspect of the topic see Part 4 Chapter 1.

[100] See Part 4 Chapter 1   [101] Product Liability Directive Art. 7(e).

[102] C-300/95 [1997] ECR I-2649.

the case had not been proven and that the development risk defence as worded in section 4(1)(e) of the 1987 Act does comply with the Directive, particularly given that, by virtue of section 1(1) of the Act,[103] the UK courts are obliged to interpret the 1987 Act in accordance with the requirements of the Directive.

Central to the defence is the requirement to establish what scientific and technical knowledge was available during the time that the product was under the control of the producer and whether that knowledge would have allowed the defect in the product to be identified. If not, and the defect is truly unknowable, then the producer will not be held liable for any injuries that it may cause.

Assessing whether the producer has satisfied the defence should be objective as it identifies the knowledge available to a reasonably diligent producer and then determines whether the producer in question matches up to that standard. However, it has been suggested that this is not necessarily the case, as the approach encompassed within the UK defence could mean that different standards might be expected from different producers, which, if true, would render the defence subjective.[104]

The court in *A v. National Blood Authority* opined that the state of scientific and technical knowledge 'is the most advanced available (to anyone, not simply to the producer in question), but it must be "accessible".'[105] This raises two issues: what constitutes scientific and technical knowledge and when is it deemed to be accessible. As to the former, one would assume that scientific and technical knowledge would include information published in leading academic and professional journals for the relevant profession or industry, but what of lesser or foreign journals?[106] Further, it is reasonable to assume that private documents belonging to individual companies would not be included, as they would not be in the public domain and thus would not form part of the body of scientific and technical knowledge available to the producing community. The same would be true of the results of experiments done in a private laboratory and included only in internal reports. The court in *Abouzaid v. Mothercare (UK) Ltd*[107] held that accident reports would not be classed as scientific and technical knowledge, Pill LJ commenting that 'The defence contemplates scientific and technical advances which throw additional light, for example, on the propensities of materials and allow defects to be discovered.'[108] This judgment gives a clear steer as to the type of information that will be considered as relevant and that which will fall outside the requisite standard.

---

[103] Consumer Protection Act 1987, s.1(1) reads 'This Part shall have effect for the purpose of making such provision as is necessary in order to comply with the Product Liability Directive and shall be construed accordingly.'
[104] See Howells and Weatherill, above n. 19.
[105] [2001] 3 All ER 289, para. 49(i).
[106] Such as in the much quoted Manchurian example set out in *EC Commission v. United Kingdom*, paras. 23–4 and referred to in *A v. National Blood Authority*, [2001] 3 All ER 289, para. 4(i). See also M. Griffiths, 'Defectiveness in EC product liability' (1987) *JBL* 222, 225.
[107] [2000] All ER (D) 2436.   [108] *Ibid.* para. 29.

Accessibility is a fraught issue but central to the defence. In addition to issues such as those mentioned above about private documentation that is not available to the general public, it raises the key concept of how wide and how deep the producer needs to research to satisfy the relevant standard such as to fall within the ambit of the defence. This would raise issues such as the geographic location of the information[109] and the practicalities and economic costs of recovering and utilising it. This might give rise, for example, to recognising:

> a conception period for the product. This period relates to the unavoidable time delay between initial discovery of a safer design and the time when the implementation is possible. It is unrealistic to imagine that a new idea could be implemented overnight. It is important though to restrict any permissible conception period to a reasonable length and not allow it to become liberal or even excessive.[110]

Concerns have been raised as to whether the defence may become subjective depending on the size and financial resources of an individual producer. A small company employing a few men and with a small production output will not have the same resources available to it as a large multinational company. However, it is questionable whether it is appropriate to take account of such factors if the rationale of the 1987 Act is to provide strict liability protection for the injured user. The background of the defendant should be irrelevant.

This highlights the real issue with the development risk defence, namely, that it effectively re-introduces negligence by the back door. The underlying rationale of the 1987 Act (and the Product Liability Directive) is the introduction of strict liability for product-related injuries, eschewing any need to consider the activities or personality of the producer. All that should be relevant is the existence of the defect, the causal link and the damage suffered by the plaintiff. However, the development risk defence expressly analyses and assesses the actions of the producer by reference to the actions and knowledge base of other producers of similar products, an approach more in line with negligence. The defence considers the blameworthiness of the defendant at the expense of the strict liability rights of the injured user. It is worth remembering that both the Pearson Commission[111] and the Joint Law Commissions[112] were against the introduction of a development risk defence because of the negative impact on the rights of the injured user, the Pearson Commission commenting in a much-quoted remark that the exclusion of development risks from any strict liability regime:

> would leave a gap in the compensation cover, through which, for example, the victims of another Thalidomide disaster might slip.[113]

---

[109] As in the much quoted Manchurian example, see above n. 106.
[110] Griffiths, above n. 106, at 225.   [111] Pearson Report, above n. 40.
[112] Joint Law Commission Report, above n. 97.
[113] Pearson Report, above n. 40, ch. 2, para. 1259.

As yet, there has been very little case law on the practical application of the defence. The court in *Abouzaid v. Mothercare (UK) Ltd* rejected an attempt by the defendant to use the defence, while in *A v. National Blood Authority*, the court held that once the risk was known, the development risk defence is no longer applicable anyway. As the defendant in the case was aware of the risk that the blood might be contaminated with Hepatitis C, the development risk defence ceased to be applicable. The fact that there was no test that allowed him to ascertain whether any individual item was defective was not relevant. Once the possibility that the product may be defective is known, the producer supplies it at his own risk.

Q11 Consider whether the inclusion of a development risk defence is acceptable in a strict product liability regime. Does it rightly protect producers from liability for unknowable defects or does it undermine the whole purpose of strict liability?

(f) Component parts

The final defence is to be found in section 4(1)(f) and deals with the issue of component parts. A component producer will be liable for injuries caused by one of his component parts proving to be defective within the meaning of section 3 of the 1987 Act. However, it is in the nature of components that they are incorporated into other products and this gives rise to the possibility that the component may prove to be faulty not because of any inherent defect in it but because of the way that it has been incorporated into the main product. Section 4(1)(f) provides the component producer with a defence when the defect in the component constitutes a defect in the final product and one of two situations has occurred.

The first is that the defect in the component is wholly attributable to the design of the final product, the implication being that the component has been used incorrectly in the main product. Thus, for example it may be that the component has been expected to withstand stresses greater than those for which it was designed,[114] a problem that may be particularly pertinent with components such as screws, which can be used in a wide variety of different products. The essence of this strand of the defence is that a component which would have functioned perfectly if used correctly, has failed in usage due to being incorporated into a product for which it was not designed. The component producer would not be liable in this instance, as the product was not defective at the time that he supplied it,[115] the defect being introduced after it left his control.

---

[114] M. Griffiths and I. Griffiths, *Law for Purchasing and Supply* (3rd edn, Pearson Education Ltd, Harlow, 2002).

[115] In this instance, he would be able to claim a defence under Consumer Protection Act 1987, s.4(1)(d), namely, that the defect did not exist at the relevant time, that time being when he supplied the component to the producer of the final product.

However, the producer of the final product would be liable in this situation as he has put a defective product into circulation.

The second possibility occurs when the component manufacturer has produced a component part to comply with instructions provided to him by the producer of the final product. In that situation, the design of the component is the responsibility of the final producer and not the component manufacturer who, presumably, will be contractually bound to produce components that comply with the requisite design. Consequently, if the component should prove defective because the design is unsuitable for the purpose for which the component is used, liability for it will lie with the final producer while the component manufacturer can claim the protection of the defence in section 4(1)(f)(ii). Of course, if the main producer can show that the design was satisfactory but that the component part in question did not comply with it, then the component manufacturer would be liable for a manufacturing defect.

Professor Miller has raised an interesting point about the application of the defence to packaging.[116] A product may be defective because the instructions for use are wrong and themselves pose the danger. In practice, the instructions to be included with and on the packaging will have been approved by the producer of the final product. As such, the second strand of the defence would seem to be available to the packer. However, if the instructions appear on the outer packaging, can it truly be said the defective component (the packaging) is 'comprised' in the final product as required by section 4(1)(f)? On a strict interpretation of the wording of that subsection, there would seem to be a lacuna and that external packaging would not be covered. Arguably, however, this is playing semantics. Professor Miller is of the view that the wording of Article 7(f) of the Product Liability Directive would cover this situation, and that section 4(1)(f)(i) would be interpreted to comply with it as required by section 1(1) of the Consumer Protection Act 1987.

Q12 Does the defence for component manufacturers provide a balanced approach between holding them liable for defective components while not holding them responsible for defects beyond their control?

6 Contributory negligence

As discussed previously when considering defences to claims under Part I of the Consumer Protection Act 1987, the rules relating to contributory negligence apply.[117] Thus, where a defect is caused partly by a defective product and partly through the fault of the person who has suffered the injury, the Law Reform (Contributory Negligence) Act 1945 and the Fatal Accidents Act 1976 apply. Thus, when contributory negligence occurs, any damages awarded to the

---

[116] Miller and Goldberg, above n. 10, para. 13.109.
[117] Consumer Protection Act 1987, s.6(4).

injured user are reduced by a percentage equivalent to the percentage responsibility that the user must bear for his part in the injury-causing event.

7 Recoverable damage

Not all damage caused to product users is necessarily recoverable under product liability, the parameters of recoverable damages being laid out in section 5 of the 1987 Act. As a basic premise, 'damages' is defined as being 'death or personal injury or any loss of or damage to any property (including land)'.[118] 'Personal injury' is defined for this purpose as including 'any disease and any other impairment of a person's physical or mental condition'[119] and, as such, would include damages for nervous shock as long as the psychiatric damage suffered satisfied the relevant criteria. Psychiatric damage suffered by the injured user himself, the 'primary' victim, would be covered automatically while psychiatric damage suffered by a 'secondary' victim, such as a person who witnessed the incident, would need to satisfy the criteria laid down in *White* v. *Chief Constable of the South Yorkshire Police*.[120] Pure economic loss is not recoverable.

Not all property damage is included and section 5 continues by specifying the various limitations to recoverable property damage. Thus, under section 5(2) no liability exists under the 1987 Act for any damage to the product itself. This is not unreasonable because damage of that type will be recoverable in contract under the Sale of Goods Act 1979 if the defect was caused by the product not being of a satisfactory quality and fit for the purpose for which it was to be used. If the injured product user purchased the product himself, he can bring an action in contract alongside his tortious claim in strict product liability for any other damage. By contrast, if the product was bought by somebody else, then clearly it is their choice as to whether to pursue a contract claim in respect of the damaged item.

Of more concern is the fact that section 5(2) goes on to restrict compensation in respect of 'the loss of or any damage to the whole or any part of any product which has been supplied with the product in question comprised in it'. Thus, if a component proves to be faulty, the claimant has no claim under the 1987 Act in respect of the whole product if it has been damaged in the incident. Thus, for example, if a component part in a television is defective and causes the television to catch fire and be destroyed, the user cannot claim under the 1987 Act against the final producer or the component manufacturer for the loss of the set. The same would be true if a car is damaged in a crash because its brakes

[118] *Ibid.* s.5(1).   [119] *Ibid.* s.45(1).
[120] [1999] 1 All ER 1. It was held in this case that for a secondary victim who has suffered psychiatric damage as the result of death or personal injury to another person to be able to recover compensation, he would need to demonstrate three things: that he had a close tie of love and affection with the person killed, injured or imperilled; that he was close to the incident in time and space; and that he perceived the relevant incident directly and did not merely hear about it.

are defective and the driver cannot stop the car safely. While the driver would be able to recover under product liability for any personal injury suffered in the accident, he would not have a claim in product liability in respect of the damage to the car and would have to pursue any claim in contract or negligence. Of course, both of these claims would be dependent on him being the owner of the car. If he is not, then the owner would pursue these particular claims.

An interesting anomaly in section 5(2) is that the ability of an injured user to recover compensation for a product depends on whether the faulty component comprised in it was supplied as part of the final product or is a replacement part. If the latter is the case, there is a strong argument for saying that the user can recover for any damage caused to the final product by the defective replacement component as the defective component was not comprised in the final product when it was supplied. In the example of the car given above, if the faulty brakes were the original ones supplied with the car, there will be no claim for damage to the vehicle if the brakes prove to be faulty. However, if the brakes have been replaced during the life of the vehicle and then prove defective, damage to the car would be recoverable under the 1987 Act although clearly there would be no claim for the replacement brakes themselves.

Section 5(3) specifies that liability is restricted to property that, at the time that it is lost or damaged, is of a type that is ordinarily intended for private use, occupation or consumption and is intended by the injured user to be used 'mainly for his own private use, occupation or consumption'. It follows that business property is not covered and any claim in respect of such property would have to be pursued in negligence or contract. The first issue to resolve is whether the product can be described as one which is 'ordinarily intended for private use or consumption', a difficult line to draw when so-called migrating products such as cars, personal computers and some tools can be used properly for business use or private use, or indeed both. The use of the word 'mainly' in strand (b) of the subsection is crucially important in this context as it allows an element of subjectivity to be introduced into the claim by considering the main intention of the injured user, while recognising that he may use the product for more than one purpose.

Section 5(4) introduces a lower financial threshold for claims for property damage namely, £275.[121] The purpose of this lower limit, as laid out in the Preamble to the Product Liability Directive, is to 'avoid litigation in an excessive number of cases'. The net effect of the provision is that if the property damage is valued at £276 the user will have a valid claim in product liability, while if the property damage is £274 no claim exists and the user would have to pursue an action in negligence. The approach of Member States to the lower threshold has differed, with some countries not allowing users to recover the threshold sum itself but only the amount by which the damage suffered exceeds that amount.

---

[121] The Product Liability Directive introduced a threshold of 500 ECU in Art. 9(b).

By contrast, in the United Kingdom, claimants are allowed to recover the full sum as long as it exceeds the threshold limit.

Q13 Are the categories of recoverable damage sufficiently comprehensive for the purposes of the 1987 Act?

8 Limitations on liability

(a) Time limits

There are two limitation periods that are relevant to a product liability claim under the Consumer Protection Act 1987. First, any claim under the Act must be brought within three years.[122] For the purposes of making the claim, loss or damage to property is deemed to have occurred at the earliest time at which a person with an interest in the property had knowledge of the material facts.[123] This will occur when a reasonable person would consider the loss or damage to be sufficiently serious to justify commencing proceedings against a defendant who does not dispute liability and is able to satisfy any judgment.[124]

In addition to the three-year limitation period, there is also a ten-year cut-off period, which provides that claims under Part I of the Consumer Protection Act 1987 cannot be commenced after the expiration of ten years from the relevant time,[125] that being the time at which the product was put into circulation. This cut-off period allows the producer to draw a line under his legal liability and, arguably, will increase his ability to get insurance cover for the product because there is a definite end to his potential liability. The producer should keep thorough records for the ten-year period to ensure that he has all the information available should he want to use this cut-off period to defeat a claim. While the ten-year cut-off period may be a pragmatic approach to product liability, commentators have suggested that it is not necessarily in the best interests of injured users.[126] Some injuries take longer than ten-years to become apparent and thus a claim may be statute-barred before the cause of action for personal injury has even accrued. Examples would include damages for drug-related injures where the damage may not become apparent for many years after the relevant incident, such as occurred in *Sindell* v. *Abbott Laboratories,*[127] the 'DES daughters' case discussed previously,[128] where the ovarian cancers suffered by the daughters of women who had used the drug during pregnancy were not apparent until the plaintiffs reached their teens or twenties. Equally, the effects of exposure to carcinogenic products may not be apparent for twenty or thirty years after the exposure has occurred. Such

---

[122] Limitation Act 1980, s.11A(4).
[123] Consumer Protection Act 1987, s.5(5).
[124] *Ibid.* s.5(6).   [125] Limitation Act 1980, s.11A(3).
[126] See Howells and Weatherill, above n. 19, at 251 and Griffiths and Griffiths, above n. 114, at 186.
[127] 26 Cal. 3d 588 (1980).   [128] See Part 4 chapter 1.

victims will be denied any claim in strict product liability and will have to rely instead on a claim in negligence.

However, there is one example of the ten-year cut-off period being circumvented. In *Horne-Roberts* v. *SmithKline Beecham plc*,[129] an extension to the period was permitted by the Court of Appeal based on the meaning of the Limitation Act 1980. The case related to damage suffered by the defendant following use of the MMR vaccine. The plaintiff's representatives issued a claim against Merck and Co. Inc., who they wrongly believed to have produced the vaccine. On discovering that the vaccine had actually been produced by SmithKline Beecham plc, they applied to have SmithKline substituted as the defendant, an application which was approved by the Court of Appeal despite the expiration of the ten-year cut-off period. The substitution was allowed on the basis that the representatives had been genuinely mistaken within the meaning of the Limitation Act 1980 and the Civil Procedure Rules 1998.[130]

(b) Global financial limit

While there is a lower financial threshold for property damage, there is no upper limit to the size of the claim that can be made in respect of death or personal injury suffered as a result of a product-related injury. Under Article 16.1 of the Product Liability Directive, Member States had the option of restricting the global liability of a producer to 70 million ECU, the restriction applying to claims of death or personal injury caused by 'identical items with the same defect'.

As discussed in the previous chapter, the difficulty with a global financial limit is that, by setting an artificial ceiling to the total compensation that can be paid, a strategy must be implemented to deal with cases where that financial limit is not sufficient to satisfy all of the legitimate claims that may be brought. There are two possible strategies, neither of which is really desirable. The first involves paying out claims on a 'first come, first served' basis. This is somewhat of a lottery and may result in some valid claims being rejected purely because the money has run out. Claimants who make their claims in the early part of the ten-year period may receive full compensation, while those whose claims arise during the latter part of the period may not receive anything. The alternative strategy is equally unsatisfactory. If claims are to be dealt with equitably, with all claimants receiving the same proportion of their claim (whether that be 100 per cent of the claim or less), it is necessary to hold on to all of the claims and not pay out on any of them until the ten-year period has expired and any further claims would be statute-barred.

---

[129] [2002] 1 WLR 1662. See also *H (a Child)* v. *Merck & Co. Inc.* (2001) WL 98168 and the discussion in Miller and Goldberg, above n. 10, para. 17.132.
[130] SI 1998/3132.

70 million ECU was designated as the lowest sum possible for such a global limit, there being no restriction on the power of a Member State to set a higher limit if they so chose. However, Article 16.1 is permissive rather than mandatory and hence there was no obligation on any Member State to adopt such a limit. The United Kingdom chose not to avail itself of this option and thus there is no global financial limit in the Consumer Protection Act 1987.

(c) Exclusion of liability

Section 7 of the 1987 Act forbids any exclusion or limitation of liability under Part I against any person who has suffered damage caused wholly or partly by a defective product. This ban on any attempt to limit or exclude liability extends to any dependant or relative of an injured person and covers contract terms, notices and any other provision.

Q14 Do the temporal and financial limits imposed by the 1987 Act, combined with the inability to exclude liability, provide a balanced approach to the liability of producers under the 1987 Act?

9 Recommended reading

Giliker, P. 'Strict liability for defective products: the ongoing debate' (2003) *Business Law Review* 87

Griffiths, M. 'Defectiveness in EC product liability' (1987) *Journal of Business Law* 222

Griffiths, M. and Griffiths, I. *Law for Purchasing and Supply* (3rd edn, Pearson Education Ltd, Harlow, 2002)

Howells, G. and Weatherill, S. *Consumer Protection Law* (2nd edn, Ashgate Publishing Ltd, Aldershot, 2005)

Miller, C.J. and Goldberg, R.S. *Product Liability* (2nd edn, Oxford University Press, 2004)

Newdick, C. 'The development risk defence of the Consumer Protection Act 1987' (1988) *Cambridge Law Journal* 455

Shears, P. 'The EU Product Liability Directive: twenty years on' (2007) *Journal of Business Law* 884

Miller and Goldberg's *Product Liability* is a specialist text on this subject which is well worth reading. In addition, readers would benefit from reading the articles by Giliker and Shears to consider the way that the law on product liability has developed.

Part 5
Unfair Commercial Practices

Introduction

Part 5 concentrates on those aspects of the criminal law which provide the framework to the everyday trading environment. In practice, criminal law plays an important, but often under-valued, role in trading matters. The tendency is to concentrate on civil law controls and remedies for matters such as breaches of sale of goods and product liability without addressing the role that compliance with criminal law can play in preventing incidents arising. This part seeks to redress that balance somewhat.

Part 5 is divided into three chapters. The first deals with the policy that lies behind the repeal and amendment of so much of the pre-existing criminal trading law. Particular reference is made to the role that the European Union has played through the Unfair Commercial Practices Directive,[1] which resulted in the passage of two sets of Regulations, the Consumer Protection from Unfair Trading Regulations 2008[2] and the Business Protection from Misleading Marketing Regulations 2008.[3] The first chapter continues by looking at the offences created by the Regulations and the available defences thereto, most notably the due diligence defence.

Chapter 2 looks specifically at the provisions of the Consumer Protection from Unfair Trading Regulations 2008. The Regulations replace much of the previous criminal law as it applied to goods and services supplied to consumers and introduces new provisions, such as those relating to aggressive commercial practices under regulation 7. In addition to analysing the requirements governing unfair commercial practices, misleading statements, misleading omissions and aggressive commercial practices, Chapter 2 also analyses the list of thirty-one commercial practices contained in Schedule 1 to the Regulations which are automatically deemed to be unfair. Examples of situations that would breach the various controls are provided throughout the chapter.

---

[1] Directive 2005/29/EC concerning unfair business-to-consumer commercial practices in the internal market.
[2] SI 2008/1277.   [3] SI 2008/1276.

The final chapter in this Part considers the provisions of the Business Protection from Misleading Marketing Regulations 2008. These Regulations provide criminal controls over misleading marketing practices as they impact on businesses and, as such, replace some of the pre-existing provisions that were repealed as a result of the passage of the Unfair Commercial Practices Directive. Further, regulation 5 provides for controls over comparative advertising and hence ensures continued compliance with Directive 2006/114/EC. These provisions replace those found previously in the Control of Misleading Advertisements Regulations 1988.[4]

---

[4] SI 1998/915.

Part 5 Chapter 1

Policy on Unfair Commercial Practices

Contents

1 Introduction

This chapter analyses the policy behind the use of criminal law controls and, more latterly, civil law enforcement to control unfair trading practices which have a negative impact on the trading framework within which both business purchasers and consumer buyers acquire goods and services. It addresses the controls previously and currently in place that protect these two disparate groups of purchasers. It is structured as follows

Section 2 provides a background to this topic and looks at the way that the law has recently developed and the introduction of two new sets of Regulations, the Consumer Protection from Unfair Trading Regulations 2008[1] and the Business Protection from Misleading Marketing Regulations 2008.[2]

Section 3 analyses the enforcement strategy that underpins the enforcement of both of these sets of Regulations, while Section 4 looks at the criminal law controls that are in place for both sets of Regulations. The first part of the section details the criminal law offences contained in the two sets of Regulations and identifies which offences require proof of *mens rea* and which are strict liability offences. The second part of the section considers the statutory defences that are open to someone charged with an offence contrary to either set of Regulations, with particular reference to the parameters of the

---

[1] SI 2008/1277. [2] SI 2008/1276.

due diligence defence and the defence of 'innocent publication'. The section concludes by looking at the liability of 'another person' for offences against the Regulations.

Section 5 considers the role of civil law enforcement as a means of promoting compliance. The first part of the section looks at civil enforcement under the Consumer Protection from Unfair Trading Regulations 2008, including enforcement orders and interim enforcement orders and undertakings. The section goes on to consider civil enforcement under the Business Protection from Misleading Marketing Regulations 2008, including injunctions and undertakings.

2 Background

For centuries, the state has had a role to play in the regulation of the trading environment in which sellers and buyers transact their business. As far back as the Assize of Cake and Ale in 1266, controls existed to regulate the quality of food and drink.[3] Likewise, criminal controls over weights and measures have been on the statute books for many centuries. Purchasers, whether traders or consumers, need to be assured that, when buying goods by weight, length or volume, they will receive the true quantity for which they have paid. Equally, purchasers must know that goods and services will be as described and advertised and that they will not be subjected to misleading or fraudulent claims about the products. Such basic regulatory controls encourage confidence in the market and create a stable trading environment in which business can flourish.

While some fundamental controls have existed for many centuries, the period since the 1960s has seen a marked upsurge in criminal trading law. The role of the state in these developments has been crucial since, as a regulator enforcing criminal legislation, it establishes the minimum standards of behaviour that will be tolerated without penalty. This helps to promote a stable trading environment in which both seller and buyer can have confidence when transacting business, whether on a commercial basis or as a consumer. The use of criminal regulation as opposed to civil law remedies is valuable from a chronological perspective, as compliance with the criminal framework should prevent problems arising while civil law remedies deal with the aftermath of an event when damage has already occurred.

The legislative developments of the last sixty years have emanated partly from Westminster and, since the United Kingdom's accession to the EC Treaty, partly from Europe. Thus, for example, the Consumer Protection Acts 1961–71, which dealt with product safety, originated in the United Kingdom. By contrast, however, current product safety legislation is to be found primarily (but

---

[3] The quality of food is now governed by the Food Safety Act 1990, which lies beyond the remit of this text.

not exclusively)[4] in the General Product Safety Regulations 2005,[5] which give effect to a European Directive.[6] Other major UK legislation since the 1960s has included the Trade Descriptions Act 1968 and pricing controls,[7] although these have also largely been overtaken by a European Directive. However, the ambit of controls in the past went far wider than this and included matters as diverse as unsolicited goods,[8] pyramid selling, bargain offers, outlawing attempts to deprive consumers of their legal rights[9] and preventing traders from concealing their commercial status.[10]

This wealth of legislation, while far-reaching, developed in a very piecemeal fashion. It is significant, therefore, that the passage of the Consumer Protection from Unfair Trading Regulations 2008, which adopt the Unfair Commercial Practices Directive 2005/29/EC, has swept away the existing multiplicity of tightly drafted specific offences and replaced them with a few holistic provisions that, arguably, speak rather more to the spirit of the law than the precise letter of it.[11] In total, twenty-two pieces of legislation were either repealed or amended to make way for the requirements of the Directive, some of the main amendments involving the repeal of the major offences in the Trade Descriptions Act 1968[12] and Part III of the Consumer Protection Act 1987, which dealt with misleading prices. The Control of Misleading Advertisements Regulations 1988[13] were also repealed. While the majority of the repealed provisions have been replaced and often enhanced for consumer buyers by the Consumer Protection from Unfair Trading Regulations 2008, the wholesale repeal and amendment of so many provisions impacted negatively on business-to-business transactions. This necessitated the passage of the Business Protection from Misleading Marketing Regulations 2008 to protect business purchasers and to ensure continued compliance with the Misleading and Comparative Advertising Directive.[14] The detailed provisions of both sets of new Regulations will be analysed in the following two chapters.

---

[4] There are some residual controls based upon Part 2 of the Consumer Protection Act 1987 but the General Product Safety Regulations 2005, SI 2005/1803 are the primary legislation in this area. A detailed analysis of the controls over product safety fall outside the remit of this text.

[5] SI 2005/1803.

[6] Directive 2001/95/EC of 3 December 2001 on general product safety.

[7] Initially in the Trade Descriptions Act 1968, s.11 and then in the Consumer Protection Act 1987, Part II.

[8] Unsolicited Goods and Services Act 1971.

[9] Consumer Transactions (Restrictions on Statements) Order 1976, SI 1976/1813.

[10] Business Advertisements (Disclosure) Order 1977, SI 1977/1918.

[11] See M. Griffiths, 'Unfair commercial practices: a new regime' (2007) 12 *Communications Law* 194.

[12] Trade Descriptions Act 1968, s. 1, which dealt with the application of false trade descriptions to goods and the supply or offer to supply goods to which a false trade description of goods had been applied, and s. 14 which dealt with the application of false trade descriptions to services, accommodation or facilities.

[13] SI 1988/915.

[14] Directive 84/450/EC, now codified in Directive 2006/114/EC. The Business Protection from Misleading Marketing (BPMM) Regulations 2008 are discussed in detail in the Part 5 Chapter 3.

The new Regulations encompass many of the malpractices regulated by the previous regime. It follows that, in some instances, existing case law may still be relevant, while in respect of the newer areas, such as the prohibition on aggressive behaviour in the Consumer Protection from Unfair Trading Regulations 2008, a new body of case law will have to develop over the coming years.

Q1 Consider the need for legislation to protect both business purchasers and consumer buyers in order to promote a sound trading framework.

3 Enforcement strategy

Article 13 of the Unfair Commercial Practices Directive[15] requires that Member States must introduce penalties that are 'effective, proportionate and dissuasive' for breaches of national legislation used to adopt the provisions of the Directive.[16] Further, Member States must take all the necessary measures to ensure that these penalties are enforced.

As with many areas of law, an effective enforcement machinery, whether via criminal offences or civil law remedies, is crucial to success. Traditionally, the primary focus for enforcement authorities in this area has been on criminal law enforcement, including, of course, the pursuit of criminal prosecutions. There will always be situations when prosecution for a criminal offence will be the most appropriate enforcement tool because, for example, of the severity of the conduct concerned and the risks that it poses to purchasers. Alternatively, it may be appropriate if the trader concerned refuses to provide an undertaking or comply with enforcement orders or refrain from the offending conduct. However, enforcement authorities might reasonably argue that resort to a criminal prosecution, while eminently justifiable in respect of rogues, fraudsters and persistent offenders, might be considered too heavy-handed when used against a genuine trader who, perhaps through carelessness rather then intent, has committed a strict liability offence. In such circumstances, a better option would be to use civil law approaches, such as the giving of undertakings by a trader not to offend in the future.

When exercising their enforcement powers under both sets of regulations, enforcement authorities must 'have regard to the desirability of encouraging [compliance] … by such established means as it considers appropriate having regard to all the circumstances of the particular case'.[17] Thus, it is clear that the paramount policy behind enforcement is to promote and ensure compliance with the Regulations rather than simply to punish transgressors.

---

[15] Directive 2005/29/EC concerning unfair business-to-consumer commercial practices in the internal market ('Unfair Commercial Practices Directive').

[16] In the United Kingdom, the Consumer Protection from Unfair Trading (CPUT) Regulations 2008.

[17] CPUT Regulations 2008 reg. 19(4) and the BPMM Regulations 2008 reg. 13(4).

Given this policy consideration, the development and use of civil law enforcement powers is particularly significant. The use of the powers in the Enterprise Act 2002 in respect of breaches of the Consumer Protection from Unfair Trading Regulations 2008, and the use of injunctions and undertakings for breaches of the Business Protection from Misleading Marketing Regulations 2008 are positive moves. This permits enforcement bodies to seek assurances from traders and obtain injunctions as a means of bringing undesirable practices to an end without incurring the expense and delay necessary to pursue a criminal prosecution. If the underlying rationale of good enforcement in this area is to protect purchasers by prohibiting and removing unfair commercial practices, a civil injunction may be more effective than a criminal prosecution.

Q2 Do you consider that the use of civil law enforcement in addition to criminal law enforcement is a positive move in enforcement strategy?

4 Criminal law controls

(a) Offences

Both the Consumer Protection from Unfair Trading (CPUT) Regulations 2008 and the Business Protection from Misleading Marketing (BPMM) Regulations 2008 create criminal law offences. The CPUT Regulations 2008 create offences in regulations 8–12 inclusive, while the BPMM Regulations 2008 contain an offence in regulation 6. In addition to these main offences, both sets of regulations contain the normal provision holding the officers of a corporation liable for the criminal actions of the corporation[18] and, also, a provision allowing enforcement authorities to prosecute another person whose act or default caused the original offender to commit the offence.[19]

The offences fall into two categories, those that require *mens rea* and those that are strict liability offences only requiring proof that the offending *actus reus* has occurred, without any need to consider the mental intent of the defendant. This is not unusual, as strict liability offences are very common in trading legislation.

The only offence requiring proof of *mens rea* is in regulation 8 of the CPUT Regulations 2008, which makes it an offence to breach the regulation 3 prohibition against unfair commercial practices. Regulation 8(1) provides that a trader commits an offence if he knowingly or recklessly engages in a commercial practice which contravenes the requirements of professional diligence under regulation 3(3)(a); and, further, that the practice materially distorts or is likely to materially distort the economic behaviour of the average consumer with regard to the product.

---

[18] CPUT Regulations 2008 reg. 15 and the BPMM Regulations 2008 reg. 8.
[19] CPUT Regulations 2008 reg. 16 and the BPMM Regulations 2008 reg. 9.

The meaning of the key concepts 'commercial practice', 'professional diligence' and 'materially distorting the economic behaviour of the consumer' will be dealt with in detail below. What concerns us here is the phrase 'knowingly or recklessly' which delineates the *mens rea* aspect necessary to prove the offence. 'Knowingly' clearly connotes actual knowledge by the defendant or someone acting on his behalf, such as an employee. By contrast, 'recklessly' is a more nebulous concept, which has been interpreted judicially in the past when considering alleged offences against the Trade Descriptions Act 1968. Arguably, 'recklessness' requires a lesser element of *mens rea*, given that the court in *MFI Warehouses Ltd* v. *Nattrass*[20] held that recklessness does not imply dishonesty, merely that the defendant has not paid due regard to his actions. This approach has been reinforced by regulation 8(2) of the CPUT Regulations 2008, which states that:

> a trader who engages in a commercial practice without regard to whether the practice contravenes the requirements of professional diligence shall be deemed recklessly to engage in the practice, whether or not the trader has reason for believing that the practice might contravene those requirements.

Knowledge is not relevant, it is the lack of care that creates the offence. It is reasonable to assume that the new law will follow the previous approach in that a defendant should not be held liable for a commercial practice that was acceptable when he did it but was rendered unfair by the subsequent act of a third party.[21]

The remainder of the offences created by the CPUT Regulations 2008 and that to be found in regulation 6 of the BPMM Regulations 2008 are strict liability offences. Hence, there is no *mens rea* requirement, and liability follows if the defendant has committed the offending action irrespective of his intentions. However, as the relevant offences are strict liability as opposed to absolute liability, defences are permitted and both sets of Regulations contain statutory defences, of which the due diligence defence is the most important.[22]

The offence provisions are relatively straight-forward, each creating a strict liability offence for contravention of a specified regulation. Thus, regulation 9 of the CPUT Regulations 2008 makes it an offence to breach the requirements of regulation 5 relating to misleading actions; regulation 10 makes it an offence to breach regulation 6 on misleading omissions; regulation 11 makes it an offence for a trader to engage in an aggressive commercial practice contrary to regulation 7; and, finally, regulation 12 makes it an offence for a trader to engage in one of the inherently unfair commercial practices detailed in paragraphs 1 to 10, 12 to 27 and 29 to 31 of Schedule 1 to the CPUT Regulations 2008.

Regulation 6 of the BPMM Regulations 2008 is also straight-forward, simply stating that it is an offence to engage in advertising which is 'misleading' under

---

[20] [1973] 1 All ER 762.   [21] *Sunair Holidays* v. *Dodd* [1970] 2 All ER 410.
[22] See below.

regulation 3 of those Regulations. The meaning of 'misleading' advertising in this context will be considered in detail below.[23]

***Q3 Are strict liability offences acceptable in trading law? Consider why the offence in regulation 8 requires* mens rea.**

(b) Defences

The criminal offence under regulation 8 of the CPUT Regulations 2008 requires proof of *mens rea*, the offence being to 'knowingly or recklessly engage in a commercial practice' which breaches regulation 3. The requirement for *mens rea* means that the due diligence defence, which is the defence commonly supplied for strict liability offences in trading law, is simply not relevant. As such, regulation 8 falls outside the regime of defences included in regulations 16 to 18 of the Regulations.

(i) Due diligence defence

The main defence to offences under regulations 9 to 12 of the CPUT Regulations 2008 and regulation 6 of the BPMM Regulations 2008 is the due diligence defence, to be found in regulation 17 and regulation 11, respectively. Unlike the due diligence defence in product safety legislation, which is a single strand defence only requiring the defendant to show that 'he took all reasonable precautions and exercised all due diligence to avoid committing the offence',[24] the version of the due diligence defence in both the CPUT Regulations 2008 and the BPMM Regulations 2008 is a two strand defence derived from the Trade Descriptions Act 1968.[25]

The defence provides that in any proceedings against a person for an offence under regulations 9 to 12 of the CPUT Regulations 2008 or regulation 6 of the BPMM Regulations 2008, it is a defence for that person to prove:

    (a) that the commission of the offence was due to:

        (i) a mistake;
        (ii) reliance on information supplied to him by another person;
        (iii) the act or default of another person;
        (iv) an accident; or
        (v) another cause beyond his control; and

    (b) that he took all reasonable precautions and exercised all due diligence to avoid the commission of such an offence by himself or anyone under his control.[26]

Given that this defence is identical to that under the Trade Descriptions Act 1968, it follows that the case law interpreting that defence is equally applicable

[23] See Part 5 Chapter 3.   [24] General Product Safety Regulations 2005, reg. 29.
[25] Trade Descriptions Act 1968, s. 24(1).
[26] CPUT Regulations 2008 reg. 17(1) and BPMM Regulations 2008 reg. 11(1).

here. Both strands of the defence, (a) and (b), must be satisfied before the defence is proved. It is not sufficient for the defendant to prove only one of them.

Under paragraph (a), the defendant must show the existence of one of the five listed criteria. The 'mistake' referred to in paragraph (a)(i) must be a mistake by the defendant and not that of some other person.[27] By contrast, the next two criteria revolve around the relationship between the defendant and 'another person'. The second criteria requires that the defendant relied on information supplied to him by another person, while the third deals with the act or default of 'another person'. This raises the key issue of who is 'another person' for these purposes. Given that the defendant will be a trader, defined as being someone 'acting for purposes relating to his business, and anyone acting in the name of or on behalf of a trader', it follows that the key issue is who will be classed as 'another person' when dealing with alleged offences committed by companies.

The leading case on this point is *Tesco Supermarkets Ltd* v. *Nattrass*.[28] The case related to a 'flash offer,' which involved the advertising and supply of cartons of soap-powder at a reduced price, there being a poster in the store advertising the offer. Unfortunately, the store ran out of the reduced price cartons and a shop assistant put some full price cartons on display without removing the advertising poster. The store manager, who was responsible for ensuring that everything was in order on the premises, did not notice this. When a customer was charged full price for the product, the enforcement authority prosecuted for an offence. The House of Lords held that the offence had been committed by the store manager who was 'another person' for the purposes of the defence. When considering the structure of companies, the company itself only comprises those persons who would be classed as the *alter ego* of the company, i.e., those persons such as the directors and company secretary who have a direct impact on the decisions and actions of the corporation. Indeed, those people can be charged separately if a body corporate has committed an offence due to their consent, connivance or neglect. Anyone, such as a store manager or employee, who falls outside the *alter ego* is 'another person' for the purposes of the defence.[29] However, if a company wants to rely on the actions of another person as part of their defence, it must identify that person to the prosecutor at least seven days before the date of the hearing.[30]

The final two criteria relate to an accident, within the normal meaning of that term, and another cause beyond the control of the defendant.

---

[27] *Birkenhead and District Cooperative Society* v. *Roberts* [1970] 3 All ER 391.

[28] [1972] AC 153.

[29] See also M. Griffiths, and I. Griffiths, *Law for Purchasing and Supply* (3rd edn, Pearson Education Ltd, Harlow, 2002); and P. Dobson, and R. Stokes, *Commercial Law* (7th edn, Sweet & Maxwell Ltd, London, 2008).

[30] CPUT Regulations 2008, reg. 17(2) and BPMM Regulations 2008, reg. 11(2).

Assuming that the defendant can satisfy the first strand of the defence, he must also prove that he took all reasonable precautions and exercised all due diligence to avoid the commission of the offence by himself or anyone under his control. This effectively requires that the defendant establish a suitable quality control system to avoid the commission of the offence and, thereafter, regularly monitor it to ensure that the system works. In practice, each case will depend on its facts, with the burden on the defendant to show that his actions satisfy the due diligence requirement. Further, setting up a suitable system may allow the defendant to claim the benefit of the defence when the failure by an employee to comply with the system has caused an offence.[31] That assumes, of course, that the defendant has issued adequate instructions to his employees about the system and the need to comply with it.[32]

The taking of 'reasonable precautions' in paragraph (b) raises issues about the onus on defendants to sample the products that they supply. The Divisional Court in *Garrett* v. *Boots Chemists Ltd*[33] felt that there is a duty on traders to carry out some random sampling even if the trader has instructed their supplier to comply with certain standards. The defendant had offered pencils for sale which exceeded the permitted levels of chromium and/or lead, despite the fact that the contract with the suppliers required compliance with the relevant regulatory standards. The defendant had not done any independent testing to ensure compliance with the contractual and regulatory requirements and was found guilty of an offence against the Pencil and Graphic Instruments (Safety) Regulations 1974.[34] Arguably, the simplest tests can always be undertaken irrespective of the size or resources of the trader.[35]

Q4 Does the two strand due diligence defence provide an appropriate level of protection for innocent traders charged with a strict liability offence?

(ii) Innocent publication

A further defence relates to the innocent publication of an advertisement.[36] This defence is available to, a publisher who demonstrates that he is a person whose business is to publish or to arrange for the publication of advertisements and, further, that he received the advertisement in question in the ordinary course of business and had no reason to either know or suspect that its publication would amount to an offence under the respective Regulations.

---

[31] *Newcastle-upon-Tyne City Council* v. *Safeway plc* (unreported, 27 June 1994, DC). See Griffiths and Griffiths, above n. 29.

[32] See Dobson and Stokes, above n. 29.   [33] Unreported, 16 July 1980, DC.

[34] SI 1974/2406.

[35] See *Sherratt* v. *Gerald's the Amercan Jewellers Ltd* (1970) 114 Sol. Jo. 117, in which the Divisional Court held that a trader, charged with an offence under s.1(1)(b) of the Trade Descriptions Act 1968 for supplying a diver's watch falsely described as 'water-proof', could easily have tested the accuracy of the statement by submerging the watch in a container of water.

[36] CPUT Regulations 2008, reg. 18.

(c) Liability of 'another person'

The final pair of regulations[37] to be considered here depend upon the commission of a *prima facie* offence by a person whose criminality is due to the act or default of another person. They both have effect irrespective of whether the primary offender is able to claim a valid statutory defence and provide that, when a *prima facie* offence has taken place and the offence is due to the act or default of another person, that other person will be guilty of the offence,[38] subject to the other person's ability to claim a valid defence. Further, liability will be visited upon that other person irrespective of whether or not they are a trader and irrespective of whether their act or default is an unfair commercial practice or misleading advertising, as appropriate. The fact that a private individual can be held criminally liable if their act or default has subsequently caused the commission of an offence reflects the original hard-line approach of the Trade Descriptions Act 1968, section 23, as evidenced in the decision in *Olgeirsson* v. *Kitching*.[39] Further, the person may be charged with and convicted of the offence irrespective of whether proceedings are taken against the primary offender.[40] It is sufficient to show that a *prima facie* offence has been committed by the primary offender, there being no requirement for proceedings to have been instituted against him. This allows for the possibility that either the primary offender has a valid defence or, alternatively, that the enforcement authority decides to take no action against him or to use an alternative strategy such as issuing a formal caution. However, if no *prima facie* offence has occurred because, for example, the main offender is not a trader, then regulation 16 or regulation 9, respectively, cannot be used to take any action against the person whose act or default has caused the main incident to take place.[41]

Q5 Consider whether it is appropriate to hold a private individual liable for an offence where their act or default has caused the primary offender to commit an offence under these provisions.

5 Civil law enforcement

(a) Consumer Protection from Unfair Trading Regulations 2008

If good enforcement in this context is about protecting consumers by prohibiting and removing unfair commercial practices, a civil law remedy may be a more effective tool than a criminal prosecution.[42] Consequently, in addition to creating criminal offences, the CPUT Regulations 2008 utilise the enforcement

---

[37] CPUT Regulations 2008, reg. 16 and BPMM Regulations 2008 reg. 9.
[38] CPUT Regulations 2008, reg. 16(2) and BPMM Regulations 2008, reg. 9(2), respectively.
[39] [1986] 1 All ER 746.
[40] CPUT Regulations 2008, reg. 16(3) and BPMM Regulations 2008, reg. 9(3), respectively.
[41] *Coupe* v. *Guyett* [1973] 2 All ER 1058. See also Griffiths and Griffiths, above n. 29
[42] Enforcement strategies and methods will be discussed in full detail below.

provisions of Part 8 of the Enterprise Act 2002.[43] There are three relevant enforcement mechanisms here: enforcement orders and interim enforcement orders under sections 217 and 218, respectively, and an undertaking under section 219. A failure to comply with any of these three enforcement mechanisms can give rise to further court action for contempt of court, which, if the trader is found guilty, can result in punishment by a fine and, if the defendant is an individual, a term of imprisonment not exceeding two years.

Breaches of the Regulations are specified to be Community infringements within the meaning of the Enterprise Act 2002, being breaches which contravene a listed Directive and harm the collective interests of consumers.[44] The 2002 Act is not concerned with the effect on an individual consumer but rather with the impact on consumers as a collective body. There is no requirement that a large number of consumers have already been affected by the practice in question, simply a realistic expectation that the continuance or repetition of the practice will impact upon consumers generally in the future. When dealing with a minimum harmonisation Directive, EEA states can provide additional protection over and above the relevant Directive,[45] the Secretary of State in the United Kingdom having the power to specify such additional powers.[46] However, the Unfair Commercial Practices Directive is a maximum harmonisation Directive and, hence, no deviation from its terms is permitted and states cannot therefore provide additional protection.

The general enforcement bodies for the purposes of the 2002 Act are the Office of Fair Trading (OFT), local weights and measures authorities and the Department of Enterprise, Trade and Investment in Northern Ireland, although the Secretary of State can appoint as a designated enforcer any person or body which has the protection of the collective interests of consumers as one of its purposes.[47]

(i) Enforcement orders and interim enforcement orders

Before applying for either an enforcement order under section 217 or an interim enforcement order under section 218, the enforcer must consult with both the OFT (assuming that the enforcer is someone other than the OFT) and the person against whom the enforcement order would be made. This is to try and ensure that any infringement will cease and that there will not be any repetition of it. However, while consultation must take place, it is subject to a time limit in that, in respect of an application for an enforcement order, the consultation period ends after fourteen days beginning with the day following the one on which the trader would have received the request for consultation from the enforcer.[48] This is reduced to seven days in respect of an application for an

---

[43] Part 8 of the Enterprise Act 2002 has replaced Part III of the Fair Trading Act 1973 and the Stop Now Orders (EC Directive) Regulations 2001, SI 2001/1422.

[44] Enterprise Act 2002, s.212.

[45] *Ibid.*   [46] *Ibid.*   [47] *Ibid.* s.213.   [48] *Ibid.* s.214(4).

interim time order.[49] This prevents traders abusing the consultation requirement by wrongfully extending the time before which an enforcer can seek an
order. Indeed, the requirement to consult will not apply at all if the OFT thinks
that an application for an order should be made without delay.[50]

The application must name the person whom the enforcer thinks has
engaged, is engaging or is likely to engage in conduct that is an infringement.[51]
The OFT has the power to decide who will apply for the relevant enforcement
order, which might be the OFT itself or such other enforcer as the OFT directs.[52]
However, if the OFT directs that only itself may apply for an order, that does
not prevent either the OFT or any other enforcer from seeking an undertaking
under section 219.

An enforcement order will be issued under section 217 if the court finds
that the person named in the application has engaged in conduct which constitutes an infringement or is likely to do so. In deciding the matter, the court
must take into account whether the person has provided an undertaking and, if
so, whether he has breached it. The order, if granted, must specify the conduct
concerned and direct the person to refrain from continuing with the conduct
or repeating it, or conniving at it when done by a body corporate. Further, the
enforcement order can require the trader to publish in a manner, form and
extent directed by the court, details of the order and a corrective statement. As
an alternative to an enforcement order, the court can accept an undertaking
instead.

It may be that an order is needed as a matter of urgency, in which case the
enforcer may decide to seek an interim enforcement order under section 218
pending the hearing of an application for an enforcement order under section 217. An application must relate to conduct that constitutes a Community
infringement, be of such a type that an application for an enforcement order
would be likely to be granted and it must be expedient to prohibit or prevent
the conduct immediately.[53] The interim order must indicate the nature of the
conduct concerned and require the trader to comply with the order. The application can be made at any time before an application for an enforcement order
has been decided[54] and will terminate when that application is determined.[55] If
it appears appropriate, the court can accept an undertaking from the trader in
lieu of issuing an interim enforcement order.[56]

(ii) Undertaking

When the enforcer is in the position to apply for an enforcement order, he can
instead accept an undertaking from the trader concerned.[57] The trader will
be someone who the enforcer believes has engaged in conduct which is an
infringement, or is engaging in such conduct, or is likely to engage in conduct

---

[49] *Ibid.*   [50] *Ibid.*   [51] *Ibid.* s.215(1).   [52] *Ibid.* s.216(2).
[53] *Ibid.* s.218.   [54] *Ibid.*   [55] *Ibid.*   [56] *Ibid.*
[57] *Ibid.* s.219(2).

which would be a Community infringement.[58] A trader providing such an undertaking will be deemed to have complied with it if he does not continue or repeat the conduct, does not engage in such conduct in his business or in another business, and does not consent to or connive at the carrying on of such conduct by a body corporate with which he has a special relationship.[59] The use of an undertaking would seem to be particularly useful if the trader has only committed an infringement on one occasion or the enforcer is satisfied that the trader did not realise that the conduct concerned was an infringement and that, in either case, an undertaking will ensure future compliance. If an enforcer accepts an undertaking, it must notify the OFT of the identity of the trader and the terms of the undertaking.[60] This allows the OFT to co-ordinate enforcement by the various enforcers and to ensure that a trader is not being required to give undertakings to a variety of enforcers when a more formal enforcement order or interim enforcement order might be more appropriate in all the circumstances.

Q6 Consider the likely effectiveness of the use of enforcement orders, interim enforcement orders and undertakings as a means of controlling future breaches of the Consumer Protection from Unfair Trading Regulations 2008.

(b) Business Protection from Misleading Marketing Regulations 2008

While criminal liability under BPMM Regulations 2008 is restricted to offences against regulation 6, civil enforcement applies to breaches of regulation 3 (misleading advertising), regulation 4 (comparative advertising) and regulation 5 (the promotion of prohibited misleading advertising and comparative advertising).

(i) Injunctions

Under regulation 15, if the enforcement authority considers that there has been a breach, or is likely to be a breach of regulations 3, 4 or 5, the authority can seek an injunction (and a interim injunction if appropriate) against any person who is concerned with or likely to be concerned with the breach. However, there is a restriction in that, before instituting proceedings, the authority must notify the OFT and then wait for fourteen days to elapse, unless the OFT consents to the proceedings in a shorter period. This allows the OFT to monitor such applications and to co-ordinate the process if more than one authority is seeking an injunction. While this is unlikely to be the case with small local companies, several authorities may be simultaneously considering proceedings against larger companies with a broader reach and a larger purchaser base. The court can require the person to justify the advertising claims that he has made

---

[58] *Ibid.*   [59] *Ibid.*   [60] *Ibid.*

and publish a corrective statement if necessary.[61] A breach of an injunction is, of course, a contempt of court and can be punished as such.

(ii) Undertakings

A less dramatic step, when an enforcement authority considers that there has been or is likely to be a breach of regulations 3, 4 or 5, is to accept an undertaking under regulation 16 from the person concerned or likely to be concerned. Such an undertaking would state that the person concerned will comply with the Regulations in the future. If the trader subsequently breaches the undertaking, the enforcement authority can seek an injunction instead, and if the trader fails to comply with the injunction, he could be prosecuted for contempt of court, which could result in imprisonment.

Q7 Consider the use of injunctions and undertakings as a means of enforcing the Business Protection from Misleading Marketing Regulations 2008.

6 Recommended reading

De Groote, B. and De Vulder, K. 'European framework for unfair commercial practices: analysis of Directive 2005/29' (2007) *Journal of Business Law* 16

Department of Trade and Industry *The Unfair Commercial Practices Directive, Consultation on a Draft EU Directive, COM(2003)356* (London, 2002)

   The Unfair Commercial Practices (UCP) Directive, Consultation on Framing and Enforcing Criminal Sanctions in the Regulations implementing the Unfair Commercial Practices Directive (London, 2006)

   Implementation of the Unfair Commercial Practices Directive, Consultation on the Draft Consumer Protection from Unfair Trading Regulations 2007 (London, 2007)

Dobson, P. and Stokes, R. *Commercial Law* (7th edn, Sweet & Maxwell Ltd, London, 2008)

Griffiths, M. 'Unfair commercial practices: a new regime' (2007) 12 *Communications Law* 194

Griffiths, M. and Griffiths, I. *Law for Purchasing and Supply* (3rd edn, Pearson Education Ltd, Harlow, 2002)

Johnson, H. 'Advertisers beware! The impact of the Unfair Commercial Practices Directive' (2005) 10 *Communications Law* 164

Ramsay, I. *Consumer Law and Policy: Text and Materials on Regulating Consumer Markets* (2nd edn, Hart Publishing, Oxford, 2007)

Shears, P. 'Overviewing the EU Unfair Commercial Practices Directive: Concentric circles' (2007) 18 *European Business Law Review* 781

Stuyck, J., Terryn, E., and Van Dyck, T. 'Confidence through fairness? The new Directive on Unfair Business-to-Consumer Commercial Practices in the internal market' (2007) 43 *Common Market Law Review* 107

Twigg-Flesner, C. 'Deep impact? The EC Directive on Unfair Commercial Practices and Domestic Consumer Law' (2005) 121 *Law Quarterly Review* 386

---

[61] BPMM Regulations 2008, reg. 18.

The passage of the Unfair Commercial Practices Directive was one of the major current developments in commercial law and, as such, has attracted a lot of academic comment. Given that the Directive has been adopted almost verbatim into the Consumer Protection from Unfair Trading Regulations 2008, readers may benefit from reading articles about the Directive and the Regulations drawn from the list above.

Part 5 Chapter 2

The Consumer Protection from Unfair Trading Regulations 2008

Contents

1 Introduction

This chapter analyses the provisions of the Consumer Protection from Unfair Trading Regulations 2008 and the new, comprehensive regime of controls that have been put in place to protect consumers from unfair and unscrupulous activities by traders. The Regulations replace many of the pre-existing provisions while also extending protection in other areas

Section 2 considers the scope of the Regulations, including what constitutes a commercial practice, the meaning of consumers and which transactions are covered by the Regulations.

Section 3 analyses the prohibition against unfair commercial practices and the criminal offence created for breaches of that regulation, and section 4 deals with the prohibition against code owners using codes of conduct to promote unfair commercial activities.

Section 5 examines the controls over misleading actions that have replaced and extended the law in this area, including the definition of a misleading action, and the regulation 5(4) factors.

Section 6 deals with the issue of misleading omissions to prevent traders from misleading consumers by omitting or hiding material information. Section 7 looks at the prohibition against aggressive commercial practices, including an analysis of the various types of activity that can be classed as aggressive.

Section 8 analyses the thirty-one commercial practices detailed in Schedule 1 to the Regulations, which are always presumed to be unfair, and section 9 discusses the offences created by the Regulations.

2 Scope of the 2008 Regulations

(a) What constitutes a 'commercial practice'

The Unfair Commercial Practices Directive 2005/29/EC, and hence the Consumer Protection from Unfair Trading (CPUT) Regulations 2008, SI 2008/1277 delineate both the transactions that fall within their remit and the categories of consumers who are to be protected. This has necessitated the introduction of new terminology. The most fundamental definition relates to the meaning of the phrase 'commercial practice', defined in regulation 2(1) of the CPUT Regulations 2008 as being:

> any act, omission, course of conduct, representation or commercial communication (including advertising and marketing) by a trader, which is directly connected with the promotion, sale or supply of a product to or from consumers, whether occurring before, during or after a commercial transaction (if any) in relation to a product.

The first point to note is that the term only covers commercial activities involving traders. Thus, activities undertaken by individuals do not fall within the remit of the Regulations while civil law remedies remain under sale of goods and other related legislation. A trader for the purposes of the Regulations is anyone 'acting for purposes relating to his business,[1] and anyone acting in the name of or on behalf of a trader'. This would encompass anyone who has a controlling interest in a business[2] and anyone else overtly acting on behalf of a business, which would include employees.[3]

The activities covered are very broad in nature and include both positive actions and omissions, also representations and commercial communications such as advertising and marketing, and extend to a trader's course of conduct.

---

[1] The Unfair Commercial Practices Directive defines a trader as someone acting for purposes relating to 'his trade, business, craft or profession', see Art. 2. However, in the United Kingdom, someone acting in the course of a business is presumed to include anyone acting in pursuit of their profession, see *Roberts* v. *Leonard, The Times*, 10 May 1995, in which veterinary surgeons were convicted of offences against s.1(1)(b) of the Trade Descriptions Act 1968 when they falsely stated on an export licence that they had inspected 557 calves.

[2] See *Warwickshire County Council* v. *Johnson* [1993] 1 All ER 299, a decision under the misleading pricing provisions of Consumer Protection Act 1987, s.20(1), in which the House of Lords held that the phrase 'in the course of any business of his' only applied where the defendant was the owner of the business or had a controlling interest in it.

[3] Employees have, in the past, been found guilty of offences under criminal trading legislation such as the Trade Descriptions Act 1968, so their inclusion in this provision does not break new ground. The Unfair Commercial Practices Directive specifically includes 'anyone acting in the name of or on behalf of a trader', see Art. 2.

Many of these actions form the basis of specific prohibitions in the Regulations, such as the control of misleading actions under regulation 5 and misleading omissions under regulation 6. However, in an attempt to encompass all potentially unfair practices and future-proof the provisions against as yet unknown practices, there is a general prohibition against unfair commercial practices under regulation 3 with the breadth of the definition of a 'commercial practice' lending strength to this catch-all regulation.

The commercial practice must be connected with the promotion, sale or supply of a product. Given the inclusion of the promotion of a product, it follows that there is no requirement that a sale or other supply has occurred. Accordingly, the provisions of the Regulations can be used as a preventative measure giving enforcement authorities the power to step in and act before a consumer has been adversely affected by the practice in question. This is in line with previous consumer legislation where the enforcement strategy has been to prevent incidents occurring rather than deal with the consequences of consumers being affected by a prohibited act.

The definition of a 'commercial practice' also extends to activities where the product is being promoted, sold or supplied both to and from the consumer. While most activity is likely to involve products being promoted, sold or supplied to a consumer, it is important to remember that sometimes products are acquired from a consumer instead. The most obvious example is the part-exchange of second-hand cars, when the consumer typically supplies his old vehicle to a trader as part-payment for a new one.[4] This approach accords with the previous position under the Trade Descriptions Act 1968, whereby in *Fletcher* v. *Budgen*[5] a trader was convicted of an offence when, while acquiring a vehicle from a customer, he described it as being unrepairable and fit only for scrap. Having bought it for £2 from the customer, the trader spent some money repairing it and sold it for £135.

The final aspect of the definition of a 'commercial practice' outlines the temporal ambit of the controls. While most of the previous controls in this area applied to activities occurring before or at the time of the supply or offer to supply the goods,[6] the scope of these controls over commercial practices extends to activities 'occurring before, during or after a commercial transaction (if any) in relation to a product'. This is significant since, in addition to promotional activities before the time of supply and during it, controls now extend to things occurring after the supply of the goods or services. Thus, from now on, after-sales service and maintenance will be covered as well as such things as complaint handling and debt collecting.[7]

---

[4] See M. Griffiths 'Unfair commercial practices: a new regime' (2007) 12 *Communications Law* 194, 195.

[5] [1974] 2 All ER 1243.

[6] See, among others, the Trade Descriptions Act 1968 and Part III of the Consumer Protection Act 1987.

[7] See D.L. Party, R. Rowell and C. Ervine, *Butterworths Trading and Consumer Law* (London, 1990) Division 1A.

It is clearly important to identify the scope of the word 'product' in this context. The CPUT Regulations 2008 define 'product' as including not merely goods but also services and immovable property such as land. While services were included in some previous enactments, such as in section 14 of the Trade Descriptions Act 1968, the inclusion of immovable property is a new departure. The Regulations will impact on a trader selling or leasing land to a consumer. This would include, for example, the initial sale of a house by a property developer to a consumer, however should that consumer subsequently sell the house to a new owner, the latter transaction would fall outside the Regulations. Similarly, the sale of immovable property between businesses is also beyond the remit of the Regulations. 'Property' also includes other rights and obligations such as, for example, a right to use a caravan for a period, membership of a club, premium rate phone calls and the provision of credit to consumers.[8]

Q1 Consider how the remit of the CPUT Regulations 2008 extends beyond that of previous controls.

(b) The meaning of 'consumers'

As previously indicated, the CPUT Regulations 2008 are intended to protect 'consumers', defined in regulation 2(1) as being 'any individual who in relation to a commercial practice is acting for purposes which are outside his business'.[9] However, having identified that the protection is limited to individuals, the Regulations go on in various places to refer to 'average' consumers and 'vulnerable' consumers, both of which require further explanation. An analysis of who is an 'average consumer' is found in regulation 2(2) to (6), with an additional explanation provided by the Office of Fair Trading (OFT).[10] The average consumer may be an individual or may be one of a group of like people affected by the commercial practice in question. Regulation 2(2) provides that when assessing the effect of a commercial practice on an average consumer, account must be taken of the main characteristics of such a consumer, including his being 'reasonably well informed, reasonably observant and circumspect'. This objective approach accords closely to the English concept of the reasonable man. No actual consumer need be involved,[11] the standard being decided by the court's interpretation of the way that a reasonable man would react or behave in the circumstances.

---

[8] See Office of Fair Trading, *Consumer Protection from Unfair Trading Regulations* 2008. *Guidance on the Implementation of the Unfair Commercial Practices Directive*, OFT 1008 (London, 2008) para. 14.18. See also *Butterworths Trading and Consumer Law*, above n. 7, Division 1A, para. 8.

[9] This makes clear that the protection is limited to individuals and does not extend to sole traders or small partnerships as occurs, for example, under some sections of the Consumer Credit Act 1974.

[10] OFT Guidance, above n. 8, paras. 14.28–14.37.   [11] *Ibid.* para. 14.28.

While the term 'average consumer' might be assumed to be the average of all consumers in the United Kingdom as a whole, this is not necessarily the case. Commercial practices can be directed at identifiable groups within society, in which case the average consumer would be construed as the average member of that group. Thus, for example, a group might be determined by age, social background, interests, employment or culture. The OFT uses as an example that the average consumer of a Welsh language magazine must be assumed to read Welsh.[12] Thus, Welsh speakers are an identifiable group for the purpose of promoting or selling this product and an average consumer would be a member of that group. Further, within an identifiable group of consumers, it is possible to target a section of that group for the purposes of promoting a particular product. Thus, to continue with the OFT's example, not all Welsh speakers would be interested in an academic journal about Welsh linguistics.[13] Such a product would, in practice, be carefully targeted, with the average consumer being a member of that particular targeted group.

Regulation 2(5) considers the position of identifiable groups of consumers who may be vulnerable to the practice[14] or the underlying product[15] because of mental or physical infirmity, age or credulity[16] which the trader could reasonably have been expected to foresee. Physical infirmity includes a variety of situations, from the person in a wheelchair who may be particularly affected by claims regarding ease of access,[17] to those suffering from a medical condition who might be affected by claims that a particular product may cure their condition or alleviate their symptoms.[18] Age is clearly relevant in relation to certain products, with the elderly and children being target groups for some products. The promotion of toys to children is an obvious example, particularly, it could be argued, at Christmas-time when children are hoping to receive more toys than at other times of the year.[19] Credulity is more difficult to quantify than 'age' but relates to those people who are, perhaps because of some misfortune, more likely than other consumers to believe claims about the practice or product in question. In determining the impact of a commercial practice on the average vulnerable consumer, account must be taken both of the vulnerability in

---

[12] *Ibid.* para. 14.33.   [13] *Ibid.*

[14] E.g. doorstep selling in sheltered accommodation See *Butterworths Trading and Consumer Law*, above n. 7, Division 1A, para. 8.

[15] E.g. funeral plans and security equipment. See *ibid.*

[16] Note that this list is exhaustive with the concept of vulnerability being limited to these three factors.

[17] OFT Guidance, above n. 8, para. 14.37.

[18] Falsely claiming that a product is able to cure illness, dysfunctions or malformations is always regarded as an unfair commercial practice under CPUT Regulations 2008, Sch. 1 para. 17. See also Griffiths, above n. 4, at 196.

[19] It is always regarded as an unfair commercial practice to use an advertisement to directly exhort children to buy advertised products or to persuade their parents or other adults to buy those products for them. See CPUT Regulations 2008, Sch. 1 para. 28. However, while all but two of the thirty-one commercial practices listed in Sch. 1 are criminal offences, a practice within para. 28 does not constitute a criminal offence.

question and whether the practice is likely to materially distort the economic behaviour of that group.[20] There must a clear link between the vulnerability and the economic impact. That said, when assessing commercial practices as they apply to vulnerable groups, it does not prevent traders using exaggerated advertising about the product which is not expected to be taken literally.[21]

Q2 Consider how the definition of a 'consumer' seeks to identify and protect those affected by the Regulations.

(c) Which transactions are covered

The CPUT Regulations 2008 introduced new definitions and concepts that are crucial to understanding the breadth and thrust of the Regulations. Three of these are 'invitation to purchase', 'transactional decision' and 'materially distort the economic behaviour'. It is only through understanding these concepts that it is possible to fully appreciate the impact of the Regulations.

In English law, we are used to the term 'invitation to treat' as the stage in contractual discussions that precedes a contractual offer. Thus, we are familiar with the idea that a display of goods in a shop window is an 'invitation to treat'[22] by virtue of which the potential buyer may acquire enough information about the goods to enable him to make an offer for them. The information provided might include colour, size, manufacturer, constituent fabric, etc., but without any requirement to include details about the price, which the potential buyer could, of course, discover relatively easily by asking a shop assistant. Technically, the same would be true of an advertisement in a magazine but, in practice, it is most unlikely, for purely practical reasons, that the price would not be included. By contrast, the related concept of an 'invitation to purchase' is to be found in regulation 2(1) of the Regulations[23] and provides that such an invitation is a 'commercial communication that includes both the characteristics of the product and the price in a way appropriate to that communication, in such a way as to permit the consumer to make a purchase'. It follows from the definition that the inclusion of the price is essential if the details provided to the consumer are to constitute an 'invitation to purchase'[24] as opposed to merely being a commercial communication and a contractual 'invitation to treat'. Equally, where there is a failure to provide details of the characteristics of the product, or where the communication does not put the consumer in a position to purchase the goods, or where it is merely an advertisement for the brand rather than for a particular item, the communication will not constitute an 'invitation to

---

[20] CPUT Regulations 2008, reg. 2(5)(b).   [21] *Ibid.* reg. 2(6)
[22] *Fisher* v. *Bell* [1961] 1 QB 394.
[23] The wording of reg. 2(1) closely follows that of Art. 2(i) of the Unfair Commercial Practices Directive.
[24] A failure to include price means that it is not an invitation to purchase, see OFT Guidance, above n. 8, para. 7.28.

purchase'.[25] The OFT Guidance provides some examples of what would constitute invitations to purchase and includes, among others, an advertisement in a newspaper that includes an order form to be sent to the seller; an interactive TV advertisement; a restaurant menu; and a webpage on a website where consumers can place an order.[26] The information must be provided in a 'clear, unambiguous, intelligible and timely manner'[27] unless the information is clear from the context, such as the name of a shop when the consumer is already in it.[28] The exact nature of the required information will be considered in depth when analysing 'misleading omissions' under regulation 6 below.

Q3 Analyse how the term 'invitation to purchase' differs from the concept of 'invitation to treat'.

The second important term is 'transactional decision' and is central to the controls over misleading actions,[29] misleading omissions[30] and aggressive commercial practices.[31] What constitutes a 'transactional decision' is defined in regulation 2 as any decision taken by a consumer whether to act or refrain from acting in respect of a contract for a product. Further, the decision must relate to whether, how and on what terms to purchase a product, whether to make payment in full or part for a product, and whether to retain or dispose of a product. Thus, it covers both decisions to take a positive action and decisions not to act at present or, indeed, at all. The transactional decision will revolve around the terms on which the purchaser is prepared to buy and, most particularly, how much he is prepared to pay. This might dictate whether to buy in a small local shop, or in a major supermarket or department store with immediate delivery or whether to delay delivery for a couple of days in order to buy the item more cheaply via the Internet. Factors such as cost and delivery times are part of the transactional decision. Whether a deposit is payable or whether the full amount must be paid immediately, and whether to pay cash for an item or pay via a credit card, with the possibility of incurring interest if the debt is not settled in full when the bill arrives, might affect the buyer's decision as to whether and where to purchase the goods. Further, the decision to purchase on credit may be affected if there are two credit card providers, one offering interest-free credit while the other charges interest.[32] While these examples all relate to the purchase of a product, the decision not to purchase an item or to retain an item rather than sell it would also constitute transactional decisions. Thus, if, for example, a consumer decides not to sell his car in part-exchange for a new one, that choice is a 'transactional decision' for this purpose.

---

[25] *Ibid.* paras. 7.27, 7.29 and 7.30, respectively.
[26] *Ibid.* para. 7.25, where other examples are also included.
[27] *Ibid.* para. 7.31.   [28] *Ibid.* para. 7.32.
[29] CPUT Regulations 2008, reg. 5(2)(b) and (3)(b)(ii).
[30] *Ibid.* reg. 6(1).   [31] *Ibid.* reg. 7(1)(b).
[32] For further examples of transactional, decisions see *Butterworths Trading and Consumer Law*, above n. 7, Division 1A, para. 8.

However, transactional decisions go wider than simply decisions whether or not to buy a product and on what terms. They also encompass whether, how and on what terms to exercise a contractual right. This might include, for example, exercising a cancellation right, or the right to terminate a contract early, such as exists under the Consumer Credit Act 1974, or deciding whether to seek a refund or a replacement for faulty goods or whether to enforce the terms of a manufacturer's guarantee. It follows that transactional decisions may occur at any time throughout the lifetime of the contract and do not simply occur when the contract is being made.

Q4 Analyse the situations that are classed as 'transactional decisions'.

The phrase 'materially distorts the economic behaviour' lies at the heart of the prohibition against unfair commercial practices in regulation 3. It should be noted that it is only the economic behaviour of the consumer that is at issue here. The CPUT Regulations 2008 are not concerned with any other aspect, such as, for example, the health and safety of the consumer. The term refers to a 'material' distortion of behaviour and not a minor one, let alone no distortion at all. The definition requires there to be an appreciable impairment of the ability of the average consumer to make an informed decision.[33] Further, the material distortion must have caused the consumer to make a transactional decision that he would not otherwise have made. Thus, a definite causal link is required and not merely the possibility of a distortion and an alternative transactional decision.

Q5 Analyse situations that would and would not be classed as 'materially distorting the economic behaviour' of the consumer.

3 Prohibition against unfair commercial practices

The basic prohibition against unfair commercial practices is to be found in regulation 3(1), which states simply that 'unfair commercial practices are prohibited'. This catch-all provision serves two useful purposes. First, it encompasses any unfair practices that do not fall within the specific prohibitions against misleading actions, misleading omissions and aggressive commercial practices to be found in regulations 5, 6 and 7, respectively. Secondly, it introduces an element of future-proofing as it is broad enough to include unfair commercial practices that have not yet been recognised and may develop in the future. This should prevent the legislation becoming dated and less relevant in the future.

A commercial practice is deemed unfair if:

(a) it contravenes the requirements of professional diligence; and
(b) it materially distorts or is likely to materially distort the economic behaviour of the average consumer with regard to the product.[34]

[33] CPUT Regulations 2008, reg. 2.   [34] *Ibid.* reg. 3(3).

The concepts of the average consumer and materially distorting have already been considered but paragraph (a) of this definition raises the concept of 'professional diligence'. This requires the trader to demonstrate a level of special skill and care towards consumers which is commensurate with either honest market practice in the trader's field of activity or the general principles of good faith in the trader's field of activity.[35] The acid test would seem to be 'Is the trader acting to a standard that a reasonable person would expect?'[36] The inclusion of this requirement for traders to act within the requirements of professional diligence when dealing with consumers is to be welcomed.

The concept of professional diligence in this context is not dissimilar from the concept of good faith to be found elsewhere in English law. However, here it is firmly embedded in the central provision of the CPUT Regulations 2008 while, in English law, the concept of good faith is more specialised in application. Of course, the average consumer will still be required to exercise care for his own safety and wellbeing, but the trader will now be expected to exercise the special skill and care appropriate to his professional ability in all of the commercial practices with which he is involved. While the definition specifically refers to the standard in the trader's field of activity, the common standard to be expected in all industries remains the same, namely, that of professional diligence. Standards do not vary depending upon the type of business with which an individual trader is involved. In assessing the relevant standard, regard may be had to things such as industry codes of practice, compliance with which is to be expected within the relevant sector. However, this does not necessarily equate with professional diligence, as the code, which is indicative only, may set a standard below that which a reasonable consumer has a right to expect. Equally, if poor standards of practice are common across a sector, a trader cannot simply comply with those low standards and then claim that he is acting in accordance with professional diligence.[37]

For a practice to be deemed an unfair commercial practice, such as to be in breach of regulation 3, the practice in question must breach both parts of the regulation. Thus, it must not merely offend against the requirements of professional diligence but must also materially distort the economic behaviour of the average consumer or be likely so to do. There is no requirement that a consumer has actually been affected by the practice; it is the likelihood of impact that is assessed and it is only the consumer's likely economic behaviour that is considered as opposed to their health and safety or any other aspect of their life. It follows that if the practice would not be likely to affect the transactional decisions of the average consumer, there will be no breach, even if the practice falls significantly below the standard of professional diligence.[38]

---

[35] *Ibid*. reg. 2.   [36] See OFT Guidance, above n. 8, para. 14.19.

[37] See *ibid*. paras. 10.4–10.7. See also Griffiths, above n. 4, at 196.

[38] *Butterworths Trading and Consumer Law*, above n. 7, Division 1A, para. 9.

If a breach does occur, there is a twofold outcome. First, a breach of regulation 3 will be a criminal offence under regulation 8(1), and, secondly, it will also constitute a Community infringement contrary to Enterprise Act 2002, Part 8.[39]

The offence under regulation 8 requires *mens rea*, unlike the other offences in the CPUT Regulations 2008, which are strict liability[40] and for which only an *actus reus* is required. Regulation 8(1) provides that:

> A trader is guilty of an offence if:
>
> (a) he knowingly or recklessly engages in a commercial practice which contravenes the requirements of professional diligence under regulation 3(3)(a); and
>
> (b) the practice materially distorts or is likely to materially distort the economic behaviour of the average consumer with regard to the product under regulation 3(3)(b).

The meaning of 'knowingly' is self-evident but the term 'recklessly' is less clear-cut and is defined in regulation 8(2) as occurring when a trader engages in a commercial practice and:

> without regard to whether the practice contravenes the requirements of professional diligence [he] shall be deemed recklessly to engage in the practice, whether or not the trader has reason for believing that the practice might contravene those requirements.

What is clear is that there is no need for full *mens rea* in that, while the trader must clearly have intended to undertake the commercial practice in question, there is no requirement that he knew that the action would be prohibited as unfair and contrary to the CPUT Regulations 2008. Each case will need to be decided on its facts, as the test is whether the act contravenes the requirements of professional diligence as defined above.

The term 'recklesly' is the same as that used previously in the Trade Descriptions Act 1968, section 14 as it related to false trade descriptions applied to services, accommodation or facilities. As such, cases decided under that section are arguably instructive here. One of the leading cases on section 14 was *MFI Warehouses Ltd* v. *Nattrass*[41] in which the court confirmed that 'recklessly' does not connote dishonesty so much as that the defendant did not pay due regard to the matter in hand, exactly the approach that is being taken to regulation 3 of the CPUT Regulations 2008. Lord Widgery CJ opined that:

> I have … come to the conclusion that 'recklessly' in the context of the 1968 Act does not involve dishonesty. Accordingly it is not necessary to prove that the statement was made with that degree of irresponsibility which is implied in the phrase 'careless whether it be true or false'.[42]

---

[39] Enforcement provisions under the Enterprise Act 2002 will be considered in more detail below.

[40] CPUT Regulations 2008, regs. 9, 10, 11 and 12, which relate to the other unfair practices, and will be discussed below.

[41] [1973] 1 All ER 762.   [42] *Ibid.* 768.

Thus, the court was satisfied that an offence could be committed where the defendant did not pay due regard to his actions, there being no need to prove either dishonesty or the high level of irresponsibility required previously.[43] Applying this approach to regulation 8 of the CPUT Regulations 2008, it seems reasonable to assume that the court will hold that there is no need to demonstrate irresponsibility in the commercial practice in question for an offence under regulation 8 to take place, it being sufficient to show that the defendant did not pay due regard to his actions. Further, recklessness, being an example of *mens rea*, must be shown to have been present at the time that the alleged unfair commercial practice took place. Applying *Sunair Holidays* v. *Dodd*,[44] it can be assumed that the actions of the defendant cannot be rendered 'reckless' retrospectively by the subsequent actions of a third party.

The regulation 8 offence has two strands, first that the unfair commercial practice was committed knowingly or recklessly, but also that the practice materially distorts or is likely to materially distort the economic behaviour of the average consumer with regard to the product in question. In short, the question is whether the practice in question will affect or be likely to affect a transactional decision of the average consumer when deciding whether or not to acquire the goods or dispose of them and, if so, on what terms. Given the wording that the practice 'might be likely to distort' the economic behaviour of the average consumer, it follows that there is no need to show that any consumer has actually been affected by the practice. After all, one of the main rationales behind criminal consumer law is to establish a trading framework that militates against consumers being adversely affected in the first place by preventing dubious or unsafe practices from occurring. One method for achieving this is by considering the likely or possible outcomes from identifiable practices or actions and forbidding them, thereby minimising the risk to consumers.

Q6 Analyse the parameters of the prohibition against unfair commercial practices under regulation 3 and the criminal offence under regulation 8.

4 Codes of practice

Codes of practice are of real value as part of a self-regulatory role within an industry. Ideally, they seek to promote good practice among signatories and members of the organisation responsible for the code of practice and thereby protect customers and promote the reputation of the industry as a whole.[45] The CPUT Regulations 2008, regulation 2 defines a code of practice as meaning:

---

[43] *Derry* v. *Peek* (1889) 14 App. Cas. 337, in which it was held that to be reckless requires total irresponsibility and a total lack of consideration.

[44] [1970] 2 All ER 410, a case decided under the Trade Descriptions Act 1968, s.14.

[45] Examples would include the ABTA (Association of British Travel Agents) Code and the SMMT (Society of Motor Manufacturers and Traders) Code.

an agreement or set of rules (which is not imposed by legal or administrative requirements), which defines the behaviour of traders who undertake to be bound by it in relation to one or more commercial practices or business sectors.

As such, codes of practice are voluntary and reflect the agreed practices of an industry. Typically, they are promoted by a professional body or trade organisation who, for the purposes of the Regulations, acts as the 'code owner', a role defined in regulation 2 as meaning 'a trader or a body responsible for the formulation and revision of a code of conduct, or monitoring compliance with the code by those who have undertaken to be bound by it.'

The role of codes of practice in consumer law has been enhanced by the involvement of the OFT in their Approved Codes of Practice Scheme, which recognises various industry codes of practice as requiring higher standards of service from their members than are required by the law. Indeed, to gain recognition as an OFT approved code of practice, the code owner must demonstrate that members complying with the code will:

- provide customers with good standards of customer service;
- give customers clear information about the goods or services they are selling;
- use clear and fair contracts;
- have user-friendly and prompt procedures for dealing with customer complaints and provide access to low cost, independent advice to resolve disputes;
- have a commitment to providing customers with adequate information about goods and services;
- use clear and fair contracts;
- ensure protection of deposits or prepayments;
- provide low cost, independent dispute resolution if a complaint is not dealt with satisfactorily.[46]

In promoting good practice, codes of practice are invaluable as part of the strategy for controlling and negating unfair commercial practices, although their role is limited to regulating the activities of their members and, in practice, it is likely to be those businesses that are not party to a professional organisation and not bound by a code of practice that will engage in unfair practices. However, as a code of practice reflects the agreed stance of the organisation's members with no requirement that it stipulates the highest standards possible, it is possible, though not likely, that a member could comply with a code and still be involved in an unacceptable and unfair commercial practice.

Regulation 4 adds some legal controls to the role of codes by prohibiting the promotion of any unfair practice by a code owner in a code of practice. Given the generally positive rationale behind codes of practice, it is to be hoped that no code would actively promote unfair practices, but regulation 4 actively

---

[46] See 'OFT Approved Codes Explained' at www.oft.gov.uk.

prohibits such behaviour. However, unlike the other prohibited unfair prac-tices, a breach of regulation 4 is not a criminal offence. Rather, it gives rise to civil enforcement under the Enterprise Act 2002, Part 8 whereby the relevant enforcement bodies can seek enforcement orders prohibiting the offender from continuing with the conduct or activity in question. As such, the use of enforce-ment orders and injunctions is intended to remedy the problem and thereby protect consumers from the offending activity in future.[47] It seeks to correct an unfair trading environment by prohibiting the use of unfair practices.

Q7 Consider the role of codes of practice in preventing unfair commercial practices.

5 Misleading actions

(a) Definition of misleading action

The first of three consecutive regulations prohibiting identifiable types of behaviour is regulation 5, which controls misleading actions.[48] It can reason-ably be argued that regulation 5, which is very extensive in impact, lies at the very heart of the new regime and is the natural successor to long-standing pro-tectionist legislation such as the Trade Descriptions Act 1968 and Part III of the Consumer Protection Act 1987, covering much the same ground as those stat-utes. It follows that, in interpreting regulation 5, recourse may be had to some of the case law which analysed the previous controls. Breaches of regulation 5 are criminal offences under regulation 9.

Regulation 5, which gives effect to Article 6 of the Unfair Commercial Practices Directive,[49] provides that a practice will be a misleading action if it satisfies the conditions in either regulation 5(2) or (3). Regulation 5(2) has two strands, both of which must be satisfied if a breach of regulation 5 is to occur. First, regulation 5(2)(a) provides that a commercial practice will be unfair when it contains false information and is therefore untruthful in relation to the mat-ters specified in regulation 5(4) or if its overall presentation in any way deceives the average consumer in relation to any of those matters even if the information is factually correct. Secondly, regulation 5(2)(b) requires that the false infor-mation must either cause or be likely to cause the average consumer to take a transactional decision he would not otherwise have taken.

The approach of regulation 5(2)(a) is reminiscent of section 1(1)(a) of the Trade Descriptions Act 1968 under which it was an offence to apply a false trade description to goods,[50] meaning in practice the making of an untrue statement

---

[47] For enforcement procedures under the Enterprise Act 2002, see Part 5 Chapter 1.
[48] The other two are reg. 6 misleading on omissions and reg. 7 on aggressive commercial practices.
[49] Directive 2005/29/EC.
[50] It was also an offence to supply goods to which a false trade description had been applied, see Trade Descriptions Act 1968, s.1(1)(b).

about the goods. The second part of regulation 5(2)(a) also follows the 1968 Act, in that it recognises that a statement may be factually correct and yet still be misleading because of the context and manner in which it is used.[51] The key question under regulation 5 is whether the way in which the information has been presented has deceived or would be likely to deceive the average consumer as to any of the relevant factors. Note that, as under regulation 3, there is no requirement that a consumer has actually been deceived, merely that the likelihood exists. While at first sight this provision is potentially very broad, it is restricted in that the falsity must relate to one of the matters listed in regulation 5(4). If it does not, there cannot be a breach of regulation 5 and no further action can be taken.

Q8 Analyse the relationship between the two strands of regulation 5(2).

(b) The regulation 5(4) factors

As the eleven matters specified in regulation 5(4) are essential to a breach of regulation 5, it is important to understand what those factors encompass. They are wide-ranging and yet go to the heart of the unfair practices concerned. Many of them are redolent of other controls that have existed previously and, as such, are not really new to the statute book so much as a re-enactment of existing controls, albeit under a different mechanism and format. Indeed, the majority of the situations that would previously have been offences under the Trade Descriptions Act 1968 or the Consumer Protection Act 1987 section 20 will now be caught by the controls under regulation 5.[52] Regulation 5(4)(b) is further qualified by the contents of regulation 5(5).

(i) The existence or nature of the product (regulation 5(4)(a))
The first factor relates to the existence or nature of the product,[53] which would include, for example, encouraging consumers to apply for a product which is not yet in existence or, indeed, a product that will never exist, which is being advertised only as a mechanism for inducing consumers into a 'bait and switch'

---

[51] Trade Descriptions Act 1968, s.3(2) provides that 'A trade description which, though not false, is misleading, that is to say, likely to be taken for such an indication of any of the matters specified in s.2 of this Act as would be false to a material degree, shall be deemed to be a false trade description'. See also *R* v. *Inner London Justices, ex parte Wandsworth London Borough Council* [1983] RTR 425, in which a car was described as having had 'one previous owner'. While technically accurate, the one owner had been a car leasing company and the car had had five different users. It was held that the statement was misleading to a material degree. For a further discussion see M. Griffiths and I. Griffiths. *Law for Purchasing and Supply* (3rd edn, Pearson Education Ltd, Harlow, 2002) and Griffiths, above n. 4.

[52] See S. Rook, '*Consumer Protection from Unfair Trading Regulations*' (2009) *Trading Standards Today* June 34.

[53] CPUT Regulations 2008, reg. 5(4)(a).

scenario.[54] Bait and switch, which is always an unfair commercial practice,[55] consists of advertising a product and then refusing to show the advertised product to consumers, or refusing to take orders for it or deliver it within a reasonable time or, alternatively, demonstrating a defective item, all of these practices being with the intention of promoting another, typically more expensive, product to the consumer. The original advertisement is only intended to attract the attention of the consumer and draw them into a trading situation which the unscrupulous trader can then exploit. Of course, for an offence under regulation 5 to have taken place, the misleading action must have resulted in the consumer taking a transactional decision that he would not otherwise have taken.

(ii) The main characteristics of the product (regulation 5(4)(b))

The second factor included in regulation 5(4) is 'the main characteristics of the product'. Examples of what this means are included in a non-exhaustive list in regulation 5(5). It must be stressed that this is a non-exhaustive list and thus the court is free to conclude that other features of the product might also be classed as 'main characteristics' for this purpose. The list, which is very broad in scope and impact, includes such obvious matters as the availability of the product, e.g., 'offer ends 31st December' or 'limited edition of 1,000 items only'; the composition of the product, e.g., cotton, wool, 22 carat gold, sterling silver, stainless steel; the method and date of manufacture, e.g., hand-made, hand-stitched, 1998, pre-1900;[56] and the delivery of the product, e.g., 'delivery within seven days', 'overnight delivery to your home'.[57] However, the list goes much wider than this and includes, among others, the benefits of the product, risks of the product, accessories of the product, after-sales customer assistance and complaint handling. The benefits of the product most obviously applies to medicinal and quasi-medicinal products, many of which make claims about their beneficial effect to the user. Any claims about such products must also be read in light of Schedule 1 paragraph 17, which stipulates that falsely claiming that a product is able to cure illnesses, dysfunction or malformation is always to be classed as an unfair commercial practice. Thus, a false claim about the curative effect of a product would be both a breach of regulation 5 (and thereby an offence against regulation 9) and an offence under Schedule 1. While medicinal products are an obvious example of claims to have a beneficial effect, they are not the only products that do this. Thus, for example, foods and drinks are regularly promoted for their health benefits, e.g., wholewheat breakfast cereals and super-food cereal

---

[54] See *Butterworths Trading and Consumer Law*, above n. 7, Division 1A, para. 11 for a comprehensive list of examples of the various matters listed under both reg. 5(4) and reg. 5(5).

[55] CPUT Regulations 2008, Sch. 1.

[56] Date of manufacture might be particularly important in respect of cars as the market value of a vehicle is directly affected by its age. Equally, dates are of particular concern when dealing with antiques, see *Butterworths Trading and Consumer Law*, above n. 7, Division 1A, para. 11.

[57] The correlation between the CPUT Regulations 2008 and the Trade Descriptions Act 1968 is very obvious here, as the descriptions used in any of these examples would have been criminal offences under the Trade Descriptions Act 1968.

bars; beauty products such as face creams and shampoos for their impact in promoting clear well-moisturised skin and silky, glossy hair; and cleaning products, such as bleach, for ensuring clean, germfree facilities and work surfaces in the kitchen and bathroom. Such claims may cross the boundary between being representations that are to be believed and relied upon, and advertising puffs which, while entertaining and drawing a consumer's attention to the product, are not intended to be relied upon by the average consumer who, in practice, would not do so. As regulation 5(2) requires that the commercial practice in question 'deceives or is likely to deceive the average consumer' it follows that an advertising puff will not give rise to a breach of regulation 5(2).

The risks of the product are clearly those unavoidable during the use of the product and, as such, should be addressed in instructions for use and warnings. This would include instructions about how to use the product safely, whether its use is affected by another product, e.g., instructions with over-the-counter medicines not to drink alcohol, and any warnings about risks inherent in the use of the product. This would clearly include any age-related warnings, such as routinely appear on toys warning of their unsuitability for children below a specified age.

The composition of the product speaks to its constituent elements and thus would include descriptions such as wool, stainless steel, copper, etc., all of which would have attracted liability previously under the Trade Descriptions Act 1968.[58] Accessories would include those additional parts which need to be included with the main product, such as cleaning tools with a vacuum cleaner, fixings with self-assembly furniture and remote controls with a television. The absence of any of these when the product has been advertised as including them would be a misleading action under regulation 5.

As products become more technical, there is the potential for greater use of after-sales services. Products such as computers and broadband, the workings of which typically lie outside the knowledge of the average consumer, give rise to a need for an efficient and effective after-sales support service. Further, consumers expect to be able to complain if the product does not work properly or, in some other way, does not match up to the description applied to it and to have their complaint handled quickly and efficiently with an appropriate outcome in a reasonable time. Both the after-sales service and the handling of complaints are included in regulations 5(5)(g)–(h) and thus are main characteristics of the product such as to give rise to liability under regulation 5(2).

Other 'main characteristics of the product' as defined in regulation 5(5) include the method and date of manufacture, the method and date of the provision of the product, delivery of the product, fitness for purpose and its usage. These factors would all have attracted liability previously under the Trade

---

[58] Trade Descriptions Act 1968, s. 2(1)(c) specifically included composition as one of the factors, the description of which would constitute a trade description for the purposes of the 1968 Act.

Descriptions 1968, with regard to either goods[59] or services,[60] and thus the new provisions merely re-inforce the pre-existing situation. The method and date of manufacture covers statements such as hand-made and organic, which make clear statements about the method of production, while the date of manufacture pins down the age of the product, which, as stated above, might be very important when supplying cars[61] or valuing and selling antiques. The method and date of provision of the product overlap to some extent with the delivery of the product and would include obvious things such as delivery dates. However, it is wider than that as product in this context includes services. Thus, it would include statements about the provision of services such as car maintenance, the installation of double glazing or the processing of photographs. Also included would be details about the method of delivery, e.g., hand delivered, sent by special delivery and air-mail; and the place of delivery, whether that involves the buyer collecting the goods from the premises of the seller or them being delivered to the home of either the buyer or that of a third party. 'Fitness for purpose' and 'usage' again repeat previous controls under the Trade Descriptions Act 1968.[62] Fitness for purpose covers a wide range of situations, which would include, for example, statements such as 'water-proof' when applied to a diver's watch,[63] or 'child-resistant' when referring to bottles for tablets, or 'rust-proof' when referring to metal tools. It would also include statements about the strength or durability of a product, each of which is an attribute relevant to the fitness for purpose of the product. Arguably, 'usage' would include both proposed usage by the buyer or any third party and its suitability for that purpose, but is also broad enough to include the past usage of the product.[64] Thus, statements such as that the product is second-hand or has had a given number of previous owners, or that a car has been involved in a prestigious road-race or a statement as to the number of miles on the clock, would all fall within the ambit of the phrase 'usage' and, as such, be subject to control and give rise to an offence if untrue.

The final group of attributes detailed in regulation 5(5), which explain the parameters of the 'main characteristics' of the product for the purposes of regulation 5(4) include the quantity of the product, the specification of the product, its geographical or commercial origins, the results to be expected from its usage and the results and material features of tests or checks carried out on the product. The quantity of the product is self-evident and would include any statement as to weight, capacity or volume while also including any statement as to

---

[59] *Ibid.* s.1.   [60] *Ibid.* s.14.

[61] Age is a determining factor when fixing the value of cars.

[62] Trade Descriptions Act 1968, s. 2(1)(d) and (j), respectively. Of course, the CPUT Regulations 2008 are actually giving effect to Art. 6.1 of the Unfair Commercial Practices Directive.

[63] See *Sherratt* v. *Gerald's the American Jeweller's Ltd* (1970) 114 Sol. Jo. 117 in which a watch described as water-proof let in water after being submerged for one hour. See also Griffiths and Griffiths, above n. 51.

[64] As previously governed by the Trade Descriptions Act 1968, s.2(1)(j), which covered 'other history, including previous ownership or use'.

the number of items provided. Thus, e.g., 1 kg of apples or twelve apples would both fall within the ambit of this provision as being details about the quantity being supplied. The specification of the product would include things such as the dimensions of the product in height, length, area, etc., but it is suggested this would also include the capacity and speed of computers and broadband.[65] The geographic origin of a product includes statements about products that have been manufactured outside the United Kingdom and European Union,[66] but is also relevant to products which are marketed with an emphasis on the fact that they have been produced in a particular part of the United Kingdom, e.g., 'made in Wales', 'produced in Cornwall', etc. The commercial origin of the product would include facts such as that the product is part of bankrupt stock[67] or is ex-catalogue or military surplus.[68]

The final two factors are, first, the results to be expected from the use of the product and, secondly, the results or material features of tests or checks carried out on the product. The former would include things such as the expected life-span of the product, e.g., of electrical goods, carpets or double glazing, but also the expected performance of products such as the speed of broadband or the quality of picture from a digital camera. This would include things such as pre-delivery checks on cars, electrical tests on second-hand electrical equipment and safety checks carried out on goods that have been repaired.[69]

Q9 Review the remit of the phrase 'main characteristics of the product' as used in regulation 5(4) and the matters that fall within it.

(iii) The extent of the trader's commitments (regulation 5(4)(c))

The third matter included in regulation 5(4) as interpretive of regulation 5(2)(a) is 'the extent of the trader's commitments'.[70] This requires the trader not to make any false or misleading statements about the extent of his obligations under the commercial practice in question. Thus, this would encompass details of exactly what will be done by the trader and, equally, what will not be done by him. Arguably, confusion about the trader's commitments is most likely to arise in respect of contracts for services where there is potentially more scope for confusion. Thus, for example, if there is preparatory work to be done on site before a conservatory can be installed, will the trader do that work or is the responsibility on the consumer to make the necessary arrangements? In a contract for car repairs, what has been agreed if the repairs are more extensive than

---

[65] *Butterworths Trading and Consumer Law*, above n. 7, Division 1A, para. 11.
[66] The place of origin is highly relevant to any civil law claim for damages in product liability under the Consumer Protection Act 1987 as, if the product is produced outside the European Union, the first importer into the EU will be liable for any injury that it causes.
[67] Given the number of companies being declared insolvent as a result of the trading downturn in the current recession, bankrupt stock may become more common.
[68] See *Butterworths Trading and Consumer Law*, above n. 7, Division 1A, para. 11.
[69] *Ibid.*   [70] CPUT Regulations 2008, reg. 5(4)(c).

expected and, as a consequence, will cost a lot more that the original estimate? The onus is on the trader to ensure that the consumer is not misled about any aspect of the agreement.

(iv) The motives for the commercial practice (regulation 5(4)(d))

The 'motives for the commercial practice'[71] includes any statement as to why the sale of goods is taking place. This will clearly encompass statements about closing down and other sales, which have always given rise to problems, such as the never-ending closing down sale in which the sale drags on and the closure never happens.[72] Such practices would previously have fallen under the Trade Descriptions Act 1968, section 14.[73] Also included within the commercial motives would be things such as 'stock clearance', stock reduction prior to moving to new premises, and a liquidator's sale where the business in question has gone into liquidation. Other examples would include the sale of damaged stock following a flood or other incident in the trader's warehouse.

(v) The nature of the sales process (regulation 5(4)(e))

The 'nature of the sales process'[74] would encompass statements such as that the property in question is to be sold at auction, and whether or not reserve prices will apply to any or all of the products for sale in that auction. It would also include statements such as 'cash only', which inform the potential purchaser about the way in which the sale of the product is to be performed.

(vi) Sponsorship or approval of the trader or the product (regulation 5(4)(f))

The use of statements or symbols about direct or indirect sponsorship of a product or the approval of the trader or the product is included in regulation 5(4)(f). This would include the usage of symbols such as the BSI Kitemark and quality marks sponsored by various trade or professional bodies, such as the mark under the 'Red Tractor' food assurance scheme launched in 2000.[75] The use of trust marks, quality marks and other equivalent indications without the proper authority is always an unfair commercial practice under Schedule 1 paragraph 2, since the use of such a mark encourages reliance on it by the consumer, which may affect a transactional decision made by that consumer as to which product to buy.

---

71 *Ibid*. reg. 5(4)(d).
72 Claims that a trader is about to cease trading or move premises when he is not are now always regarded as an unfair commercial practice under *ibid*. Sch.1 para. 15.
73 It was an offence against Trade Descriptions Act 1968, s.14 for a trader to make a statement which he knew to be false, or to recklessly make a statement which is false, as to the provision in the course of a business of any services, accommodation or facilities, their nature, the time at which they were to be provided, the examination, approval or evaluation of them, or the location or amenities of any accommodation so provided.
74 CPUT Regulations 2008, reg. 5(4)(e).
75 Over 78,000 farmers and growers are now members of the scheme, all committed to maintaining high standards of food safety and hygiene, animal welfare and environmental protection. The

(vii) Price (regulation 5(4)(g),(h))

The next two factors both relate to the price at which the product is being sold. Price is an extremely important factor in the making of any transactional decision, whether the decision is to buy, not buy, sell or not sell. It follows that stringent controls are needed over pricing and all matters relating to pricing. Prior to the CPUT Regulations 2008, issues regarding misleading statements about price were governed by the Consumer Protection Act 1987, Part III, with additional guidance provided by the Code of Practice for Traders on Price Indications.[76] The first of the two price-related paragraphs refers to the price or manner in which the price is calculated.[77] Clearly, this refers to straight-forward statements about price but also would include unit pricing by, for example, weight, length or capacity whereby the actual price for the product concerned is calculated by reference to the unit price. This would include everything from cheese and fruit sold by the kilogramme to curtain fabric sold by the metre or drink sold by volume. The Code of Practice for Traders on Price Indications, which explained and gave examples of pricing controls under the Consumer Protection Act 1987, has been repealed and replaced by a new guidance, the BERR Pricing Practices Guide.[78] This provides traders with examples of good practice in a multiplicity of pricing situations, such as comparison with their own previous price, references to value or worth, prices relating to particular sizes, the sale of entertainment tickets and credit facilities.

The guidance also addresses pricing issues that are closely connected to the second of the two pricing controls included in regulation 5(4)(h), namely, the existence of a specific price advantage. Typically, this might relate to a comparison of the prices charged by a trader with those charged by a competitor[79] or might relate to some special price, such as an introductory offer price or an 'after-sale' or 'after promotion' price,[80] or comparisons relating to different circumstances such as 'when perfect' comparisons.[81]

Q10 Consider the scope of the criteria discussed in paragraphs (c) to (h) of regulation 5(4).

Red Tractor logo can be spotted on thousands of products such as beef, lamb, pork, chicken, turkey, milk, cheese, cream, cereals, vegetables, sugar, flour, fruit and salads in shops and supermarkets everywhere. See www.redtractor.org.uk/rtassurance/assurance/about/rta.eb.

[76] In addition to the 1987 Act, there were also some statutory instruments dealing with particular aspects of pricing controls. These SIs were repealed along with Part III of the 1987 Act by the CPUT Regulations.

[77] CPUT Regulations 2008, reg. 5(4)(g).

[78] Department for Business, Enterprise and Regulatory Reform *Pricing Practices Guide: Guidance for Traders on Good Practice in Giving Information about Prices* (London, 2008).

[79] For example, it is common practice in supermarkets for shelf edge tickets to show not merely the price at which the trader is selling the goods but also the price, usually higher, at which a major competitor is selling the same item. See BERR *Pricing Practices Guide*, above n. 78, Part 1.5.

[80] *Ibid.* Part 1.3.   [81] *Ibid.* Part 1.4.

(viii) The need for a service, part, replacement or repair (regulation 5(4)(i))

This is most likely to relate to contracts for the provision of a service where a consumer is falsely told that the item is in need of repair or replacement, such as new parts for a car or an electrical appliance, or where a product is faulty and the trader informs the consumer that the item cannot be repaired and will have to be replaced. The obvious motive in both of these situations is to persuade the consumer to pay for a service or repair that the product does not need or, alternatively, to persuade the consumer to buy an unnecessary new replacement item instead of retaining or repairing the one that they already possess. In either instance, the practice is intended to encourage the consumer to believe that the item they already own is in a poorer condition than is really the case. It must be remembered that the CPUT Regulations 2008 apply not only when the trader is supplying the product in question but also when they are acquiring it and, hence, false or deceptive statements made about the need for a repair to an item when the trader is acquiring it will be covered by this provision.[82] The most obvious scenario would be undervaluing a car during a part-exchange deal by suggesting that the vehicle needs repairs when this is not the case.

(ix) The nature, attributes and rights of the trader (regulation 5(4)(j))

Regulation 5(4)(j) addresses the nature, attributes and rights of the trader. This paragraph is qualified by the contents of regulation 5(6), which details various aspects of the trader's person, qualifications and business attributes. Thus, on a personal level, it considers the trader's qualifications and his identity, whether as an individual or as the representative of a company. Identity may be important in that the consumer may want to deal with only one person or company[83] and would not be prepared to contract with anyone else. Qualifications are significant in that they make a statement about the ability and professionalism of the person in question. Thus, for a trader to falsely suggest that he possesses qualifications may encourage a consumer to employ that trader, a decision he would not have made had he known that the trader lacked a relevant qualification.[84] Other factors that are relevant in respect of the nature of the trader and his attributes and rights are his assets, both physical and financial, the status of his business and any approvals that he claims to have, together with any affiliations or connections that he may have to trade bodies or organisations, the

---

[82] For an example of a decision under the Trade Descriptions Act 1968, see *Fletcher* v. *Budgen* [1974] 2 All ER 1243, in which a trader, when buying a car from a consumer, falsely told the consumer that the car was unrepairable and only worth scrap value.

[83] Mistakes as to identity arising from fraudulent actions of a buyer pretending to be somebody else have given rise to numerous civil law cases in which the innocent purchaser has sought to have a contract declared void or voidable for mistake as to identity. See, e.g., *Cundy* v. *Lindsay* (1878) 3 App. Cas. 459, HL; *Kings Norton Metal Co. Ltd* v. *Edridge, Merrett & Co. Ltd* (1897) 14 TLR 98, CA; *Lewis* v. *Averay* [1971] 3 All ER 907; *Citibank NA* v. *Brown Shipley & Co. Ltd* [1991] 2 All ER 690.

[84] For a decision made under the Trade Descriptions Act 1968, see *R* v. *Breeze* [1973] 2 All ER 1141, in which the defendant stated that he was a qualified architect when this was not the case.

ownership of any industrial, commercial or intellectual property rights and any awards or distinctions that he, his business or his product may possess.

(x) The consumer's rights or the risks he may face (regulation 5(4)(k))

The final factor to be included in regulation 5(4) are the rights of a consumer or the risks that he may face. Consumers have a wide variety of rights, including the most well-known, such as rights under the Sale of Goods Act 1979[85] and the corresponding rights under the Supply of Goods and Services Act 1982.[86] In addition, other rights would include, among many others, rights under the Supply of Goods (Implied Terms) Act 1973 in relation to hire-purchase contracts, rights under the Consumer Credit Act 1974, rights under the Consumer Protection (Distance Selling) Regulations 2000[87] and rights under the Cancellation of Contracts made in a Consumer's Home or Place of Work etc. Regulations 2008.[88] A statement that suggested that these rights did not exist or had wrongfully been excluded would be classed as a misleading statement such as to give rise to liability under regulation 5(2)(a), as would any statement that a consumer's rights are a distinctive feature of the trader's product.[89] The risks that a consumer might face would include what remedies would be available to him if the product failed after the guarantee period had expired.[90]

Breaches of regulation 5 of the CPUT Regulations 2008 may result in a two-fold outcome, namely, the commission of a strict liability criminal offence under regulation 9 with the consequent penalties of a fine up to the statutory maximum on summary conviction and an unlimited fine or imprisonment for up to two years or both for a conviction on indictment,[91] and also the possibility of a Community infringement under the Enterprise Act 2002 leading to civil law enforcement via undertakings, enforcement orders and interim enforcement orders.[92]

---

[85] The most well publicised rights under the Sale of Goods Act 1979 are undoubtedly those relating to the right to pass title, sale by description, satisfactory quality and fitness for purpose, and sale by sample which give rights on breach to rescission of the contract and damages, see Part 2 Chapter 2. Alternative remedies of repair, replacement, reduction of the purchase price and rescission are also available under s.48 of the 1979 Act. These statutory remedies cannot be excluded against a person dealing as a consumer (Unfair Contract Terms Act 1977, s.6(2)) and can only be excluded against a person who is not dealing as a consumer when the exclusion clause is reasonable (Unfair Contract Terms Act 1977, s.6(3)). Notices which purported to give effect to a term which would offend s.6 were prohibited previously by the Consumer Transactions (Restrictions on Statements) Order 1976, SI 1976/1813, which was repealed by the CPUT Regulations 2008.

[86] The Supply of Goods and Services Act 1982 provides for implied conditions in contracts for the transfer of goods other than by sale or hire purchase and implied conditions in contracts of hire. It also provides for the inclusion of implied terms in contracts for services of reasonable care and skill, stipulations as to time of performance and stipulations as to contractual consideration. See Part 2 Chapter 4.

[87] SI 2000/2334.   [88] SI 2008/1816.   [89] CPUT Regulations 2008 Sch. 1 para. 10.

[90] See *Butterworths Trading and Consumer Law*, above n. 7, Division 1A, para. 11.

[91] CPUT Regulations 2008, reg. 13.

[92] Enforcement under the Enterprise Act 2002, Part 8 was discussed in Part 5 Chapter 1.

Q11 Consider the impact of the factors contained in paragraphs (i) to (k) of regulation 5(4) on the meaning of the phrase 'misleading action'.

6 Misleading omissions

Regulation 6 introduces the concept of a misleading omission, although in *R* v *Haesler*,[93] deliberately hiding information was held to be an offence contrary to section 1 of the Trade Descriptions Act 1968.[94] Regulation 6(1) describes the scenarios that will give rise to a misleading omission, namely, that the commercial practice either omits or hides material information,[95] or it provides material information in a manner which is unclear, unintelligible, ambiguous or untimely,[96] or the commercial practice fails to identify its commercial intent unless it is already obvious from the context.[97] In respect of any of these, there is also a requirement that the misleading omission causes or is likely to cause the average consumer to take a transactional decision that he would not otherwise have taken. However, whether information has been deliberately omitted, hidden, etc. must be considered in its factual context.[98] The parameters of that context are laid out in regulation 6(2) as encompassing the features and circumstances of the practice, the limitations of the medium used to communicate it and, where that medium imposes limitations of time or space, what steps the trader has taken to make the information available to consumers. Thus, for example, the size of the product may restrict the amount of information that can be given, e.g., a chocolate bar wrapper provides far less space for information than a cereal box or the outer cardboard box containing flat-packed furniture. In a situation such as the chocolate bar, additional information relating to offers might be included either on a point-of-sale flyer or on a website belonging to the manufacturer. Similarly, a time limitation will be imposed when dealing with television advertisements that might only last fifteen or thirty seconds, with additional information being supplied separately via a website. By contrast, such information might have been readily available in a magazine advertisement for the same product. With either the chocolate bar or the television advertisement, a statement that terms and conditions apply will notify the prospective purchaser that more information is available and, typically, where it can be found.

---

[93] [1973] RTR 486.

[94] *R* v. *Haesler* [1973] RTR 486, in which a car was re-registered when being brought to the mainland from the Channel Islands. The statement 'Ex Channel Islands', which appeared in the registration document and indicated that the car had been previously registered elsewhere and so was older than its current registration suggested, was erased by the defendant car dealer before selling the vehicle. It was held that this amounted to a false trade description contrary to the Trade Descriptions Act 1968 s.1.

[95] CPUT Regulations 2008, reg. 6(1)(a) and (b), respectively.

[96] *Ibid*. reg. 6(1)(c).   [97] *Ibid*. reg. 6(1)(d).

[98] *Ibid*. reg. 6(1) See OFT Guidance, above n. 8, para. 7.19 and *Butterworths Trading and Consumer Law*, above n. 7, Division 1A, para. 12.

In analysing and applying regulation 6(1), the concept of omitting material information is relatively straight-forward as it simply requires that the information is not included and there is no specified alternative way to access it. By contrast, hiding material information is more complicated in that the relevant information is present but the trader has deliberately attempted to prevent the consumer from seeing it. Thus, it has been suggested that hiding material information at the end of a long contract or in very small print or, even, in a separate document would, depending on the context, constitute hiding it contrary to regulation 6(1)(b).[99] The requirement that material information be provided in a manner that is clear, intelligible, unambiguous and timely is an obvious demand for clarity whether it be in the way that the information is drafted or in the way that it is presented. Thus, arguably, it requires plain English as opposed to technical jargon, with unambiguous wording. Further, it must be legible, which calls into play aspects of presentation such as the size and colour of any lettering or diagram and the background colour of the paper on which it is displayed.[100] The paragraph also requires that the information be provided in a timely manner, which must be before the consumer makes any transactional decision, otherwise the requirement is redundant.

Regulation 6(1)(d) is slightly different in its approach in that it requires the commercial intent of the practice to be identified unless that is obvious from the context. The clear implication of this is that the fact that the trader is acting with commercial intent is always material information. Certainly, previous legislation required traders to disclose their business status, with it being an offence to withhold or secrete that information[101] and hence this is not a totally new approach. The commercial intent of the practice will often be obvious if, for example, it occurs in a shop or is included in a catalogue published by a trader or appears on a website belonging to a trader. But it would be less obvious if it is disguised as a market survey or as an editorial in a magazine or a consumer item on the television or radio, or where the trader is deliberately masquerading as a private individual with the intention of hiding his commercial credentials.[102]

The regulation 6(1) controls revolve around the omission of material information, which is defined as being the information which the average consumer needs, according to the context, to make an informed transactional decision[103] and includes any information required as the result of a Community

---

[99] See *Butterworths Trading and Consumer Law*, above n. 7, Division 1A, para. 12.

[100] *Ibid.*

[101] Business Advertisements (Disclosure) Order 1977, SI 1977/1918. See also *Stainethorpe* v. *Bailey* [1980] RTR 7 for a decision under the Trade Descriptions Act 1968 on a related point.

[102] This would be important in relation to claims under the Sale of Goods Act 1979, s.14, which deals with satisfactory quality and fitness for purpose. As that section only applies where the sale was in the course of a business, a trader could try to avoid all liability under that section by pretending to be a private individual involved in a private sale.

[103] CPUT Regulations 2008, reg. 6(3)(a).

obligation.[104] What information is required will largely depend on the circumstances of the sale and the product in question. It is reasonable to assume that, in most situations, the price of the product will constitute material information. Further, if the rationale behind the material information is to allow the consumer to make an informed transactional decision, then clearly it must be provided before the decision is made and, as such, must be provided in a timely manner.[105]

This definition of what constitutes material information is extended considerably when the commercial practice in question involves an invitation to purchase.[106] When that is the case, certain specified information will always be deemed to be material unless it is already apparent from the context and it must be provided in addition to any information already required by virtue of regulation 6(3) as discussed above. The required material information includes the main characteristics of the product to the extent appropriate to the product and to the medium being used to communicate the invitation to purchase. For a simple product that requires no additional information as to its characteristics and when the price is included with the product, it may be that there is no other material information needed.[107] This may vary depending on whether the consumer is purchasing in a shop with the opportunity to see and perhaps handle the product prior to sale, or is purchasing products that are advertised in a magazine or on a website when additional information might be needed.

The identity of the trader, including his trading name and the name of any trader on whose behalf he is trading, together with their geographical addresses,[108] is classed as material information. This is important as it allows the consumer to be certain of the identity of the person responsible for the commercial practice and how to contact them should the need arise. The geographical address is crucial in this regard as, of course, merely knowing a website address does not, of itself, allow the consumer to contact the trader. While the suffix at the end of a web address may identify the country in which the trader is based, it does not do any more than that. If a consumer is to be able to enforce their legal rights, they must be able to identify the location of the trader and the jurisdiction to which they are subject.

---

[104] *Ibid*. reg. 6(3)(b). For a useful chart listing those provisions in English law that give effect to relevant EU Directives, see *Butterworths Trading and Consumer Law*, above n. 7, Division 1A, para. 12.

[105] See, e.g., OFT Guidance, above n. 8, para. 7.17, which gives as an example the need for restaurants to provide details of the prices of food and drink to consumers before they order.

[106] An invitation to purchase is defined in reg. 2(1) as a 'commercial communication that includes both the characteristics of the product and the price in a way appropriate to that communication in such a way as to permit the consumer to make a purchase'.

[107] See OFT Guidance, above n. 8, para. 7.34, which gives an example of a pencil being sold in a shop. The colour and thickness of the lead are apparent from looking at it and the price is given. The identity of the trader is obvious and there are no special requirements relating to delivery or complaint handling.

[108] CPUT Regulations 2008, reg. 6(4)(b) and (c), respectively.

The price of the goods is also material information. Hence, there is a stipulation that either the price (including taxes) or, alternatively, the method by which the price can reasonably be calculated must be provided.[109] This would include price lists on display in cafes, restaurants, etc., but would also include unit pricing on shelf edge tickets that allow consumers to calculate the price for goods that they wish to buy. Where appropriate, material information will also include all additional freight, delivery or postal charges and, where that sum cannot be calculated beforehand, a statement that such charges will be payable.[110]

The trader is expected to act within the confines of, and in the manner to be expected by the demands of professional diligence. Where matters relating to arrangements for payment, delivery, performance and complaint handling depart from the normal requirements of professional diligence, any information about them will be deemed to be material for the purposes of regulation 6, with any withholding of relevant information being a material omission. Finally, when dealing with products and transactions which attract a right of cancellation, the existence of that right is material information for this purpose and so must be disclosed if the trader is to avoid liability under regulation 6.

Non-compliance with regulation 6 may lead to enforcement bodies providing advice and guidance to encourage compliance but can also lead to criminal prosecution for a strict liability offence under regulation 10 for summary offences or offences on indictment. It can also give rise to enforcement action under the Enterprise Act 2002, Part 8, with enforcement bodies seeking undertakings, enforcement orders and interim enforcement orders.[111]

Q12 Consider what constitutes 'material information' for the purposes of regulation 6 and the ways in which it can be withheld from a prospective purchaser.

7 Aggressive commercial practices

A well-known, though hopefully not common, problem is the use by some traders of aggressive commercial practices in order to force a consumer to buy goods or services, typically against their will. In this regard, doorstep selling has always attracted particular comment and criticism for practices such as refusing to leave a consumer's house until the consumer has signed a contract for the goods being sold, even if this involved the trader refusing to leave for several hours or even until late at night. It was against this background that cancellation

---

[109] *Ibid.* reg. 6(4)(d).   [110] *Ibid.* reg. 6(4)(e).
[111] Enforcement strategies and processes are dealt with in Part 5 Chapter 1.

rights were introduced for consumers in respect of contracts signed away from business premises[112] so as to allow the consumer to think again, both in the cold light of day and when the oppressive influence of the salesman had been removed.

The definition of aggressive practices under regulation 7 goes far wider than merely suggesting a threat of physical violence and includes practices that might not, at first glance, be classed as aggressive within the traditional meaning of the word. Regulation 7(1) defines an aggressive commercial practice as one which, in its factual context and taking account of all its features and circumstances, significantly impairs or is likely to significantly impair the freedom of choice of the average consumer or his conduct in relation to the product concerned through the use of harassment, coercion or undue influence. It should be noted that the impairment of freedom of choice or of conduct must be significant.[113] It follows that if the impact is only slight there will not be a breach of regulation 7. As with the other controlled practices, there is no requirement that a consumer has actually been affected, merely the likelihood that the commercial practice in question would have an impact on a consumer. The impact must be caused by harassment, coercion or undue influence. Neither harassment not coercion are defined in the regulation, although coercion is stated to include the use of physical force and the OFT expressly stated that the terms 'harassment' and 'coercion' include both physical and non-physical pressure, including psychological pressure.[114] In the absence of definitions, the words must be taken to have their usual meaning, with the courts having the opportunity to refine the terms in context.

Undue influence is defined as meaning 'exploiting a position of power in relation to the consumer so as to apply pressure, even without using or threatening to use physical force, in a way which significantly limits the consumer's ability to make an informed choice'.[115] This covers the situation where the consumer does not have an equality of bargaining power because of a level of influence achieved and used by the trader. This would include, for example, the repairer of goods who has done additional work without the agreement of the consumer but who refuses to return the goods to the consumer until the latter has paid for the additional unauthorised repairs.[116] Because the trader has possession of the goods, he can use that position of power to wrongfully influence the behaviour of the consumer.[117] Similarly, a creditor can misuse his influence over a debtor

---

[112] See Cancellation of Contracts made in a Consumer's Home or Place of Work etc. Regulations 2008, SI 2008/1816, which replaced the previous provisions under the Consumer Protection (Cancellation of Contracts Concluded away from Business Premises) Regulations 1987, SI 1987/2117.

[113] The example given above of a trader staying in a consumer's home until he feels compelled to sign a contract for foods or services would be classed as a significant impairment, see OFT Guidance, above n. 8, para. 8.6.

[114] *Ibid.* para. 8.3.   [115] CPUT Regulations 2008, reg. 7(3)(b).

[116] OFT Guidance, above n. 8, para. 8.4.

[117] *Ibid.*

to pressure the debtor to take out a further loan[118] by, for example, encouraging the debtor to take out a new consolidation loan to cover his existing debts and to get additional usable credit.

When analysing whether any given activity is harassment, coercion or undue influence within the meaning of regulation 7, the commercial practice must be considered in the context of the facts and of all its features and circumstances.[119] Regulation 7(2) outlines what those factors include. Thus, consideration must be given to the timing, location, nature or persistence of the practices.[120] Timing would include, for example, late night telephone calls or visits to the consumer's house, while location would include calling on the consumer at his place of work or isolating the consumer at a location which it is impossible for him to leave until he signs a contract.[121] Timing might also relate to surrounding circumstances, such as immediately following a bereavement or redundancy when the consumer may be vulnerable, and location would include approaches made in a hospital.[122] The nature of the commercial practice would include the way and medium by which the consumer is approached, which includes approaching the consumer's employer or a member of his family, while persistence would clearly encompass repeated visits, phone calls, texts or emails or other methods of contact.[123]

As might be expected, the use of threatening or abusive language or behaviour[124] will be considered when assessing whether coercion, harassment or undue influence exists. Whether such language or behaviour has occurred will be a question of fact for the court to determine.

The third factor to be weighed in the balance is whether the trader has exploited a specific misfortune or circumstance of such gravity as might affect the judgement of the consumer when deciding upon the proposed transaction.[125] The relevant misfortune or circumstance must be known to the trader who has used it to influence the decision made by the consumer about the product. This clearly requires the trader to act knowingly. Examples of exploiting a

---

[118] *Ibid.*

[119] CPUT Regulations 2008, reg. 7(1).   [120] *Ibid.* reg. 7(2)(a).

[121] The OFT gives the example of a holiday club presentation being made at a distant location with no opportunity for return transport until the consumer signs a contract, see OFT Guidance, above n. 8, para. 8.11. Containing a consumer in a location and restricting his ability to leave might also constitute false imprisonment for which the trader could be held liable to pay damages.

[122] *Butterworths Trading and Consumer Law*, above n. 7, Division 1A, para. 13. An example of an approach in a hospital would include, e.g., an accident claims company signing up injured and traumatised patients in the casualty department of a hospital. While there is no objection to such companies advertising their services in a hospital casualty department, representatives speaking to and signing up clients might constitute undue influence. The same would be true of funeral directors approaching recently bereaved families while they are still in the hospital following the patient's death.

[123] Such persistence would constitute harassment.

[124] CPUT Regulations 2008, reg. 7(2)(b).   [125] *Ibid.* reg. 7(2)(c).

misfortune would include exploiting a recently bereaved family,[126] or someone who has been the victim of a burglary[127] or a violent crime.[128]

The fourth factor to be considered is any onerous or disproportionate non-contractual barrier imposed by the trader when the consumer wants to exercise his rights under the contract.[129] This would include termination rights and the right to switch to another trader, both of which are expressly included in regulation 7(2)(d) but would also include such things as the enforcement of rights relating to faulty goods and the exercise of cancellation rights. Non-contractual barriers would include requiring the consumer to return goods to a place some distance from their residence, as this would involve postal charges or travelling costs, either of which might be significant.[130] A gloss on this practice would be a demand that the consumer return the goods in person.[131]

The final factor referred to in regulation 7(2) is any threat to take any action which cannot legally be taken. This would include threats to take legal action to enforce a contract or recover a debt where no right of action exists, e.g., a threat by a debt collector to use bailiffs to recover money for unenforceable debts.[132] In a time of recession when personal debts are running high[133] and redundancy[134] may bring about serious financial pressures on consumers, the chances that a consumer may fall behind with debt repayments will rise, with a consequent upturn in the use of debt collectors and court actions. While enforcement of legitimate debts is to be expected, the attempted recovery of unenforceable

---

[126] Examples of such exploitation would include the example given by the OFT of staff in a funeral parlour persuading the relatives of a recently deceased person to avoid the potential for family shame by buying a more expensive coffin than they might otherwise have done, see OFT Guidance, above n. 8, para. 8.11. A similar example might involve pressure by a funeral director to buy the best coffin available because the deceased would deserve the best. Another unfair commercial practice that might arise out of bereavement would be the practice by some estate agents of scouring the bereavement notices in local papers and then visiting the bereaved partner or delivering marketing material offering to buy their property, typically at an undervalue, so that the bereaved person will not have the worry and stress of maintaining the property and paying the bills.

[127] Such exploitation might involve a company selling burglar alarms which contacts the victims of recent burglaries, exploiting their shock and vulnerability at having their home invaded, and perhaps ransacked, by a stranger and who might be seeking therefore to improve their household security.

[128] For other examples see *Butterworths Trading and Consumer Law*, above n. 7, Division 1A, para. 13.

[129] CPUT Regulations 2008, reg. 7(2)(d).

[130] This would be particularly relevant if the item is either very bulky or very heavy.

[131] See *Butterworths Trading and Consumer Law*, above n. 7, Division 1A, para. 13.

[132] See OFT Guidance, above n. 8, para. 8.11.

[133] In July 2011, UK personal debt stood at £1,452 billion with consumer credit lending standing at £210 billion. Household debt was £8,076 (excluding mortgage) while every individual in the United Kingdom owed £55,862 (including mortgage). A house was being repossessed every 14 minutes. See www.creditaction.org/helpful-resources/debt-statistics.html.

[134] In July 2011, 1,271 people were being made redundant every day. One person was being declared insolvent or bankrupt every 4.36 minutes. See www.creditaction.org/helpful-resources/debt-statistics.html.

debts would put added pressure on consumers and would constitute an aggressive commercial practice.

For liability to arise under regulation 7, the commercial practice in question must not simply involve harassment, coercion or undue influence sufficiently serious to impair or be likely to impair the consumer's freedom of choice or conduct, it must also have caused or be likely to cause the consumer to take a different transactional decision from the one that he would have taken or would be likely to have taken in the absence of the unfair commercial practice.[135] As with the other unfair commercial practices under regulations 3, 5 and 6, the impact upon the transactional decision of the consumer is central to establishing the existence of an aggressive commercial practice.

A breach of regulation 7 may give rise to a strict liability offence under regulation 11 and will also constitute a Community infringement within the meaning of the Enterprise Act 2002 and, as such, be enforceable via undertakings, enforcement orders and interim enforcement orders.

Q13 Analyse whether the provisions controlling aggressive behaviour successfully address the unfair practices concerned.

8 Commercial practices which are automatically unfair

In addition to the categories of unfair commercial practices contrary to regulations 3 to 7 of the CPUT Regulations 2008, Schedule 1 lists thirty-one commercial practices which are considered to be unfair in all circumstances. As the practices are always classed as unfair and are automatically prohibited, it follows that there is no need to consider the impact or likely impact of these practices on a consumer[136] and, equally, no need to consider whether the relevant practice has affected any transactional decision. With two exceptions – the use of advertorials[137] and an exhortation to children to buy or get others to buy advertised products[138] – a breach of any of the specified commercial practices is a strict liability offence under regulation 12. In addition to criminal liability, breach of any of the thirty-one commercial practices listed is a Community infringement under the Enterprise Act 2002 and can be enforced via undertakings, enforcement orders and interim enforcement orders. In addition, depending on the facts, any of the practices concerned might also offend against one of the prohibitions contained in the Regulations and give rise to liability under that provision as well.

Many of the practices listed have long been recognised as undesirable or exploitative practices and have been regulated through a range of legal provisions. Thus, while Schedule 1 officially gives effect to Annex 1 to the Unfair Commercial Practices Directive,[139] it can be viewed as bringing together many

---

[135] CPUT Regulations 2008, reg. 7(1)(b).   [136] See OFT Guidance, above n. 8, para. 6.1
[137] CPUT Regulations 2008, Sch. 1 para. 11.   [138] *Ibid.* Sch. 1 para. 28.
[139] Directive 2005/29/EC.

of the anti-consumer commercial practices that have caused problems in the past. Many of the Acts and Regulations that controlled them previously have either been repealed or amended by the CPUT Regulations 2008.

Although there are thirty-one unfair commercial practices listed in Schedule 1, some of them have been grouped together here for ease of analysis.

(a) Nature of services or facilities

The first four of the prohibited practices (paragraphs 1 to 4) relate in some way to claims regarding the nature of services or facilities, which, prior to the advent of the CPUT Regulations 2008, would have constituted an offence under the Trade Descriptions Act 1968.[140] The first practice is committed by a trader claiming to be a signatory of a code of practice when he is not. This provision applies both to OFT approved codes of practice and also to other codes of practice promulgated by professional organisations and bodies. A trader who professes to be a signatory of a code of practice is encouraging the consumer to believe that he is trustworthy and will uphold the values promulgated by the organisation, and that as such, the consumer can rely upon him to perform the work concerned to a good standard within a reasonable time and for a reasonable price.

The remaining three practices in this group relate to claims regarding endorsements or approval by some body. Thus, the display of a trust mark, quality mark or equivalent without having the requisite authorisation is always unfair,[141] as is claiming that a code of conduct has an endorsement from a public or other body when this is not the case. The last of the four relates to false claims that a trader, his commercial practices and/or his products have been approved, endorsed or authorised by a public or private body when they have not been, or where he is making such a claim while not complying with the terms of any approval, endorsement or authorisation. Paragraph 4 would be breached if, for example, a gas-installer professes to be CORGI-registered when he is not.[142]

(b) Advertising goods that are not available

The next three unfair commercial practices relate to situations in which the trader is advertising goods without having a realistic possibility, or even the intention, of being able to supply them to some or all of the prospective purchasers. Paragraph 5 of Schedule 1 states that it is an unfair commercial practice for a trader to issue an invitation to purchase without revealing whether

---

[140] Trade Descriptions Act 1968, s. 14.

[141] This would occur if a trader were to wrongly include a trust or quality mark on his product or in his advertising literature, as it fraudulently claims a level of approval for his product that does not exist.

[142] See OFT Guidance, above n. 8, para. 6.1.

he has reasonable grounds for believing that he will be able to offer those goods for supply, or alternatively be able to get another trader to supply them, at that price for a reasonable period. The period must be assessed by reference to the product, the scale of the advertising and the price at which it is being offered. Further, the trader must be able to establish that he will be able to offer the goods in sufficient quantities bearing those factors in mind. Thus, a trader would breach this provision if he placed an advertisement knowing that he would not be able to satisfy likely demand for the relevant product at the price offered. If he is aware of this probability, he should qualify the advertisement with a statement such as 'limited quantities only'.

When discussing misleading actions under regulation 5, reference was made to the practice of 'bait and switch' whereby a trader advertises an item with no real intention of supplying it but rather using the advertisement as a means of persuading the consumer to buy an alternative, typically more expensive, item. In addition to that possibility, bait and switch is assumed automatically to be an unfair commercial practice by virtue of Schedule 1 paragraph 6. It provides that the practice occurs when a trader makes an invitation to purchase, which necessarily includes the price, and then either refuses to show the advertised item to the consumer, or refuses to take orders for it within a reasonable time, or demonstrates a defective sample of it with the intention of promoting a different product. The intention of the trader to promote an alternative product is important, suggesting a degree of under-lying fraud in his actions. Thus, in the example given by the OFT Guidance,[143] a trader who advertises a television in his window for £300 and then dem-onstrates a defective television with the intention of persuading a consumer to buy an alternative set, probably one attracting a higher profit margin, will breach this provision.

When making purchases, it is natural for purchasers to want the opportun-ity to think about their prospective purchase. However, in situations where the product will only be available for a limited time, there is less opportunity for reflection and, arguably, consumers are more likely to impulse buy rather than risk not being able to get the product in the future. Thus, their freedom of choice may be affected by statements such as 'closing down sale', 'last few days' and 'must end Saturday'. All of these slogans indicate that the product is only available for a limited period and, hence, that if the consumer wants to buy one, he must do so quickly. Given this premise, falsely making a state-ment that the product will either only be available for a limited period or only available on those terms for a limited period, in order to elicit an immedi-ate decision depriving the consumer of sufficient opportunity or time to make an informed choice,[144] is automatically an unfair commercial practice (paragraph 7).

---

[143] *Ibid.*   [144] CPUT Regulations 2008, Sch. 1 para. 7.

(c) Language

One of the underlying rationales behind EU consumer law is harmonisation and from that comes the opportunity to promote cross-border trade.[145] Cross-border trade necessarily brings into play the whole issue of language and the consequent importance of consumers being provided with all of the relevant information about a product in a language that they understand. Schedule 1, paragraph 8 deals with some of the implications of the language issue. It relates to the provision of after-sales service to a consumer where the trader has communicated with the consumer prior to the transaction in a language which is not an official language in the EEA state in which the trader is based, but has not informed the consumer prior to him being committed to the transaction that the after-sales service will actually be provided in a different language. Thus, to quote the example proffered by the OFT, a trader in England who communicates with a consumer in German prior to the sale but fails to inform him that the after-sales service for the product will only be available through the medium of English would fall foul of this provision.[146]

(d) No legal right of sale

Schedule 1 paragraph 9 deals with the situation where the trader creates the impression that the product can be sold legally when this is not the case. This does not necessarily imply that the goods are inherently illegal but, rather, that the seller does not have the legal right to sell them. This echoes the provisions of the Sale of Goods Act 1979, section 12, which deals with the implied condition in contracts for the sale of goods that the seller has the right to sell the goods in question.[147] Thus, it might be because the goods have been stolen and, as such, the seller has no title to them or, alternatively, because to sell them would involve the breach of intellectual property rights belonging to another person.[148] In either instance, or indeed in any similar scenario in which the trader wrongly states or implies an ability to sell the goods legally which is not true, paragraph 9 will apply.

(e) Falsely claiming that legal rights are a distinctive feature of the product

Schedule 1 paragraph 10 deals with the legal rights of the consumer and any attempt by a trader to suggest that those legal rights are, in some way,

---

[145] The consumer *acquis*, which encompasses the eight major EU Directives affecting consumer law, is currently under review with the likelihood that some of the Directives will be amended.

[146] See OFT Guidance, above n. 8, para. 6.1.

[147] Other Acts contain similar provisions applicable to different types of contract, e.g., Supply of Goods and Services Act 1982, Part 1, which implies a similar condition into contracts for the transfer of goods other than by sale or hire-purchase.

[148] *Niblett Ltd* v. *Confectioners' Materials Co.* [1921] 3 KB 387; *contra Microbeads AG* v. *Vinehurst Road Haulage Ltd* [1975] 1 All ER 529. For a full discussion of Sales of Goods Act 1979, s.12 see Part 2 Chapter 2.

a distinctive feature of the offer being made by the trader. Thus, for example, the rights of the consumer under the implied conditions contained in sections 12–15 of the Sale of Goods Act 1979 are implied by statute and cannot be excluded against a consumer. As such, the rights will always exist irrespective of any action or conduct by the trader. The consumer has a right to expect that the goods will comply with any description applied to them and that they will be of a satisfactory quality and fit for their intended purpose, with any breach of those conditions giving rise to a right of rescission. Any suggestion by a trader that the right to a refund in that situation is a distinctive feature of his product is untrue and is potentially misleading to a consumer, who might wrongly believe that those rights would not exist if he were to buy the item elsewhere. Further, it is possible that the consumer might have paid a higher price for the goods in the erroneous belief that he was getting some extra protection as part of the deal.

Q14 Analyse the ambit of the first ten commercial practices listed in Schedule 1 (section 8(a)–(e) above) which are automatically deemed to be unfair.

(f) Advertorials

Schedule 1 paragraph 11 addresses the issue of advertorials and it is one of only two unfair commercial practices listed in Schedule 1 that does not attract criminal liability. Practices falling within paragraph 11 only trigger civil law enforcement under Part 8 of the Enterprise Act 2002. Essentially, an advertorial is an advertisement masquerading as an independent publication. Typically, it takes the format of an editorial, which encourages consumers to rely upon it believing it to be independent of the manufacturer and, as such, the consumer is more likely to take its content at face value rather than recognising it as an advertisement in which the manufacturer has a vested interest. To avoid the potential for the consumer to be misled, a trader who has paid for an advertorial must make that clear to the consumer in the content, or by images or sounds that the consumer will identify. Failure to do so brings the practice within paragraph 11.

(g) Exploiting fears about personal safety

Schedule 1 paragraph 12 seeks to prevent unscrupulous traders from exploiting any fear that a consumer may have about his personal safety or that of his family. The fear of crime is well documented and a consumer may seek to minimise any perceived risk to himself or his family by purchasing personal safety alarms, or burglar alarms, or security cameras for his property. As long as these items are sold objectively there is no problem. However, if the trader exaggerates the risk to the consumer by, for example, overstating the risk of burglaries in the area in which the consumer lives, then paragraph 12 may apply. However, to be actionable, the claim must be materially inaccurate and must relate to the nature and extent of the risk to the consumer if he does not buy the item in question. The requirement for a material inaccuracy means that advertising puffs are not included and acceptable levels of exaggeration are permitted as part of the sales process.

(h) Passing off and pyramid selling

The next two paragraphs (13 and 14) deal with issues that are already well recognised as being illegal, first, passing off and, secondly, pyramid selling. Passing off occurs when a consumer is misled into buying goods believing that they have been manufactured by one person when they have, in fact, been produced by somebody else. This would arise if, for example, trader A deliberately produces goods of the same type and dimensions as goods produced by trader B and also packages them in a way so similar to the packaging used by trader B that a consumer would be misled into thinking that they are buying goods produced by trader B. This practice is fraudulent, as the trader is deliberately presenting the goods in a way intended to deceive. Under the tort of passing off, trader B may sue trader A for damages in respect of the imitation of his goods by the latter and any loss of business that resulted. However, paragraph 13 is more concerned with protecting the consumer from this undesirable practice, as opposed to protecting the innocent trader who has lost the opportunity to do business and make a profit.

Pyramid selling has been recognised as an undesirable and unscrupulous practice for many years. The practice works by encouraging consumers to invest in a product or service with the promise that they will make a significant profit by introducing other consumers to the pyramid. Thus, for example, the consumer may have to introduce four new customers; each of whom has to introduce another four customers, etc., with each level of new customers paying a fee to join. Some of the fee is then paid to consumers higher up the pyramid, with the remainder going as profit to the person organising the practice. It works exactly like a chain letter. As the first customer rises up the pyramid he will ultimately reach the top, at which point he should theoretically receive a significant profit on his original investment. However, this assumes that sufficient people will join the scheme to maintain it and, in practice, such schemes quickly run out of potential new customers and existing consumers end up losing their money. Paragraph 14 automatically makes it an unfair commercial practice to establish, operate or promote a pyramid promotional scheme where a consumer gives consideration for the chance to receive compensation which is mainly derived from introducing other consumers to the scheme, as opposed to selling or consuming products.

(i) Making false claims

The unfair practices addressed in paragraphs 15 to 17 all relate to the making of false claims with the intent of inducing the consumer into a transactional decision which he would not make otherwise. The first of the three, paragraph 15, relates to claims that the trader is about to cease trading or move premises when he is not.[149] Typical among these is the never-ending 'closing down sale' in which the business never closes.[150] The purpose behind such claims, and equally claims about the trader moving premises, is to force the consumer into an early transaction because of his perceived fear that the goods may not be available much longer. The net result is that the consumer makes a purchase without necessarily taking the time to think the matter over in the way that they would do otherwise. It forces an impulse buy which the consumer may regret later, either because they did not need the product or they could have purchased it at a better price elsewhere.

The second type of false claim (paragraph 16) prohibits the making of claims that the product in question is able to facilitate winning in a game of chance. Thus, the OFT Guidance gives an example of an advertisement for a computer program that claims to be able to help the purchaser 'win money on scratch-card lotteries'.[151] Such a statement would be classed automatically as an unfair commercial practice.

The third type of prohibited statement in this group is covered by paragraph 17 and forbids falsely claiming that a product is able to cure illness, dysfunction or malformation. It is reasonable to assume that consumers suffering with an illness, dysfunction or malformation are particularly vulnerable to advertisements for products which they believe may alleviate their suffering, either by curing the ailment or, at least, militating against the effects of the condition. This might be, for example, the relief of constant pain. Someone suffering with painful arthritis would be vulnerable to advertisements for chairs, orthopaedic beds or specialised mattresses that promise greater comfort when sitting or sleeping. Equally, someone suffering with a skin condition such as eczema or psoriasis would be vulnerable to claims about skincare products that might ease the inflammation and itching or cure the condition completely. Paragraph 17 is aimed at advertisements relating to cures as opposed to those that might alleviate symptoms, but the latter will still need to be accurate as otherwise they will constitute misleading actions and give rise to a breach of regulation 5(2) as regards the provision of false information about the fitness for purpose of the product.

---

[149] As discussed above, such a claim would also be relevant to a misleading action contrary to reg. 5 as it would be classed as a statement relating to the 'motives for the commercial practice' under reg. 5(4)(d).

[150] See *Butterworths Trading and Consumer Law*, above n. 7, Division 1A, para. 58 for an interesting point about the possibility that a 'closing down sale' notice might be qualified by the addition in small letters of a phrase such as 'for a refurbishment'. The sign is only indicating a temporary closure and consumers will need to take care that they are not misled.

[151] See OFT Guidance, above n. 8, para. 6.1.

(j) Inaccurate statements about market conditions

Paragraph 18 returns to the issue of misleading statements that are intended to induce the consumer into a transaction that they would not otherwise make. It prohibits the passing on of materially inaccurate information about market conditions or about the possibility of the consumer being able to find the product. The intention of the action must be to induce the consumer into acquiring the product upon less favourable terms than would be available in the market under normal conditions. Thus, there are three essential requirements here. First, the information given must be materially inaccurate; hence, as in the discussion above regarding paragraph 12, it is clear that information that might constitute an advertising puff or normal advertising language may not fall within the paragraph. Secondly, it must have been provided with the intention of inducing the consumer to acquire the product. If there is no intention, there cannot be a breach. Finally, it must induce the consumer to acquire the goods on conditions less favourable than the normal market conditions. Thus, if the consumer acquires the goods on the current market conditions, the material inaccuracy of the information provided will not cause paragraph 18 to apply, although, of course, it might still be a breach of the controls over misleading actions under regulation 5. In considering the type of behaviour that would fall within paragraph 18, the OFT gives an example of an estate agent who falsely states that he has sold several houses in an area at a particular price, with the intention of making the customer buy a property at an inflated price.[152] The same would be true of a trader who, for example, falsely tells a consumer that a Christmas toy is out of stock everywhere and thus the consumer should buy the one he is selling rather than risk not getting the item at all, who then charges a higher price for the item than the price charged generally for the toy, which, despite what he has said, is available elsewhere at the normal price.

(k) Free products

Paragraphs 19 and 20 of Schedule 1 relate to the availability of products and opportunities which are supposedly free to the consumer. The first situation relates to the provision of prizes in competitions or prize promotions. It is always an unfair commercial practice under paragraph 19 to claim to offer such a competition or prize promotion without then awarding either the prizes described or a reasonable equivalent. This is to prevent the fraudulent enticement of a consumer to buy a product on the basis that their purchase will guarantee them entry into a free competition. In practice, the entry is not truly free as the consumer has to buy the product in order to acquire the opportunity to be entered into the competition. If the prizes will not be awarded, then it follows that the competition is a sham and the consumer has been fraudulently

---

[152] *Ibid.*

induced into the purchase. The OFT Guidance gives the example of consumers purchasing scratch-cards for which the advertised top prize in never awarded, either because winning tickets are never printed or are never circulated, the net result being that the top prize cannot be won.[153]

In much the same vein, it is fraudulent to describe a product as being 'gratis', 'free', 'without charge' or similar if this is not truly the case and some charge will be made for the item. The exception is that the trader can describe the product as being free even though the consumer may incur the inevitable costs of responding to the advertisement, e.g., returning a coupon by post, and the cost of collecting or paying for the delivery of the item. These costs are effectively ancillary to the cost of the product itself and, thus, the product can be described as free despite the need to incur these ancillary charges. However, if the delivery charges exceed the true cost of that facility and are a disguised method of charging the consumer an amount towards the cost of the product, then paragraph 20 would apply.

Q15 Analyse the scope of the unfair commercial practices listed in Schedule 1 paragraphs 11–20 (section 8(f)–(k) above).

(l) Unsolicited goods

The provision of unsolicited goods and services has been an issue for many years, with such practices being a criminal offence contrary to the Unsolicited Goods and Services Acts 1971, as amended. One such practice is sending an invoice to a person implying that they have either ordered or received the goods in question and that payment is now due. This is a practice that can be perpetrated against both consumers and businesses.[154] In the present context, the CPUT Regulations 2008 are concerned with protecting consumers and, under paragraph 21, prohibits the provision of marketing material to consumers where that material includes any invoice or similar document seeking payment which wrongly gives the consumer the impression that he has already ordered the product in question. This practice fraudulently seeks payment from a consumer for goods or services that he has not ordered or received and hence now constitutes a commercial practice which is always deemed to be unfair.

(m) Statements about the commercial nature of the seller

The legal rights available to a consumer depend to some extent on the character of the seller or supplier. Thus, for example, the character of the seller is paramount in both section 14 of the Sale of Goods Act 1979 and in sections 13 and

---

[153] *Ibid.*

[154] One of the prohibited practices in relation to businesses relates to the sending of an invoice to a company for a fictitious entry in a trade catalogue.

14 of the Supply of Goods and Services Act 1982. In both instances the relevant Act stipulates that the obligation on the seller/supplier only arises where he is acting in the course of a business. Thus, it is to the advantage of an unscrupulous seller/supplier to pretend that they are not in business at all but are acting in a private capacity, thereby misleading the consumer as to the legal rights that he possesses in the event of the goods or service proving to be unsatisfactory. Schedule 1, paragraph 22 now automatically renders such deception an unfair commercial practice and, as such, a criminal offence.[155] It is prohibited for a trader to falsely claim or create the impression that he is not acting for the purposes relating to his trade, business, craft or profession or, alternatively, to falsely represent himself as a consumer.

(n) Cross-border trading

The promotion of cross-border trade among consumers is one of the objectives of the European Union and of the reform of the consumer *acquis*. It follows that if cross-border trade is to be encouraged either through the promotion of web-based trading or through consumers buying goods while abroad and then bringing them back to the United Kingdom, consumers will be concerned about the enforcement of their rights if something goes wrong and equally about what level of after-sales service will be available. Schedule 1 paragraph 23 makes it an unfair commercial practice to create a false impression about the availability of after-sales service in an EEA[156] state other than the one in which the consumer buys the product. Thus, for example, it would apply where a trader in the United Kingdom sold goods to consumers from another EEA country, e.g., Germany, Italy or Iceland, by falsely stating that after-sales service will be available in Germany, Italy or Iceland, respectively.

(o) Aggressive commercial practices

The next three practices prohibited under Schedule 1 and thus classed as unfair commercial practices relate to the use of aggressive commercial practices to force a consumer to enter into a transaction that he would not do otherwise. Aggressive commercial practices are, of course, prohibited under regulation 7 of the CPUT Regulations 2008 but Schedule 1 paragraphs 24 to 26 address specified aggressive practices. Paragraph 24 prohibits a trader from creating the impression that a consumer cannot leave the premises until a contract has been signed. The OFT Guidance quotes an example of a holiday company providing a presentation at a hotel with doormen posted at all the doors, creating the impression that a consumer has no choice but to sign a contract if he wants

---

[155] This practice was illegal previously under the provisions of the Business Advertisements (Disclosure) Order 1977, SI 1977/1918.

[156] The EEA comprises all of the EU Member States plus Iceland, Norway and Lichtenstein.

to be able to leave the premises. This activity would interfere with the right of the consumer to make up his mind without fear of consequences and to decide objectively whether he wishes to contract for the product concerned.

While paragraph 24 controls practices occurring in trade premises, the practices prohibited under paragraphs 25 and 26 are more intrusive in that they affect the consumer when he is at his home, which, necessarily, makes them more difficult to avoid. Paragraph 25 prohibits the trader from making personal visits to the house of a consumer and then ignoring his requests to leave or not to return. Thus, a doorstep seller who refuses to leave until the consumer makes a purchase, or a trader who, having responded to a request from the consumer to visit his house to talk about a product, then refuses to leave without an order, or a trader who repeatedly calls back despite being asked not to return, all fall under the provisions of paragraph 25. Each of these examples would constitute an aggressive commercial practice under regulation 7 and would be an unfair commercial practice under paragraph 25. That said, conducting personal visits on the consumer's premises despite requests not to do so is permissible to the extent that it is justified to enforce a contractual obligation, although the behaviour of the trader must be justifiable as opposed to oppressive.

Paragraph 26 deals with the related issue of persistent and unwanted solicitations by phone, fax, email or other remote media. While these practices do not involve the physical presence of the trader, they do, nonetheless, interfere with the ability of the consumer to enjoy the undisturbed quiet of his own premises. Persistent contact by phone, fax, etc., may constitute harassment and, as such, is unacceptable in that it interferes with the right of the consumer to make an objective decision about a transaction. Again, as with personal visits by the trader, persistent phone calls or contact via email, fax or other remote media is permitted to the extent justified to enforce a contractual obligation.

(p) Insurance contracts

Insurance contracts are contracts *uberrimae fidei*, i.e., contracts of the utmost good faith. When taking out insurance policies, consumers are required to act in good faith and to bring to the attention of the insurance company any information that may be material to the decision by the insurance company whether to underwrite the risk. The insurance company has to be in a position to evaluate the risk posed by the consumer. It is not unreasonable, therefore, for the consumer to expect that the insurance company will also act in good faith and, most particularly, will pay out legitimate claims in full within a reasonable period and not create artificial barriers to any such claim. It is against this background that Schedule 1 paragraph 27 takes effect. It provides that it will be an unfair commercial practice for an insurance company to require a consumer who wants to make a claim on a policy to produce documentation which cannot reasonably be considered to be relevant as to whether or not the claim is valid. In short, insurance companies must not ask for irrelevant documentation as a tactic to dissuade a consumer from enforcing his legitimate contractual rights. Likewise, insurance companies are prohibited from systematically failing to reply to pertinent correspondence from consumers in order to dissuade consumers from enforcing their contractual rights.

(q) Exerting pressure on children

It is well recognised that children can bring pressure to bear on their parents or other adults to buy them toys, magazines, etc. that they have seen advertised on the television or in comics or the like. This makes children an obvious target for focused advertising so that they will respond to an advertisement by bringing pressure to bear on the parent or other adult who will buy the product for them. While such pressure will always exist, whether as a result of advertisements or consequent upon peer pressure, the CPUT Regulations 2008 make it an unfair commercial practice to use an advertisement to directly exhort children to buy products or to get them to persuade their parents or other adults to buy the advertised product for them. Thus, an advertisement cannot include a statement such as 'get Mum or Dad to buy it for you' without falling within Schedule 1 paragraph 28. This practice is the second of the unfair commercial practices listed in Schedule 1 that does not give rise to criminal liability and is only enforceable via civil law enforcement under the Enterprise Act 2003 Part 8.

(r) Unsolicited goods

Schedule 1 paragraph 29 returns to the issue of unsolicited goods by addressing the problem of traders making demands for payment for products that have been supplied unsolicited to consumers. Previously regulated by the Unsolicited Goods and Services Act 1971, paragraph 29 prohibits traders from demanding immediate or deferred payment from consumers for such unsolicited products. Likewise, the trader cannot require the consumer either to return the goods or to keep them safe, as either of these activities would allow the trader to place an unsolicited obligation on a consumer. If a consumer has received goods as the result of a contract, then clearly he is a contractual bailee in respect of those goods and would be under a legal obligation to take care of them and not to allow them to become damaged as a result of any negligence on his part. Thus, if a consumer has received goods as a substitute product within the provisions of regulation 19(7) of the Consumer Protection (Distance Selling) Regulations 2000, SI 2000/2334, he is under an obligation to care for them until such time as they are returned to the trader.

(s) Falsely suggesting that the trader's livelihood is at risk

Pressure to purchase can be brought to bear upon a consumer in varying ways. One method which is expressly forbidden by Schedule 1 paragraph 30 and classed as an unfair commercial practice is where the trader expressly informs a consumer that if he does not buy the product or service in question, the trader's job or livelihood will be in jeopardy. Such a statement is a straight-forward and blatant attempt to pressurise the consumer and thereby to remove his ability to make an objective and independent decision about whether to purchase the relevant product.

(t) False statements about prizes

The last of the thirty-one practices listed in Schedule 1 which will always be classed as an unfair commercial practice relates to statements made to a consumer that they have won or will win a prize or other benefit. It encompasses creating a false impression that a consumer either has won, will win or, on the doing of a specified act will win, a prize or other benefit, when the truth is either that the prize or benefit does not exist or that claiming the prize or other benefit requires the consumer to pay some money or incur a cost. The OFT Guidance gives an example of a trader sending out letters to consumers which are headed 'You have won our top prize of £3,000' when the back of the letter states in small letters that the consumer must buy a product before being entered into a draw for the money.[157]

All of the thirty-one practices listed in Schedule 1 have a common feature in that they attempt to take advantage of the consumer and use unfair, fraudulent and aggressive methods to try and influence any transactional decision that the consumer may make to the benefit of the trader. The Schedule evidences the intention of the law to step in to protect the consumer from such practices. Enforcement of the provisions of the Schedule is the responsibility of the relevant enforcement authority.

Q16 Analyse the ambit of the unfair commercial practices listed in Schedule 1 paragraphs 21–31(section 8(l)–(t) above).

9 Offences

Regulations 8 to 12 of the CPUT Regulations 2008 create criminal law offences. Regulation 8 makes it an offence to breach the regulation 3 prohibition against unfair commercial practices, while regulations 9 to 12 deal with the strict liability offences for breaches of regulations 5 to 7 and for the unfair commercial practices listed in Schedule 1.[158]

The criminal offence under regulation 8 requires proof of *mens rea*, the offence being to 'knowingly or recklessly engage in a commercial practice'

---

[157] See OFT Guidance, above n. 8, para. 6.1.
[158] A breach of any of the practices listed in Sch.1 is a strict liability criminal offence, with the exception of breaches of paras. 11 and 28, which deal with advertorials and exhortations directed to children, respectively, and which are enforceable through civil law enforcement only.

which breaches regulation 3. The requirement for *mens rea* means that the due diligence defence, which is the defence commonly supplied for strict liability offences in trading law, is simply not relevant. As such, regulation 8 falls outside the regime of defences included in regulations 16 to 18 of the Regulations.[159]

10 Recommended reading

Department for Business, Enterprise and Regulatory Reform *Explanatory Memorandum to the Consumer Protection from Unfair Trading Regulations 2008 and the Business Protection from Misleading Marketing Regulations 2008* (London, 2008)

Pricing Practices Guide: Guidance for Traders on Good Practice in Giving Information about Prices. (London, 2008)

Department of Trade and Industry *The Unfair Commercial Practices Directive, Consultation on a Draft EU Directive COM(2003)356* (London, 2002)

The Unfair Commercial Practices Directive, Consultation on Framing and Enforcing Criminal Sanctions in the Regulations Implementing the Unfair Commercial Practices Directive (London, 2006)

Implementation of the Unfair Commercial Practices Directive. Consultation on the Draft Consumer Protection from Unfair Trading Regulations 2007 (London, 2007)

Griffiths, M. 'Unfair commercial practices: a new regime' (2007) 12 *Communications Law* 194

Griffiths, M. and Griffiths, I. *Law for Purchasing and Supply* (3rd edn, Pearson Education Ltd, Harlow, 2002)

Hart, H. 'The end of sharp practice' (2007) 157 *New Law Journal* 796

Johnson, H. 'Advertisers beware! The impact of the Unfair Commercial Practices Directive' (2005) 10 *Communications Law* 164

Office of Fair Trading *Consumer Protection from Unfair Trading Regulations 2008, Guidance on the Implementation of the Unfair Commercial Practices Directive*, OFT 1008 (London, 2008)

Party, D.L., Rowell, R. and Ervine, C. (eds.), *Butterworths Trading and Consumer Law* (London, 1990) Division 1A

Ramsay, I. *Consumer Law and Policy: Text and Materials on Regulating Consumer Markets* (2nd edn, Hart Publishing, Oxford, 2007)

Rook, S. 'Consumer Protection from Unfair Trading Regulations' (2009) *Trading Standards Today* (June 2009) 34

Shears, P. 'Overviewing the EU Unfair Commercial Practices Directive: concentric circles' (2007) 18 *European Business Law Review* 781

The Consumer Protection from Unfair Trading Regulations 2008 introduced significant amendments to the law in this area. The OFT's Guidance and the BERR's Explanatory Memorandum are comprehensive and provide good background and explanation to the Regulations. In addition, the articles by Griffiths, Hart, Johnson and Shears are instructive.

---

[159] See Part 5 Chapter 1 for a full discussion of the offences under the CPUT Regulations 2008 and the statutory defences thereto.

Part 5 Chapter 3

Business Protection from Misleading Marketing

Contents

1 Introduction

If traders are to compete in a fair market, it is important to ensure that there are comprehensive and effective controls over both misleading and comparative advertising.

This chapter looks at the current controls over misleading advertising as it affects business purchasers and, also, at the latest legal controls over comparative advertising whereby traders are permitted to include reference to competitors in their advertisements subject to satisfying certain controls.

Section 2 includes a brief background to the issue of misleading and comparative advertising and details the genesis of the current provisions. Section 3 considers the controls over misleading advertisements including: the remit of the controls and the situations that they are designed to cover, and the definition of the phrase 'misleading advertisements' and the criteria upon which it depends.

Section 4 considers the new controls over comparative advertising and addresses: the remit of the controls and the criteria that must be satisfied if a comparative advertisement is to be legal. Section 5 considers the prohibition of misleading or comparative advertising by code owners.

2 Background

Directive 2006/114/EC[1] states that 'misleading and unlawful comparative advertising can lead to distortion of competition within the internal market'.[2] Misleading advertising has 'a direct effect on the smooth functioning of the internal market',[3] while differing national controls over both misleading and comparative advertising can affect the free circulation of goods and services. By contrast, legal comparative advertising can promote competition between suppliers to the benefit of purchasers, both business purchasers and consumers.

UK controls over misleading advertisements directed at traders and comparative advertisements are currently found in the Business Protection from Misleading Marketing Regulations 2008,[4] which were enacted following the passage of the Unfair Commercial Practices Directive.[5] The repeal of significant parts of the Trade Descriptions Act 1968 left businesses less well protected than previously,[6] while the repeal of the Control over Misleading Advertisements Regulations 1988[7] required alternative provisions to be made to ensure the United Kingdom's continued compliance with Directive 2006/114/EC. The Business Protection from Misleading Marketing (BPMM) Regulations 2008 address both of these issues, with regulation 3 prohibiting advertising which misleads traders, thereby dealing with the legal lacuna created by the repeal of parts of the Trade Descriptions Act 1968, while regulation 4 controls comparative advertising in compliance with the requirements of Directive 2006/114/EC.

3 Controls over misleading advertising

(a) Remit of the controls

Regulation 3(1) of the BPMM Regulations 2008 prohibits misleading advertising. For the purposes of the Regulations, 'advertising' means 'any form of representation which is made in connection with a trade, business, craft or profession in order to promote the supply or transfer of a product' and '"advertiser" is to be construed accordingly'.[8] This broad definition encompasses a wide variety of advertising methods, including print advertisements (e.g., billboards, newspapers, magazines, catalogues, flyers, statements on packaging, etc.), broadcasts, web-based advertisements and oral representations made on

---

[1] Directive 2006/114/EC concerning misleading and comparative advertising.
[2] *Ibid.* recital 3.   [3] *Ibid.* recital 2.
[4] SI 2008/1276, effective from 26 May 2008.
[5] Directive 2005/29/EC concerning unfair business-to-consumer commercial practices in the internal market. For a discussion of this Directive and the Consumer Protection from Unfair Trading Regulations 2008, see Part 5 Chapter 2.
[6] The Trade Descriptions Act 1968 provided protection to both businesses and consumers, while the Consumer Protection from Unfair Trading Regulations 2008 only protect consumers and exclude businesses.
[7] SI 1988/915.   [8] BPMM Regulations 208, reg. 2(1).

behalf of the trader. The advertisement must have been made for the purposes of the trade or business and been intended to promote a product. It follows that an advertisement placed by a trader for his private purposes falls outside the remit of these controls, as do advertisements placed by private individuals.

Implicit in the fact that the offending advertisement must be for the purposes of a trade or business is the assumption that it will have been placed by a trader, defined for the purposes of the Regulations as being 'any person who is acting for purposes relating to his trade, craft, business or profession and anyone acting in the name of or on behalf of a trader'.[9] This would include the owner of a business,[10] professional people[11] and employees acting on behalf of a trader.[12]

The definition refers to the 'supply or transfer' of a product and, thus, extends beyond mere sale and includes other methods of transfer such as part-exchange or barter.

(b) Definition of misleading advertisements

Regulation 3(1) prohibits misleading advertising. An advertisement becomes misleading for these purposes when it:

   (a) in any way, including its presentation, deceives or is likely to deceive the traders to whom it is addressed or whom it reaches; and by reason of its deceptive nature, is likely to affect their economic behaviour; or

   (b) for those reasons, injures or is likely to injure a competitor.[13]

First, it must be noted that the offending advertisement must either have been addressed to traders or reach traders, as previously defined. Thus, the controls cover business-to-business advertisements and do not encompass advertisements addressed to consumers, which are dealt with under the Consumer Protection from Unfair Trading (CPUT) Regulations 2008.[14]

The underlying requirement is that the advertisement deceives or is likely to deceive the trader to whom it is addressed or who it reaches. Therefore, if the advertisement would not deceive the trader in question, there will not be any contravention of the BPMM Regulations 2008. It should be noted that the question of deception is considered from the perspective of the trader to whom it is addressed and not from the viewpoint of the advertiser. Thus, the advertiser may genuinely believe that the advertisement is acceptable but still fall foul of the Regulations if the advertisement is likely to deceive the trader to whom it is addressed or who it reaches. That said, it is unlikely that this would occur in practice.

---

[9] *Ibid.* reg. 2(1).

[10] *Warwickshire County Council* v. *Johnson* [1993] 1 All ER 299.

[11] E.g., veterinary surgeons, see *Roberts* v. *Leonard, The Times,* 10 May 1995, in which veterinary surgeons were held liable for offences against s.1(1)(b) of the Trade Descriptions Act 1968.

[12] Traders are also vicariously liable in civil law for the actions of their employees while undertaking their employment duties.

[13] BPMM Regulations 2008, reg. 3(2).   [14] SI 2008/1277. See Part 5 Chapter 2.

Deception requires that things are not as they seem, so an advertisement will be deceptive if it is misleading in some way. It may contain a statement that is untrue because of something it says, or perhaps, does not say. Statements can be rendered misleading through both commission and omission.[15] Concealing an important fact is potentially as deceptive as a straight-forward misstatement.[16] Further, the context of the statement can also be relevant, as a statement that is 100 per cent accurate may be rendered misleading by the manner and/or context in which it is made.[17] Incorrect or misleading statements may involve the nature and characteristics of the goods or services being advertised, e.g., an item not being as described. However, statements may also refer to the intended behaviour of the trader, e.g., as to when he will dispatch the goods. If a statement is untrue because the trader promises to do something that he has no intention of doing, e.g., meeting delivery dates, that is sufficient to render the advertisement misleading.[18]

Having established that the advertisement deceives or is likely to deceive, one of two things must be proven. It must be shown either that the deception is likely to affect the economic behaviour of the trader to whom it was addressed or, alternatively, that the deception injures or is likely to injure a competitor. In respect of the former, it is only the economic behaviour of the trader that is relevant and other factors such as his health and safety are irrelevant in this context.[19] The economic behaviour of a trader will be affected if, for example, he decides to purchase the goods or services advertised, on the basis of the information in the misleading advertisement.[20] The most obvious injury to the advertiser's competitor occurs when the recipient of the advertisement buys the relevant goods or services from the advertiser in reliance on the advertisement and in the mistaken belief that he is buying the goods from the advertiser's competitor, i.e., where he purchases goods advertised by A in the erroneous belief that he is purchasing them from B. The injury in

---

[15] Compare CPUT Regulations 2008, reg. 5 (misleading actions) and reg. 6 (misleading omissions). See Part 5 Chapter 2.

[16] See *R* v. *Haesler* [1973] RTR 486 and *R* v. *Southwood* [1987] 3 All ER 556, both of which were decided under the Trade Descriptions Act 1968. In *R* v. *Haesler*, the defendant removed the words 'ex Channel Islands' from the registration document of a vehicle to suggest that the vehicle was newer than it was, while in *R* v. *Southwood*, the odometer on a car was adjusted to conceal the true mileage of the vehicle.

[17] Compare Trade Descriptions Act 1968, s.3(2), which stipulated that a statement which, though not false, was misleading was to be deemed to be a false trade description and, as such, capable of giving rise to criminal liability if false to a material degree.

[18] See OFT, *Busines to Business Promotions and Comparative Advertisements: A Quick Guide to the Business Protection from Misleading Marketing Regulations 2008*, OFT 1058 (London, 2009).

[19] This is narrower than the previous controls under the Trade Descriptions Act 1968, where it was only the falsity of the statement that was relevant and not its impact on the person to whom the statement was directed. However, this concentration on the economic interests of the person who has been misled accords with the approach in the CPUT Regulations 2008, reg. 3(3), which stipulates that a commercial practice is unfair if it affects the economic behaviour of the consumer.

[20] OFT Guide, above n. 18, at 5.

this scenario is obvious: trader B has been denied the sale and the consequent opportunity to make a profit.

Q1 *Analyse the scope and impact of the controls over misleading advertisements.*

(c) Definition of 'misleading'

Having recognised that it is the impact and content of the advertisement that dictates whether it is misleading for the purposes of the BPMM Regulations 2008, it is clearly important to understand the meaning and parameters of the term 'misleading'. Regulation 3(3) to (5) provide a non-exhaustive definition and list of factors that are relevant to interpreting the term 'misleading' as used here. Regulation 3(3) requires that account be taken of all the features of the advertisement, with particular regard to any information about the characteristics of the product, the price or manner in which the price is calculated, the conditions on which the product is supplied or provided and the nature, attributes and rights of the advertiser.[21] The use of the phrase 'all its features' is, of course, a catch-all term and hence interpretation is not restricted to the four factors specifically mentioned.

Regulation 3(4) addresses the meaning of the phrase 'characteristics of the product' as used in regulation 3(3)(a) and includes many of the factors that were included previously in the Trade Descriptions Act 1968, section 2. This list is also non-exhaustive and hence other factors can be considered if relevant. The factors specifically quoted include, first, the availability of the product, which requires that the product is available on the market and that the trader has a supply of it or can access a supply without delay.[22] Other factors detailed in paragraph (4) include the nature, execution and composition of the product,[23] which covers such things as the general description of the product itself, how the product or service is to be provided, and the materials or fabrics from which it is made, e.g., copper, wool, stainless steel.

The next two factors encompass the date and method of the manufacture of the product and of its provision. This includes statements relating to the age of the product[24] and the method by which it was made, e.g., hand-made and organic. The method and date of provision of the product will include statements relating to the intended delivery date and whether the product must be collected by the purchaser or will be delivered to him and, if so, at what cost.

---

[21] These factors bear a marked resemblance to some of those adopted in the CPUT Regulations 2008, reg. 5(4) in respect of misleading statements made to consumers.

[22] It is possible that misleading advertisements relating to limited editions and limited stock availability would fall within this paragraph. See D.L. Parry, R. Rowell and C. Ervine (eds.) *Butterworths Trading and Consumer Law* (London, 1990) Division 5, para. 228

[23] BPMM Regulations 2008, reg. 3(4)(b)–(d).

[24] Which may be significant in assessing the value of the item, be it a second-hand van or a valuable antique.

The next two factors address the fitness for purpose of the item and the uses for which it is intended. Clearly, there are echoes here of the civil law requirement of fitness for purpose in the Sale of Goods Act 1979, section 14(3). Fitness for purpose includes any reference to particular facets of the product which impact on its use, e.g., being water-proof or shock-proof, while uses of the product can reflect not only the intended uses of the product in the future but, it is argued, also any references to its previous usage, e.g., the number of previous owners of a vehicle or its recorded mileage.[25]

The next three factors cover the quantity of goods, their specification, such as capacities and dimensions, and their geographic origin, such as 'made in Wales'. The last two factors relate to the results to be expected from usage of the product and, finally, the details of any tests or checks that have been carried out on the product.

Having considered the parameters of the phrase 'the characteristics of the product', it must be remembered that this is only the first of the four aspects of a product that is specifically listed in regulation 3(3), the other three being the price or manner in which the price is calculated, the conditions on which the product is supplied or provided, and the nature, attributes and rights of the advertiser.

The price or manner by which it will be calculated is a self-explanatory factor, indicating either that an actual price has been quoted or that a mechanism for calculating it has been provided, e.g., that the goods will be sold by reference to a unit price such as per lb, kg, tonne, etc, or alternatively by reference to a price prevailing on a particular date. It would also include details of special offers and details about delivery charges.[26] The conditions on which the product is supplied or provided relates to the contractual terms on which the goods are being supplied and would include details of delivery times, exclusion and limitation clauses, liquidated damages clauses, the duration of the contract, termination clauses, etc.

The last of the four aspects is the nature, attributes and rights of the advertiser, which include his identity, assets, qualifications, his ownership of industrial, commercial or intellectual property rights, and any awards or distinctions that he may possess. Thus, it would include claims that he works for a particular company, or that he has specified qualifications[27] or that he has received named industry awards.

Q2 Analyse whether the four aspects of the product referred to in regulation 3(3) provide a comprehensive approach to this topic.

---

[25] See *Butterworths Trading and Consumer Law*, above n. 22, Division 5, para. 28.

[26] *Ibid.*

[27] See *R* v. *Breeze* [1973] 2 All ER 1141, CA, in which the defendant falsely claimed that he was a qualified architect contrary to the Trade Descriptions Act, 1968.

4 Comparative advertising

(a) Remit of the controls

The legal parameters of comparative advertising are laid down in regulation 4 of the BPMM Regulations 2008, which implements Directive 2006/114/EC, Article 4 and replaces the controls contained previously in the now repealed Control of Misleading Advertisements Regulations 1988.[28]

Comparative advertising is defined as being 'advertising which in any way, either explicitly or by implication, identifies a competitor or a product offered by a competitor'.[29] Explicit comparisons involve those where competitors are referred to by name, the most common example being the advertisements regularly used by supermarkets in which they compare their prices to those of a named competitor. The purpose behind such advertisements is typically to prove their superiority, usually in relation to the price of identified products, and may include things such as a guarantee of lower prices. By contrast, implied comparisons relate to situations where the product being advertised is compared to a 'leading brand' as opposed to a named product but where the market is such that it is clear which leading product is being used as the comparator. The OFT uses an example of a supermarket comparing a cola product to a 'leading brand', when there is an obvious brand leader for cola products.[30] Both types of comparisons are valuable and can provide purchasers, both business buyers and consumers, with relevant and useful information to guide them when making purchasing decisions. Given their potential influence, it is crucial that such advertisements are accurate and not misleading.

Regulation 4 allows comparative advertising on condition that the advertisements comply with specified criteria. These criteria are cumulative and thus comparative advertisements must comply with all of them and not merely some of them. A failure to comply can result in enforcement authorities seeking an undertaking under BPMM Regulations 2008, regulation 16 or an injunction under regulation 15. If a trader breaches an undertaking, the enforcement authority can seek an injunction instead, the breach of an injunction is a contempt of court and can be punished as such.

(b) The regulation 4 criteria

There are nine criteria listed in regulation 4 although the first two merely require that the comparative advertisement is not misleading contrary to regulation 3 of the BPMM Regulations 2008[31] and, likewise, is neither a misleading action nor a misleading omission contrary to regulations 5 and 6, respectively, of the CPUT Regulations 2008.[32] As such, these two criteria do not make any

---

[28] SI 1998/915.   [29] BPMM Regulations 2008, reg. 2.
[30] See OFT Guide, above n. 18.   [31] BPMM Regulations 2008, reg. 4(a).
[32] *Ibid.* reg. 4(b).

new demands upon the advertiser, although it follows that any comparative advertisement that is misleading under BPMM Regulations 2008, regulation 3 or breaches regulations 5 or 6 of the CPUT Regulations 2008 will also be in breach of regulation 4 and can be enforced as such.

Regulation 4(c) requires that the goods being compared in a comparative advertisement must meet the same needs or be intended for the same purpose. Like must be compared with like. Thus, it would not be acceptable for a supermarket to claim a price advantage by comparing the prices of their basic range with those of the prestige range of a competitor. However, it would be permissible to compare the same product from two basic ranges or, indeed, the cost of a selection of products from the comparable ranges as long as the individual products selected are themselves comparable.[33] Equally, it would not be acceptable for a financial institution to compare the interest rates of their mortgages with those of the interest rates applicable to credit cards issued by a competitor.[34] Mortgages and credit cards, while both financial products, have different characters and serve different purposes and, as such, are not amenable to direct comparison.

Regulation 4(d) requires that there must be an objective comparison of one or more material, relevant, verifiable and representative features of the products, which can include the price. Thus, it requires a comparison of factors that are capable of being verified, such as dimensions, capacity, origin, method of manufacture and price. It deals with facts, not opinions or marketing claims. Thus, subjective comment such as 'best value' or 'lower prices' cannot be used in comparative advertising as they are not verifiable facts, merely opinions. Shop A cannot place an advertisement simply stating 'We are cheaper than Shop B' without backing that comment with verifiable facts about the cost of comparable products in both shops.[35]

The next criteria, contained in regulation 4(e), only relates to comparative advertising that misleads traders as opposed to consumers. It addresses situations in which a business purchaser is misled into thinking that goods advertised and produced by the advertiser were, in fact, produced by one of his competitors. Thus, it relates to causing confusion in the mind of a business purchaser between the advertiser and his competitor, whether by name, trade mark, trade name, etc., such that the prospective business purchaser is confused as to who produced the product in question.[36] Clearly, such confusion may result in the business purchaser purchasing goods from a supplier other than the one that he intended to use and therefore not getting the product that

---

[33] See *Lidl Belgium GmbH & Co. KG* v. *Etalbissementen Franz Colruyt NV* C-356/04 [2007] 1 CMLR 9, as quoted in *Butterworths Trading and Consumer Law*, above n. 22, Division 5, para. 229.

[34] See OFT Guide, above n. 18.

[35] See *Lidl Belgium GmbH & Co. KG* v. *Etalbissementen Franz Colruyt NV* C-356/04 [2007] 1 CMLR 9, as quoted in *Butterworths Trading and Consumer Law*, above n. 22, Division 5, para. 229.

[36] This provision only relates to business purchasers. Consumer buyers are given similar protection under the CPUT Regulations 2008, see Part 5 Chapter 2.

he really wanted. Equally, the advertiser's competitor has lost the opportunity to make a sale with the consequent loss of the opportunity to make a profit from that sale.

Comparative advertising allows the advertiser to objectively and directly compare his products or services with those of a competitor. It follows that, if the advertisement is to be an objective comparison, traders should not be allowed to use such advertisements as a means to denigrate or discredit their competitors. Regulation 4(f) stipulates that a comparative advertisement must not 'discredit or denigrate the trademarks, trade names, other distinguishing marks, products, activities or circumstances of a competitor'. Advertisements must not be used as a vehicle for making derogatory comments about a competitor, they are only to be used for legitimate comparisons within the meaning of the BPMM Regulations 2008.

One verifiable factor of a product is its designation of origin, whether it be Double Gloucester cheese, Welsh lamb or Scotch whisky. While these examples are all foodstuffs, many other products can also include an express statement of origin as part of their verifiable characteristics. The Regulations require[37] that when a product has a designated origin, it must be compared with products of the same designation. This approach negates the potential for misleading advertisements based on the price difference between similar goods produced in different places, e.g., the difference between champagne and sparkling wine produced elsewhere by the same method. Thus, if a supplier wishes to compare the cost of his Italian sparkling wine with wine sold by a competitor, he must compare it with similar wine from the same origin and not with champagne being sold by his competitor, which will necessarily command a higher price and give the misleading impression that the competitor's product is more expensive. However, if both products have an indication of origin, it must be the same one if the comparison is to be permitted. The European Court of Justice has held that where one product does not have an indication of origin it is acceptable to compare it to a product that does have an indication, e.g., comparing beer to champagne.[38]

As already discussed, regulation 4(e) seeks to prevent any confusion arising in the minds of trader-purchasers about which person has produced the goods they are intending to buy, so as to prevent producer A from passing off his goods as being made by producer B, thereby depriving producer B of the opportunity to make a sale and make some profit from that sale. Regulation 4(h) takes this approach a step further by stipulating that a comparative advertisement must not take unfair advantage of the reputation of a trade mark, trade name or other distinguishing mark of a competitor or of the designation

---

[37] BPMM Regulations 2008, reg. 4(g).

[38] See *De Landtsherr Emmanuel SA* v. *Comité Interprofessional du Vin de Champagne, Veuve Cliquot Ponsardin SA* C-381/05 ECJ, [2008] All ER (EC) 1068 as quoted in *Butterworths Trading and Consumer Law*, above n. 22, Division 5, para. 229.

of origin of competing products. Thus, if a producer uses a trade mark, trade name, etc., that is so similar to that of his competitor that it will cause confusion in the minds of potential purchasers, there will be a breach of this provision as it takes advantage of the reputation of his competitor. Further, it may, for example, make an implicit statement about the quality of the product, suggesting that it is of a comparable quality to that produced by the competitor. Of course, if the product is in any way technical or needs to fit another item, it may be that the use of the same design and possibly the same part number as the original is necessary, e.g., if a producer is making computer printer cartridges to fit particular printers. In this example, the producer will need to indicate the make and model of the printer that it will fit; however, while the cartridge must be identical in size to one produced by the original printer manufacturer, it does not necessarily require the use of the same part number – to use the same part number might be taking advantage of the printer manufacturer's reputation. It will, as always, depend on the facts of the particular case. It is noticeable that this paragraph does not expressly require that any confusion has been caused but, in practice, unfair advantage implies that a purchaser has been misled. This can apply equally to business purchasers and consumers and it may be that the use of a logo or part number would not have misled a business purchaser but would mislead a consumer who is less familiar with the particular industry.

Finally, regulation 4(i) prohibits an advertiser from presenting a product as being an imitation or replica of any product which carries a protected trade mark or trade name. This goes further than merely addressing the issue of counterfeit goods, where the advertiser seeks to pass off counterfeit goods as being the genuine article. This paragraph considers those situations where the advertiser openly states that the goods are imitations but, nonetheless, they look like the real thing. Arguably, the most common examples are to be found in imitation designer jewellery, clothing, handbags and football strip. The aim of such imitations is not to mislead the purchaser, who is usually fully aware that the goods are replicas, but, nonetheless, the advertiser is taking unfair advantage of the reputation of the genuine trade mark and any resultant supply and profit will be regarded as having arisen through unfair competition contrary to regulation 4(i).

Q3 Do the controls over comparative advertising provide a balanced and fair approach to the topic?

5 Promotion of misleading or comparative advertising

Regulation 5 prohibits a code owner from using a code of conduct to promote misleading advertising contrary to regulation 3 or comparative advertising contrary to regulation 4. A 'code owner' is defined for this purpose as being 'a trader or body responsible for the formulation and revision of a code of conduct; or [for] monitoring compliance with the code by those who have undertaken to be bound by it'.[39] Codes of conduct in any given industry are usually voluntary and are promulgated by professional organisations seeking to promote good practice among their members. In practice, therefore, it seems unlikely that any code owner would deliberately promote unfair comparative advertising, but regulation 5 adds legal controls to the self-regulation contained in a code of practice. A breach of regulation 5 is not a criminal offence but the code owner could be subject to civil enforcement through a local authority seeking an undertaking under regulation 16 or an injunction under regulation 17. The potential advantage of this approach to an enforcement authority is that taking action against a code owner and thereby changing a code of conduct impacts on all of the members of that professional body and negates the need to deal with each member individually. Of course, offending traders who do not subscribe to a code of conduct will still need to be dealt with on an individual basis.

6 Recommended reading

Department for Business, Enterprise and Regulatory Reform *Explanatory Memorandum to the Consumer Protection from Unfair Trading Regulations 2008 and the Business Protection from Misleading Marketing Regulations 2008* (London, 2008)

Griffiths, M. 'Unfair commercial practices: a new regime' (2007) 12 *Communications Law* 194

Office of Fair Trading *Business to Business Promotions and Comparative Advertisements: A Quick Guide to the Business Protection from Misleading Marketing Regulations 2008*, OFT 1058 (London, 2009)

Party, D.L., Rowell, R. and Ervine, C. (eds.), *Butterworths Trading and Consumer Law* (London, 1990)

Ramsay, I. *Consumer Law and Policy: Text and Materials on Regulating Consumer Markets* (2nd edn, Hart Publishing, Oxford, 2007)

There has been relatively little written on this topic, hence the brevity of the reading list. Readers may benefit from reading the official guidance and also the comment by Griffiths.

---

[39] BPMM Regulations 2008, reg. 2. This definition is identical to that used in the CPUT Regulations 2008, reg. 2 and is drawn from Directive 2006/114/EC.

Part 6
Banking and Finance Law

Introduction

Part 6 deals with banking and finance law. Chapter 1 identifies and explains the policies adopted by the United Kingdom government towards the banking sector. The chapter begins by providing a brief historical account of the development of banking regulation from the creation of the Court of Alderman in the seventeenth century to the Financial Services Bill (2011). The chapter identifies the contrasting policies adopted by the Labour government (1997–2010) and those proposed by the Coalition government.

Chapter 2 sets out to provide a detailed overview of the law relating to banks. The chapter begins by attempting to answer what in theory should be a very simple question – what is a bank? However, it will become clear that this is quite a difficult question to answer. Chapter 2 goes onto define a 'customer' and then progresses to highlight the very complicated relationship between a bank and its customers. Particular attention is paid to the duties a bank owes to its customers, including, for example, the duty of confidentiality. The chapter also outlines the different types of bank accounts offered to customers and deals with some of the legal issues relating to cheques, e-banking and the regulation of bank accounts.

Chapter 3 provides an overview of the United Kingdom's financial regulation provisions. The chapter begins by briefly highlighting the influence of EU legislative provisions on the UK financial regulation system. This includes a discussion of the various Banking Directives, the Basel Accord and the Basel Committee on Banking Supervision. The chapter then concentrates on the current system of regulation imposed by the Financial Services Authority (FSA) via its Handbook and the provisions of the Financial Services and Markets Act 2000. The chapter finally turns its attention to financial crime and identifies the relevant statutory provisions relating to money laundering, insider dealing, market abuse, terrorist financing and fraud.

Part 6 Chapter 1

Government Policy

Contents

The regulation of the financial services industry in the United Kingdom has developed piecemeal over time.[1]

1 Introduction

This chapter identifies and explains the policies adopted by the UK government towards the banking sector. The chapter begins by providing a brief historical account of the development of banking regulation from the creation of the Court of Alderman in the seventeenth century to the Financial Services Bill (2011). The chapter identifies the contrasting policies adopted by the Labour government (1997–2010) and those proposed by the Coalition government.

2 History of banking regulation: early policy initiatives

The first attempt to regulate financial activity in the United Kingdom occurred in 1697 when legislation was enacted that required those who worked within the 'City of London' to be licensed annually by the Court of Alderman.[2] The regulatory regime required licensees to take an oath that they would undertake

[1] D. Scott and J. Herbst. 'The Financial Services and Markets Bill: regulation and the 21st century' (1999) 1(1) *Journal of International Financial Markets* 33, 33.
[2] J. Fisher and J. Bewsey. *The Law of Investor Protection* (London, 1997) 13.

transactions honestly and without fraud. Gilligan took the view that the 1697 Act 'was a crucial legislative initiative because it was the first attempt by any government to impose certain standards of probity and competence upon those dealing in the embryonic securities market'.[3] The next piece of legislation enacted was the Bubble Act 1720, which was followed by an Act to Prevent the Infamous Practice of Stock-Jobbing in 1734.[4] However, this legislation only lasted until the early part of the eighteenth century and was replaced by the Joint Stock Companies Act 1844 and the Limited Liability Act 1855.[5] It was not until 1939 that any direct legislation applied to the financial services industry. The Prevention of Fraud (Investments) Act 1939 was the first piece of legislation that aimed to protect investors. The 1939 Act was amended by the Prevention of Fraud (Investments) Amendment Act 1958, which gave the Board of Trade the authority to appoint inspectors to investigate the administration of unit trusts. Gilligan noted that these two pieces of legislation 'were notable for the improvements they brought in licensing standards'.[6] Conversely, Fisher and Bewsey argued that they 'were of very limited scope in practice, regulating only a fraction of investment business'.[7] The impact of this legislation was negligible and it resulted in the City of London becoming self-regulating.[8] This is a stance supported by other commentators, who noted that financial markets in the United Kingdom have a 'long-held traditions of self-regulation',[9] as influenced by the 'essentially private character of the Bank of England and the Stock Exchange'.[10]

The next major reform was the Financial Services Act 1986, which represented a complete statutory overhaul of the Prevention of Fraud (Investments) Acts. The reform process began in 1981, when Professor L.C.B. Gower was appointed by the government to undertake a review of the legislative protection required by investors, following (according to Professor Gower himself) 'the collapse, in close succession, of two major firms of the new breed of investment managers. The second and more sensational of these left both the Department of Trade and the Bank of England with egg on their faces.'[11] He published his initial views in a discussion document in 1982 and indicated that he would have preferred to recommend the creation of a 'US-style securities commission, but acknowledged that political constraints made it impossible. Instead he recommended a new Securities Act which would establish wide-ranging self regulatory authorities which would be funded by the industry.'[12] Professor Gower also stated that

---

[3] G. Gilligan. 'The origins of UK financial services regulation' (1997) 18(6) *Company Lawyer* 167, 171.

[4] *Ibid.*   [5] *Ibid.* 174.   [6] *Ibid.* 176.

[7] See Fisher and Bewsey, above n. 2, at 13.

[8] C. Blair. *Financial Services and Markets Bill,* House of Commons Research Paper 99/68 (London, 1999) 7. For an excellent discussion of self-regulation and its application to the financial services sector, see A. Page, 'Self-regulation: the constitutional dimension' (1986) 49(2) *Modern Law Review* 141.

[9] See Gilligan, above n. 3, at 169.   [10] *Ibid.* 170.

[11] L. Gower, 'Big bang and city regulation' (1988) 51(1) *Modern Law Review* 1, 7.

[12] See Gilligan, above n. 3 at 173. In 1981, Gower wrote 'the main City bodies were livid. They denounced me for having, exceeded my brief by suggesting regulation of the elite merchant

he wanted statutory regulation of investment business under the guidance of a financial regulatory agency.[13] He admitted that this would be almost impossible to achieve because the sector was committed to the concept of self-regulation.[14] However, 'revelations about the scandals at Lloyd's, misdeeds by some Stock Exchange members and criminal behaviour and the collapse of many commodity firms tarnished the City's reputation both nationally and internationally'.[15] On producing his final report in 1983, Professor Gower recommended that the Prevention of Fraud (Investments) Acts should be replaced by a new Investor Protection Act, the aim of which would be to provide the framework for a comprehensive system of regulation of investment business based upon self-regulation, subject to government surveillance.[16] Following the publication of the report, two groups were created; one under the guidance of the Governor of the Bank of England to advise on the structure and operation of the self-regulatory groupings, the other under the Parliamentary Under-Secretary of State for Corporate and Consumer Affairs to advise on the prospectus for practitioner-based regulation of the marketing of life insurance and unit trusts.

In October 1984, the government published a White Paper, which endorsed a majority of the recommendations made by Professor Gower.[17] The White Paper stated that its proposals comprised a system of 'self regulation within a statutory framework'.[18] However, Professor Gower argued that 'a more accurate description of what has emerged is statutory regulation monitored by self-regulatory organisations recognised by, and under the surveillance of, a self-standing Commission'.[19] Gilligan was highly critical of the proposals, which upheld the independence of the City of London rather than protected investors.[20] The White Paper envisaged two practitioner bodies, the Securities and Investments Board (SIB), covering the regulation of securities and investments, and the Marketing of Investments Board (MIB), covering the marketing of investments. After the publication of the White Paper, the MIB was established in the form of an organising committee, but it was subsequently decided that it should merge to form a single body, the SIB. Lomnicka took the view that 'the SIB was incorporated in … anticipation of the [Financial Services Act], 1986'.[21] The SIB exercised both legislative and administrative functions, and was described as an 'umbrella organisation'.[22] It supervised self-regulating organisations (SROs),

---

banks and Stock Exchange firms when all that was needed was effective regulation of the fringe operators'. Gower, above n. 11, at p.8.

[13] See Gower, above n. 11, at 8. FSA 1986, s.114(1) permits the Secretary of State to create a 'designated body' if he wishes to delegate his powers under the Act.

[14] Gower, above n. 11.   [15] See *Ibid.* 8.

[16] *Review of Investor Protection*, Cmnd. 9125 (1984).

[17] *Financial Services in the UK: A New Framework for Investor Protection*, Cmnd. 9432.

[18] See Gower, above n. 11, at 11.   [19] *Ibid.*

[20] See Gilligan, above n. 3, at 169.

[21] E. Lomnicka, 'Making the Financial Services Authority accountable' (2000) *Journal of Business Law* 65, 66.

[22] *Ibid.* 67.

which were legal bodies, supervising their members and operating in different sectors of the investment industry.[23] In order to be recognised, a prospective SRO had to apply to the SIB for recognition and, if the application satisfied the statutory conditions, it must be accepted. A recognised professional body (RPB) regulated the practice of a profession rather than having as its main purpose the regulation of investment business.[24]

The Financial Services Act (FSA) 1986 came into effect on 29 April 1988 and it continued the traditional self-regulation system of financial regulation.[25] The aim of the Act was to regulate investment business and some elements of the occupational pension schemes.[26] According to Professor Gower, 'the scope of the Act is wide – much wider than that of the Prevention of Fraud (Investments) Acts'.[27] However, the FSA 1986 did not apply to all aspects of the financial services sector; for example, the banking sector was regulated by the Bank of England under the Banking Act 1987. The FSA 1986 remained on the statute books until it was replaced by the Financial Services and Markets Act (FSMA) 2000.

3 New Labour and a new policy

Three weeks after the 1997 general election, Gordon Brown, then Chancellor of the Exchequer, announced that work would begin on the reform of the regulatory structure created under the FSA 1986.[28] The government had outlined its intention to reform the system in 1995,[29] and proclaimed that 'we propose to make the SIB directly responsible for the regime broadly covered by the 1986 Act'.[30] This was emphatically re-emphasised in 1997 when the Labour Party pledged that 'as the guardians of other people's money there needs to be effective supervision and regulation of the industry'.[31] However, it must be noted that the Conservative government had previously asked the then Chairman of the SIB, Andrew Large, to conduct a review of its effectiveness in 1992.[32] Similarly, in 1994 the Treasury Select Committee also conducted a broad enquiry into financial services regulation.[33] Following the announcement in May 1997, the

---

[23] A self-regulating organisation was defined as an organisation that 'regulates the carrying on of investment business of any kind by enforcing rules which are binding on persons carrying on business of that kind either because they are members of that body or because they are otherwise subject to its control'. FSA 1986, s.8(1).

[24] Fisher and Bewsey above, n 2 at 28.

[25] For a more detailed discussion of self regulation under the FSA 1986 see Gower above, n 11, at 13–17.

[26] Fisher and Bewsey, above n. 2, at 16.   [27] Gower, above n. 11, at 18.

[28] HC. Debs. cols. 508–11, 20 May 1997. See also S. Bazley, 'The Financial Services Authority: risk based regulation, principles based rules and accountability' (2008) 23(8) *Journal of International Banking Law and Regulation* 422.

[29] HC Debs. cols. 1184–5, 14 December 1995, Alistair Darling.   [30] *Ibid.*

[31] *Labour's Manifesto: Equipping Britain for the Future* (London, 1997).

[32] Securities and Investment Board, *Financial Services Regulation: Making the Two Tier System work* (London, 1993).

[33] Treasury and Civil Service Committee *The Regulation of Financial Services in the UK*, HC 332-I, 1994–1995 (London, 1995).

Conservative Party, then in opposition, expressed its concerns over the statement and subsequent uncertainty arising from it.[34] However, this view was
in the minority, as the proposals were supported by the *Financial Times*,[35]
the Consumers Association[36] and the Chief Executive of Lloyds TSB.[37] One
of the most interesting responses was from the Bank of England, whose official response was 'studiously guarded'.[38] It took the view that 'what matters
is not the Bank's position but the whole structure of financial regulation and
what is best for depositor, investor and policy-holder protection'.[39] Following
the announcement, 'the government lost no time in beginning to implement
its ambitious proposals. A new Chairman of the SIB was appointed in August
1997, and in anticipation of its new role, the SIB was renamed the Financial
Services Authority (FSA) in October 1998'.[40] The reforms were published in the
Financial Services and Markets Bill 1998. The next part of the chapter identifies
the factors that influenced the government to alter its policy from self-regulation towards creating a sole financial regulatory agency.

(a) Importance of the banking sector to the United Kingdom economy

An important reason why the self-regulatory stance of the FSA 1986 was
reformed is the contribution made by the financial services sector towards the
economy. The economic functions of the financial services sector can be divided
into three broad categories: matching savers, borrowers and investments
through the investment chain; risk pooling; and managing and facilitating payments.[41] London's importance as the centre of the global financial services sector can be traced back to the twelfth century.[42] Blair noted that 'the process of
internationalisation received an important boost in London's "bid bang" in the
mid-1980s. In particular, deregulation made it possible for non-UK acquisition
of firms, and led to enormous inward investment.'[43] Similarly, Professor Gower
noted that 'London, thanks to the Euro-market, was still a major international
financial centre and the national interest demanded that it remained'.[44]

---

[34] HC Debs. cols 509–11,20 May 1997, Kenneth Clarke.
[35] 'All change for the super-SIB', *Financial Times*, 21 May 1997, available at www.ft.com.
[36] 'Brown signals overhaul of City regulation', *Independent*, 21 May 1997, available at www.
independent.co.uk.
[37] 'One watchdog to monitor all City dealings', *The Times*, 21 May 1997, available at www.
thetimesonline.co.uk.
[38] Blair, above n. 8, at 23.
[39] 'Transfer of banking supervision', *Bank of England Press Release*, 20 May 1997, available at www.
bankofengland.co.uk.
[40] E. Lomnicka, 'Reform of the UK financial services regulation: the creation of a single regulator'
(1999) *Journal of Business Law* 480, 481.
[41] HM Treasury, *The UK Financial Services Sector: rising to the Challenges and Opportunities of
Globalisation* (London, 2005) 5.
[42] Fisher and Bewsey, above n. 2, at 167.
[43] W. Blair, 'The reform of financial regulation in the UK' (1998) *Journal of International Banking
Law* 43.
[44] Gower, above n. 11, at 2.

In addition to its historical significance, the following statistics highlight the importance of the financial services sector to the economy.[45] In 1996, the financial intermediation sector contributed 6.4 per cent, or £42.7 billion to the United Kingdom's gross domestic product.[46] In 1999, over 1.17 million people were employed in the financial intermediation sector.[47] In 1998, the typical daily turnover of foreign exchange in the United Kingdom was approximately £380 billion. This was almost more than that of the United States, Japan and Singapore combined.[48] It is also interesting to note that more companies are listed on the London Stock Exchange than on the Tokyo or New York Stock Exchanges.[49] In 1998, the annual turnover of the London Stock Market was £1,037.1 billion, making it the world's third largest stock market. In 2003, the United Kingdom produced over 40 per cent of the world's turnover in cross-border foreign equity trading.[50] The UK private equity industry accounted for 47 per cent of the total annual European private equity investment in 2003.[51] According to a 2005 study by the Centre for Economic and Business Research, the City of London accounted for '41 per cent of all city-type financial services in the EU'.[52] In 2005, HM Treasury reported that:

> the UK financial services sector also contributes directly to output, employment, trade and productivity in the UK. It accounts for over 5 per cent of UK gross value added, one million jobs and a trade surplus of 1.6 per cent of GDP. Moreover, there is evidence that it is a source of higher-than-average productivity within the UK, and that productivity within the sector is growing faster than in the economy as a whole.[53]

The British Bankers Association (BBA) reported that 'the UK's financial industry has grown faster than any other business sector over the past ten years'.[54] The Chief Executive of the BBA, Angela Knight, stated that 'financial services are the powerhouse of the UK economy: a massive contributor to the Exchequer through tax, an employer of more than a million people directly and one of the UK's last acknowledged world-leading industries'.[55]

In light of the above evidence, it is essential that the United Kingdom has an effective financial regulatory environment that protects investors and safeguards a significant contributor to the economy.

---

[45] HM Treasury Financial Services Report, above n. 41, at 5.   [46] Blair, above n. 8, at 14.

[47] International Financial Services, *International Financial Markets in the UK* (London, 2004).

[48] Blair, above n. 8, at 7.

[49] HM Treasury Financial Services Report, above n. 41, at 9.

[50] *Ibid.*   [51] *Ibid.* 10.

[52] Centre for Economics and Business Research, *The City's Importance to the EU Economy 2005* (Corporation of London, 2005) 35.

[53] HM Treasury Financial Services Report, above n 41, at 18.

[54] British Bankers Association Press Release, 'Financial services sector tops UK growth tables'; 18 January 2008, available at www.bba.org.uk. See also National Statistics News Release 'Financial services top growth sector 1996 to 2006', *Economic and Labour Market Review*, 14 January 2008, available at www.statistics.gov.uk.

[55] BBA Press Release, above n. 54.

***Q1 What was the former Labour government's policy towards banking regula-
tion between 1997 and 2010?***

(b) Ineffective legislative framework

The regulatory system under the FSA 1986 was extremely fragmented and often
confusing for consumers and the financial services sector. The high level of
fragmentation is illustrated by the fact that there were several pieces of legislation relating to the regulation of the financial services and banking sector. This
caused uncertainty and an unsatisfactory division of responsibility between
the regulators.[56] Blair commented that 'the proliferation of agencies was over-
complex'.[57] Similarly, McDowall noted that 'the structure of financial services
regulation was certainly confusing given that there are twenty bodies conducting financial services regulation'.[58] The problems resulting from this fragmentation were graphically highlighted by the lack of action, co-operation and
communication between the regulatory agencies during the pensions mis-
selling crisis in the 1990s.[59] Therefore, the creation of a single agency would present 'opportunities for developing a rational and coherent regulatory system'.[60]
It has also been argued that the creation of a single regulatory agency 'brings
with it the obvious benefits of economies of scale'.[61] Lomnicka concluded 'it is
clear that regulatory functions which affect the whole financial sector can best
be undertaken on a unified and co-ordinated basis'.[62]

   There are numerous examples of the failures of the FSA 1986 regulatory system. For example, the level of supervision and the enforcement policies of the
SROs and the SIB were inconsistent,[63] which clearly indicated the failings of the
system and damaged the confidence of investors.[64]

   One of the most important innovations introduced by the FSA 1986 was the
creation of the SIB. The FSA 1986 introduced a higher level of regulation, which
imposed more obligations on the regulated sector. To enforce these higher
standards of behaviour, the SIB was given enhanced statutory enforcement

---

[56] HM Treasury, *Financial Services and Markets Bill: A Consultation Document,* Part 1, *Overview
of Financial Regulatory Reform* (London, 1998) 1. See also see R. McDowall, 'Financial services
authority: progress or pragmatism?' (1998) 13(4) *Journal of International Banking Law* 123, 124.
The relevant agencies were the Building Societies Commission, Friendly Societies Commission,
Insurance Directorate of the Department of Trade and Industry, Investment Management
Regulatory Organisation, Personal Investment Authority, Registry of Friendly Societies,
Securities and Futures Authority, SIB and the Supervision and Surveillance Division of the Bank
of England.

[57] See Blair, above n. 43, at 45.   [58] See McDowall, above n. 56, at 124.

[59] See Lominicka, above, n. 40, at 488. For a more detailed discussion of the pensions mis-selling
crisis, see R. Nobles, and J. Black, 'Personal pensions misselling: the causes and lessons from
regulatory failure' (1998) 61(6) *Modern Law Review* 789 and J. Virgo, and P. Ryley, 'Mis-selling of
personal pension plans: a legal perspective' (1999) 5(1) *Journal of Pensions Management* 18.

[60] See Lominicka, above n. 40, at 486.   [61] *Ibid.*   [62] *Ibid.* 488.

[63] See HM Treasury Consultation document, above n. 56, at 124..

[64] See Bazley, above n. 28, at 423.

powers combined with tougher criminal sanctions.[65] As pointed out by Grey, 'in order to ensure efficacious enforcement of the FSA [1986], the SIB had an impressive range of investigatory powers'.[66] The SIB could apply for either an injunction or a restitution order against unauthorised investment businesses.[67] The SIB had the power to bar financial practitioners from operating in the financial services industry.[68] FSA 1986, section 61 provided comparable powers to those in section 6 to act against unacceptable ways of carrying our investment business.[69] Finally, the SIB could apply to the court to wind up either an authorised person or an appointed representative.[70] However, the prosecutorial role of the SIB was limited to breaches relating to the authorisation to conduct investment business and insider dealing.[71] Its enforcement performance was hampered by its unwillingness to take on a larger prosecutorial role.[72] The enforcement performance of the SIB can be criticised because it paid little or no attention to supervision or improving its statutory investigatory mechanisms and it did little to tackle or prevent commercial fraud.[73] Conversely, it has been argued that during its lifespan, the SIB did ensure that the financial sector and markets were effectively regulated.[74]

In summary, the regulatory system under the FSA 1986 had several fundamental flaws. First, the Act created too many financial regulatory agencies.[75]

[65] J. Fishman, 'A comparison of enforcement of securities law violations in the UK and US' (1993) 14(9) *Company Lawyer* 163.

[66] For a more detailed commentary on these provisions of the FSA 1986 see J. Grey, 'Financial Services Act 1986 Reforms: Part 2' (1991) 9(9) *International Banking Law* 412, 415.

[67] FSA 1986, s.6.

[68] *Ibid.* s.59. For a critical commentary on these powers see R. Davies, 'Powers granted to the SIB under FSA 1986, s.59' (1994) 15(4) *Company Lawyer* 119.

[69] For a more detailed commentary of these powers see H. McVea, 'Fashioning a system of civil penalties for insider dealing: sections 61 and 62 of the Financial Services Act 1986' (1996) *Journal of Business Law* (July) 344 and D. Capps, 'The UK Securities and Investments Board: how it can and does protect investors' (1993) 8(6) *Journal of International Banking Law* 248.

[70] FSA, ss.71 and 72. For a more detailed discussion and analysis of the powers of the SIB see R. Harwood, 'The SIB's exercise of its enforcement powers' (1995) 16(9) *Company Lawyer* 271 and C. Currie, 'Civil enforcement as a regulatory device: the use of the civil law as a means of enforcing securities law violations' (1996) 17(5) *Company Lawyer* 139.

[71] For a more detailed discussion of the enforcement of the insider dealing provisions of the FSA 1986, see E. Lomnicka, 'Curtailing section 62 accountability' (1991) *Journal of Business Law* (July) 353 and A. Alcock, 'Insider dealing: how did we get here' (1994) 15(3) *Company Lawyer* 67.

[72] It should be noted that the FSA 1986 did provide the SIB with fraud enforcement powers under s.47. For a more detailed analysis see W. Barnett, 'Fraud enforcement in the Financial Services Act 1986: an analysis and discussion of section 47' (1996) 17(7) *The Company Lawyer* 203.

[73] See B. Rider, 'Policing the city: combating fraud and other abuses in the corporate securities industry' (1988) 41 *Current Legal Problems* 47 and J. Long, 'Policing the markets: SIB's role' (1994) 15(3) *Company Lawyer* 83.

[74] See Blair, above n. 43, at 49. This view is also supported by I. MacNeil, 'The future for financial regulation: the financial services and markets bill' (1999) 62(5) *Modern Law Review* 725 and M. Taylor, 'Redrawing the regulatory map: why the Financial Services Act must not be reformed in isolation' (1996) 11(10) *Journal of International Banking Financial Law* 463.

[75] Fishman, in particular, noted that the approach adopted towards the enforcement of the FSA 1986 has been 'marked by overlapping authority and lack of co-ordination'. See above n. 65, at 171.

Secondly, the provisions of the Act were not effectively enforced. Thirdly, this period of financial regulation was blighted by a number of high profile financial scandals. Fourthly, the FSA 1986 was poorly drafted and very difficult for consumers to understand.[76]

Q2 Briefly outline some of the criticisms of the Financial Services Act 1986.

(c) Independence of the Bank of England

The Labour government adopted a two-stage legislative approach towards reforming financial services regulation. In May 1997, Gordon Brown announced the first part of the reform process: changes to the role, powers and function of the Bank of England.[77] The Bank of England was to concentrate upon its role of curbing inflation, which according to Arora 'would bring it in line with the Bundesbank and the Federal Reserve Bank'.[78] The Bank of England Act 1998 gave the Bank of England independence in determining the United Kingdom's monetary policy.[79] The objectives of the monetary policy of the Bank of England are to maintain price stability, and to support the economic policy of the government through growth and employment.[80] The legislation also created a Monetary Policy Committee, which has the responsibility of formulating monetary policy.[81] McDowall took the view that 'the creation of the Financial Services Authority was the flipside of UK Chancellor Gordon Brown's announcement that UK interest rate and money supply management would devolve from the UK Treasury to the Bank of England'.[82] He added 'the changes are progress but they do seem to have come from a desire to change the role of the Bank of England rather then an altruistic desire to improve financial services regulation'.[83] Blair *et al.* took the view that the '1998 Act reflects a new policy consensus in favour of taking the conduct of monetary policy out of direct political control'.[84]

The second stage was the formal transfer of banking supervision from the Bank of England to the FSA. Since the Bank of England Act 1696 'the Bank has had a virtual monopoly as regards the carrying on of fully fledged banking business by a corporation'.[85] The Banking Acts 1979 and 1987 granted the Bank

[76] Justice compared attempting to understand the Act to 'wading through blancmange'. See Justice, *The Protection of the Small Investor* (Cambridge, 1992).

[77] HM Treasury, 'The Chancellor's statement to the House of Commons on the Bank of England', 49/97, 20 May 1997, available at www.hm-treasury.gov.uk.

[78] A. Arora, 'Changes to the powers of the Bank of England' (1997) 16(3) *Journal of International Banking and Financial Law* 21. For a more detailed discussion of this see M. Blair, R. Cranston, C. Ryan, and M. Taylor, *Blackstone's guide to the Bank of England Act 1998* (London, 1998) 13–18.

[79] This amended the provision under the Bank of England Act 1946 that HM Treasury were able to direct the Bank of England where the public interest demanded it. Bank of England Act 1946, s.4(1).

[80] Bank of England Act 1998, s.11.   [81] Bank of England Act 1998, s.13.

[82] See McDowall, above n. 56, at 123.   [83] *Ibid.* 127.   [84] M. Blair *et al.*, above n. 78, 10.

[85] E. Ellinger, E. Lomnicka, and R. Hooley, *Modern Banking Law* (Oxford University Press, 2002) 29.

of England the power and the duty to supervise the banks authorised by it to carry on a deposit-taking business in the United Kingdom.[86] Part III of the 1998 Act transferred the Bank of England's powers and responsibilities for the supervision of the banking sector and wholesale money market institutions to the FSA.[87] The FSA inherited the regulatory function of the Insurance Directorate of HM Treasury, the Building Societies Commission, the Friendly Societies Commission and the Registry of Friendly Societies. Arora concluded that the 'the changes announced … will have an unprecedented effect on the powers of the Bank of England'.[88] Taylor took the view that 'the Bank of England Act 1998 amounts to one of the most significant changes to the Bank's governance, role and functions in its 300-year history. It is certainly the most significant legislative change to affect the Bank since nationalisation in 1946.'[89]

(d) Ineffective consumer protection and financial scandals

One of the most important reasons why the Labour government created the FSA was the lack of protection afforded to investors. Banking regulation under the stewardship of the Bank of England was beset with financial scandals, including the secondary banking crisis, and the banking collapses of Johnson Matthey Bank, Barlow Clowes, Bank of Credit and Commerce International (BCCI) and Barings Bank, and of Equitable Life. The Labour government felt that there was a genuine need for effective regulation because these scandals undermined confidence within the banking and financial services industry. The collapse of any financial institution will have a major impact on customers, both individual and businesses, and it is therefore unsurprising that successive governments have attempted to safeguard the stability of the banking and financial services system by imposing tougher regulation. The next section briefly highlights the inadequacies of the performance of the Bank of England and how these contributed towards the change of policy by the Labour government.

(i) The secondary banking crisis
The secondary banking crisis of the 1970s was preceded by a 'period of UK financial liberalisation, [during which] a number of smaller or "secondary"

---

[86] For a more detailed commentary on how the Bank of England regulated the banking sector, see D. Singh, *Banking Regulation of UK and US financial markets* (Ashgate, 2007) 8–17 and more specifically on its role under the Banking Act 1987, see A. Arora, 'The Banking Act 1987: Part 1' (1988) 9(1) *The Company Lawyer*, 8.

[87] Bank of England Act 1998, s.21. The Act transferred to the FSA the Bank of England's supervision powers under the Banking Act 1987, the Banking Coordination (Second Council Directive) Regulations 1992, SI 1992/3218 Building Societies Act 1985, s.101(4) FSA 1986, s.43 and the Investment Services Regulations 1995, SI 1995/3275.

[88] Arora, above n. 78, 21.

[89] *Ibid.*, 17. For a more detailed commentary of the history of the Bank of England, see J. Wood, *A History of Central Banking in Great Britain and the United States* (Cambridge University Press, 2005) 32–116.

banks rapidly expanded their lending to property companies in the early 1970s'.[90] However, the growth was short lived when the government decided to implement a restrictive financial policy in 1973. As a result, the public's confidence in the secondary banking sector began to wane, and depositors began to withdraw their savings. The Bank of England responded by creating the 'Control Committee of the Bank of England and the English and Scottish Clearing Banks', which provided financial support and became known as the 'lifeboat'.[91] In practice, this meant that any lending risks were equally shared amongst all members of the Committee. Dale pointed out that 'by August 1974 total lifeboat support approached £1.2 billion, representing 40 per cent of the participating banks' capital. Beyond this, the banks were not prepared to go, with the result that any further assistance had to be provided by the Bank of England at its own risk. During this period some banks that had received liquidity support now faced insolvency.'[92]

(ii) Johnson Matthey Bank

Johnson Matthey Bank faced collapse in 1984 and highlighted the inadequacies of banking regulation under the Banking Act 1979.[93] This bank began to have financial problems in 1984 after it decided to lend to a small number of customers who faced financial problems.[94] The Bank of England became aware of the difficulties in 1984 when it was informed that the bank needed extensive financing to prevent its collapse. The Bank of England decided that this bank could not be allowed to collapse and it formulated a financial rescue package of £245 million. Additionally, Johnson Matthey Bank was able to raise £130 million from its own diminishing resources.[95] The light-touch approach adopted by the Bank of England had resulted in Johnson Matthey Bank being able to breach the safeguards put in place by the Banking Act 1979 by distracting the Bank of England's attention away from its financial problems.[96] Ellinger et al. took the view that 'if JMB had been subjected to the more stringent supervision which applies to licensed deposit-takers, its financial difficulties would have been discovered earlier'.[97] They added that 'following the JMB affair, the question of bank supervision was reviewed by a Committee set up by the Chancellor in 1984 and chaired by the governor of the Bank of England'.[98] It is important to note that Johnson Matthey Bank's difficulties led to the enactment of the Banking Act 1987.

---

[90] R. Dale, 'Bank crisis management: the case of the United Kingdom' (1995) 10(8) *Journal of International Banking Law* 326, 327.

[91] *Ibid.*   [92] *Ibid.*

[93] E. Ellinger, E. Lomnicka, and R. Hooley, *Ellinger's Modern Banking Law* (Oxford University Press, 2006) 33.

[94] Dale, above n. 90, at 327.   [95] *Ibid.* 328.

[96] D. Lewis, 'The Banking Bill: between Charybdis and Scylla' (1987) 2(1) *Journal of International Banking Law* 49, 50.

[97] Ellinger *et al.*, above n. 85, at 98.

[98] *Ibid.* 33.

(iii) Barlow Clowes

A graphic illustration of the inadequacies of the approach towards financial regulation was the collapse of Barlow Clowes. The company was created in 1973 by Peter and Elizabeth Clowes,[99] and operated out of Jersey due to a loophole in the UKs tax regime. When the loophole was closed by the Finance Act 1985, the company was renamed Barlow Clowes International and moved to Gibraltar. Barlow Clowes International offered investors a tax efficient and low risk scheme which proved to be extremely popular, more so than its predecessor. A large percentage of the money that was invested in Barlow Clowes International 'found its way into loans made to companies connected with Clowes and his associates or was used to buy yachts and property'.[100] The Department of Trade and Industry (DTI) appointed inspectors to investigate the operations of Barlow Clowes International when it became disturbed about its activities.[101] The evidence collected by the inspectors resulted in the SIB obtaining a court order that compelled Barlow Clowes International to be wound up and it was subsequently placed into liquidation in 1988.[102] Johnson described the incident as 'a sorry tale of how thousands of investors, many of them elderly and retired, stand to lose substantial sums of money'.[103] The two companies had amassed £190 million from approximately 20,000 misled investors.

Following the collapse of the company, many MPs referred complaints from local constituents to the Parliamentary Commissioner for Administration (Ombudsman).[104] The nature of the complaints related to actions by the DTI under the Prevention of Fraud (Investments) Act 1958.[105] The report by the Parliamentary Ombudsman highlighted several areas 'in which there had been significant maladministration by the DTI'.[106] These included an error by the DTI, who on four separate occasions allowed Barlow Clowes to continue operating without a licence as required under the Prevention of Fraud (Investments) Act 1958.[107] By 1984, when the DTI had finally accepted that Barlow Clowes International had been operating without a licence, its decision to allow the company to continue trading also amounted to maladministration.[108] In

---

[99] G. Drewry, and R. Gregory, 'Barlow Clowes and the Ombudsman: Part 1' (1991) *Public Law* (Summer) 192, 193.

[100] *Ibid.*

[101] The inspectors were appointed under the FSA 1986, s.106.

[102] Drewry and Gregory, above n. 99, at 193.

[103] H. Johnson, 'The Barlow Clowes affair and government regulation' (1989) 7(8) *Journal of International Banking Law* 114 114.

[104] V. Younghusband, 'Financial regulation: the Barlow Clowes affair' (1990) 5(3) *Journal of International Banking Law* 7676. For a full commentary on the findings of the Parliamentary Ombudsman, see Parliamentary Commissioner for Administration, *Second Report of the PCA: the Barlow Clowes Affair*, HC 76 (London, 1989/1990).

[105] For a more detailed discussion of the potential liability of the DTI, see S. Vaughan, and P. May, 'The Barlow Clowes affair' (1988) 7(3) *International Banking Law* 34, 36–7.

[106] Younghusband, above n. 104, at 76.

[107] Prevention of Fraud (Investments) Act 1958, s.1.

[108] Younghusband, above n. 104, at 76.

December 1989, the then Conservative government, without admitting liability, announced that it was prepared to make significant payments to those people who had lost money after investing in the two companies.[109]

(iv) BCCI

One of the most infamous banking collapses in the United Kingdom was Bank of Credit and Commerce International (BCCI) in 1991. The bank was established in Pakistan, incorporated in Luxembourg in 1972 and in 1976 it opened its first office in the United Kingdom.[110] BCCI applied to the Bank of England to be legally recognised as a bank under the Banking Act 1979. The Bank of England refused to do so, but nonetheless granted it a licence as a deposit-taking institution under the Banking Act 1979.[111] The Bank of England mistakenly relied on regulation provided by the Luxembourg regulatory authorities and decided not formally to regulate BCCI itself.[112] Arora pointed out that during this period further memoranda passed between the officials of the bank, drawing attention to the fact that the real place of business of BCCI SA was London and that the Bank of England should be its primary supervisor.[113]

The first concerns regarding the operations of BCCI were raised by an international group called 'the College'. According to Arora 'this group expressed concerns about a large concentration of exposures due to the group's lending and the effect on the group's activities of the arrest of seven of its officials in Tampa, Florida, in October 1988, on charges of drug trafficking, conspiracy and money laundering'.[114] The Bank of England was informed by Price Waterhouse Coopers (PWC) that the auditors were unable to sign BCCI's 1989 accounts due to financial irregularities.[115] Towards the end of 1990, PWC became aware of the fraudulent activities of BCCI's directors and were asked by the Bank of England to investigate the allegations.[116] Some seven months later, the Bank of England sought to close down BCCI,[117] and in 1991 the bank collapsed, leaving a vast amount of debt under a shadow of allegations of fraud. Hemraj noted that 'BCCI was deliberately rigged to avoid effective regulation. Generally speaking, despite being an

---

[109] For a more detailed commentary on the government's response to the findings of the Parliamentary Ombudsman, see G. Drewry, and R. Gregory, 'Barlow Clowes and the Ombudsman: Part 2' (1991) *Public Law* (Autumn) 408, 415.

[110] A. Arora, 'The statutory system of bank supervision and the failure of BCCI' (2006) *Journal of Business Law* (August) 487, 490.

[111] *Ibid.* 490.

[112] This was permitted under the Banking Act 1979, s.3(5). This was amended by the Banking Act 1987, s.9(3), which however, continued to allow the Bank of England to rely upon the regulators in Luxembourg.

[113] Arora, above n. 110, at 490–1.   [114] *Ibid.*   [115] *Ibid.* 490–2.

[116] Price Waterhouse Coopers were asked to investigate the activities of BCCI under the Banking Act 1987, s.41.

[117] Arora, above n. 110, at 492.

international financial centre, Britain has failed to create an effective regulatory structure.'[118] Arora added that 'the failure of BCCI was clearly a failure of both domestic and international banking regulation. Rarely was BCCI hindered by regulators or law enforcement officials: even after the bank was shut down, response from bank regulators was sluggish'.[119] Indeed, in his report on the collapse of BCCI, Lord Bingham concluded that 'on more than one occasion the Bank's supervision was not up to scratch'.[120] The collapse of BCCI 'in July 1991 sent shockwaves around the banking world and left thousands of depositors out of pocket with little prospect of seeing their money again'.[121]

In 1993, over 6,000 claimants sued the Bank of England. According to Grey, 'the liquidators' claim related to the Bank of England's discharge of supervisory and regulatory responsibilities over the United Kingdom operations of the BCCI banking group over a period which spanned 1980 through to 1991 when action was taken by the Bank of England'.[122] The claimants alleged that the Bank of England had committed the tort of misfeasance and were liable for negligence in a public office.[123] Zuckerman noted that when the case ended in 2005, 'the claimants abandoned their action on day 256 of the trial. In the intervening 12 years a great deal of litigation took place requiring numerous court hearings occupying an extraordinary amount of judicial time in the High Court, Court of Appeal and House of Lords (involving at least 63 days of hearings) and costing the defendants some £80 million.'[124] The case was lengthy and the costs of both parties spiralled. It has been estimated that Deloitte spent approximately £38 million, while the Bank of England spent around £170 million on the case.[125] The collapse of BCCI influenced the decision by the government to create a new financial services regulatory regime and tarnished the regulatory reputation of the Bank of England.

---

[118] M. Hemraj, 'The regulatory failure: the saga of BCCI' (2005) 8(4) *Journal of Money Laundering Control* 346, 350.

[119] Arora, above n. 110, at 509.

[120] K. McGuire, 'Banking supervision after the Bingham Report on BCCI: the end of an era?' (1993) 4(3) *Journal of International Company and Commercial Law* 118. For a commentary on the response of the Bank of England to the collapse of BCCI, see M. Stallworthy, 'BCCI: Bank of England response' (1992) 11(4) *Journal of International Banking and Financial Law* 44.

[121] *Ibid.*

[122] J. Grey, 'Lessons from BCCI saga for the current accountability debate surrounding Northern Rock?' (2008) 23(2) *Journal of International Banking Law and Regulation* 37, 38.

[123] See M. Andenas, 'Liability for supervisors and depositor's rights: the BCCI and the Bank of England in the House of Lords' (2001) 22(8) *The Company Lawyer* 226.

[124] M. Zuckerman, 'A colossal wreck – the BCCI – Three Rivers litigation' (2006) 25 *Civil Justice Quarterly* (July) 287.

[125] Editorial, 'BCCI liquidators drop Bank of England claim' (2006) 27(3) *Company Lawyer* 91. For a more detailed commentary regarding the potential liability of the FSA, see E. Cavalli, and T. Blyth, 'The liability of the Financial Services Authority after Three Rivers' (2001) 3(5) *Journal of International Financial Markets* 199.

(v) Barings Bank

The collapse of Barings Bank in 1995, one of the United Kingdom's oldest banks,[126] with approximately £927 million in losses, is associated with the illegal actions of Nicholas Leeson, otherwise known as the 'rogue trader'. Nicholas Leeson opened the famous '88888' account to offset losses and unauthorised transactions he made whilst undertaking unlicensed trading on the Singapore, Osaka and Tokyo Stock Exchanges between 1992 and 1995.[127] Kane and DeTrask took the view that proprietary trading by Nicholas Leeson destroyed Barings Bank.[128] Kornert stated that 'the Barings crisis of 1995 is regarded as one of the most spectacular international events in the banking world in recent years'.[129] According to Dale, '[a]t the end of February 1995 Barings, an old-established United Kingdom merchant banking group with total assets of around £6 billion and deposits of some £3 billion, faced collapse, having incurred massive losses on unauthorised derivatives transactions undertaken through its Singapore trading unit'.[130] The outcome for Barings can be contrasted with the collapse of Johnson Matthey Bank because the Bank of England refused to bail out the bank. Following its collapse it was sold to the Dutch bank ING in 1995 for a symbolic £1.

Barings Bank was regulated by the Bank of England under the Banking Act 1987 and although it was not directly responsible for regulating the overseas subsidiaries of Barings, the Bank of England had to rely upon the reputation and the financial stability of the parent company.[131] The Bank of England can be criticised because it 'knew about Barings' extraordinary profitable activities in Asia, [but] it accepted the bank's explanation of volatile arbitrage trading between the Asian Exchanges'.[132] Dale argued that 'there could be no doubt that the collapse of Barings, with ensuing losses to depositors, would inflict considerable damage both on London's reputation as a banking centre and on the credit standing – and therefore competitiveness – of UK merchant banks'.[133] The collapse of Barings Bank clearly demonstrated fundamental weaknesses in the regulatory approach of the Bank of England.

(vi) Equitable Life

The near collapse of Equitable Life straddles the regulation of the Bank of England and the FSA. The firm misled its policy-holders over a ten-year period

---

[126] J. Kornert, 'The Barings crisis of 1890 and 1995: causes, courses, consequences and the danger of domino effects' (2003) 13(3) *International Financial Markets, Institutions and Money* 187, 189.

[127] *Ibid.* 197.

[128] E. Kane, and K. DeTrask, 'Breakdown of accounting controls at Barings and Daiwa: benefits of using opportunity-cost measures for trading activity' (1999) 7(3–4) *Pacific-Basin Finance Journal* 203, 206.

[129] See Kornert, above n. 126, at 196.   [130] See Dale, above n. 90, at 330–1.

[131] See Kornert, above n. 126, at 204.

[132] *Ibid.* 204. For a more detailed discussion of the regulatory failure behind the collapse of Barings Bank, see L. Proctor, 'The Barings collapse: a regulatory failure, or a failure of supervision' (1997) 22 *Brooklyn Journal of International Law* 735.

[133] See Dale, above n. 90, at 330–1.

about the amount of money it had. In 2000, Equitable Life stated that the value of its customers' polices was £3 billion more than the total amount of the assets of the company. Equitable Life's position worsened when the House of Lords handed Equitable Life a bill of more than £1.5 billion to pay for annuity guarantees.[134] Singh took the view that 'the difficulties surrounding Equitable Life occurred because of the gross failures of management to mitigate the problems arising from its approach to calculating annuity rates'.[135]

The near collapse of Equitable Life resulted in several public investigations, including the Baird Report,[136] the Penrose Report,[137] and one by the Parliamentary Ombudsman.[138] The Baird Report highlighted and commented upon a number of inadequacies in the approach adopted by the FSA towards the scandal.[139] The Penrose Report criticised the FSA for failing to keep abreast of the problems that Equitable Life was facing. It must be noted, however, that the vast majority of the problems associated with Equitable Life occurred under the watchful eye of the Department of Trade and Industry and HM Treasury.[140] According to Singh, the FSA was also criticised because it did not 'notify consumers fully about the problems associated with Equitable Life so they could avoid buying policies that were relatively unmarketable by other providers without some sort of financial penalty'.[141]

Q3 How effective was the Bank of England's approach to banking regulation prior to 1997?

Q4 What is meant by the concept of 'self-regulation'?

4 The Financial Services Authority

The purpose of the FSMA 2000 is to provide a single legal framework for the FSA, replacing the different frameworks under which the various regulators operated. The Act contains a number of important provisions and policies that aim to overcome some of the inadequacies highlighted above. The FSA is responsible for the authorisation and prudential supervision of members of the financial services sector.

---

[134] *Equitable Life Assurance Society* v. *Alan David Hyman* [2000] 1 All ER 961. For a more detailed commentary see L. Roach, 'Equitable Life and non-executive directors: clarification from the High Court?' (2005) 26(8) *The Company Lawyer* 253.

[135] See Singh, above n. 86, at 29.

[136] Financial Services Authority, *Report of the Financial Services Authority on the Review of the Regulation of Equitable Life Assurance Society from 1 January 1999 to 8 December 2000* (London, 2001) (Baird Report).

[137] Lord Penrose, Return to an Order of the House of Commons dated 8 March 2004 for the Report of the Equitable Life Inquiry, HC 290, (Penrose Report).

[138] Parliamentary Ombudsman, *The Prudential Regulation of Equitable Life,: Overview and Summary of Findings*, HC 809–1 (London, 2002).

[139] See above n. 136, at 187.   [140] *Ibid.*

[141] Singh, above n. 86, at 29. The impact of the near collapse of Northern Rock will be discussed below.

The FSMA 2000 has a number of distinctive features. First, it provides the FSA with four statutory objectives and requires them to adopt an open and responsive approach. In order to meet this requirement, the FSA has established a Consumer Panel,[142] with a brief to monitor the extent to which the FSA is meeting its objectives in relation to consumers. The FSA has also created an independent Practitioner Forum, which publishes its views on the work of the FSA.[143]

The FSA has the power to grant,[144] refuse,[145] or withdraw the authorisation,[146] or restrict the business of firms.[147] The FSA also has five main types of standard-setting powers: to make rules,[148] which are applicable to regulated firms; to state principles in the form of a code of practice; to make evidential provisions, which will assist to demonstrate observance or breach of binding requirements; to endorse codes of regulated firms; and to issue guidance. The FSA also has the ability to fine firms for breaches of its rules and procedures.

(a) Statutory objectives

The most innovative aspect of the FSMA 2000 was its four statutory objectives. The FSA is required to carry out its regulatory functions in a way that, as far as is reasonably possible,[149] is compatible with the four statutory objectives: (i) to maintain market confidence in the financial system;[150] (ii) to increase public awareness;[151] (iii) to ensure consumer protection;[152] and (iv) to prevent and reduce financial crime.[153]

(i) Maintaining market confidence

The statutory objective of maintaining confidence in the UK financial system is shared jointly with the Bank of England. This co-operation is further enhanced by the cross-membership arrangements made by HM Treasury, between the FSA and the Bank of England.[154] Market confidence is defined as 'maintaining confidence in the financial system',[155] whilst the financial system includes financial markets and exchanges, regulated activities and connected activities.[156] The stance taken by the FSA is that maintaining market confidence 'involves preserving both the actual stability in the financial system and the reasonable expectation that it will remain stable'. [157] The FSA is also alert to the reality that market confidence can be threatened not just as a result of financial failure. As stated by Howard Davies, the then Chairman of the FSA, 'it is not just financial failure that can threaten market confidence. Widespread market misconduct can be just as serious. So too can financial crime – either because its form is so serious, or so widespread within the system'. [158]

---

[142] FSMA 2000, s.10.   [143] *Ibid.* s.9.   [144] *Ibid.* s.42.   [145] *Ibid.* s.54.
[146] *Ibid.* s.33.   [147] *Ibid.* s.48.   [148] *Ibid.* s.138.   [149] *Ibid.* s.2(1).
[150] *Ibid.* s.3.   [151] *Ibid.* s.4.   [152] *Ibid.* s.5.   [153] *Ibid.* s.6.
[154] *Ibid.* s.3.   [155] *Ibid.* s.3(1).   [156] *Ibid.* s.3(2).
[157] Financial Services Authority, *A New Regulator for the New Millennium* (London, 2000) 6.
[158] Howard avies, FSA, 'The role of financial regulators in promoting financial stability', speech at IOSCO Conference, 23–29 June 2001, available at www.fsa.gov.uk.

The FSA has not expressed the aim of preventing all collapses, or all lapses in the conduct of the financial system, as achieving zero market failure is held to be impossible and undesirable.[159] However, the FSA aims to minimise the impact of any failure. In a financial system in which the financial services industry constitutes more than 7 per cent GDP and forms a crucially important sector of the UK economy, the maintenance of market confidence is pivotal to its success. However, it is wholly unrealistic to believe that, if the FSA fulfils their role to the utmost degree, we will suddenly witness the advent of a revolutionary financial system that boasts zero market failure and not even a whisper of a financial scandal. This type of regime would be suicidal to the industry; as stated by the FSA, 'any such regime … would be likely to damage the economy as a whole and would be uneconomic from a cost-benefit point of view; it would stifle innovation and competition'. [160] As demonstrated above, the FSA were unable to prevent the near collapse of Northern Rock (see further below) and the Equitable Life scandal, the latter of which led to a radical policy rethink by then Labour government and the implementation of the Banking Act 2009 and the Financial Services Act 2010.

(ii) Promotion of public awareness

The second statutory objective relates to promoting public awareness and understanding of the financial system.[161] This includes increasing the awareness of the benefits and risks associated with different kinds of investment or other financial dealings,[162] and the provision of appropriate information and advice.[163] This is an extremely innovative and timely objective and never before has a financial regulator been explicitly charged with the significant role of educating consumers. Taylor states that assigning this role to the FSA 'represents an innovation in the sense that this type of regulation serves a social purpose as well as contributing to the efficient working of financial markets'.[164]

In order to achieve this statutory obligation, the FSA has stated that two objectives need to be fulfilled: to improve general financial literacy and the quality of the information and advice that is available to consumers. The reasoning behind the objective is that there is evidence that consumers do not understand how the financial services system works.[165] In principle, it is a major step forward for consumers that a regulator has been charged with the role of increasing public awareness of the ever-increasingly complex financial system. However, to what extent the FSA will actually be able to fulfil its role is unknown. A core problem that needs to be overcome with regard to today's consumers is the psychological barriers that appear to

---

[159] See above n. 157, at 6.   [160] *Ibid.*   [161] FSMA 2000, s.4.

[162] *Ibid.* s.4(2)(a).   [163] *Ibid.* s.4(2)(b).

[164] M. Blair, M. Minghella, L. Taylor, M. Threipland and G. Walker, *Blackstone's Guide to the Financial Services and Markets Act 2000* (London, 2001) 33.

[165] See above n. 157, at 7.

exist, with many people appearing to believe that they do not need financial education.[166]

(iii) Consumer protection

The FSA is charged with the role of 'securing the appropriate degree of protection for consumers'.[167] When considering the degree of protection that is appropriate, the FSA must have regard to four points:

(a) the differing degrees of risk involved in different kinds of investment or other transaction;[168]
(b) the differing degrees of experience and expertise those different consumers may have in relation to different kinds of regulated activity;[169]
(c) the needs that consumers may have for advice and accurate information;[170] and
(d) that consumers should take responsibility for their decisions.[171]

The imposition of the objective of consumer protection was a welcome step in such a complex and evolving financial system. The general ethos of this objective is that, although consumers need to be protected and adequate mechanisms for protection need to be established, the FSA has to strike a balance between the expectations for protection that consumers have and the level of responsibility that they must accept for their own actions. The aim of the objective is not to protect consumers from every possible risk that they may face. The most obvious example of how the FSA intends to achieve this statutory objective is via the Financial Services Compensation Scheme and Ombudsman Scheme.

The purpose of the Compensation Scheme is to compensate customers who have suffered loss as a consequence of the inability of an authorised firm to meet its liabilities. It also acts as a safety net for customers of authorised firms and compensation is payable if such a firm is unable, or likely to be unable, to pay claims against it. In general, this is when a firm is insolvent or has gone out of business. The Scheme covers business conducted by firms regulated by the FSA and is funded by levies on authorised firms. However, it should be noted that the Scheme is not intended to compensate people where a regulatory breach has occurred. Customers may also make a claim against an authorised person even if the claim arises in relation to an activity which the authorised person did not have permission to do under the FSMA 2000.[172] The FSA claim that membership of both Schemes could significantly benefit the financial services sector unions, because members will have access to a compensation scheme. This means that if a firm were to fail, members are protected and will be refunded a significant proportion of their savings. Following the near collapse of Northern Rock, the FSA announced in October 2008 that the level of

---

[166] For an in-depth commentary see Financial Services Authority, *Better Informed Consumers* (London, 2000).
[167] FSMA, s.5(1).   [168] *Ibid.* s.5(2)(a).   [169] *Ibid.* s.5(2)(b).
[170] *Ibid.* s.5(2)(c).   [171] *Ibid.* s.5(2)(d).   [172] *Ibid.* s.213.

compensation for bank deposits was to be increased from £35,000 to £50,000 for each customer.[173] This also means that joint account holders are eligible to claim up to £100,000.[174]

The Financial Ombudsman Service has been created with the aim of solving disputes between authorised firms and customers. The Ombudsman Scheme is the largest of its kind in the world.[175] All authorised firms are required to submit to the jurisdiction of the scheme.[176] If a claim against an authorised person is upheld, the respondent may be ordered to pay compensation up to a maximum that may be set by the FSA.[177] The Ombudsman may recommend an amount exceeding the limit as fair compensation and the respondent may also be ordered to take such steps as are necessary to rectify the matter complained of.[178] The Scheme operator has the ability to create rules regarding costs that can be awarded by the Ombudsman.[179] The Ombudsman Service is an independent body which acts as a free service to consumers to help settle individual disputes between consumers and financial firms. The Ombudsman Service can be contacted only after the individual has complained to the firm first and has exhausted that avenue. The decision made is binding on the firm concerned but not on the complainant, who still has the option to go to court instead. The service is completely confidential and the names of firms and consumers whose complaints are handled are not published.

The Financial Ombudsman Service commissioned the Hunt Review as part of its continuing corporate strategy.[180] The Hunt Review made a series of recommendations aimed at improving accessibility and the transparency of the Ombudsman Scheme.[181] The first set of recommendations related to raising the profile of the Ombudsman Service: a funded marketing strategy, advertising campaigns and a combined outreach strategy.[182] The Review also suggested

[173] Financial Services Authority Press Release, 'Compensation Scheme to cover savers' claims up to £50,000', 3 October 2008, available at www.fsa.gov.uk.

[174] For a more detailed discussion of these changes see Financial Services Authority, *Financial Services Compensation Scheme: Review of Limits* (London, 2008) and HM Treasury, *Financial Stability and Depositor Protection: Special Resolution Regime* (London, 2008).

[175] P. Morris, 'The Financial Ombudsman Services and the Hunt Review: continuing evolution in dispute resolution' (2008) *Journal of Business Law* 785, 786.

[176] The scheme's compulsory jurisdiction may only be applied to persons who were authorised at the time the activity to which the complaint relates was carried out, and the rules must have been in force at the time, FSMA 2000, s.226. It is important to note that the jurisdiction of the Ombudsman was extended to include certain types of consumer credit arrangements. See Consumer Credit Act 2006, ss.59 and 61.

[177] FSMA 2000, s.229.

[178] This can be enforced through the courts by the complainant if necessary.

[179] FSMA 2000, s.230.

[180] Financial Ombudsman Service, *Corporate Plan and 2008–2009 Budget* (London, 2008) 5 and 12.

[181] Lord Hunt, *Opening Up, Reaching Out and Aiming High: An Agenda for Accessibility and Excellence in the Financial Ombudsman Services* (London, 2008). For other reports on the Ombudsman see E. Kempson, S. Collard and N. Moore, *Fair and Reasonable: An Assessment of the Financial Ombudsman Service* (Personal Finance Research Centre, Bristol University, 2004).

[182] *Ibid.* paras. 2.11–2.15.

a change of name to the 'Financial Complaints Service'.[183] Other recommendations were aimed at streamlining the decision-making process of the Ombudsman Service.[184]

As mentioned above, the imposition of the objective of consumer protection is a welcome step in such a complex financial system. For many consumers, however, the inclusion of this objective has come far too late, with many of them facing the consequences of investments made as a result of poor and misleading advice. Nevertheless, in an age where e-banking and the like is becoming the norm, it is extremely advantageous that mechanisms are beginning to be implemented to protect consumers.

(iv) The reduction of financial crime

The final objective of the FSA is to prevent and reduce financial crime.[185] This statutory duty combines the efforts of financial regulation with those of criminal law intelligence, investigation and the prosecution agencies. The function of the FSA here is to ensure that financial institutions have systems and practices in place to protect themselves against being used as vehicles by financial criminals.[186]

(b) Enforcement powers

As previously argued, one of the criticisms of the FSA 1986 was the enforcement policy adopted by the SIB. FSMA 2000 provides the FSA with the power to ensure that people who work with authorised persons for particular purposes are both fit and proper to perform the functions for which they were employed. Enforcement within the context of FSMA 2000 incorporates two broad concepts: first, preventing those who are not so authorised from conducting banking or investment business; and secondly, ensuring that those who are authorised to conduct such businesses do so properly.[187] The FSMA 2000 states that the FSA has the power to require information or documents that may reasonably be required in connection with the discharge of its functions under the Act.[188] The information or documents can be required from any person, including a legal person. This would include an authorised person, a formerly authorised person, a person connected with an authorised person, an operator, a recognised investment exchange and a recognised clearing house. FSMA 2000 also provides that the FSA has the power to require an authorised person or a formerly authorised person to commission a report and provide it to the FSA in any manner in which the FSA might specify.[189] The FSA is also provided with

---

[183] *Ibid.* para. 2.30.   [184] *Ibid.* paras. 3.14–3.4.   [185] FSMA 2000, s.6.

[186] For a more detailed discussion of how the FSA intends to reduce and prevent financial crime see Part 6, Chapter 3.

[187] J. Bagge, 'The future for enforcement under the new Financial Services Authority' (1998) 19(7) *Company Lawyer* 194, 196.

[188] FSMA 2000, s.165.   [189] *Ibid.* s.166.

powers to issue public statements or impose financial penalties where the rules under the FSMA 2000 have been contravened. For example, the FSA has the power to issue a public statement concerning a breach by an authorised person of any requirement that is imposed by the Act.[190]

Under the FSMA 2000, the FSA has become a prosecuting authority in respect of certain financial criminal offences, such as money laundering. It should be noted, however, that the FSA does not have any direct power to prosecute for fraud or dishonesty offences. These powers apply whether or not the entity to be prosecuted is actually regulated by the FSA and they are therefore the most important aspects of the FSA's obligation to reduce financial crime.[191] The FSA also has the power to impose a financial penalty where it establishes that there has been a contravention by an authorised person of any requirement imposed under FSMA 2000.[192] The FSA has imposed a series of fines on firms who have breached their anti-money laundering obligations under the FSA Handbook, even where there was no evidence of money laundering. For example, the FSA fined the Royal Bank of Scotland £750,000,[193] Investment Services UK Ltd £175,000,[194] Raiffeisen Zentralbank £150,000,[195] Northern Bank £1.25 million,[196] the Bank of Ireland £375,000[197] and the Abbey National £2.2 million.[198]

Since 2006, there has been a significant increase in the frequency of financial penalties imposed by the FSA where it has determined that a firm has inadequate anti-fraud controls. First, in March 2006, the FSA fined Capita Financial Administration Ltd (CFAL) £300,000 for poor anti-fraud controls over client identities and account details.[199] After an investigation, the FSA found that CFAL had inadequately considered the threat posed by fraud and had not maintained effective systems and controls to mitigate this risk.[200] The failures

---

[190] *Ibid.* s.205.   [191] *Ibid.* s.402 (1)(a).

[192] *Ibid.* s.206(1). Ellinger *et al.* noted that 'the FSA has imposed heavy "penalties" on a number of banks for non-compliance with the ML Module'. See above n. 93, at 113.

[193] Financial Services Authority Press Release, 'FSA fines Royal Bank of Scotland £750,000 for money laundering control failings', FSA/PN/123/2002, 17 December 2002, available at www.fsa.gov.uk.

[194] Financial Services Authority Press Release, 'FSA fines bond broker and managing director for anti-money laundering failures', FSA/PN/117/2005, 9 November 2005, available at www.fsa.gov.uk.

[195] Financial Services Authority Press Release, 'FSA fines Raiffeisen Zentralbank £150,000 for money laundering control failings', FSA/PN/035/2004, 6 April 2004, available at www.fsa.gov.uk.

[196] Financial Services Authority Press Release, 'FSA fines Northern Bank £1,250,000 for money laundering control failings', FSA/PN/084/2003, 7 August 2003, available at www.fsa.gov.uk.

[197] Financial Services Authority Press Release, 'FSA fines Bank of Ireland £375,000 for money laundering control failings', 2 FSA/PN/077/2004, September 2004, available at www.fsa.gov.uk.

[198] Financial Services Authority Press Release, FSA fines Abbey National £2,320,000 for money laundering control failings, FSA/PN/132/2003, 10 December 2003, available at www.fsa.gov.uk.

[199] Financial Services Authority Press Release, 'FSA fines Capita Financial Administrators Limited £300,000 in first anti-fraud controls case', FSA/PN/019/2006, 16 March 2006, available at www.fsa.gov.uk.

[200] In this instance, the attempted frauds amounted to £417,321 and the actual fraud totalled £328,241.

by CFAL resulted in a small number of attempted and actual frauds against its customers, which were allegedly facilitated by CFAL employees.

Secondly, in May 2007 the FSA fined BNP Paribas Private Bank (BNPP) £350,000 for weaknesses in its systems and controls which allowed a senior employee to fraudulently transfer £1.4 million out of the firm's clients' accounts without permission. This was the first time that the FSA has fined a private bank for weaknesses in its anti-fraud systems.[201] The FSA also determined that BNPP's anti-fraud procedures did not make clear provision about the precise role of senior management in checking significant transfers prior to payment, and therefore, a number of fraudulent transactions were not independently checked.

Thirdly, the FSA fined the Nationwide Building Society £980,000 for 'failing to have effective systems and controls to manage its information security risks'.[202] The failings highlighted by the FSA related to a laptop stolen from the home of an employee of the building society. After undertaking an investigation, the FSA determined that the Nationwide did not have adequate safety measures in place to protect customers from an increased risk of fraud.

Fourthly, in December 2007, the FSA fined Norwich Union Life £1.26 million for not 'having effective systems and controls in place to protect customers' confidential information and manage its financial crime risks'.[203] The inadequate systems that Norwich Union had in place permitted fraudsters to access and use personal information from customers to 'impersonate customers and obtain sensitive customer details from its call centres'.[204] The fraudsters were able to obtain confidential customer information including addresses and bank account details. The fraudsters used this information to request the surrender of seventy-four customers' policies totalling £3.3 million in 2006.

Also, in 2008, the FSA fined and/or banned several mortgage brokers for submitting false mortgage applications: Amjad Ali Malik,[205] Tahir Mahmood,[206] Isah Mohammed,[207] Rafiu Akanbi,[208] Erinma Didi Jordan,[209] Byron Brown,[210]

---

[201] Financial Services Authority, *Financial Services Authority Annual Report* 2007/2008 (London, 2008) 23.

[202] Financial Services Authority Press Release, 'FSA fines Nationwide £980,000 for information security lapses', FSA/PN/021/2007, 14 February 2007, available at www.fsa.gov.uk.

[203] Financial Services Authority Press Release, 'FSA fines Norwich Union Life £1.26m', FSA/PN/130/2007, 17 December 2007, available at www.fsa.gov.uk.

[204] *Ibid.*

[205] Financial Services Authority, *Final Notice: Mr Amjad Ali Malik* (London, 2008), available at www.fsa.gov.uk.

[206] Financial Services Authority Press Release, 'FSA bans mortgage brokers for submitting false loan applications', 21 February 2008, available at www.fsa.gov.uk.

[207] Financial Services Authority, *Final Notice: Mr Isah Attayi Mohammed* (London, 2008), available at www.fsa.gov.uk.

[208] Financial Services Authority Press Release, 'FSA bans South London mortgage brokers for submitting false loan applications', 9 June 2008, available at www.fsa.gov.uk.

[209] *Ibid.*

[210] See above n. 208.

Muhammad Adnan Ashraf,[211] Muhammad Asim Iqbal,[212] Mohammed Atif Mayo,[213] Andrew Talai Kiplimo,[214] John Paul Keay,[215] Gerard McStravick,[216] Sadia Nasir[217] and Ian Sanderson.[218]

In addition to the ability to impose a financial penalty, the FSA also has the power to ban authorised persons and firms from undertaking any regulated activity.[219] For example, in April 2008, the FSA banned John Paul Keay, who operated as Jack Keay Mortgage Services 'for not being competent or capable to perform any functions related to regulated activities, including giving advice'.[220] The FSA determined that Mr Keay 'failed to maintain adequate control over [the business], which made the business a target for mortgage fraudsters' and that his business was 'used for the submission of mortgage applications containing false information and supported by falsified pay slips, bank statements and employer references'.[221] Another illustration of the FSA using these powers related to Mr Amjad Malik and Mr Tahir Mahmood.[222] The FSA banned the two partners of a mortgage broker firm for their involvement in submitting false mortgage applications to lenders. The FSA determined that the partners had submitted bogus loan applications on behalf of clients that contained misleading information relating to their annual income and means of employment.[223]

(c) Accountability mechanisms

One of the main concerns regarding financial regulation has been the ineffective mechanisms to ensure the accountability of regulatory agencies. Instead of being addressed and corrected, the concern has once again reared its head with the creation of the FSA.[224] Omoyele took the view that 'the need

---

[211] Financial Services Authority Press Release, 'FSA bans East London brokers for involvement in mortgage fraud', 23 June 2008, available at www.fsa.gov.uk.

[212] *Ibid.*   [213] *Ibid.*

[214] Financial Services Authority Press Release, 'FSA bans introducer for making false mortgage applications', 5 March 2008, available at www.fsa.gov.uk.

[215] Financial Services Authority, *Final Notice: Mr John Paul Keay, Trading as Jack Keay Mortgage Services* (London, 2008), available at www.fsa.gov.uk.

[216] Financial Services Authority Press Release, 'FSA bans Belfast mortgage broker for involvement in fraud', 8 June 2008, available at www.fsa.gov.uk.

[217] Financial Services Authority, Press Release FSA bans and fines mortgage broker £129,000 for involvement in mortgage fraud, 7 July 2008, available from www.fsa.gov.uk.

[218] Financial Services Authority Press Release, 'FSA fines a mortgage firm £11,900 and bans adviser in relation to false mortgage applications', 15 July 2008, available at www.fsa.gov.uk.

[219] FSMA 2000, s.56.

[220] Financial Services Authority, *Final Notice to Mr John Paul Keay trading as Jack Keay Mortgage Services*, 21 April 2008, available at www.fsa.gov.uk.

[221] *Ibid.*

[222] Financial Services Authority Press Release, 'FSA bans mortgage brokers for submitting false loan applications', 21 February 2008, available at www.fsa.gov.uk.

[223] *Ibid.*

[224] For an excellent commentary on the legal accountability of financial regulators see Singh, above n. 86 at 181–210.

for accountability of the Financial Services Authority arises almost innately out of the unprecedented nature of its powers'.[225] Lomnicka stated that 'a body exercising such enormous authority over such a major sector clearly needs to be "accountable" in the sense of having suitable constraints placed on its wide discretion so that it operates appropriately'.[226] The Joint Parliamentary Scrutiny Committee raised concerns about the accountability of the FSA.[227] In response to these concerns, the then Chairman of the FSA, Howard Davies, boldly asserted:

> the second crucial advantage of the new regime is that it incorporates clear lines of accountability. There is clearly no doubt about who is responsible in the event of a regulatory failure. I may live to regret that clarity of responsibility, but at least as a theoretical proposition it is attractive.[228]

The first method of accountability is the statutory objectives of the FSA. In the Financial Services and Markets Bill Progress Report, it was stated that the creation of the four statutory objectives would ensure 'transparency and accountability', with the FSA's activities being assessed against them.[229] The FSA is required to carry out its regulatory functions in a way that, as far as is reasonably possible, is compatible with the four statutory objectives.[230] The FSA must also take into account the general regulatory principles.[231] Then Chancellor of the Exchequer, Gordon Brown, stated that 'the objectives will give the new regulator a clear sense of priorities and will provide a benchmark against which the performance of the regulator can be measured. They will form the basis of the regulator's annual report.'[232] Howard Davies described the statutory objectives as the capstone of the FSMA 2000.[233] However, the extent to which the statutory objectives provide a mechanism for accountability is debatable. Lomnicka argued that the 'objectives and principles operate at a very general level and do not apply to specific decisions'.[234] The effectiveness of the statutory objectives

[225] O. Omoyele, 'Accountability of the Financial Services Authority: a suggestion of corporate governance' (2006) 27(7) *The Company Lawyer* 194.

[226] E. Lomnicka, 'Making the Financial Services Authority accountable' (2000) *Journal of Business Law* 65, 66.

[227] Joint Parliamentary Scrutiny Committee, *Draft Financial Services and Markets Bill: First Report* (London, 1999).

[228] Howard Davies, FSA, 'Building the Financial Services Authority: what's new?', Travers Lecture, London Guildhall University Business School, 11 March 1999, available at www.fsa.gov.uk.

[229] HM Treasury, *Financial Services and Markets Bill, Progress Report* (London, 1999) para. 4.1.

[230] FSMA 2000, Sch. 1, para. 10(1)(b). It has been argued that the term 'general functions' under s.2(4) is too narrow and as such 'the objectives only operate at a general level and do not impose specific statutory duties on the FSA'. See G. Bevers, 'The accountability of the Financial Services Authority under the Financial Services and Markets Act 2000' (2001) 22(7) *The Company Lawyer* 220.

[231] FSMA 2000, s.2(3).

[232] HM Treasury Press Release, 'NEWRO gets new name', 28 October 1997, available at www.hm-treasury.gov.uk.

[233] See above n. 228.

[234] See Lomnicka, above n. 226. Bevers described the statutory objectives as merely a 'self assessment exercise'. See above n. 230, at 220.

as an accountability mechanism also needs to be assessed against the FSA's requirement to produce an annual report.[235] The FSA must report on the extent to which, in its opinion, the regulatory objectives have been met. Whilst this requirement appears, on the face of it, to re-inforce the idea of the statutory objectives being used as an accountability mechanism, the problem lies in the fact that it is up to the FSA to assess its own effectiveness in this area. No outside agency or independent body is given the task of assessing the FSA's activities against its objectives. Therefore, the integrity of the FSA's assessment may need to be questioned. As a final point, it is also worth noting that no specific weighting has been applied to the statutory objectives nor has it been stated that they apply with equal force. This may lead to the FSA placing more emphasis on one objective over another as they see fit, affecting their suitability as an accountability mechanism for the FSA.

The FSA is not directly accountable to Parliament; therefore, it is through the role of HM Treasury that some level of accountability to Parliament is achieved. Under this second means of accountability of the FSA, HM Treasury has the power to appoint and dismiss the board and chairman of the FSA.[236] The FSA is required to produce an annual report to HM Treasury detailing the discharge of its functions; the extent to which, in its opinion, the regulatory objectives have been met; its consideration of the restraining principles; and any other matters required by HM Treasury.[237] The report must be laid before Parliament within three months and a public meeting must also be held within this time-frame at which the report can be discussed and the FSA questioned on its performance.[238] HM Treasury also has the power to appoint an independent person to conduct a review and compile a written report on any element of the economy, efficiency and effectiveness with which the FSA has used its resources to discharge its functions.[239] Furthermore, HM Treasury also has the power to launch certain inquiries in certain circumstances;[240] it may determine the scope of the inquiry and must lay the report before Parliament. As with the power of review, HM Treasury may also publish all or part of the report unless it would seriously prejudice a particular person or would breach international obligations. If the FSA informs HM Treasury that private persons have suffered or will suffer as a result of widespread breach of its rules by authorised firms, HM Treasury can require the FSA to establish and operate a past business review and compensation scheme by statutory instrument subject to affirmative resolutions of both Houses of Parliament.[241]

The Consumer Panel and Practitioner Panel have varying roles to play in acting as a third mechanism of accountability for the FSA. The Consumer Panel in particular plays a role in monitoring the extent to which the FSA achieves its statutory objectives in relation to consumers. The Practitioner Panel plays a

[235] FSMA 2000, Sch. 1, para. 10(1)(b).   [236] *Ibid.* Sch. 1 para. 2(3).
[237] *Ibid.* Sch. 1, para. 10.   [238] *Ibid.* Sch. 1, paras. 11 and 12.   [239] *Ibid.* s.12.
[240] *Ibid.* ss.14–18.   [241] *Ibid.* ss.404 and 429(1).

similar role to the Consumer Panel but also has to consider to what extent the FSA are giving due regard to the considerations set out in the legislation. FSMA 2000 imposes a general duty on the FSA to consult practitioners and consumers 'on the extent to which its general policies and practices are consistent with its general duties', this covers both the statutory objectives and the principles of the FSA.[242] The consultation arrangements must include a Practitioner Panel and a Consumer Panel, the membership of which must follow the requirements specified in the Act.[243] The FSA must consider all representations from these panels and provide written explanations if it disagrees with their views.[244] This therefore acts as a mechanism of accountability, with the FSA having to be formally accountable to both panels for its decisions. Both the Consumer Panel and the Practitioner Panel are independent of the FSA and are free to publish their views. The Consumer Panel can also commission research into consumer views. Both panels also produce annual reports on their activities and an assessment of the FSA's effectiveness each year. However, Bevers noted that the FSMA 2000 'puts a limit on the influence that the Panels have, by stating that the FSA must consider the representations made by the Panels. They are merely consultative.'[245]

The FSA is a body conducting public functions and as such can be subject to judicial review, which provides a fourth accountability mechanism. It should be noted, however, that when drafted, the FSMA 2000 was designed to limit the instances of an action for judicial review. The FSA, as the United Kingdom's sole financial regulator, undoubtedly needs to have in place clear lines of accountability without at any time losing its position as an independent regulatory body. Omoyele concluded 'it is apparent, however, from a detailed examination of these existing accountability mechanisms that they do not go far enough to ensure the FSA's accountability'.[246]

(d) The credit crunch and Northern Rock

The following highlights the impact of the performance of the FSA. The first signs of a global recession appeared between 2005 and 2006, when the United States' financial markets showed signs of weakening. This was preceded by a period of economic prosperity that was fuelled by the sub-prime market for low cost mortgages, which also began to falter. The sub-prime market permitted the granting of mortgages to people who were generally unable to afford such loans and as such the loans represented a greater level of risk for the lender. The impact of the sub-prime crisis on the US banking and mortgage market was catastrophic. Freddie Mac (an organisation that was set up to encourage the growth of the US secondary mortgage market) and Fannie Mac (an organisation

---

[242] *Ibid.* s.8.   [243] *Ibid.* ss. 9 and 10.   [244] *Ibid.* s.11.

[245] Bevers also noted that the FSA appoints the Chairperson of both Panels and provides their funding. See above n. 230, at 221.

[246] See Omoyele, above n. 225, at 195.

that provides funding for the US mortgage sector) encountered severe financial problems, as did American International Group, the Bank of America and Lehman Brothers. These events had a domino effect across the Atlantic, and the first United Kingdom bank to be adversely affected was Northern Rock. Other banks affected included Bradford and Bingley, which went into administration in September 2008, the Royal Bank of Scotland and HBOS.

Northern Rock was established in the middle of the nineteenth century, demutualised in 1997 and by 2006 it was worth over £100 billion.[247] By September 2007, following the sub-prime crisis, the bank was unable to acquire loans from other financial institutions via the inter-bank lending market ('the Libor').[248] The Bank of England agreed to lend Northern Rock £25 billion, which it promised to repay by 2010.[249] This led Tomasic to conclude 'the rescue of Northern Rock Plc by the Bank of England in September 2007 has been a significant event in the history of British banking and in the wider application of corporate rescue ideas'.[250] After the loan was made public, thousands of Northern Rock's customers queued in desperation to withdraw their savings, despite their savings being protected by the Financial Services Compensation Scheme. HM Treasury announced that it would cover all the deposits of Northern Rock.[251] In February 2007, the share price of Northern Rock was 1,200 pence, by January 2008 the price had fallen below 200 pence and its shares were suspended in February 2008.[252] The bank was later nationalised after emergency legislation was rushed through the House of Commons.[253] As a result of this financial scandal, the FSA has been severely criticised and in March 2008 it published a review of its actions.[254] The review highlighted four areas of concern:

(1) a lack of sufficient supervisory engagement with the firm, in particular the failure of the supervisory team to follow up rigorously with the management of the firm on the business model vulnerability arising from changing market conditions;

(2) a lack of adequate oversight and review by FSA line management of the quality, intensity and rigour of the firm's supervision;

---

[247] R. Tomasic, 'Corporate rescue, governance and risk taking in Northern Rock' (2008) 29(11) *The Company Lawyer* 330.

[248] See X. Lok, 'LIBOR and market disruption: the future of LIBOR' (2008) 23(8) *Journal of International Banking and Financial Law* 421.

[249] BBC News, 'Rock pledges to repay tax payers', 31 March 2008, available at www.bbc.co.uk. For a more detailed discussion of the options available to the Bank of England when a bank collapses, see C. Bamford, 'Northern Rock and the single market' (2008) 29(3) *The Company Lawyer* 65.

[250] R. Tomasic, 'Corporate rescue, governance and risk-taking in Northern Rock' (2008) 29(10) *Company Lawyer*, 297.

[251] HM Treasury, Statement by the Chancellor of the Exchequer on financial markets, 17 September 2007, available at www.hm-treasury.gov.uk.

[252] BBC News, 'Northern Rock, in facts and figures', 18 February 2008, available at www.bbc.co.uk.

[253] Banking (Special Provisions) Act 2008.

[254] Financial Services Authority, *Executive Summary of Review* (London, 2008).

(3) inadequate specific resources directly supervising the firm;

(4) a lack of intensity by the FSA in ensuring that all available risk information was properly utilised to inform its supervisory actions.[255]

The review upheld the FSA's principles-based regulation as opposed to a rules-based approach. The review also concluded that responsibility for the collapse of Northern Rock rested with its senior management team. The review made several important recommendations:

- the FSA senior management to have increased engagement with high impact firms;
- the FSA to increase the rigour of its day-to-day supervision;
- the FSA to increase its focus on prudential supervision, including liquidity and stress testing;
- the FSA to improve its use of information and intelligence in its supervision;
- the FSA to improve the quality and resourcing of its financial and sectoral analysis;
- the FSA to strengthen its supervisory resources, and
- the FSA senior management to increase the level of oversight of firms' supervision.

Rosemary Hilary stated that the aim of the recommendations are to 'ensure that the framework is properly applied, with good record-keeping, good information flows, the appropriate levels of challenge and the right amount of engagement and supervision of front-line staff by management. Whilst the recommendations are designed to apply to the supervision of all high impact firms, many are more generally applicable.'[256] HM Treasury Select Committee took the view that 'the FSA was asleep on the job … A very clear signal of a bank running a big risk is rapid expansion. Northern Rock was giving that signal quite clearly; it is remarkable that [the FSA] missed it.'[257]

However, it must be noted that the Bank of England and the SIB also got it wrong during the collapses of financial institutions outlined above. It is impossible for the FSA to implement a regulatory regime that will achieve a zero failure rate. The FSA must learn lessons from this incident and ensure that it does more to maintain market confidence and protect the consumers who have been adversely affected by Northern Rock.

The 'credit crunch' highlighted the inadequacies of the regulatory regime created by the Labour government in 1997 and resulted in the introduction of the Financial Services Act (FSA) 2010, which received Royal Assent on 8 April 2010. The Act contains a number of important provisions, which include the extension of the statutory objectives of the FSA to include 'financial stability'.[258]

---

[255] *Ibid.*

[256] Financial Services Authority Press Release, 'FSA moves to enhance supervision in the wake of Northern Rock', 26 March 2008, available at www.fsa.gov.uk.

[257] HM Treasury Select Committee, *Northern Rock on the Run* (London, 2007) 22.

[258] FSA 2010, s.1.

More specifically, the amendments introduced by the FSA 2010 can be summarised as follows: [259]

(1) The FSA was granted innovative powers to establish rules regarding the payment mechanisms of financial services firms.[260]
(2) The FSA was directed to create rules relating to recovery and resolution plans.[261]
(3) The FSA was empowered to make rules prohibiting bank short selling.[262]
(4) The FSA's powers of intervention against a financial services firm were increased.[263]
(5) The FSA was granted additional disciplinary powers.[264]
(6) The FSA 2010 introduced a new form of consumer redress scheme.[265]
(7) The FSA was given new powers to force the production of more information by the financial services sector.[266]

Q5 Why was the Financial Services Authority created in 1997?

5 The Coalition government

The 2010 General Election resulted in the United Kingdom's first coalition government in nearly a century. Following the poor performance of the FSA during the 'credit crunch' it became clear that the Coalition government would instigate an extensive review of the United Kingdom's banking policies and regulation. The Coalition Agreement stated 'we will reform the regulatory system to avoid a repeat of the financial crisis. We will bring forward proposals to give the Bank of England control of macro-prudential regulation and oversight of micro-prudential regulation.'[267]

In June 2010, the Chancellor of the Exchequer, George Osborne, outlined in greater detail the Coalition government's financial services policy. Of particular relevance to this chapter was the proposal to abolish the FSA and transfer its supervisory powers to the Bank of England;[268] create a Financial Policy Committee within the Bank of England; establish a Prudential Regulation Authority that would be responsible for the day-to-day supervision of financial institutions; establish a Consumer Protection Markets Authority that would regulate the conduct of all financial services firms; establish the Economic Crime Agency; create an Independent Commission on Banking; and introduce

---

[259] N. Willmott, P. McGowan, M. Ghusn, V. Brocklehurst, R. Aikens, S. Bailey, M. Scodie and J. Palme. 'Equipping the modern regulator: assessing the new regulatory powers under the Financial Services Act 2010' (2010) 78 *Compliance Officer Bulletin* (July/August) 1, 3.
[260] FSA 2010, ss.3–6.   [261] *Ibid.* s.7.   [262] *Ibid.* s.8.
[263] *Ibid.* ss.9–13.   [264] *Ibid.*   [265] *Ibid.* ss.14–17.   [266] *Ibid.* ss.18–19.
[267] HM Government, *The Coalition: our programme for government* (London, 2010) 9.
[268] See HM Treasury, *A New Approach to Financial Regulation: Consultation on Reforming the Consumer Credit Regime* (London, 2010).

a specific bank levy.[269] In February 2011, the Coalition government published details of Project Merlin, which resulted in the United Kingdom banks agreeing to increase the levels of lending to businesses; that each bank's senior management salary will be associated with its lending commitments; to pay lower bonuses; to introduce new disclosure arrangements regarding the salaries of a bank's senior management; and to make a contribution of £1.2 billion to the Business Growth and the Big Society Bank.

In June 2011, the Coalition government published another consultation paper and White Paper that included the draft Financial Services Bill,[270] which contains three major proposals:

- a specific statutory objective governing the Prudential Regulation Authority's responsibilities for the insurance sector;
- an updated and enhanced competition regime under a Financial Conduct Authority; and
- steps to strengthen the handling of cases of widespread consumer detriment, including mis-selling.[271]

It appears that the policy adopted by the Coalition government is to revert back to regulation by the Bank of England, which is very similar to that adopted by the former Conservative governments, as outlined at the start of this chapter.

Q6 What is the Coalition government's policy towards banking regulation?

6 Conclusion

As stated above, the main issues highlighted by the government which influenced its decision to create the FSA were ineffective regulation and inadequate investor protection. The FSMA 2000 contained several mechanisms aimed at improving the levels of financial regulation and enhancing the level of protection offered to investors. Sadly, the effectiveness of these measures must be questioned in light of the near collapse of Northern Rock and Equitable Life. Following the Northern Rock crisis, the government decided to introduce the Banking Act 2009, which permits the Bank of England to intervene when a bank is in financial difficulties and creates a 'financial stability objective'.[272] Prior to the creation of the FSA in 1997, the former Conservative government left the regulation of the banking sector in the hands of the Bank of England. This proved to be a very ineffective model, as the performance of the Bank of England was blighted by several high profile financial scandals. The policy

---

[269] HM Treasury, Financial services policy agenda, available at www.hm-treasury.gov.uk/fin_policy_agenda_index.htm.

[270] HM Treasury, *A New Approach to Financial Regulation: the Blueprint for Reform* (London, 2011).

[271] HM Treasury, 'Government publishes financial regulation White Paper and draft Bill', 16 June 2011, available at www.hm-treasury.gov.uk/press_59_11.htm.

[272] FSA 2010, s.1.

adopted by the former Labour government towards banking laws was to create one of the largest financial regulatory agencies, the FSA, to encourage the growth of the banking sector. However, largely due to the 'Credit Crunch', the Coalition government seems to have reverted back to regulation by the Bank of England.

7 Recommended reading

Bevers, G. 'The accountability of the Financial Services Authority under the Financial Services and Markets Act 2000' (2001) 22(7) *Company Lawyer* 220

Gower, L. 'Big bang and city regulation' (1988) 51(1) *Modern Law Review* 1

Grey, J. 'Lessons from BCCI saga for the current accountability debate surrounding Northern Rock?' (2008) 23(2) *Journal of International Banking Law and Regulation* 37

HM Government *The Coalition: Our Programme for Government* (London, 2010)

HM Treasury *A New Approach to Financial Regulation: Consultation on Reforming the Consumer Credit Regime* (London, 2010)

A New Approach to Financial Regulation: the Blueprint for Reform (London, 2011)

Lomnicka, E. 'Making the Financial Services Authority accountable' (2000) *Journal of Business Law* 65

Page, A. 'Self-regulation: the constitutional dimension' (1986) 49(2) *Modern Law Review* 141

Tomasic, R. 'Corporate rescue, governance and risk taking in Northern Rock: Part 2' (2008) 29(11) *Company Lawyer* 330

Part 6 Chapter 2

Banking and Finance Law

Contents

1 Introduction

The purpose of this chapter is to provide a detailed overview of the law relating to banks. The chapter begins by attempting to answer what in theory should be a very simple question. What is a bank? However, it will become clear that this is quite a difficult question to answer. The chapter goes on to define a customer and then progresses to highlight the very complicated relationship between a bank and its customers. Particular attention is paid to the duties a bank owes to its customers, including the duty of confidentiality. The chapter also outlines the different types of bank accounts offered to customers and deals with some of the legal issues relating to cheques, e-banking and the regulation of bank accounts.

2 What is a bank?

The first question faced by students studying the law relating to banks is how do you define a bank? This is not an easy question to answer, a point raised by Wadsley and Penn, who took the view that:

[The question is] notoriously difficult to answer. The question has become much harder to answer in recent years, with the advent of telephone and Internet banking as well as banks in supermarkets. The traditional idea of a bank with many local branches dealing with customers face to face (core retail banking) seems odd and out of date.[1]

The common law definitions of a bank are varied, summed up in the comments by Salmon J, who in *Woods* v. *Martins Bank Ltd* stated 'what may have been true of the Bank of Montreal in 1918 is not necessarily true of Martins Bank in 1959 … the question "what is a bank" will be answered differently from time to time and place to place'. The nature of banking business at any particular time depends on the surrounding circumstances, and is a matter of fact as well as of law.[2] In *Bank of Chettinand Ltd of Colombo* v. *Commissioners of Income Tax, Colombo*, the court stated 'the words "banking" and "banker" may bear different shades of meaning at different periods of history and their meaning may not be uniform today'.[3] This was a point recognised by Azzouni who noted that:

Banking has indeed been a developing area in which new changes and developments have been taking place every decade. Legislators have always been required to study the efficiency and capability of the existing laws to solve any ambiguity or difficulty associated with any new change. With regard to Internet banking, although the major problems can be handled either through traditional legislation or through the recent regulations designed for Internet problems in general, there are still some gaps in these legal controls.[4]

One of the most authoritative definitions of a bank is that adopted in *United Dominions Trust Ltd* v. *Kirkwood*.[5] Here, Lord Denning MR provided a useful list of features of banking practices:

Bankers accept money from and collect cheques for their customers and place them to their credit; honour cheques or orders drawn on them by their customers when presented for payment and debit their customers accordingly, and keep current accounts in which credits and debits are entered.[6]

---

1   J. Wadsley and P. Penn, *Penn and Shea, The Law relating to Domestic Banking* (Sweet and Maxwell, London, 2000) 89.
2   [1959] 1 QB 55, 56.
3   [1948] AC 378, 383.
4   A. Azzouni, 'Internet banking and the law: a critical examination of the legal controls over Internet banking in the UK and their ability to frame, regulate and secure banking on the Net' (2003) 18(9) *Journal of International Banking Law and Regulation* 351, 362.
5   [1966] 2 QB 431, CA.
6   *Ibid.* 461. The definition provided by Lord Denning has been cited and used in numerous cases, such as *Hafton Properties Ltd* v. *McHugh* (1987) 84 LSG 342. For a more detailed discussion see P. Skitmore, 'Case comment: Hafton Properties Ltd v McHugh (1987) 84 LSG 342' (1987) 8(5) *Company Lawyer* 231. The definition has also been used by the Inland Revenue, as illustrated in V. Magurie and M. Walton, 'The ordinary course of banking business and deduction of tax at source' (1992) 7(1) *Journal of International Banking Law* 29.

Therefore, 'a bank must have only two distinctive elements, namely deposit tak-ing and cheque collection'.[7] However, Hsiao stated that:

> This definition is by no means helpful in answering the question: 'what is a bank?' Banks are classified in different ways. Some institutions will fall into the banking category despite not having the two elements stated in the *Kirkwood* case. By the same token, the building society, which is generally regarded as having a bank-ing status, is excluded by the [Banking Act 2009], and so is the credit union. The bank in the Act is any United Kingdom institution falling under the FSMA 2000 with authorisation or exemption to carry on the regulated activities of accepting deposits. The Act is only applicable to institutions incorporated or formed under the law of the United Kingdom.[8]

In addition to the common law definitions, there are several statutory defi-nitions that will assist us to answer the question of what is a bank. For example, according to the European Union, a bank can be defined as 'an undertaking the business of which is to receive deposits or other repayable funds from the public and to grant credits for its own account'.[9] Ellinger *et al.* noted that 'Parliament has found it necessary to provide a generally applicable functional definition that distinguishes banks from other types of financial institution. Different pieces of legislation do, however, define the term "bank" for their own specific purposes.'[10] Thus, the Banking Act 2009 provides that; 'bank' 'means a UK institution which has permission under of the Financial Services and Markets Act 2000 to carry on the regulated activity of accepting deposits (within the meaning of section 22 of that Act, taken with Schedule 2 and any order under section 22)'.[11] According to the explanatory notes, 'this section defines a bank as a UK institution that has a regulatory permission, granted by the FSA under the Financial Services and Markets Act 2000, to accept depos-its'. For the purposes of the FSMA 2000, a bank does not include a building society,[12] a credit union[13] or 'any other class of institution excluded by an order made by the Treasury'. The Bills of Exchange Act 1882 provides that a 'banker includes a body of persons whether incorporated or not who carry on the busi-ness of banking'.[14]

Wadsley and Penn stated that 'many commentators have pointed out that the circularity of these words leaves courts with the same question to answer as they started with'.[15]

---

[7] M. Hsiao, 'Legitimised interference with private properties: Banking Act 2009' (2010) 25(5) *Journal of International Banking Law and Regulation*, 227, 229–30.

[8] *Ibid.* 230.   [9] EU Banking Directive 2006/48/EC, Art. 4.

[10] E. Ellinger, E. Lomnicka and C. Hare, *Ellinger's Modern Banking Law* (Oxford University Press, 2011) 7.

[11] Banking Act 2009, s.2.   [12] As defined by the Building Societies Act 1986, s.119.

[13] As defined by the Credit Unions Act 1979, s.31.

[14] Bills of Exchange Act 1882, s.2.

[15] Wadsley and Penn, above n. 1, at 96.

Q1 Briefly outline the judicial attitude towards the definition of a bank. Does this approach take into account modern banking practices?

3 What is a customer?

The interpretation of the phrase 'customer' is similar to the definition of a 'bank', because it is a very difficult term to define. Why is it important to define the term? Cranston noted that 'the conventional view is that "customer" has a technical meaning, which leads to lengthy discussions on who is or is not a bank's customers'.[16] One reason advocated by Wadsley and Penn is that 'the concepts "bank" and "customer" are interdependent, and the one cannot be completely understood without reference to the other'.[17] There is no statutory definition of the term 'customer', and 'it is not specifically defined in the Bills of Exchange Act 1882 or the Cheques Act 1957'.[18] Cranston added that inconsidering the provisions of both of the Acts 'the courts have decided that anyone who opens an account, rogue or angel, is a customer for the purposes of statutory protection'.[19] Indeed, Andrew noted that 'the word "customer" is used in the Bills of Exchange Act 1882 and the Cheques Act 1957 but the word is not defined in these statutes. These days therefore when banks invite the public to consult them on a whole range of financial products and services large areas of the public can be drawn into a bank's customer net.'[20] Therefore, although several academics have offered some useful comments on what amounts to a customer, there is no clear all-embracing statutory definition of the term.

An important question that needs to be considered is when does someone become a customer? It has been argued that one of the main circumstances in which a person becomes a customer of a bank is when he or she opens an account.[21] Indeed, it has been described as 'the touchstone of whether a person is a customer of a bank'.[22] This was the decision reached by the court in *Woods* v. *Martins Bank Ltd*,[23] where the plaintiff had been given investment advice by the bank's manager to invest money in a company, which was heavily in debt to the bank. The plaintiff had not been informed by the bank manager about the level of debt or the bank's pre-existing contractual arrangements with this company. In this instance, Salmon J stated that the bank manager 'ought never to have advised the plaintiff at all – certainly not without making a full disclosure to the plaintiff of the conflicting interests between the plaintiff and the defendant bank and the plaintiff and the defendant bank's other customers'.[24] The decision

---

[16] R. Cranston, *Principles of Banking Law* (Oxford University Press, 2002) 130.
[17] Wadsley and Penn, above n. 1, at 96.   [18] Ellinger *et al.*, above n. 10.
[19] Cranston, above n. 16, at 130.
[20] E. Andrew, 'Customer care and banking law' (1989) 4(3) *Journal of International Banking Law* 101.
[21] Wadsley and Penn, above n. 1, at 97.   [22] Ellinger *et al.*, above n. 10, at 116.
[23] [1959] 1 QB 55.
[24] N. Clayton, 'Banks as fiduciaries: the UK position' (1992) 7(8) *Journal of International Banking Law* 315, 317.

in Woods was approved by the Privy Council in *Mutual Life and Citizens' Assurance Co. Ltd* v. *Evatt*.[25] Here, the court 'succeeded in imposing liability on a bank by holding that the bank owed a fiduciary duty to a non-customer (a prospective customer) who sought investment advice'.[26]

The court in *Commissioners of Taxation* v. *English, Scottish and Australian Bank* offered a useful discussion of when a person becomes a customer.[27] Here, the court determined that once the person had opened an account they were deemed to be a customer of the bank. In *Great Western Railway* v. *London and County Banking Co.*, the House of Lords determined that a rate collector who habitually cashed cheques in the bank, which would pay some of the proceeds to the district council and the remainder to the rate collector, was not a customer. The House of Lords decided that the bank 'collected money on their own behalf, not for him as a customer'.[28] It is possible to argue that a person only becomes a client when a bank ascertains the identity of the prospective client. This is a view advocated by the Wolfsberg Principles, which according to Haynes means that 'the bank will take reasonable measures to establish the identity of its clients and beneficial owners and will *only* accept clients when this process has been completed'.[29] A similar approach was referred to in *Ladbroke* v. *Todd*,[30] about which Haynes noted that 'it was traditionally regarded as necessary for a bank to check both the identity of a new client and to ascertain whether they were a suitable person to hold an account'.[31]

More recently, the situation has become more complex, and a customer may 'include persons who receive services from a bank without necessarily holding an account'.[32] The FSMA 2000 follows this approach and provides that a customer 'in relation to an authorised person, means a person who is using, or who is or may be contemplating using, any of the services provided by the authorised person'.[33] Further guidance on the term 'customer' is offered by the FSA's Banking: Conduct of Business Sourcebook, which resulted in the adoption in the FSA Handbook of the term 'banking customer'. This term includes a customer, a micro-enterprise and charities with an annual income of less than £1 million. It has also been argued that 'banking customers' include households and small to medium-sized enterprises.[34] The Handbook also defines a 'customer' as including 'a client who is not an eligible counterparty for the relevant purposes, a person who is a policyholder, or even a prospective policyholder'.

---

[25] [1971] AC 793, 805.
[26] T. Shea, 'Liability of banks for erroneous status opinions' (1986) 1(1) *Journal of International Banking Law*, 20, 21–2.
[27] [1920] AC 683, PC.
[28] [1901] AC 414, as cited in Wadsley and Penn, above n. 1, at 98.
[29] Emphasis added. A. Haynes, 'The Wolfsberg Principles: an analysis' (2004) 7(3) *Journal of Money Laundering Control* 207, 208.
[30] (1914) 30 TLR 433.   [31] Haynes, above n. 29, at 208.
[32] Ellinger *et al.*, above n. 10, at 110.   [33] FSMA 2000, s.59(11).
[34] A. Mullineux, 'The regulation of British retail banking utilities' (2009) 17(4) *Journal of Financial Regulation and Compliance*, 453, 464.

Q2 What is a customer? How has this definition been impacted by the FSA?

4 Bank accounts

A Bank account has been described as 'a chose in action in which a customer deposits money with a bank and the bank recognises that money is credited to the customer's account. The bank owes the contractual duties of creditor and debtor to its customer.'[35] Cranston noted that the 'most basic service a bank can provide to members of the public is to act as a depository for their money'.[36] Cranston took the view that 'these days multifunctional banks hold the people's money in other forms – in various collective investment schemes, funds, and insurance products. In many senses these are functionally equivalent to bank accounts and may be economically more advantageous for customers.'[37]

(a) The Current account

One of the most popular bank accounts in the United Kingdom is a current account, which is used by 'customers for their regular financial transactions'.[38] Hudson noted that 'a current account is the ordinary account held between banker and customer'.[39] Wadsley and Penn noted that 'the current account is still regarded as a basic element in the banker customer relationship. It is thought of as supplying liquid funds, and is used for day to day payments in and out. Legally … it is a debt owing to the customer by the bank, not the actual money of the customer.'[40] The purpose of a credit account is to enable the customer to pay for goods and/or services by 'cheque, debit card, or other funds transfer, amounts due from him, and to arrange for the collection of cheques payable to him and other receivables'.[41] Once the money has been deposited into the current account, it becomes the property of the bank, which means it has a contractual relationship with its customer.[42] Current accounts play a pivotal role in the relationship between a bank and its customers: current accounts offer access to deposit-holding services (and potential access to savings services), money transmission through cheques and debit facilities and potentially act as a vehicle for credit through overdraft.'[43] the money deposited in this bank account is 'payable on demand, either by withdrawal or by the customer instructing the bank to make payment to a third party'.[44] Furthermore, a customer is able to 'use his current account for the purpose of discharging his

---

[35] A. Hudson, *The Law of Finance* (Sweet and Maxwell, London, 2009) 795.
[36] Cranston, above n. 16, at 159.   [37] *Ibid.* 130.
[38] Ellinger *et al.*, above n. 10, at 223.   [39] Hudson, above n. 35, at 729.
[40] Wadsley and Penn, above n. 1, at 253.   [41] Ellinger *et al.*, above n. 10, at 226.
[42] Hudson, above n. 35, at 729.
[43] C. Gondat-Larralde and E. Nier, *The Economics of Retail Banking: an Empirical Analysis of the UK Market for Personal Current Accounts* (FSA, London, 2003) 2.
[44] Cranston, above n. 16, at 130.

liabilities. This can be done either by drawing cheques that he dispatches to his creditors, by using a debit card that operates directly on his current account, or by using some other form of giro transfer, such as a standing order or direct debit.'[45]

The association between a bank and its customer via a current account is that of a creditor and debtor.[46] The approach adopted by the common law to this relationship was outlined in *Joachimson* v. *Swiss Bank Corp.* by Atkin LJ:

> The bank undertakes to receive money and to collect bills for its customer's account. The proceeds so received are not to be held in trust for the customer, but the bank borrows the proceeds and undertakes to repay them. The promise to repay is to repay at the branch of the bank where the account is kept, and during banking hours. It includes a promise to repay any part of the amount due against the written order for the customer addressed to the bank at the branch, and as such written orders may be outstanding in the ordinary course of business for two or three days, it is a term of the contract that the bank will not cease to do business with the customer except upon reasonable notice. The customer on his part undertakes to exercise reasonable care in executing his written orders so as not to mislead the bank or facilitate forgery. I think it is necessarily a term of such contract that the bank is not liable to pay the customer the full amount of his balance until he demands payment from the bank at the branch at which the current account is kept. Whether he must demand it in writing it is not necessary now to determine.[47]

When faced with a prospective new customer, a bank must comply with a number of legal obligations.[48] For example, a bank must perform certain 'customer due diligence' requirements under the Money Laundering Regulations 2007 prior to entering into a business relationship, which includes opening a current account and undertaking intermittent transactions for its customer.[49] Additionally, a bank is required to comply with the Banking and Payments Service Regime, which comprises the Banking Conduct of Business Sourcebook[50] and the Payment Services Regulations 2009.[51] The Payment Services Regulations 2009 were introduced as a result of the passage of the EU Payment Services Directive 2007/64/EC,[52] and their implementation will be

---

[45] Ellinger *et al.*, above n. 10, at 223.   [46] Cranston, above n. 16, at 160.

[47] [1921] 3 KB 110, 127.   [48] Ellinger *et al.*, above n. 10, at 226.

[49] SI 2007/2157. For a more detailed discussion of the Money Laundering Regulations 2007, see C. Stott. and Z. Ullah, 'Money Laundering Regulations 2007, Part 1 (Legislative Comment)' (2008) 23(3) *Journal of International Banking Law and Regulation*, 175; 'Money Laundering Regulations 2007 Part 2 (Legislative Comment)' (2008) 23(5) *Journal of International Banking Law and Regulation* 283 and P. Snowdon and S. Lovegrove,. 'Money Laundering Regulations 2007' (2008) 54 *Compliance Officer Bulletin* (March), 1.

[50] For a more detailed discussion of the Banking Conduct of Business Sourcebook, see P. Cartwright 'Retail depositors, conduct of business and sanctioning' (2009) 17(3) *Journal of Financial Regulation and Compliance* 302.

[51] SI 2009/209.

[52] See R. Bollen. 'European regulation of payment services: the story so far' (2007) 22(9) *Journal of International Banking Law and Regulation* 451 and R. Bollen, 'European regulation of payment

supported by the Financial Services Authority.[53] Brandt and Graham stated that:

> The Payment Services Directive began life as a European Commission legislative proposal in December 2005. The draft Directive was subject to a significant amount of negotiation. Political support from the European Parliament and the Council of Ministers was received in April 2007 with the Directive being adopted formally on 13 November 2007.[54]

According to Ellinger *et al.* this system of regulation is twofold. First, the '[current] account can be used by the customer as a means of satisfying any payment instructions that he gives to his bank and is, therefore, the means whereby a bank can provide payment services to its customer'.[55] Secondly, 'a current account enables a bank to receive deposits made by, or on behalf of, its customer'.[56] The Payment Services Regulations 2009 stipulate that once the customer deposits cash into the current account, the funds must be attributed to the account and made available to the customer immediately.[57] If the cash is deposited by a different type of customer, the account must be accredited 'no later than the end of the business day after the receipt of the funds'.[58]

(b) Deposit account

A deposit account is often used for 'longer term deposits'[59] and they are often referred to as savings accounts or extra interest accounts. Hudson noted that 'a deposit account can be an account in relation to which the deposit can be withdrawn, in relation to which the deposit can only be withdrawn on specified notice, or in relation to which the deposit can only be withdrawn after the effluxion of a period of time'.[60] Wadsley and Penn noted that 'funds in deposit accounts may be withdrawable on demand, but are often withdrawable only on specified notice or after a fixed time; it depends on the terms on which the contract is made. Because they are less liquid than current accounts, deposit accounts attract higher rates of interest.'[61] Traditionally, a cheque book is not provided for a deposit account as outlined by J. Mocatta in *Barclays Bank v. Okenarhe*, who also took the view that 'I am quite unable to accept than an overdrawn deposit account is a concept known to the law'.[62]

services: recent developments and the proposed Payment Services Directive, Part 2' (2007) 22(10) *Journal of International Banking Law and Regulation* 532.

[53] P. Brandt, and P. Graham, 'An update on the UK's implementation of the Payment Services Directive' (2009) 64 *Compliance Officer Bulletin*, (March) 1, 3.

[54] *Ibid.* 2.   [55] Ellinger *et al.*, above n. 10, at 227.   [56] *Ibid.*

[57] SI 2009/909, reg. 72(a).   [58] Ellinger *et al.*, above n. 10, at 227.

[59] Wadsley and Penn, above n. 1, at 254.   [60] Hudson, above n. 35, at 796.

[61] Wadsley and Penn, above n. 1, at 254.   [62] [1966] 2 Lloyd's Rep. Bank. 87, 94.

(c) Joint account

Ellinger *et al.* stated that 'a joint account is opened in the name of two or more customers. It is distinguishable from accounts, such as corporate or administrator's accounts, on the ground that, although more than one person might be required to sign cheques drawn upon the latter type of account, they do so in a representative or fiduciary capacity. In contrast joint account holders sign as principals, whether jointly or severally'.[63] A joint account 'constitutes a debt owed to the account holders jointly by the bank'.[64] 'Liability may either be joint or joint and several, although bank mandates are normally in joint and several form'.[65] 'There is also the question whether the bank owes a duty jointly and severally to the account holders. This problem has sometimes arisen where the bank has paid wrongly. The question is whether, if liability is joint, the other (injured party) can sue the bank.'[66]

(d) Minor's account

'Minors may only make valid contracts under certain conditions. Contracts made by minors are void unless they are for the supply of goods and services that are necessaries.'[67]

(e) Overdraft

An overdraft is regarded as a loan between the bank and its customer.[68] An overdraft has been defined as 'permission granted to an account holder to draw on the facility expressed by the bank account – with its payment cards, cheques … above the amount of any credit which the account holder may have in the account'.[69] When a customer opens a bank account, the bank can agree to permit an overdraft facility,[70] which allows the customer to use this facility once all of their money in the account has been used.[71] Overdrafts are regarded as one of the most traditional means of borrowing in the United Kingdom, normally over a short period of time.[72] An overdraft works where the credit balance of the account is depleted and the customer is allowed, through an agreement with the bank, to overdraw the account. If there is no prior agreement between the bank and the customer, and the customer seeks to make a payment/withdrawal from the account, this can be deemed by the bank as a request for an overdraft. However, a bank is not required to permit a customer to overdraw an account unless it is contractually obliged to do so.[73] Once a customer is overdrawn or

---

[63] Ellinger *et al.*, above n. 10, at 755.   [64] Wadsley and Penn, above n. 1, at 260.
[65] *Ibid.*   [66] *Ibid.* 261.   [67] *Ibid.* 270.
[68] For a brief outline of the practical nature of obtaining an overdraft see Ellinger *et al.*, above n. 10, at 755.
[69] Hudson, above n. 35, at 796.   [70] Cranston, above n. 16, at 160.
[71] Hudson above, n 35 at 796.   [72] Cranston, above n. 16, at 255.
[73] See, e.g. *Office of Fair Trading* v. *Abbey National plc* [2008] EWHC 8758 (Comm.), paras. 45, 55.

surpasses his overdraft limit without the bank's prior agreement, banks often charge higher rates of interest and extra bank charges. Davies stated that 'banks regularly levy charges for unarranged overdrafts. Even if a customer's attempt to become overdrawn on an account without prior arrangement is blocked by a bank, the customer may still incur a charge'.[74]

The issue of bank charges was recently tested in the Supreme Court in *Office of Fair Trading* v. *Abbey National plc*,[75] where the 'Office of Fair Trading attempted to challenge some of the charges levied by the high street banks under the Unfair Terms in Consumer Contracts Regulations 1999'.[76] Mulheron took the view that this case was also influenced by the furore involving allegedly unauthorised bank charges, which involved over 46,000 claims to the Financial Ombudsman Service, and approximately 53,000 claims filed against defendant banks between March 2006 and August 2007 (including almost 9,000 county court claims commenced in May 2007 alone).[77] At first instance and in the Court of Appeal, the OFT successfully contended that the bank charges could be challenged under the Unfair Terms in Customer Contracts Regulations 1999, SI 1999/2083, because they were 'collateral or subsidiary to the main price of the contract'.[78] The Supreme Court determined that the bank charges were not subject to the Regulations because they were 'part of the price paid for the services provided by the banks'.[79] In particular, the Supreme Court ruled that 'regulation 6(2)(b) covers any price or remuneration terms and that unarranged overdraft bank charges, being price terms, are thus exempt from the unfairness assessment'.[80] However, Lord Phillips stated that the 'OFT could still try to scrutinise bank charges under other parts of the consumer protection regulations'.[81]

Montague noted that:

> This decision, described as 'sensational' and 'unexpected' in the media reports, has been much misunderstood. In the wake of the banking scandals of the past year, it has been generally viewed as further proof of the establishment's protection of the banks' profits. However, the Supreme Court was *not* saying that charges of up to £39 a day were acceptable, but only that there was no legal ground to challenge them via the route chosen by the OFT. The view of the Supreme Court was that the lower courts had over-complicated a relatively simple question of interpretation.[82]

---

[74] P. Davies, 'Case comment: bank charges and unfair terms' (2008) 67(3) *Cambridge Law Journal* 466.

[75] See above n. 73.

[76] J. Montague,. 'Case comment: Office of Fair Trading v Abbey National Plc: contract – bank levies unfair terms – Office of Fair Trading' (2009) 14(2), *Coventry Law Journal*, 44.

[77] R. Mulheron. 'Recent milestones in class actions reform in England: a critique and a proposal' (2011) 127 *Law Quarterly Review* (April) 288, 298–9.

[78] Montague, above n. 76, at 44.   [79] *Ibid.*

[80] Chen-Wishart, M. 'Case comment: transparency and fairness in bank charges' (2010) 126 *Law Quarterly Review* (April) 157.

[81] B. McDonnell, O. Bell, J. Butler, D. Crehan, E. Heaton and N. Lindsay, 'Annual review' (2009) 72 *Compliance Officer Bulletin*, (December/January) 1, 38.

[82] Montague, above n. 76, at 44.

Importantly, an overdraft presents a reversal of roles from a current account, where the bank becomes the creditor and the customer is the debtor.[83] The Court of Appeal in *Crimpfil Ltd* v. *Barclays Bank Plc* held that a bank was 'not entitled to withdraw the overdraft facility during the year of its currency and were in breach of contract in doing so'.[84]

5 Cheques

Despite the technological advances, cheques remain an important part of the relationship between a bank and its customer,[85] and have two well-documented functions. First a cheque permits the account holder to obtain or withdraw cash from their own bank account.[86] Secondly, a cheque allows the transmission of money from one bank account to another, or from the payer to the payee.[87] A cheque is a type of money transfer form,[88] and it has also been defined as 'a means of facilitating payment'.[89] A cheque has been described as a 'non-transferable payment order, because the cheque, technically a bill of exchange drawn on a banker payable on demand, in fact has been deprived of its negotiability'.[90] A bill of exchange can be defined as:

> an unconditional order in writing, addressed by one person to another, signed by the person giving it, requiring the person to whom it is addressed to pay on demand or at a fixed or determinable future time a sum certain in money to or to the order of a specified person, or to bearer.[91]

Hudson noted that a bill of exchange has five important features. First, 'it must be unconditional in the sense that there must not be any condition precedent before the bill is payable'. Secondly, 'it involves a transfer of money's worth by one person to another in that the bill itself expresses one person as being payer and the other being payee'. Thirdly, 'the person expressed on the bill as being the person to whom it is addressed is entitled to be paid'. Fourthly, 'the payment date may either be on a fixed date, or at a time to be fixed in the future'. Fifthly, the bill may either be paid to the original payee named on the bill itself, or the bill may be 'indorsed' by the payee.[92] The Bills of Exchange Act 1882 also defines a cheque as a 'bill of exchange drawn on a banker payable on demand. Except otherwise provided by in this Part, the provisions of this Act applicable to a bill of exchange payable on demand apply to a cheque.'[93] Therefore, Wadsley

---

[83] Cranston, above n. 16, at 255.

[84] [1995] CLC 385, as cited in 'Case comment: whether overdraft repayable on demand' (1995) 8(7) *Insolvency Intelligence* 3, 54.

[85] Wadsley and Penn, above n. 1 at 417.   [86] Hudson, above n. 35, at 805.

[87] *Ibid.*

[88] A. Rahmatian, 'Must cheques disappear by 2018?' (2011) 26(7) *Journal of International Banking Law and Regulation* 310.

[89] Hudson, above n. 35, at 803.   [90] Rahmatian, above n. 88, at 311.

[91] Bills of Exchange Act 1882, s.3(1).   [92] Hudson, above n. 35, at 903.

[93] Bills of Exchange Act 1882, s.73(1).

and Penn noted that if you combine these two definitions 'a cheque is an unconditional order in writing, signed by the person giving it, requiring the bank to whom it is addressed to pay on demand a sum certain in money to, or to the order of, a specified person or bearer'.[94]

The applicable law relating to cheques is to be found in the Bills of Exchange Act 1882, the Cheques Act 1957 and the Cheques Act 1992.[95] Alexander described the Cheques Act 1957 as a 'major reform in commercial and banking law and practice'.[96] The 1957 Act was amended by the Cheques Act 1992, the objective of which was to 'settle the problems respecting crossings accompanied by the words "Not-Negotiable – Account Payee only"'.[97] The 1992 Act amended the Bills of Exchange Act 1882 by inserting a new section 81, which now provides:

(1) Where a cheque is crossed and bears across its face the words 'account payee' or 'a/c payee', either with or without the word 'only', the cheque shall not be transferable, but shall only be valid as between the parties.

(2) A banker is not to be treated for the purposes of section 80 above as having been negligent by reason only of his failure to concern himself with any purported indorsement of a cheque which under subsection (1) above or otherwise is not transferable.[98]

In essence, this means that:

Subsection (1), effectively, applies the provisions of section 8(1) to cheques bearing a crossing accompanied by the words 'a/c payee only'. Such a cheque now has the same effect as one in which the words 'not transferable' appear on the cheque or a cheque on which the word 'only' is added after the payee's name. Under section 8(1) and the new section 81A, the title to an instrument bearing any of these formulas cannot be passed by its negotiation. Consequently, the original payee, to whom the instrument has been issued, remains its owner notwithstanding his attempt to transfer the instrument. The transferee, thus, has no enforceable title and cannot bring an action to enforce the cheque in his own name.[99]

This represents the culmination of decades of debate on the subject of non-transferable cheques. While transferability and negotiability have always been essential features of bills of exchange which are used not only as a means of payment but also as a source of credit (and must be capable of circulating freely in the discount markets prior to maturity) cheques by contrast are generally used simply as a means of instruction to transfer funds from the bank account of the payer to the bank account of the payee and the instrument's transferability is, in the vast majority of cases, an unwanted feature exposing both the payer and the payee to the risk of fraud by third parties.[100]

---

[94] Wadsley and Penn, above n. 1 at 418.   [95] Cranston, above n. 16 at 258–9.

[96] J. Alexander, 'Cheques Act, 1957' (1957) 23(3) *Arbitration*, 142.

[97] 'Legislative Comment: the Cheques Act 1992' (1992) *Journal of Business Law* (May) 270.

[98] Bills of Exchange Act 1882, s.81A.

[99] See above n. 97, at 270.

[100] J. Fox, 'Legislative comment: the Cheques Act 1992' (1992) 7(7) *Journal of International Banking Law* 280.

The Cheques Act 1992 'amends certain provisions of the Bills of Exchange Act 1882 and of the Cheques Act 1957, and gives effect to a recommendation made in the White Paper presented by the Chancellor of the Exchequer to Parliament in March 1990 in the wake of the Report of the Review Committee on Banking Services Law'.[101]

6 Payment cards

There is a vast array of different payment cards in existence in the United Kingdom and they are an extremely convenient way for customers to pay for goods and services.[102] According to Ellinger *et al.*, there are six different types of payments cards:

(1) credit card;[103]
(2) charge card;
(3) cheque card;
(4) debit card;
(5) cash card; and
(6) electronic purse or digital cash card.[104]

The legal classification of these cards also differs, depending on the type of card. For example, if a card is regulated by the Consumer Credit Act 1974, the card must be classified as a consumer credit agreement or a credit token. Hudson noted that it is possible to obtain some clarity on the legal classification of cards from the decision in *Re Charge Card Services Ltd*.[105] Here, Millet J stated:

> As the cases cited to me demonstrate, the approach of the courts to this question has not been conceptual or based on any such supposed principle, but has been strictly pragmatic. As each new method of payment has fallen to be considered, its nature and the surrounding circumstances have been examined to see whether a presumption of conditional payment should be made. Indeed, only in this way is it possible to identify those special circumstances which may take an individual case out of the general rule applicable to payments by a particular method.[106]

---

[101] See above n. 97, at 270.
[102] B. Bisping, 'The case against s.75 of the Consumer Credit Act 1974 in credit card transactions' (2011) 5 *Journal of Business Law* 457.
[103] See further Part 7.
[104] Ellinger *et al.*, above n. 10, at 649–51.
[105] [1989] Ch. 497, CA. For an interesting discussion of this case see S. Deane, 'Re Charge Card Services Ltd and Hong Kong's section 15A' (1991) 6(8) *Journal of International Banking Law* 332 and R. Goode, 'Case comment: setting off contingent claims' (1986) *Journal of Business Law* (September) 431. This case has been described as a 'welcome development' by Shea, above n. 26, at 57 and as 'very welcome in casting some light into a legally obscure area' in Editorial, 'Credit cards: our flexible friends and legal relations' (1988) 7(6) *International Banking Law* 82.
[106] [1987] Ch. 150, 166.

(a) Charge card

According to Wadsley and Penn, charge cards 'are not classed as credit cards, because the total balance outstanding has to be repaid regularly on the due date'.[107] Conversely, it has been argued that a charge card is a 'variant of the credit card', which requires the card holder to pay the outstanding balance punctually or regularly.[108] Charge cards are governed by the Consumer Credit Act 1974 and the Payment Services Regulations 2009.[109] It has also been argued by some commentators that a charge card is very similar to a debit card, yet the card is not necessarily issued by the customer's bank.[110]

(b) Debit card

Debit cards were first introduced in 1987 and have 'become increasingly popular, particularly for smaller payments'.[111] Hudson noted that when payment is made via a debit card 'the amount paid is taken directly from the customer's bank account'.[112] They perform a very similar purpose to a cheque, in that the money is debited from the card holder's bank account by the Electronic Funds Transfer at Point of Sale (EFTPOS) Sustem.[113] This system 'authenticates the card as being valid at first and then the customer enters a [four digit] personal identification number to authorise the transaction'.[114] Writing in 1986, Arora took the view that EFTPOS has the:

> result that a customer of the connected business will be able to pay for goods and services by giving direct instructions to his bank to debit his account for a specified amount and simultaneously to credit the retailer's account with an equivalent amount.[115]

(c) Automated teller machine card and cash card

These cards were first introduced in 1967 and are used by bank customers to obtain cash and other services from what is often referred to as a 'hole in the wall'.[116] Once the transaction has been completed, the customer's bank account is debited with the amount of cash withdrawn. There are two different types of cash cards: (a) offline, and (b) online.[117] An offline cash card 'operates by means of identification of the PIN, which is encoded on the card itself, by the automatic teller machine'.[118]

---

[107] Wadsley and Penn, above n. 1, at 466.   [108] Ellinger *et al.*, above n. 10, at 650.
[109] SI 2009/209.   [110] Hudson, above n. 35, at 817.
[111] Wadsley and Penn, above n. 1, at 466.   [112] Hudson, above n. 35, at 817.
[113] For a description of the operation of this scheme see C. Reed, 'Consumer electronic banking' (1994) 9(11) *Journal of International Banking Law* 451.
[114] Hudson, above n. 35, at 817.
[115] A. Arora, 'Electronic funds transfer and the law' (1986) 7(5) *Company Lawyer* 195, 198.
[116] Wadsley and Penn, above n. 1, at 466.   [117] Ellinger *et al.*, above n. 10, at 661.
[118] *Ibid.*

(d) Cheque card

A cheque card 'is a card issued by a bank to its customer which purports to guarantee that the bank will honour a single cheque up to that maximum amount'.[119] Ellinger *et al.* noted that 'in this type [of card], the issuer warrants to the payee that a cheque, drawn by the card holder for not more than a stated amount, will be paid on presentation, as long as a number of conditions, including that the signature on the cheque corresponds to that on the card, are met'.[120] Millet J in *Re Charge Card Services* stated that:

> A cheque is a revocable mandate by the customer to his bank which authorises the bank, as his agent, to make payment out of moneys standing to the credit of his account or which the bank is willing to advance to him. The obligation undertaken by the bank to the supplier, which it enters into through the agency of its customer when he uses the bank card, is not to dishonour the cheque on presentation for want of funds in the account, so that it is obliged if necessary to advance moneys to the customer to meet it. If the cheque is met, the bank honours its own undertaking as principal to the supplier and, as agent for the customer, makes payment on its behalf out of his own moneys, whether or not these have been advanced to him for the purpose.[121]

(e) Store card

Store cards have become an extremely popular method of payment. Hudson noted that 'store cards are not of a generic type but rather may be charge cards or they may be credit cards but they are issued by a retail shop, usually a retail chain of shops'.[122]

(f) Electronic purse or digital cash card

Ellinger *et al* described electronic money as being where 'monetary value in the form of digital information ("digital cash") is loaded onto a smart card and the corresponding deduction is made from the customer's bank or credit card account'.[123] Ramage stated:

> This is how electronic money works: a prepaid monetary value may be stored in a computer chip on a smart card or stored on a computer chip in a wireless device, or on a computer disk drive. One can transfer money through card reader/writers, or using computers or wireless devices over the Internet. Cards, wireless devices, and computers can be used to authorise monetary transfers from one account to another. These accounts may be bank accounts or reserve assets held in non-bank institutions. Stock, bond, mutual fund, and gold deposit accounts allow ownership transfer of assets to be made by computer or wireless devices.

---

[119] Hudson, above n. 35, at 816.   [120] Ellinger *et al.*, above n. 10, at 657.
[121] [1987] Ch. 150, 166.   [122] Hudson, above n. 35, at 821.
[123] Ellinger *et al.*, above n. 10, at 651.

For security reasons, transfers are protected by cryptographic codes and can even be anonymous if the user so chooses.[124]

7 Banker's duty of confidentiality

The banker's duty of confidentiality is one of the most important aspects of their relationship with a customer. It has also been argued that this duty applies to non-customers 'by giving an express undertaking to that effect, such as when a business plan is presented to the bank to secure finance'.[125] The duty of confidentiality in the United Kingdom is based on judicial precedent, whilst in many other countries the duty is statute based.[126] A bank's duty of confidentiality is based on an implied term of the contract between itself and its customer. A bank's duty of confidentiality was established in the famous case of *Tournier* v. *National Provincial Union Bank of England*.[127] This case has been described as the 'locus classicus' of the bank's duty of confidentiality towards its customers.[128] It has also been referred to as 'the leading case in respect of the bank's duty of confidentiality'.[129] The court imposed a duty of confidentiality in this case after the National Provincial Union Bank of England disclosed to Tournier's employer his overdraft facility and that he had failed to meet the weekly repayments of £1. The Court of Appeal awarded damages to the customer.[130] The extent of the duty of confidentiality was outlined by Atkin LJ, who stated:

> It clearly goes beyond the state of the account, that is, whether there is a debit or credit balance, and the amount of the balance. It must at least extend to all transactions that go through the account, and to the securities, if any, given in respect of the account; and in respect of such matters it must, I think, extend beyond the period when the account is closed, or ceases to be an active account. I further think that the obligation extends to information obtained from other sources than the customer's actual account, if the occasion upon which the information was obtained arose out of the banking relations of the bank and its customers – for example, with a view to assisting the bank in conducting the customer's business, or in coming to decisions as to its treatment of its customers.[131]

It is important to note the dissenting judgment of Scrutton LJ, who 'expressed the contrary view, holding that the bank's duty to respect its customer's

---

[124] S. Ramage, 'Legislative comment: digital money, electronic fraud, new regulations and the old money laundering regulations' (2011) 200 *Criminal Lawyer* 1, 2.

[125] Ellinger *et al.*, above n. 10, at 176.   [126] Wadsley and Penn, above n. 1, at 89.

[127] [1924] 1 KB 461.

[128] R. Goode, 'The banker's duty of confidentiality' (1989) *Journal of Business Law* (May) 269.

[129] S. Chew, 'Disclosure of information by the bank: protection of the guarantor's rights or a threat to the doctrine of confidentiality' (2009) 24(6) *Journal of International Banking Law and Regulation* 313, 316. For a similar view see A. Olukonyinsola, 'International securities regulation' (1992) 7(5) *Journal of International Banking Law* 191, 192.

[130] Ellinger *et al.*, above n. 10, at 176.

[131] *Tournier* v. *National Provincial Union Bank of England* [1924] 1 KB 461, 485, as cited in Goode, above n. 128, at 269.

confidence did not apply "to knowledge derived from other sources during the continuance of the relation".[132] However, the courts have sided with the approach of Atkin LJ. In *Barclays Bank plc* v. *Taylor,* Lord Donaldson MR stated 'the banker-customer relationship imposes upon the bank a duty of confidentiality in relation to information concerning its customer and his affairs which it acquires in the character of his banker'.[133] Wadsley and Penn noted that 'the Court of Appeal held that it is an implied term of the banker-customer contract that bankers owe their customers a duty of secrecy or non-disclosure, and that in this case, the duty had been breached'.[134] Arora noted that the Jack Committee 'recommended the statutory codification of the rule in *Tournier* v. *National Provincial & Union Bank of England* … where the court established a duty of confidentiality in respect of the customer's affairs'.[135] Stokes stated:

> Thus the concept of banking confidentiality was born and quickly established itself at the heart of the banker-customer relationship. Consequently a traditional account of the banker's duty of confidentiality would state that, generally, the duty of confidentiality is owed to the customer of the bank and begins upon the opening of the account.[136]

Therefore, a 'bank may not disclose to any other person any document or other information it has obtained in the course of the relationship with a customer without the consent of the customer'.[137]

However, there are a number of exceptions to this rule, which were outlined by Banks LJ in *Tournier.* who famously stated:

> On principle, I think the qualifications can be classed under four heads: (a) where disclosure is under compulsion by law: (b) where there is a duty to the public to disclose; (c) where the interests of the bank require disclosure: (d) where disclosure is made by express or implied consent of the customer.[138]

Banks LJ offered an interesting commentary on the longevity of the duty of confidentiality and stated that:

> I certainly think that the duty does not cease the moment a customer closes his account. Information gained during the currency of the account remains confidential unless released under circumstances bringing the case within one of the classes of qualification I have already referred to.[139]

These qualifications have been described as being 'almost universally regarded in the jurisprudence as exceptions to the duty and as if they have statutory

---

[132] As cited in Ellinger *et al.*, above n. 10, at 177.   [133] [1989] 1 WLR 1066, 1070, CA.

[134] Wadsley and Penn, above n. 1, at 105.

[135] A. Arora, 'Code of Banking Practice: Part A' (1992) 10(12) *International Banking and Financial Law* 177, 179.

[136] R. Stokes, 'The banker's duty of confidentiality, money laundering and the Human Rights Act' (2007) *Journal of Business Law* (August) 502, 508.

[137] Wadsley and Penn, above n. 1, at 89.   [138] [1924] 1 KB 461.   [139] *Ibid.*

force'.[140] Furthermore, they have also been referred to as the 'central statement of the bank's duty of confidentiality'.[141]

The first exemption, 'compulsion by law', applies to both civil and criminal proceedings,[142] and is illustrated by the Bankers Books Evidence Act 1879, which provided:

> On the application of any party to a legal proceeding a court or judge may order that such party be at liberty to inspect and take copies of any entries in a banker's book for any of the purposes of such proceedings. An order under this section may be made either with or without summoning the bank or any other party, and shall be served on the bank three clear days before the same is to be obeyed, unless the court or judge otherwise directs.[143]

Other examples include orders for disclosure, witness summons, writs of sequestration, garnishee orders, cross-border disclosure and disclosure to investigators.[144] Indeed, Ellinger et al., took the view that the amount of legislation permitting courts to order the inspection and disclosure of bank documents or otherwise requiring bank disclosure in specific circumstances has burgeoned, making major inroads into the bank's duty of confidentiality.[145] The FSMA 2000 empowers the Financial Services Authority to compel a bank to provide confidential information provided four conditions are met:

(1) he is the person under investigation or a member of that person's group;[146]
(2) the person to whom the obligation of confidence is owed is the person under investigation or a member of that person's group;[147]
(3) the person to whom the obligation of confidence is owed consents to the disclosure or production;[148] or
(4) the imposing on him of a requirement with respect to such information or document has been specifically authorised by the investigating authority.[149]

It is important to note that this exception has been subject to criticism from several commentators.[150]

The importance of the second exception, a bank's duty to the public, was illustrated following the infamous collapse of the Bank of Credit and Commerce International (BCCI).[151] In *Pharaon* v. *Bank of Credit and Commerce International SA*, the court ruled that 'having access to that institution's accounts

140 Cranston, above n. 16, at 174.   141 Hudson, above n. 35, at 824.
142 A. Silvertown, 'Bankers' duty of confidentiality' (1988) 7(5) *International Banking Law* 72.
143 Bankers Books Evidence Act 1879, s.7.
144 This exception also applies to requests by financial regulatory agencies and government departments. See *Libyan Arab Foreign Bank* v. *Bankers Trust Co.* [1989] 3 All ER 252.
145 Ellinger et al., above n. 10, at 178–9.   146 FSMA 2000, s.175(5)(a).
147 *Ibid.*, s.175(5)(b).   148 *Ibid.* s.175(5)(c).
149 *Ibid.* s.175(5)(d).   150 See, e.g., Cranston, above n. 16, at 174.
151 See, e.g., *Price Waterhouse* v. *BCCI Holdings (Luxembourg)* [1992] BCLC 583, Ch. D, for a discussion of this rule. Other examples of this exception include trading with the enemy and suspected terrorist links.

overrode the duty of banker-customer confidentiality'.[152] The third exception, the interests of the bank, could apply where a bank sues its customer for debt. Ellinger *et al.* took the view that 'this qualification will most obviously cover the situation where a bank commences proceedings against its customer to recover an unpaid loan or overdraft facility and the bank has to disclose in the pleadings the extent of the customer's liabilities.[153] The final exception is where the customer authorised the bank to disclose certain information. It has, however, also been suggested that a further very important restriction on a bank's duty of confidentiality arises in relation to reporting allegations of money laundering. Under the Proceeds of Crime Act 2002 and the Money Laundering Regulations 2007, a banker is required to report any suspicious activity to the bank's money laundering reporting officer (MLRO), who will then file a suspicious activity report with the Serious Organised Crime Agency. Failure to comply with these reporting obligations could result, if convicted, in a custodial sentence and/or the imposition of a financial penalty by the FSA. However, it has been argued that the money laundering reporting provisions of the Proceeds of Crime Act 2002 are 'vulnerable to attack through the Human Rights Act 1998 and in particular, through Article 8 of the European Convention on Human Rights'.[154]

Q3 What is the significance of the decision in **Tournier v. National Provincial Union Bank of England***?*

8 Banking Conduct Regime

In November 2009, the Banking Conduct Regime, which covers the regulated activity of accepting deposits, supplanted the similar provisions of the self-regulatory Banking Code and Business Banking Code. It was argued in Part 6 Chapter 1 that self-regulation is an unsatisfactory means of managing the activities of banks in the United Kingdom, although several commentators have pointed out that self-regulation does contain a number of benefits.[155] The FSA identified several problem areas in the previous Banking Codes, which included:

(a) the lack of an equivalent to the FSA's requirement in Principle 6;
(b) weaknesses in the Banking Code and Business Banking Code's disciplinary powers;
(c) the implementation in November 2009 of the Payment Services Directive, which applies to the majority of retail banks and replaced large parts of the existing Codes.[156]

[152] [1998] 4 All ER 455.
[153] Ellinger *et al.*, above n. 10, at 191.
[154] Stokes, above n. 136, at 508.
[155] See, e.g., the excellent commentary by Cartwright, above n. 50, at 303–6.
[156] P. Richards-Carpenter, E. Sautter, A. Hayes, N. Kynoch, P. Stark, M. Baker, S. Dehra, S. Rosser, V. Plange, and M. Ali, 'Annual Review for 2008' (2008) 62 *Compliance Officer Bulletin* (December/January) 1, 18.

The Banking Conduct Regime consists of three very important parts: the full application of the FSA's Principles for Businesses; the conduct of business requirements of the Payment Services Regulations 2009, SI 2009/209; and the Banking Conduct of Business Sourcebook.

(a) Banking Conduct of Business Sourcebook

The Banking Conduct of Business Sourcebook applies to all firms that accept deposits from banking customers and those who provide current and savings accounts. The FSA published a consultation paper in 2008 that outlined its proposed structure as to how banks should treat their customers.[157] Richards-Carpenter *et al.*, stated:

> These proposals follow the speech made in July 2007 by John Tiner, the former chief executive of FSA, at a meeting of the High Level City Group in which he indicated that, among other things, FSA should bring the conduct of deposit-taking business solely under its 'umbrella'. The reasoning being that this would eliminate the 'regulatory gaps' that existed.[158]

Cartwright noted that the Banking Conduct of Business Sourcebook:

> is concerned, therefore, with conduct of business requirements in areas of retail banking that are not circumscribed by the Directive. The FSA uses the language of 'retail banking services' to encapsulate the activities covered by [the Banking Conduct of Business Sourcebook] BCOBS. This covers many of the services which are not dictated by the Regulations, but which involve retail banking, such as accepting deposits and providing related services such as foreign exchange. Some areas are currently covered by COBS and would largely be carried forward. In other areas, BCOBS will introduce new high-level rules. Many of these issues were previously incorporated into the Banking Code, and one area of concern has been whether protection would be lost in a move to BCOBS. BCOBS is intended to apply to UK branches of credit institutions authorised in other European Economic Area states, credit unions and e-money issuers.[159]

The Banking Conduct of Business Sourcebook contains rules and guidance on a wide range of activities including:

- communications with banking customers and financial promotions;
- distance communications, including the requirements of the Distance Marketing Directive 2002/65/EC and E-commerce Directive 2000/31/EC;
- information to be communicated to banking customers, including appropriate information and statements of account;

---

[157] Financial Services Authority Consultation Paper 08/19, *Regulating Retail Banking Conduct of Business* (London, 2008) and its response to the views received in 2009, FSA, Policy Statement regulating retail banking conduct of business, feedback on CP08/19 and final rules.

[158] Richards *et al.*, above n. 156.

[159] Cartwright, above n. 50, at 302–3.

- post-sale requirements on prompt, efficient and fair service, moving accounts and lost and dormant accounts;
- unauthorised and incorrectly executed payments; and
- cancellation, including the right to cancel and the effects of cancellation.[160]

Q4 Outline the approach towards banking regulation adopted by the Banking Conduct of Business Sourcebook.

9 Payment Services Regulations 2009

The Payment Services Directive 2007/64/EC was implemented in the United Kingdom on 1 November 2009 via the Payment Services Regulations 2009.[161] The FSA was designated the competent authority to implement the Directive through the 2009 Regulations.[162] The Payment Services Directive applies to a wide range of firms that supply payment services to their customers, including banks, building societies, e-money issuers, money remitters, non-bank credit card issuers and non-bank merchant acquirers. A firm that provides payment services must comply with two requirements:

(1) it must be authorised or registered with the FSA, unless it is eligible for an exemption; and
(2) it must satisfy the Payment Services Regulations 2009 conduct of business requirements.[163]

The Payment Services Regulations 2009 established a new type of regulated institution, a payment institution, which is compelled to be authorised or registered with the FSA. If a firm is seeking to provide a payment service, even if it is eligible to take advantage of the FSA's transitional provisions, the payment institution is still required to comply with the conduct of business requirements of the 2009 Regulations.[164] A firm may be registered as

(a) a small payment institution;
(b) an authorised payment institution; or
(c) an agent of a payment institution.

A firm seeking registration as a small payment institution must satisfy four requirements:

---

[160] FSA, The Banking Conduct Regime, available at www.fsa.gov.uk/Pages/Doing/Regulated/ banking/bcobs/index.shtml.
[161] SI 2009/209.
[162] For a more detailed discussion of the role of the FSA in relation to the Payment Services Regulations 2009, see FSA, *The FSA's Role under the Payment Services Regulations 2009: Our Approach* (London, 2010).
[163] FSA, Payment Services Regulations, available at www.fsa.gov.uk/pages/Doing/Regulated/ banking/psd/index.shtml.
[164] For a more detailed overview of these obligations, see FSA, above n. 162, at 15–34.

(1) its average monthly payment transactions (over the preceding twelve months) must not exceed €3 million;

(2) none of the individuals responsible for managing the business has been convicted of offences relating to money laundering or terrorist financing or other financial crimes;

(3) its head office, registered office or place of residence must be in the United Kingdom; and

(4) it must comply with the registration requirements of the Money Laundering Regulations 2007, where those requirements apply to it.[165]

The second option for a firm is to become an authorised payment institution, which requires the applicant to provide the FSA with a wide range of information about its payment services, including:

• details of the payment services business the applicant carries out;
• the governance arrangements and internal procedures in place;
• how the firm will meet the capital requirements;
• details of the individuals responsible for payment services; and
• details of any persons with qualifying holdings.[166]

The final option available for a firm is to become an agent of a small payment institution or an authorised payment institution.

Once a payment institution is authorised or registered with the FSA, it is legally obliged to comply with the FSA's prudential requirements and with the Payment Services Regulations 2009 conduct of business requirements. Furthermore the payment institution is required to provide the FSA with certain types of information, which have been categorised as reports and notifications. The reporting information is required by the FSA on a regular basis so that the payment institution can conform to the FSA's supervisory obligations and EU reporting obligations. The payment institution is also obliged to provide the FSA with notifications if the information it has already provided needs to be altered. The FSA require this information to be provided within twenty-eight days of the change.

10 Conclusion

This chapter has discussed the interpretation of important terms such as a 'bank' and 'customer' and provided an overview of the relationships between a bank and its customers. What becomes clear is that, not only the definition of a bank and the practices it is involved with, but also the bank's relationship with its customers have both dramatically altered. Part 6 Chapter 3 deals with various aspects of banking regulation.

---

[165] FSA, 'Becoming a small payment institution', available at www.fsa.gov.uk/pages/Doing/ Regulated/banking/psd/applying/small/index.shtml.

[166] FSA, 'Becoming an authorised payment institution', available at www.fsa.gov.uk/pages/Doing/ Regulated/banking/psd/applying/authorised/index.shtml.

11 Recommended reading

Bollen, R. 'European regulation of payment services: recent developments and the proposed Payment Services Directive, Part 2' (2007) 22(10) *Journal of International Banking Law and Regulation* 532

'European regulation of payment services: the story so far' (2007) 22(9) *Journal of International Banking Law and Regulation* 451

Brandt, P. and Graham, P. 'An update on the UK's implementation of the Payment Services Directive' (2009) 64 *Compliance Officer Bulletin* (March) 1, 3

Cartwright, P. 'Retail depositors, conduct of business and sanctioning' (2009) 17(3) *Journal of Financial Regulation and Compliance* 302

Chen-Wishart, M. 'Case comment: transparency and fairness in bank charges' (2010) 126 *Law Quarterly Review* (April) 157

Cranston, R. *Principles of Banking Law* (Oxford University Press, 2002)

Davies, P. 'Case comment: bank charges and unfair terms' (2008) 67(3) *Cambridge Law Journal* 466

Ellinger, E., Lomnicka, E. and Hare, C. *Ellinger's Modern Banking Law* (Oxford University Press, 2011)

Hsiao, M. 'Legitimised interference with private properties: Banking Act 2009' (2010) 25(5) *Journal of International Banking Law and Regulation* 227

Hudson, A. *The Law of Finance* (Sweet and Maxwell, London, 2009)

Mulheron, R. 'Recent milestones in class actions reform in England: a critique and a proposal' (2011) 127 *Law Quarterly Review* (April) 288

Mullineux, A. 'The regulation of British retail banking utilities' (2009) 17(4) *Journal of Financial Regulation and Compliance* 453

Rahmatian, A. 'Must cheques disappear by 2018?' (2011) 26(7) *Journal of International Banking Law and Regulation* 310

Ramage, S. 'Legislative comment: digital money, electronic fraud, new regulations and the old money laundering regulations' (2011) 200 *Criminal Lawyer* 1.

Stokes, R. 'The banker's duty of confidentiality, money laundering and the Human Rights Act' (2007) *Journal of Business Law* (August) 502

Wadsley, J. and Penn, P. *Penn and Shea, The Law relating to Domestic Banking* (Sweet and Maxwell, London, 2000)

Part 6 Chapter 3

Banking Regulation

Contents

1 Introduction

The purpose of this chapter is to provide an overview of the United Kingdom's financial regulation provisions. The chapter begins by briefly highlighting the influence of legislative provisions on the United Kingdom's financial regulation system. This includes a discussion of the various Banking Directives,[1] the Basel Accord and the Basel Committee on Banking Supervision. The next part of the chapter concentrates on the current system of regulation imposed by the Financial Services Authority through its Handbook and the provisions of the Financial Services and Markets Act 2000. The chapter then turns its attention to financial crime and identifies the relevant statutory provisions dealing with money laundering, insider dealing, market abuse, terrorist financing and fraud.

2 European banking regulation

Like many aspects of law, banking regulation laws and policy have been heavily influenced by the European Union. This influence and levels of international

[1] Set out in section 2 below.

co-operation will continue to grow as the global economy attempts to recover from the 2007 crash. One of the most important legislative instruments is the Second Consolidated Banking Directive.[2] The aim of the Directive is to 'harmonise banking laws across the EU and to provide a "single licence" for banks to be passported from their home State across the EU'.[3] This has been described as a mutual recognition system so that 'freedom of establishment and freedom to provide services is applied in the banking context, so that credit institutions established and authorised in one Member State are generally permitted to operate in other Member States without the need for re-authorisation'.[4] The Directive also seeks to 'ensure competition between banks and safeguard depositors'.[5] However, the Directive does not apply in assessing the financial soundness or solvency of a credit institution.[6] The European Union has implemented several statutory measures aimed at regulating banking activities. These include, for example, the Prospectus Directive 2003/71/EC, the Recast Banking Consolidation Directive 2006/48/EC, the Markets in Financial Instruments Directive 2004/39/EC, the Recast Capital Adequacy Directive 2006/49/EC, the Financial Conglomerates Directive 2002/87/EC, UCITS Directives 2009/-65/EC, the Deposit Guarantee Schemes Directive 94/19/EC, the Investor Compensation Scheme Directive 97/9/EC, the Market Abuse Directive 2003/6/EC and the Transparency Directive 2004/109/EC. It is important to note that the European Union's approach toward banking regulation has been heavily influenced by the Basel Committee on Banking Supervision and Basel III, which is an international regulatory framework for banks that seeks to improve the levels of 'regulation, supervision and risk management of the banking sector'.[7] Basel III has three objectives:

(1) to improve the banking sector's ability to absorb shocks arising from financial and economic stress, whatever the source;
(2) to improve risk management and governance; and
(3) to strengthen banks' transparency and disclosures.[8]

These objectives target two specific issues:

(a) bank-level, or microprudential, regulation, which will help raise the resilience of individual banking institutions to periods of stress; and
(b) macroprudential regulation of system-wide risks that can build up across the banking sector as well as the procyclical amplification of these risks over time.[9]

---

[2] 2006/48/EC (14 June, 2006).

[3] A. Hudson, *The Law of Finance* (Sweet and Maxwell, London, 2009) 165.

[4] R. Bollen, 'European regulation of payment services: the story so far' (2007) 22(9) *Journal of International Banking Law and Regulation* 451, 457.

[5] See Hudson, above n. 3, at 165.   [6] *Ibid.*

[7] Bank of International Settlements, 'International regulatory framework for banks (Basel III)', available at www.bis.org/bcbs/basel3.htm.

[8] *Ibid.*   [9] *Ibid.*

The next part of the chapter identifies the relevant international institutions that perform very important roles in the regulation of banking activities. Many of these institutions have no formal law-making powers, although some produce 'best practice 'or 'guidance' notes. Nonetheless, they all play a very important role and have direct influence over the United Kingdom's banking regulation laws.

(a) International Monetary Fund

The International Monetary Fund (IMF) consists of 187 countries. It seeks to develop international co-operation to maintain financial stability, to encourage and assist international trade, to encourage high levels of employment, advance sustainable economic progress and reduce global poverty. The principal objective of the IMF is to 'ensure stability in the international system', and this is achieved in three ways:

(1) keeping track of the global economy and the economies of member countries;
(2) lending to countries with balance of payments difficulties; and
(3) giving practical help to members.

Furthermore, the IMF manages the international monetary system and monitors the financial and economic policies of its 187 members. Importantly, it monitors the economic performance on a national, regional and global level and it provides members with financial policy advice. The IMF provides low and middle income countries with education and training facilities to devise and implement suitable financial policies. The IMF also provides loans to countries which are unable to repay their international financial commitments and cannot secure funding from other sources.

(b) World Bank

The World Bank, like the IMF, is a very important financial resource for developing countries that consists of 187 members. Its mission is to reduce poverty, to encourage people to become self-sufficient through a series of partnerships between the private and public sector. Unlike the IMF, the World Bank is not a lending institution and it is made up of two development organisations, the International Bank for Reconstruction and Development (IBRD) and the International Development Association (IDA). These are supported by the International Finance Corporation (IFC), Multilateral Investment Guarantee Agency (MIGA) and the International Centre for the Settlement of Investment Disputes (ICSID).

(c) Bank of International Settlements

The role of the Bank of International Settlements (BIS) is to support central banks to maintain monetary and financial stability, to encourage international co-operation and to act as a bank for central banks. The BIS seeks to achieve these objectives by:

(a) promoting discussion and facilitating collaboration among central banks;
(b) supporting dialogue with other authorities that are responsible for promoting financial stability;
(c) conducting research on policy issues confronting central banks and financial supervisory authorities;
(d) acting as a prime counterparty for central banks in their financial transactions; and
(e) serving as an agent or trustee in connection with international financial operations.

(d) Basel Banking Supervision Committee

The Basel Committee on Banking Supervision acts as a medium for recurring co-operation on banking supervisory matters. The Committee's objective is to improve awareness and knowledge of important banking supervisory matters and to enhance the levels of banking supervision. This is partly achieved by promoting best practices, and by exchanging information on national, regional and international supervisory matters. Importantly, the Committee issues best practice notes and guidelines, which have become known as the Core Principles for Effective Banking Supervision; and the Concordat on Cross-border Banking Supervision. The work of the Basel Banking Supervision Committee is divided into four sub-committees:

(1) the Standards Implementation Group;
(2) the Policy Development Group;
(3) the Accounting Task Force; and
(4) the Basel Consultative Group.

(e) International Organisation of Securities Commission

The International Organisation of Securities Commission (IOSC) consists of a number of different agencies that seek to expand and put into practice international standards of regulation and enforcement in order to protect investors. Specifically, the IOSC seeks to promote and maintain investor protection and confidence in the securities market. This is achieved through the exchange of information and increased levels of co-operation in enforcement actions against illegal activities.

(f) Financial Stability Forum

The Financial Stability Forum (FSF) has been established to co-ordinate at the international level the work of national financial authorities and international standard-setting bodies and to develop and promote the implementation of effective regulatory, supervisory and other financial sector policies. It brings together national authorities responsible for financial stability in significant international financial centres, international financial institutions, sector-specific international groupings of regulators and supervisors, and committees of central bank experts.

(g) Financial Action Task Force

The Financial Action Task Force (FATF) is an intergovernmental body that was created in 1989 to develop and promote the use of national and international strategies to combat money laundering. In 1990, it published the '40 Recommendations', which have served as a precedent for countries seeking to introduce money laundering policies and legislative frameworks. Its remit was extended to include terrorist financing following the al Qaeda attacks in the United States in September 2001.

Q1 What is the role of the Basel Committee on Banking Supervision?

3 The Financial Services Authority

As outlined in the Part 6 Chapter 1, the FSA is the United Kingdom's financial regulatory agency. It was created in October 1997 by the former Labour government and it will probably cease to exist in its current format by the end of 2012 when the Financial Services Bill is expected to be enacted. The relevant legislative framework of the FSA consists of the provisions of the Financial Services and Markets Act (FSMA) 2000 and the FSA's extensive Handbook and it is to these that the chapter now turns.

(a) Financial Services and Markets Act 2000

The FSMA 2000 received Royal Assent on 14 June 2000. The purpose of the FSMA 2000 was to provide a single legal framework for the FSA, replacing the different frameworks under which the various regulators had previously operated.[10] Many of the provisions in the FSMA 2000 represent consolidation of existing law or self-regulatory requirements. Such provisions would include arrangements for authorisation of firms, making arrangements for approval of individuals, providing for rule-making powers, for information gathering and investigation powers and the ability to impose financial penalties on those authorised firms which breach the regulatory framework. The main powers conferred on the FSA in the FSMA 2000 are the powers to impose financial penalties upon those who abuse investment markets, and to take on the role

---

[10] Financial Services Authority, *Legal Framework* (London, 2000).

of the UK Listing Authority, which it undertook under substantially the same parameters as previously exercised by the London Stock Exchange.

Importantly, the FSA was given four statutory objectives: to maintain market confidence, to promote the public's understanding of the financial services sector, to maintain consumer protection and to reduce financial crime.[11] The purpose of the FSMA 2000 was to provide the FSA with an adequate statutory framework within which to operate, and to provide for the regulation and authorisation of businesses, including banks, building societies, insurance companies, friendly societies, credit unions, Lloyd's, investment and pension advisers, stockbrokers, professional firms, fund managers and derivatives traders. Also under the provisions of the FSMA 2000, a Financial Services and Markets Tribunal was created, a single ombudsman was provided for under the new law and an improved compensation scheme was established to provide further protection for consumers.

A central objective of the FSMA 2000 was to modernise the financial regulatory arrangements that were contained in numerous pieces of legislation. Previously, financial services providers were regulated under the Credit Unions Act 1979, the much criticised Financial Services Act 1986, the Building Societies Act 1986, the Banking Act 1987 and the Friendly Societies Act 1992. The FSMA 2000 provides that if a person intends to undertake a regulated activity in the United Kingdom, they must either be authorised to do so by the FSA or exempt under the provision of the Act.[12] If a person undertakes a regulated activity without authorisation by the FSA or an exemption, they are liable to criminal prosecution and could be subject to a custodial sentence of two years and/or a fine. The definition of a regulated activity is contained in the Financial Services and Markets Act 2000 (Regulated Activities) Order 2001.[13] Examples of regulated activities include accepting deposits, issuing e-money, dealing in investments, arranging home finance activities, managing investments, safeguarding and administering investments, advising on investments, advising on home finance activities, entering into funeral plan contracts, and agreeing to do most of the above activities. In order for an activity to be a regulated activity it must be carried on 'by way of business'.[14]

(b) FSA Handbook

The FSMA 2000 provides that the FSA is required to exercise its rule-making powers in writing through 'rule-making instruments'.[15] This is more commonly referred to as the FSA Handbook. This is an extremely extensive and detailed document that outlines the FSA's rules and guidance, which have been issued

[11] For a more detailed discussion of these objectives and the amendments introduced by the Financial Services Act 2010, see Part 6 Chapter 1.
[12] FSMA 2000, s.19.   [13] SI 2001/544.
[14] FSMA 2000, s.22.   [15] Ibid. s.153.

under the provisions of the FSMA 2000. The Handbook is divided into Blocks, which has been sub-divided into modules:

- Block 1 (High Level Standards) deals with the overarching requirements for all authorised persons (firms) and approved persons.
- Block 2 (Prudential Standards) outlines the prudential requirements that affect regulated firms.
- Block 3 (Business Standards) covers a majority of the requirements that relate to a firm's day-to-day business.
- Block 4 (Regulatory Processes) outlines the process of the FSA's supervisory and disciplinary functions.
- Block 5 (Redress) deals with the mechanisms for dealing with complaints and compensation.
- Block 6 (Specialist Sourcebooks) applies to specified parts of the regulated sector such as credit unions.[16]
- Block 7 (Listing, Prospectus and Disclosure Rules) outlines the requirements for issuers seeking admission to the Official List of the UK Listing Authority, rules that relate to a sponsor and a person applying for approval as a sponsor, along with the prospectus and disclosure documents.

The FSA publishes Handbook guides which are aimed at certain types of regulated firms. This has included, for example, the Energy Markets Participants (EMP), Oil Markets Participants (OMP) and Service Companies (SERV). The FSA also publishes regulatory guides for certain regulatory aspects of the Handbook. This has included, for example:

- Building Societies Regulatory Guide (BSOG), which offers guidance to building societies on constitutional matters under the Building Societies Act 1986;
- Collective Investment Schemes Regulatory Guide (COLLG), which provides useful facts on the regulation of collective investments schemes in the United Kingdom;
- Enforcement Guide (EG), which outlines and describes the FSA's policy towards utilising its enforcement powers;
- Perimeter Guidance Manual (PERG), which contains guidance about the circumstances in which authorisation is required, or exempt person status is available, including guidance on the activities regulated under the FSMA 2000 and the exemptions that are available;
- Responsibilities of Providers and Distributors for the Fair Treatment of Customers (RPPD), which set out these responsibilities under the FSA's Principles and rules;

---

[16] There are fourteen tailor-made handbooks for smaller firms, which are considerably smaller than the full scope of the Handbook, which apply, e.g., to asset managers, general insurance brokers and small friendly societies.

- Unfair Contract Terms Regulatory Guide (UNFCOG), which sets out the FSA's powers under the Unfair Terms in Consumer Contract Regulations 1999, SI 1999/2083 and explains the FSA's approach to using them.

The Handbook uses a series of letters to categorise its rules and provisions. For example, the letter R refers to general rules made under the FSMA 2000,[17] specialised rules[18] and listing rules.[19] The great majority of the rules in the Handbook impose legal obligations on a regulated firm and, if breached by a firm, the FSA is entitled to utilise its extensive array of enforcement powers. The letter E relates to evidential provisions,[20] and is also used in the Code of Practice for Approved Persons[21] and in certain circumstances in the Code of Market Conduct.[22] The letter G is utilised in relation to guidance under the FSMA 2000.[23] D refers to directions and requirements under the 2000 Act.[24]

(c) FSA Principles for Business

In October 1998, the FSA published a consultation paper that outlined its views on the creation of its Principles for Business.[25] The FSA proposed to establish eight Principles for Business:

(1) Integrity: a firm must conduct its business with integrity;
(2) Skill, care and diligence: a firm must conduct its business and organise its affairs with due skill, care and diligence;
(3) Management and control: a firm must organise and control its affairs effectively;
(4) Prudence: a firm must conduct its business;
(5) Market conduct: a firm must observe proper standards of market conduct;
(6) Customers – general: a firm must pay due regard to the interests of its customers and treaty them fairly;
(7) Customers – relationships of trust: a firm must keep faith with any customer who is entitled to rely upon its judgement;
(8) Relations with regulators: a firm must deal with its regulators in an open and co-operative way.[26]

In October 1999, the FSA revised the principles and extended the number from eight to eleven.[27] The current principles are:

1. A firm must conduct its business with integrity.
2. A firm must conduct its business with due skill, care and diligence.

---

[17] FSMA 2000, s.138. [18] *Ibid.* ss.140–7. [19] *Ibid.* s.73A.
[20] *Ibid.* s.149. [21] *Ibid.* s.64. [22] *Ibid.* s.119. [23] *Ibid.* s.157. [24] See, e.g., *ibid.* s.51(3).
[25] FSA, *The FSA Principles for Business* (London, 1998). [26] *Ibid.*
[27] FSA, *The FSA Principles for Businesses, Response on Consultation Paper 13* (London, 1999) 4. See also K. Connolly, 'FSA response paper on principles for business' (1999) 11(7) *Journal of International Financial Markets* N86.

3. A firm must take reasonable care to organise and control its affairs responsibly and effectively, with adequate risk management systems.
4. A firm must maintain adequate financial resources.
5. A firm must observe proper standards of market conduct.
6. A firm must pay due regard to the interests of its customers and treat them
   fairly.
7. A firm must pay due regard to the information needs of its clients, and
   communicate information to them in a way which is clear, fair and not
   misleading.
8. A firm must manage conflicts of interest fairly, both between itself and its
   customers and between a customer and another client.
9. A firm must take reasonable care to ensure the suitability of its advice and
   discretionary decisions for any customer who is entitled to rely upon its
   judgement.
10. A firm must arrange adequate protection for clients' assets when it is
    responsible for them.
11. A firm must deal with its regulators in an open co-operative way, and must
    disclose to the FSA appropriately anything relating to the firm of which the
    FSA would reasonably expect notice.

The Principles have been described as a 'keystone in the FSA Handbook',[28]
and they 'articulate the actions and behaviours that [the FSA] expect from
firms'.[29] The importance of the Principles is highlighted in the FSA Handbook.[30]

(d) Risk-based approach

One of the most important and controversial aspects of the regulatory approach
adopted by the FSA is its risk-based approach. The FSA outlined its risk-based
approach towards financial regulation in 1997 when it stated that it would
assume an adaptable method of supervision by targeting specific business practices and the level of risk associated with certain markets and firms. This means
that a firm will be able to allocate its resources in a cost-effective and proportionate way so that it can focus on the most relevant risks from money laundering that it faces. The FSA has adopted a two stage policy. First, it has devised a
list of services and products that categorise risk status, and secondly, it has put
in place a new set of procedures to ensure that firms verify the identity of a client. The risk-based approach of the FSA towards the regulated sector will vary
between the 'highest' and 'lowest' at-risk firms. According to the FSA, the most
at-risk sections of the financial services industry are international banking in

---

[28] FSA, *Principles for Business*, above n. 25, at 6.
[29] FSA, 'Principles-based regulation: looking to the future', speech by John Tiner, Chief Executive
    Officer FSA, FSA Insurance Sector Conference, 21 March 2007, available at www.fsa.gov.uk/
    pages/Library/Communication/Speeches/2007/0321_jt.shtml.
[30] *The Full Handbook* (London, 2011) Principle 2.1.

high risk jurisdictions, domestic banking, independent financial advisers, online stockbrocking, spread betting and credit unions. The highest risk firms will benefit from what is best described as a 'continuous relationship'

(e) Principles-based regulation

Principles-based regulation has been defined by the FSA as 'placing greater reliance on principles and outcome focussed, high level rules as a means to drive the regulatory aims they want to achieve, and less reliance on prescriptive rules'.[31] This means that financial regulation would move away from a comprehensive and dictatorial approach towards a high-level Principles approach.[32] The FSA has stated that this approach 'requires firms to take reasonable care to organise and control their affairs responsibly and effectively, with adequate risk management systems'.[33] The move towards a Principles-based approach towards financial regulation is generally regarded as having begun in 2005 when the FSA published its Better Regulation Action Plan,[34] although Samuels argued that the move towards a Principles-based approach in fact began in 2004.[35] This movement towards a Principles-based regulator comprised five core elements:

(a) dependence on existing Principles rather than establishing new rules;
(b) incorporation of the Principles more explicitly into the FSA's supervisory work;
(c) that the rules should be high level and outcome-focused;
(d) when implementing EU Directives, they should not be 'goldplated'; and
(e) development of FSA staff to ensure that they were better able to operate in a Principles-based system.[36]

The adoption of a Principles-based approach allows the regulated sector to adopt a greater level of flexibility to achieve the regulatory objectives of the FSA. This has been achieved by moving away from a system of burdensome rules to allow firms to adopt a more flexible approach. The FSA stated that its 'rulebook is becoming much less detailed and prescriptive with the regulator relying more on its Statements of Principle and high-level rules'.[37] An important part of this approach is that the accountability for important regulatory decisions falls

---

[31] FSA *Principles-based Regulation: Focusing on Outcomes that Matter* (London, 2007).
[32] Herbert Smith, *Principles-based regulation, in principle and in Practice; preliminary observations* (Herbert Smith, London, 2007) 4.
[33] FSA 'Regulatory principles in a principles-based world', speech by Sarah Wilson, Director FSA, ILAG Annual General Meeting, 15 June 2006, available at www.fsa.gov.uk/pages/Library/Communication/Speeches/2006/0615_sw.shtml.
[34] FSA *Better Regulation Action Plan* (London, 2005).
[35] A. Samuel, 'Principles-based regulation, MiFID and the new financial promotion rules' (2007) 49 *Compliance Officer Bulletin* (September) 1, 2.
[36] M. Hopper, and J. Stainsby, 'Principles-based regulation: better regulation?' (2006) 21(7) *Journal of International Banking Law and Regulation* 387, 388.
[37] Freshfields, *FSA Principles-based Regulation* (London, 2007) 1.

on senior management. From a consumer's point of view, a Principles-based approach can cultivate a culture of improvement and competition in the financial services sector.[38] The Principles-based approach represents a move away from a risk-based approach, but the FSA has stated that 'risk-based regulation will remain central to determining how we prioritise our resources, as principles-based regulation steers our expectations of firms and the way we deal with them.'[39]

Q2 What is the risk-based approach of the FSA towards banking regulation?

(f) Authorisation

In order for a regulated firm to undertake an activity or range of activities under the FSMA 2000, it generally has to be authorised by the FSA.[40] Section 19 of FSMA 2000 provides that a person who undertakes a regulated activity must be authorised to do so, and may be liable to criminal proceedings and/or a fine if they perform such activities and are not authorised.[41]

(g) Enforcement powers

Part II of the FSMA 2000 empowers the FSA and the Secretary of State to require the production of information and documents, to require reports to be prepared, to conduct investigations and to gain access to premises with a warrant. The powers provided in this Part of the FSMA 2000 are in addition to the specific powers that the FSA has under the Act. These provisions allow the FSA to obtain information on an ad hoc basis and therefore supplement the FSA's ability to make rules that require an authorised person to provide it with information on a routine basis under its general rule-making power. Section 165 of the FSMA 2000 provides that the FSA has the power to require information or documents that may reasonably be required in connection with the discharge of its functions under the FSMA 2000. The information or documents can be required from any person, including a legal person; this would include an authorised person, a formerly authorised person, a person connected with an authorised person, an operator, a recognised investment exchange and a recognised clearing house. Section 166 confers on the FSA the power to require an authorised person or a formerly authorised person to commission a report and provide it to the FSA in any manner which the FSA might specify. This is an important power for the FSA, as it enables them to require such reports from other persons carrying on a business who are, or were, connected to the

---

[38] See FSA speech by John Tiner, above n.29.   [39] FSA, *Focusing on Outcomes*, above n. 31, at 4.

[40] The activities are those listed in the Financial Services and Markets Act 2000 (Regulated Activities) Order 2001, SI 2001/3544.

[41] For a more detailed discussion of the authorisation mechanisms under FSMA 2000 see Financial Services Authority, 'How do I get authorised' (n/d), available at www.fsa.gov.uk/pages/doing/how/index.shtml.

authorised or formerly authorised person.[42] The FSA has become a prosecuting authority for allegations of money laundering and insider dealing.[43]

Q3 What are the enforcement mechanisms of the FSA?

4 Financial Services Compensation Scheme

The Financial Services Compensation Scheme (FSCS) was created to compensate customers who have suffered loss as a consequence of the inability of an authorised person to meet its liabilities. However, it should be noted that the FSCS is not intended to compensate people where a regulatory breach has occurred. Under FSMA 2000, section 213, customers may make a claim against an authorised person even if the claim arises in relation to an activity for which the authorised person did not have permission under the FSMA 2000. In respect of lost deposits, an eligible depositor with a bank is entitled to claim up to £85,000, with joint account holders able to claim £85,000 each.[44]

5 Financial Ombudsman Scheme

Under Part XVI of the FSMA 2000, a single compulsory Ombudsman scheme has been created with the aim of solving disputes between authorised firms and their customers. Under section 226, all firms that are authorised by the FSA are required to submit to the jurisdiction of the scheme.[45] The FSA is empowered to make rules to determine which activities of authorised persons fall within its jurisdiction. If a claim against an authorised person is upheld, the respondent may be ordered to pay compensation up to a maximum amount set by the FSA.[46] Furthermore, the Ombudsman may recommend an amount exceeding the limit as fair compensation and the respondent may also be ordered to take such steps as are necessary to rectify the matter complained of.[47] Under section 230, the scheme operator has the ability to create rules regarding costs that can be awarded by the Ombudsman.

6 Financial Services and Markets Tribunal

The Financial Services and Markets Tribunal is an independent tribunal established by section 132 of the FSMA 2000, and it has been described as one of the

---

[42] FSMA 2000, s.166(2).

[43] See, e.g., N. Ryder, 'The Financial Services Authority and Proceeds of Crime Act; too little too late?' (2010) *Financial Regulation International* (September) 8–9.

[44] For more information on this, see www.FSCA.org.uk.

[45] The scheme's compulsory jurisdiction may only be applied to persons who were authorised at the time the activity to which the complaint relates was carried out, and the rules must have been in force at the time.

[46] FSMA 2000, s.229.

[47] This can be enforced through the courts by the complainant if necessary.

Act's key features.[48] Its role is to provide an impartial review mechanism of the decisions made by the FSA, including, for example, decisions:

(a) to discipline authorised firms and approved persons;[49]
(b) to vary a firm's permission to conduct certain or all regulated activities;
(c) relating to market abuse;[50]
(d) to withdraw individual approval, and
(e) to make prohibition orders banning people from employment relating to certain or all regulated activities.

The Tribunal may either uphold the decision of the FSA, instruct the FSA not to take any action, or direct them to take a different enforcement action, and it may make recommendations on the FSA's regulatory measures and requirements. The operation and procedure of the Tribunal is regulated by the Financial Services and Markets Tribunal Rules 2001.[51] The Tribunal may give a direction regarding the running of the case, which may be granted at any time during the hearing and could apply, for example, to the time limits, disclosure of certain documents and the suspension of an FSA notice. The hearings before the Tribunal are normally held in public unless there are valid reasons for it to direct otherwise and its decision may be overturned where an error has been made by the Tribunal's staff or additional evidence has been presented.[52] A party to a case may appeal on a point of law to the Court of Appeal.

7 The Bank of England

As referred to in Part 6 Chapter 2, the Bank of England is the United Kingdom's central bank. It was established in 1694, nationalised in 1946 and gained self-determination in 1997.[53] The Bank of England has two primary or 'core' objectives: monetary stability and financial stability. Monetary stability includes maintaining steady prices and confidence in sterling, whilst financial stability requires the Bank of England to identify and reduce the threats posed to the UK financial system. In order to achieve its objectives the Bank of England works with other central banks, international organisations such as the World Bank

---

[48] P. Bourke, and A. Henderson, 'The first decision of the Financial Services and Markets Tribunal' (2002) 23(12) *Company Lawyer* 381.

[49] See in particular Editorial 'Case comment: Financial Services and Markets Tribunal rules on applications for authorisation and approved person status' (2005) 13(3) *Journal of Financial Regulation and Compliance* 278.

[50] See, e.g., J. Gray, 'Case comment: first market abuse ruling from Financial Services and Markets Tribunal' (2005) 13(3) *Journal of Financial Regulation and Compliance* 272.

[51] SI 2001/2476.

[52] For a more detailed discussion of this see S. Orton, 'When will hearings of the Financial Services and Markets Tribunal be held in private' (2003) 18(3) *Journal of International Banking Law and Regulation* 141.

[53] Bank of England, 'About the bank', available at www.bankofengland.co.uk/about/index.htm. See Bank of England, 'Core purposes', available at www.bankofengland.co.uk/about/corepurposes.

and IMF, HM Treasury and the FSA. The Bank of England has nine areas of strategic priority:[54]

(1) to keep inflation on track to meet the 2 per cent target;

(2) to ensure the Bank has the policies, tools and infrastructure in place to implement monetary policy and issue banknotes;

(3) to sustain public support for the monetary policy framework and the benefits of low inflation;

(4) to maintain stability and improve the resilience of the financial system;

(5) to develop the framework and instruments for the Bank's role in macroprudential policy, operating through the Financial Policy Committee (FPC);

(6) to prepare for the transition to the Bank of responsibility for microprudential supervision (through the Prudential Regulation Authority) and infrastructural oversight;

(7) to build and sustain public support for the micro- and macroprudential frameworks;

(8) to ensure that the Bank of England has the correct people and processes to carry out its core purposes; and

(9) to promote public trust and confidence in the Bank's activities.

The regulatory function of the Bank of England was fundamentally altered by the Bank of England Act 1998. The Act removed the Bank of England's regulatory and supervisory functions and transferred them to the FSA,[55] but it conferred the management of monetary policy on the Bank's Monetary Policy Committee (MPC). Further changes to the regulatory role of the Bank of England were made by the Banking Act 2009, including the Bank being given a statutory objective of financial stability,[56] the creation of the Financial Stability Committee[57] and the Bank of England being given supervisory control over the inter-bank payment systems.[58]

8 Bank insolvency

In light of the impact of the 'credit crunch', the former Labour government deemed it necessary to introduce new measures to deal with bank insolvency. The Banking Act 2009 deals with banks experiencing financial problems by capturing the complex set of risks of a bank in distress, in order to minimise the consequences of a bank failure for the financial system as a whole and to compensate depositors as efficiently as possible.[59] It is important to note that the Banking Act 2009 is very different from its predecessors in that it deals

---

[54] See Bank of England, 'Core purposes', available at www.bankofengland.co.uk/about/corepurposes.

[55] Bank of England Act 1998, s.21.   [56] Banking Act 2009, s.238.

[57] *Ibid.*   [58] *Ibid.* s.181.

[59] See generally D. Singh, 'The UK Banking Act 2009, pre-insolvency and early intervention: policy and practice' (2011) 1 *Journal of Business Law* 20.

with banking failure.[60] The Act 'adds the new banking insolvency and banking administration respectively to the existing Insolvency Act 1986'.[61] Singh noted that the 'existing insolvency regime was considered inadequate to deal with a bank in distress, albeit that it has been used on a number of occasions with relative success'.[62] The 2009 Act 'strengthen[ed] the statutory framework for financial stability and depositor protection; it introduces new insolvency and administration regimes for banking companies'.[63] The Act introduced the Special Resolution Regime,[64] a new bank insolvency procedure involving the making of a 'bank insolvency order' [65] and a new bank administration procedure for use where there has been a partial transfer of business from a failing bank.[66] The Special Resolution Regime 'is designed to address some or all of the business of a bank that is likely to encounter difficulties'.[67] The Banking Act 2009 provides that the Special Resolution Regime will be utilised 'where all or part of the business of a bank has encountered, or is likely to encounter, financial difficulties'.[68] The Act also empowers the authorities to use one of three stabilisation options,[69] the bank insolvency procedure[70] and the bank administration procedure.[71] The three stabilisation options are transfer to a private sector purchaser,[72] transfer to a bridge bank[73] and transfer to temporary public ownership.[74] The Special Resolution Regime has five objectives:

(1) to protect and enhance the stability of the financial systems of the United Kingdom;[75]
(2) to protect and enhance public confidence in the stability of the banking systems of the United Kingdom;[76]
(3) to protect depositors;[77]
(4) to protect public funds;[78] and
(5) to avoid interfering with property rights in contravention of an ECHR right.[79]

The 2009 Act has given the financial regulators more power to intervene in a bank's operation. It enables the authorities to step in much more quickly to rescue a troubled institution, for instance, through temporary nationalisation or selling it on to a rival, because the authorities have realised they need triggers to cut in earlier after the Northern Rock debacle.[80] The Banking Act 2009

---

[60] M. Hsiao, 'Legitimised interference with private properties: Banking Act 2009' (2010) 25(5) *Journal of International Banking Law and Regulation* 227.
[61] *Ibid.*   [62] See Singh, above n. 59, at 21.
[63] Editorial 'Banking Act 2009 introduces new bank insolvency/administration procedures' (2009) 247 *Company Law Newsletter* 5.
[64] Banking Act 2009, Part 1.   [65] *Ibid.* Part 2.
[66] *Ibid.* Part 3.   [67] See Hsiao, above n. 60, at 229.
[68] Banking Act 2009, s.1(1).   [69] *Ibid.* s.1(2)(a).   [70] *Ibid.* s.1(2)(b).
[71] *Ibid.* s.1(2)(c).   [72] *Ibid.* s.1(3)(a).   [73] *Ibid.* s.1(3)(b).
[74] *Ibid.* s.1(3)(c).   [75] *Ibid.* s.4(4).   [76] *Ibid.* s.4(5).
[77] *Ibid.* s.4(6).   [78] *Ibid.* s.4(7).   [79] *Ibid.* s.4(8).   [80] See Singh, above n. 59.

'provides stabilisation powers that consist of a transfer to the private sector, bridge banks and public ownership'.[81] These provisions are administered by the Bank of England,[82] HM Treasury[83] and the FSA.[84]

9 Illicit finance

The problems posed by financial crime to financial services providers merit their inclusion in this book. From a regulation perspective, firms are expected to have in place a number of what are referred to as 'preventive measures'. This part of the chapter briefly reviews the financial crime regulations that banks are required to comply with. Particular attention is given to money laundering, insider dealing, market abuse, fraud and the financing of terrorism.

(a) Money laundering

Money laundering can be defined as the concealment of the profits from illegal activity. It is a global problem and its extent in the United Kingdom has been estimated at £25 billion. The United Kingdom's anti-money laundering (AML) policy has been led by HM Treasury, a point illustrated by the publication of its 'Anti-money laundering strategy'.[85] In its policy document, HM Treasury stated that its strategy was based on three objectives: effectiveness, proportionality and engagement.[86] HM Treasury outlined how it aims to achieve these objectives:

> the existing regime consists of measures ranging from provisions in the criminal law to punish money launderers and to deprive them of their proceeds, to the obligation on the financial services industry and certain other sectors and professions to identify their customers and to report suspicious activities when necessary.[87]

The primary money laundering legislation is contained in Part 7 of the Proceeds of Crime Act (PCA) 2002 and the Money Laundering Regulations 2007.[88] The three principal money laundering offences created by the 2002 Act are:

(i) concealing, disguising, converting, transferring or removing from the jurisdiction any criminal property;[89]

---

[81] See Hsiao, above n. 60, 227.   [82] Banking Act 2009, s.1(5)(a).
[83] *Ibid.* s.1(5)(b).   [84] *Ibid.* s.1(5)(c).
[85] HM Treasury, *Anti-money Laundering Strategy* (HM Treasury, London, 2004).
[86] *Ibid.* 12.
[87] HM Treasury, above n. 85, at 11. For a similar view see A. Leong, (2007) 'Chasing dirty money: domestic and international measures against money laundering' (2007) 10(2) *Journal of Money Laundering Control* 140, 141–2.
[88] SI 2007/2157. It is important to note that drug money laundering was initially criminalised by the Drug Trafficking Offences Act 1986, while money laundering was criminalised by virtue of the CJA 1993.
[89] PCA 2002, s.327.

(ii) entering into or becoming concerned in an arrangement knowing or sus-
      pecting it to facilitate the acquisition, retention, use or control of criminal
      property on behalf of another person;[90] and

(iii) acquiring, using or possessing criminal property.[91]

These offences may be committed by any person, whether or not they work
within the 'regulated sector' or undertake a 'relevant business'. Other offences
created by the 2002 Act include failing to disclose information about money
laundering which comes to a person carrying on business in the regulated
sector,[92] failure to disclose such information by nominated officers in the regulated sector,[93] failure to disclose by other nominated officers,[94] tipping off,[95] and
prejudicing an investigation.[96]

The second part of the United Kingdom's AML policy is reliant on the regulations imposed by the FSA, which has extensive rule-making powers to impose
regulations on the regulated sector.[97] In January 2006, the FSA adopted a
Principles-based approach in the Senior Management Arrangements, Systems
and Controls (SYSC) part of the Handbook. Part 3 provides that firms must
have in place systems and controls which are appropriate for the firm to conduct
its business.[98] In particular, a firm is required to 'take reasonable care to establish and maintain effective systems and controls for compliance with applicable
requirements and standards under the regulatory system and for countering the
risk that the firm might be used to further financial crime'.[99] Therefore, firms are
required to carry out regular assessments of the adequacy of the anti-money
laundering systems they have in place to prevent themselves from being used to
further financial crime;[100] to allocate a director or senior manager with overall
responsibility for establishing and maintaining the anti-money laundering system; and to appoint a money laundering reporting officer.[101]

The FSA has extensive investigative and enforcement powers. For example, it
has the ability to require information from firms,[102] to appoint investigators,[103]
to obtain the assistance of overseas financial regulators[104] and provide appointed
investigators with additional powers.[105] Furthermore, it has become a prosecuting authority for certain money laundering offences.[106] The FSA also has the
power to impose a financial penalty where it establishes that there has been a
contravention by an authorised person of its rules.[107] The FSA has imposed a
series of fines on firms which have breached AML provisions even where there
was no evidence of money laundering.[108] More recently, it has fined a firm's

[90] *Ibid.* s.328.   [91] *Ibid.* s.329.   [92] *Ibid.* s.330.   [93] *Ibid.* s.331.
[94] *Ibid.* s.332.   [95] *Ibid.* s.333A.   [96] *Ibid.* s.342.   [97] FSMA 2000, s.146.
[98] FSA Handbook, above n. 30, SYSC 3.1.1.   [99] *Ibid.* SYSC 3.2.6 R.
[100] *Ibid.* SYSC 3.2.6 C.   [101] *Ibid.* SYSC 3.2.6 H and I.   [102] FSMA 2000, ss.165–6.
[103] *Ibid.* ss.167–8.   [104] *Ibid.* s.169.   [105] *Ibid.* s.172.
[106] *Ibid.* s.402(1)(a). The scope of the FSA's prosecutorial powers were approved by the Supreme
      Court in *R* v. *Rollins* [2010] UKSC 39.
[107] FSMA 2000, s.206(1).
[108] See generally N. Ryder, 'The Financial Services Authority and money laundering: a game of cat
      and mouse' (2008) 67(3) *Cambridge Law Journal* 67(3) 635.

money laundering reporting officer.[109] The FSA also implements the Money Laundering Regulations 2007, the purpose of which is to prevent businesses based in the United Kingdom from being abused by criminals and terrorists for the purposes of money laundering.[110]

The final part of the United Kingdom's AML strategy is the use of suspicious activity reports (SARs) to gather financial intelligence, which are to be found in the PCA 2002 and the Money Laundering Regulations 2007.[111] The PCA 2002 provides that SARs should be submitted if a firm 'suspects'[112] or has 'reasonable grounds for suspecting' that an offence has been committed.[113] If a firm has 'reasonable suspicion'[114] or considers it in any way possible (provided that it is more than 'fanciful') that the firm is being used for the purposes of money laundering, it is required to notify its money laundering reporting officer, who will complete a SAR and send it to the Serious Organised Crime Agency (SOCA), who will then determine if further action is to be taken.[115] The interpretation of the term 'suspicion' has been considered by courts in England and Wales on many occasions, and is seen by many commentators as limiting the effectiveness of money laundering reporting requirements.[116] In the decision of the Court of Appeal in *Shah* v. *HSBC Private Bank (UK) Ltd*,[117] Longmore LJ stated 'I cannot see why, rather than submit to summary judgment dismissing the claim, Mr Shah cannot require the bank to prove its case that it had the relevant suspicion and be entitled to pursue the case to trial so that the bank can make good its contention in this respect'.[118]

A common criticism of the reporting requirements is that they have created a 'fear factor', which has resulted in a significant increase in the number of SARs

---

[109] See, e.g., FSA 'FSA fines firm and MLRO for money laundering controls failings', 29 October 2008, www.fsa.gov.uk/pages/Library/Communication/PR/2008/125.shtml, and FSA, 'FSA fines Alpari and its former money laundering reporting officer, Sudipto Chattopadhyay, for anti-money laundering failings' 5 May 2008, available at www.fsa.gov.uk/pages/Library/Communication/PR/2010/077.shtml.

[110] Money Laundering Regulations 2007, SI 2007/2157.

[111] The reporting obligations imposed by the PCA 2002 have been severely criticised by the Court of Appeal in *UMBS Online Ltd* [2007] EWCA Civ 406.

[112] PCA 2002, ss.328(1), 330(2)(a) and 331(2)(a).

[113] *Ibid.* ss.330(2)(b) and 331(2)(b).

[114] The Court of Appeal in *R* v. *Da Silva* [2006] EWCA Crim 1654 rejected the argument by Da Silva that the court 'could not imply a word such as "reasonable" into the relevant statutory provision' (1655).

[115] *K Ltd* v. *National Westminster Bank plc* [2007] 1 WLR 311.

[116] Further guidance on the definition of 'suspicion' is offered by Joint Money Laundering Steering Group, *Prevention of Money Laundering/Combating Terrorist Financing: Guidance for the UK Financial Sector* (London, 2007), Part 1, Guidance 6.9. Longmore LJ in *R* v. *Da Silva* [2006] EWCA Crim. 1654 stated 'It seems to us that the essential element of the word suspect and its affiliates, in this context, is that the defendant must think that there is a possibility, which is more than fanciful, that the relevant facts exist. A vague feeling of unease would not suffice.'

[117] [2010] EWCA Civ 31, [2010] Lloyd's Rep. FC 276, CA. For an analysis of the impact of this case see P. Marshall, 'Does Shah v HSBC Private Bank Ltd make the anti-money laundering consent regime unworkable?' (2010) 25(5) *Journal of International Banking and Financial Law* 287.

[118] *Ibid.* 22.

submitted.[119] The number of SARs submitted between 1995 and 2002 increased from 5,000 to 60,000, and SOCA reported that it had received 228,834 SARs between October 2008 and September 2009.[120] This increase is associated with the threat of sanctions by the FSA, and it has led to the regulated sector adopting a tactic that has been referred to as 'defensive' or 'preventative' reporting.[121]

Q4 What is money-laundering?

(b) Insider dealing

It was not until the Companies Act 1980 that insider dealing was properly criminalised and later consolidated into the Company Securities (Insider Dealing) Act 1985. Further reform was introduced by the Insider Dealing Directive,[122] which was enacted as Part V of the Criminal Justice Act (CJA) 1993. The Act contains three offences of insider dealing,[123] covering an 'insider' who deals in price affected securities;[124] encouraging another to deal in price affected securities;[125] and a disclosure offence relating to the passing on of inside information by one party to another otherwise than in the proper performance of the functions of their employment, office or performance.[126] The fundamental nature of the offence is where an 'insider' is in possession of 'inside information' and undertakes prohibited activities as set out in the Act.[127] The list of relevant securities contained in the legislation include such securities as shares, debt securities, warrants, depository receipts, options, futures and contracts for differences.[128] One of the factors restricting the legislation in scope is that the offence must take place on a regulated market,[129] defined as 'any market, however operated'.[130] This focus on regulated markets precludes face to face deals between individuals, presumably leaving it up to the individuals concerned to ensure equality of information.[131] Key in the legislation is the notion of 'inside information', as to be in breach of the provision the 'insider' must be in possession of such 'inside information'. The definition of 'inside information' is information that relates to particular securities or to a particular issuer of securities;[132] is specific or precise;[133] has not been made public;[134] and if it

---

[119] R. Sarker, 'Anti-money laundering requirements: too much pain for too little gain' (2006) 27(8) *Company Lawyer* 250, 251.

[120] Serious Organised Crime Agency, *The Suspicious Activity Reports Regime Annual Report 2008* (London, 2008) 14.

[121] Leong, above n. 87, at 142.   [122] Directive 89/592/EC.

[123] CJA 1993, s.52.   [124] *Ibid.* s.52(1).   [125] *Ibid.* s.52(2)(a).

[126] *Ibid.* s.52(2)(b).

[127] M. Stallworthy, 'The United Kingdom's new regime for the control of insider dealing' (1993) 4(12) *International Company and Commercial Law Review* 448.

[128] *Ibid.*   [129] CJA 1993, s.52(3).   [130] *Ibid.* s.60(1).

[131] Contrast this with the early regulation in the United States, where only face to face deals and not anonymous markets were caught by the Securities and Exchange Act 1934.

[132] CJA 1993, s.56(1)(a). This does not include securities generally or issuers of securities generally.

[133] *Ibid.* s.56(1)(b).   [134] *Ibid.* s.56(1)(c).

were made public would be likely to have a significant effect on the price of any securities.[135]

The CJA 1993 outlines in some detail when it would be considered that the information was in the public domain, and thus no longer inside information.[136] A key element here is that research and diligence is rewarded. 'Made public' does not have to mean an overt statement made by the issuer of securities, it could be information and data contained in accessible reports that one diligent market participant has found and used. This would not be caught by the prohibition. Another important element in the legislation is that the prohibition relates only to insiders who are in possession of 'inside information', knowing that it is inside information;[137] and to a person who has received it, and knows that he has received it, from an inside source.[138] The Act goes on to provide that an insider has information from an inside source if, and only if, he has it through being a director, employee or shareholder of an issuer of securities;[139] or having access to the information by virtue of his employment, office or profession;[140] or the direct or indirect source of his information is a director, employee or shareholder of an issuer of securities.[141]

While not specified in the legislation, the term 'insider' itself is sub-divided into primary and secondary insider. The primary insider is one who receives or has the information by virtue of being the issuer or closely connected with the issuer, and would include people who in the ordinary course of their business acquire price sensitive information. In essence, a primary insider is one who acquires inside information about price sensitive information likely to have a significant impact on the price of securities by virtue of their relationship with the company. Classes of people who would fall into this category include directors, employees and shareholders. Secondary insiders acquire inside information from a primary insider knowing that it is unpublished price sensitive information, and commits the offence if they then deal or encourage others to deal. An example of this could be an office cleaner. The criminal justice provisions arguably have a narrow focus, applying only to an individual who is an 'insider' in possession of 'inside information', 'dealing' or 'encouraging' other individuals to deal, in 'prescribed securities', on a 'regulated market'.

The sanctions for insider dealing are contained in CJA 1993, section 61 and are a maximum of six months' imprisonment and/or a fine on summary conviction, and seven years' imprisonment and/or a fine for conviction on indictment. The Act does provide a number of defences: (a) that the 'insider' did not expect the dealing to result in a profit attributable to the fact that the information in question was price sensitive information in relation to the securities;[142] or (b) that he believed on reasonable grounds that the information had been disclosed widely enough to ensure that none of those taking part in the dealing

---

[135] *Ibid.* s.56(1)(d).   [136] *Ibid.* s.59.   [137] *Ibid.* s.57(1)(a).
[138] *Ibid.* s.57(1)(b).   [139] *Ibid.* s.57(2)(a)(i).   [140] *Ibid.* s.57(2)(a)(ii).
[141] *Ibid.* s.57(2)(b).   [142] *Ibid.* s.53(1)(a).

would be prejudiced by not having the information;[143] or (c) that he would have done what he did even if he had not had the information.[144] Further defences are listed in Schedule 1 to the Act.[145]

In addition to the criminal insider dealing provisions discussed above, English law also criminalises the intentional misleading of financial markets. Such a provision is contained in FSMA 2000, section 397, which makes it an offence to make statements, promises or forecasts knowing that they are materially misleading, false or deceptive; to dishonestly conceal material facts; or to recklessly make a statement, promise or forecast which is materially misleading, false or deceptive.[146]

(c) Market abuse regime

A new approach to tackling abuse is the Market Abuse Regime. One of its key objectives is to give the FSA maximum flexibility in its task by requiring a lower standard of proof than needed to secure a criminal conviction.[147] The Code of Market Abuse[148] section of the Handbook will play a central role in controlling market abuse. Reference must also be made to the Handbook generally, in particular the High Level Standards such as Principles of Business,[149] Senior Management Arrangement, Systems and Controls,[150] and other specific regulation such as the Supervision Manual,[151] Decision Procedures and Penalties Manual,[152] Disclosure Rules and Transparency Rules[153] and the Listing Rules.[154] The new regime is designed to complement the criminal provisions of the CJA 1993, to run in parallel and in addition to, not to replace and substitute them.[155] While the regime only came into force in 2001, it has already been subject to a major revision by virtue of the passage of the Market Abuse Directive, which aims to set a minimum standard across EU markets.[156] The revised Market Abuse Regime came into force on 1 July 2005.[157] The FSMA 2000 provides that market abuse can take a number of forms and that it comprises behaviour that:

   (a) occurs in relation to:

      (i) qualifying investments admitted to trading on a prescribed market;

      (ii) qualifying investments in respect of which a request for admission to trading on such a market has been made; or

---

[143] *Ibid.* s.53(1)(b).   [144] *Ibid.* s.53(1)(c).   [145] *Ibid.* Sch. I.

[146] For an analysis of FSMA 2000, s.397 and its predecessor provision, Financial Services Act 1986, s.47, see W. Barnett, 'Fraud enforcement in the Financial Services Act 1986: an analysis and discussion of s.47' (1996) 17(7) *Company Lawyer* 203.

[147] See E. Swan, 'Market abuse: a new duty of fairness' (2004) 25(3) *Company Lawyer* 67.

[148] MAR.   [149] PRIN.   [150] SYSC.   [151] SUP.

[152] DEPP.   [153] DTR.   [154] LR.

[155] See A. Sykes, 'Market abuse: a civil revolution' (1999) 1(2) *Journal of International Financial Markets* 59.

[156] Directive 2003/6/EC.

[157] Amendments made to FSMA 2000 by the Financial Services and Markets Act 2000 (Market Abuse) Regulations 2005, SI 2005/381.

    (iii) … investments which are related investments in relation to such qualify-
        ing investments, and

    (b) falls within any one or more of the types of behaviour set out in [section
        118] (2) to (8).[158]

Part VIII of the FSMA 2000 applies to all persons whose actions have an
effect on the market, irrespective of whether they are required to seek authorisation or have an exemption.

The first three types of behaviour relate to the misuse of inside information or
of information which is not yet generally available, while the second four relate
to various types of market manipulation. Unlike the criminal provisions of the
CJA 1993, the market abuse regime does not require the prosecuting authority
to show intent on the part of the market participant,[159] a cause for initial concern, explained by the government on the basis that the market abuse regime
was not primarily about catching errant individuals but about providing clean
and efficient financial markets. This lack of a requirement to prove intent has
now been confirmed by the Court of Appeal.[160]

The FSA is required to publish a code of conduct outlining what the FSA's
responsibilities are in respect of guarding against market abuse.[161] The Code of
Market Conduct (MAR) in the FSA Handbook is central to the operation of the
Market Abuse Regime. The Code is designed to provide assistance and guidance in ascertaining whether behaviour amounts to market abuse.[162] The Code
makes it clear that it is not an exhaustive description of all types of behaviour
amounting to market abuse,[163] nor is it an exhaustive description of all factors
to be taken into account in the determination of whether behaviour is market
abuse.[164]

What then amounts to behaviour that would be regarded as market abuse?
The first of the seven types of behaviour is the classic offence of insider dealing,[165] requiring an 'insider' to deal, or try to deal on the basis of 'inside information'. The second form of behaviour caught by the regime is improper
disclosure,[166] where the 'insider' discloses 'inside information' to another person without permission. The third type of behaviour caught by the legislation
is misuse of information[167] not generally available, which would have an effect
on an investor's decision about the terms on which to deal. The fourth type of
behaviour is manipulating transactions,[168] where trades or the placing of orders
to trade give a false or misleading impression of the supply of, or demand for,
one or more investments, thus raising the price of the investment to an artificial

---

[158] FSMA 2000, s.118.   [159] MAR1.2.6G.

[160] *Winterflood Securities Ltd and others* v. *Financial Services Authority* [2010] EWCA Civ 423,
   [2010] WLR (D) 101.

[161] FSMA 2000, s.119.

[162] MAR1.1.2G. Note that anything marked with a 'C' is behaviour that does not constitute market
   abuse, see MAR1.1.4G.

[163] MAR1.1.6G.   [164] MAR1.1.7G.   [165] FSMA 2000, s.118(2).

[166] *Ibid.* s.118(3).   [167] *Ibid.* s.118(4)(a), (b).   [168] *Ibid.* s.118(5)(a), (b).

or abnormal level.[169] The fifth type of behaviour is manipulating devices,[170] where a person trades or places orders to trade, employing fictitious devices or any other form of deception or contrivance. The sixth form of behaviour comprises dissemination[171] of information, where a person gives out information conveying a false or misleading impression about an investment or issuer of an investment knowing that this information is false and misleading. The final type of behaviour is distortion and misleading behaviour[172] that gives a false and misleading impression of either the supply of, or demand for, an investment; or behaviour that otherwise distorts the market in an investment.

The primary function of the Market Abuse Regime is to punish market abusers, and Part VIII of the FSMA 2000 is indeed entitled 'Penalties for Market Abuse.' To this end, the FSA has considerable power to undertake investigations into alleged market abusers. These powers are contained in Part XI of the FSMA 2000, which empowers the FSA to appoint professionals to undertake general investigations under section 167 or investigations in particular cases under section 168. The types of cases relevant to section 168 include insider dealing[173] and market abuse.[174] To bring a disciplinary action the FSA must be satisfied that a person has engaged in market abuse,[175] or has encouraged another person to undertake behaviour which if he had engaged in such action, would amount to market abuse.[176] The FSA retains the power to bring criminal prosecutions for insider dealing[177] under the CJA 1993; however, it is arguable that the FSA has been slow in progressing down this route preferring to use financial penalties as its main enforcement mechanism, thereby attracting criticism,[178] with some commentators wondering if the FSA would ever get round to commencing criminal prosecutions for insider dealing at all.

Q5 What is market abuse?

(d) Fraud

Prior to 2006, the law relating to fraud was comprised of eight statutory deception offences in the Theft Acts 1968 and 1978 and the common law offence of conspiracy to defraud.[179] The offences created by Theft Act were difficult to enforce.[180] This, therefore, led to the introduction of the Theft Act 1978, which

---

[169] See, e.g., *R* v. *Disciplinary Appeal Tribunal of the Securities and Futures Authority Ltd, ex parte Bertrand Fleurose* [2001] EWHC Admin 292, [2001] 2 All ER (Comm) 481.

[170] FSMA 2000, s.118(6).   [171] *Ibid.* s.118(7).   [172] *Ibid.* s.118(8).

[173] *Ibid.* s.168(2)(a).   [174] *Ibid.* s.168(2)(d).   [175] *Ibid.* s.123(1)(a).

[176] *Ibid.* s.123(1)(b).   [177] *Ibid.* s.402(1)(a).

[178] J. Haines, 'FSA determined to improve the cleanliness of markets: custodial sentences continue to be a real threat' (2008) 29(12) *Company Lawyer* 370.

[179] Other noteworthy attempts to tackle fraud before and after the Theft Act 1968 were the Prevention of Fraud (Investments) Act 1958 and the Financial Services Act 1986.

[180] See generally P. Kiernan, and G. Scanlan, 'Fraud and the law commission: the future of dishonesty' (2003) 10(3) *Journal of Financial Crime* 199.

however did little to rectify the problems.[181] In 1999, the Law Commission published a Consultation Paper, which distinguished between two types of fraudulent offences, dishonesty and deception.[182] The Law Commission published its final report in 2002 with the Fraud Bill. The Fraud Act 2008 came into force on 15 January 2007;[183] it overhauled and widened the criminal offences available in respect of fraudulent and deceptive behaviour.[184] The new offence of fraud, punishable by imprisonment of up to ten years and/or an unlimited fine, can be committed in one of three ways: fraud by false representation,[185] fraud by failing to disclose information, [186] and fraud by abuse of position.[187]

There are a broad range of regulatory agencies that attempt to combat fraud. The most prominent agency is the Serious Fraud Office (SFO), which was established following the 'era of financial deregulation' in the 1980s.[188] The impetus for introducing the Criminal Justice Act 1987 and creating the SFO was the Fraud Trials Committee Report ('Roskill Report'). The Roskill Committee considered the introduction of more effective means of fighting fraud through changes to the law and criminal proceedings.[189] The Roskill Committee made 112 recommendations, of which all but two were implemented.[190] Its main recommendation was the creation of a new unified organisation responsible for the detection, investigation and prosecution of serious fraud cases. The result was the SFO, which has jurisdiction in England, Wales and Northern Ireland, but not Scotland.[191] It is headed by a Director, who is appointed and accountable to the Attorney General. Under the 1987 Act, the SFO has the power to search property and compel persons to answer questions and produce documents, provided its officers have reasonable grounds to do so.[192]

[181] R. Wright, 'Developing effective tools to manage the risk of damage caused by economically motivated crime fraud' (2007) 14(1) *Journal of Financial Crime* 17, 18.
[182] Law Commission, *Legislating the Criminal Code Fraud and Deception*, Law Commission Consultation Paper no 155 (London, 1999).
[183] Fraud Act 2006 (Commencement) Order 2006, SI 2006/3500.
[184] For a detailed commentary and analysis of the Fraud Act, 2006 see D. Ormerod, 'The Fraud Act 2006: criminalising lying?' (2007) *Criminal Law Review* (March) 193. However, it is important to note that not all of the offences under the Theft Act 1968 have been abolished, e.g., false accounting (Theft Act 1968, s.17); liability of company directors (*ibid.* s.18); false statements by company directors (*ibid.* s.19); and dishonest destruction of documents (*ibid.* s.20(1)).
[185] Fraud Act 2006, s.2.   [186] *Ibid.* s.3.   [187] *Ibid.* s.4.
[188] R. Bosworth-Davies, 'Investigating financial crime: the continuing evolution of the public fraud investigation role – a personal perspective' (2009) 30(7) *Company Lawyer* 195, 196.
[189] The Roskill Committee was asked to 'consider in what ways the conduct of criminal proceedings in England and Wales arising from fraud can be improved and to consider what changes in existing law and procedure would be desirable to secure the just, expeditious and economical disposal of such proceedings'. See Fraud Trials Committee Report (HMSO, 1986).
[190] For a detailed commentary of the Roskill Commission see M. Levi, 'The Roskill Fraud Commission revisited: an assessment' (2003) 91(1) *Journal of Financial Crime* 38.
[191] CJA 1987, s.1.
[192] *Ibid.* s.2. It is important to note that the SFO has other investigative and prosecutorial powers under the Fraud Act 2006, the Theft Act 1968, the Companies Act 2006, the Serious Crime Act 2007, the Serious Organised Crime and Police Act 2005, the Proceeds of Crime Act 2002 and the Regulation of Investigatory Powers Act 2000.

The FSA's fraud policy can be divided into four parts: a direct approach;[193] increased supervisory activity;[194] promoting a more joined up approach; [195] and Handbook modifications.[196] The FSA requires a firm's senior management to take responsibility for managing the risk of fraud, and firms are required to have in place effective controls and instruments that are proportionate to the risk the firm faces. The FSA sees its role as encouraging firms to maintain their systems and controls, thematic work, improving whistle-blowing arrangements, amending the financial crime material in the FSA Handbook and ensuring that the financial services sector, trade associations and the government continue to communicate the risk of fraud to customers.[197]

To implement this policy, the FSA has been given an extensive array of enforcement powers, some of which it has utilised to combat fraud. It has the power to impose a financial penalty where it establishes that there has been a contravention by an authorised person of any requirement.[198] The FSA fined Capita Financial Administration Ltd £300,000 for poor anti-fraud controls,[199] and in May 2007 fined BNP Paribas Private Bank £350,000 for weaknesses in its systems and controls which allowed a senior employee to fraudulently transfer £1.4 million out of the firm's clients' accounts without permission.[200] The FSA also has the power to ban authorised persons and firms from undertaking any regulated activity.[201]

The most recent agency created to tackle fraud is the National Fraud Authority (NFA).[202] The objectives of the NFA include creating a criminal justice system that is sympathetic to the needs of victims of fraud by ensuring that the system operates more effectively and efficiently;[203] discouraging organised criminals from committing fraud in the United Kingdom and increasing the public's confidence in the response to fraud. An important measure introduced

[193] It is intended that the FSA should focus its efforts on specific types of fraud or dishonesty which constitute the greatest areas of concern, and where they can make a difference.

[194] This would include, for example, considering the firms' systems and controls against fraud in more detail in the FSA's supervisory work, including how firms collect data on fraud and dishonesty.

[195] This involves the FSA liaising closely with the financial sector and other interested parties in order to achieve a more effective approach towards fraud prevention in the financial services sector.

[196] This would include codification and clarification of the relevant fraud risk management provisions of the Handbook.

[197] FSA Handbook, above n. 30, *SYSC* 3.2.6 R.

[198] FSMA 2000, s.206(1).

[199] FSA Press Release, 'FSA fines Capita Financial Administrators Limited £300,000 in first anti-fraud controls case', 16 March 2006, www.fsa.gov.uk/pages/Library/Communication/PR/2006/019.shtml.

[200] FSA, *Financial Services Authority Annual Report* 2007/2008 (London, 2008) 23.

[201] FSMA 2000, s.56.

[202] National Fraud Authority. *The National Fraud Strategy: A New Approach to Combating Fraud* (London, 2010) 10.

[203] For a more detailed discussion of how this is to be achieved see Attorney General's Office, *Extending the Powers of the Crown Court to Prevent Fraud and Compensate Victims: A Consultation* (London, 2008).

by the NFA was the publication of the National Fraud Strategy, which is an integral part of the government's fraud policy.[204]

The Office of Fair Trading 'is chiefly concerned with the protection of consumers. It also regulates competition amongst businesses but this is approached from a consumer protection perspective.'[205] The OFT has three regulatory objectives: investigation of whether markets are working well for consumers; enforcement of competition laws; and enforcement of consumer protection laws. It is important to note that the OFT has its own fraud policy.[206] The objectives of the OFT are to inform and protect consumers from fraudulent scams.[207] The OFT also works and co-operates with other agencies such as the SFO,[208] and it also liaises with overseas agencies.[209]

If a suspected fraud is committed against a bank, it should be reported to its money laundering reporting officer (MLRO). Successful frauds should be reported to SOCA. However, it is a decision for the individual bank to determine whether or not to report the fraud to the police. In 2007, the Home Office announced that victims of credit card, cheque and online banking fraud should report the matter to banks and financial institutions.[210] The obligation to report allegations of fraud is not as straight-forward, but nonetheless still important. The primary statutory obligation for reported instances of fraud is contained in the PCA 2002.[211] It is a criminal offence under the 2002 Act to fail to disclose by means of a SAR when there is knowledge, suspicion or reasonable grounds to know or suspect, that a person is laundering the proceeds of criminal conduct. Successful fraud is defined as money laundering for the purpose of the 2002 Act.[212] Furthermore, the Act specifies that members of the regulated sector are required to report their suspicions 'as soon as reasonable practical' to SOCA via their MLRO. There is no legal obligation to report unsuccessful or attempted frauds to the authorities because attempted frauds will not give rise to the criminal proceedings that are available for money laundering, and fall outside the scope of the mandatory reporting obligations under the PCA 2002. Ultimately, the decision lies with the police whether or not an investigation will be conducted.

A firm in the regulated sector is obliged to report fraud to the FSA in the following circumstances:

---

[204] National Fraud Authority, above n. 202, at 3.

[205] P. Kiernan, 'The regulatory bodies: fraud and its enforcement in the twenty-first century' (2003) 24(10) *Company Lawyer* 293, 295.

[206] OFT, *Prevention of Fraud Policy* (London, n/d).

[207] See, e.g., OFT, *Scamnesty 2010 Campaign Strategy* (London, 2009).

[208] See, e.g., OFT, *Memorandum of Understanding between the Office of Fair Trading and the Director of the Serious Fraud Office* (London, 2003).

[209] See, e.g., OFT, 'OFT and Nigerian financial crime squad join forces to combat spam fraud', 4 November 2005, available at www.oft.gov.uk/news-and-updates/press/2005/210–05.

[210] Home Office. 'Fraud', available at www.crimereduction.homeoffice.gov.uk/fraud/fraud17.htm.

[211] PCA 2002, s.330.

[212] The PCA 2002 applies to serious crime, which includes fraud.

(1) it becomes aware that an employee may have committed a fraud against one of its customers; or

(2) it becomes aware that a person, whether or not employed by it, may have committed a fraud against it; or

(3) it considers that any person, whether or not employed by it, is acting with intent to commit a fraud against it; or

(4) it identifies irregularities in its accounting or other records, whether or not there is evidence of fraud; or

(5) it suspects that one of its employees may be guilty of serious misconduct concerning his honesty or integrity and which is connected with the firm's regulated activities or ancillary activities.[213]

In determining whether or not the matter is significant, the firm must consider:

(1) the size of any monetary loss or potential monetary loss to itself or its customers (either in terms of a single incident or group of similar or related incidents);

(2) the risk of reputational loss to the firm; and

(3) whether the incident or a pattern of incidents reflects weaknesses in the firm's internal controls.[214]

The FSA Handbook states that 'the notifications under SUP 15.3.17 R are required as the FSA needs to be aware of the types of fraudulent and irregular activity which are being attempted or undertaken, and to act, if necessary, to prevent effects on consumers or other firms'.[215] Therefore, 'a notification under SUP 15.7.3 G should provide all relevant and significant details of the incident or suspected incident of which the firm is aware'.[216] Furthermore, 'if the firm may have suffered significant financial losses as a result of the incident, or may suffer reputational loss, the FSA will wish to consider this and whether the incident suggests weaknesses in the firm's internal controls'.[217] If the fraud is committed by a firm's representatives or other approved persons, the FSA has the power to withdraw its authorisation and there is also the possibility of prosecution.

Q6 What constitutes fraud?

(e) Terrorist financing

The Prevention of Terrorism (Temporary Provisions) Act 1989 criminalised terrorist financing and allowed the government to seek the forfeiture of any money or other property which, at the time of the offence, the terrorist had

---

[213] FSA Handbook, above n. 30, SUP 15.3.17R.   [214] *Ibid.* SUP 15.3.18G.
[215] *Ibid.* SUP 15.3.19G.   [216] *Ibid.* SUP 15.3.19G.   [217] *Ibid.* SUP 15.3.20G.

in his possession or under his control.[218] The provisions were amended by the Terrorism Act 2000, which created five offences. Section 15 make it a criminal offence for a person to solicit,[219] or to receive,[220] or provide money or property on behalf of terrorists if the person knows or has reasonable cause to suspect that such money may be used for the purpose of terrorism.[221] Under section 16, a person commits an offence if he uses money or other property for terrorist purposes.[222] Section 17 provides that a person commits an offence if he enters into or becomes concerned in an arrangement in which money[223] or property is made available to another and the person knows or has cause to suspect that it may be used for terrorism.[224] A person breaches section 18 if he enters into or becomes concerned in an arrangement which facilitates the retention or control by or on behalf of another person of terrorist property by concealment,[225] by removal from the jurisdiction,[226] by transfer to nominees[227] or in any other way.[228] It is a defence for a person charged under section 18 to prove that they either did not know, or had no reasonable cause to suspect that the arrangement related to terrorist property.[229]

The Terrorism Act 2000 grants law enforcement agencies additional investigative powers, including financial information orders and account monitoring orders.[230] The purpose of an account monitoring order is to permit law enforcement agencies to discover and recognise relevant bank accounts whilst undertaking a terrorist investigation. In order to obtain an account monitoring order, an application must be made by a police officer, of at least the rank of superintendent,[231] before a Circuit judge,[232] who must be satisfied that (a) the order is sought for the purposes of a terrorist investigation; (b) the tracing of terrorist property is desirable for the purposes of the investigation; and (c) the order will enhance the effectiveness of the investigation.[233] Once an order has been granted, it will enable the police to require a financial institution to provide customer information for the purposes of the investigation.[234] It is provided that if a person is convicted of an offence under Part III of the 2000 Act,[235] any property connected with the offence may be the subject of a forfeiture order.[236] This is referred to as criminal forfeiture.[237] The person subject to the order, once granted by a court, is required to give to a designated police officer any property specified in the order.[238] Under the 2000 Act, Orders in

---

[218] Prevention of Terrorism (Temporary Provisions) Act 1989, s.13. See also M. Levi, 'Combating the financing of terrorism: a history and assessment of the control of threat finance' (2010) 50(4) *British Journal of Criminology* 650, 652.

[219] Terrorism Act 2000, s.15(1).   [220] *Ibid.* s.15(2).   [221] *Ibid.* s.15(3).

[222] *Ibid.* s.16(1).   [223] *Ibid.* s.17(1).   [224] *Ibid.* s.17(2).   [225] *Ibid.* s.18(1)(a).

[226] *Ibid.* s.18(1)(b).   [227] *Ibid.* s.18(1)(c).   [228] *Ibid.* s.18(1)(d).   [229] *Ibid.* s.18(2).

[230] *Ibid.* Sch. 6.   [231] *Ibid.* Sch. 6 para. 2(a).   [232] *Ibid.* Sch. 6 para. 2(b).

[233] *Ibid.* Sch. 6 para. 3.

[234] J. Peddie, 'Anti-terrorism legislation and market regulation' in W. Blair and R. Brent (eds.), *Banks and Financial Crime: the International Law of Tainted Money* (Oxford University Press, 2008) 437–58, 440.

[235] Terrorism Act 2000, ss.15–19.   [236] *Ibid.* s.23.

[237] *Ibid.* s.28.   [238] *Ibid.* Sch. 4.

Council may also be made to permit foreign forfeiture orders to be recognised in England.[239]

The Anti-terrorism, Crime and Security Act 2001 amended the provisions for account monitoring orders, financial information orders and disclosure information orders. Under the 2001 Act, an account monitoring order may be granted by a Crown Court judge provided that the court is satisfied that (a) the order is sought for the purposes of a terrorist investigation; (b) the tracing of terrorist property is desirable for the purposes of the investigation; and (c) the order will enhance the effectiveness of the investigation.[240] The Anti-terrorism, Crime and Security Act 2001 provides that a court may grant a financial information order to compel a financial institution to disclose certain types of customer information for a terrorist investigation. A disclosure of information order allows for the disclosure of certain types of information and is very wide-ranging.

The Counter-Terrorism Act 2008 contained a number of provisions which the government states were designed to enhance counter-terrorism powers. Under the Act, HM Treasury gained additional powers to direct financial institutions to impose a graduated range of financial restrictions on businesses connected with jurisdictions of concern regarding money laundering and terrorist financing.[241] If HM Treasury is of the opinion that a country poses a considerable threat to the United Kingdom's national interests due to an increased threat of money laundering of terrorist financing, it may issue a direction.[242]

The Anti-terrorism Crime and Security Act 2001 authorises the seizure of terrorist cash anywhere in the United Kingdom;[243] the freezing of funds at the start of an investigation;[244] the monitoring of suspected accounts;[245] the imposition of requirements on people working within financial institutions to report where there are reasonable grounds to suspect that funds are destined for terrorism; and permits HM Treasury to freeze assets of foreign individuals and groups. Part II of the 2001 Act permits HM Treasury to freeze the assets of overseas governments or residents who have taken, or are likely to take, action to the detriment of the United Kingdom's economy or action constituting a threat to the life or property of a national or resident of the UK.[246] HM Treasury may make a freezing order if two statutory requirements are met. First, they must reasonably believe that action threatening the UK economy or the life or property of UK nationals or residents has taken place or is likely to take place.[247] Secondly, the persons involved in the action must be resident outside the

---

[239] Peddie, above n. 234, at 443.   [240] Terrorism Act 2000, s.38A.
[241] Counter-Terrorism Act 2008, Sch. 7.   [242] *Ibid.* Sch. 7 para. 3.
[243] Anti-terrorism, Crime and Security Act 2001, Sch. 1 Part 2.
[244] *Ibid.* ss. 4–16.   [245] *Ibid.* Sch. 1 Part 1.
[246] This provision repealed the Emergency Laws (Re-enactments and Repeals) Act 1964, s.2.
[247] The Anti-terrorism, Crime and Security Act 2001 provides that HM Treasury is not required to prove actual detriment to freeze the assets of a suspected terrorist, but that a threat is sufficient.

United Kingdom or be an overseas government.[248] A freezing order prevents all persons in the United Kingdom from making funds available to, or for the benefit of, a person or persons specified in the order.[249] HM Treasury is also required to keep the freezing order under review and to determine whether it should be enforced continually over a period of two years.[250] HM Treasury has frozen the assets of individuals and organisations who were suspected of financing terrorism.[251] The government regularly updates a list of organisations and individuals whose accounts have been frozen.[252]

In October 2007, HM Treasury's Asset Freezing Unit was created, which is responsible for legislation on financial sanctions; the implementation and administration of domestic financial sanctions; the designation of terrorist organisations; the implementation and administration of international financial sanctions in the United Kingdom, liaising with the Foreign and Commonwealth Office and collaborating with international partners to develop international frameworks for asset freezing.

The United Kingdom has implemented the Terrorism (United Nations Measures) Order 2006 to give legal effect to UN Security Council Resolution 1373.[253] The Order also gives effect to EU Regulation 2580/2001, which provides for the designation of persons and entities for the purposes of measures that relate, among other things, to the freezing of funds, financial assets and economic resources.[254] The legality of the Terrorism (United Nations Measures) Order 2006 was challenged in *A* v. *HM Treasury*.[255] The matter finally came before the Supreme Court, who also considered the legitimacy of the Al-Qaeda and Taliban (United Nations Measures) Order 2006, SI 2006/2952. The Supreme Court determined that both of the Orders were *ultra vires*.

Schedule 2 Part III to the Anti-terrorism, Crime and Security Act 2001 inserted section 21A into the Terrorism Act 2000 and created the offence of failure to disclose information regarding offences which came to the person in the course of a business in the regulated sector. A person commits an offence under this section if three conditions are met: (a) that the accused knows or suspects, or has reasonable grounds for knowing or suspecting, that a person has committed an offence under sections 15 to 18 of the Terrorism Act 2000;[256] (b) that the information or other matter upon which the accused has based his knowledge or suspicion, or which gives reasonable grounds for such knowledge of suspicion, came to him in the course of a business that operates within the regulated sector;[257] and (c) that the

---

[248] Terrorism Act 2000, s.4(1)(a) and (b).
[249] *Ibid.* s.5.   [250] *Ibid.* ss.7 and 9.
[251] The freezing of assets is permitted by the Terrorism (United Nations Measures) Order 2006, SI 2006/2657.
[252] Terrorism Act 2000, Part II, Sch. 1.   [253] SI 2006/2657.
[254] Regulation 2580/2001 on specific restrictive measures directed against certain persons and entities with a view to combating terrorism.
[255] [2008] EWHC 869.   [256] Terrorism Act 2000, s.21A(2).
[257] *Ibid.* s.21A(3).

accused does not disclose the information or other matter to a constable or nominated officer, usually a money laundering reporting officer, as soon as practicable after he received the information.[258] Since the introduction of the new section 21A, there have been no trials in which the section has been tested. A person does not commit an offence if he has a reasonable excuse for not disclosing the information or other matter or he is a professional legal adviser and the information or other matter came to him in privileged circumstances.[259]

The 2001 Act also inserted section 21B into the Terrorism Act 2000, which created a defence of protected disclosures.[260] In order for this defence to apply, three conditions must be met: (a) that the information or other matter disclosed came to the person making the disclosure (the discloser) in the course of a business in the regulated sector;[261] (b) that the information or other matter causes the discloser to know or suspect, or gives him reasonable grounds for knowing or suspecting, that a person has committed an offence as outlined above under sections 15 to 18 of the Terrorism Act 2000;[262] (c) that the disclosure is made to a constable or a nominated officer as soon as is practicable after the information or other matter comes to the discloser.[263]

A new section 21ZA was inserted into the Terrorism Act 2000 in December 2007.[264] This amendment permits people to undertake unlawful acts provided there is consent by an authorised officer and its aim is to facilitate the discovery of offences. Section 21ZB aims to shield disclosures where such disclosures are made after a person has entered into such arrangements. Section 21ZC provides a further defence of reasonable excuse for not disclosing.

Q7 Discuss the measures to combat the financing of terrorism.

10 Conclusion

The regulation of the banking sector in the United Kingdom has undergone a series of significant reforms since the 1980s. More recently, the regulatory effectiveness of the FSA has been questioned as a result of its ineffective performance The Coalition government have proposed to reform the FSA, though this has led to accusations by some commentators that this would merely result in a rebranding of the FSA.

The United Kingdom has adopted a tough stance towards combating the threat posed by financial crime and is largely fully compliant with its international obligations in relation to these matters.

---

[258] *Ibid.* s.21A(4).   [259] *Ibid.* s.21A(5).   [260] *Ibid.* s.21B.
[261] *Ibid.* s.21B(2).   [262] *Ibid.* s.21B(3).   [263] *Ibid.* s.21B(4).
[264] Terrorism Act 2000 and Proceeds of Crime Act 2002 (Amendment) Regulations 2007, SI 2007/3398.

11 Recommended reading

Cartwright, P. 'Retail depositors, conduct of business and sanctioning' (2009) 17(3) *Journal of Financial Regulation and Compliance* 302

Cranston, R. *Principles of Banking Law* (Oxford University Press, Oxford, 2002)

Ellinger, E., Lomicka, E. and Hare, C. *Ellinger's Modern Banking Law* (Oxford University Press, Oxford, 2011)

Hsiao, M. 'Legitimised interference with private properties: Banking Act 2009' (2010) 25(5) *Journal of International Banking Law and Regulation* 227

Hudson, A. *The Law of Finance* (Sweet and Maxwell, London, 2009)

Mullineux, A. 'The regulation of British retail banking utilities' (2009) 17(4) *Journal of Finance Regulation and Compliance* 453

Stokes, R. 'The banker's duty of confidentiality, money laundering and the Human Rights Act' (2007) *Journal of Business Law* (August) 502

Wadsley, J. and Penn, P. *Penn and Shea, The Law relating to Domestic Banking* (Sweet and Maxwell, London, 2000)

Part 7
Consumer Credit

Introduction

The seventh part of this book deals with consumer credit and is divided into two chapters. The first chapter outlines how the relaxation of the consumer credit legislative frameworks resulted in an increase in the availability of 'convenient credit', which is defined as 'credit that is granted by the creditor with little or no reference to the creditworthiness of the debtor'. This chapter identifies several problems that have arisen from access to 'convenient credit', including record levels of consumer debt, financial exclusion and over-indebtedness; an increase in irresponsible lending practices and ineffective legislative protection of consumers. These have contributed towards a dramatic U-turn by the government towards promoting access to 'affordable credit'. Affordable credit contains five basic elements: access to loans that are simple and transparent; lenders that are sympathetic towards low income consumers' circumstances; simple loan application procedures; small loans over a short period of time; and affordable repayments. Chapter 1 then identifies several government initiatives aimed at promoting access to affordable credit, including the creation of the Social Exclusion Unit, the promotion of credit unions, the development of the Saving Gateway and the Financial Inclusion Fund.

Chapter 2 focuses on the Consumer Credit Act 1974 as amended by the Consumer Credit Act 2006. It begins by briefly highlighting the importance of the recommendations of the Crowther Committee on Consumer Credit 1971 and how it influenced the introduction of the Consumer Credit Act 1974. The second part of the chapter provides a general discussion of the aims and objectives of the Consumer Credit Act 1974 and comments on its scope and application. It then provides an overview of the interpretation of several important concepts and terms within the Act. The remainder of the chapter provides a detailed discussion of its main provisions and highlights the significant amendments introduced by the Consumer Credit Act 2006. In particular, the chapter concentrates on the interpretation of key phrases; the formalities of a consumer credit agreement; the cancellation of such an agreement; the pre-contract information obligations; the documentation of credit and hire agreements; credit advertising; credit licensing; and the unfairness test. The latter part of the chapter also considers the role and scope of the Financial Ombudsman Service; the increased enforcement powers of the Office of Fair Trading; and the impact of the Consumer Credit Directive 2008/48/EC.

Part 7 Chapter 1

The Government's Policy towards Consumer Credit

Contents

1 Introduction

Since the introduction of the first credit card in 1966, the influential recommendations of the Crowther Committee on Consumer Credit (1971)[1] and the introduction of the Consumer Credit Act 1974,[2] creditors now allow debtors to access credit twenty-four hours a day and 365 days a year. The number of creditors and credit products has grown at an unprecedented rate. The evolution of the credit market was hastened by the deregulation of consumer credit legislation in the 1980s and 1990s. This chapter outlines how the relaxation of the consumer credit legislative frameworks resulted in an increase in the availability of 'convenient credit', which is defined as 'credit that is granted by the creditor with little or no reference to the creditworthiness of the debtor'. This chapter identifies several problems that have arisen from access to 'convenient credit' (record levels of consumer debt, financial exclusion and over-indebtedness, an increase in irresponsible lending practices and ineffective legislative protection of consumers), which has resulted in a dramatic U-turn by the government towards

---

[1] Known as the Crowther Committee.   [2] See below.

promoting access to 'affordable credit'. Affordable credit comprises five basic elements: (i) access to loans that are simple and transparent; (ii) lenders that are sympathetic towards low income consumers' circumstances; (iii) simple loan application procedures; (iv) small loans over a short period of time; and (v) affordable repayments.[3] The chapter identifies several government initiatives aimed at promoting access to affordable credit, including the creation of the Social Exclusion Unit (SEU), the promotion of credit unions, the development of Saving Gateway and the Financial Inclusion Fund.

2 Evolution of the consumer credit market

Access to consumer credit, which 'less than a century ago barely existed' has dramatically altered.[4] Consumers are able to access credit over the World Wide Web, their interactive television sets, through telephone banking and retail outlets. This development is summarised by the National Association of Citizens Advice Bureau (NACAB):

> In 1979 bank customers wanting to arrange a loan had to ensure that they were able to visit their branch office on a weekday between 9.30 a.m. and 3.30 p.m. Today the proliferation of telephone and Internet banking provides 24-hour access 365 days a year. An ever increasing number of companies have entered the personal finance market offering an ever more bewildering choice of products.[5]

The increased use of credit initially had a positive impact for consumers, a view initially held by the Crowther Committee, who concluded that 'on balance consumer credit is beneficial, since it makes a useful contribution to the living standards and social wellbeing of the majority of the British people.'[6] Similarly, Borrie commented on the benefits afforded by access to credit:

> as inflation began to rise in the 1970s, it made no sense to wait before buying: the price would inevitably be higher if you did so. Two-digit inflation was a great boost to buying on credit, and buying a house on credit made the greatest sense of all because inflation ensured that the capital value of your house increased while your repayments took a gradually smaller percentage of your income. So the enormous expansion of credit in the 1960s and 1970s met a very real demand by the public which was expressed not in the ballot box but in the shops and in the bank manager's parlour.[7]

---

[3] National Consumer Council, *Affordable Credit: a Model that Recognises Real Needs* (National Consumer Council, London, 2005) 1.

[4] M. Richards, P. Palmer and M. Bogdanova, 'Irresponsible lending? A case study of a UK credit industry reform initiative' (2008) 81(3) *Journal of Business Ethics* 499, 501.

[5] National Association of Citizens Advice Bureau, *Daylight Robbery: The CAB Case for Effective Regulation of Extortionate Credit* (London, 2000).

[6] Crowther Committee on Consumer Credit, as cited in C. Ironfield-Smith, K. Keasey, B. Summers, D. Duxbury and R. Hudson, 'Consumer debt in the UK: attitudes and implications' (2005) 13(2) *Journal of Financial Regulation and Compliance* 132,134.

[7] G. Borrie, 'The credit society: its benefits and burdens' (1986) *Journal of Business Law* (May) 181, 184.

Furthermore, Scott and Black argued that:

> from the customer's viewpoint buying on credit has its advantages. It may simply be convenient either at the point of sale or in enabling payment to be made for something over a period. With major purchases consumers can obtain the present employment of products, services and property without the need for immediate payment; there is a good argument that the use of credit in this way is a desirable forms of forced saving for some people.[8]

The consumer credit market has undergone a revolution since the 1970s when the government's legislative control over the sector was extremely restrictive.[9] Indeed, prior to the publication of the Crowther Committee Report and the introduction of the Consumer Credit Act (CCA) 1974, the consumer credit legislative framework consisted of the restrictive and unsuitable Pawnbrokers Acts 1872–1960,[10] the Moneylenders Acts 1900–1927 and the Hire-Purchase Act 1965.[11] The Griffiths Commission stated that 'there were strict quantitative limits imposed on the banks by the government. Building societies supplied mortgages for house purchases, but again these were rationed on the basis of rigid and conservative debt to income ratios'.[12]

The 1980s and 1990s saw the deregulation of the restrictive consumer credit legislation.[13] Such measures included the abolition of controls on transactions in foreign exchange in 1979, the restrictions on banking lending being lifted, the removal of the reverse asset ratio in 1981 and the abolition of hire purchase controls in 1982.[14] Keasey *et al.* noted that this deregulation 'transformed borrowing into an acceptable, and necessary, part of many consumers' lives … making buying on credit more attractive when compared with saving for consumer goods'.[15] Other important measures included the move to allow banks to offer mortgages;[16] the Building Societies Act 1986 liberalised the interest rate fixing agreements; the demutualisation of building societies occurred and

---

[8] C. Scott and J. Black, *Cranston's Consumers and the Law* (Butterworths, London, 2000) 231. The Griffiths Commission stated that the 'credit markets have grown to their present size because the services they have provided have responded to consumer demands. The result has been that consumers have been able to enjoy a higher standard of living than would have been the case if these markets had not existed'. *The Griffiths Commission on Personal Debt: What Price Credit?* (Centre for Social Justice, London, 2005) 1.

[9] Richards *et al.,* above n.4.

[10] For a more detailed discussion of this legislative framework J. Macleod, 'Pawnbroking: a regulatory issue' (2005) *Journal of Business Law* (March) 155.

[11] S. Brown, 'The Consumer Credit Act 2006: real additional mortgagor protection?' (2007) *Conveyancer and Property Lawyer* (July/August) 316, 317.

[12] Griffiths Commission, above n. 8, at 21.

[13] E. Fernandez-Corugedo and J. Muellbauer, *Consumer Credit Conditions in the United Kingdom,* Bank of England Working Paper No. 314 (London, 2006) 4.

[14] NACAB, above n. 5, at 6.

[15] See Ironfield-Smith *et al.,* above n. 6, at 134.

[16] During this period mortgage borrowing increased by 300 per cent, largely due to the introduction of 'right to buy' legislation under the Housing Act 1980. See E. Kempson, *Over-indebtedness in Britain: A Report to the Department of Trade and Industry* (Personal Finance Research Centre, Bristol, 2002).

the number of Internet mortgage providers increased in the latter part of the
1990s.[17] All these legislative amendments resulted in an increase in the availability of credit.[18] The then Department of Trade and Industry (DTI) shared this
view and stated that the consumer credit market had fundamentally changed
and that the variety of credit commodities available had grown at an unparal-
leled velocity.[19] Similarly, HM Treasury stated that a majority of households had
witnessed a significant increase in ease of access to credit products.[20]

However, there is a 'dark side' to the consumer credit market, fuelled by
access to convenient credit and increased competition within the sector. This
'dark side' of the credit market is illustrated by record levels of consumer
debt,[21] increasing evidence of irresponsible lending practices,[22] the imposition
of extortionate interest rates,[23] and ineffective legislative protection of consumers.[24] This was a point recognised by Ziegel, who in 1973 wrote that 'even
under the most favourable circumstances a consumer credit orientated economy is bound to produce a number of casualties. These are the debtors who, for
one reason or another, have over-committed themselves and are unable to pay
their debts.'[25] Despite an increase in the availability of convenient credit, there
are an increasing number of households who are forced to obtain credit from
sub-prime providers, who traditionally charge higher interest rates than banks
or building societies.[26] Sub-prime providers of credit can be divided into three
categories: commercial cash loans,[27] non-commercial cash loans[28] and credit
tied to the purchase of goods.[29] It has been estimated that 2.25 million people
are at risk in terms of access to affordable credit.[30] Research conducted by the

---

[17] Fernandez-Corugedo and Muellbauer, above n. 13, at 8–9.
[18] E. Lomnicka, 'The reform of consumer credit in the UK' (2004) *Journal of Business Law* 129.
[19] DTI White Paper, *Fair, Clear and Competitive: the Consumer Credit Market in the 21st Century* (London, 2003).
[20] HM Treasury, *Promoting Financial Inclusion* (London, 2004).
[21] Credit Action, *Debt Facts and Figures* (Lincoln, 2011).
[22] HM Treasury, above n. 20.
[23] See E. Kempson and C. Whyley, *Extortionate Credit in the UK*, (DTI, London, 1999). Collard and Kempson took the view that people on low income would borrow from lenders who would charge annual percentage rates between 100 and 400 per cent. See S. Collard and E. Kempson, *Affordable credit: the Way Forward* (Joseph Rowntree Foundation, Bristol, 2005) 1.
[24] Lomnicka, above n. 18, at 129.
[25] J. Ziegel, 'Recent developments in Canadian consumer credit law' (1973) 36(5) *Modern Law Review* 479, 480.
[26] FSA, *In or Out? Financial Exclusion: a Literature and Research Review* (London, 2000) 42.
[27] This includes home credit companies, pawn brokers, sale and buy back, payday loans and unlicensed money lenders. For a graphic illustration of the consequences of using home credit companies see HM Treasury, *Review of Christmas Savings Schemes* (London, 2007).
[28] This includes the government run Social Fund and Budgeting Loan Scheme, credit unions, savings and loan schemes, community-based loan schemes, family and friends and informal savings and loan schemes.
[29] This includes agency mail order companies and rental purchase outlets.
[30] P. Davis and C. Brockie, 'A Mis-signalling problem? The troubled performance relationship between credit unions and local government in the UK' (2001) 27(1) *Local Government Studies* 1.

Financial Services Authority (FSA) suggested that 40 per cent of the population have no savings at all.[31]

However, it must be noted that there has been a constant increase in people's use of financial services products. For example, in 1975 only 45 per cent of adults used a current account but that figure had increased to 85 per cent by 1998.[32] A factor that has also contributed towards the increased use of sub-prime lenders is the decline in the number of financial services outlets. This has restricted people's access to affordable credit and it has been suggested by some commentators that up to 23 per cent of the population lack access to a current account,[33] although conversely, the Office of Fair Trading (OFT) estimated that only 12 per cent of the country did not have access to a current account.[34] These figures suggest that an increasing number of people are being forced to gain credit from sub-prime providers. In practical terms this means that people are compelled to enter into short-term credit agreements that attract higher levels of interest payments from pawn brokers, catalogues, sale and buyback shops and illegal money lenders.[35] The next part of this chapter comments on the problems associated with access to convenient credit and it illustrates how they have influenced a change of policy by the government towards promoting affordable credit.

Q1 How has the consumer credit market evolved over time?

3 Consumer debt, financial exclusion and over-indebtedness

Due to the diversity and unpredictable nature of the consumer credit market, there has been a momentous increase in the levels of consumer debt. The Department for Work and Pensions (DWP) reported that the average level of outstanding consumer credit per household has increased from £2,088 in 1995 to £6,464.[36] Similarly, NACAB stated that the number of people facing financial liquidity problems has increased by approximately 50 per cent since 1998.[37] They added that the average level of debt per client was £16,971, almost two-thirds higher than in 2001, and that these clients would take an average of ninety-three years to pay off their debts.[38] In 2009, the Department for Business

---

[31] FSA, *Levels of Financial Capability in the UK: Results of a Base-line Survey* (London, 2006), 43.
[32] FSA, above n. 26, at 11.
[33] E. Kempson and C. Whyley, *Access to Current Accounts* (British Bankers Association, London, 1998).
[34] OFT, *Vulnerable Consumers and Financial Services*, Report of the Director General's Inquiry (London, 1999).
[35] HM Treasury, above n. 20. HM Treasury estimate that there are 3 million 'regular users' of the alternative credit market.
[36] DWP, *Tackling Over-Indebtedness Action Plan 2004* (London, 2004) 13.
[37] As cited in S. Bridges and R. Disney, 'Use of credit and arrears of debt among low-income families in the United Kingdom' (2004) 25(1) *Fiscal Studies* 1, 2.
[38] NACAB, *A Life in Debt: the Profile of CAB Debt Clients in 2008* (London, 2009) 1.

Innovation and Skills (DBIS) stated that 'consumers currently owe around £1.4 trillion to banks and other financial institutions. The vast majority of this borrowing is for mortgages on houses. However, £230 billion is unsecured borrowing, which includes personal loans, overdrafts, credit cards, store cards and some other forms of specialist lending.'[39] Credit Action reported that the total level of personal debt in November 2010 was £1,454 billion; the average level of household debt was £8,495 (excluding mortgages), £16,336 if based on the number of households who actually have an unsecured loan and £57,706 (including mortgages). Therefore, the average owed by every United Kingdom adult was £29,875.[40]

High levels of consumer debt have been exacerbated by the global financial crisis or 'credit crunch'.[41] The uncertainty in the global financial system has led to a dramatic reduction in the availability of affordable credit. These problems have been partly fuelled by the sub-prime mortgage crisis in the United States.[42] Sub-prime mortgage loans are designed for persons with poor credit histories and, as such, they carry a significantly higher interest rate than prime loans.[43] Baker described them as 'being more expensive in respect of interest and charges as a result of the credit and repayment histories of the borrower'.[44] The growth in the level of sub-prime lending in the United States is staggering.[45] The total amount of outstanding loans for the sub-prime mortgage market has increased at an unprecedented rate and has resulted in a 75 per cent increase in the number of repossessions in the United States.[46] It is the global contraction of credit that has caused turmoil in the United Kingdom credit market and has resulted in the near collapse and part-nationalisation of several banks.[47]

---

[39] DBIS, *Review of the Regulation of Credit and Store Cards, a Consultation: Initial Equality Impact Assessment* (London, 2009) 7.

[40] Credit Action, above n. 21, at 1.

[41] For an excellent, albeit, brief comment on the impact of the credit crunch see R. Disney, S. Bridges and J. Bathergood. *Drivers of Over-indebtedness,* Report to the Department for Business, Enterprise and Regulatory Reform DBERR (London, 2008) 34–5.

[42] For a detailed discussion of the sub-prime mortgage market see C. Foote,K. Gerardi,L. Goette and P. Willen, 'Just the facts: an initial analysis of subprime's role in the housing crisis' (2008) 17(4) *Journal of Housing Economics* 291.

[43] A sub-prime mortgage loan is defined as 'a mortgage loan to a borrower with sub-standard credit'. See V. *Henry, Lehman Commercial Paper, Inc.,* 471 F.3d 977, 984 (9th Cir. 2006) as cited in K. Johnston, J. Greer, J. Biermacher, and J. Hummel, 'The subprime mortgage crisis: past, present, and future' (2008) 5(12) *North Carolina Banking Institute* 125.

[44] A. Baker, 'Banks and the communities they serve: time to legislate' (2008) 29(2) *Liverpool Law Review* 165, 173.

[45] A. Jacobson, 'The burden of good intentions: intermediate-sized banks and thrifts and the Community Reinvestment Act' (2006) 6 *UC Davis Business Law Journal* 16. Also see G. Udell, 'Wall Street, main street, and a credit crunch: thoughts on the current financial crisis' (2009) 52(2) *Business Horizons* 117.

[46] For a more detailed commentary on the predicted decline in the US mortgage sector, see Mortgage Bankers Association, 'Mortgage Finance Forecast', 14 January 2008, 8 January 2007, 10 January 2006, available at www.mortgagebankers.org.

[47] For a more detailed discussion of this see Part 6 Chapter 1.

The changes in the consumer credit market have also contributed towards financial exclusion. Financial exclusion has been present in the United Kingdom for some time, yet it has only received political attention since 1997.[48] According to the European Commission, the term 'was first coined in 1993 by geographers who were concerned about limited physical access to banking services as a result of bank branch closures'.[49] Financial exclusion has been defined as a person's inability to access financial products, bank accounts and money transmission facilities.[50] The European Commission offered a broader definition and described it as a 'process whereby people encounter difficulties accessing and/or using financial services and products in the mainstream market that are appropriate for their needs and enable them to lead a normal social life in the society to which they belong'.[51] The extent of financial exclusion is difficult to determine and it has led several commentators to argue that its full extent and impact will never be fully known or understood.[52] It is also said to be geographically concentrated and it has been suggested that '68 per cent of the financially excluded reside in 10 per cent of the most financially excluded post codes districts'.[53] There are several different types of financial exclusion: access exclusion;[54] condition exclusion;[55] price exclusion; marketing exclusion; and self-exclusion.[56] HM Treasury identified other types of financial exclusion, including 'geographical exclusion, exclusion on the grounds that charges and prices are prohibitively high, or exclusion from marketing efforts'.[57] Financial exclusion is not unique to the United Kingdom; it can also be found in many countries in the European Union.[58]

Over indebtedness is another problem resulting from the diversity of the consumer credit market. It can be defined as a 'debt which has become a

---

[48] N. Ryder, 'Out with the old and in with the new? A critical analysis of contemporary policy towards the development of credit unions in Great Britain' (2005) *Journal of Business Law* (September 617) 627.

[49] European Commission, *Financial Services Provision and Prevention of Financial Exclusion* (Brussels: 2008) 9.

[50] For a more detailed discussion of the impact of financial exclusion see E. Kempson, and C. Whyley, *Kept Out or Opted Out? Understanding and Combating Financial Exclusion* (Policy Press, London, 1998) and E. Mayo, T. Fisher, T. Conaty, J. Doling and A. Mullineux, *Small is Bankable: Community Reinvestment in Great Britain* (Joseph Rowntree Trust, York, 1998).

[51] European Commission, above n. 49, at 9.

[52] J. Ford and K. Rowlinson, 'Low-income households and credit: exclusion, preference and inclusion' (1996) 28 *Environment and Planning* 1345.

[53] D. McKillop, A. Ward and J. Wilson, 'The development of credit unions and their role in tackling financial exclusion' (2007) 27(1) *Public Money and Management* 37.

[54] This occurs where people are excluded through risk assessment procedures.

[55] This occurs where conditions attached to financial products and services make them inappropriate.

[56] Marketing exclusion occurs as a consequence of targeted marketing and sales campaigns and self-exclusion occurs when people do not apply for financial goods and services as they feel they might be rejected.

[57] HM Treasury, above n. 20 at 2. For a more detailed discussion of the different types of financial exclusion see European Commission, above n. 49, at 11–14.

[58] *Ibid*. 58–60.

major burden for the borrower'.[59] It has been argued that 'lack of access to affordable credit is one of the factors leading to over-indebtedness amongst low-income households'.[60] Approximately 7 per cent of households in the United Kingdom have levels of credit associated with over-indebtedness and 13 per cent of households are in arrears on either consumer credit or household bill commitments.[61] A report by the Centre for Policy Evaluation noted that 'the ratio of household indebtedness both on secured housing and unsecured, relative to income, has increased by approximately 50 per cent'.[62] The DWP recognised that the 'costs of over-indebtedness can be substantial, including loss of the family home, depression and relationship breakdown … in addition over-indebtedness imposes costs on creditors, government and society as a whole'.[63] NACAB concluded that 'over-indebtedness is a persistent and possibly growing feature of the consumer sector of the United Kingdom'.[64]

Another problem that consumers face from the diversity of the consumer credit market and the 'credit crunch' is the increase in the number of company insolvencies. According to the Insolvency Service, there was a 14 per cent increase in the number of insolvencies in the third quarter of 2009 when compared to the same period in 2008.[65] Similarly, Credit Action reported that every day 372 people are declared insolvent or bankrupt, which is the equivalent of one person every fifty-two seconds.[66]

Despite such problems, the increase in the amount of consumer credit has been sustainable for some people due to the increased value of property.[67] Many of such home owners have utilised this equity to support increased use of credit.[68] However, HM Treasury warned that if property prices continue to increase it will pose a serious threat to the United Kingdom's social and economic success.[69] Spiralling property prices and the contraction of credit have prevented first time buyers purchasing properties and this position has worsened over the last thirty years.[70] Richards *et al.* took the view that 'since the early 1990s low unemployment, reasonably stable inflation and base rates, and rising house prices in the United Kingdom have increased consumer confidence. Consumer spending has followed this period of economic stability unchecked

---

[59] DWP, above n. 36, at 6.

[60] J. Rossiter and N. Cooper, *Scaling Up for Financial Inclusion* (Debt on our Doorstep, Manchester, 2005). Over-indebtedness, like financial exclusion, is not unique to the United Kingdom and is to be found in many Member States of the European Union. See, e.g., G. Betti,N. Dourmashkin, C. Ross, and Y. Yin, 'Consumer in the EU: measurement and characteristics' (2007) 34(2) *Journal of Economic Studies* 136.

[61] DWP, above n. 36, at 3.   [62] Disney *et al.*, above n. 41, at 7.

[63] DWP, above n. 36, at 6.   [64] NACAB, above n. 5, at 4.

[65] Insolvency Service Policy Directorate of Statistics, 'Statistics release: insolvencies in the third quarter 2009', INS/COM/50, 6 November 2009, available at www.insolvency.gov.uk.

[66] Credit Action, above n. 21, at 1.

[67] HM Treasury, *Barker Review of Housing Supply, Final Report* (London, 2004).

[68] HM Treasury, *Housing Policy: an Overview* (London, 2005) 6.

[69] FSA, above n. 26, at 5.   [70] HM Treasury, above n. 68, at 6.

by any controls.'[71] The next part of the chapter outlines how irresponsible lending practices resulted in a change of government policy from access to convenient credit to access to affordable credit.

*Q2 What are the factors which have contributed to the record levels of con-
sumer debt?*

4 Irresponsible lending

Creditors and financial institutions must accept some of the blame for the
increase in consumer debt, financial exclusion and over-indebtedness due to
their lending practices. This has been referred to as irresponsible or predatory
lending.[72] It has also been called 'socially harmful lending', which can include
such practices as targeting low-income households at Christmas, targeting
people who are facing financial problems and soliciting credit on the doorstep.[73] The OFT stated that irresponsible lending is a business practice that it
would consider deceitful, oppressive, unfair and improper for the purposes of
revoking a consumer credit licence.[74] Creditors have been accused of irresponsible lending practices and have been subject to much criticism.[75] Inderst stated
that 'in the United Kingdom various reports and taskforces on consumer lending practices have brought up the issue of irresponsible lending.'[76]

What practices constitute irresponsible lending? Examples include increasing
credit card and overdraft limits without the customer's consent; not requesting
proof of income when determining the level of credit to be offered; and providing loans and credit cards to the unemployed and people who are dependent on
state benefits.[77] Other examples of irresponsible lending practices are the speed
and simplicity of credit applications; the prominence given to very high credit
limits; the importance given to very low interest rates for cards, incentives to use
a particular brand of credit card; unwanted mail shots for credit card cheques;

---

[71] Richards *et al.*, above n. 4. See also National Audit Office, *HM Treasury Asset Protection Scheme*
(London, 2010) 27.

[72] For a more detailed discussion of predatory lending in the United States, see A. Penningto-Cross
and G. Ho, 'Predatory lending laws and the cost of credit' (2008) 36(2) *Real Estate Economics*
175–211 and M. Spector, 'Taming the beast: payday loans, regulatory efforts, and unintended
consequences' (2008) 57 (4) *Depaul Law Review* 961.

[73] Kempson and Whyley, above n. 23, at 8.

[74] For a more detailed discussion of how irresponsible lending is regulated under the CCA Act
2006, see Part 7, Chapter 2.

[75] See, e.g., the predicament of Wendy and Derek Dickerson who were lent £100,000 by Lloyds
TSB in spite of having a combined annual income of £5,000. See E. Simon. 'Banks face
crackdown on irresponsible lending', *Daily Telegraph*,18 (2005) May 18 2005, available at www.
telegraph.co.uk.

[76] R. Inderst, 'Irresponsible lending with a better informed lender' (2008) 118 (532) *Economic
Journal* 1499, 1500.

[77] Insolvency Helpline, 'Debt from irresponsible lending', available at www.insolvencyhelpline.
co.uk.

important information in small print and the indiscriminate targeting of direct mail shots.[78] In relation to such activities, HM Treasury Select Committee took the view that 'issuers should never raise credit limits without carrying out appropriate internal and external credit checks. Lenders also need to recognise that in many cases, for over-indebted consumers, increases in credit limits are wholly inappropriate.'[79]

Worryingly, there is an increasing amount of evidence that creditors have contributed toward irresponsible lending practices. For example, uSwitch.com reported that 88 per cent of credit card applicants were not asked to provide any proof of their income.[80] Furthermore, uSwitch.com suggested that credit card providers had issued over £8.8 billion in unrequested credit to customers; approximately 5.7 million people had their credit limit extended without providing any consent; the average increase in credit was £1,538 and the overall average credit limit increased from £5,129 to £6,667. Despite having an additional £8.8 billion to spend, consumers faced an overall increase in interest charges from £800 to £1,047, amounting annually to £5.9 billion.[81] These practices have resulted in a significant increase in the amount of bad debt written off by financial institutions.[82] The Insolvency Helpline argued that 'the root cause of irresponsible lending is the staff of credit companies who are given incentives such as bonuses or commission to actively sell credit cards and loans. These staff are paid on the volume of loans they sell which itself is irresponsible.'[83] This resulted in Richards et al. concluding 'that there is public support for governmental or financial industry regulation to prevent people from getting into unmanageable debt situations.'[84]

5 Regulation of irresponsible lending

As a result of these concerns, a self-regulation system has been proposed by the banks which includes a voluntary Responsible Lending Index that seeks to encourage best practice in credit lending.[85] However, Ironfield-Smith et al. noted that:

---

[78] HM Treasury Select Committee, *Transparency of Credit Card Charges: First Report of Session 2003–04* (London, 2004) 43.

[79] *Ibid.* 38.

[80] uSwitch, 'Affordability study, Lamsons Digital Media, 6–11 January 2006', available at www. creditaction.org.uk. As cited in Richards *et al.*, above n. 4.

[81] uSwitch, 'Credit card providers throw £8.8billion of unrequested credit at consumers', 2 July 2009, available at www.uswitch.com.

[82] A. Cattermole, 'UK banks write off bad debt', Monetary and Financial Statistics, Bank of England, September 2004, pp. 1–4, available at www.bankofengland.co.uk.

[83] Insolvency Helpline, above n. 77, at 1.

[84] Richards *et al.*, above n. 4, at 502, citing Ironfield *et al.*, above n. 6, at 134.

[85] *Ibid.* 500. Richards *et al.* were highly critical of the Responsible Lending Index and the role of the Association for Payment Clearing Services. For an alternative viewpoint see P. Rodford, 'APACS response to irresponsible lending? A case study of a credit industry reform initiative' (2009) 86(4) *Journal of Business Ethics* 535.

The problem the credit industry faces, however, is that it needs debt levels to keep increasing if it is to meet its ongoing profit targets. Consequently, transforming an industry, built on pushing credit, into one that is responsible in its lending will not be an easy task and if this proves to be the case, then this may have to be an area for yet further regulation over and above that which is already scheduled and planned.[86]

Another example of a voluntary attempt to promote responsible lending is contained in Part 13 of the Banking Code.[87] This provides that 'before we lend you any money or increase your overdraft, we will assess whether we feel you will be able to repay it'.[88] Cartwright noted that 'the Banking Code was created as a result of recommendations made by the Jack Committee which had been established to examine the law relating to the provision of banking services to personal and business customers'.[89] However, from 1 November 2009, retail bank deposit taking has fallen under the regulatory umbrella of the FSA and the Banking Code is no longer used.[90]

The FSA have implemented a number of measures aimed at tackling irresponsible lending. For example, it introduced a mortgage affordability test for lenders, which provides that lenders are responsible for assessing and determining the ability of consumers to meet their monthly repayments; the banning of so-called 'toxic combination' loans, i.e., loans worth more than 90 per cent of the value of a house for people with poor credit histories; the banning of charges for borrowers who are behind on payments, but are at least able to maintain an arrangement to repay these debts; and the broadening of the scope of FSA regulation to all mortgage advisers and arrangers.[91] In November 2010, the FSA imposed its first financial penalty for irresponsible lending. Bridging Loans Ltd a mortgage lender, was fined £42,000, and its director Joseph Cummings £70,000, for 'serious failures relating to lending practices and for failing to treat customers in arrears fairly'. The importance of this ground-breaking financial penalty by the FSA cannot be overstated. It is the first reported instance of a firm being fined by a regulatory body for irresponsible lending practices.[92] The FSA must be commended for tackling the problems associated with irresponsible lending, an issue that had previously received little regulatory attention.

---

[86] See Ironfield Smith *et al.,* above n. 6, at 141.

[87] For a more detailed commentary on the Banking Code see Part 6 Chapter 1.

[88] British Bankers Association, *The Banking Code* (London, 2008) para. 13.1.

[89] P. Cartwright, 'Retail depositors, conduct of business and sanctioning' (2009) 17(3) *Journal of Financial Regulation and Compliance* 302.

[90] This process began in 2008 when the FSA published a consultation paper which proposed a new regime for regulating retail banking conduct of business. See FSA, *Regulating Retail Banking Conduct of Business,* Consultation Paper No. 89/19 (London, 2008). For a more detailed discussion of this see Part 6 Chapter 1.

[91] See generally, FSA, *Mortgage Market Review: Responsible Lending* (London, 2010).

[92] FSA Press Release, 'FSA fines mortgage lender and its director for irresponsible lending and unfair treatment of customers in arrears', 4 November 2010, available at www.fsa.gov.uk/pages/Library/Communication/PR/2010/159.shtml.

In addition to the measures taken by the FSA, the OFT stated that creditors:

> should undertake proper and appropriate checks on the potential borrower's creditworthiness and ability to repay the loan and to meet the terms of the agreement. The checks should be proportionate, taking account of the type of agreement, the amounts involved, the nature of the lender's relationship with the consumer, and the degree of risk to the consumer.[93]

The Consumer Credit Act (CCA) 2006 provides that irresponsible lending is a business practice that the OFT would take into account for the purposes of revoking a consumer credit licence.[94]

The Consumer Credit Directive 2008/43/EC requires Members States to guarantee that 'before the conclusion of the credit agreement, the creditor assesses the consumers' creditworthiness on the basis of sufficient information, where appropriate obtained from the consumer and, where necessary, on the basis of a consultation of the relevant database'.[95] This obligation was initially proposed by HM Treasury Select Committee in 2004, stating that 'it is important that lenders assess a consumer's ability to repay based on as complete as possible a picture of their current income and credit commitments and not just on their payment history'.[96]

Q3 What is irresponsible lending?

6 Irresponsible borrowing

Despite such practices of lenders outlined above, it is necessary to consider whether debtors are also culpable for irresponsible borrowing.[97] This was a point raised by the DTI who stated:

> creditors should be expected to undertake enquiries that are proportionate, having regard to the type of agreement, their relationship with the customer, and the costs and risks involved. The obligation on the lender must also be balanced with an obligation on borrowers to provide true and accurate information about their financial circumstances.[98]

---

[93] OFT, *Irresponsible Lending: A Scoping Paper* (London, 2008) para, 2.14.
[94] The OFT had published guidance notes on irresponsible lending, which provided that creditors should employ appropriate business practices and procedure; there should be transparency in dealings between creditors and borrowers; there should be proportionality in dealings between creditors and borrowers; and creditors should not treat borrowers unfairly. See OFT, *Irresponsible Lending: OFT Guidance for Creditors* (London, 2010).
[95] Directive on credit agreements for consumers 2008/43/EC, Art.8 [2008] OJ L133/66. These obligations were introduced by the Consumer Credit (EU Directive) Regulations 2010, SI. 2010/1010.
[96] HM Treasury Select Committee, above n. 78, at 40.
[97] For a more detailed discussion of the problems directly associated with irresponsible borrowing see Kempson, above n. 16, at 44–9.
[98] DTI White Paper, above n. 19, at 57.

This was a point raised by HM Treasury Select Committee, who pointed out that 'despite all the sophisticated scoring techniques used, it must be recognised that the borrowers themselves have an important contribution to make in the decision'.[99] Ironfield-Smith *et al.* took the view that:

> Improving consumer financial capability and awareness will rely in large part on the availability of better and more accessible information and a number of changes to legislation and voluntary codes of conduct have been made or are in the pipeline to facilitate this, including a number of reforms to the Consumer Credit Act.[100]

Is there a need to increase the level of financial education or even debtor education?[101] The FSA has been charged with improving the public's awareness and understanding of the financial system.[102] This includes promoting the awareness of the benefits and risks associated with different kinds of investment or other financial dealings,[103] and the provision of appropriate information and advice.[104] This is an extremely innovative objective and never before has a financial regulator been explicitly charged with the significant role of educating consumers. Taylor states that assigning this role to the FSA 'represents an innovation in the sense that this type of regulation serves a social purpose as well as contributing to the efficient working of financial markets'.[105]

In order to achieve the statutory objective two aims need to be fulfilled: to improve general financial literacy and to improve the quality of the information and advice that is available to consumers. The rationale behind the statutory objective is that evidence suggests that consumers do not understand how the financial services system works. Theoretically, the objective should be a major step forward for consumers now that a regulator has been charged with the role of increasing public awareness of the increasingly complex financial system. However, to what extent will the FSA actually be able to fulfil its role? A core problem that needs to be addressed regarding consumers is the psychological barriers that appear to exist, with many people appearing to believe that they do not need financial education.[106] A major task facing the FSA is getting consumers actually to realise that they have financial information and education needs. How successful they can be in achieving this will only be seen with time,

---

[99] HM Treasury Select Committee, above n. 78, at 38.
[100] See Ironfield Smith *et al.,* above n. 6 at 139.
[101] For a more detailed commentary on these issues see J. Tribe, 'Personal insolvency law: debtor education, debtor advice and the credit environment: Part 1' (2007) 27(2) *Insolvency Intelligence* 23.
[102] FSMA 2000, s.4. For a general discussion of this issue see N. Ryder, 'Two plus two equals financial education: the Financial Services Authority and consumer education' (2001) 35(2) *Law Teacher* 216.
[103] FSMA 2000, s.4(2)(a).
[104] *Ibid.*, s.4(2)(b).
[105] M. Blair, M. Minghella, L, Taylor, M. Threipland, and G. Walker, *Blackstone's Guide to the Financial Services and Markets Act 2000* (London, 2001) 33.
[106] See generally FSA, *Better Informed Consumers* (London, 2000).

though it is welcome that the FSA is also of this opinion: 'we are under no illusions about quick fixes. This is inevitably a long-term process.'[107]

The FSA is also charged with the role of 'securing the appropriate degree of protection for consumers'.[108] When considering the degree of protection that is appropriate, the FSA must have regard to four considerations:

(1) the differing degrees of risk involved in different kinds of investment or other transaction;[109]
(2) the varying levels of experience and expertise those different consumers may have in relation to different kinds of regulated activity;[110]
(3) the needs that consumers may have for advice and accurate information;[111]
(4) that consumers should take responsibility for their decisions.[112]

The creation of the objective of consumer protection is again a welcome step in such a complex and evolving financial system. For many consumers, the inclusion of this objective has come too late for those facing the consequences of investments made as a result of poor and misleading advice. The general ethos of this objective is that although consumers need to be protected and adequate mechanisms for protection need to be established, the FSA has to strike the balance between the expectations for protection that consumers have and the level of responsibility that they must accept for their own actions. This objective is not to protect consumers from every possible risk that they face.

The FSA published a paper in 2006 which explained how these two objectives are going to be achieved for consumers through its Treating Customers Fairly initiative.[113] It should be noted that this campaign only applies to the regulated sector and personal loans fall outside the scope of the Financial Services and Markets Act (FSMA) 2000. However, the Financial Ombudsman Service has indicated that they are prepared to investigate claims made by customers who have been lent money that they feel they are unable to repay. Instances of irresponsible lending are regulated by the unfair relationship test created by the CCA 2006. This measure is a substitute for the ineffective extortionate credit bargain regime under the CCA 1974, which will be discussed below.[114]

Q4 What is irresponsible borrowing?

7 Ineffective legislative protection for consumers

Reform of the CCA 1974 was an important part of the government's policy aimed at increasing people's access to affordable credit.[115] NACAB expressed

---

[107] FSA Press Release, 'Clued up consumers are FSA goal', FSA/PN/012/2001, 25 January 2001, available at www.fsa.gov.uk/Pages/Library/Communication/PR/2001/012.shtml.
[108] FSMA 2000, s.5(1).   [109] *Ibid.* s.5(2)(a).   [110] *Ibid.* s.5(2)(b).
[111] *Ibid.* s.5(2)(c).   [112] *Ibid.* s.5(2)(d).
[113] FSA, *Treating Customers Fairly: Towards Fair Outcomes for Consumers* (London, 2006).
[114] For a more detailed discussion of the unfairness test see Part 7 Chapter 2.
[115] HM Treasury, above n. 20.

the view that 'the dynamic changes in the consumer credit sector have not been matched by changes in the legislation intended to protect consumers from abuse'.[116] There was a consensus of opinion amongst commentators that the CCA 1974 was in desperate need of reform. The DTI stated that 'the laws governing this market were set out a generation ago … the regulatory structure that was put in place … is not the same as the regulatory structure required today'.[117] The Griffiths Commission also pointed out that 'since the introduction of the Act, the credit market has been wholly transformed and the current credit market bears little resemblance to that which existed in 1974'.[118] Brown noted that:

> within a few years of the final implementation orders of the Consumer Credit Act being issued, which incidentally was not until the mid-1980s, general dissatisfaction with the working of the Consumer Credit Act was beginning to surface. Although no reform took place at that time, further suggestion for change was again mooted a few years later, resulting in the Consumer Credit Review set up by the Government in 2001.[119]

Melanie Johnson MP, the then Consumer Minister, stated that 'our credit laws are 30 years old and need a radical overhaul to protect people in today's credit market'.[120]

The CCA 1974 was outdated and had not kept pace with the complexity and diversity of the consumer credit market. The Act contained a number of inadequacies: the extortionate credit provisions;[121] the consumer credit licensing regime; and the limited enforcement powers of the OFT.[122] Indeed, the DTI took the view that:

> The Act has not provided sufficient protection for consumers where they have been unfairly treated by consumer credit businesses. The rights that the Act accords to consumers and the avenues it provides to them to challenge unfair conduct are restricted. Furthermore, the Act has provided regulators with insufficient powers to tackle improper or unfair conduct by consumer credit businesses.[123]

---

[116] NACAB, above n. 5, at 1.

[117] The DTI stated 'in 1971, there was only one credit card available; now there are 1,300. 30 years ago, £32 million was owed on credit cards, now it is over £49 billion'. DTI White Paper, above n. 19 at 12.

[118] Griffiths Commission, above n. 8, at App. 2.3.   [119] Brown, above n. 11, at 318.

[120] DTI, Press Notice P/2001/398, 'Johnson announces biggest overhaul of credit laws for a generation', 25 July 2001.

[121] For an excellent commentary on relevant judicial precedent see L. Bently and G. Howells, 'Judicial treatment of extortionate credit bargains, Part I' (1989) *Conveyancer and Property Lawyer* 164 and 'Loan sharks and Extortionate Credit Bargain, Part II', (1989) *Conveyancer and Property Lawyer* 234.

[122] Kempson and Whyley, above n. 23, at 36–37. For a more detailed commentary on consumer credit licences see OFT, *Consumer Credit Licensing: General Guidance for Licences and Applicants on Fitness and Requirements* (London, 2008).

[123] DTI, *Consumer Credit Bill: Full Regulatory Impact Assessment* (London, 2004) 4. Further support for this view is offered by Lomnicka, above n. 18, at 132.

The reform process began with the publication of a White Paper in 1999, in which, the government announced its intention to modernise the CCA 1974 and to ensure that it provided adequate protection for consumers.[124] In October 2000, a Task Force was created with the remit of achieving responsible lending and borrowing.[125] Later that year, the DTI published a consultation paper which sought the opinions of interested parties on the general effectiveness of the CCA 1974.[126] A second White Paper was published in December 2003, with the aim of creating 'a more transparent regime so consumers can make better informed decisions and get a fairer deal'.[127] In conjunction with the White Paper, the DTI published another consultation paper on how the legislative changes were to be implemented.[128] Subsequently, several Statutory Instruments were introduced to implement some of the proposed amendments to the 1974 Act.[129]

However, a majority of the reforms were introduced by the CCA 2006, which came into effect on 1 October 2008. The scope of this Act is extensive and applies to the regulation of consumer credit agreements and consumer hire agreements; the provision of information to debtors and hirers after the agreement is made; unfair relationships between debtors and creditors; the licensing of consumer credit and hire businesses and ancillary credit businesses; the powers of the OFT in relation to the licensing of consumer credit and hire businesses and ancillary credit businesses; appeals from decisions of the OFT in relation to the licensing of consumer credit and hire businesses and ancillary credit businesses; and the extension of the jurisdiction of the Financial Ombudsman Service.[130]

However, successive governments are still not satisfied with the measures introduced by the CCA 2006 and believe that that there is still the need for further legislative intervention. In May 2008, the government initiated a Review of Consumer Law,[131] the aim of which was to achieve a balance between protecting consumers, reducing the unwarranted burdens imposed on businesses, and seeking to promote and endorse fair and competitive markets. The Review sought views on four particular areas: the case for reform; options for reform; consumer empowerment and redress; and securing compliance with the law. As a result of this Review, the DBIS took the view that:

> the law is complex, fragmented and inflexible. This can lead to higher levels of consumer detriment as well as unnecessary costs for business and less effectiveness for enforcers. The Government is committed to a fundamental

---

[124] DTI White Paper, *Modern Markets: Confident Consumers* (London, 1999).
[125] DTI, *Report by the Task Force on Tackling Overindebtedness* (London, 2001).
[126] DTI, *Tackling Loan Sharks – and more! – Consultation Document on Modernising the Consumer Credit Act 1974* (London, 2001).
[127] DTI White Paper, above n. 19, at 5.
[128] DTI, *Establishing a Transparent Market* (London, 2003).
[129] For a more detailed discussion of these measures see Part 7 Chapter 2.
[130] For a more detailed commentary on these issues see Part 7 Chapter 2.
[131] DBIS, *Consumer Law Review: Call for Evidence* (London, 2008).

modernisation of the consumer law framework to fit the modern, interconnected and interdependent world. This will ensure consumer rights are fit for purpose in the age of the Internet. It will provide consumers, business and enforcers with the clarity and confidence to explain, to exercise and to enforce the protections and responsibilities we all have as consumers.[132]

In July 2009, the government published another White Paper,[133] the aim of which was to review the regulations that govern consumer credit and store cards. In 2004, HM Treasury Select Committee had warned that 'store cards charge much higher rates of interest even than credit cards. Although in part this may flow from a pricing model which places all the costs of the operation on the minority who pay interest, there is also evidence to suggest that competition is not working properly'.[134] The 2009 White Paper concentrated on four areas relating to credit and store cards:

> firstly, the requirement that repayments to a credit or store card are allocated to debts attracting the highest interest rates first; secondly, the level of minimum payments; thirdly, the issue of unsolicited credit limits; and finally, the ability of lenders to raise interest rates on existing debts.[135]

It could be argued that a review of the regulations that apply to credit and store cards is rather timely given the adverse impact of the credit crunch and record levels of consumer debt. Indeed, the DBIS took the view that:

> Consumers value the flexibility that credit and store cards offer and their use has risen dramatically in the past two decades. However, a significant minority of consumers carry high levels of debt on their credit and store cards with no prospect of paying it off within a reasonable amount of time, if at all. Store cards account for a much smaller proportion of unsecured borrowing than credit cards, but are of particular concern because of the high interest rates they charge. Many consumers are facing financial pressures as a result of the downturn and are now having to deal with unsustainable debts built up on their credit and store cards during the years of easy credit.[136]

The proposals in the 2009 white paper have been largely welcomed by consumer groups. For example, Which? expressed the view that 'for too long, card companies have been allowed to apply the tricks of their trade to the detriment of millions of consumers', adding that 'we think it's simply wrong to entice people into spending more than they can afford and then to squeeze as much money out of them as possible'.[137] Similarly, Malcolm Hurlston of the Consumer Credit Counselling Service stated that 'the government has put its finger on the four main problems that consumers have with credit card debt.

[132] DBIS, *A Better Deal for Consumers: Delivering Real Help Now and Change for the Future* (London, 2009) 77.
[133] *Ibid.*   [134] HM Treasury Select Committee, above n. 78, at 46.
[135] DBIS, above n. 39, at 3.   [136] *Ibid.*
[137] BBC News, 'Credit card terms "to be curbed"', 27 October 2009, available at http://news.bbc.co.uk/1/hi/business/8326485.stm.

We believe that the banks should be able to change their practices on each of these but if they can't, regulation will be necessary.'[138] The DBIS published a paper in July 2009 entitled *A Better Deal for Consumers: Delivering Real Help Now and Change for the Future*. According to this publication, there are six key principles that underpin the government's consumer strategy: these are protection, responsibility, enforcement, change, proportionality and competition.[139] The Coalition government also published a number of consultation papers in 2010.[140] In a joint consultation paper published by HM Treasury and the DBIS, the government proposes to transfer the regulation of credit from the OFT to the Consumer Protection and Markets Authority (CPMA).[141] The government claim that this reform is necessary in order to 'improve the way consumer credit is regulated and to create a simpler, more responsive regime'.[142]

Q5 Briefly identify some reasons for the ineffective protection of consumers under the Consumer Credit Act 1974.

8 A change of policy

There are several reasons underpinning the unprecedented level of government intervention within the consumer credit market. First, consumer credit forms an important part of a successful, modern and efficient economy. The importance of consumer credit to the economy has been highlighted by the DWP, who described it as 'the most energetic and competitive consumer credit market in Europe'.[143] Similarly, the DTI has also stated that the consumer credit market is central to the United Kingdom economy and is an 'important part of economic stability'.[144] This view was also supported by Rossiter and Cooper who argued that the economy 'depends on the functioning of the consumer credit market'.[145] The consumer credit market is 'often cited as the most developed in Europe and no single firm has more than a 10 per cent share of the market'.[146] The importance of the consumer credit market to the United Kingdom economy was clearly illustrated by the unprecedented actions taken by the government during the 'credit crunch'.[147] Accordingly, an effective and versatile consumer credit market is an integral part of the government's economic agenda. Convenient credit is not currently available to all households, with many of them suffering

---

[138] *Ibid.*   [139] DBIS, above n. 132, at 13.

[140] HM Treasury, *A New Approach to Financial Regulation: Consultation on Reforming the Consumer Credit Regime* (London, 2010).

[141] The creation of the CPMA was announced by HM Treasury in July 2010 as part of a wider programme to reform financial regulation in the United Kingdom.

[142] www.bis.gov.uk/Consultations/consultation-reforming-consumer-credit.

[143] DWP, above n. 36, at 6.   [144] DTI White Paper, above n. 19, at 57.

[145] Rossiter and Cooper, above n. 60, at 4.

[146] DTI White Paper, above n. 19, at 19.

[147] For a discussion of the measures implemented by the government to support the UK banking sector see Part 6.

high levels of debt and over-indebtedness. It has been argued that these problems were largely ignored by the previous Conservative government,[148] which has been described as contributing towards them.[149] Conversely, the Labour government initiated several initiatives aimed at improving access to affordable credit.

(a) Non-legislative reforms

The evolution of government policy stemmed from the creation of the Social Exclusion Unit (SEU) in 1997. The Unit was given the broad remit of reducing financial exclusion,[150] and attempted to develop a number of ground-breaking initiatives to tackle financial exclusion. At first, the Unit formed part of the Cabinet Office and it then moved to the Office of the Deputy Prime Minister in 2002. Some of the solutions proposed by the SEU have been seen as important and worthwhile; indeed, one independent assessment suggested that the efforts made by the government since 1997 represented the first concerted attempt by any European government to tackle financial exclusion.[151] HM Treasury listed five significant developments since the creation of the SEU: – the creation of Policy Action Team 14 (PAT 14); the introduction of measures to encourage savings; the launch of the Saving Gateway; the introduction of the CCA 2006, and the creation of the Financial Inclusion Fund.[152] However, the SEU's overall effectiveness has been questioned because of its failure to meet the initial aspirations of its supporters and the limited resources it has received from the government.[153]

Particular note should be taken of the 1999 Report of Policy PAT 14. PAT 14 were asked to consider the scope for the development of credit unions; the availability of insurance services; and the role of retail banks, the Post Office and other organisations in providing access to and delivery of financial services in deprived neighbourhoods.[154] PAT 14 suggested a number of measures designed to address financial exclusion and promote access to affordable credit. In relation to the provision of insurance, PAT 14 recommended that the insurance industry should improve access to insurance in deprived communities.[155] They also recommended that all major high street banks should offer a

---

[148] M. Wallace, 'A new approach to neighbourhood renewal in England' (2001) 38(12) *Urban Studies* 2163.
[149] *Ibid.*
[150] P. Watt, and K. Jacobs, 'Discourses of social exclusion: an analysis of Bringing Britain Together: A National Strategy for Neighbourhood Renewal' (2000) 17(1) *Housing, Theory and Society.*
[151] M. Drakeford, and D. Sachdev, 'Financial exclusion and debt redemption' (2001) 21(2) *Critical Social Policy* 215.
[152] HM Treasury, *Financial Inclusion: the Way Forward* (London, 2007) 27.
[153] R. Geyer, 'Can EU social policy save the Social Exclusion Unit and vice versa?' (1999) 19(3) *Politics* 159, 161.
[154] HM Treasury, *Access to Financial Services, Report of Policy Action Team 14* (London, 1999).
[155] *Ibid.* 53.

basic bank account and that HM Treasury should continue with its policy of deregulation of the Credit Unions Act 1979.[156] PAT 14 has been described as a 'landmark' report,[157] and as 'the first strategic review of the problems of financial exclusion'.[158] PAT 14's Report played a significant role in terms of the government's policy towards affordable credit. It contained several innovative recommendations aimed at assisting people and communities to gain access to affordable credit.

(b) The Saving Gateway

The government has created several mechanisms aimed at encouraging people to save. The Saving Gateway is a savings account for employed individuals on low income. The aim is to encourage people to save through a government-backed scheme. The government announced that it intended to contribute 50p for every pound saved within the scheme.[159] A number of such schemes were successfully piloted between 2002 and 2007 in Cambridge, Cumbria, East London, Manchester, Hull and South Yorkshire.[160] The government piloted the Saving Gateway as a tool for encouraging saving amongst lower income households and for promoting financial inclusion. The account is designed to be flexible and permit account holders to vary their financial payments. The scheme was given a legislative footing by the Saving Gateway Accounts Act 2009, which, among other things, outlines the eligibility criteria for the Saving Gateway, imposes an obligation on HM Revenue and Customs to issue notices to those people who are eligible for the Saving Gateway, and to pay the government's contribution under the scheme. Membership of the scheme is open to people who are on benefits, including income support, job-seeker's allowance and child tax credit. Eligible people are permitted to open accounts, for a fixed period of time, with financial institutions that have been approved to offer Saving Gateway accounts by HM Revenue and Customs.

(c) Credit unions

A credit union is a self-help financial co-operative that provides accessible and inexpensive savings and loans facilities.[161] The principle purpose of a credit

---

[156] For a more detailed discussion of the legislative amendments made to the Credit Unions Act 1979, see N. Ryder, 'Credit union legislative frameworks in the United States of America and the United Kingdom: a flexible friend or a step towards the dark side?' (2008) 31(2) *Journal of Consumer Policy* 147.

[157] Welsh Affairs Select Committee, *Social Exclusion in Wales, Report of the Welsh Affairs Select Committee* (London, 2001).

[158] S. Collard, 'Towards financial inclusion in the UK: progress and challenges' (2007) *Public Money and Management* (February) 13.

[159] HM Treasury, *Pre-Budget Report* 2004 (London, 2004).

[160] HM Treasury and HM Revenue and Customs, *The Saving Gateway: Operating a National Scheme* (London, 2008) 8–9.

[161] Davis and Brockie, above n. 30, at 3.

union is to encourage members to save regularly and facilitate the borrowing of money at lower interest rates than those normally charged by other financial institutions.[162] Credit unions are based on a number of important concepts that distinguish them from other financial institutions such as banks and building societies. For example, membership of a credit union is based upon a common bond, which means that members must share something in common, such as working for the same employer or living within specified geographical areas.[163] Credit unions can also be distinguished because they are based on a set of unique co-operative operating principles. These principles are open membership, democracy, distribution of refunds on a patronage basis, limited interest payments for the use of capital, political and religious neutrality, cash trading, and the promotion of financial education. It is the self-help ethos that has led to the government viewing credit unions as a perfect institution to combat financial exclusion. Since 1997, credit unions are perceived by policy-makers as an ideal vehicle for redeveloping struggling economies and meeting the credit needs of the financially excluded. There are several factors which have limited the development of credit unions in the United Kingdom: a restrictive legal framework, ineffective financial regulation, inappropriate credit union development models, an overdependence on state subsidies and a disunited credit union movement. The next section briefly outlines the measures introduced to promote the growth of credit unions.

The Credit Unions Act 1979 was regarded by many commentators as the most restrictive of its kind in the world. In recognition of the Act's limitations, the government introduced a series of legislative amendments aimed at encouraging the growth of the sector.[164] For example, the interpretation of the membership criteria was widened, and credit unions were allowed to offer mortgages, individual savings accounts,[165] child trust funds,[166] and transaction accounts.[167] These were intended to help credit unions become over time a 'one stop shop' for the financial services of their members, who would benefit from

---

[162] R. Donnelly and A. Haggett, *Credit Unions in Britain: A Decade of Growth* (The Plunkett Foundation, Oxford 1997).

[163] For a more detailed commentary on the common bond see N. Ryder and A. Baker, 'The enemy within? A critical analysis of the Credit Unions Act 1979 and the common bond' (2003) 36(2) *Journal of Co-operative Studies* 117.

[164] See, e.g., Credit Unions (Increase in Limits on Deposits by Persons Too Young to be Members and of Periods for the Repayment of Loans) Order 2001, SI 2001/811; FSMA 2000 (Permissions and Applications) (Credit Unions etc) Order 2002, SI 2002/704; FSMA 2000 (Consequential Amendments and Transitional Provisions) (Credit Unions) Order 2002, SI 2002/1501; Regulatory Reform (Credit Unions) Order 2003, SI 2003/256; Civil Partnership Act 2004 (Overseas Relationships and Consequential, etc. Amendments) Order 2005, SI 2005/3129); Individual Savings Account (Amendment No. 3) Regulations 2005, SI 2005/3350; and Child Trust Funds (Amendment No. 2) Regulations 2005, SI 2005/909.

[165] Individual Savings Account (Amendment No. 3) Regulations 2005, SI 2005/3350, reg. 3.

[166] Child Trust Funds (Amendment No. 2) Regulations 2005, SI 2005/909, reg. 3.

[167] See HM Treasury Select Committee, *Banking and Unbanked: Banking Services, the Post Office Card Account and Financial Inclusion, 13th Report of Session 2005–2006* (London, 2006) 43.

saving what they could afford, borrowing what they could afford to repay, and using direct debit facilities and ATM machines in the LINK network.

Ineffective regulation was another important issue limiting the growth of credit unions in the United Kingdom. Prior to the Credit Union Act (CUA) 1979, credit unions were regulated under the Companies Act 1948 or the Industrial and Provident Societies Act 1965, both of which were deemed inappropriate.[168] The government announced in November 1999 that credit unions were to be brought within the scope of the FSMA 2000.[169] From July 2002, credit unions have been subject to an increased level of regulation by the FSA. As a result of this, credit unions are members of the Financial Services Compensation Scheme (FSCS),[170] a timely change, and one which was considered central to the credibility and viability of the movement more generally. Members will benefit because their savings are protected and a large proportion will be refunded in the event of a collapse.

9 Lessons from the United States

It is suggested that one way in which the government could improve access to affordable credit is to follow the legislative approach adopted in the United States. It was estimated that approximately 20 per cent of US households lacked access to affordable credit and that 22 per cent of adults did not have either a current or savings account.[171] In order to overcome this problem, the Community Reinvestment Act (CRA) 1977 required financial institutions to take steps to meet the credit needs of their entire community. In practical terms, the principle objective of the Act was to persuade banks and savings associations to meet the financial needs of borrowers in designated moderate and low income communities. This legislation was enacted to prevent financial institutions from 'red-lining', or refusing to offer loans to, low and moderate income communities. Swindle noted that 'the concern was that banks would treat entire geographic areas as off limits for financing'.[172] The CRA 1977 was introduced as part of a large and ambitious reform programme that covered a whole range of housing and community issues. This legislation requires banks to meet the credit needs of communities, including low and moderate income neighbourhoods. No specific criteria are set out in the Act for assessing the performance of banks and savings associations. However, the extent to which a financial

---

[168] R. Berthoud and T. Hinton, *Credit Unions in the United Kingdom* (Pinter Publishers, London, 1989).

[169] HM Treasury Press Release, 'Enhanced role for credit unions', 16 November 1999, available at www.hm-treasury.gov.uk.

[170] FSMA 2000, ss. 212–14.

[171] E. Kempson, A. Atkinson and O. Riley, *Policy Level Response to Financial Exclusion in Developed Countries: Lessons for Developing Countries* (Personal Finance Research Centre, Bristol University, 2004).

[172] G. Swidler, 'Making the Community Reinvestment Act work' (1994) 69 *New York University Law Review* 387.

institution complies with the Act's requirements will be taken into account by financial regulatory agencies if the bank or savings association wishes to expand, merge or acquire another like institution. The CRA 1977 is enforced by agencies that are required to evaluate the bank's record of meeting the credit needs of its designated communities and to 'take such record into account in its evaluation of an application for a deposit facility by such institution'.[173]

Swidler noted that 'the CRA 1977 is a controversial piece of legislation',[174] a view supported by Dahl *et al.* who commented that the CRA 1977 'played a controversial role in encouraging financial institutions to make loans in neighbourhoods with low or moderate incomes'.[175] The CRA 1977 is still politically popular and it has been argued that 'the legislation has had a major influence on reinvestment activity throughout the country and has brought greater attention to local needs, especially in low-income and minority areas'.[176] Brooke-Overby described this legislation as 'a crucial step toward, if not a key to, solving the problems of inadequate housing, urban decay, and violence that have become issues of national importance'.[177]

Could a similar law be introduced in the United Kingdom? The introduction of such a controversial piece of legislation remains unlikely because it represents a radical step toward imposing a series of social and moral obligations on providers of credit. However, despite the best efforts of the government to improve people's access to consumer credit, it could be argued that the best way for such access to be improved would be by primary legislation based upon the CRA 1977.

Q6 *Outline the key measures which have been introduced to promote access to affordable credit.*

10 Conclusion

The chapter began by identifying the problems that have been caused by access to convenient credit: high levels of personal debt, over-indebtedness and financial exclusion. These problems have been exacerbated by the irresponsible lending practices of creditors and the inappropriate level of protection provided by the CCA 1974. Accordingly, the government has introduced several initiatives aimed at improving people's access to affordable credit. Lack of access to affordable credit 'imposes significant costs on individuals ... and society as a whole'.[178]

---

[173] R. Art, 'Social responsibility in bank credit decisions: the community reinvestment act one decade later', (1987) 18 *Pacific Law Journal* 1071.

[174] See Swidler, above n. 172.

[175] D. Dahl, D. Evanoff, and M. Spivey, 'Community reinvestment act enforcement and changes in targeted lending' (2002) 25(3) *International Regional Science Review* 307.

[176] G. Garwood and D. Smith, 'The Community Reinvestment Act: evolution and current issues' (1993) 79 *Fed. Res. Bull* 251.

[177] House of Commons Votes and Proceedings, 5th July 2000.

[178] HM Treasury, *Spending Review* 2004 (London, 2004).

For individuals it can lead to higher credit charges, limited access to financial products and services and lack of security, and it can inhibit employment.[179] Furthermore, lack of access to affordable credit contributes to child poverty, imposes additional costs on the state benefit system and is directly linked to social exclusion.[180] Social exclusion has been described as 'complex and multi-dimensional' and it creates problems for families, the economy and 'for society as a whole'.[181] The previous Labour government must be commended for attempting to tackle this issue, which was largely ignored by a succession of Conservative administrations. The SEU has been hailed as a success, but did it achieve its objective in relation to access to affordable credit? There is little evidence to suggest a reduction in the number of people who are financially excluded.

The long-term solution could be legislation on community reinvestment based on the CRA 1977 in the United States. Unfortunately, it appears that the Coalition government does not have the political will to implement such a controversial piece of consumer legislation. It appears that the government's policy towards the provision of credit in the United Kingdom has reverted to the position prior to the recommendations of the Crowther Committee and the introduction of the CCA 1974. After three decades of what can best be described as a 'laissez faire' approach towards the regulation of the consumer credit market, the government has decided, no doubt influenced by the impact of the 'credit crunch' and increasing levels of consumer debt, to restrict the amount of credit available through a series of legislative measures. In this author's opinion, such measures will have a minimal impact on the problems faced by an ever-increasing percentage of the population in accessing affordable credit.

11 Recommended reading

Borrie, G. 'The credit society: its benefits and burdens' (1986) *Journal of Business Law* (May) 181

Brown, S. 'The Consumer Credit Act 2006: real additional mortgagor protection?' (2007) *Conveyancer and Property Lawyer* (July/August) 316

'Using the law as a usury law: definitions of usury and recent developments in the regulation of unfair charges in consumer credit transactions' (2011) 1 *Journal of Business Law* 91

Howells, G. 'The consumer credit litigation explosion' (2010) 126 *Law Quarterly Review* (October) 617

Lomnicka, E. 'The reform of consumer credit in the United Kingdom' (2004) *Journal of Business Law* 129

---

[179] *Ibid.*   [180] HM Treasury, *Child Poverty Review* (London, 2004)

[181] The government defines social exclusion as 'a shorthand term for what can happen when people and areas suffer from a combination of linked problems such as unemployment, poor skills, low income, unfair discrimination, poor housing, high crime, bad health and family breakdown'. See Social Exclusion Unit, *Tackling Social Exclusion: Taking Stock and Looking to the Future* (ODPM Publications, London, 2004).

Nield, S. 'Responsible lending and borrowing: whereto low-cost home ownership?' (2010) 30(4)*Legal Studies* 610

Patient, J. 'The Consumer Credit Act 2006', (2006) 21(6) *Journal of International Banking Law and Regulation* 309

Ryder, N. 'The credit crunch: the right time for credit unions to strike?' (2009) 29(1) *Legal Studies* 75

Part 7 Chapter 2

The Consumer Credit Act 1974

Contents

1 Introduction

This chapter begins by briefly highlighting and commenting on the importance of the recommendations of the Crowther Committee on Consumer Credit 1971 and how it influenced the enactment of the Consumer Credit Act (CCA) 1974. The second part of the chapter provides a general discussion of the aims and objectives of the CCA 1974 and comments on its scope and application. It then provides an overview of the interpretation of several important concepts and terms within the Act. The remainder of the chapter provides a detailed discussion of the Act's main provisions and highlights the significant amendments introduced by the Consumer Credit Act (CCA) 2006. The latter part of the chapter considers the role and scope of the Financial Ombudsman Service (FOS), the increased enforcement powers of the Office of Fair Trading (OFT) and the impact of the Consumer Credit Directive.[1]

2 Crowther Committee on Consumer Credit

The introduction of the CCA 1974 is associated with the recommendations of the Crowther Committee, which in 1968 was given the broad remit to investigate and explore all forms of credit.[2] The Committee identified several weaknesses within the then-existing consumer credit legislative framework,[3] and it recommended the introduction of two statutes, a Lending and Security Act and a Consumer Sale and Loan Act.[4] The proposed Lending and Security Act would 'apply to all credit transactions … it would deal not just with the rights of the parties under the loan contract, but also with registration of the security interest and conflicts between the secured party and any third party'.[5] Macleod commented that this recommendation 'would fuse together all the various existing forms of legislation relating to consumer credit into one rationally coherent enactment'.[6] However, the proposal to implement a Lending and Security Act was not acted on due to its complex nature and high cost implications,[7] and the recommendation to introduce a Consumer Sale and Loan Act resulted in the implementation of the CCA 1974 as the 'basis of regulation for consumer credit'.[8] It is important to note that the principal objective of the recommendations was to provide consumers with a higher level of protection, as discussed in Part 7 Chapter 1.[9] Indeed, the Crowther Committee stated that the main objective of its proposed reforms was 'to provide for the small individual borrower the protection he unquestionably needs without setting up artificial barriers between one sort of credit and another'.[10] This is a view supported by Scott and Black who argued that the 'main thrust of the Committee's exhaustive analysis was directed to improving consumers' rights and to rationalising the law into a new coherent framework'.[11]

---

[1] Directive 2008/48/EC..

[2] *Report of the Committee on Consumer Credit* (Chairman: Lord Crowther) (Cmnd. 4596, 1971) ('Crowther Committee Report').

[3] See J. Macleod, *Consumer Sales Law* (Routledge, Oxford, 2007) 175; S. Brown, 'The Consumer Credit Act 2006: real additional mortgagor protection?' (2007) *Conveyancer and Property Lawyer* 316, 317–18. The existing framework included, e.g., the Pawnbrokers Act 1872, Bill of Sales Acts 1878 and 1882, Moneylenders Acts 1900–1927, Hire Purchase Act 1964 and Advertisements (Hire Purchase) Act 1967.

[4] Crowther Committee Report, above n. 2, at 183.

[5] Macleod, above n. 3, at 175.   [6] *Ibid.*

[7] See C. Scott and J. Black, *Cranston's Consumers and the Law* (Butterworths, London, 2000) 238.

[8] Brown, above n. 3, at 317.

[9] G. Borrie, 'The credit society: its benefits and burdens' (1986) *Journal of Business Law* (May) 181, 184.

[10] Crowther Committee Report, above n. 2, at 6.6.3–6.4.

[11] Scott and Black, above n. 7, at 238.

Q1 What were the main recommendations of the Crowther Committee?

3 Consumer Credit Act 1974

The CCA 1974 was a radical piece of legislation that amended the Moneylenders Acts 1900–1927 and the Hire-Purchase Act 1965.[12] The CCA 1974 sought to protect borrowers in five areas: consumers were to be given a cooling-off period; creditors would not be able to demand early payment; if the borrower had paid one-third of the total price of the goods under a hire-purchase agreement, then the creditor could not take the goods back without first obtaining a court order; if a credit agreement was extortionate, then the borrower could apply to the court for a review of the agreement; and certain written information had to be provided to the borrower.[13] In order to afford this level of protection, the CCA 1974 made provision for the creation of specific regulations covering such areas as the form and content of consumer credit agreements, the advertising of credit, the calculation of the annual percentage rate of interest (APR), credit licensing provisions, extortionate credit bargains and the procedures to be adopted in the event of default, termination or early settlement. Despite its laudable aims, the CCA 1974 failed to fulfil its objective of increasing the level of consumer protection and it was consequently amended by the CCA 2006. The 2006 Act was implemented on 1 October 2008 and modified and updated its 1974 predecessor. The Department for Business Innovation and Skills (DBIS) boldly asserted that the CCA 2006 would 'establish a fairer, more transparent and competitive credit market, updating consumer credit legislation that had been in place since the 1970s, making it more relevant to today's consumers'.[14] At the heart of the legislation was the aim to increase the level of protection afforded to consumers. This was to be achieved by strengthening the credit licensing system, improving the ability of consumers to challenge unfair lending, and broadening the enforcement powers of the OFT. Furthermore, consumers would benefit from receiving clearer pre- and post-contractual information about their credit agreements. Patient commented that the CCA 2006 would:

> establish … further protection for consumer credit customers by providing, *inter alia*, further stringent informational requirements, the ability to have the agreement set aside or altered in the event of an unfair credit relationship, and the extension of the Consumer Credit Act to all credit agreements regardless of the size of the loan.[15]

---

[12] See F. Philpott, 'E-commerce and consumer credit' (2001) 3(4) *Journal of International Financial Markets* 131.

[13] See Department of Trade and Industry White Paper, *Fair, Clear and Competitive: the Consumer Credit Market in the 21st Century* (London, 2003) 114.

[14] See Department for Business Innovation and Skills, 'Consumer Credit Act 2006' (n/d), available at www.berr.gov.uk.

[15] Brown, above n. 3, at 317.

Further important reforms were introduced by the Consumer Credit Directive 2008/48/EC,[16] which was implemented in February 2011.

The amendments introduced by the CCA 2006 have been directly incorporated into the CCA 1974, and it is these amended provisions that will be referred to throughout the remainder of the chapter.

(a) Scope and key definitions

The CCA 1974 is divided into two parts and deals with the following areas:

(1) the OFT;[17]
(2) credit agreements, hire agreements and linked transactions;[18]
(3) licensing of credit and hire businesses;[19]
(4) seeking business;[20]
(5) entry into credit or hire agreements;[21]
(6) matters arising during currency of credit or hire agreements;[22]
(7) default and termination;[23]
(8) security;[24]
(9) judicial control;[25]
(10) ancillary credit businesses;[26]
(11) enforcement of the Act;[27] and
(12) supplemental issues.[28]

(i) Creditor, debtor and credit

One of the most important definitions in the consumer credit legislative framework is that of a 'creditor'. A creditor is defined as 'the person providing credit under a consumer credit agreement or the person to whom his rights and duties under the agreement have passed by assignment or operation of law, and in relation to a prospective consumer credit agreement, includes the prospective creditor'.[29] Dobson and Stokes noted that 'the creditor means the person who provides the credit, that is, in the case of a hire-purchase agreement, the owner, in the case of a direct loan, the lender and in the case of a credit sale agreement, the seller'.[30] The creditor does not need to be an individual, so it can include, for example, an artificial person.[31] Conversely, a debtor is defined as 'the individual receiving credit under a consumer credit agreement or the person to whom his rights and duties under the agreement have passed by assignment or operation

---

[16] Directive 2008/48/EC on credit agreements for consumers of the European Parliament and of the Council, 23 April 2008, [2008] OJ L133/66. A copy of the Directive is available at http://eur-lex.europa.eu/LexUriServ/LexUriServ.do?uri=OJ:L:2008:133:0066:0092:EN:PDF.
[17] CCA 1974, ss.1–7.   [18] Ibid. ss.8–20.   [19] Ibid. ss.21–42.
[20] Ibid. ss.43–54.   [21] Ibid. ss.55–74.   [22] Ibid. ss.75–86.   [23] Ibid. ss.87–104.
[24] Ibid. ss.105–26.   [25] Ibid. ss.127–44.   [26] Ibid. ss.145–60.
[27] Ibid. ss.161–73.   [28] Ibid. ss.174–93.   [29] Ibid. s.189(1).
[30] P. Dobson and R. Stokes, Commercial Law (Sweet and Maxwell, Gosport, 2008) 289.
[31] Macleod, above n. 3, at 200.

of law and in relation to a prospective consumer credit agreement includes the prospective debtor'.[32] However, the definition of an individual was broadened by the CCA 2006 and an individual now includes 'a partnership consisting of two or three persons not all of whom are bodies corporate; and an unincorporated body of persons which does not consist entirely of bodies corporate and is not a partnership'.[33]

An equally important term to define is 'credit', which includes 'cash,[34] a loan and any other form of financial accommodation'.[35] There is no definition of 'financial accommodation' and it has been said that 'the definition of "credit" in the CCA 1974 is not as precise and unambiguous as one might have wished'.[36]

(ii) Regulated agreements

In order to determine whether a transaction falls within the scope of the CCA 1974 it is important to ascertain if it is a regulated agreement.[37] A regulated agreement is defined as 'a consumer credit agreement, or consumer hire agreement, other than an exempt agreement, and "regulated" and "unregulated" shall be construed accordingly'.[38] The CCA 1974 also refers to a 'consumer credit agreement'[39] and a 'consumer hire agreement'.[40] A consumer credit agreement is defined as an agreement between an individual who is referred to as the debtor and another individual, the creditor, who provides the debtor with credit.[41] This definition originally had to be read in conjunction with CCA 1974, section 8(2), which limited the definition of a personal credit agreement to an agreement by which the creditor provided the debtor with credit not exceeding a given sum (£25,000 in 2008), but this financial limit was removed by CCA 2006, section 2.[42]

Macleod noted that the definition of a consumer credit agreement contains four elements: there must be an agreement, for the provision of credit, between the debtor and the creditor.[43] A consumer credit agreement embraces a wide range of contractual credit, including hire purchase, conditional sale, credit trading, credit cards, budget accounts, overdrafts, personal loans, mortgages and pledges.[44] The CCA 1974 only controlled consumer credit agreements;

---

[32] CCA 1974, s.189(1).   [33] *Ibid.*, as amended by CCA 2006, s.1.

[34] CCA 1974, s.189(1).

[35] *Ibid.* s.9(1). For a discussion of the courts' approach to the definition of credit see *Dimond v. Lovell* [2000] 2 All ER 897. See I. McLaren, 'Dimond v Lovell: the spot rate issue' (2000) 150(6944) *New Law Journal* 1066, 1068.

[36] D. Rosenthal, *Guide to Consumer Credit Law and Practice* (Butterworths, London, 2002) 6.

[37] Macleod, above n. 3, at 185.   [38] CCA 1974, s.189(1).

[39] *Ibid.* s.8.   [40] *Ibid.* s.15.

[41] *Ibid.* s.8. For a general discussion of the interpretation of a consumer credit agreement see *TRM Copy Centres (UK) Ltd* v. *Lanwall Services Ltd* [2009] UKHL 35.

[42] Dobson and Stokes, above n. 30, at 295. For an interesting (historical) discussion of the different approaches adopted by the courts to the interpretation of the financial limit, see *Humberclyde Finance Ltd* v. *Thompson* [1997] CCLR 23; *London North Securities Ltd* v. *Meadows* [2005] EWCA Civ 956; and *Wilson* v. *Robertsons (London) Ltd* [2005] 3 All ER 873.

[43] Macleod, above n. 3, at 193.   [44] *Ibid.* 192.

it did not apply to credit provided where the debtor is an 'artificial' person. However, its provisions might apply where the debtor is 'not a body corporate' as defined by the Companies Acts or under a Royal Charter or Act of Parliament.[45]

A consumer hire agreement is defined as 'an agreement made by a person with an individual (the "hirer") for the bailment or (in Scotland) the hiring of goods to the hirer, being an agreement which (a) is not a hire-purchase agreement, and (b) is capable of subsisting for more than three months'.[46]

The scope of these terms has been limited by the introduction of a number of exemptions,[47] which has resulted in the current position that regulated agreements will either be non-exempt consumer credit agreements or non-exempt consumer hire agreements.[48] These two categories of agreements were thought to be mutually exclusive, but this understanding was invalidated by the House of Lords in *Dimond* v. *Lovell*.[49]

(iii) Restricted use and unrestricted-use agreements

The CCA 1974 provides that credit is either restricted-use credit or unrestricted-use credit. It defines a restricted-use credit agreement as a 'regulated consumer credit agreement (a) to finance a transaction between the debtor and the creditor, whether forming part of that agreement or not; or (b) to finance a transaction between the debtor and a person (the "supplier") other than the creditor; or (c) to refinance any existing indebtedness of the debtor's, whether to the creditor or another person, and "restricted-use credit" shall be construed accordingly'.[50] An unrestricted-use credit agreement is a regulated consumer credit agreement not falling within the above provisions.

(iv) Debtor-creditor-supplier agreements

A regulated consumer credit agreement will either be a debtor-creditor-supplier agreement or a debtor-creditor agreement. A debtor-creditor-supplier agreement is defined as a regulated agreement that is a restricted-use credit agreement, that is made by the creditor under an already existing credit agreement, or in the consideration of future arrangements between himself and the supplier; or an un-restricted use credit agreement which is made by the creditor under pre-existing arrangements between himself and the supplier other than the debtor in the knowledge that the credit is to be used to finance a transaction between the debtor and the supplier.[51] Conversely, a debtor-creditor agreement is defined as a restricted-use credit agreement that is not made by the creditor under pre-existing arrangements, or in contemplation of future arrangements, between himself and the supplier, or a restricted-use credit agreement, or an unrestricted-use credit agreement which is not made by the creditor under

---

[45] *Ibid*. 198.   [46] CCA 1974, s.15(1).   [47] *Ibid*. s.8(3).
[48] Macleod, above n. 3, at 194.   [49] [2000] 2 All ER 897.
[50] CCA 1974, s.11(1).   [51] *Ibid*. s.12(1).

pre-existing arrangements between himself and a person other than the debtor in the knowledge that the credit is to be used to finance a transaction between the debtor and the supplier.[52]

(b) Exempt agreements

The CCA 1974 provides for a number of exemptions from its provisions.[53] A consumer credit agreement is exempt from the Act if it is a short-term consumer credit agreement;[54] low cost credit;[55] financing for foreign trade;[56] a house mortgage which is regulated by the Financial Services Authority (FSA) under the Financial Services and Markets Act (FSMA) 2000; or a loan from a responsible mortgage lender such as a local authority[57] or a housing association.[58] Other exemptions include certain second charge mortgages, which depend on the nature of the agreement and the identity of the lender; agreements for goods or services where the consumer has to repay the credit within twelve months in four payments or fewer; charge cards and similar agreements where the consumer has to repay the outstanding balance in full at the end of each period;[59] credit union agreements where the APR does not exceed 26.9 per cent; credit agreements offered to a limited group of borrowers where the APR does not exceed a specified 'low cost' rate (set by reference to average base rates); and certain agreements relating to overseas finance.[60] Other agreements exempt under the CCA 1974 are those contained in the Consumer Credit (Exempt Agreements) Order 1989, as amended.[61] As mentioned above, the financial limit of £25,000 imposed by CCA 1974, section 8(2) was removed in 2008.[62] The exemptions available under the CCA 1974 were further altered by the implementation of Consumer Credit Directive 2008/48/EC on 1 February 2011, which narrowed the range of exempt agreements[63] as regards matters including the number of payments, relevant charges payable for the credit, insignificant charges, the rate of the total charge for credit and certain agreements in countries outside the United Kingdom.

Additional exemptions were provided by the CCA 2006, the Consumer Credit (Exempt Agreements) Order 2007[64] and the Legislative Reform (Consumer Credit) Order 2008.[65] The CCA and the 2007 Order introduced two exemptions that related to lending to high net worth individuals who have a net income that exceeds £150,000 or net assets that exceed £500,000 and business lending over £25,000 where the loan is wholly or principally for business

---

[52] *Ibid.* s.13.   [53] *Ibid.* s.189(1).   [54] *Ibid.* s.16(5)(a).   [55] *Ibid.* s.16(5)(b).

[56] *Ibid.* s.16(5)(c).   [57] *Ibid.* s.16(1), (2).   [58] *Ibid.* s.16(6A).   [59] *Ibid.* s.16(5)(a).

[60] See *ibid.* s.16 and the Consumer Credit (Exempt Agreements) Order 1989, SI 1989/869.

[61] SI 1989/869, as amended by Consumer Credit (Exempt Agreements) Order 2007, SI 2007/1168.

[62] See SI 2007/1168 and CCA 1974, ss.16A and 16B.

[63] Department for Business Innovation and Skills, *Consumer Credit Regulations: Guidance on the Regulations Implementing the Consumer Credit Directive* (London, 2010) 14.

[64] SI 2007/1168.   [65] SI 2008/2826.

purposes.[66] The 2008 Order provided for the creation of an additional exempt agreement relating to 'buy-to-let' which came into effect from 31 October 2008.[67] The OFT stated that the CCA 2006 amended the exemption provisions of the 1974 Act 'to bring certain previously exempt agreements into the category of regulated agreements, by removing the upper financial limit beyond which an agreement was not subject to regulation, and to provide for new exemptions'.[68]

The CCA 1974 does not apply to a regulated mortgage contract or a regulated home purchase plan;[69] or to an agreement where the creditor is a housing authority which is secured by a land mortgage of a dwelling.[70]

(c) Multiple agreements

An important concept in the CCA 1974 is a multiple agreement, which was intended 'as an anti-avoidance provision'.[71] A multiple agreement is defined as one whose terms are such as '(a) to place a part of it within one category of agreement mentioned in this Act, and another part of it within a different category of agreement so mentioned, or within a category of agreement not so mentioned, or (b) to place it, or a part of it, within two or more categories of agreement so mentioned'.[72] These agreements have caused 'much academic controversy'[73] and have 'caused havoc for those devising and drafting multifunctional agreements such as flexible mortgages'.[74] Howells noted that the interpretation of this phrase has raised 'some of the most intricate interpretative issues that have given rise to fierce debate between the drafter of the CCA, Francis Bennion, and one of its leading commentators, Sir Roy Goode'.[75]

(d) Ancillary credit businesses

The CCA 1974 seeks to regulate a wide range of other types of business which participate in the credit and hire industry. The Act terms these 'other ancillary credit businesses'.[76] These are defined by the Act as including credit brokerage,[77] debt-adjusting,[78] debt-counselling,[79] debt-collecting,[80] or the operation of a credit reference agency.[81] The definition of these businesses must be combined

---

[66] These exemptions were introduced by CCA 2006, s.3 and Consumer Credit (Exempt Agreements) Order 2007, SI 2007/1168, arts. 2–5.

[67] Legislative Reform (Consumer Credit) Order 2008, SI 2008/2826.

[68] OFT, *Consumer Credit: Regulated and Exempt Agreements* (London, 2008) 4.

[69] CCA 1974, s.16(6C).   [70] *Ibid.* s.16(6A).   [71] Macleod, above n. 3, at 202.

[72] CCA 1974, s.18(1). For a practical illustration of the interpretation of this section see *Heath* v. *Southern Pacific Mortgage Ltd* [2009] EWCA Civ 1135.

[73] Macleod, above n. 3, at 202.

[74] E. Lomnicka, 'The reform of consumer credit in the UK' (2004) *Journal of Business Law* 129, 132.

[75] G. Howells, 'The consumer credit litigation explosion' (2010) *Law Quarterly Review* 617, 625.

[76] Macleod, above n. 3, at 198.   [77] CCA 1974, s.145(1)(a).

[78] *Ibid.* s.145(1)(b).   [79] *Ibid.* s.145(1)(c).   [80] *Ibid.* s.145(1)(d).

[81] *Ibid.* s.145(1)(e).

with the extensive range of exceptions contained in the Act.[82] Two other categories of ancillary credit business have been added by amendments made by
the CCA 2006: debt administration[83] and the provision of credit information
services,[84] and the operation of a credit reference agency.[85]

(e) Non-commercial agreements

The CCA 1974 defines a non-commercial agreement as 'a consumer credit
agreement or a consumer hire agreement not made by the creditor or owner
in the course of a business carried on by him'.[86] Thus, Dobson and Stokes commented that 'an agreement for a loan between friends or from a father to his son
would be a non-commercial agreement'.[87]

(f) Linked transactions

The CCA 1974 provides that 'a transaction entered into by the debtor or hirer or
a relative of his, with any other person, except one for the provision of security, is
a linked transaction in relation to an actual or prospective regulated agreement
of which it does not form part if'[88] one of the following conditions are met:

(a) the transaction is entered into in compliance with a term of the principal
    agreement; or
(b) the principal agreement is a debtor-creditor-supplier agreement and the
    transaction is financed, or to be financed, by the principal agreement; or
(c) the other party is a person mentioned in subsection (2).[89]

The Act restricts the use of linked transactions and provides that 'a linked
transaction entered into before the making of the principal agreement has no
effect until such time (if any) as that agreement is made'.[90] The CCA 1974 thus
affects regulated agreements but also satellite or linked agreements.[91] Dobson
and Stokes pointed out that these provisions 'enable later sections to provide for
what will be the effect on linked transactions in the event of the debtor or hirer
withdrawing an offer to enter into a regulated agreement or exercising his right
of cancellation of a regulated agreement'.[92]

(g) Total charge for credit

The CCA 1974 does not define 'total charge for credit' although it requires the
Secretary of State to make regulations 'for determining the true cost to the
debtor of the credit'.[93] This was done by the Consumer Credit (Total Charge for

[82] *Ibid.* s.146.   [83] *Ibid.* s.145(1)(da).   [84] *Ibid.* s.145(1)(db).
[85] *Ibid.* s.145(1)(e).   [86] *Ibid.* s.189(1).   [87] Dobson and Stokes, above n. 30, at 303.
[88] CCA 1974, s.19(1).   [89] *Ibid.* s.19.   [90] *Ibid.* s.19(3).
[91] Macleod, above n. 3, at 202.   [92] Dobson and Stokes, above n. 30, at 304.
[93] CCA 1974, s.20.

Credit) Regulations 1980,[94] regulation 3 of which defines the total charge for credit as the sum of charges specified in regulation 4 less those charges specified in regulation 5. Regulation 4 refers, in particular, to interest payments and, somewhat blandly, to 'other charges … payable under the transaction'. The concept of the 'total charge for credit' is not all-encompassing; some costs do not come within this concept. The selection of the costs which constitute the 'total charge for credit' is essentially a matter of legislative policy.[95] These provisions were amended by the Consumer Credit (Total Charge for Credit) Regulations 2010.[96] The Regulations implement a number of provisions of the Consumer Credit Directive 2008/48/EC and outline the method of calculation of the APR and the total charge for credit.

Q2 How were the main recommendations of the Crowther Committee implemented by the Consumer Credit Act 1974?

4 Formalities

The CCA 1974 outlines the formalities that must be complied with when making a regulated agreement. The purpose of these formalities is to ensure that the debtor is fully aware of the nature and content of the transaction he is about to enter into and that the written agreement gives him a clear account of his rights and obligations.

The relevant sections specify that the regulated agreement is not properly executed unless the document is signed by the debtor or hirer and on behalf of the creditor or owner;[97] the document includes all the terms of the agreement;[98] and all of the terms are readily legible.[99] The Act also contains provisions as to copies, stipulating those points in the contractual process at which the debtor/hirer is entitled to receive a copy of the agreement.[100] A failure to provide the relevant copies at the relevant times will make the contract unenforceable.[101] The Act also imposes a duty to give notice of cancellation rights.[102] These requirements apply to regulated agreements but not to any non-commercial agreement.[103]

Furthermore, a regulated agreement must comply with the requirements of the Consumer Credit (Agreements) Regulations 2004, which require the insertion of the names and address of the parties to the consumer credit agreement;

---

[94] SI 1980/51. See also F. Bennion, 'Consumer credit: the narrowing of "linked transactions" in relation to the total charge for credit' (1986) *Journal of Business Law* (July) 294 and S. Bone and L. Rutherford, 'Consumer credit, defects in the linked transactions Regulations' (1985) *Journal of Business Law* 209.

[95] Macleod, above n. 3, at 283.   [96] SI 2010/1011.

[97] CCA 1974, s.61(1)(a). For a general commentary on s.61 of the Act see *Brophy* v. *HFC Bank* [2011] EWCA Civ 67 and in particular the statement by Clarke LJ in *Watchtower Investments Ltd* v. *Payne* [2001] EWCA Civ 1159.

[98] CCA 1974, s.61(1)(b).   [99] *Ibid.* s.61(1)(c).   [100] *Ibid.* ss.62 and 63.

[101] *Ibid.* s.65.   [102] *Ibid.* s.64.   [103] *Ibid.* s.74(2).

the cash price; the amount of any deposit or advance payment required of the customer; the credit limit; the APR; the total amount payable; the amount of each payment and when payable; details of default charges and details of any security provided by the debtor or hirer.[104] If these obligations are not complied with, then the agreement is 'improperly executed'.[105]

The CCA 1974 also provides that the consumer credit agreement must be signed (i) by the debtor or hirer and (ii) by or on behalf of the creditor. Dobson and Stokes pointed out that 'the debtor must sign in person, unless the debtor or hirer is a partnership or other unincorporated body in which case [the agreement] can be signed by one person on behalf of the debtor or hirer. It is not sufficient that the debtor or hirer signs it when it is still blank.'[106] It is also important to note that the Consumer Credit (Agreements) Regulations 1983 provide that the credit agreement must include a signature box, which must contain the signature of the debtor or hirer.[107]

The Consumer Credit Directive has also amended the formalities requirements of the CCA 1974. Regulations 8 and 9 of the Consumer Credit (EU Directive) Regulations 2010, SI 2010/1010, inserted new provisions into the CCA 1974 which impose a duty to supply a copy of the executed credit agreement[108] and a duty to supply a copy of any overdraft agreement.[109]

5 Cancellation of agreements

The CCA 1974 provides that a regulated agreement can be cancelled by the debtor or hirer unless 'the agreement is secured on land, or is a restricted-use credit agreement to finance the purchase of land or is an agreement for a bridging loan in connection with the purchase of land',[110] or 'the unexecuted agreement is signed by the debtor or hirer at premises at which any of the following is carrying on any business (whether on a permanent or temporary basis): (i) the creditor or owner; (ii) any party to a linked transaction (other than the debtor or hirer or a relative of his); (iii) the negotiator in any antecedent negotiations'.[111] The Act also provides for a cooling-off period from 'the end of the fifth day following the day on which [the debtor or hirer] received a copy under section 63(2) or a notice under section 64(1)(b)',[112] or 'the end of the fourteenth day following the day on which he signed the unexecuted agreement'.[113]

6 Pre- and post-contract information

The CCA 1974 outlines the information that creditors are obliged to provide to people before they enter into a consumer credit or hire agreement. There are two sets of regulations that apply to this area, the Consumer Credit

---

[104] SI 2004/1482.   [105] Dobson and Stokes, above n. 30, at 350.
[106] *Ibid.* 347.   [107] SI 1983/1553.   [108] CCA 1974, s.61A.
[109] *Ibid.* s.61B.   [110] *Ibid.* s.67(1)(a).   [111] *Ibid.* s.67(1)(b).
[112] *Ibid.* s.68(1)(a).   [113] *Ibid.* s.68(1)(b).

(Disclosure of Information) Regulations 2004,[114] and the Financial Services (Distance Marketing) Regulations 2004.[115] The Consumer Credit (Disclosure of Information) Regulations 2004 apply to face-to-face advice situations and apply to all consumer credit agreements with the exception of distance agreements and contracts secured on land. The Regulations specify that a creditor must provide the debtor with the same type of information as required in the credit agreement so the debtor can consider the information before entering into the agreement. If the Regulations are not complied with, the creditor is permitted to enforce the agreement against the debtor by obtaining a court order. Furthermore, local authorities or the OFT are able to initiate enforcement proceedings against the creditor under Part 8 of the Enterprise Act 2002. The Financial Services (Distance Marketing) Regulations 2004 apply to financial services contracts and credit agreements agreed at a distance, that is to say, without any face-to-face communications. These Regulations stipulate that explicit information must be provided to the consumer prior to entering into the agreement. If it relates to a consumer credit agreement the information must include the name and address of the creditor, the main characteristics of the credit, the total price payable for the credit, the collection of payment, and information relating to the cancellation or termination of the agreement. Importantly, the Regulations allow a right of cancellation where the contract is entered into at a distance and the fourteen-day period of cancellation is from the conclusion of the contract or from the date on which the consumer obtained the terms and conditions.

Further amendments were introduced by the Consumer Credit (Disclosure of Information) Regulations 2010, which apply to unsecured credit including loans, hire-purchase, credit cards and overdrafts.[116] These Regulations provide that certain information must be revealed to the borrower 'in good time' prior to entering into the credit agreement.[117] In the vast majority of instances this will be communicated via the pre-contract credit information form. If these Regulations are not complied with the agreement is unenforceable. Furthermore, the 2010 Regulations also provide that creditors must provide an adequate explanation to the borrower pre-contract. This is to allow the borrower to evaluate the proposed agreement. The explanation must include:

- any features of the credit which may make it unsuitable for particular types of use;
- how much the borrower will pay periodically and in total;
- features which may have a significant adverse effect in a way that the borrower is unlikely to foresee;
- the principal consequences of failure to make repayments, including legal proceedings and repossession where applicable;
- the right of withdrawal and how/when this can be exercised.

---

[114] SI 2004/1481. These Regulations were made pursuant to CCA 1974, s.55.
[115] SI 2004/2095.   [116] SI 2010/1013.   [117] *Ibid.* reg. 10.

The CCA 1974 contained several provisions that related to the post-contract information and stipulated that certain types of information should be given to debtors during the credit agreement, including, for example, regular statements of the credit account, notification of any variations of the credit agreement, default notices, enforcement and termination and what information is to be provided upon request. The CCA 2006 introduced new measures covering the post-contract information so that consumers are able to manage their borrowing. This is an important amendment to the CCA 1974 and any statutory provision that seeks to empower debtors with more information about their financial commitments must be applauded. Since the introduction of the CCA 2006, creditors are required to provide debtors with annual statements in relation to regulated agreements for fixed-sum credit.[118] Furthermore, creditors are also required to include supplementary information in periodic statements for running-account credit. This now includes the outcome of only making minimum repayments; the result of not making minimum repayments; a statement of the order of payment allocation; what happens if the balance is not repaid in full and the implications for future interest charges; the dispute resolution mechanisms available; and that complaints can be made to the Financial Ombudsman Service (FOS).[119] Additionally, creditors are also required to provide debtors with notice of sums in arrears under fixed-credit agreements where the debtor is in arrears by more than a certain amount.[120] Debtors must receive notice from the creditor in a specified form where a default sum becomes payable under a regulated credit agreement.[121] Furthermore, creditors are required to provide more information regarding default notices. Creditors are required to notify the debtor if they intend to charge post-judgment interest under a regulated agreement in connection with a sum that is required to be paid under a court judgment.[122] Finally, debtors are also required to have copies of the OFT information sheets to accompany arrears notices and default notices.[123] These provisions have been amended following the implementation of the Consumer Credit Directive in February 2011. The Consumer Credit (EU Directive) Regulations 2010 introduced several provisions that related to the notification of interest rate charges, periodic information on overdraft rates and charges, information on non-significant overrunning, rights to request an amortisation table and notification of assignment of rights.[124]

Q3 What pre- and post-contract information must be provided by a creditor to a debtor under the Consumer Credit Act 1974?

[118] CCA 1974, s.77A, as inserted by CCA 2006, s.6.
[119] CCA 1974, s.78(4A), as inserted by CCA 2006, s.7.
[120] CCA 1974, s.86B, as inserted by CCA 2006, s.9.
[121] CCA 1974, s.86E, as inserted by CCA 2006, s.12.
[122] CCA 1974, s.130A, as inserted by CCA 2006, s.17.
[123] Consumer Credit (Information Requirements and Duration of Licences and Charges) Regulations 2007, SI 2007/1167, as amended by SI 2008/1751.
[124] SI 2010/1010.

7 Documentation of credit and hire agreements

The CCA 1974 includes conditions on how regulated agreements are to be documented.[125] These rules were originally implemented by the Consumer Credit (Agreements) Regulations 1983,[126] as amended by the Consumer Credit (Agreements) (Amendment) Regulations 2004.[127] The scope of these Regulations is broad, and they apply to all consumer credit agreements and consumer hire agreements that fall within the CCA 1974. In relation to a credit agreement, the Regulations specify that the following information must be documented: the type of agreement; the parties involved; important information, including the amount of credit and the duration of the agreement; and there must be a signature box.

8 Matters arising during the currency of credit or hire agreements

The CCA 1974 provides that a creditor may be held responsible for any breach of contract or misrepresentation by a supplier of goods or services on credit.[128] Section 75 provides that a creditor will be 'jointly and severally liable' with the supplier if:

- the cash price of the item is more than £100 but not more than £30,000;[129]
- the credit agreement is regulated under the Act;[130] and
- credit is advanced under arrangements between the credit provider and the supplier.[131]

This section applies to purchases on credit cards (depending upon the cash price of the goods or services) and also retail credit. The provisions of section 75 were amended by the Consumer Credit Directive, which inserted a new section 75A in the Act, which provides that the creditor may be liable in a small number of instances where section 75 does not apply, i.e., where:

- the cash price of the item exceeds £30,000 but the amount of credit does not exceed £60,260;[132]
- the credit agreement is a linked agreement;[133] and
- the supplier cannot be traced or is insolvent or does not respond or the consumer has taken reasonable steps to pursue the supplier but has not obtained satisfaction (this need not include court action).

Borrowers and hirers are permitted to request the creditor to send them information about their credit agreements. If this is not provided within twelve working days, the debt becomes unenforceable until they receive the

---

[125] CCA 1974, s.179.
[126] SI 1983/1553, as amended by SIs 1984/1600, 1985/666, 1988/2047, 1999/3177 and 2001/3649.
[127] SI 2004/1482.   [128] CCA 1974, s.75.
[129] *Ibid.* s.75(3)(b), as amended by SI 1983/1878.
[130] *Ibid.* s.75(3).   [131] *Ibid.*   [132] *Ibid.* s.75A(6)(a).   [133] *Ibid.* s.75A(6)(b).

information they asked for. The CCA 1974 outlines the information that creditors are required to provide to debtors under fixed-term, running account and hire agreements.[134] Under the Act, a debtor is permitted to obtain a copy of their agreement, copies of some of the other documents mentioned in their agreement and a statement of account.[135] Furthermore, where the regulated agreement is for a fixed sum, the creditor must provide the debtor with a statement.[136]

If the creditor fails to provide the information, the creditor will not be permitted to require the debtor to pay the debt before it is due, obtain a court judgment against the debtor or take back anything hired or bought on credit, or take anything used as security in the agreement. However, the creditor will be allowed to ask the debtor to pay what they owe, send a default notice, pass information on to a credit reference agency, pass information on to a debt collector, sell the debt to someone else or take the case to court. The OFT took the view that 'the sanction under the Act for non-compliance with an information request is unenforceability of the credit or hire agreement for so long as the creditor or owner fails to comply with his duty. Where there is such a failure, the courts have no discretion to allow enforcement.'[137]

9 Credit advertising

For the purpose of the CCA 1974, an advertisement is defined as:

> including every form of advertising, whether in a publication, by television or radio, by display of notices, signs, labels, showcards or goods, by distribution of samples, circulars, catalogues, price lists or other material, by exhibition of pictures, models or films, or in any other way, and references to the publishing of advertisements shall be construed accordingly.[138]

The CCA 1974 applies to any advertisement published for the purposes of a business carried on by the advertiser which indicates[139] that he is willing either to provide credit or enter into an agreement for bailment or the hiring of goods by him.[140] Casanova stated that:

> the threshold question is to consider whether the advertisement indicates that the creditor is willing to provide credit. Generally, an advertisement which consists

---

[134] *Ibid.* ss.77, 78 and 79. For a judicial discussion of these sections see *Carey* v. *HSBC Bank plc* [2009] EWHC 3417 (QB).

[135] CCA 1974, s.77(1). This will cost the debtor a £1 payment.

[136] *Ibid.* s.77A.

[137] OFT, *Guidance on Sections 77, 78 and 79 of the Consumer Credit Act 1974: the Duty to Give Information to Debtors and the Consequences of Non-compliance on the Enforceability of the Agreement* (London, 2010) 2.

[138] CCA 1974, s.189(1).

[139] For a discussion of the meaning of 'indicating' under the CCA 1974 see *Jenkins* v. *Lombard North Central Plc* [1985] RTR 21.

[140] CCA 1974, s.43(1)(a) and (b).

simply of the name or logo of the creditor would not be an advertisement falling within section 43(1), as it would not indicate that the advertiser was willing to provide credit.[141]

The advertisement is exempt from the CCA 1974 if the advertiser does not carry on a consumer credit business or consumer hire business,[142] a business in the course of which he provides credit to individuals secured on land[143] or a business which comprises or relates to unregulated agreements.[144] Furthermore, the Act enables the Secretary of State to introduce and implement regulations that control and administer both the manner and substance of the subject matter of the credit advertisement.[145] The CCA 1974 made it a criminal offence for an advertisement to convey 'information which in a material respect is false or misleading'.[146] However, this was repealed by the Consumer Protection from Unfair Trading Regulations 2008.[147] The Act also makes it a criminal offence for a person, with a view to financial gain, to send a document to a minor inviting him to borrow money,[148] obtain goods on credit or hire,[149] obtain services on credit,[150] or to apply for information or advice on borrowing money.[151] Furthermore, the CCA 1974 imposes restrictions on the provision of credit card cheques.[152]

The first Regulations applying to consumer credit advertising were introduced in 1980.[153] These were subsequently revoked and replaced by the Consumer Credit (Advertisements) Regulations 1989, which applied to advertisements by people who undertook consumer credit businesses, consumer hire business and business in the course of which credit secured on land was provided to individuals.[154] The Regulations set down the requirements for the form and content of three categories of advertisements: simple,[155] intermediate[156] and full.[157]

The 1989 Regulations were replaced by the Consumer Credit (Advertisements) Regulations 2004, as part of a series of amendments that preceded the implementation of the CCA 2006.[158] The 2004 Regulations came into effect on 31 October 2003 and apply to all credit advertisements and hire advertisements irrespective of the form in which they are published. The Regulations provide, *inter alia*, that the advertisements must be clear and understandable; the advertisement must contain information about the credit on offer; other types of information are also required to be displayed and important information about the annual percentage rate should be easily identifiable.[159] The

---

[141] J. Casanova, 'Establishing Internet credit card programmes in the United Kingdom' (2001) 16(3) *Journal of International Banking Law* 70, 74.

[142] CCA 1974, s.43(2)(a).   [143] *Ibid*. s.43(2)(b).   [144] *Ibid*. s.43(2)(c).

[145] *Ibid*. s.44(1).   [146] *Ibid*. s.46(1).   [147] SI 2008/1277, Sch. 4 para. 1.

[148] CCA 1974, s.50(1)(a).   [149] *Ibid*. s.50(1)(b).   [150] *Ibid*. s.50(1)(c).

[151] *Ibid*. s.50(1)(d). See *Alliance & Leicester Building Society* v. *Babbs* [1993] CCLR 77.

[152] CCA 1974, s.51A.

[153] Consumer Credit (Advertisements) Regulations 1980, SI 1980/54.

[154] SI 1989/1125.   [155] *Ibid*. reg. 2(2)(a).   [156] *Ibid*. reg. 2(2)(b).

[157] *Ibid*. reg. 2(2)(c).   [158] SI 2004/1484.   [159] OFT, *Credit Advertising* (London, 2008) 2.

Regulations aim to make certain that credit advertisements provide a transparent and even-handed view of the nature and costs of the credit available. Importantly, the 2004 Regulations apply to all forms of advertising, whether in print, on television, the radio, the Internet, teletext or by telephone canvassing. The Regulations provide that all credit advertisements are required to contain the name of the lender, and where the interest rate is provided, the APR is also to be exhibited.[160] The 2004 Regulations do not apply to advertisements for loans or the hire of goods to businesses, to financial promotions or to advertisements for mortgages which are a first charge on the borrower's home.[161] The Regulations contain a list of information that is to be included in credit advertisements[162] and a matching list for inclusion in hire advertisements.[163] Importantly, the 2004 Regulations also apply to the APR and the advertiser is required to stipulate the characteristic APR in any advertisement that contains certain financial information. The characteristic or 'typical APR' is the rate the advertiser would expect to charge in at least two-thirds of the transactions he will enter into as a result of the advertisement.[164] The definition of 'typical APR' was amended in 2007 and it is now provided that 'the typical APR is an APR at or below which the advertiser reasonably expects, at the date on which the advertisement is published, that credit would be provided under at least 66% of the agreements which will be entered into as a result of the advertisement'.[165] It is a criminal offence to publish a consumer credit advertisement that breaches the obligations contained in the 2004 Regulations.[166]

The 2004 Regulations were amended by the Consumer Credit (Advertisements) Regulations 2010,[167] which apply to unsecured credit, including credit cards, loans and hire-purchase agreements. They also apply to all forms of advertising on the television or radio, the Internet, teletext or telephone canvassing. The Regulations provide that if an advertisement includes an interest rate or any amount relating to the cost of the credit, this triggers the requirement to include a 'representative example', including a 'representative APR'. This must be representative of agreements expected to be entered into as a result of the advertisement, and at least 51 per cent of borrowers must be expected to receive the advertised APR or better. The representative APR is also triggered by reference to a non-status or comparative indication or incentive. Furthermore, the OFT have stated that 'the representative example must include, in addition to the representative APR, the annual rate of interest, any non-interest charges required to be paid for the credit, and the amount of credit. In addition, where applicable, it must include the duration of credit, the total amount payable, the periodic instalments, and the cash price of goods or services financed by the credit. All of this information must be shown together and of equal

---

[160] See SI 2004/1484.   [161] *Ibid.* reg. 10.   [162] *Ibid.* Sch. 2.
[163] *Ibid.* Sch. 3.   [164] *Ibid.* reg. 8.
[165] See Consumer Credit (Advertisements) (Amendment) Regulations 2007, SI 2007/827.
[166] CCA 1974, s.167.   [167] SI 2010/1012 and SI 2010/1970.

prominence, and must be more prominent than any other cost information and any trigger.'[168]

10 Credit licensing

The CCA 1974 stipulates that a licence is required to provide a consumer credit business or a consumer hire business.[169] The licence application must be made in writing together with the fee.[170] There are two types of licence that can be granted by the OFT: a standard and a group licence. A standard licence is 'issued by the OFT to a person named in the licence on an application made by him, which, during the prescribed period, covers such activities as are described in the licence'.[171] This type of credit licence is the one most commonly granted by the OFT, whilst a group licence is normally granted for companies. A group licence is one 'issued by the OFT (whether on the application of any person or of its own motion), which, whilst the licence is in effect, covers such persons and activities as are described in the licence'.[172] The OFT must grant a group licence 'only if it appears to it that the public interest is better served by doing so than by obliging the persons concerned to apply separately for stand-ard licences'.[173] This is referred to as the 'public interest test'.

The OFT has the power to renew or vary on request the terms of a group licence;[174] refuse, revoke or suspend a group licence;[175] compulsorily vary the group licence;[176] grant a group licence in different terms from those applied for[177] and exclude individual members from the cover of the group licence.[178]

The CCA 1974 provides that 'a person who engages in any activities for which a licence is required when he is not a licensee under a licence covering those activities commits an offence'.[179] Therefore, if someone fails to obtain a licence to offer credit that person commits an offence.

The consumer credit licensing system as originally set up by the CCA 1974 was criticised as ineffective, prompting reform in the CCA 2006. Indeed, Brown took the view that 'the main body of the 2006 Act is concerned primarily with further requirements for information provision and a considerable overhaul of the licensing system. With regard to the latter, the 2006 Act gives the OFT more power to manage the licensing system more efficiently, for example, in terms of the application procedure, requirements imposed on licensees and duties with regard to information.'[180]

Importantly, the CCA 2006 amended the definition of both a standard licence and group licence and allowed the OFT to grant an indefinite standard

---

[168] OFT, 'Credit advertising' (n/d), available at www.oft.gov.uk/about-the-oft/legal-powers/legal/cca/guidance.

[169] CCA 1974, s.21(1).   [170] *Ibid.* s.6(2).   [171] *Ibid.* s.22(1)(a).

[172] *Ibid.* s.22(1)(b).   [173] *Ibid.* s.22(5).   [174] *Ibid.* s.30.

[175] *Ibid.* s.32(1).   [176] *Ibid.* s.30(2).   [177] *Ibid.* s.30(1).

[178] *Ibid.* s.30(3).   [179] *Ibid.* s.39(1).   [180] Brown, above n. 3, at 320.

licence.[181] The purpose of this provision was to allow the OFT to issue either an indefinite standard licence or one for a certain period of time.

The CCA 2006 also amended the application process for a standard credit licence.[182] Applicants for a standard licence must state whether they are applying for the licence to cover the carrying on of that type of business with no limitation; or for the licence to cover the carrying on of that type of business only so far as it falls within one or more descriptions of business.[183] The OFT has the power under the CCA 2006 amendments[184] to vary a standard licence and even wind up the standard licensee's business.[185] Professor Macleod took the view that 'it would appear that an applicant has a right to the issue of a standard licence provided only that there are satisfied the two conditions as to type of business and fitness, rather than that issue being in the discretion of the OFT'.[186]

The CCA 2006 also altered the test used to determine whether or not a person applying for a licence is 'fit' to do so. Under its original provisions (retained in amended form by the CCA 2006), the CCA 1974 provided that, when considering an application for a licence, the OFT must be satisfied that the applicant is a 'fit person' having 'regard to any circumstances appearing to it to be relevant', including any evidence tending to show that the applicant or any of the applicant's past or present employees, agents or associates or, or where the applicant is a corporation, any person that appears to be a controller of such an entity, has committed any offence of fraud or dishonesty or violence,[187] breached any provision of the CCA 1974,[188] practised discrimination on grounds of sex, colour, race or ethnic or national origins in, or in connection with, the carrying on of any business,[189] or has engaged in business practices which appear to be deceitful or oppressive, or otherwise unfair or improper.[190]

Under the CCA 2006 reforms, the OFT stated that it had adopted a more demanding fitness test which would vary depending upon the level of risk faced by consumers. Businesses and individuals applying for licences for riskier credit businesses would be required to demonstrate to the OFT that they were both 'fit' and 'competent' to do so. Once a licence has been granted by the OFT, it was imperative that the licensee maintained the standard of fitness expected. The CCA 2006 reforms attempted to strengthen the unfitness test by adding 'some positive criteria of competence'.[191] It is now provided:

> In determining whether an applicant for a licence is a fit person for the purposes of this section the OFT shall have regard to any matters appearing to it to be relevant including (amongst other things):

---

[181] CCA 1974, s.22(1), as amended by CCA 2006, s.34.
[182] CCA 1974, s.24A, as inserted by CCA 2006, s.28.
[183] *Ibid.* s.24A(1)(a) and (b).   [184] CCA 1974, s.30(1), as amended by CCA 2006, s.31.
[185] CCA 1974, s.34A, as inserted by CCA 2006, s.32.
[186] Macleod, above n. 3, at 206.
[187] CCA 1974, s.25(2A)(a), as amended by CCA 2006, s.29.
[188] *Ibid.* s.25(2A)(b).   [189] *Ibid.* s.25(2A)(d).   [190] *Ibid.* s.25(2A)(e).
[191] Macleod, above n. 3, at 245.

    (a) the applicant's skills, knowledge and experience in relation to consumer credit businesses, consumer hire businesses or ancillary credit businesses;

    (b) such skills, knowledge and experience of other persons who the applicant proposes will participate in any business that would be carried on by him under the licence;

    (c) practices and procedures that the applicant proposes to implement in connection with any such business;

    (d) evidence of the kind mentioned in subsection (2A) [i.e., the negative criteria listed above].'[192]

Furthermore, the CCA 2006 also specifically provided that the business practices that the OFT could consider to be deceitful, oppressive, unfair or improper 'include practices … that appear to the OFT to involve irresponsible lending'.[193] Indeed, the OFT stated in its 2009 Annual Report that 'the fitness test was extended explicitly to cover irresponsible lending'.[194]

The OFT is under a statutory obligation to publish guidance notes on how it establishes the 'fitness' of the credit licence application.[195] When determining whether or not a person or business is fit for the purposes of obtaining a credit licence, the OFT considers any relevant circumstances, which can include any evidence of past misconduct, the skills and knowledge of the people managing and running the business in relation to the licensed activity (this includes any relevant experience) and the practices and procedures that they operate in the organisation of the business.[196] Having adopted a risk-based approach towards the licensing application system (see above), the OFT has stated that it will focus on two particular issues.[197] First, their assessment will concentrate on 'evidence that raises doubts about the personal integrity of individuals running or controlling a licensed business.'[198] Examples of such evidence include, amongst other things, criminal offences for fraud or dishonesty, any breach of the CCA 1974 and its regulations, any breach of consumer protection laws, or any breach of the rules or principles of the FSA. Secondly, the OFT will also consider any 'business activities that because of either their nature or past association with high levels of complaint have a greater potential for consumer detriment'.[199] In addition, the OFT will consider a list of positive factors whilst determining whether or not to issue a credit licence. This includes, for example, membership of an OFT approved consumer code scheme, authorisation or approval by the

---

[192] CCA 1974, s.25, as amended by CCA 2006, s.29.

[193] CCA 1974, s.29(2A), as amended by CCA 2006, s.29.

[194] OFT, *Flexibility for Changing Markets, Annual Report and Resources Report 2008–2009* (London, 2009) 26.

[195] CCA 1974, s.25A.

[196] OFT, *Consumer Credit Licensing: General Guidance for Licensees and Applicants on Fitness and Requirements* (London, 2008) 3.

[197] For a useful comparative discussion of the risk-based approach adopted by the FSA see S. Stewart, 'Coping with the FSA's risk-based approach' (2005) 13(1) *Journal of Financial Regulation and Compliance* 43.

[198] OFT, above n. 196, at 3.   [199] *Ibid.* 4.

FSA, a record of fair dealing over a significant amount of time and a record of liaising with local authority trading standards services.[200]

If the OFT refuses an application for a consumer credit licence, from 6 April 2008 the applicant was entitled to appeal to the Consumer Credit Appeals Tribunal. The functions of that Tribunal were transferred to the First-tier Tribunal on 1 September 2009, which now hears and decides appeals against decisions of the OFT relating to its licensing decisions under the CCA 1974 and the imposition of a financial penalty on a licensee under the CCA 2006.[201] The Tribunal has a wide range of powers at its disposal. For example, it may confirm the determination appealed against; quash that determination; vary that determination; remit the matter to the OFT for reconsideration and determination in accordance with the directions (if any) given to it by the Tribunal; and give the OFT directions for the purpose of giving effect to its decision. However, the Tribunal does not have the power to increase the level of the penalty imposed, or extend the time within which the penalty must be paid.

Examples of appeals from disgruntled credit licence applicants which have been heard by the Tribunal include: *Road Angels Non-fault Accident Management Ltd* v. *Office of Fair Trading*, where the Tribunal granted an appeal against a decision to refuse a standard licence application;[202] *Finance Select (UK) Ltd* v. *Office of Fair Trading*, where the Tribunal determined that the OFT had failed to comply with the notice provisions of the CCA 1974;[203] *Mark Cooper* v. *Office of Fair Trading*,[204] where the Tribunal upheld the decision of the OFT to revoke the licence of the applicant due to a conviction for obtaining property by deception; and *Vrajilal Laxmias Sodha (trading as V. L. Sodha, M. N. S. Financial and M. N. S. Consultancy)* v. *Office of Fair Trading*,[205] where the Tribunal upheld the decision of the OFT to renew a standard credit licence.

The OFT emphasised that 'the Consumer Credit Act 2006 amends the CCA 1974 to include new provisions to improve and strengthen the licensing regime administered by the OFT'.[206] In line with the amendments already discussed above, the OFT has a wide range of enforcement powers for breaches of a consumer credit licence. Indeed, Patient took the view that 'some of the most significant changes to be introduced by the [2006] Act relate to the powers of the OFT'.[207] She pointed out how the OFT has been given additional enforcement powers: 'when issuing licences the OFT will be able to publish guidance in relation to how it determines whether persons are "fit" to hold a licence; where the OFT is dissatisfied with any matter in connection with a business carried on or proposed to be carried on by a licensee it may by notice require a licensee to do

[200] *Ibid.* 3.
[201] CCA 1974, s.41A, repealed by Transfer of Functions of the Consumer Credit Tribunal Order 2009, SI 2009/1835, an Order made under the Tribunals, Courts and Enforcement Act 2007.
[202] CCA/2008/0003.   [203] CCA/2008/0002
[204] CCA/2008/0006.   [205] CCA/2008/0005.
[206] OFT, *Consumer Credit Licensing: Statement of Policy on Civil Penalties* (London, 2008) 1.
[207] J. Patient, 'The Consumer Credit Act 2006' (2006) 21(6) *Journal of International Banking Law and Regulation* 309, 314.

or refrain from doing something specified in the notice; the OFT will be able to impose a financial penalty on anyone who fails to comply with a requirement imposed on them. The fines may be up to £50,000.'[208]

The OFT has the ability to suspend, vary and revoke a licence; it can refuse applications, impose requirement on existing and new licences and grant licences on different terms. The ability to impose requirements on a licence is a new enforcement power for the OFT.[209] CCA 1974, section 33A provides that the OFT is entitled to impose a requirement on a licence where it is dissatisfied with any matter in connection with '(a) a business being carried on, or which has been carried on, by a licensee or by an associate or a former associate of a licensee',[210] or in connection with '(b) a proposal to carry on a business which has been made by a licensee or by an associate or a former associate of a licensee',[211] or with '(c) any conduct not covered by paragraph (a) or (b) of a licensee or of an associate or a former associate of a licensee'.[212] The requirement imposed may compel or stop the licensee from doing something which the OFT is dissatisfied with.[213]

In addition, the OFT has the ability to impose a financial sanction of up to £50,000 when a licensee fails to observe a requirement that has been imposed on a standard licence or as a reasonable person in relation to a group licence.[214] In January 2008, the OFT published a statement on its policy towards the imposition of financial penalties for breaches of the credit licensing regime.[215] There are four issues that the OFT will focus on before imposing a penalty: proportionality; changing behaviour; no (or limited) financial benefit obtained from non-compliance; and consistency.[216] The OFT will also consider a nondefinitive list of other factors. This includes, for example, whether or not the non-compliance is simply a one-off breach or a series of habitual breaches? Has the licensee taken the necessary measures to ensure that the non-compliance has stopped. Has the licensee co-operated with the OFT? Was the firm's senior management or controlling mind aware of the non-compliance?[217]

Prior to imposing a financial penalty, the OFT is required to inform the recipient of the penalty that is to be imposed.[218] Professor Macleod stated that 'the Office of Fair Trading may give a person notice that it is minded to impose such a penalty, what may be termed a "yellow card", so that the alleged defaulter may make representations to try to dissuade it'.[219] The notice must state the anticipated amount of the penalty;[220] justify the reasons for imposing a penalty;[221] state the proposed period for payment of the penalty;[222] and invite him to make representations in accordance with CCA 1974, section 34.[223]

---

[208] *Ibid.*   [209] CCA 1974, s.33A, as inserted by CCA 2006, s.38.
[210] *Ibid.* s.33A(1)(a).   [211] *Ibid.* s.33A(1)(b).
[212] *Ibid.* s.33A(1)(c).   [213] *Ibid.* s.33A(2)(a) and (b).
[214] Under *ibid.* ss.33A, 33B, or 36A. See CCA 1974, s.39A, as inserted by CCA 2006, s.52.
[215] OFT, above n. 206.   [216] *Ibid.*   [217] *Ibid.* 7–8.
[218] CCA1974, s.39A(1).   [219] Macleod, above n. 3, at 253.   [220] CCA 1974, s.39A(2)(a).
[221] *Ibid.* s.39A(2)(b).   [222] *Ibid.* s.39A(2)(c).   [223] *Ibid.* s.39A(2)(d).

Additionally, the OFT can impose a financial sanction if a licensee fails to provide it with information as specified.[224] This is also referred to as a 'penalty notice' or a 'red card', which outlines the reasons for the imposition of a financial penalty and the methods and time period within which the payment must be made.[225]

Q4 What is the legislative approach of the Consumer Credit Act 1974 towards granting a credit licence?

Q5 What are the enforcement powers of the OFT if the credit licence provisions of the CCA 1974 are breached and are these powers effective? How do they compare with the enforcement powers of the FSA as outlined in Part 6?

11 Unfairness test

(a) Extortionate credit bargains

One of the most controversial and ineffective means of consumer protection afforded by the CCA 1974 were the extortionate credit bargain provisions (subsequently repealed by the CCA 2006, see below).[226] These provisions permitted a court to intervene in consumer credit agreements.[227] However, this was not the first statutory provision that allowed the courts to perform such a function. For example, the Moneylenders Acts 1900–1927 provided that an interest rate above 48 per cent was 'excessive and the credit transaction harsh and unconscionable'.[228] The phrase 'harsh and unconscionable', according to Browne-Wilkinson J, meant that 'the terms of the credit transaction [were] imposed in a morally reprehensible manner'.[229] Scott and Black pointed out that interest 'rate regulation has a long history deriving from the suspicion with which money lending has always been regarded'.[230] Similarly, Brown noted that:

> the question of an interest rate ceiling is one that has engaged law reformers for many years. Indeed it was the control of choice under the Usury Laws until their abolition in 1854. When reform of pawnbroking legislation and the establishment of the money-lending legislation were considered, interest rate controls were still seen as appropriate. It was only with the Crowther Committee Report and the passing of the CCA [1974] that interest rate controls were finally abandoned.[231]

---

[224] *Ibid.* s.36A, as inserted by CCA 2006, s.45.
[225] CCA 1974, s.39C(6), as inserted by CCA 2006, s.47.
[226] Brown, above n. 3, at 326.   [227] Lomnicka, above n. 74, at 137.
[228] National Association of Citizens Advice Bureau, *Daylight Robbery: the CAB Case for Effective Regulation of Extortionate Credit* (London, 2000) 6.
[229] *Multiservice Bookbinding Ltd* v. *Marden* [1979] Ch. 84, 110.
[230] Scott and Black, above n. 7, at 254.   [231] Brown, above n. 3, at 326.

The extortionate credit bargain provisions of the CCA 1974 were far-reaching. They applied to all credit agreements between individuals and creditors and not simply regulated agreements. The Act stipulated that 'if the court finds a credit bargain extortionate it may reopen the credit agreement so as to do justice between the parties'.[232] A credit bargain was defined as follows: 'where no transaction other than the credit agreement is to be taken into account in computing the total charge for credit, [credit bargain] means the credit agreement',[233] or 'where one or more other transactions are to be so taken into account, [it] means the credit agreement and those other transactions, taken together'.[234]

A credit bargain was considered to be extortionate if it required the debtor or a relative of his to make payments which were grossly exorbitant or otherwise grossly contravened ordinary principles of fair dealing.[235] The court was permitted to take into account several factors when determining whether or not the credit bargain was extortionate, including the interest rates prevailing at the time the credit agreement was made;[236] other factors in relation to the debtor;[237] factors in relation to the creditor;[238] whether or not a colourable cash price was quoted for any goods or services included in the credit bargain;[239] and issues relating to any linked transaction, including the question as to how far the transaction was reasonably required for the protection of debtor or creditor, or was in the interest of the debtor.[240]

(b) Unfair relationship

It was widely accepted by most commentators that the extortionate credit bargain provisions were ineffective. Scott and Black, for example, noted 'the wide discretion given to the courts in considering bargains for their extortionate character', and opined that 'the fact that so much can depend upon individual circumstances of a credit transaction, means that little control of credit charges has resulted from the enactment of this provision'.[241] Consequently, the provisions were repealed by the CCA 2006[242] and replaced by new 'unfair relationship' provisions, which apply to agreements from 6 April 2007. Any agreement that was made before the provisions came into effect is covered by the extortionate credit bargain provisions.

---

[232] CCA 1974, s.137(1).   [233] *Ibid.* s.137(2)(i).   [234] *Ibid.* s.137(2)(ii).

[235] *Ibid.* s.138(1)(a) and (b).   [236] *Ibid.* s.138(2)(a).

[237] *Ibid.* s.138(2)(b). This includes the debtor's age, experience, business capacity, state of health, the degree to which, at the time of making the credit bargain, he was under financial pressure, and the nature of that pressure.

[238] *Ibid.* s.138(4). This includes the degree of risk accepted by him, having regard to the value of any security provided, his relationship to the debtor and whether or not a colourable cash price was quoted for any goods or services included in the credit bargain.

[239] *Ibid.* s.138(4).   [240] *Ibid.* s.138(5).

[241] Scott and Black, above n. 7, at 256.   [242] Macleod, above n. 3, at 1013–16.

Under the 'unfair relationship' test, a court may make an order in connection with a credit agreement if it is of the opinion that the relationship between the creditor and the debtor arising out of the agreement is unfair.[243] Under the terms of the provisions, a court may decide that the relationship between the parties is unfair because of one or more of the following:

(a) any of the terms of the credit agreement or a related agreement;[244]
(b) the way in which the lender has exercised or enforced its rights under the credit agreement or a related agreement;[245] or
(c) any other thing done (or not done) by or on behalf of the lender either before or after the making of the credit agreement or a related agreement.[246]

According to the OFT conduct that would fall under the last category includes 'pre-contract business practices (such as advertising) and post-contract actions not based on a right (such as demanding sums of money the consumer has not agreed to pay). Relevant omissions might include failure to provide key information in a clear and timely manner (or at all), or to disclose material facts. Category (c) would also encompass acts or omissions which are non-commercial.'[247]

It is provided that if the debtor (or a surety) asserts that the credit agreement breaches the unfair relationship test, the burden of proof is on the creditor to illustrate that the relationship was not unfair.[248]

If the court concludes that the agreement is unfair, it has a broad range of powers which include:

• requiring the creditor, or any associate or former associate of his, to repay (in whole or in part) any sum paid by the debtor or by a surety by virtue of the agreement or any related agreement (whether paid to the creditor, the associate or the former associate or to any other person);[249]
• requiring the creditor, or any associate or former associate of his, to do or not to do (or to cease doing) anything specified in the order in connection with the agreement or any related agreement;[250]
• reducing or discharging any sum payable by the debtor or by a surety by virtue of the agreement or any related agreement;[251]
• directing the return to a surety of any property provided by him for the purposes of a security;[252]
• otherwise setting aside (in whole or in part) any duty imposed on the debtor or on a surety by virtue of the agreement or any related agreement;[253]

---

[243] CCA 1974, s.140A, as inserted by CCA 2006, s.19.
[244] *Ibid.* s.140A(1)(a).   [245] *Ibid.* s.140A(1)(b).
[246] *Ibid.* s.140A(1)(c). For a more detailed discussion of these provisions see *Harrison* v. *Black Horse Ltd* [2010] EWHC 3152 (QB) and *Shaw* v. *Nine Regions Ltd* [2009] EWHC 3514 (QB).
[247] OFT, *Unfair Relationships: Enforcement Action under Part 8 of the Enterprise Act 2002* (London, 2008) 12.
[248] CCA 1974, s.140B(9), as inserted by CCA 2006, s.20.
[249] *Ibid.* s.140B(1)(a).   [250] *Ibid.* s.140B(1)(b).   [251] *Ibid.* s.140B(1)(c).
[252] *Ibid.* s.140B(1)(d).   [253] *Ibid.* s.140B(1)(e).

- altering the terms of the agreement or of any related agreement;[254]
- directing accounts to be taken, or (in Scotland) an accounting to be made, between any persons.[255]

(c) Enterprise Act 2002 powers

In addition to its powers under the CCA 1974, the OFT may take appropriate enforcement measures under the Enterprise Act 2002 where it believes that an unfair relationship harms the collective interests of consumers.[256] The OFT has stated that these powers 'cover situations where businesses infringe their legal obligations and as a result harm the collective interests of consumers'.[257] However, the scope of these powers is limited because the OFT is prevented from dealing with individual grievances from consumers and its role is therefore strictly limited to regulatory issues. This means that the OFT is only entitled to act in the public interest or on the public's general behalf.[258] The CCA 1974 stipulates that the OFT is required to publish guidance on how it expects the operation of the unfair relationship test to interact with its enforcement provisions under Part 8 of the Enterprise Act 2002.[259]

In order for the OFT to exercise its powers under the Enterprise Act 2002 one of two types of infringement must occur: a domestic infringement or a community infringement. Under section 211(1) of the Act, a domestic infringement is an act or omission carried out by a person who acts in the course of a business,[260] which falls within subsection (2)[261] and harms the collective interests of consumers in the United Kingdom.[262] An act or omission falls within the scope of subsection (2) if it is specified by the Secretary of State and consists of:

(a) a contravention of an enactment which imposes a duty, prohibition or restriction enforceable by criminal proceedings;[263]
(b) an act done or omission made in breach of contract;[264]
(c) an act done or omission made in breach of a non-contractual duty owed to a person by virtue of an enactment or rule of law and enforceable by civil proceedings;[265]
(d) an act or omission in respect of which an enactment provides for a remedy or sanction enforceable by civil proceedings;[266]
(e) an act done or omission made by a person supplying or seeking to supply goods or services as a result of which an agreement or security relating to the supply is void or unenforceable to any extent;[267]
(f) an act or omission by which a person supplying or seeking to supply goods or services purports or attempts to exercise a right or remedy relating to

---

[254] *Ibid.* s.140B(1)(f).   [255] *Ibid.* s.140B(1)(g).   [256] Enterprise Act 2002, Part 8.
[257] OFT, above n. 247, at 1. See also Enterprise Act 2002, s.211(1)(c).
[258] OFT, above n. 247, at 10.   [259] CCA 1974, s.140D, as inserted by CCA 2006, s.22.
[260] *Ibid.* s.211(1)(a).   [261] *Ibid.* s.211(1)(b).   [262] *Ibid.* s.211(1)(c).
[263] *Ibid.* s.211(2)(a).   [264] *Ibid.* s.211(2)(b).   [265] *Ibid.* s.211(2)(c).
[266] *Ibid.* s.211(2)(d).   [267] *Ibid.* s.211(2)(e).

the supply in circumstances where the exercise of the right or remedy is restricted or excluded under or by virtue of an enactment;[268]

(g) or an act or omission by which a person supplying or seeking to supply goods or services purports or attempts to avoid (to any extent) liability relating to the supply in circumstances where such avoidance is restricted or prevented under an enactment.[269]

A community infringement is an act or omission that also harms the collective interests of consumers and which contravenes a listed Directive or breaches laws that provide additional protection for consumers.[270]

In determining whether or not to bring an action under Part 8 of the Enterprise Act 2002, the OFT will consider the contract terms of the agreement, the rates and charges, business practice, practices in breach of the law, the Consumer Protection from Unfair Trading Regulations 2008,[271] practices not necessarily in breach of the law and other relevant matters.[272]

(d) Meaning of 'unfair'

CCA 1974, section 140A specifically refers to the credit agreement being 'unfair'. How this phrase will be interpreted is extremely difficult to determine, although the phrase is well used in both primary and secondary legislation. The FSA noted that 'the use of "fairness" in this way has a very long history in English law, going back centuries to principles of conscience and "equity". Today, it is a concept which appears in one form or other in legislation, for example, in the Sale of Goods Act 1979, the Control of Misleading Advertising Regulations 1988, the Consumer Credit Act 1974 and the Unfair Contract Terms Act 1977.'[273]

Gerry Sutcliffe, MP, the then Consumer Affairs Minister, stated that it was 'important that the test does not constrain or impede the courts' ability to do justice in every case. That is why I will not try to define an unfair relationship. It is for the courts to determine such things according to the relevant facts of each case. Unfairness is not a new concept for the industry, and fair lenders have nothing to fear from its introduction.'[274] Thus, 'the government has repeatedly refused to define what is meant by "unfair relationship" and has adopted the position that it will be for the courts to decide'.[275]

---

[268] *Ibid.* s.211(2)(f).   [269] *Ibid.* s.211(2)(g).   [270] *Ibid.* s.212(1)(a) and (b).

[271] SI 2008/1277. These Regulations implemented the Unfair Commercial Practices Directive 2005/29/EC. For a more detailed commentary on this Directive see G. Howells, 'The end of an era: implementing the Unfair Commercial Practices Directive in the United Kingdom – punctual criminal law gives way to a general criminal/civil law standard' (2009) 2 *Journal of Business Law* 183.

[272] OFT, above n. 247, at 16–32.

[273] FSA, *Treating Customers Fairly after the Point of Sale*, Discussion Paper (London, 2001) Annex A3.

[274] *Ibid.* 313.   [275] Patient, above n. 207, at 312.

This stance has been criticised by several commentators. For example, Patient expressed the opinion that 'avoiding a debate on the meaning of "unfair relationship" will leave many creditors in a position of uncertainty as to whether their agreements or standard practices will fall foul of the test. This has been recognised as a particular concern for those who securitise portfolios and may lead to requirements for additional credit enhancement where a ratings agency expresses concerns.'[276]

Parker took the view that 'it may for instance be viewed as a question of good faith … [which] is certainly now a requirement that affects consumer credit agreements indirectly in that it is included'.[277] The concept of 'good faith' has been incorporated into such agreements by the Unfair Terms in Consumer Contracts Regulations 1999,[278] the Consumer Protection (Distance Selling) Regulations 2000[279] and the Financial Services (Distance Marketing) Regulations 2004.[280] Patient noted that 'fairness is a relatively new concept in English law although in the consumer context the Unfair Terms in Consumer Contracts Regulations 1999 may prove a helpful guide. Even in this context there is little judicial guidance as again few cases have reached the courts.'[281] The interpretation of 'good faith' has been considered in several cases. For example, in *Director General of Fair Trading* v. *First National Bank*,[282] Lord Bingham stated that:

> a term … is unfair if it causes a significant imbalance in the parties' rights and obligations under the contract to the detriment of the consumer in a manner or to an extent which is contrary to the requirement of good faith. The requirement of significant imbalance is met if a term is so weighted in favour of the supplier as to tilt the parties' rights and obligations under the contract significantly in his favour … the requirement of good faith in this context is one of fair and open dealing. Openness requires that the terms should be expressed fully, clearly and legibly, containing no concealed pitfalls or traps. Appropriate prominence should be given to terms which might operate disadvantageously to the customer. Fair dealing requires that a supplier should not, whether deliberately or unconsciously, take advantage of the consumer's necessity, indigence, lack of experience, unfamiliarity with the subject matter of the contract, [or] weak bargaining position … Good faith … looks to good standards of commercial morality and practice.[283]

The concept of 'fairness' is also central to the regulation of the financial services sector by the FSA. Patient noted that 'fairness is core to the principles of the FSA which stipulate that a firm must pay due regard to the interests of its

---

[276] *Ibid.* 313.   [277] *Ibid.*   [278] SI 1999/2083.

[279] SI 2000/2334.   [280] SI 2004/2095.

[281] Patient, above n. 207, at 313.

[282] [2002] 2 AC 481. For a more detailed discussion of this case see P. Nebbia, 'Director General of Fair Trading v First National Bank Plc, House of Lords, [2001] 3 W.L.R. 1297' (2003) 40(4) *Common Market Law Review* 983.

[283] [2002] 1 AC 481, 494.

customers and treat them fairly; a firm must pay due regard to the information needs of its clients, and communicate information to them in a way which is clear, fair and not misleading; and a firm must manage conflicts of interest fairly, both between itself and its customers and between customers and another client'.[284] The FSA itself has stated that within the context of the financial services sector, 'fairness' includes such concepts as honesty, openness, transparency, acting with integrity; acting with reasonable competence and diligence, and acting in good faith.[285]

12 Other powers of the court

The CCA 1974 permits a court to grant a time order allowing the debtor more time to repay the debt under a regulated consumer credit or consumer hire agreement.[286] Further, the terms of any agreement or security may be amended as the court considers just over a period of time, which could result, for example, in reducing the rate of interest or even extending the terms of the agreement.[287]

Q6 Compare and contrast the different regulatory approaches of the extortionate credit bargain provisions as originally enacted in the Consumer Credit Act 1974 and the unfairness test introduced by the Consumer Credit Act 2006.

13 Financial Ombudsman Service

One of the most innovative reforms introduced by the CCA 2006, through amendments to the FSMA 2000, was provision of an 'alternative dispute resolution system ... [which] ... would benefit both firms and consumers'.[288] The FOS is an independent dispute resolution service that was established under the FSMA 2000 to help settle individual disputes between consumers and those firms which are regulated by the FSA.[289] Patient noted that 'The [2006] Act contains an amendment to the FSMA [2000] which will extend the scope of the financial ombudsman scheme to all consumer credit businesses. Although many mainstream institutions will already fall within the scope of scheme, a significant number of areas will be added to the jurisdiction of the ombudsman, allowing consumers a quick, straightforward and readily accessible route to redress. Areas where this may be of particular impact will be the home shopping market and debt collecting.'[290]

---

[284] Patient, above n. 207, at 313.

[285] FSA, above n. 273, Annex A3 and A4. The interpretation of the term 'fair' is integral to the FSA's 'Towards fair outcomes for consumers' policy. For a more detailed discussion see FSA, *Treating Customers Fairly: Towards Fair Outcomes for Consumers* (London, 2006).

[286] CCA 1974, s.129. The court will grant such an order where it is 'just' to do so. For a commentary on this section see *Director General of Fair Trading* v. *First National Bank Plc* [2001] UKHL 52.

[287] CCA 1974, s.136.   [288] DTI White Paper, above n. 13, at 61.

[289] FSMA 2000, Part XVI.   [290] Patient, above n. 207, at 311.

Access to the FOS will make it considerably easier for consumers to question whether or not their credit agreement breached the unfairness test of the CCA 1974. It should also be more cost-effective for consumers to challenge credit agreements through the FOS than incurring expensive legal fees in the court system.[291] The CCA 2006 amendments broaden the authority of the FOS to hear complaints concerning licensed creditors under the CCA 1974.[292] FSMA 2000, section 226A now provides that a claimant may bring a complaint before the FOS which relates to an act or omission by the respondent provided that six conditions are met:

(a) the complainant is entitled and willing to have the complaint referred to the FOS;[293]
(b) the complaint falls within the description specified in consumer credit rules;[294]
(c) at the time of the complaint the respondent was in receipt of a standard licence or was authorised to undertake activity as specified by the CCA 1974;[295]
(d) the act or omission was of a type specified by the FSMA 2000;[296]
(e) at the time of the act or omission that type of business was specified in an order made by the Secretary of State; and[297]
(f) the complaint cannot be dealt with under the compulsory jurisdiction.[298]

The FOS will only consider a complaint if the subject matter of the complaint occurred on or after 6 April 2007 and if the creditor was licensed under the CCA 1974. Further, the FOS will not investigate a complaint unless the creditor was provided with an opportunity to handle the complaint and has issued a final response, and a period of more than eight weeks has passed since the complaint was received.[299] The official complaints-handling rules for consumer credit businesses are contained in the FSA Handbook.[300]

The availability of this alternative dispute resolution scheme for consumer credit disputes has proved to be very popular, and has resulted in many credit-related disputes being referred to the FOS.[301] The most common types of such

---

[291] DTI White Paper, above n. 13, at 61.
[292] FSMA 2000, s.226A, as inserted by CCA 2006, s.59. The Financial Ombudsman Service jurisdiction 'included all existing categories of consumer credit standard licence holders on 6 April 2007'. See FOS, *Rules for the New Consumer Credit Jurisdiction* (London, 2006) 4.
[293] FSMA 2000, s.226A(2)(a).   [294] *Ibid.* s.226A(2)(b)   [295] *Ibid.* s.226A(2)(c).
[296] *Ibid.* s.226A(2)(d). The types of businesses covered by this provision are consumer credit business; consumer hire business; and a business so far as it comprises or relates to credit brokerage; debt-adjusting; debt-counselling; debt-collecting; debt administration; the provision of credit information services; or the operation of a credit reference agency.
[297] FSMA 2000, s.226A(2)(e).   [298] FSMA 2000, s.226A(2)(f).
[299] OFT, 'Alternative dispute resolution scheme' (n/d), available at www.oft.gov.uk/about-the-oft/legal-powers/legal/cca/CCA2006/alternative/.
[300] See FSA, *FSA Handbook Dispute Resolution: Complaints* (London, n/d).
[301] FOS, 'Consumer credit complaints and the ombudsman service' (2008) 68 *Ombudsman News* (March/April) 1, 12.

complaints received by the FOS in respect of businesses with a consumer credit licence relate to 'hire purchase, debt collection and store cards'.[302]

14 Enforcement

The OFT is an independent and non-ministerial government department, funded by HM Treasury, and it has the dual function as the United Kingdom's competition and consumer authority. Its objective is to ensure that 'markets work well for consumers'. It aims to achieve this objective through a number of measures including carrying out research, advising the government, promoting consumer and business education, promoting self-regulation, and by enforcement of competition and consumer law. It is to this last measure that this chapter now turns. The OFT has a wide range of enforcement duties and enforcement powers under the Estate Agents Act 1979,[303] the Unfair Terms in Consumer Contracts Regulations 1999,[304] the Consumer Protection (Distance Selling) Regulations 2000,[305] the Consumer Protection from Unfair Trading Regulations 2008,[306] the Business Protection from Misleading Marketing Regulations 2008,[307] and the Enterprise Act 2002. The OFT also has enforcement duties under the Money Laundering Regulations 2007.[308]

Following the review of the operation of the CCA 1974, the OFT was granted an extensive array of enforcement powers under the provisions of the CCA 2006 and the Consumer Protection from Unfair Trading Regulations 2008.[309] The OFT stated that these new instruments:

> mark a fundamental move away from prescriptive regulation towards a principle-based consumer protection regime which encourages targeted, risk-based enforcement geared to the efficient operation of the market. At the same time, they also increase the range of enforcement tools available to enforcers, strengthening investigative powers and enabling OFT to take criminal proceedings and to seek financial penalties, alongside existing civil enforcement and compliance tools.[310]

These new measures formed part of the Labour government's 'better regulation' policy, which was based upon a series of reports published by the government, including the Hampton Review,[311] the Arculus Review[312] and the Macrory

---

[302] *Ibid*. 13.

[303] This has since been amended by the Consumers, Estate Agents and Redress Act 2007. For a more detailed discussion of this Act see F. Ratcliffe, 'Redressing the lack of professional standards' (2007) 151(34) *Solicitors Journal* 1150.

[304] SI 1999/ 2083. For a discussion of these Regulations see E. Macdonald, 'Scope and fairness of the Unfair Terms in Consumer Contracts Regulations' (2002) 65(5) *Modern Law Review* 763.

[305] SI 2000/2334.   [306] SI 2008/1277.   [307] SI 2008/1276.

[308] SI 2007/2157.   [309] SI 2008/1277.

[310] OFT, 'Consumer protection from Unfair Trading Regulations 2008' (n/d), available at www.oft.gov.uk/business-advice/treating-customers-fairly/protection.

[311] DBIS, *Reducing Administrative Burdens: Effective Inspection and Enforcement* (London, 2005).

[312] DBIS, *Regulation—Less is More: Reducing Burdens, Improving Outcome* (London, 2005).

Review.[313] Several of the recommendations of these reports were implemented by the Legislative and Regulatory Reform Act 2006, which obliged the OFT and other regulators to consider the principles of good regulation.[314] In particular, the Act specified that regulatory functions should be undertaken in such a way that they are transparent, answerable, proportionate and consistent, and aimed at instances where action is needed. The OFT is also under an obligation to comply with the Regulators' Compliance Code, which came into force on 6 April 2008.[315] In addition, the Regulatory Enforcement and Sanctions Act 2008 stipulates that the OFT is required to review its performance of its regulatory functions and eliminate any superfluous burdens that they may be imposing.[316]

In response to these measures, the OFT published a statement that outlined its enforcement policy.[317] Prior to initiating any enforcement measures, the OFT seeks to persuade businesses to comply by adopting two approaches; first, by 'ensuring businesses have clear, targeted and timely information and guidance on legal requirements relating to our functions, and especially on changes to those requirements';[318] and secondly, by 'providing incentives to improved trading practice: we rely, where appropriate, on "established means" as a way of dealing with consumer complaints about, for example, misleading advertising and we promote the voluntary adoption of good trading practice through our Consumer Codes Approval Scheme'.[319]

In relation to its approach towards utilising its enforcement powers, the OFT explained that 'when it is necessary to use enforcement action to achieve compliance, we aim to ensure that such interventions deliver high impact results, for example, by changing market behaviour, clarifying laws or providing the necessary level of deterrence to those who would deliberately flout their legal obligations'.[320] The statement went on to clarify that the OFT 'have wide ranging duties and functions in relation to Consumer Protection. The OFT takes a risk based, intelligence led approach to enforcement using all its available tools in innovative and holistic ways to address market malpractice. These tools include targeted enforcement, the encouragement of self-regulation, liaison with private industry and other regulators to encourage positive change and consumer and business education initiatives.'[321] The OFT pointed out that 'enforcement is used to protect consumers, and particularly vulnerable consumers, from rogue traders, unfair practices and other instances where businesses disregard their legal obligations. We do not hesitate to act where it is clearly appropriate to do so. We expect to prosecute where offences have occurred and there is serious

---

[313] DBIS, *Regulation—Regulatory Justice: Making Sanctions Effective* (London, 2006).
[314] For a more detailed discussion of the introduction of the Legislative and Regulatory Reform Act 2006, see V. Keter, *The Legislative and Regulatory Reform Bill*, House of Commons Research Paper 06/06 (London, 2006).
[315] DBIS, *Regulators Compliance Code: Statutory Code of Practice for Regulators* (London, 2007).
[316] Keter, above n. 314.
[317] OFT, *Statement of Consumer Protection Enforcement Principles* (London, 2008) 7.
[318] *Ibid*. 8.   [319] *Ibid*.   [320] *Ibid*. 8–9.   [321] *Ibid*.

consumer harm or where other factors such as fraud or other dishonesty warrant the use of criminal process.'[322]

15 Consumer Credit Directive

The first Consumer Credit Directive was adopted in December 1986.[323] MacLeod noted that 'since the late 1970s the EEC has been moving towards the harmonising of consumer credit laws. The first Directive on this subject was dated 1987; and in 1990 that Directive was amended to add provisions on the computation of annual percentage rate.'[324] He added that 'the Directive was modelled on the Consumer Credit Act [1974], but was short and general in character. It was a minimum Directive, in that it allowed Member States to introduce more stringent provisions to protect consumers, so that it did not prove necessary to make any alterations to the Consumer Credit Act 1974.'[325] It was subsequently amended twice, but remained virtually unchanged during the following two decades.

By the start of the new millennia, the European Commission decided that the first Consumer Credit Directive was out of touch and needed considerable updating and amending to keep pace with the ever-expanded consumer credit market. After an extensive period of consultation, including consideration of amendments tabled by the European Parliament, the Consumer Credit Directive 2008/48/EC was adopted by the European Commission in May 2008.[326] All EU Member States were required to fully implement the Consumer Credit Directive by June 2010. The objectives of the Consumer Credit Directive were expressed to be seeking to achieve a maximum level of harmonisation and to maintain and improve the high levels of consumer protection within the European Union.[327]

Article 2 of the Directive provides that its purpose is to 'harmonise certain aspects of the laws, regulations and administrative provisions of the Member States concerning agreements covering credit for consumers'.[328] The Directive applies to all forms of consumer credit agreements but does contain several exemptions. This includes, amongst other things, mortgage agreements,[329] credit agreements where the amount of credit is less than 200 euros or more than 75,000 euros,[330] interest free credit agreements,[331] and credit agreements where the credit is granted by an employer to its employee.[332]

---

[322] *Ibid.* 9.
[323] Council Directive 1987/102/EC on consumer credit, 22 December 1986.
[324] Macleod, above n. 3, at 183.   [325] *Ibid.*
[326] Directive 2008/48/EC on credit agreements for consumers of the European Parliament and of the Council, 23 April 2008. A copy of the Directive is available at http://eur-lex.europa.eu/ LexUriServ/LexUriServ.do?uri=OJ:L:2008:133:0066:0092:EN:PDF.
[327] DBERR, *Impact Assessment of Consumer Credit Directive* (London, 2009) 1.
[328] Directive 2008/48/EC, Art. 2.   [329] *Ibid.* Art. 2(a).
[330] *Ibid.* Art. 2(c).   [331] *Ibid.* Art. 2(f).   [332] *Ibid.* Art. 2(g).

The Directive provides some definitions of key terms such as 'consumer', 'creditor', 'credit agreement', 'annual percentage rate' and 'fixed borrowing rate'.[333] Importantly, the Directive stipulates that any advertisement for the purposes of consumer credit that refers to an interest rate or any figures illustrating the costs of the available credit to a consumer must contain 'standard information'.[334] The standard information must be specified 'in a clear, concise and prominent way by means of a representative example' and will include the borrowing rate;[335] the total amount of credit;[336] the APR;[337] if appropriate, the duration of the credit agreement;[338] in the case of credit in the form of deferred payment for a specific good or service,[339] the cash price and the amount of any advance payment; and again, if applicable, the total amount payable by the consumer and the amount of the instalments.[340] The Consumer Credit Directive states that before a consumer is bound by a credit agreement, the creditor must 'provide the consumer with the information needed to compare different offers in order to take an informed decision on whether to conclude a credit agreement'.[341] Such information should include, amongst other things, the type of credit;[342] the identity and address of the creditor and credit intermediary;[343] the total amount of credit and relevant conditions;[344] the length of the credit agreement; in the case of credit in the form of deferred payment for a specific good or service and linked credit agreements, that good or service and its cash price; the borrowing rate of interest;[345] the APR and the total amount repayable by the debtor;[346] the amount, number and frequency of payments that are to be made by the debtor;[347] the interest rate applicable in the case of late payments;[348] a warning regarding the consequences of missing payments;[349] and the consumer's right to be supplied, on request and free of charge, with a copy of the draft credit agreement.[350]

The Consumer Credit Directive imposes a long overdue obligation on the creditor to assess the creditworthiness of the consumer,[351] which it is hoped will lead to a reduction in such practices as predatory and irresponsible lending. Article 8(1) provides that 'Member States shall ensure that, before the conclusion of the credit agreement, the creditor assesses the consumer's creditworthiness on the basis of sufficient information, where appropriate obtained from the consumer and, where necessary, on the basis of a consultation of the relevant database'.[352] Furthermore, 'Member States shall ensure that, if the parties agree to change the total amount of credit after the conclusion of the credit agreement, the creditor updates the financial information at his disposal concerning

---

[333] *Ibid.* Art. 3.   [334] *Ibid.* Art. 4.
[335] *Ibid.* Art. 4(2)(a).   [336] *Ibid.* Art. 4(2)(b).
[337] *Ibid.* Art. 4(2)(c). Member States may specify that the APR does not need to be included.
[338] *Ibid.* Art. 4(2)(d).   [339] *Ibid.* Art. 4(2)(e).   [340] *Ibid.* Art. 4(2)(f).
[341] *Ibid.* Art. 5.   [342] *Ibid.* Art. 5(1)(a).   [343] *Ibid.* Art. 5(1)(b).
[344] *Ibid.* Art. 5(1)(c).   [345] *Ibid.* Art. 5(1)(f).   [346] *Ibid.* Art. 5(1)(g).
[347] *Ibid.* Art. 5(1)(h).   [348] *Ibid.* Art. 5(1)(l).   [349] *Ibid.* Art. 5(1)(m).
[350] *Ibid.* Art. 5(1)(r).   [351] *Ibid.* Art. 8.   [352] *Ibid.* Art. 8(1).

the consumer and assesses the consumer's creditworthiness before any signifi-cant increase in the total amount of credit'.[353] The Directive further provides that 'each Member State shall in the case of cross-border credit ensure access for creditors from other Member States to databases used in that Member State for assessing the creditworthiness of consumers. The conditions for access shall be non-discriminatory.'[354] Furthermore, 'if the credit application is rejected on the basis of consultation of a database, the creditor shall inform the consumer immediately and without charge of the result of such consultation and of the particulars of the database consulted'.[355]

Article 10 of the Directive prescribes the type of information to be included in credit agreements.[356] This includes, for example, the type of credit agree-ment, contact details of the creditor, length of the agreement, total amount of credit, the borrowing rate and the APR. Of equal importance is Article 14, which concerns the ability of the debtor to withdraw from the credit agree-ment. The Article provides that 'the consumer shall have a period of 14 calen-dar days in which to withdraw from the credit agreement without giving any reason',[357] although the fourteen days may be reduced at the explicit request of the consumer.[358]

Article 16 of the Directive states that 'the consumer shall be entitled at any time to discharge fully or partially his obligations under a credit agreement. In such cases, he shall be entitled to a reduction in the total cost of the credit, such reduction consisting of the interest and the costs for the remaining duration of the contract.'[359] However, 'in the event of early repayment of credit, the cred-itor shall be entitled to fair and objectively justified compensation for possible costs directly linked to early repayment of credit provided that the early repay-ment falls within a period for which the borrowing rate is fixed'.[360] Furthermore, Article 16(2) provides that 'such compensation may not exceed 1% of the amount of credit repaid early, if the period of time between the early repayment and the agreed termination of the credit agreement exceeds one year. If the period does not exceed one year, the compensation may not exceed 0.5% of the amount of credit repaid early.'

In April 2009, DBIS published a consultation paper seeking views from interested parties to ensure that the Consumer Credit Directive was fully implemented. A broad range of issues were consulted upon, including the pre-contractual, contractual and post-contractual information that must be given to consumers; information to be included in advertisements; rights for consumers to repay an agreement early, in full or in part; calculation of the APR; the duty on the lender to provide adequate explanations about the credit on offer to the consumer; the obligation on the lender to check creditworthiness before offer-ing or increasing credit; and the right for consumers to withdraw from a credit

---

[353] *Ibid.* Art. 8(2).   [354] *Ibid.* Art. 9(1).   [355] *Ibid.* Art. 9(2).
[356] *Ibid.* Art. 10.   [357] *Ibid.* Art. 14(1).   [358] *Ibid.* Art. 14(2).
[359] *Ibid.* Art. 16(1).   [360] *Ibid.* Art. 16(2).

agreement within fourteen days without giving any reason.[361] While it was clear that there was a great deal of overlap in respect of many of these issues with some of the measures introduced by the CCA 2006, nonetheless, a number of measures contained in the Consumer Credit Directive were new to consumer credit law in the United Kingdom. These included, for example, the duty on the lender to provide adequate explanations about the credit on offer to the consumer; the obligation on the lender to check creditworthiness before offering or increasing credit; requirements concerning credit reference databases; the right for consumers to withdraw from a credit agreement within fourteen days without giving any reason; requirements to inform consumers when debts are sold on; and requirements for credit intermediaries to disclose fees and links to creditors.[362]

The Consumer Credit Directive was finally fully implemented in the United Kingdom in February 2011 through a number of Statutory Instruments, including the Consumer Credit (EU Directive) Regulations 2010,[363] the Consumer Credit (Total Charge for Credit) Regulations 2010,[364] the Consumer Credit (Disclosure of Information) Regulations 2010,[365] the Consumer Credit (Agreements) Regulations 2010[366] and the Consumer Credit (Advertisements) Regulations 2010.[367]

16 Conclusion

Since the recommendations of the Crowther Committee and the introduction of the CCA 1974, the consumer credit market continued to expand and evolve to such an extent that by 2006 the levels of protection afforded in 1974 were completely out of touch with the needs of consumers—the ineffectiveness of the extortionate credit bargain regime and the weak enforcement powers of the OFT were clear illustrations of this. The CCA 2006 consequently introduced several important amendments to the CCA 1974, including the extension of the scope of the FOS, the introduction of the fairness test and tougher enforcement powers for the OFT. These measures, when considered in conjunction with the provisions of the Consumer Credit Directive 2008/48/EC, have, to some extent at least, transformed an ineffective piece of legislation into one which has increased the levels of protection afforded to consumers.

17 Recommended reading

Bisping, C. 'The case against s.75 of the Consumer Credit Act 1974 in credit card transactions' (2011) 5 *Journal of Business Law* 457

---

[361] DBERR, *Consultation on Proposals for Implementing the Consumer Credit Directive* (London, 2009).
[362] *Ibid.* 4.   [363] SI 2010/1010.   [364] SI 2010/1011.
[365] SI 2010/1013.   [366] SI 2010/1014.   [367] SI 2010/1970.

Brown, S. 'The Consumer Credit Act 2006: real additional mortgagor protection?' (2007) *Conveyancer and Property Lawyer* 316

'Using the law as a usury law: definitions of usury and recent developments in the regulation of unfair charges in consumer credit transactions' (2011) 1 *Journal of Business Law* 91

Carter, R. 'Statutory interpretation using legislated examples: Bennion on multiple consumer credit agreements' (2011) 32(2) *Statute Law Review* 86

Department for Business Innovation and Skills *Consumer Credit Regulations: Guidance on the Regulations Implementing the Consumer Credit Directive* (London, 2010)

Devenney, J. and Ryder, N. 'The cartography of the concept of "total charge for credit" under the Consumer Credit Act 1974' (2006) *Conveyancer and Property Lawyer* (September/October) 475

Dobson, P. and Stokes, R. *Commercial Law* (Sweet and Maxwell, Gosport, 2008)

Howells, G. 'The end of an era: implementing the Unfair Commercial Practices Directive in the United Kingdom – punctual criminal law gives way to a general criminal/civil law standard' (2009) 2 *Journal of Business Law* 183

'The consumer credit litigation explosion' (2010) *Law Quarterly Review* 617

Lomnicka, E. 'The reform of consumer credit in the UK' (2004) *Journal of Business Law* 129

Macleod, J. 'Credit hire in the House of Lords' (2001) *Journal of Business Law* (January) 14

Consumer Sales Law (Routledge, Oxford, 2007)

McMurty, L. 'Consumer Credit Act mortgages: unfair terms, time orders and judicial discretion' (2010) 2 *Journal of Business Law* 107

Patient, J. 'The Consumer Credit Act 2006' (2006) 21(6) *Journal of International Banking Law and Regulation* 309

Scott, C. and Black, J. *Cranston's Consumers and the Law* (Butterworths, London, 2000)

Bibliography

Aaronberg, D. and Higgins, N. 'The Bribery Act 2010: all bark and no bite…?' (2010) 5
    Archbold Review 6

Alcock, A. 'Insider dealing: how did we get here' (1994) 15(3) *Company Lawyer* 67

Andenas, M. 'Liability for supervisors and depositor's rights: the BCCI and the Bank of
    England in the House of Lords' (2001) 22(8) *Company Lawyer* 226

Andrew, E. 'Customer care and banking law' (1989) 4(3) *Journal of International Banking
    Law* 101

Anon. 'Legislative comment: Cheques Act 1992' (1992) 11(2) *International Banking and
    Financial Law* 17

    'Legislative comment: The Cheques Act 1992' (1992) *Journal of Business Law* (May)
    270

    'Case comment: whether overdraft repayable on demand' (1995) 8(7) *Insolvency
    Intelligence* 53

Arora, A. 'The dilemma of an issuing bank: to accept or reject documents under a letter
    of credit' (1984) *LMCLQ* 81

    'Electronic funds transfer and the law' (1986) 7(5) *Company Lawyer* 195

    'The Banking Act 1987: Part 1' (1988) 9(1) *Company Lawyer* 8

    'Code of Banking Practice: Part A' (1992) 10(2) *International Banking and Financial
    Law* 177

    Practical Banking and Building Society Law (Blackstone Press Ltd, London, 1997)

    'Changes to the powers of the Bank of England' (1997) 16(3) *International Banking
    and Financial Law* 21

    'The statutory system of bank supervision and the failure of BCCI' (2006) *Journal of
    Business Law* (August) 487

Art, R. 'Social responsibility in bank credit decisions: the Community Reinvestment Act
    one decade later', (1987) 18 *Pacific Law Journal* 1071

Atiyah, P.S., Adams, J. and MacQueen, H. *The Sale of Goods* (11th edn, Pearson
    Education Ltd, Harlow, 2005)

    The Sale of Goods (12th edn, Pearson Education Ltd, Harlow, 2010)

The Attorney General's Office *Extending the Powers of the Crown Court to Prevent Fraud
    and Compensate Victims, a Consultation* (London, 2008)

Azzouni, A. 'Internet banking and the law: a critical examination of the legal con-
    trols over internet banking in the UK and their ability to frame, regulate and
    secure banking on the net' (2003) 18(9) *Journal of International Banking Law and
    Regulation* 351

Babiak, A. 'Defining fundamental breach under the United Nations Convention on Contracts for the International Sale of Goods' (1992) 6 *Temple Int'l* and *Comp. LJ* 113

Bagge, J. 'The future for enforcement under the new Financial Services Authority' (1998) *19(7) Company Lawyer* 194

Bailey, J. 'Facing the truth: seeing the Convention on Contracts for the International Sale of Goods as an obstacle to a Uniform Law of International Sales' (1999) 32 *Cornell International Law Journal* 273

Baker, A. 'Banks and the communities they serve: time to legislate' (2008) 29(2) *Liverpool Law Review* 165

Bamford, C. 'Northern Rock and the single market' (2008) 29(3) *Company Lawyer* 65

Bank of England, 'Transfer of banking supervision', Press Release 20 May 1997
'About the bank' (n/d) available at www.bankofengland.co.uk/about/index.htm

Barclay, C. 'Technical aspects of unseaworthiness' (1975) *LMCLQ* 288

Barnett, W. 'Fraud enforcement in the Financial Services Act 1986: an analysis and discussion of section 47' 17(7) (1996) *Company Lawyer* 203

Baughen, S. 'Does deviation still matter' (1991) *LMCLQ* 70
'Defining the limits of the carrier's responsibilities' (2005) *LMCLQ* 153

Bazley, S. 'The Financial Services Authority: risk based regulation, principles based rules and accountability' (2008) 23(8) *Journal of International Banking Law and Regulation* 422

Beale, N. and Mitchell, R. 'Retention of title clauses and s.25 of the Sale of Goods Act 1979' (2009) 25(7) *Construction Law Journal* 498

Bennion, F. 'Consumer credit: the narrowing of "linked transactions" in relation to the total charge for credit' (1986) *Journal of Business Law* (July) 294

Bently, L. and Howells, G. 'Judicial treatment of extortionate credit bargains, Part I' (1989) *Conveyancer and Property Lawyer* 164

Berthoud, R. and Hinton, T. *Credit Unions in the United Kingdom* (Pinter Publishers, London, 1989)

Betti, G., Dourmashkin, N., Ross, C. and Yin, Y. 'Consumer in the EU: measurement and characteristics' (2007) 34(2) *Journal of Economic Studies* 136

Bevers, G. 'The accountability of the Financial Services Authority under the Financial Services and Markets Act 2000' (2001) 22(7) *Company Lawyer* 220

Bianca, C.M. and Bonell, M.J. (eds.) Commentary on the International Sales Law: the 1980 Vienna Sales Convention (Giuffre, Milan, 1987)

Bisping, B. 'The case against s.75 of the Consumer Credit Act 1974 in credit card transactions' (2011) 5 *Journal of Business Law* 457

Blair, C. *Financial Services and Markets Bill, House of Commons Research Paper 99/68* (London, 1999)

Blair, M., Cranston, R., Ryan, C. and Taylor, M. *Blackstone's Guide to the Bank of England Act 1998* (London, 1998).

Blair, M., Minghella, M., Taylor, L., Threipland, M. and Walker, G. *Blackstone's Guide to the Financial Services and Markets Act 2000* (London, 2001).

Blair, W. 'The reform of financial regulation in the UK' (1998) *Journal of International Banking Law* 43

Bollen, R. 'European regulation of payment services: recent developments and the proposed Payment Services Directive, Part 2' (2007) 22(10) *Journal of International Banking Law and Regulation* 532

'European regulation of payment services: the story so far' (2007) 22(9) *Journal of International Banking Law and Regulation* 451

Bone, S. and Rutherford, L. 'Consumer credit, defects in the linked transactions regulations' (1985) *Journal of Business Law* 209

Borrie, G. 'The credit society: its benefits and burdens' (1986) *Journal of Business Law* (May) 181

'Law and morality in the market place' (1987) *Journal of Business Law* (November) 433

Bosworth-Davies, R. 'Investigating financial crime: the continuing evolution of the public fraud investigation role – a personal perspective' (2009) 30(7) *Company Lawyer*, 195

Bourke, P. and Henderson, A. 'The first decision of the Financial Services and Markets Tribunal' (2002) 23(12) *Company Lawyer* 381

Bourne, N. *Bourne on Company Law* (Routledge Cavendish, Abingdon, 2011)

Bradgate, R. *Commercial Law* (3rd edn, Butterworths, London, 2000)
Commercial Law (Oxford University Press, Oxford, 2005)

Bradgate, R., and Twigg-Flesner, C. *Blackstone's Guide to Consumer Sales and Associated Guarantees* (Oxford University Press, Oxford, 2003)

Brahms, M. 'No fault in Finland: paying patients and drug victims' (1998) 138 *New Law Journal* 678

Brandt, P. and Graham, P. 'An update on the UK's implementation of the Payment Services Directive' (2009) 64 *Compliance Officer Bulletin* (March) 1

Breslin, B., Ezickson, D. and Kocoras, J. 'The Bribery Act 2010: raising the bar above the US Foreign Corrupt Practices Act' (2010) 31(11) *Company Lawyer* 362

Bridge, M. *The Sale of Goods* (Oxford University Press, Oxford, 1997)

Bridges, S. and Disney, R. 'Use of credit and arrears on debt among low-income families in the United Kingdom' (2004) 25(1) *Fiscal Studies* 1

British Bankers Association *The Banking Code* (London, 2008)
'Financial services sector tops UK growth tables' Press Release, 18 January 2008

Brown, I. 'Divided loyalties in the law of agency' (1993) 109 *Law Quarterly Review* (April) 206

'The agent's apparent authority: paradigm or paradox?' (1995) *Journal of Business Law* (July) 360

'The significance of general and special authority in the development of the agent's external authority in English law' (2004) *Journal of Business Law* (July) 391

Brown, S. 'The Consumer Credit Act 2006: real additional mortgagor protection?' (2007) *Conveyancer and Property Lawyer* (July/August) 316

Buckley, R.P. 'Potential pitfalls with letters of credit' (1996) 70 *ALJ* 217

Busch, D. and Macgregor, L. 'Apparent authority in Scots law: some international perspectives' (2007) 11(3) *Edinburgh Law Review* 349

Butler, M. and Darnley, A. 'Consumer acquis: proposed reform of B2C regulation to promote cross-border trading' (2007) *Computer and Telecommunications Law Review* 109

Capps, D. 'The UK Securities and Investments Board: how it can and does protect investors' (1993) 8(6) *Journal of International Banking Law* 248

Cartwright, P. 'Retail depositors, conduct of business and sanctioning' (2009) 17(3) *Journal of Financial Regulation and Compliance* 302

Casanova, J. 'Establishing Internet credit card programmes in the United Kingdom' (2001) 16(3) *Journal of International Banking Law* 70

Cattermole, A. 'UK banks write off bad debt' Monetary and Financial Statistics, (Bank of England, September 2004), available at www.bankofengland.co.uk

Cavalli, E. and Blyth, T. 'The liability of the Financial Services Authority after Three Rivers' (2001) 3(5) *Journal of International Financial Markets* 199

Centre for Economics and Business Research *The City's Importance to the EU Economy 2005* (London, 2005)

Chen-Wishart, M. 'Case comment: transparency and fairness in bank charges' (2010) 126 *Law Quarterly Review* 157

Cheng-Han, T. 'Undisclosed principals and contract' (2004) 120 *Law Quarterly Review* (July) 480

Chew, S. 'Disclosure of information by the bank: protection of the guarantor's rights or a threat to the doctrine of confidentiality' (2009) 24(6) *Journal of International Banking Law and Regulation* 313

Chissick, M. and Kelman, A. *Electronic Commerce Law and Practice* (3rd edn, Sweet and Maxwell, London, 2002)

Clark, A.M. 'The conceptual basis of product liability' (1985) 48 *Modern Law Review* 325

Clarke, M. 'Seaworthiness in time charters' (1977) *LMCLQ* 493

Clayton, N. 'Banks as fiduciaries: the UK position' (1992) 7(8) *Journal of International Banking Law* 315

Collard, S. 'Towards financial inclusion in the UK: progress and challenges' (2007) *Public Money and Management* (February) 13

Collard, S. and Kempson, E. 'Affordable credit: the way forward' (Joseph Rowntree Foundation, Bristol, 2005)

Conaglen, M. 'Public-private intersection: comparing fiduciary conflict doctrine and bias' (2008) *Public Law* (Spring) 58

Connal, R. 'Compensation under the Commercial Agents (Council Directive) Regulations 1993' (2007) 28 *Scots Law Times* 211

Connolly, K. 'FSA response paper on principles for business' (1999) 11(7) *Journal of International Financial Markets* N86

Cowan, D. '*Lister & Co.* v. *Stubbs*: who profits?' (1996) *Journal of Business Law* (January) 22

Cranston, R. *Principles of Banking Law* (Oxford University Press, Oxford, 2002)

Credit Action *Debt facts and figures* (Lincoln, 2011)

Crowther Committee, *Report of the Committee on Consumer Credit* (Cmnd. 4596, 1971)

Creed, N. 'The governing law of letter of credit transactions' (2001) 16 *JIBL* 41

Cummings, C. 'A practitioner's guide to mortgage regulation' (2008) 16(1) *Journal of Financial regulation and Compliance* 93

Currie, C. 'Civil enforcement as a regulatory device: the use of the civil law as a means of enforcing securities law violations' 17(5) (1996) *Company Lawyer* 139

Dahl, D., Evanoff, D. and Spivey, M. 'Community Reinvestment Act enforcement and changes in targeted lending' (2002) 25(3) *International Regional Science Review* 307

Dale, R. 'Bank crisis management: the case of the United Kingdom' (1995) 10(8) *Journal of International Banking Law* 326

Davies, P. 'Case comment: bank charges and unfair terms' (2008) 67(3) *Cambridge Law Journal* 466

Davies, R. 'Powers granted to the SIB under FSA 1986, s.59' (1994) 15(4) *Company Lawyer* 119

Davis, P. and Brockie, C. 'A mis-signalling problem? The troubled performance relationship between credit unions and local government in the UK' (2001) 27(1) *Local Government Studies* 1

Deane, S. '*Re Charge Card Services Ltd* and Hong Kong's section 15A' (1991) 6(8) *Journal of International Banking Law* 332

De Groote, B. 'European framework for unfair commercial practices: Analysis of Directive 2005/29' (2007) 16 *Journal of Business Law*

Department for Business, Enterprise and Regulatory Reform *Consultation on EU Proposals for a Consumer Rights Directive* (London, 2008)

   Explanatory Memorandum to the Consumer Protection for Unfair Trading Regulations 2008 and the Business Protection from Misleading Marketing Regulations 2008 (London, 2008)

   Pricing Practices Guide: Guidance for Traders on Good Practice in Giving Information about Prices (London 2008)

   Consultation on Proposals for Implementing the Consumer Credit Directive (London, 2009)

   Impact Assessment of Consumer Credit Directive (London, 2009)

Department for Innovation Business and Skills *Regulation: Less Is More, Reducing Burdens, Improving Outcome* (London, 2005)

   Regulatory Justice: Making Sanctions Effective (London, 2006)

   Statutory Code of Practice for Regulators (London, 2007)

   Consumer Law Review: Call for Evidence (London, 2008)

   A Better Deal for Consumers: Delivering Real Help Now and Change for the Future (London, 2009)

   Guidance for Business on the Provision of Services Regulations 2009 (London, 2009)

   Review of the Regulation of Credit and Store Cards: a Consultation, Initial Equality Impact Assessment (London, 2009)

   Consumer Credit Regulations: Guidance on the Regulations Implementing the Consumer Credit Directive (London, 2010)

Department of Trade and Industry *White Paper Modern Markets: Confident Consumers* (London, 1999)

   Report by the Task Force on Tackling Overindebtedness (London, 2001)

   Tackling Loan Sharks: and More! Consultation Document on Modernising the Consumer Credit Act 1974 (London, 2001)

   'Johnson announces biggest overhaul of credit laws for a generation' Press Notice P/2001/398, 25 July 2001

   A Consultation Document on Making the Extortionate Credit Provisions within the CCA More Effective (London, 2003)

   Consultation on the Licensing Regime of the Consumer Credit Act 1974 (London, 2003)

   Establishing a Transparent Market (London, 2003)

   Fair, Clear and Competitive: the Consumer Credit Market in the 21st Century (Cm 6040, London, 2003)

   The Unfair Commercial Practices Directive: Consultation on a Draft EU Directive (London, 2003)

   Consultation on an EC Directive on Unfair Business-to-Consumer Commercial Practices in the Internal Market: Government Response (London, 2004)

   Full Regulatory Impact Assessment: Consumer Credit Bill (London, 2004)

The Consumer Credit (Disclosure of Information) Regulations 2004 and *the Consumer Credit (Agreements) (Amendment) Regulations 2004 Guidance Notes* (London, 2004)

The Unfair Commercial Practices (UCP) Directive: Consultation on Framing and Enforcing Criminal Sanctions in the Regulations Implementing the Unfair Commercial Practices Directive (London, 2006)

Explanatory Memorandum to the Consumer Credit (Advertisements) (Amendment) Regulations 2007 (London, 2007)

Implementation of the Unfair Commercial Practices Directive: Consultation on the draft Consumer Protection from Unfair Trading Regulations 2007 (London, 2007)

Implementation of the Unfair Commercial Practices Directive: Government Response to the Consultation on How to Frame Criminal Offences (London, 2007)

Department for Work and Pensions *Tackling Over-Indebtedness Action Plan 2004* (London, 2004)

Devenney, J. and Ryder, N. 'The cartography of the concept of "total charge for credit" under the Consumer Credit Act 1974' (2006) *Conveyancer and Property Lawyer* (September/October) 475

Devonshire, P. 'Pre-emptive orders against evasive dealings: an assessment of recent trends' (2004) *Journal of Business Law* (May) 355

Dickinson, M. 'New Banking Act comes into effect' *Independent*, 21 February 2009

Dimatteo, L. 'The CISG and the presumption of enforceability: unintended contractual liability in international business dealings' (1997) 22 *Yale Journal of International Law* 111

Disney, R., Bridges, S. and Bathergood, J. *Drivers of Over-indebtedness, Report to the Department for Business, Enterprise and Regulatory Reform* (DBERR, London, 2008)

Dobson, P. and Stokes, R. *Commercial Law* (7th edn, Sweet and Maxwell, London, 2008)

Dockray, M. 'Deviation: a doctrine all at sea' (2000) *LMCLQ* 76

Dolan, J. 'Strict compliance with letters of credit: striking a fair balance' (1985) *BLJ* 18

Donnelly, R. and Haggett, A. *Credit Unions in Britain: a Decade of Growth* (Plunkett Foundation, Oxford, 1997)

Dowrick, F. 'The relationship of principal and agent' (1954) 17(1) *Modern Law Review* 24

Drakeford, M. and Sachdev, D. 'Financial exclusion and debt redemption' (2001) 21(2) *Critical Social Policy* 209

Drewry, G. and Gregory, R. 'Barlow Clowes and the Ombudsman, Part 1' (1991) *Public Law* (Summer) 192

'Barlow Clowes and the Ombudsman, Part 2' (1991) *Public Law* (Autumn) 408

Dundas, H. 'Case comment: EU law versus New York Convention – who wins? *Accentuate Ltd* v. *Asigra Inc*' (2010) 76(1) *Arbitration* 159

Eccles, A. 'Legislative comment: investing in the future' (2006) 5 *Scots Law Times* 23

Editorial 'Credit cards: our flexible friends and legal relations' (1988) 7(6) *International Banking Law* 82

'Case comment: financial services and markets tribunal rules on applications for authorisation and approved person status' (2005) 13(3) *Journal of Financial Regulation and Compliance* 278

'BCCI liquidators drop Bank of England claim' (2006) 27(3) *Company Lawyer* 91

'Legislative comment: unfair competition and comparative advertising – new regulations criminalise misleading marketing and unfair commercial practices and regulate comparative advertising' (2008) 30(9) *European Intellectual Property Review* N71

'Banking Act 2009 introduces new bank insolvency/administration procedures' (2009) 247 *Company Law Newsletter* 5

'Proving goods are defective: the six month requirement' (2009) 32(2) *Consumer Law Today* 1

'Satisfactory quality and the right of rejection' (2010) *Consumer Law Today* (April) 1

Ellinger, E.P. 'The uniform customs and practice for documentary credits (UCP): their development and the current revisions' (2007) *LMCLQ* 152

Ellinger, E., Lomnicka, E. and Hare, C. *Ellinger's modern banking law* (Oxford University Press, Oxford, 2011)

Ellinger, E., Lomnicka, E. and Hooley, R. *Ellinger's Modern Banking Law* (Oxford University Press, Oxford, 2006)

European Commission *Report to the European Parliament and the Council on the Experience Acquired in the Application of Directive 92/59/EEC on General Product Safety,* COM(2000)140 final

Report from the Commission on the Application of Directive 85/374 on Liability for Defective Products, COM(2000)893 final

Proposal for a Directive of the European Parliament and the Council on Consumer Rights, COM(2008)614 final

Financial Services Provision and Prevention of Financial Exclusion (Brussels, 2008)

Enonchong, N. 'The autonomy principle of letters of credit: an illegality exception?' (2006) *LMCLQ* 404

Evans, P. 'FOB and CIF Contracts' (1993) *ALJ* 844

Farnsworth, A. 'The Eason-Weinmann Colloquim on International and Comparative Law: duties of good faith and fair dealing under the UNIDROIT Principles, relevant international Conventions, and national laws' (1995) 3 *Tulane Journal of International and Comparative Law* 54

Fennell, E. '*Yasuda Fire & Marine Insurance Co. of Europe Ltd* v. *Orion Marine Insurance Underwriting Agency Ltd and another*: case comment' (1995) 3(4) *Journal of Financial Regulation and Compliance* 391

Fernandez-Corugedo, E. and Muellbauer, J. *Consumer Credit Conditions in the United Kingdom, Bank of England Working Paper No. 314* (London, 2006)

Financial Ombudsman Service *Rules for the New Consumer Credit Jurisdiction* (London, 2006)

Rules for the New Consumer Credit Jurisdiction from 6 April 2007 Feedback Statement (London, 2006)

Corporate Plan and 2008–2009 Budget (London, 2008)

'Consumer credit complaints and the ombudsman service' (2008) 68 *Ombudsman News* (March/April) 1

Annual Review 2008–2009 (London, 2009)

'Consumer credit complaints and the ombudsman service' (2009) 75 *Ombudsman News* (January/February) 1

Financial Services Authority *The FSA Principles for Business* (London, 1998)

The FSA Principles for Business: Response on Consultation Paper 13 (London, 1999)

Better Informed Consumers (London, 2000)

In or Out? Financial Exclusion: a Literature and Research Review (London, 2000)

Treating Customers Fairly after the Point of Sale, Discussion Paper (London, 2001)

Report of the Financial Services Authority on the Review of the Regulation of Equitable Life Assurance Society from 1 January 1999 to 8 December 2000 (London, 2001)

Better Regulation Action Plan (London, 2005)

Treating Customers Fairly: Towards Fair Outcomes for Consumers (London, 2006)

Levels of Financial Capability in the UK: Results of a Base-Line Survey (London, 2006)

'Regulatory principles in a principles-based world', speech by Sarah Wilson, Director, ILAG Annual General Meeting, 15 June 2006 available at www.fsa.gov.uk/pages/Library/Communication/Speeches/2006/0615_sw.shtml

Principles-based Regulation Focusing on the Outcomes that Matter (London, 2007)

'Principles-based regulation: looking to the future', speech by John Tiner, Chief Executive Officer, FSA Insurance Sector Conference, 21 March 2007, available at www.fsa.gov.uk/pages/Library/Communication/Speeches/2007/0321_jt.shtml

Regulating Retail Banking Conduct of Business, Consultation Paper 08/19 (London, 2008)

Executive Summary of Review (London, 2008)

Financial Services Authority Annual Report 2007/2008 (London, 2008)

Financial Services Compensation Scheme: Review of Limits (London, 2008)

Regulating Retail Banking Conduct of Business, Consultation Paper 89/19 (London, 2008)

The FSA's Role under the Payment Services Regulations 2009: Our Approach (London, 2010)

Mortgage Market Review: Responsible Lending (London, 2010)

The Full Handbook (London, 2011)

'Becoming a small payment institution' (n/d), available at www.fsa.gov.uk/pages/Doing/Regulated/banking/psd/applying/small/index.shtml

'Becoming an authorised payment institution' (n/d), available at www.fsa.gov.uk/pages/Doing/Regulated/banking/psd/applying/authorised/index.shtml

'The Banking Conduct Regime' (n/d), available at www.fsa.gov.uk/Pages/Doing/Regulated/banking/bcobs/index.shtml

'Payment Services Regulations' (n/d), available at www.fsa.gov.uk/pages/Doing/Regulated/banking/psd/index.shtml

'Clued up consumers are FSA goal', Press Release, FSA/PN/012/2001, 25 January 2001

'FSA fines Royal Bank of Scotland £750,000 for money laundering control failings', Press Release, FSA/PN/123/2002, 17 December 2002

'FSA fines Northern Bank £1,250,000 for money laundering control failings', Press Release FSA/PN/084/2003, 7 August 2003

'FSA fines Abbey National £2,320,000 for money laundering control failings', Press Release, FSA/PN/132/2003, 10 December 2003

'FSA fines Raiffeisen Zentralbank £150,000 for money laundering control failings', Press Release, FSA/PN/035/2004, 6 April 2004

'FSA fines Bank of Ireland £375,000 for money laundering control failings', Press Release, FSA/PN/077/2004, Press Release, 2 September 2004

'FSA fines bond broker and managing director for anti-money laundering failures', Press Release, FSA/PN/117/2005, 9 November 2005

'FSA fines Capita Financial Administrators Limited £300,000 in first anti-fraud controls case', Press Release, 16 March 2006

'FSA fines Nationwide £980,000 for information security lapses', Press Release, FSA/PN/021/2007, 14 February 2007

'FSA fines Norwich Union Life £1.26m', Press Release, FSA/PN/130/2007, 17 December 2007

'FSA bans mortgage brokers for submitting false loan applications, Press Release, 21 February 2008

'FSA bans introducer for making false mortgage applications', Press Release, 5 March 2008

'FSA moves to enhance supervision in the wake of Northern Rock', Press Release, 26 March 2008

'FSA bans Belfast mortgage broker for involvement in fraud', Press Release, 8 June 2008

'FSA bans South London mortgage brokers for submitting false loan applications', Press Release, 9 June 2008

'FSA bans East London brokers for involvement in mortgage fraud', Press Release, 23 June 2008

'FSA bans and fines mortgage broker £129,000 for involvement in mortgage fraud', Press Release, 7 July 2008

'FSA fines a mortgage firm £11,900 and bans adviser in relation to false mortgage applications', Press Release, 15 July 2008

'Compensation scheme to cover savers' claims up to £50,000', Press Release, 3 October 2008

'FSA fines firm and MLRO for money laundering controls failings', Press Release, 29 October 2008

'FSA fines Alpari and its former money laundering reporting officer, Sudipto Chattopadhyay, for anti-money laundering failings', Press Release 5 May 2010

'FSA fines mortgage lender and its director for irresponsible lending and unfair treatments of customers in arrears', Press Release, 4 November 2010

Fisher, J. *Fighting Fraud and Financial Crime: a New Architecture for the Investigation and Prosecution of Serious Fraud, Corruption and Financial Market Crimes* (Policy Exchange, London, 2010)

Fisher, J. and Bewsey, J. *The Law of Investor Protection* (London, 1997)

Fishman, J. 'A comparison of enforcement of securities law violations in the UK and US' (1993) 14(9) *Company Lawyer* 163

Foote, C., Gerardi, K., Goette, L. and Willen, P. 'Just the facts: an initial analysis of subprime's role in the housing crisis' (2008) 17(4) *Journal of Housing Economics* 291

Ford, J. and Rowlinson, K. 'Low-income households and credit: exclusion, preference and inclusion' (1996) 28 *Environment and Planning* 1345

Fox, J. 'Legislative comment: the Cheques Act 1992' (1992) 7(7) *Journal of International Banking Law* 280

French, D., Mayson, S. and Ryan, C. *Mayson, French and Ryan on Company Law* (Oxford University Press, Oxford, 2010)

Freshfields *FSA Principles-based Regulation* (London, 2007)

Garwood, G. and Smith, D. 'The Community Reinvestment Act: evolution and current issues', (1993) 79 *Fed. Res. Bull.* 251

Gentle, S. 'Legislative comment: the Bribery Act 2010, Part 2: the corporate offence' (2011) 2 *Criminal Law Review* 101

Geyer, R. 'Can EU social policy save the Social Exclusion Unit and vice versa?' (1999) 19(3) *Politics* 159

Giliker, P. 'Strict liability for defective products: the ongoing debate' (2003) 87 *Business Law Review*

Gilligan, G. 'The origins of UK financial services regulation' (1997) 18(6) *Company Lawyer* 167

Gondat-Larralde, C. and Nier, E. *The Economics of Retail Banking: an Empirical Analysis of the UK Market for Personal Current Accounts* (London, 2003)

Goode, R. 'Case comment: setting off contingent claims' (1986) *Journal of Business Law* (September) 431

   'The banker's duty of confidentiality' (1989) *Journal of Business Law* (May) 269

Gorton, L. 'Ship management agreements' (1991) *Journal of Business Law* (November) 562

Gower, L. 'Big bang and city regulation' (1988) 51(1) *Modern Law Review* 1

Gray, J. 'Case comment: first market abuse ruling from Financial Services and Markets Tribunal' (2005) 13(3) *Journal of Financial Regulation and Compliance* 272

Grey, J. 'Financial Services Act 1986 Reforms, Part 2' (1991) 9(9) *International Banking Law* 412

   'Lessons from BCCI saga for the current accountability debate surrounding Northern Rock?' (2008) 23(2) *Journal of International Banking Law and Regulation* 37

Griffiths Commission *The Griffiths Commission on Personal Debt: What Price Credit?* (Centre for Social Justice, London, 2005)

Griffiths, M. 'Defectiveness in EEC product liability' (1987) *Journal of Business Law* 222

   'A year of consumer credit judicial decisions in 1993' (1994) 12(12) *International Banking and Financial Law* 122

   'Consumer credit advertising: transparent at last?' (2006) 11(3) *Communications Law* 75

   'Unfair commercial practices: a new regime' (2007) 12 *Communications Law* 194

Griffiths, M. and Griffiths, I. *Law for Purchasing and Supply* (3rd edn, Pearson Education Ltd, Harlow, 2002)

Grunfeld, C. 'Affreightment-unseaworthiness-causation' (1949) *MLR* 372

Haines, J. 'FSA determined to improve the cleanliness of markets: custodial sentences continue to be a real threat', (2008) 29(12) *Company Lawyer* 370

Hall, E. 'Cancellation rights in distance-selling contracts for services: exemptions and consumer protection' (2007) *Journal of Business Law* 683

Harrington, J. 'Information society services: what are they and how relevant is the definition?' (2001) *Journal of Business Law* 190

Harris, J. 'Sale of goods and the relentless march of the Brussels 1 Regulation' (2007) 123 *Law Quarterly Review* 522

Hart, H. 'The end of sharp practice?' (2007) 157 *New Law Journal* 796

Harwood, R. 'The SIB's exercise of its enforcement powers' (1995) 16(9) *Company Lawyer* 271

Haynes, A. 'The Wolfsberg Principles: an analysis' (2004) 7(3) *Journal of Money Laundering Control* 207

Hemraj, M. 'The regulatory failure: the saga of BCCI' (2005) 8(4) *Journal of Money Laundering Control* 346

Herbert Smith *Principles-based Regulation, in Principle and in Practice: Preliminary Observations* (Herbert Smith, London, 2007)

Hicks, A. 'The remedial principle of *Keech* v. *Sandford* reconsidered' (2010) 69(2) *Cambridge Law Journal* 287

HM Customs and Excise *Oils Fraud Strategy: Summary of Consultation Responses Regulatory Impact Assessment* (London, 2002)

HM Government *The Coalition: Our Programme for Government* (London, 2010)

HM Revenue and Customs *Renewal of the 'Tackling Alcohol Fraud' Strategy* (London, 2009)

HM Treasury *Financial Services and Markets Bill: Overview of Financial Regulatory Reform* (London, 1998)

Access to Financial Services, Report of Policy Action Team 14 (London, 1999)

'Enhanced role for credit Unions', Press Release, 16 November 1999

Financial Services and Markets Bill: Progress Report (London, 1999)

Anti-money Laundering Strategy (London, 2004)

Barker Review of Housing Supply, Final Report (London, 2004)

Child Poverty Review (London, 2004)

Pre-budget Report 2004 (London, 2004)

Promoting Financial Inclusion (London, 2004)

Spending Review 2004 (London, 2004)

Transparency of Credit Card Charges, First Report of Session 2003–04 (London, 2004)

Housing Policy: an Overview (London, 2005)

The UK Financial Services Sector: Rising to the Challenges and Opportunities of Globalisation (London, 2005)

Banking and Unbanked: Banking Services, the Post Office Card Account and Financial Inclusion, 13th Report of Session 2005–2006 (London, 2006)

Financial Inclusion: the Way Forward (London, 2007)

Northern Rock on the Run (London, 2007)

Review of Christmas Savings Schemes (London, 2007)

Financial Stability and Depositor Protection: Special Resolution Regime (London, 2008)

2008 Pre-Budget Report (London, 2008)

A New Approach to Financial Regulation: Consultation on Reforming the Consumer Credit Regime (London, 2010)

A New Approach to Financial Regulation: the Blueprint for Reform (London, 2011)

'Financial services policy agenda', (n/d), available at www.hm-treasury.gov.uk/fin_policy_agenda_index.htm

HM Treasury and Civil Service Committee *The Regulation of Financial Services in the UK* (HC 332-I, London, 1995)

HM Treasury and HM Revenue and Customs *The Saving Gateway: Operating a National Scheme* (London, 2008)

Honeyball, S. and Pearce, D. 'Contract, employment and the contract of employment' (2006) 35(1) *Industrial Law Journal* 30

Hopper, M. and Stainsby, J. 'Principles-based regulation: better regulation?' (2006) 21(7) *Journal of International Banking Law and Regulation* 387

Howells, G. 'The end of an era: implementing the Unfair Commercial Practices Directive in the United Kingdom – punctual criminal law gives way to a general criminal/civil law standard' (2009) 2 *Journal of Business Law* 183

'The consumer credit litigation explosion' (2010) 126 *Law Quarterly Review* (October) 617

Howells, G. and Bently, L. 'Judicial treatment of extortionate credit bargains, Part 1' (1989) *Conveyancer and Property Lawyer* (May/June) 164

'Loansharks and extortionate credit bargains, Part 2' (1989) *Conveyancer and Property Lawyer* 234

Howells, G. and Weatherill, S. *Consumer Protection Law* (2nd edn, Ashgate Publishing Ltd, Aldershot, 2005)

Hsiao, M. 'Legitimised interference with private properties: Banking Act 2009' (2010) 25(5) *Journal of International Banking Law and Regulation* 227

Hudson, A. *The Law of Finance* (Sweet and Maxwell, London, 2009)

Hunt, O. *Opening Up, Reaching Out and Aiming High: An Agenda for Accessibility and Excellence in the Financial Ombudsman Service* (London, 2008)

Inderst, R. 'Irresponsible lending with a better informed lender' (2008) 118(532) *Economic Journal* 1499

Ironfield-Smith, C., Keasey, K., Summers, B., Duxbury, D. and Hudson, R. 'Consumer debt in the UK: attitudes and implications' (2005) 13(2) *Journal of Financial Regulation and Compliance* 132

Jacobson, A. 'The burden of good intentions: intermediate-sized banks and thrifts and the Community Reinvestment Act' (2006) 6 *UC Davis Business Law Journal* 16

Johnson, H. 'The Barlow Clowes affair and government regulation' (1989) 7(8) *International Banking Law* 114

'Consumer credit: less advertising more advice?' (1990) 8(12) *International Banking Law* 190

'Fair credit' (1991) 10(6) *International Banking and Financial Law* 94

'Dealing with bribes' (1994) 12(9) *International Banking and Financial Law* 94

'Advertisers beware! The impact of the Unfair Commercial Practices Directive' (2005) 10 *Communications Law* 164

Johnston, K., Greer, J., Biermacher, J. and Hummel, J. 'The subprime mortgage crisis: past, present, and future' (2008) 5(12) *North Carolina Banking Institute* 125

Joint Parliamentary Scrutiny Committee *Draft Financial Services and Markets Bill: First Report* (London, 1999)

Jones. S. 'Credit cards, card users and account holders' (1988) *Journal of Business Law* (November) 457

Kane, E. and DeTrask, K. 'Breakdown of accounting controls at Barings and Daiwa: benefits of using opportunity-cost measures for trading activity' (1999) 7(3/4) *Pacific-Basin Finance Journal* 203

Kempson, E. *Over-indebtedness in Britain: a Report to the Department of Trade and Industry* (Personal Finance Research Centre, Bristol, 2002)

Kempson, E., Atkinson, A. and Riley, O. *Policy Level Response to Financial Exclusion in Developed Countries: Lessons for Developing Countries* (Personal Finance Research Centre, Bristol University, 2004)

Kempson, E., Collard, S. and Moore, N. *Fair and Reasonable: An Assessment of the Financial Ombudsman Service* (Personal Finance Research Centre, Bristol, 2004)

Kempson, E. and Whyley, C. *Access to Current Accounts* (British Bankers Association, London, 1998)

Kept Out or Opted Out? Understanding and Combating Financial Exclusion (Policy Press, London, 1998)

Extortionate Credit in the UK (DTI, London, 1999)

Keter, V. *The Legislative and Regulatory Reform Bill, House of Commons Research Paper 06/06* (London, 2006)

Kiernan, P. 'The regulatory bodies fraud: its enforcement in the twenty-first century' (2003) 24(10) *Company Lawyer* 293

Kiernan, P. and Scanlan, G. 'Fraud and the law commission: the future of dishonesty' (2003) 10(3) *Journal of Financial Crime* 199

Kirkpatrick, J. 'Product liability law: from negligence to strict iability in the US' (2009) 30 *Business Law Review 48*

Kono, T., Paulus, C.G. and Rajak, H. (eds.) *Selected Legal Issues of E-Commerce* (Kluwer Law International, the Hague, 2002)

Kornert, J. 'The Barings crisis of 1890 and 1995: causes, courses, consequences and the danger of domino effects' (2003) 13(3) *International Financial Markets, Institutions and Money* 187–209, at 189.

Kozolchyk, B. 'Strict compliance and the reasonable document checker' (1990) 56 *BLR* 48

Labour Party *Labour's Manifesto: Equipping Britain for the Future* (London, 1997)

Law Commission *Law of Contract: Implied Terms in Contracts for the Supply of Services* (Report No. 156) (London, 1986)

Sale and Supply of Goods (Report No. 160) (London, 1987)

Legislating the Criminal Code: Fraud and Deception (Consultation Paper No. 155) (London, 1999)

Reforming Bribery (Consultation Paper No. 18532) (London, 2007)

Consumer Remedies for Faulty Goods (Law Comm. No. 317, Scot Law Comm. No. 216) (London, 2009)

Law Commission and Scottish Law Commission *Liability for Defective Products* (Law Comm. No. 82, Scot Law Comm. No. 45) (London, 1977)

Consumer Remedies for Faulty Goods (Law Comm. No. 317, Scot Law Comm. No. 216) (London, 2009)

Lee, R. 'The UN Convention on Contracts for the International Sale of Goods: OK for the UK?' (1993) 37 *Journal of Business Law* 131

'Rethinking the content of the fiduciary obligation' (2009) 3 *Conveyancer and Property Lawyer* 236

Leong, A. 'Chasing dirty money: domestic and international measures against money laundering' (2007) 10(2) *Journal of Money Laundering Control* 140

Levi, M. 'The Roskill Fraud Commission revisited: an assessment' (2003) 11(1) *Journal of Financial Crime* 38

'Combating the financing of terrorism: a history and assessment of the control of threat finance' (2010) 50(4) *British Journal of Criminology* 650

Lewis, D. 'The banking bill: between Charybdis and Scylla' (1987) 2(1) *Journal of International Banking Law* 49

Lodder, A.R. and Kaspersen, H.W.K. (eds.) *eDirectives: Guide to the European Union Law on E-Commerce* (Kluwer Law International, London, 2002)

Lok, X. 'LIBOR and market disruption: the future of LIBOR' (2008) 23(8) *Journal of International Banking and Financial Law* 421

Lomnicka, E. 'Curtailing section 62 accountability' (1991) *Journal of Business Law* (July) 353

'Reform of UK financial services regulation: the creation of a single regulator' (1999) *Journal of Business Law* 480

'Making the Financial Services Authority accountable' (2000) *Journal of Business Law* 65

'The reform of consumer credit in the UK' (2004) *Journal of Business Law* 129

Macdonald, E. 'Scope and fairness of the Unfair Terms in Consumer Contracts Regulations' (2002) 65(5) *Modern Law Review* 763

MacInnes, T., Kenway, P. and Parekh, A. *Monitoring Poverty and Social Exclusion* 2009 (Joseph Rowntree Foundation, York, 2009)

'Credit hire in the House of Lords' (2001) *Journal of Business Law* (January) 14

'Pawnbroking: a regulatory issue' (2005) *Journal of Business Law* (March) 155

Consumer Sales Law (2nd edn, Routledge, Oxford, 2007)

MacNeil, I. 'The future for financial regulation: the financial services and markets bill' (1999) 62(5) *Modern Law Review* 725

Magurie, V. and Walton, M. 'The ordinary course of banking business and deduction of tax at source' (1992) 7(1) *Journal of International Banking Law* 29

Mark, M. *Chalmers Sale of Goods* (18th edn, Butterwirths, London, 1981)

Markesinis, B. and Munday, R. *An Outline of the Law of Agency* (Butterworths, London, 1992)

Marshall, P. 'Does Shah v. HSBC Private Bank Ltd make the anti-money laundering consent regime unworkable?' (2010) 25(5) *Butterworths Journal of International Banking & Financial Law* 287

Mayo, E., Fisher, T., Conaty, T., Doling, J. and Mullineux, A. *Small is Bankable: Community Reinvestment in Great Britain* (Joseph Rowntree Trust, York, 1998)

McCormack, G. 'The remedial constructive trust and commercial transactions' (1996) 17(1) *Company Lawyer* 3

'Conflicts of interest and the investment management function' (1999) 20(1) *Company Lawyer* 2

McDonnell, B., Bell, O., Butler, J. Crehan, D., Heaton, E. and Lindsay, N. 'Annual review' (2009) 72 *Compliance Officer Bulletin* 1

McDowall, R. 'Financial services authority: progress or pragmatism?' (1998) 13(4) *Journal of International Banking Law* 123

McGuire, K. 'Banking supervision after the Bingham Report on BCCI: the end of an era?' (1993) 4(3) *International Company and Commercial Law* 118

McKillop, D., Ward, A. and Wilson, J. 'The development of credit unions and their role in tackling financial exclusion' (2007) 27(1) *Public Money and Management* 37

McVea, H. 'Fashioning a system of civil penalties for insider dealing: sections 61 and 62 of the Financial Services Act 1986' (1996) *Journal of Business Law* (July) 344

Merrett, L. 'The importance of delivery and possession in the passing of title' (2008) 67(2) *Cambridge Law Journal* 376

Miller, C.J. and Goldberg, R.S. *Product Liability* (2nd edn, Oxford University Press, Oxford, 2004)

Mills, C. 'The future of deviation' (1983) 4 *LMCLQ* 587

Montague, J. 'Case comment: *Office of Fair Trading* v. *Abbey National Plc*: contract – bank levies unfair terms, Office of Fair Trading' (2009) 14(2) *Coventry Law Journal* 44

Morris, P. 'The Financial Ombudsman Services and the Hunt Review: continuing evolution in dispute resolution' (2008) *Journal of Business Law* 785

Mortimer, A. 'Trustees and investment management, Part 2' (1994) 3 *Private Client Business* 160

Mulheron, R. 'Recent milestones in class actions reform in England: a critique and a proposal' (2011) 127 *Law Quarterly Review* (April) 288

Mullineux, A. 'The regulation of British retail banking utilities' (2009) 17(4) *Journal of Financial Regulation and Compliance* 453

Munday, R. *Agency: Law and Principles* (Oxford University Press, Oxford, 2010)

Murray, J. 'An essay on the formation of contracts and related matters under the United Nations Convention on Contracts for the International Sale of Goods' (1988) 8 *Journal of Law and Commerce* 11

A Life in Debt: the Profile of CAB Debt Clients in 2008 (London, 2009)

National Association of Citizens Advice Bureau *Daylight Robbery: The CAB Case for Effective Regulation of Extortionate Credit* (London, 2000)

National Audit Office *HM Treasury Asset Protection Scheme* (London, 2010)

National Consumer Council *Affordable Credit: a Model that Recognises Real Needs* (National Consumer Council, London, 2005)

National Fraud Authority *The National Fraud Strategy: A New Approach to Combating Fraud* (London, 2010)

National Statistics, 'Financial services top growth sector 1996 to 2006', Economic and Labour Market Review, News Release, 14 January 2008

Nebbia, P. '*Director General of Fair Trading* v. *First National Bank Plc*, House of Lords, [2001] 3 WLR 1297' (2003) 40(4) *Common Market Law Review* 983

Newdick, C. 'The development risk defence of the Consumer Protection Act 1987' (1988) *Cambridge Law Journal* 455

Nobles, R. and Black, J. 'Personal pensions misselling: the causes and lessons from regulatory failure' (1998) 61(6) *Modern Law Review* 789

Nolan, R. 'Conflicts of duty: helping hands from the Privy Council?' (1994) 15(2) *Company Lawyer* 58

Noonan, C. and Watson, S. 'Examining company directors through the lens of de facto directorship' (2008) 7 *Journal of Business Law* 587

Office of Fair Trading *A General Duty to Trade Fairly, Discussion Paper* (London, 1986)

Trading Malpractices: a Report by the Director General of Fair Trading following Consideration of Proposals for a General Duty to Trade Fairly (London, 1990)

Unjust Credit Transactions, a Report by the Director General of Fair Trading on the provisions of ss. 137–140 of the Consumer Credit Act 1974 (London, 1991)

Vulnerable Consumers and Financial Services, Report of the Director General's Inquiry (London, 1999)

Memorandum of Understanding between the Office of Fair Trading and the Director of the Serious Fraud Office (London, 2003)

Consumer Credit Act 1974: Review of the Group Licensing Regime, a Consultation Paper (London, 2004)

'OFT and Nigerian financial crime squad join forces to combat spam fraud', Press Release, 4 November 2005

Delivering Better Regulatory Outcomes: A Joint FSA and OFT Action Plan (London, 2006)

Credit Advertising (London, 2008)

Consumer Credit Licensing: General Guidance for Licensees and Applicants on Fitness and Requirements (London, 2008)

Consumer Credit Licensing: Statement of Policy on Civil Penalties (London, 2008)

Consumer Credit: Regulated and Exempt Agreements (London, 2008)

Consumer Protection from Unfair Trading Regulations 2008: Guidance on the Implementation of the Unfair Commercial Practices Directive (London, 2008)

Irresponsible Lending, a Scoping Paper (London, 2008)

Statement of Consumer Protection Enforcement Principles (London, 2008)

Unfair Relationships: Enforcement Action under Part 8 of the Enterprise Act 2002 (London, 2008)

Business to Business Promotions and Comparative Advertisements: A Quick Guide to the Business Protection from Misleading Marketing Regulations 2008 (London, 2009)

Financial Services Strategy, a Consultation Document (London, 2009)

Flexibility for Changing Markets: Annual Report and Resources Report 2008–2009 (London, 2009)

High Cost Consumer Credit: Scope and Reasons for a Review (London, 2009)

OFT Anti Money Laundering Registration Policy (London, 2009)

Scamnesty 2010 Campaign Strategy (London, 2009)

Guidance on Sections 77, 78 and 79 of the Consumer Credit Act 1974: the Duty to Give Information to Debtors and the Consequences of Non-compliance on the Enforceability of the Agreement (London, 2010)

Irresponsible Lending: OFT Guidance for Creditors (London, 2010)

Olukonyinsola, A. 'International securities regulation' (1992) 7(5) *Journal of International Banking Law* 191

Omar, P. 'A delicate balance of interests: the power of sale and the duty to maximise asset values' (2005) *Conveyancer and Property Lawyer* (September) 380

Omoyele, O. 'Accountability of the Financial Services Authority: a suggestion of corporate governance' (2006) 27(7) *Company Lawyer* 194

Ormerod. D. 'The Fraud Act 2006: criminalising lying?' (2007) *Criminal Law Review* (March) 193

Ortego, J. and Krinick, E. 'Letters of credit: benefits and drawback of the independence principle' (1998) 115 *BLJ* 487

Orton, S. 'When will hearings of the Financial Services and Markets Tribunal be held in private' (2003) 18(3) *Journal of International Banking Law and Regulation* 141

Page, A. 'Self-regulation: the constitutional dimension' (1986) 49(2) *Modern Law Review* 141

Parliamentary Ombudsman *Second Report of the PCA: the Barlow Clowes Affair* (HC 76, London, 1989/1990)

The Prudential Regulation of Equitable Life, Part 1, Overview and Summary of Findings (HC 809–1, London, 2002)

Pary, D.L., Rowell, R. and Ervine, C. (eds.), *Butterworths Trading and Consumer Law* (London, 1990)

Patient, J. 'The Consumer Credit Act 2006' (2006) 21(6) *Journal of International Banking Law and Regulation* 309

Peddie, J. 'Anti-terrorism legislation and market regulation' in W. Blair and R. Brent (eds.) *Banks and Financial Crime: the International Law of Tainted Money* (Oxford University Press, Oxford, 2008) 437–58

Penningto-Cross, A. and Ho, G. 'Predatory lending laws and the cost of credit' (2008) 36(2) *Real Estate Economics* 175

Philpott, F. 'E-commerce and consumer credit' (2001) 3(4) *Journal of International Financial Markets* 131

Pope, T. and Webb, T. 'The Bribery Act 2010 (legislative comment)' (2010) 25(10) *Journal of International Banking Law and Regulation* 480

Proctor, L. 'The Barings collapse: a regulatory failure, or a failure of supervision' (1997) 22 *Brooklyn Journal of International Law* 735

Rahmatian, A. 'Must cheques disappear by 2018?' (2011) 26(7) *Journal of International Banking Law and Regulation* 310

Ramage, S. 'Legislative comment: digital money, electronic fraud, new regulations and the old money laundering regulations' (2011) 200 *Criminal Lawyer* 1

Ramberg, J. *Guide to INCOTERMS 1990* (ICC, 1991)

Ramsay, I. *Consumer Law and Policy: Texts and Materials on Regulating Consumer Markets* (2nd edn, Hart Publishing, Oxford, 2007)

Ratcliffe, F. 'Redressing the lack of professional standards' (2007) 151(34) *Solicitors Journal* 1150

Reynolds, F. 'Fiduciary duties of estate agents' (1994) *Journal of Business Law* (March) 147

Rider, B. 'Policing the City: combating fraud and other abuses in the corporate securities industry' (1988) 41 *Current Legal Problems* 47

Richards, M., Palmer, P. and Bogdanova, M. 'Irresponsible lending? A case study of a UK credit industry reform initiative' (2008) 81(3) *Journal of Business Ethics* 499

Richards-Carpenter, P., Sautter, E., Hayes, A., Kynoch, N., Stark, P., Baker, M., Dehra, S., Rosser, S., Plange, V. and Ali, M. 'Annual Review for 2008' (2008) 62 *Compliance Officer Bulletin* 1

Roach, L. 'Equitable Life and non-executive directors: clarification from the High Court?' (2005) 26(8) *Company Lawyer* 253

Rodford, P. 'APACS response to irresponsible ending? A case study of a credit industry reform initiative' (2009) 86(4) *Journal of Business Ethics* 535

Rook, S. 'Consumer protection from Unfair Trading Regulations' *Trading Standards Today*, June 2009

Rosenthal, D. *Guide to Consumer Credit Law and Practice* (Butterworths, London, 2002)

Rossiter, J and Cooper, N. *Royal Commission on Civil Liability and Compensation for Personal Injury* (Cmnd. 7054, HMSO, London, 1978)

Scaling up for Financial Inclusion (Debt on our Doorstep, Manchester, 2005)

Ryder, N. 'Two plus two equals financial education: the Financial Services Authority and consumer education' (2001) 35(2) *Law Teacher* 216

'Out with the old and in with the new? A critical analysis of contemporary policy towards the development of credit unions in Great Britain' (2005) *Journal of Business Law* (September) 617

'The Financial Services Authority and money laundering: a game of cat and mouse' (2008) 67(3) *Cambridge Law Journal* 635

'The credit crunch: the right time for credit unions to strike?' (2009) 29(1) *Legal Studies* 75

'The Financial Services Authority and Proceeds of Crime Act: too little too late?' (2010) *Financial Regulation International* (September) 8

Ryder, N. and Baker, A. 'The enemy within? A critical analysis of the Credit Unions Act 1979 and the common bond' (2003) 36(2) *Journal of Co-operative Studies* 117

Salinger, F. 'International factoring and conflicts of law' (2007) 1(1) *LFMR* 7

Samuel, A. 'Principles-based regulation, MiFID and the new financial promotion rules' (2007) 49 *Compliance Officer Bulletin* (September) 1

Sarker, R. 'Anti-money laundering requirements: too much pain for too little gain' (2006) 27(8) *Company Lawyer* 250

Sasse, S. and Whittaker, J. 'An assessment of the impact of the UK Commercial Agents (Council Directive) Regulations 1993' (1994) 5(3) *International Company and Commercial Law Review* 100

Sassoon, D.M. 'Application of FOB and CIF sales in common law countries' (1981) *ETL* 50

Savirimuthu, J. 'Pre-incorporation contracts and the problem of corporate fundamentalism: are promoters proverbially profuse?' (2003) 24(7) *Company Lawyer* 196

Schlechtriem, P. *Commentary on the UN Convention on the International Sale of Goods (CISG)* (2nd edn, Clarendon Press, Oxford, 1998)

Schofield, J. *Laytime and Demurrage* (4th edn, Lloyd's of London, 2000)

Schulze, R., Schulte-Nölke, H. and Jones, J. (eds.) *A Casebook on European Community Law* (Hart Publishing, Oxford, 2002)

Scott, C. and Black, J. *Cranston's Consumers and the Law* (Butterworths, London, 2000)

Scott, D. and Herbst, J. 'The Financial Services and Markets Bill: regulation and the 21st century' (1999) 1(1) *Journal of International Financial Markets* 33

Sealy, L.S. and Hooley, R.J.A. *Commercial Law: Text, Cases and Materials* (4th edn, (Oxford University Press, Oxford, 2009)

Securities and Investment Board *Financial Services Regulation: Making the Two Tier System Work* (London, 1993)

Serious Organised Crime Agency *The Suspicious Activity Reports Regime Annual Report 2008* (London, 2008)

Shea, T. 'Liability of banks for erroneous status opinions' (1986) 1(1) *Journal of International Banking Law* 20

'Statutory set-off' (1986) 1(3) *Journal of International Banking Law* 152

Shears, P. 'Overviewing the EU Unfair Commercial Practices Directive: concentric Circles' (2007) 18 *European Business Law Review* 781

'The EU Product Liability Directive: twenty years on' (2007) *Journal of Business Law* 884

Sheppard, J.C. 'The rule against deduction from freight reconsidered' (2006) JBL 1

Silvertown, A. 'Bankers' duty of confidentiality' (1988) 7(5) *International Banking Law* 72

Singh, D. *Banking regulation of UK and US financial markets* (Ashgate, Aldershot, 2007)

'The UK Banking Act 2009, pre-insolvency and early intervention: policy and practice' (2011) 1 *Journal of Business Law* 20

Singleton, S. *eCommerce: a Practical Guide to the Law* (Gower Publishing Ltd, Aldershot, 2003)

'Proposed Consumer Rights Directive' (2008) 10(8) *Consumer Law Today*

'Draft consumer: Rights Directive and unfair terms' (2008) *Consumer Law Today* (December) 8

'Proposed changes to distance-selling rules' (2009) *Consumer Law Today* (February) 2009 8

'Proving goods are defective – the six-month rule.' (2009) 32(2) *Consumer Law Today* 1

'The Consumer Protection from Unfair Trading Regulations (legislative comment)' (2009) 15(3) *Computer and Telecommunications Law Review* 77

Skitmore, P. 'Case comment: *Hafton Properties Ltd* v. *McHugh* (1987) 84 LSG 342' (1987) 8(5) *Company Lawyer* 231

Snowdon, P. and Lovegrove, S. 'Money Laundering Regulations 2007' (2008) 54 *Compliance Officer Bulletin* 1

Social Exclusion Unit *Tackling Social Exclusion: Taking Stock and Looking to the Future* (ODPM Publications, London, 2004)

Solvang, T. 'Laytime, demurrage and multiple charterparties' (2001) *LMCLQ* 285

Spector, M. 'Taming the beast: payday loans, regulatory efforts, and unintended consequences' (2008) 57 *Depaul Law Review* 961

Stallworthy, M. 'BCCI: Bank of England response' (1992) 11(4) *International Banking and Financial Law* 44

'The United Kingdom's new regime for the control of insider dealing' (1993) *International Company and Commercial Law Review* 448

Stewart, S. 'Coping with the FSA's risk-based approach' (2005) 13(1) *Journal of Financial Regulation and Compliance* 43

Stokes, R. 'The banker's duty of confidentiality, money laundering and the Human Rights Act' (2007) *Journal of Business Law* (August) 502

Stone, R. 'Usual and ostensible authority: one concept or two?' (1993) *Journal of Business Law* (July) 325

Stott, C. and Ullah, Z. 'Money Laundering Regulations 2007, Part 1 (Legislative Comment)' (2008) 23(3) *Journal of International Banking Law and Regulation* 175

'2007 Money Laundering Regulations 2007, Part 2 (legislative comment)' (2008) 23(5) *Journal of International Banking Law and Regulation* 283

Street, A. 'Ostensible authority and ratification' (2006) 119 *Insurance and Reinsurance Law Briefing* (September) 1

Stuyck, J., Terryn, E. and Van Dyck, T. 'Confidence through fairness? The new Directive on unfair business-to-consumer commercial practices in the internal market' (2007) 43 *Common Market Law Review* 107

Swan, E. 'Market abuse: a new duty of fairness' (2004) 25(3) *Company Lawyer* 67

Swidler, G. 'Making the Community Reinvestment Act work' (1994) 69 *New York University Law Review* 387

Sykes, A. 'Market abuse: a civil revolution' (1999) 1(2) *Journal of International Financial Markets* 59

Taylor, M. 'Redrawing the regulatory map: why the Financial Services Act must not be reformed in isolation' (1996) 11(10) *Butterworths Journal of International Banking Financial Law* 463

Tettenborn, A. 'Insurers and undisclosed agency: rough justice and commercial expediency' (1994) 53(2) *Cambridge Law Journal* 223

'Principals, sub-agents and accountability' (1999) 115 *Law Quarterly Review* (October) 655

Thurston, J. 'Partnership Act 1890: time for reform' (1988) *Journal of Business Law* (March) 155

Todd, P. 'The peculiar position of freight' (1989) 8(4) *Int. Bank. L* 56
'Start of laytime' (2002) *JBL* 217

Tomasic, R. 'Corporate rescue, governance and risk taking in Northern Rock, part 2' (2008) *Company Lawyer* 330

Treitel, G.H. 'Rights of rejection under CIF sales' (1984) *LMCLQ* 565

Tribe, J. 'Personal insolvency law: debtor education, debtor advice and the credit environment, Part 1' (2007) 27(2) *Insolvency Intelligence* 23

Twigg-Flesner, C. 'Deep impact? The EC Directive on unfair commercial practices and domestic consumer law.' (2005) 121 *Law Quarterly Review* 386

Udell, G. 'Wall Street, main street, and a credit crunch: thoughts on the current financial crisis' (2009) 52(2) *Business Horizons* 117

uSwitch 'Affordability study: Lamsons Digital Media, 6–11 January 2006', available at www.creditaction.org.uk
'Credit card providers throw £8.8billion of unrequested credit at consumers', 2 July 2009, available at www.uswitch.com

Van Alstine, M. 'Dynamic treaty interpretation' (1998) 146 *University of Pennsylvania Law Review* 687

Vass, J. *A Guide to the Provision of Financial Services Education for Consumers* (FSA, London, 1998)

Virgo, J. and Ryley, P. 'Mis-selling of personal pension plans: a legal perspective' (1999) 5(1) *Journal of Pensions Management* 18

Wadsley, J. and Penn, P. *Penn and Shea, the Law Relating to Domestic Banking* (Sweet and Maxwell, London, 2000)

Wallace, M. 'A new approach to neighbourhood renewal in England' (2001) 38(12) *Urban Studies* 2163

Ward, D. and Jones, J. 'Agents as permanent establishments under the OECD Model Tax Convention' (1993) 5 *British Tax Review* 341

Warner, J. 'The new EC Regulations' (2002) *Company Lawyer* 313

Watt, P. and Jacobs, K. 'Discourses of social exclusion: an analysis of Bringing Britain Together: A National Strategy for Neighbourhood Renewal' (2000) 17(1) *Housing, Theory and Society* 14

Watts, P. 'Illegality and agency law: authorising illegal action' (2011) 3 *Journal of Business Law* 213

Welsh Affairs Select Committee *Social Exclusion in Wales* (London, 2001)

Whittaker, S. 'The application of the "broad principle of Hedley Byrne" as between parties to a contract' (1997) 17(1) *Legal Studies* 169

Wood, J. *A History of Central Banking in Great Britain and the United States* (Cambridge University Press, Cambridge, 2005)

Wright, R. 'Developing effective tools to manage the risk of damage caused by economically motivated crime fraud' (2007) 14(1) *Journal of Financial Crime* 17

Younghusband, V. 'Financial regulation: the Barlow Clowes affair' (1990) 5(3) *Journal of International Banking Law* 76

Ziegel, J. 'Recent developments in Canadian consumer credit law' (1973) 36(5) *Modern Law Review* 479

Zuckerman, M. 'A colossal wreck: the BCCI-Three Rivers litigation' (2006) 25 *Civil Justice Quarterly* (July) 287

Index